World War II

World War II

The Essential Reference Guide

Priscilla Roberts

 ABC-CLIO

Santa Barbara, California • Denver, Colorado • Oxford, England

Copyright 2012 by ABC-CLIO, LLC

Library of Congress Cataloging-in-Publication Data

World War II : the essential reference guide / [edited by] Priscilla Roberts.
    p. cm.
  Includes bibliographical references and index.
  ISBN 978-1-61069-101-7 (hardcopy : acid-free paper) — ISBN 978-1-61069-102-4 (ebook)
1. World War, 1939–1945.   I. Roberts, Priscilla.
  D743.W6658 2012
  940.53—dc23   2012014149

ISBN: 978-1-61069-101-7
EISBN: 978-1-61069-102-4

16 15 14 13 12   1 2 3 4 5

This book is also available on the World Wide Web as an eBook.
Visit www.abc-clio.com for details.

ABC-CLIO, LLC
130 Cremona Drive, P.O. Box 1911
Santa Barbara, California 93116-1911

This book is printed on acid-free paper ∞

Manufactured in the United States of America

For My Brave Friend
Dyan Francis

CONTENTS

OVERVIEW OF WORLD WAR II

World War II was the most destructive enterprise in human history. It is sobering to consider that more resources, material, and human lives (approximately 50 million) were expended on the war than on any other human activity. Indeed, this conflict was so all-encompassing that very few "side" wars took place simultaneously, the 1939–1940 Finnish–Soviet War (Winter War) being one of the few exceptions.

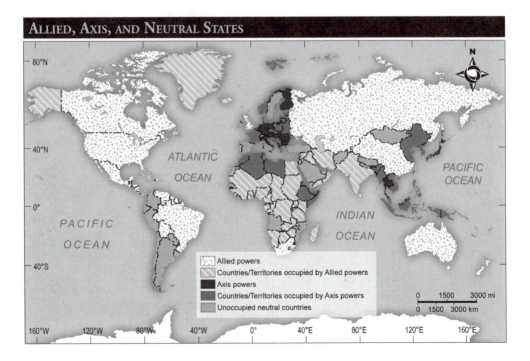

ALLIED, AXIS, AND NEUTRAL STATES

THE EARLY PHASES OF THE WAR

The traditional and widely accepted date for the start of World War II is September 1, 1939, with the quick but not quite blitzkrieg-speed German invasion of Poland. This action brought France and Great Britain into the conflict two days later in accordance with their guarantees to Poland. (The Soviet Union's invasion of eastern Poland on September 17 provoked no such reaction.)

The Germans learned from their Polish Campaign and mounted a true blitzkrieg offensive against the Low Countries and France that commenced on May 10, 1940. The Allies were simply outmaneuvered, losing France in six weeks. The Germans found that the French Routes Nationales (National Routes), designed to enable French forces to reach the frontiers, could also be used in the opposite direction by an invader. The Germans themselves would relearn this military truth on their autobahns in 1945.

Germany suffered its first defeat of the war when its air offensive against Great Britain, the world's first great air campaign, was thwarted in the Battle of Britain. The main advantages of the Royal Air Force (RAF) in this battle were radar and the geographic fact that its pilots and their warplanes were shot down over home territory. German pilots and

Although Italy was one of the Axis powers, in September 1939, Italy—still recovering from its war with Ethiopia and its involvement in the Spanish Civil War—remained a nonbelligerent in the European war. On June 10, 1940, as it became clear that German forces were about to defeat France, Benito Mussolini declared war on France, Britain, and their allies. He thought the war would soon be over, and hoped to take over assorted French and British territories in Africa and the Mediterranean. One week later, Mussolini visited Munich, Germany, to meet in person with Adolf Hitler, his fellow Fascist dictator and wartime ally. (National Archives)

aircraft in a similar predicament were out of action for the duration of the war, and they also had farther to fly from their bases. But Britain's greatest advantage throughout this stage of the war was its prime minister, Winston Churchill, who gave stirring voice and substance to the Allied defiance of Adolf Hitler.

Nonetheless, by spring 1941, Nazi Germany had conquered or dominated all of the European continent, with the exception of Switzerland, Sweden, and Vatican City. Greece, which had held off and beaten back an inept Italian offensive, finally capitulated to the German Balkan blitzkrieg in spring 1941.

Nazi Germany then turned on its erstwhile ally, the Soviet Union, on June 22, 1941, in Operation BARBAROSSA. Josef Stalin's own inept generalship played a major role in the early Soviet defeats, and German forces drove almost to within sight of the Kremlin's towers in December 1941 before being beaten back.

THE UNITED STATES ENTERS THE WAR

Early that same month, war erupted in the Pacific with Japan's coordinated combined attacks on the U.S. naval base at Pearl Harbor and on British, Dutch, and American imperial possessions. With the Soviet Union holding out precariously and the United States now a belligerent, the Axis had lost the war, even though few recognized that fact at the time. The United States' "great debate" as to whether and to what extent to aid Britain was silenced in a national outpouring of collective wrath against the new enemy.

Japanese forces surprised and outfought their opponents by land, sea, and air. British and Dutch forces in Asia, superior only in numbers, had been routed in one of the most successful combined-arms campaigns in history. Singapore, the linchpin of imperial European power in Asia, surrendered ignominiously on February 16, 1942. Only the Americans managed to delay the Japanese seriously, holding out on the Bataan Peninsula and then at the Corregidor fortifications until May. The end of imperialism, at least in Asia, can be dated to the capitulation of Singapore, as Asians witnessed other Asians with superior technology and professionalism completely defeat European and American forces.

And yet, on Pearl Harbor's very "day of infamy," Japan actually lost the war. Its forces missed the American aircraft carriers there, as well as the oil tank farms and the machine shop complex. On that day, the Japanese killed many U.S. personnel, and they destroyed mostly obsolete aircraft and sank a handful of elderly battleships. But, above all, they outraged Americans, who determined to avenge the attack. Japan would receive no mercy in the relentless land, sea, and air war that the United States was now about to wage against it. More significantly, American industrial and manpower resources vastly surpassed those Japan could bring to bear in a protracted conflict.

The tide would not begin to turn until the drawn-out naval-air clash in the Coral Sea (May 1942), the first naval battle in which neither side's surface ships ever came within sight of the opponent. The following month, the U.S. Navy avenged Pearl Harbor in the Battle of Midway, sinking no fewer than four Japanese carriers, again without those surface ships involved ever sighting each other. The loss of hundreds of superbly trained, combat-experienced naval aviators and their expert maintenance crews was as great a blow to Japan as the actual sinking of its invaluable carriers. The Americans could make up their own losses far more easily than the Japanese.

By this time, U.S. production was supplying not only American military needs but also those of most of the Allies. Everything from aluminum ingots and the canned-meat product Spam to Sherman tanks and finished aircraft crossed the oceans to the British Isles, the Soviet Union, the Free French, the Nationalist Chinese, the Fighting Poles, and others. Moreover, quantity was not produced at the expense of quality. Although some of the Allies might have had reservations in regard to Spam, the army trucks, the boots, the small arms, and the uniforms provided by the United States were unsurpassed. The very ships that transported the bulk of this war material—the famous mass-produced Liberty ships ("rolled out by the mile, chopped off by the yard")—could still be found on the world's oceanic trade routes decades after they were originally scheduled to be scrapped.

THE WAR IN EUROPE

Although considered a sideshow by the Soviets, Operation TORCH was of the utmost strategic importance, and until mid-1943, it was the only continental land campaign that the Western Allies were strong enough to mount. Had North Africa, including Egypt, fallen to the Axis, the Suez Canal could not have been held and German forces could have gone through the Middle East, mobilizing Arab nationalism, threatening the area's vast oil fields, and even menacing the embattled Soviet Union. Not until the British commander in North Africa, General Bernard Montgomery, amassed a massive superiority in armor was Germany's General Erwin Rommel defeated at El Alamein in October 1942 and slowly pushed back toward Tunisia. U.S. and British landings in Algeria and Morocco to the rear of Rommel's forces were successful, but the American troops received a bloody nose at Kasserine Pass. The vastly outnumbered North African Axis forces did not capitulate until May 1943.

After the North African Campaign ended in 1943, the Allies drove the Axis forces from Sicily, and then, in September 1943, they began the interminable Italian Campaign. It is perhaps indicative of the frustrating nature of the war in Italy that the lethargic Allies allowed the campaign to begin with the escape of most Axis forces from Sicily to the Italian peninsula. The Germans conducted well-organized retreats from one mountainous fortified line to the next. The Italian Campaign was occasionally justified for tying down many German troops, but the truth is that it tied down far more Allied forces—British, Americans, Free French, Free Poles, Brazilians, Canadians, Indians, and British and French African colonials among them. German forces in Italy ultimately surrendered in late April 1945, only about a week before Germany itself capitulated.

The aftermath of World War II proved considerably different from that of World War I, with its prevailing spirit of disillusionment. Amazingly, all of World War II's belligerents, winners and losers alike, could soon look back and realize that the destruction of the murderous, archaic, racialist Axis regimes had genuinely cleared the way to a better world. All enjoyed peace and the absence of major war. Even for the Soviets, the postwar decades were infinitely better than the prewar years, although much of this measure of good fortune might be attributed simply to the death of Stalin. The United States and much of the British Commonwealth emerged from the war far stronger than when they entered it. By the 1950s, both war-shattered Western Europe and Japan were well on their way to becoming major economic competitors with the United States. The uniquely sagacious and farsighted Western Allied military occupations of Germany, Japan, and Austria in many ways laid the foundations for the postwar prosperity of these former enemy nations. (For the most part, however, similar good fortune bypassed the less developed nations.) Within a few years, former belligerents on both sides could agree that, despite its appalling casualties and destruction, World War II had been if not perhaps "the Good War" then at least something in the nature of a worthwhile war.

H. P. Willmott and Michael Barrett

CAUSES OF WORLD WAR II

IMMEDIATE CAUSES

Sino-Japanese War

In autumn 1938, the Japanese captured Canton and the Wuhan cities and, in effect, brought to an end what was the first phase of the Sino-Japanese War. In this phase the Japanese had overrun much of northern China, Inner Mongolia, the middle Yangtze River Valley, and certain coastal areas. Japan had acquired for itself control of the richest and most advanced areas of China. The Kuomintang (Nationalist) regime was limited to southwest China with its capital at Chungking and was virtually bereft of outside support, the Soviet Union excepted. But the government of Jiang Jieshi (Chiang Kai-shek) had committed itself to a protracted war, and by autumn 1938 Japan indeed found itself committed to a prohibitively expensive war that it could not win either politically or militarily. Determined to reserve economic power for itself, Japan would not sponsor any genuine alternative to the Chungking clique for fear that any new force within China might be turned against it. Japan lacked the military numbers to conquer and occupy while its 1939 and 1940 air offensives, the first strategic air offensives in history, could not win a victory that had eluded Japanese ground forces. Japan was caught with a war that it could not win and which, by its own 1941 study, would result in collapse and defeat in 5 to 10 years.

Munich Conference

Autumn 1938 also saw the greatest of the European interwar crises: the Munich Conference. It was a conference that in a sense marked the end of a Eurocentric world. It involved just four powers, the United States and the Soviet Union having been excluded from the proceedings. It was a crisis that has attracted endless condemnation for three reasons. First, in terms of Anglo-French intent, it failed in that it did not produce the basis for peace but merely postponed war. Second, it postponed war for only a year, in which time the Anglo-French position relative to Germany worsened. Third, at Munich the British and French abandoned a democracy, and in fact the only democracy east of the Rhine (Denmark and Scandinavia excepted). This was something that was morally dubious, and Prime Minister Neville Chamberlain's infamous comment about Czechoslovakia—"a far-away country of which we know nothing"—merely compounded that element of ex post facto moral disapproval of the Anglo-French action.

Munich came as the culmination of a process that is perhaps best summarized by the scene "Tomorrow Belongs to Me" in the famous film *Cabaret*. What was clearly at work was a German political, economic, and military revival and a resurgence to which the British and French had no effective response. France sought and secured a military arrangement with the Soviet Union in what was clearly intended as an attempt to recreate the pre-1914 arrangements, but with no common border between Germany and the Soviet Union the latter could not bring a balance in central and eastern Europe into play because the various states of this area were not prepared to associate themselves in any way with the Stalinist state. Germany, under Adolf Hitler, was opportunist rather than very deliberate, with a set timetable and program, and it used a series of crises to destroy French military primacy within Europe, to reacquire its own armed forces and territorial integrity, and to secure Austria and the Sudetenland. But Germany's occupation of the Czech homeland in March 1939 brought home to Great Britain the futility of both the arrangements that had been made at Munich and seeking any further arrangement with Germany: Poland was guaranteed for the very simple reason that it was seen as Hitler's next target.

Many inhabitants of the Sudetenland, a Czech border region with a substantial German population that Czechoslovakia ceded to Germany under the September 1938 Munich Agreement, were unhappy over their transfer to German rule. Here one Czech woman attempts to hide her tears while offering a reluctant Nazi salute to German leader Adolf Hitler. (National Archives)

Expansion of the War

The British attempts to avoid war by a combination of inducing some concessions to Germany and the attempt to enlist Soviet support without any form of reciprocal arrangement can be cast in a very unworthy light, but the Soviet Union's deal with Nazi Germany in August 1939 marked the final step before the outbreak of war: Hitler had hoped that Britain and France would give way without war, but the Polish Campaign soon became a general war in September 1939. With Britain and France having to plan for a two- to three-year mobilization, Germany chose to move in 1940 against first Denmark and Norway and then in northwestern Europe. These victories were the basis of two greater conflicts. First, German primacy within Europe and Britain's ineffectiveness paved the way for the real German war in the east. Second, the collapse of the three greatest imperial powers exposed Southeast Asia and provided Japan with maximum temptation at seemingly minimal risk. Moreover, Japan could foresee that by 1941 it would stand at the peak of its strength relative to a United States that in the summer of 1940, after Germany's victory in northwestern Europe, had authorized naval programs that could only result in Japan's eventual eclipse. For Japan, 1941 was a case of "go now or never," and in its decision to try to fight the United States to a negotiated settlement, it initiated a conflict that drew together all the elements that go under the name of World War II.

INTERMEDIATE CAUSES

In seeking to determine the causes of, and responsibility for, World War II, there is a very plausible argument that asserts that the British and French played a negative role in the rise of Adolf Hitler and Nazism. The French prevailed in the 1920s when they sought to enforce the Versailles settlement when there was no real threat to it, and the British prevailed in the 1930s when they sought to revise the Versailles settlement when the threat to it had emerged. The argument is attractive in its simplicity, not least because the British effort not only "whetted the appetite of the insatiable," but also compromised France's power of resistance.

Events in the Far East

Whatever the merits of this particular argument, the fact was that the first challenges to the existing international order came in the Far East and in eastern Africa from Japan and Italy, respectively—not within Europe from Hitler's Germany. The three nations would become intertwined, but the initial challenge to the international system created in the aftermath of World War I predated Hitler's coming to power in January 1933. The fact that Japanese aggression in Manchuria in 1931–1932 elicited no response set the scene for what was to follow. Great Britain and France, beset by the problems of the Great Depression and denied any form of help or cooperation by an isolationist United States, could not contemplate opposition to, still less a preventative war against, Japan. Japan's conquests of 1931–1932 were followed by the occupation of Jehol in 1933 and then a series of encroachments that had the effect of eliminating the political and military presence of the Kuomintang regime in Inner Mongolia and the provinces north of the Great

Wall. For the Kuomintang, the process of being obliged to make concessions proved impossible to halt once it had begun. It is important to note, however, that after 1927 the Kuomintang, which had established its primacy within China by a dual process of conquest and compromise with certain provincial leaders, was involved in a campaign against the communists and by 1934–1935 had come within reach of final and decisive victory. The communists' celebrated Long March to Shenshi Province seemed certain to have done no more than postpone final defeat and annihilation, but the refusal of Manchurian forces to complete the Kuomintang victory in December 1936 spelled an end to the Chinese Civil War. It was now possible to present a united front against further Japanese aggression. For their part, there were certain Japanese officials who saw in the Chinese move a reason to act before Chinese intent could assume substance.

Events in Europe and Africa

By this stage, the estrangement of Britain and France on the one hand and Italy on the other had come to pass, in part because of Anglo-French ineffectiveness in opposing Italian ambitions in Abyssinia. Also at work was the Italian attempt to exploit what was, with the emerging German challenge to Britain and France, the division and balance of power within Europe. In 1934–1935, Italy associated itself with Britain and France in opposing German designs on Austria, but thereafter Italy began taking after Germany on ideological grounds. This was compounded by the two countries' intervention in the Spanish Civil War on the side of Francisco Franco's fascist uprising. With the Soviet Union moving to support what was initially a democratic government in Spain but which during the civil war in effect became a communist-dominated dependency, Anglo-American nonintervention smacked of weakness. Such perceived weakness seemed to resemble France's lack of an effective response to the German military occupation of the demilitarized Rhineland in March 1936, which had led to Belgium ending its military alliance with France in October 1936. Thereafter, with the onset of general war in China after July 1937, the crisis within Europe moved to center stage. This crisis had three main features: a weakening of a badly divided France, the questioning of French commitment to its allies in eastern and southeast Europe (which now promised not to be additions to strength but liabilities to be supported), and Germany's possession of the political and moral initiative.

LONG-TERM CAUSES

Great Depression

In one sense, the origins and causes of World War II can be summarized in the person of Adolf Hitler, and for good and obvious reason. The outbreak of war in Europe in 1939, Germany, and Hitler cannot be separated. But, on the other hand, the origins of the war in Europe can be assigned alternative starting points. One would be the result of World War I (not the Versailles Treaty or the general provisions of the Versailles settlement, but the actual result of the conflict), and the other would be the Great Depression that followed in the wake of the stock market crash of October 29–November 13, 1929. The latter is the more immediately relevant in the sense that had Hitler died in 1928 history would never have afforded him and Nazism anything more substantial than a footnote.

Once in power, the Nazis staged huge annual rallies at Nuremberg, lasting several days, that became prestigious symbols of their regime, a focus for national pride in Germany's regeneration. Hundreds of thousands of Nazi Party supporters of all kinds took part in these spectacles, which featured Hollywood-style pageantry of every kind, klieg lights, orchestras, mock battles, mass marches, and speeches by Hitler and his closest associates. Hitler is the center figure of the three men in the foreground. (AP/Wide World Photos)

The Great Depression brought Hitler to power and precipitated the eclipse of democracy not just in Germany but throughout Europe. By 1938, there was but one democracy (other than Denmark) east of the Rhine. The impact of the Great Depression was also instrumental in pushing Japan into the campaign of conquest with reference to Manchuria that proved to be the precursor to Japan's wars in eastern Asia and the western Pacific.

Effects of World War I

In a wider sense, however, World War II followed from World War I in one sense that is seldom properly defined. In the aftermath of Germany's defeat, the victorious powers attempted to create a new international order on the basis of increasingly fragmented nationalism. Two of the great multinational empires—Austria-Hungary and Turkey—disappeared. The third great multinational empire, Russia, was held together by the Bolshevik victory in the civil war but was nonetheless obliged to shed Finland, the Baltic states, and part of Poland. The point, however, was that in Europe the increase in the number of states was not matched by economic, demographic, and military credibility on the part of these new states. The general peace of Europe after 1919 was good just as long as there was no real threat to it.

France, by virtue of its massive military advantage over a largely disarmed Germany and its series of alliances with Belgium, Poland, Czechoslovakia, Romania, and Yugoslavia, dominated Europe throughout the 1920s, and after the Locarno rapprochement Germany was prepared to work within the status quo. It is often asserted that the whole process of German revenge was based on a reaction to Versailles, but by 1939 the Versailles settlement was dead: Germany had absorbed Austria and had acquired the Sudetenland, and in terms of physical size it was greater than in 1914. The war that came in 1939 was not the result of Versailles, but in some measure the reality of Germany's defeat in 1918—which German nationalism wished to reverse—and to a larger extent the product of that ideological perversion that is called Nazism. Hitler did not want war in 1939; he wanted victory. He wanted victory in a series of campaigns that would be but the prelude to the real war—against the Slavic *untermenschen* of Eastern Europe and in the *volksgemeinschaft*, the struggle for racial purity within the German master race.

The Far East

A similar set of circumstances were—albeit with substantial differences—at work in the Far East. World War I, by reducing European states' regional presence and strength, and the Washington Treaties (1921–1922), had created a balance of power in the general area but had left Japan with a marked local superiority that was largely unused in the 1920s. The Great Depression, the collapse of its overseas trade, and the widespread distress throughout the countryside after 1929 served to encourage those within the Japanese military who saw conquest and acquisition—specifically of Manchuria, Mongolia, and northern China—as the sine qua non of Japan's political, social, economic, and military survival. These areas would provide Japan with the raw materials and markets essential to its survival as a great power. Those who were to provoke the Manchurian Crisis of 1931–1932 and those who were to play leading roles in the process that led to general war with China after 1937 generally believed that war with the United States was inevitable. What was happening in the long term was that the onset of the Great Depression brought the parallel discrediting of political and economic liberalism and the rise of dictatorships and increasingly militant nationalism, specifically on the part of revisionist states determined to overturn the existing international order.

H. P. Willmott and Michael Barrett

Consequences of World War II

IMMEDIATE CONSEQUENCES

Global War

World War II was probably the most destructive war in history. In relative terms, the fourth century BC and the 13th century were probably more destructive than the 20th century, and the Taiping Rebellion in 19th-century China was certainly more deadly than World War II in relative terms, and perhaps even in numbers. But World War II is still considered the most destructive war in history, chiefly for three reasons. First, it was a global war that inflicted itself on Europe; northern, northwestern, and eastern Africa; and the Middle East. It reached into the Arctic and North Atlantic oceans; the Mediterranean, Baltic, and Black seas; and the South Atlantic and Indian oceans. It spread into Australian waters, the western Pacific, eastern and southeastern Asia, the whole of the Pacific north of the Equator, and the southwest Pacific. World War I had reached China, Chilean waters, the Falklands, and the Indian Ocean, but it was primarily a war fought and decided in Europe and the Middle East. World War II was very different in terms of reach, in large measure because it was a two-part conflict.

Widespread Destruction

Second, in World War I there had been strips of murdered nature, specifically the Western Front, which had been subject to protracted stalemate. There was movement and destruction in other theaters, most obviously on the Eastern Front and in the Balkans, but also in the Middle East. But in World War I there was no destruction that rivaled the level of ruinous waste that characterized World War II. Europe was very largely destroyed. From Brest to the Volga and from the Baltic to Calabria, the devastation of Europe was all but complete. It has been estimated that 97% of the French rail system was destroyed in the course of the war. European industry and road, rail, and canal transport systems had all but ceased to exist by 1945. In China, destruction was perhaps less total and widespread, but many provinces had been devastated as a result of Japanese military ruthlessness and wanton destruction. In Japan, American bombing had destroyed almost half of Japan's 65 major cities.

Rise of the United States

Third, the death toll exceeded 60 million, and the European total would represent one death every four seconds between September 1, 1939 and May 12, 1945. The devastation wrought on Soviet, Polish, and Yugoslav societies is staggering. But beyond this destructiveness and appalling slaughter was another kind of destructiveness: the destruction of Europe itself. For more than 400 years, Europe, the smallest of the continents, had been considered by Europeans to be the greatest, and the world had come to bear the mark of Europe in terms of overseas settlement, societies and borders, industry and trade, and science and technology. By the beginning of the 20th century, the United States had emerged as the greatest industrial power in the world, and European primacy had passed in the course of World War I. But the European empires survived that war, and in many ways Europe remained the greatest of the continents until 1938. By 1945, Europe's fate was in the hands of two powers that were not European. The Soviet Union was part of Europe but it was also extra-European, and the United States had been transformed in the course of the war. In 1939, the United States was a North Atlantic power with a continental interior, but by 1945 it was a continental power that reached across two oceans and was incomparably the greatest power in the world on two counts. First, it was the only power in the world with atomic weapons, and it possessed a navy and an air force that were so large and advanced that they were literally unchallengeable. Second, in September 1945, something like three quarters of all industrial manufacture was American. In 1938, the United States had accounted for only about 32% of worldwide industrial output, but by 1945 it utterly dominated the world in industrial and financial terms. It was American money that would form the basis of the world trading system that was to be put in place over the next few years.

INTERMEDIATE CONSEQUENCES

Allies are not necessarily friends, and those divisions and differences held in check by common need invariably come to the fore with the approach of victory. The very real danger presented by Germany in Europe and then, by 1943–1944, the American need to recruit Soviet support for a Japanese war that it was believed might reach into 1947–1948 had the effect of holding the Allies together. But in reality deep divisions and differences were already in position even by the time of Japan's surrender in September 1945.

Soviet Buffer Zone

In this process, two matters were crucially important. The first was the Soviet determination to establish for itself a buffer zone throughout Eastern Europe and to hold a part of Germany as its first line of defense. After so destructive a war as the one that was then coming to an end, the Soviet intention was to secure a buffer zone of such depth that it would ensure that no future war would be fought on its soil. As the Cold War took shape, however, what in 1945 was a manipulation of the electoral processes throughout Eastern Europe became straightforward Soviet control of client states that had their own communist regimes and which were underwritten by Soviet military forces.

Atomic Weaponry and Limited War

The second matter was the manner in which the Japanese war ended, or at least appeared to have ended. Japan's final defeat was comprehensive and manifested itself in the annihilation of the Japanese Navy; the virtual collapse of all overseas trade; defeat at Soviet hands in northern China, Manchuria, and the Kuriles; local but irreversible defeats in Burma, New Guinea, and the Philippines; and the devastation of the Japanese home islands by the American strategic bombing offensive that reached its apogee with the attacks on Hiroshima and Nagasaki. The latter was to usher onto center stage something that was unprecedented. Military services had always had a deterrence role in the sense that they were state instruments capable of being used as deterrents, but with first atomic and then thermonuclear weapons, this deterrence would be ensured through the threat of the total and absolute destruction of society itself. Furthermore, the threat could manifest itself, and total destruction of a society could be achieved, in a matter of days, if not hours.

This development would not manifest itself right away, but within a very short time—less than four years after the end of the European war—the impact of developments was demonstrated in two ways. The United States and then the North Atlantic Treaty Organization (NATO) organized themselves on the basis of permanent readiness in order not to fight a war, but instead to ensure that no war was forthcoming. This was a rather strange development, but it went hand in hand with something that was no less strange. The weapons that were used to deter could not be employed in defense if deterrence failed, while defensive (conventional) forces in effect had no significance in terms of strategic deterrence. It took time for the implications of these developments to be understood, but at the same time strategic deterrence encouraged the search for other forms of conflict (that is, below the deterrence level). In terms of great powers, this search was to result in the concept of limited war, which was fitted into place in the mid-1950s in the aftermath of the Korean War.

European Integration

But there was one other development at work in these same years, but at a very different level and to a very different end. After the Thirty Years' War, the French Revolutionary and Napoleonic Wars, and World War I, the states of Europe deliberately sought to secure the means whereby such disastrous events might be avoided in the future. Results, inevitably, were mixed, but the limited warfare of the 18th century and then the long period of general peace in Europe after 1815 were evidence of intent and success. After 1945, however, there was within Europe the move to ensure the peace of Europe through economic and industrial integration that would prevent the European states from resorting to war with one another. There was, of course, an additional motive in the sense that for Europeans this was the means of ensuring against a resurgent Germany. In a sense, this new European integration was embodied by French foreign minister Robert Schuman—born in Luxembourg, raised in Lorraine, a soldier in the German Army during World War I, and in 1950 the proponent of Franco-German and a wider European industrial integration. This was a development unthinkable before 1939 but that was, in very large measure, the direct result of World War II.

LONG-TERM CONSEQUENCES

The distinction between immediate, intermediate, and long-term consequences is very fine indeed, and whatever classification one adopts is certain to be challenged and on good and possibly unanswerable terms of reference. One would suggest that the most important single consequence of the war was the emergence of the United States as the world's greatest power—industrial and financial, in terms of naval and air power, and by virtue of its possession and use of atomic weapons. It was in 1945 the only country in the world with global reach. Great Britain and France had global presence, but the United States was unique in its ability to project power across the whole globe.

The End of European Colonialism

But the citing of Britain and France, and their global presence, brings into play the subject of their colonial empires, and in this matter there were both immediate and long-term consequences. With reference to the latter, World War II saw the mobilization of the colonial empires and the raising of military formations that saw service. Both the British and the French came to be wary of committing black formations to battle because of their awareness of the fates of those taken prisoner by German and Japanese enemies, but the basic point was that the British and French colonial territories made contributions to the imperial cause in terms of manpower, economic resources, and position. For example, Kenya served as one of the bases for the British effort in eastern Africa and housed Italian prisoners, while two regiments raised in Africa saw service in Burma in 1944–1945.

World War II also saw a series of campaigns in the colonial empires: Italian Libya after 1940, British and Italian Somaliland and Abyssinia in 1940–1941, Syria and Lebanon in 1941, Madagascar and French Northwest Africa in 1942, and, of course, the whole of Southeast Asia after December 1941. In these areas, the primacy of colonial control was broken and never fully reestablished (although in Malaya the returning British received a welcome that was in very marked contrast to that afforded the French in Indochina and the Dutch in the East Indies). But the basic point was that World War II represented the supreme crisis for the colonial empires, and the various efforts that were made in the common cause had to be recognized accordingly. The British were singularly slow to grasp this new situation, but within a decade of the end of the war the Dutch had been forced to abandon the East Indies (western New Guinea excepted), the French had experienced bitter defeat in Indochina and were on the point of abandoning Morocco and Tunisia, and the British had been brought to the brink of reality in terms of Ghana's independence.

Power Vacuum in the Far East

In this sense, the European and Japanese wars were very different in consequence in one respect. In Europe the comprehensiveness of Axis defeat and the immediate reality of a new balance of power precluded further war, but in the Far East the end of the Japanese war ushered in a period of upheaval and revolution that was to last some 30 years before the local forces of nationalism and communism and great power interests resolved themselves in such a way as to produce some form of settled, recognized order. In this way, World War II was but one part of, and in its own right a major cause in, a process that saw

The Declaration of the United Nations is signed by representatives of 26 Allied nations, who pledged to continue fighting the Axis powers, in Washington, DC, on January 1, 1942. They also committed themselves to promoting freedom, democracy, human rights, and social justice in their own countries and abroad. U.S. president Franklin D. Roosevelt (seated, second from left) first used the term "United Nations" in this declaration. (Corel)

the passing of empires and the division of virtually the entire land surface of the world between indigenous sovereign states.

Creation of the United Nations and Focus on Humanitarianism

The end of World War II also saw the creation of the United Nations (UN). The ambiguity of its role—whether it was there to preserve the existing status quo or to change it—was unresolved, and it was beset by Cold War divisions and the selfishness of the great powers. But the creation of new states ran in parallel with changes in the nature of the state. The lesson of World War II was that states that could mobilize in order to wage total war could mobilize in order to wage peace, specifically to fight and defeat the scourges of unemployment, lack of health care and social security, lack of educational opportunities, and bad housing. For more than 20 years after the end of World War II, these issues dominated the political agenda in Europe and North America, and with considerable success. The generation that grew up after 1945 for the most part did not know primary poverty. Things were to change with the 1970s, but by that time the process of decolonization was complete and a new world order was in the making.

H. P. Willmott and Michael Barrett

Africa

Africa was an important theater of operations in World War II. The continent offered war materials and important routes for air and sea communications. Essential to Allied strategic planning was control of the Suez Canal in Egypt, and despite the demands of the Battle of Britain, British prime minister Winston Churchill had to divert scant British military resources there. Had the Axis powers taken that vital waterway, all British shipping to and from India would have been forced to detour around the Cape of Good Hope, doubling the length of the voyage.

Securing the vital oil supplies of the Middle East was another important consideration for Allied planners. From Cairo, the British Middle East Command directed operations to secure the Suez Canal and then to take the offensive against Italian forces invading from Libya and resident in East Africa.

Unlike World War I, World War II saw no fighting in southern Africa. The Union of South Africa, a British dominion, rallied to the British cause and made major contributions to the Allied war effort. The French African empire was another situation entirely. Following the defeat of France, most of the empire remained loyal to the new Vichy regime, although Chad declared early for Free French leader General Charles de Gaulle.

Allied operations occurred at Dakar and Madagascar and in the Horn of Africa in Italian East Africa, but most of the fighting took place in French North Africa and in northeast Africa. The road from Tripoli in western Libya through Benghazi and east to Alexandria, Egypt—the Benghazi Handicap—was the primary scene of fighting as Allied and Axis ground forces engaged in tactical patterns, advancing and retreating along the narrow coastal band of desert. Benito Mussolini's Italian forces invaded Egypt from Libya in September 1940. The fighting there seesawed back and forth with both sides increasing the stakes. Finally, with the British offensive at El Alamein and simultaneous British and U.S. landings in French North Africa, Axis forces there were caught in a vise. The continent was cleared of Axis troops in the Battle of Tunis in May 1943.

The war had tremendous influence on African nationalism, often because of the role African troops played in the war effort. General Charles de Gaulle acknowledged during the conflict that France owed a special debt of gratitude to its African empire for providing France the base and resources that enabled it to reenter the war in its final phases. It was thanks to the French colonial empire that the independent existence of France was continuously preserved. De Gaulle pledged a new relationship between metropolitan France and its colonies after the conflict.

Although Churchill was very much an imperialist, he could not override the strong anti-colonial attitudes expressed by the governments of the United States and the Soviet Union. U.S. president Franklin D. Roosevelt had often declared himself opposed to European colonialism, and when he attended the Casablanca Conference in early 1943, Roosevelt denounced French imperial practices. Soviet leader Josef Stalin often condemned Western imperialism, although this stance did not prevent him from practicing it himself in the case of Eastern and Central Europe, nor did it keep him from requesting bases in Libya.

Nationalism found fertile ground in those African states that had been cut off from the mother countries during the war, especially in the case of the French and Belgian African possessions. Serious uprisings against French rule occurred both in Madagascar and at Sétif in Algeria. French authorities put these down with significant loss of life. Repression only temporarily quieted nationalism, which continued to feed on the lack of meaningful political reform.

After the war, Italy lost its African empire save Italian Somaliland as a mandate; Libya became independent. Nationalism also affected the colonial African empires of Britain, Belgium, France, and Portugal. In 1945, Ethiopia, Egypt (nominally), Liberia, and the Union of South Africa were the only free states in Africa. Over the next two decades, however, most of the African states secured independence. Sometimes this occurred peacefully and sometimes with significant loss of life.

In a very real sense, World War II was a great watershed for Africa. Its outcome led to a fulfillment of the nationalism that had first washed over the continent in World War I. Unfortunately, the governments of many of the newly independent states seemed incapable of managing effectively the development of the continent's vast resources and the education of its people.

Spencer C. Tucker

See also

Churchill, Sir Winston Leonard Spencer; De Gaulle, Charles; North Africa Campaign; Rommel, Erwin Johannes Eugen; Roosevelt, Franklin D.; Stalin, Josef

References

Albertini, Rudolf von. *Decolonization: The Administration and Future of the Colonies, 1919–1960.* Translated by Francisca Garvie. Garden City, NY: Doubleday, 1971.

Barbour, Nevill, ed. *A Survey of French North Africa [The Maghrib].* New York: Oxford University Press, 1962.

Osborne, Richard E. *World War II in Colonial Africa: The Death Knell of Colonialism.* Indianapolis, IN: Riebel-Roque Publishing, 2001.

Atlantic, Battle of the

The Battle of the Atlantic was the longest campaign of World War II. In it, the German Navy tried to sever the Allied sea lines of communication along which supplies necessary

Keeping the Atlantic shipping routes open was vital for the Allies. Throughout the war Britain and Russia received massive quantities of supplies from North America. Most of the U.S. troops who fought in North Africa and Europe also arrived by sea. Allied warships and merchant vessels in the Atlantic quickly became prime targets for German submarines (U-boats). On September 17, 1939, the Royal Navy aircraft carrier *HMS Courageous* was hit by a torpedo from the German submarine U29, southwest off Ireland, and sank within 20 minutes, with the loss of almost half of the crew. (AP/Wide World Photos)

to fight the war were sent to Great Britain. To carry out the battle, the Germans employed a few surface raiders, but principally they used U-boats.

At the beginning of the war, the German Navy possessed not the 300 U-boats deemed necessary by Kommodore (Commodore) Karl Dönitz (he was promoted to rear admiral in October 1939), but 57 boats, of which only 27 were of types that could reach the Atlantic from their home bases. Although an extensive building program was immediately begun, only in the second half of 1941 did U-boat numbers begin to rise.

On the Allied side, British navy leaders were at first confident that their ASDIC (for Allied Submarine Detection Investigating Committee) location device would enable their escort vessels to defend the supply convoys against the submerged attackers, so that shipping losses might be limited until the building of new merchant ships by Britain, Canada, and the United States could settle the balance. However, Dönitz planned to concentrate groups of U-boats (called "wolf packs" by the Allies) against the convoys and to jointly attack them on the surface at night. It took time, however, before the battles of the convoys really began. The Battle of the Atlantic became a running match between numbers of German U-boats and the development of their weapons against the Allied merchant ships, their sea and air escorts (with improving detection equipment), and new weapons.

The Battle of the Atlantic may be subdivided into eight phases. During the first of these, from September 1939 to June 1940, a small number of U-boats, seldom more than 10 at a time, made individual cruises west of the British Isles and into the Bay of Biscay to intercept Allied merchant ships. Generally, these operated independently because the convoy system, which the British Admiralty had planned before the war, was slow to take shape. Thus the U-boats found targets, attacking at first according to prize rules by identifying the ship and providing for the safety of its crew. However, when Britain armed its merchant ships, the German submarines increasingly struck without warning. Dönitz's plan to counter the convoy with group or "pack" operations of U-boats—also developed and tested before the war—was put on trial in October and November 1939 and in February 1940. The results confirmed the possibility of vectoring a group of U-boats to a convoy by radio signals from whichever U-boat first sighted the convoy. However, at this time, the insufficient numbers of U-boats available and frequent torpedo failures prevented real successes.

The German conquest of Norway and western France provided the U-boats with new bases much closer to the main operational area off the Western Approaches and brought about a second phase from July 1940 to May 1941. In this phase, the U-boats, operated in groups or wolf packs, were directed by radio signals from the shore against the convoys, in which was now concentrated most of the maritime traffic to and from Great Britain. Even if the number of U-boats in the operational area still did not rise to more than 10 at a time, a peak of efficiency was attained in terms of the relationship between tonnage sunk and U-boat days at sea. This was made possible partly by the weakness of the convoy escort groups because the Royal Navy held back destroyers to guard against an expected German invasion of Britain. In addition, British merchant shipping losses were greatly augmented during this phase by the operations of German surface warships in the north and central Atlantic; by armed merchant raiders in the Atlantic, Pacific, and Indian Oceans; by the attacks of German long-range bombers against the Western Approaches; and by heavy German air attacks against British harbors. The Germans were also aided by Italian submarines based at Bordeaux and sent into the Atlantic, the numbers of which in early 1941 actually surpassed the number of German U-boats.

In late 1940 and spring of 1941, when the danger of an invasion of the British Isles had receded, London released destroyers for antisubmarine operations and redeployed Coastal Command aircraft to support the convoys off the Western Approaches. Thus, in the third phase of the Battle of the Atlantic, from May to December 1941, the U-boats were forced to operate at greater distances from shore. Long lines of U-boats patrolled across the convoy routes in an effort to intercept supply ships. This in turn forced the British in June to begin escorting their convoys along the whole route from Newfoundland to the Western Approaches and—when the U-boats began to cruise off West Africa—the route from Freetown to Gibraltar and the United Kingdom as well.

In March 1941, the Allies captured cipher materials from a German patrol vessel. Then, on May 7, 1941, the Royal Navy succeeded in capturing the German Arctic meteorological vessel *München* and seizing her Enigma machine intact. Settings secured from this encoding machine enabled the Royal Navy to read June U-boat radio traffic practically currently. On May 9, during a convoy battle, the British destroyer *Bulldog* captured the German submarine *U-110* and secured the settings for the high-grade officer-only German naval signals. The capture on June 28 of a second German weather ship, *Lauenburg*, enabled British decryption operations at Bletchley Park (BP) to read July German home-waters radio traffic currently. This led to interception of German supply ships in the Atlantic and cessation of German surface ship operations in the Atlantic. Beginning in August 1941, BP operatives could decrypt signals between the commander of U-boats and his U-boats at sea. The Allies were thus able to reroute convoys and save perhaps 1.5 million gross tons of shipping. During this third phase, the U.S. Atlantic Fleet was first involved in the battle.

The entry of the United States into the war after the Japanese attack on Pearl Harbor ushered in the fourth phase of the battle, presenting the U-boats with a second golden opportunity from January to July 1942. Attacking unescorted individual ships off the U.S. East Coast, in the Gulf of Mexico, and in the Caribbean, German U-boats sank greater tonnages than during any other period of the war.

But sightings and sinkings off the U.S. East Coast dropped off sharply after the introduction of the interlocking convoy system there, and Dönitz found operations by individual U-boats in such distant waters uneconomical. Thus, in July 1942, he switched the U-boats back to the North Atlantic convoy route. This began the fifth phase, which lasted until May 1943. Now came the decisive period of the conflict between the U-boat groups and the convoys with their sea and air escorts. Increasingly, the battle was influenced by technical innovations. Most important in this regard were efforts on both sides in the field of signals intelligence.

On February 1, 1942, the Germans had introduced their new M-4 cipher machine, leading to a blackout in decryption that lasted until the end of December 1942. This accomplishment was of limited influence during the fourth phase, because the German U-boats operated individually according to their given orders, and there was no great signal traffic in the operational areas. And when the convoy battles began again, the Germans could at first decrypt Allied convoy signals.

But when Bletchley Park was able to decrypt German signals anew, rerouting of the convoys again became possible, although this was at first limited by rising numbers of German U-boats in patrol lines. In March 1943, the U-boats achieved their greatest successes against the convoys, and the entire convoy system—the backbone of the Allied strategy against "Fortress Europe"—seemed in jeopardy. Now Allied decryption allowed the dispatch of additional surface and air escorts to support threatened convoys. This development, in connection with the introduction of new weapons and high-frequency direction finding, led to the collapse of the U-boat offensive against the convoys only eight weeks later, in May 1943.

This collapse came as a surprise to Dönitz. Allied success in this regard could be attributed mainly to the provision of centimetric radar equipment for the sea and air escorts and the closing of the air gap in the North Atlantic. In a sixth (intermediate) phase from June to August 1943, the U-boats were sent to distant areas where the antisubmarine forces were weak, while the Allied air forces tried to block the U-boat transit routes across the Bay of Biscay.

The change to a new Allied convoy cipher in June, which the German decryption service could not break, made it more difficult for the U-boats to locate the convoys in what was the seventh phase from September 1943 to June 1944. During this time, the German U-boat command once more tried to deploy new weapons (acoustic torpedoes and increased antiaircraft armament) and new equipment (radar warning sets) to force a decisive outcome to the war by eliminating the convoys, first in the North Atlantic and then on the Gibraltar routes. After short-lived success, these operations failed and tapered off as the Germans tried to pin down Allied forces until new, revolutionary U-boat types became available for operational deployment.

The final, eighth phase, from June 1944 to May 1945, began with the Allied invasion of Normandy. The U-boats, now equipped with "snorkel" breathing masts, endeavored to carry out attacks against individual supply ships in the shallow waters of the English Channel and in British and Canadian coastal waters. The U-boats' mission was to pin down Allied supply traffic and antisubmarine forces to prevent the deployment of warships in offensive roles against German-occupied areas. But construction of the new U-boats (of which the Allies received information by decrypting reports sent to Tokyo by the Japanese embassy in Berlin) was delayed by the Allied bombing offensive, and the German land defenses collapsed before sufficient numbers of these boats were ready.

The Battle of the Atlantic lasted without interruption for 69 months, during which time German U-boats sank 2,850 Allied and neutral merchant ships, 2,520 of them in the Atlantic and Indian Oceans. The U-boats also sank many warships, from aircraft carriers to destroyers, frigates, corvettes, and other antisubmarine vessels. The Germans lost in turn one large battleship, one pocket battleship, some armed merchant raiders, and 650 U-boats, 522 of them in the Atlantic and Indian Oceans.

The Allied victory in the Battle of the Atlantic resulted from the vastly superior resources on the Allied side in shipbuilding and aircraft production (the ability to replace lost ships and aircraft) and from superior antisubmarine detection equipment and weapons. Allied signals intelligence was critical to the victory.

Jürgen Rohwer

See also
Germany, Navy; Great Britain, Navy; Signals Intelligence; United States, Navy

References

Beesly, Patrick. *Very Special Intelligence: The Story of the Admiralty's Operational Intelligence Centre, 1939–1945*. London: Greenhill Books, 2000.

Blair, Clay. *Hitler's U-Boat War*. 2 vols. New York: Random House, 1996, 1998.

Gardner, W. J. R. *Decoding History: The Battle of the Atlantic and Ultra*. Annapolis, MD: Naval Institute Press, 1999.

Howarth, Stephen, and Derek Law, eds. *The Battle of the Atlantic, 1939–1945*. London and Annapolis, MD: Greenhill Books and Naval Institute Press, 1994.

Milner, Marc. *The Battle of the Atlantic*. Stroud: Tempus Books, 2003.

Niestlé, Axel. *German U-Boat Losses during World War II: Details of Destruction*. Annapolis, MD: Naval Institute Press, 1998.

Offley, Edward. *Turning the Tide: How a Small Band of Allied Sailors Defeated the U-Boats and Won the Battle of the Atlantic*. New York: Basic Books, 2011.

Rohwer, Jürgen. *The Critical Convoy Battles of March 1943*. Annapolis, MD: Naval Institute Press, 1977.

Rohwer, Jürgen. *Axis Submarine Successes of World War Two: German, Italian and Japanese Submarine Successes, 1939–1945*. London: Greenhill Books, 1999.

Runyan, Timothy J., and Jan M. Copes, eds. *To Die Gallantly: The Battle of the Atlantic*. Boulder, CO: Westview Press, 1994.

Sebag-Montefiore, Hugh. *Enigma: The Battle for the Code*. London: Weidenfeld and Nicolson, 2000.

Snow, Richard. *A Measureless Peril: America in the Fight for the Atlantic, the Longest Battle of World War II*. New York: Scribner's, 2010.

Syrett, David. *The Defeat of the German U-Boats: The Battle of the Atlantic*. Columbia: University of South Carolina Press, 1994.

Williams, Andrew. *The Battle of the Atlantic: The Allies, Submarine Fight against Hitler's Grey Wolves of the Sea*. London: BBC Books, 2002.

Wynn, Kenneth. *U-Boat Operations of the Second World War*. Vol. 1: *Career Histories, U1-U510*; Vol. 2: *Career Histories, U511-UIT25*. London: Chatham Publishing, 1998, 1999.

Atomic Bomb, Decision to Employ

It could be argued that the decision to use the atomic bomb was actually made on December 6, 1941, when the first money was approved to fund its development. At the time, American leaders assumed the new invention would be a legitimate weapon in the war, and they never questioned that assumption afterward. Although there were extensive consultations about the employment of the atomic bomb, discussions always focused on how to use the new weapon, not whether to use it. The primary aim of Allied decision-makers was to achieve the unconditional surrender of Japan as quickly as possible at the lowest cost in lives, and everyone of importance assumed that if the MANHATTAN Project could produce a workable weapon, that weapon would be expended against an enemy target.

Although President Franklin D. Roosevelt's key advisers on the project concluded in May 1943 that the first operational bomb should be dropped on Japan, the choice of targets really did not receive systematic attention until two years later. A special Target Committee for the MANHATTAN Project began meeting in April 1945, and by the next month it had selected a shortlist of cities including Kyoto and Hiroshima. On May 31, a blue-ribbon Interim Committee appointed by Secretary of War Henry L. Stimson began meeting to discuss how best to use the new weapon. A suggestion made at lunch to try a warning and noncombat demonstration was quickly rejected for many practical reasons, and the committee recommended that the bomb be dropped without warning on a target that would make the largest possible psychological impression on as many inhabitants as possible.

A mushroom cloud of smoke rose more than 60,000 feet into the air above the Japanese port city of Nagasaki on August 9, 1945, after the dropping of the second atomic bomb. Three days earlier the United States had dropped the first atomic bomb on the city of Hiroshima. Five days later, on August 14, 1945, Japan surrendered unconditionally. (National Archives)

Eventually, military planners came up with a target list of Hiroshima, Kokura, Kyoto, and Nigata. Stimson persuaded the planners to substitute Nagasaki for the shrine city of Kyoto and then presented the list to President Harry S. Truman in late July. Truman approved the directive without consulting anyone else and wrote in his diary that the bomb would be used between July 25 and August 10. The new weapon offered the possibility of ending the war sooner, and he had no compelling reason not to employ it. Despite some historians' claims to the contrary, there was no reliable evidence of any imminent Japanese collapse or surrender. Although some leaders did perceive a display of the atomic bomb's power as a potential tool to intimidate the Soviet Union in the future, this was a secondary benefit of its employment and not a factor in operational decisions.

No single government document shows Truman's decision to use the bomb, but there were two relevant military directives from the Joint Chiefs to the U.S. Army Air Forces. The first, to General Henry "Hap" Arnold on July 24, designated the four possible targets. The next day, a similar order to General Carl Spaatz, who was commanding strategic air forces in the Pacific, added a date: "after about August 3, 1945." That document also directed that other bombs were to be delivered against targets as soon as they were ready. On the basis of these orders, Spaatz selected Hiroshima and then Kokura to be the targets for the first and second atomic missions. (Cloud cover on the day of the second raid caused the shift to the secondary target of Nagasaki.)

Some critics have questioned why there was not more deliberation about whether to use the terrible new weapon. The main concern for decision-makers was to win the war quickly while avoiding a bloody invasion or losing public support for unconditional surrender. Under the conditions in 1945, which had already produced fire raids that had killed far more Japanese civilians than did the attacks on Hiroshima and Nagasaki, no U.S. president or general could have failed to employ the atomic bomb.

Conrad C. Crane

See also

Hiroshima and Nagasaki, Bombing of; Roosevelt, Franklin D.; Truman, Harry S.; United States, Army Air Force

References

Kagan, Donald. "Why America Dropped the Bomb." *Commentary* 100 (1995): 17–23.

Merrill, Dennis. *The Decision to Drop the Atomic Bomb on Japan.* Vol. 1: Documentary History of the Truman Presidency. Bethesda, MD: University Publications of America, 1995.

Miscamble, Wilson D. *The Most Controversial Decision: Truman, the Atomic Bombs, and the Defeat of Japan.* Cambridge: Cambridge University Press, 2011.

Sherwin, Martin J. *A World Destroyed: Hiroshima and Its Legacies.* 3rd ed. Stanford, CA: Stanford University Press, 2000.

Wainstock, Dennis D. *The Decision to Drop the Atomic Bomb.* Westport, CT: Praeger, 1996.

Walker, J. Samuel. *Prompt and Utter Destruction: Truman and the Use of Atomic Bombs against Japan.* 2nd ed. Chapel Hill, NC: University of North Carolina Press, 2004.

Australia, Role in War

Australia played an important role in Allied operations in all theaters of World War II. Although its population was only about 7 million people, Australia covered 3 million square miles of territory and was strategically located in the Southwest Pacific. The war, however, caught Australians unprepared. As with the other Commonwealth nations, Australia followed Britain's lead, and Prime Minister Robert Menzies announced a declaration of war on Germany on September 3, 1939.

The exuberance that had marked the nation's entry into war in 1914 was sadly lacking in 1939. Australians remembered the heavy losses sustained in World War I. Many had suffered in the Great Depression, and ties with Britain had grown weaker. Initially, the nation's war effort was directed at supporting Britain in the European Theater of Operations, but after Japan's entry into the war, Australia became the principal Allied staging point in the Pacific, and during the conflict Australians served in virtually every theater of war.

With 10 percent of its population unemployed, Australia could easily raise men for the war effort, but weapons and equipment were in desperately short supply. In 1939, Australian defense spending was only 1 percent of its gross national product (GNP); not until 1942 did the level of Australian defense spending approach that of the other warring powers. In 1943–1944, Australia was spending 37 percent of GNP on the war effort, in large part from higher taxes and the sale of low-interest government bonds.

During the course of the war, the Australian economy shifted over to military production, and real industrial expansion was achieved. For example, during the war Australia produced 3,486 aircraft. Although new defense spending was concentrated on production of equipment including guns, ammunition, aircraft, and ships, measures were also put in place to increase the reserves. The government introduced conscription, but only for home service, which included assignments to Papua and the mandate of New Guinea. As part of the mobilization for war, industrialist Essington Lewis was placed in charge of the production of munitions, and newspaper publisher Keith Murdoch headed propaganda.

In October 1941, the Labour Party took power; John Curtin was prime minister until his death in July 1945. Labour would govern Australia for the remainder of the war. The generally ambivalent popular attitude toward the war changed when Japan joined the conflict in December 1941. The widespread rapid early Japanese victories raised the possibility that Australia itself might be invaded. This led to more government control over the economy, including the right for the government to order men and women to work in any occupation. Wages and prices were controlled, and rationing was introduced. The government also increased efforts at civilian defense and the improvement of coastal defenses. An even greater blow for Australians was the February 1942 fall of Singapore and the loss of two brigades of the Australian 8th Division there. The Japanese raid on Darwin later that month—the first time since the arrival of Europeans in Australia that Australians had been killed on their own soil by an invader—caused great anxiety.

Curtin then called for the return of Australian troops and naval assets from the Mediterranean Theater. Gradually most of these forces were released, but British prime minister Winston Churchill was loath to see so many fine fighting men lost at once from the North African Theater, and he called on Washington to take up the slack. The United States then became Australia's chief ally. Many thousands of U.S. servicemen arrived in Australia (eventually some 10,000 Australian women married U.S. military personnel). This influx required construction of bases and facilities, creating an acute labor shortage and necessitating the discharge of some personnel from the Australian armed forces. Italian prisoners of war were also pressed into labor service.

The labor shortage was also the result of the extensive Australian armaments program, which included an indigenous tank—the excellent medium cruiser Sentinel—that entered production in 1943, and a large shipbuilding program that produced three destroyers and 56 corvettes in addition to some 30,000 small craft and amphibious vehicles. Australian shipyards also repaired or refitted thousands of Australian and Allied ships. To alleviate labor shortages, women's auxiliary units were created for each branch of the military, and large numbers of women went to work in industrial occupations.

In March 1942, the Australian government agreed to the formation of the Southwest Pacific Command with American General Douglas MacArthur as commander in chief and General Sir Thomas Blamey as the commander of land forces. Australia became the principal logistics base for Allied military actions, particularly in the campaigns in New Guinea and the Solomon Islands. The Australian conscripts proved an embarrassment for the government; under pressure from MacArthur, who believed Americans were doing an unfair share of the fighting, the Curtin government secured in February 1943 what became known as the Militia Bill. It permitted deployment of conscripts overseas, although this was to be limited to the Southwest Pacific Area. In August 1943, the Australian Labour Party scored a resounding election victory.

Tensions developed (largely behind the scenes) between MacArthur and the Australian government and armed forces, especially given MacArthur's tendency to take credit himself for any successes and blame others for anything that went wrong. His disparaging attitude toward Australians notwithstanding, Australians distinguished themselves in every theater of war, including North Africa and the Mediterranean and also with the Royal Australian Air Force in Bomber Command. Australian troops scored important successes on the ground in New Guinea and Papua, and they also helped garrison Allied island conquests. In 1945, Australian troops led the invasions of Borneo and Tarakan. They were also in garrison on New Britain Island. The July 1945 invasion of Balikpapan was marked the largest amphibious operation undertaken by Australian forces during the war.

By the end of the fighting, 993,000 Australian men and women had served in the army, air force, and navy, and more than half of them had been deployed overseas. In addition, the nation had suffered 27,073 military dead (including prisoners of war who died in captivity) and 23,467 wounded.

World War II had a profound effect on the Australian nation. During the conflict, Australia established formal diplomatic ties with many more nations, and after the conflict it took pride in its place as a principal Pacific power. The war also enhanced Australian relations with the United States at the expense of existing ties with Great Britain.

Thomas Lansford and Spencer C. Tucker

See also

Casualties; Churchill, Sir Winston Leonard Spencer; Japan, Air Force; Japan, Army; Japan, Navy; MacArthur, Douglas; Southeast Pacific Theater; Southwest Pacific Theater

References

Beaumont, Joan, ed. *Australia's War, 1939–45*. St. Leonard's, NSW, Australia: Allen and Unwin, 1996.

Beaumont, Joan, and Ilma Martinuzzi O'Brien, eds. *Under Suspicion: Citizenship and Internment in Australia during the Second World War*. Canberra: National Museum of Australia Press, 2008.

Curran, James. *Curtin's Empire*. Cambridge: Cambridge University Press, 2012.

Day, David. *The Great Betrayal: Britain, Australia and the Onset of the Pacific War, 1939–42*. New York: W. W. Norton, 1989.

Day, David. *John Curtin: A Life*. Sydney: Angus and Robertson, 1999.

Day, David. *Reluctant Nation: Australia and the Allied Defeat of Japan, 1942–45*. New York: Oxford University Press, 1992.

Horner, D. M. *Inside the War Cabinet: Directing Australia's War Effort 1939–45*. St. Leonard's, NSW, Australia: Allen and Unwin, 1996.

Jackson, Ashley. *The British Empire in World War II*. New York: Hambledon Continuum, 2006.

Johnston, George Henry. *The Toughest Fighting in the World: The Australian and American Campaign for New Guinea in World War II*. Yardley, PA: Westholme Publishing, 2011.

Potts, E. Daniel, and Annette Potts. *Yanks Down Under 1941–45: The American Impact on Australia.* New York: Oxford University Press, 1985.

Robertson, John, and John McCarthy. *Australian War Strategy, 1939–1945: A Documentary History.* Brisbane, Australia: University of Queensland Press, 1985.

Sarantakes, Nicholas Evan. *Allies against the Rising Sun: The United States, the British Nations, and the Defeat of Imperial Japan.* Lawrence, KS: University Press of Kansas, 2009.

Thompson, Robert Smith. *Empires on the Pacific: World War II and the Struggle for the Mastery of Asia.* New York: Basic Books, 2001.

Waters, Christopher. *Australia and Appeasement: Imperial Foreign Policy and the Origins of World War II.* London: I. B. Tauris, 2011.

Balkans Theater

The Balkan Peninsula lies between the Black Sea and the Sea of Marmara to the east, the Mediterranean Sea to the south, the Ionian Sea to the southwest, and the Adriatic Sea to the west. The northern boundary of the Balkans is generally considered to be formed by the Sava and Danube Rivers. In 1939, there were six states south of that line: Albania, Greece, Bulgaria, European Turkey, most of Yugoslavia, and southeastern Romania.

With the exception of Turkey—which remained neutral—the Axis powers of Germany and Italy gained the allegiance of some of the Balkan states and then invaded and conquered the remainder in 1940 and 1941. This move ensured that the Axis powers had control over the eastern side of the Mediterranean, and it provided the security on the southern flank that was a prerequisite to a German invasion of the Soviet Union. With

BALKANS, 1944–1945

the rapid collapse of France between May and June 1940, Soviet leader Josef Stalin moved swiftly to secure gains promised him under the August 1939 Soviet-German pact. The Red Army occupied Lithuania, Latvia, and Estonia. This development was expected, but Adolf Hitler professed himself surprised by the subsequent Soviet moves in the Balkans.

In late June 1940, Stalin ordered the annexation of the Romanian provinces of Bessarabia and Northern Bukovina. Bessarabia had been assigned to the Soviet sphere under the nonaggression pact, but Northern Bukovina had not. Also, unlike Bessarabia, Bukovina had never been part of Imperial Russia, and it was the gateway to the Romanian oil fields at Ploesti, vital to the German war machine.

Italy also sought to take advantage of the defeat of France as well as of Britain's weakness by opening new fronts in Africa and in Greece. In April 1939, Italian dictator Benito Mussolini had ordered Italian forces to seize Albania. Then, on October 28, 1940, he sent his army into Greece from Albania, without informing Hitler in advance. Hitler most certainly knew of the Italian plans but did not act to restrain his ally, nor did he reproach him. Mussolini's decision, taken on short notice and against the advice of his military leaders, had immense repercussions. Not only did the Greeks contain the Italians, they also drove them back and began their own counterinvasion of Albania. That winter, the campaign became deadlocked, which caused Hitler to consider sending in German troops to rescue the Italians.

Meanwhile, Hitler acted aggressively in the Balkans to counter the Soviet moves and shore up his southern flank before the German invasion of the Soviet Union. In November 1940, he forced both Hungary and Romania to join the Axis powers and accept German troops. Bulgaria followed suit at the beginning of March 1941. Hitler took advantage of irredentist sentiment but also used hardball tactics to secure the allegiance of these countries. He pressured Yugoslavia, and in late March, under German threats, Prince Regent Paul reluctantly agreed to join the Axis powers.

Meanwhile, early in March 1941, honoring the pledge to defend Greece, British prime minister Winston Churchill dispatched to that country two infantry divisions and an armored brigade. He hoped thereby to forestall a German invasion, but this step also forced the British Middle East commander, General Sir Archibald Wavell, to halt his offensive against the Italians in North Africa.

On March 27, elements in the Yugoslavian army carried out a coup in Belgrade that overthrew Paul and repudiated the German alliance. This move was motivated, above all, by popular sentiment among the Serbs against the alliance. Furious at the turn of events, Hitler ordered German forces to invade Yugoslavia. Marshal Wilhelm List's Twelfth Army and Generaloberst (U.S. equiv. full general) Ewald von Kleist's 1st Panzer Group, positioned in Hungary and Romania for the forthcoming invasion of the Soviet Union, now shifted to southwestern Romania and Bulgaria.

The German invasion of Yugoslavia began on April 6, 1941, with a Luftwaffe attack on Belgrade that claimed 17,000 lives. Eleven German infantry divisions and four tank divisions invaded from the north, east, and southeast. Other Axis troops, including the Third Hungarian Army, took part, but Hungarian premier Pál Teleki committed suicide rather than dishonor himself by participating in the invasion of neighboring Yugoslavia. The invasion was conducted so swiftly that the million-man Yugoslav army was never completely mobilized. Yugoslavia surrendered unconditionally on April 17.

Simultaneous with their move into Yugoslavia, the Germans came to the aid of the hard-pressed Italians by invading Greece. This move caught the Greeks with 15 divisions in Albania and only three divisions and border forces in Macedonia, where the Germans attacked. Also, the scratch British Expeditionary Force (BEF) in Greece was woefully unprepared to deal with German armor and the Luftwaffe, and between April 26 and April 30, it precipitously evacuated Greece. Many of the roughly 50,000 troops taken off were then landed on Crete. During the evacuation of Greece, British naval units were savaged by the Luftwaffe, with the Royal Navy losing more than two dozen ships to German air attack; many other vessels were badly damaged.

In May 1941, the Germans continued their push south by occupying the island of Crete in the eastern Mediterranean in the first airborne invasion in history. The invasion turned out to be the graveyard of German paratroop forces. Hitler saw the action only as a cover for his planned invasion of the Soviet Union, securing the German southern flank against British air assault and helping to protect the vital oil fields of Ploesti. The German invasion, conducted by parachutists and mountain troops carried to the island by transport aircraft, began on May 20 and was soon decided in favor of the attackers. Again, the Royal Navy suffered heavy losses, although it did turn back a German seaborne landing effort. Churchill's decision to try to hold Crete, unprepared and bereft of Royal Air Force (RAF) fighter support, ignored reality. But Hitler, by his aggressive Balkan moves, barred Soviet expansion there and secured protection against a possible British air attack from the south. These goals accomplished, he was ready to move against the Soviet Union.

Masses of German parachutists nearing the ground during the invasion of Crete, Greece, on June 26, 1941. This was the first large-scale airborne invasion in history. (AP/Wide World Photos)

From the very beginning of the Axis occupation, the Balkans were a theater for guerrilla warfare until the Red Army invaded in August 1944. In both Greece and Yugoslavia, there were Communist and non-Communist resistance groups, which often fought among themselves as well as against their Greek and Italian occupiers. In Greece, the lead was taken by the National People's Liberation Army (ELAS), which came to be dominated by the Communists, and the National Republican Greek League (EDES). In Yugoslavia, the Chetniks were led by former army officers. Soon, a rival resistance group, known as the Partisans, came to the fore, dominated by the Communists. As in Greece, these two groups would become bitter enemies, even to the point of fighting one another. Ultimately, the British, who oversaw Allied aid to the Yugoslav resistance, decided to back only the Partisans, a decision that helped bring Josip Broz (Tito) to power in Yugoslavia after the war. The Yugoslav resistance largely freed the country from German control.

When Italy left the war in September 1943, Germany had to provide the occupying forces on its own, severely straining resources in men and material. The Allies also conducted a number of commando raids in the Balkans, including the German-occupied islands of the eastern Mediterranean.

In late August 1944, the Red Army's second and third Ukrainian Fronts launched an offensive in Romania against Army Group Südukraine. Romania and Bulgaria soon capitulated and then switched sides, declaring war on Germany. In the case of Romania, these events occurred on August 23 and September 4, and for Bulgaria, they took place on August 25 and December 8, 1944. In Greece, the Communists made three attempts to seize power: the first came during the 1943–1944 Axis occupation in anticipation of an early end to the war; the second occurred in Athens in December 1944; and the third effort came in the form of a bloody and prolonged civil war from 1946 to 1949. World War II in the Balkans was extremely costly in terms of human casualties, both directly—in actual military losses and civilian casualties resulting from warfare—and indirectly, stemming from shortages of food and other necessities.

In the immediate postwar period, the alignment of the Balkans actually worked out by and large along the lines of the agreement made between Churchill and Stalin at Moscow in October 1944. The Soviet Union dominated Romania and Bulgaria, whereas Greece ended up in the Western camp. Yugoslavia, which was to have been a fifty-fifty arrangement, freed itself from Moscow's grip in 1949.

Thomas J. Weiler and Spencer C. Tucker

See also

Churchill, Sir Winston Leonard Spencer; Collaboration; Greece, Role in War; Hitler, Adolf; Italy, Air Force; Italy, Army; Italy, Navy; Mussolini, Benito; Resistance; Soviet Union, Army; Stalin, Josef

References

Beevor, Anthony. *Crete: The Battle and the Resistance.* Boulder, CO: Westview Press, 1994.

Blau, George E. *Invasion Balkans! The German Campaign in the Balkans, Spring 1941.* Shippensburg, PA: Burd Street Press, 1997.

Catherwood, Christopher. *The Balkans in World War II: Britain's Balkan Dilemma.* New York: Palgrave Macmillan, 2004.

Glantz, David M. *Red Storm over the Balkans: The Failed Soviet Invasion of Romania, Spring 1944*. Lawrence, KS: University Press of Kansas, 2006.

Glenny, Misha. *The Balkans: Nationalism, War, and the Great Powers, 1804–1999*. New York: Viking Penguin, 2000.

Kennedy, Robert M. *Hold the Balkans! German Antiguerrilla Operations in the Balkans, 1941–1944*. Shippensburg, PA: White Mane Press, 2001.

Lucas, Peter. *The OSS in World War II Albania: Covert Operations and Collaboration with Communist Partisans*. Jefferson, SC: McFarland, 2007.

Mazower M. *Inside Hitler's Greece: The Experience of Occupation, 1941–1944*. New Haven, CT: Yale University Press, 1993.

Shepherd, Ben. *Terror in the Balkans: German Armies and Partisan Warfare*. Cambridge, MA: Harvard University Press, 2012.

Tomasevich, Jozo. *War and Revolution in Yugoslavia, 1941–1945: Occupation and Collaboration*. Stanford, CA: Stanford University Press, 2002.

Bradley, Omar Nelson (1893–1981)

Omar Nelson Bradley, a U.S. Army general, commanded 12th Army Group. Born in Clark, Missouri, on February 12, 1893, Omar Bradley secured an appointment to the U.S. Military Academy in 1911. He graduated in 1915, a member of what would become known as the "class the stars fell on," and was commissioned a second lieutenant of infantry.

Assigned to the 14th Infantry Regiment in Spokane, Washington, Bradley saw service along the Mexican border during the 1916 crisis that followed Pancho Villa's raid on Columbus, New Mexico. Like his classmate Dwight D. Eisenhower, Bradley missed combat in World War I. During the interwar period, his career followed a familiar pattern, with a number of troop commands interspersed with assignments at various military schools, including West Point. His most significant assignment was as chief of the Weapons Section during Colonel George C. Marshall's tenure as deputy commandant at the Infantry School at Fort Benning, Georgia.

Bradley graduated from the Army War College in 1934. Following service in General Marshall's secretariat of the General Staff between 1939 and 1941, he was promoted to brigadier general in February 1941 and assigned command of the Infantry School. Promotion to major general followed in February 1942, and Bradley successively commanded the 82nd Infantry Division and the 28th National Guard Division. In February 1943, Marshall dispatched him to North Africa, where General Eisenhower assigned him as deputy commander of Lieutenant General George S. Patton's II Corps in the wake of the Kasserine Pass debacle. When Patton assumed command of Seventh Army, Bradley took command of II Corps and led it with great distinction both in Tunisia and in Sicily.

In October 1943, Bradley assumed command of First Army and transferred to England to prepare for the cross-Channel invasion. He commanded U.S. ground forces on D-Day in Operation OVERLORD and during the ensuing Normandy Campaign. On July 26, First Army broke the German lines outside Saint-Lô in Operation COBRA, Bradley's operational masterpiece. On August 1, 1944, he assumed command of 12th Army

General Omar Bradley, shown here around 1943, commanded II Corps in North Africa and Sicily in 1943. During the invasion of Western Europe, he commanded 12th Army Group, the largest army deployed by the United States in World War II. He later served as chief of staff of the army and then first chairman of the Joint Chiefs of Staff, when he was advanced to general of the armies, the last U.S. soldier to be made a five-star general. (Library of Congress)

Group, which then encompassed General Courtney Hodges's First Army and General George Patton's Third Army.

During the subsequent drive across France, Bradley performed well but not spectacularly. His failure to close the Falaise–Argentan gap reflected poorly on his ability as a strategist and undoubtedly extended the war in the West. When Hitler launched the Ardennes counteroffensive, Bradley was slow to react, but in the subsequent campaign, he renewed Marshall's and Eisenhower's confidence by carefully orchestrating the advance of the American armies on Field Marshal Bernard L. Montgomery's right flank. By war's end, Bradley had clearly emerged as Eisenhower's most trusted military adviser. As 12th Army Group grew to include four separate armies, the largest purely American military force in history, Bradley was promoted to full general in March 1945, on the eve of Germany's capitulation.

Following the war, Bradley headed the Veterans' Administration, and in February 1948, he succeeded Eisenhower as army chief of staff. In this post, he championed the continued unification of the nation's armed forces. One year later, he became the first chairman of the Joint Chiefs of Staff and was subsequently promoted to the five-star rank of General of the Army in September 1950. During the Korean War, Bradley supported President Harry S. Truman's relief of General Douglas MacArthur and opposed expansion of the war. Bradley retired from active military service in August 1953 to become chairman of the board of Bulova Watch Corporation. During the Vietnam War, he served as an adviser to President Lyndon Johnson. Bradley died on April 8, 1981, in Washington, DC.

Cole C. Kingseed

See also

Eisenhower, Dwight D.; France, Role in War; Italy Campaign; Marshall, George Catlett; Montgomery, Sir Bernard Law; North Africa Campaign; Patton, George Smith, Jr.; Truman, Harry S.; Western European Theater of Operations

References

Axelrod, Alan. *Bradley*. New York: Palgrave Macmillan, 2007.

Bradley, Omar N. *A Soldier's Story*. New York: Henry Holt, 1951.

Bradley, Omar N., and Clay Blair. *A General's Life*. New York: Simon and Schuster, 1983.

DeFelice, Jim. *Omar Bradley: General at War*. Washington, DC: Regnery Publishing, 2011.

Jordan, Jonathan W. *Brothers, Rivals, Victors: Eisenhower, Patton, Bradley and the Partnership that Drove the Allied Conquest in Europe*. New York: New American Library, 2011.

Weigley, Russell F. *Eisenhower's Lieutenants*. Bloomington, IN: Indiana University Press, 1981.

Burma Theater (1941–1945)

As part of Japan's southern offensive in the aftermath of its December 7, 1941, attack on Pearl Harbor, its forces landed on the Isthmus of Kra and moved down Malaysia to take the great British naval base of Singapore. Thereafter, Japan repositioned forces used in the attack on Malaysia and moved into Burma to threaten the British in India. The location and topography of Burma helped determine that it would be a minor theater of action in World War II. As with much of Southeast Asia, the country features mountains and rivers running mostly north and south, and thus, it presented difficult topographical barriers for the Japanese forces advancing from east to west and for the British seeking to move from west to east. Terrain, climate, and disease remained formidable obstacles in the China–Burma–India (CBI) Theater of War.

Despite these problems, the Japanese sought to secure Burma in order to cut the so-called Burma Road and further the isolation of China and to bring about an end to the Sino-Japanese War, as well as to stir up nationalist opposition to the British in India. The British government, meanwhile, wanted to keep China in the war and contain Japanese military forces sufficiently to the east to prevent them from encouraging Indian nationalist sentiment.

On December 8, 1941, Japanese Lieutenant General Iida Shōjirō sent the 33rd and 55th Divisions that comprised his Fifteenth Army into Thailand. Then, on January 20, 1942, Iida's reinforced divisions, with air support, crossed into Burma, driving west toward Moulmein and Tavoy. The Japanese had some success in mobilizing Burmese nationalists (notably Aung San) to their cause, promising them independence from British rule. Some uprisings occurred against the British.

A mixed force of U.S. troops and Kachin scouts advance through the jungles of Burma. Kachin operations against occupying Japanese forces were among the most successful operations mounted by the Office of Strategic Services (OSS). (Library of Congress)

The British defenders, initially commanded by Lieutenant General Thomas Hutton, believed the difficult terrain would limit the Japanese to roads and cleared areas. The British suffered early and serious defeats because of this mistaken preconception. On January 30–31, 1942, the Japanese drove Hutton's ill-equipped force—equivalent to two understrength divisions of British, Indian, and Burmese troops—from Moulmein, inflicting heavy casualties in the process. The faster-moving Japanese then forded the Salween River and outflanked the British left. In the February 18–23 Battle of the Sittang, they nearly surrounded Hutton's entire force, destroying 12 British battalions and virtually all heavy equipment.

On March 5, 1942, Lieutenant General Sir Harold Alexander arrived in Rangoon and took command from Hutton but without markedly different results. Reinforcements from India restored British strength to two small divisions, but Alexander knew he could not hold back the Japanese, and on March 7, after hard fighting, he abandoned Rangoon and vast storehouses of supplies to the advancing Japanese; Alexander himself barely evaded capture. The Japanese occupied Rangoon the next day.

At that point, the understrength Nationalist Chinese Fifth and Sixth Armies, nominally commanded by U.S. Lieutenant General Joseph Stilwell, entered northern Burma along the Burma Road to help the retreating British. The British held the right (southern) side of a rough defensive line across Burma; the two Chinese armies held the center and left. Major General William Slim, who arrived in Burma in mid-March, took command of the Burma Corps, as the British units were titled. Slim turned out to be one of the top field commanders of the war. However, the British continued to move along roads, and the Japanese continued to move through jungle trails and thus were able to outflank and defeat them.

General Iida made plans to attack first at Yenangyaung. He intended to occupy the Chinese Fifth Army, leave the Sixth Army to the east alone, and then mass against the Burma Corps at Yenangyaung to secure the oil fields there.

On March 21, 1942, the Japanese struck the Fifth Army at Toungoo, cutting off the entire Chinese 200th Division. Chinese counterattacks under Stilwell, supported by Slim's British troops, allowed the 200th Division to fight its way free. Allied forces were slowly driven back, however. Although both Chinese armies at times fought well, they and the British did not cooperate effectively. Both sides were then reinforced, leading to a temporary pause in the fighting. The addition of part of the Chinese Fifty-Sixth Army permitted Stilwell to strengthen his defense of the Rangoon-Mandalay Railroad. Slim and Stilwell now laid plans for a counteroffensive, but Iida had also been reinforced, in the form of two additional divisions freed up by the surrender of Singapore.

The Japanese struck first, attacking the Burma Corps, defending Yenangyaung, and holding elsewhere. In the ensuing Battle of Yenangyaung (April 10–19, 1942), the Japanese temporarily trapped the 1st Burma Division, but British counterattacks, assisted by pressure from the Chinese 38th Division on the Japanese flank, allowed the 1st Division to escape. At this point, the Japanese 56th Division surprised the Chinese Sixth Army in the Loikaw–Taunggyi area and defeated it. On April 29, troops of the Japanese 56th Division entered Lashio and cut the Burma Road to China. Alexander now ordered his troops to withdraw across the Irrawaddy River.

General Slim continued to retreat under heavy Japanese pressure until he reached the Indian border and Imphal, with the Japanese pursuit halting at the Chindwin River. Meanwhile, the Chinese Sixth Army largely disintegrated under Japanese attacks, and other Chinese forces withdrew into Yunnan.

The rainy season beginning in May brought a welcome lull in operations for both sides. The Japanese now occupied four-fifths of Burma and needed time to organize their vast gains there and elsewhere, and the British wanted the respite to prepare a defense of eastern India. The cost of the fighting had been high, particularly for the British. A Japanese army of 50,000 men had beaten 40,000 British and Indian troops and inflicted on them some 30,000 casualties. The Japanese had also defeated 95,000 Nationalist Chinese troops, and only Major General Sun Li-jen's 38th Division withdrew as a fighting unit. At the same time, the Japanese had suffered only some 7,000 casualties themselves.

Allied air support had been largely ineffective. Colonel Claire Chennault's American Volunteer Group (AVG, the Flying Tigers) and Royal Air Force (RAF) fighters did what they could, claiming a high kill ratio against Japanese aircraft. But a surprise Japanese raid on Magwe on March 21, 1941, destroyed most British and American planes there and forced the RAF to withdraw to airfields in India. Although the RAF and Flying Tigers continued to try to assist the withdrawing Allied troops, ground–air communications were poor, and the long distance from their airfields and thus the limited time over target rendered their efforts largely ineffective. The arrival of long-range Spitfires for the RAF helped somewhat. And in June 1942, with land resupply to China through Burma no longer possible, Stilwell, now commanding the CBI Theater, began aerial resupply by transport aircraft flying from airfields in northeastern India to Kunming. The planes were forced to fly over the eastern Himalayas, known to the American pilots as "the Hump."

General Archibald Wavell, now commanding in India, worked to prepare defenses against a possible Japanese invasion of that country from Burma. Wavell realized that it would be a year or more until he would have trained troops and sufficient matériel to assume the offensive, but at the same time, he worried about the effects of inaction on British, Indian, and Burmese morale. As a consequence, he decided to conduct a limited offensive action during the 1942–1943 dry season. Accordingly, in December 1942, the British launched a counterattack by the 14th Indian Division of Indian and British units against Arakan, the northwest coastal province of Burma and an area largely separated from the rest of the country by rugged mountains. Although the Japanese there were badly outnumbered, the 14th Division moved too slowly, allowing the Japanese time to build up their strength and to fortify. Iida rushed in reinforcements, and in March 1943, troops of the Japanese 55th Division went on the offensive and worked their way over the mountains to hit the British in the flank and force their troops back to India by May. The British had again been proven wrong in their assumption that the Japanese would stick to existing roadways.

Meanwhile, Brigadier General Orde Wingate secured Wavell's approval to try "long-range penetration attacks" with his 77th Indian Brigade, known later as the Chindits (their emblem was a *chinthe*, a mythical Burmese beast resembling a lion, and they operated beyond the Chindwin River). This move was a British effort to try to beat the Japanese at their own game in using infiltration tactics. The Chindits would operate deep behind enemy lines in an effort to damage Japanese communications, destroy supplies, and sow confusion. The force of 3,000 Chindits would rely entirely on aerial resupply for food, clothing, medicines, and arms.

The first Chindit raid began with a crossing of the Chindwin River in February 1943. The force managed to cut sections of the Mandalay–Myitkyina and Mandalay–Lashio railroads, and in mid-March, they crossed the Irrawaddy River. This latter move brought major Japanese reaction, forcing a Chindit withdrawal in April. Newspapers in the Allied countries claimed a great victory, but in reality, the raid had been a failure militarily. The damage to Japanese troops and positions was slight, and the raiders lost half of their force.

Although the British fared poorly on land, the Royal Navy continued to control the Indian Ocean, which was immensely important for the long supply lines to the Middle East and to the Soviet Union. Meanwhile, to secure the loyalty of Indian nationalists, the British held out the promise of eventual sovereignty after the war. The major Allied problems in the Burma Theater remained the nearly complete lack of cooperation between the British and Chinese strategists, the inability to cope with Japanese tactics, and inadequate resources and supplies for a fighting front far down the Allied priority list.

Stilwell now mounted a drive into northern Burma. In February 1943, he committed the American-trained reconstituted Chinese 38th Division in upper Assam on the Burma–India border, where U.S., Chinese, and Indian engineers were building a road from Ledo. The 38th Division drove the few Japanese from the area. In late October, having secured the reluctant support of General Wavell and the agreement of Chinese Nationalist leader

Jiang Jieshi (Chiang Kai-shek) to employ his forces to reopen a land route to China, Stilwell committed the 38th Division south into the Hukawng Valley, where it was resupplied entirely by air. At the same time, the Chinese 22nd Division moved up from Ramgarh to Ledo. Meanwhile, Stilwell pushed construction of the road from Ledo.

In late November, Japanese forces struck the 38th and subjected it to punishing attacks, completely cutting off some of its units. U.S. aerial resupply prevented the Japanese from overrunning the troops, however. At the end of December, Stilwell arrived, along with light artillery, and the Chinese then counterattacked, driving the Japanese from the Hukawng Valley.

During January and February 1944, there was stalemate in the Hukawng Valley. Japanese Major General Tanaka Shinichi's 18th Division halted the advance of the Chinese 38th and 22nd Divisions. The Chinese resumed their advance in late February.

Much of the rest of Burma had remained quiet throughout 1943. In a considerable engineering feat, the Japanese built a 250-mile-long railroad across Burma, in the process employing as slave labor British prisoners captured at Singapore and some American captives. The Japanese utilized the railroad to mass supplies for an attack on eastern India. On August 1, 1943, they also granted Burma its "independence," although this step did not resonate sufficiently with the Japanese-installed Burmese government to enable Japan to exploit fully Burmese rice and petroleum resources.

The Japanese reorganized their forces in Burma, which were under the overall command of the Southern Resources Area commander, Field Marshal Count Terauchi Hisaichi, in Saigon. In March 1943, Lieutenant General Kawabe Masakazu had assumed command from General Iida of the six Japanese divisions in Burma. Kawabe had direct supervision of the two divisions in southwest Burma; the other four Japanese divisions were in the north under Lieutenant General Mutaguchi Renya. Kawabe directed Mutaguchi to invade eastern India with three of his divisions, and toward that end, the Japanese amassed some 100,000 troops. The Japanese intended to seize the Imphal–Kohima plain of Manipur, the logical British staging area for an invasion of Burma from central India. Their second major goal was to take and hold the rail line into Assam that passed through Manipur. Along it flowed most of the supplies that were ferried into China, as well as those destined for Stilwell's divisions in north Burma.

On the night of February 3, 1944, the Japanese attacked in the south, and once again, they surprised the British with the size and speed of the assault. But the now experienced British and Indian troops held their positions even when surrounded and did not surrender their supply dumps, which the Japanese needed to support their advance. British and U.S. aircraft flew supplies to the defenders in Imphal, and other aircraft strafed the Japanese. General Slim also organized a relief column, drove it to Imphal, and broke the siege after 88 days on June 22. After desperate fighting by both sides, the Japanese, short of supplies and facing the onset of the monsoon season, called off the attack, and Fifteenth Army began to withdraw.

In October 1943, Vice Admiral Lord Louis Mountbatten had taken up his post as commander of the new South-East Asia Command, although command ambiguities remained. He and Slim agreed that British forces could not do much until the next dry season, although they were willing to organize some spoiling attacks to take pressure off a larger offensive sought by General Stilwell for his Chinese units. Wingate, now a major general and enjoying British prime minister Winston Churchill's full support, planned a second and even more audacious raid for his Chindits that would include three brigades supported logistically by the U.S. Army Air Forces. The operation involved 25,000 men, of whom 3,000 were Americans. Led briefly by Brigadier General Frank Merrill, the U.S. force was known as Merrill's Marauders.

The March 1944 raid began with high promise, but the whole venture was doomed from the start because its success rested on the active participation of Chinese divisions. These forces were being husbanded by Jiang Jieshi, who drove his chief of staff, Stilwell (also commanding all U.S. forces in the CBI Theater), to distraction. In secret instructions to his generals, Jiang sharply limited Chinese military involvement, which in any case proved to be ineffectual. Another factor that contributed to the failure of the raid was the death of Wingate in a plane crash in India on March 24, whereupon Stilwell controlled operations. Wingate and Stilwell were much alike—both eccentric and dynamic—but they seldom disclosed their intentions, and as a result, there were serious failures in planning and staff work. Stilwell, in fact, disliked the British and did not use the Chindits effectively. Nor did he understand the difficulties facing guerrilla forces while dependent on aerial resupply but operating as conventional units.

The Japanese, heavily outnumbered in the air and lacking other modern weapons, fought back with considerable tenacity. Finally, the monsoon rains that began in mid-May slowed the offensive and brought more malaria. By June, the chief Allied enemies were not the Japanese but exhaustion, malnutrition, and disease. Although the raid inflicted 50,000 Japanese casualties against only 17,000 for the British, Allied forces were obliged to withdraw from Burma in July. Since it was ultimately unsuccessful, the 1944 Burma Campaign has remained a controversial subject. Unfortunately for all involved, it had no practical effect on the outcome of the war.

The lack of Chinese support in this operation displeased U.S. leaders, who had hoped that Nationalist armies would tie down the Japanese forces. Jiang, however, seemed more preoccupied with building up his own strength so that he could do battle with his domestic opposition, the Chinese Communists, after the war. Washington's realization that it could not count on Jiang to fight the Japanese resulted in increased support for forces under Admiral Chester Nimitz in the central Pacific and General Douglas MacArthur in the southwest Pacific.

As the Japanese offensive ended, the Allies began their own offensive in October 1944, with the British largely in support of a Chinese attack. Stilwell employed five American-trained and American-equipped Chinese divisions to take Myitkyana. Opposing them was the Japanese Thirty-Third Army, composed of three depleted divisions commanded by Lieutenant General Honda Masaki. Stilwell hoped to be able to trap the Thirty-Third Army between the five divisions in Burma and the Y-Force in Yunnan. However, Stilwell's poor relationship with Jiang and the situation in China after the Japanese attacked to remove the threat of U.S. strategic bombers there led Jiang to demand that Washington replace Stilwell. This change occurred on October 18, with Stilwell succeeded by Lieutenant General Daniel Sultan. Jiang's recall of two of the Chinese divisions from Burma to help stop the Japanese offensive in south China brought the Chinese offensive against the Japanese in Burma to a halt in December.

By fall 1944, the Allied position in Burma had improved considerably and the Japanese position had weakened, reflecting the relative fortunes of each side in the larger conflict. General Slim followed up his successful relief of Imphal, and in October, the British crossed the Chindwin River. The new Japanese commander in Burma, Lieutenant General Kimura Heitaro, had 10 divisions. He wanted to let the British advance in the center and outrun their supplies; then, he would counterattack to cut off and surround the British. This approach set the stage for the climactic battles of 1945.

In December 1944, the Allies assumed the offensive in the south (assisted by landing craft no longer needed for the invasions of France), in the center, and from China in the north. The southern advance required crossing many rivers and canals, and the going was naturally rather slow, although the Anglo-Indian forces regained the port of Akyab and Ramree Island as Kimura withdrew. Meanwhile, two Chinese divisions advanced into north Burma, reopened the Burma Road against negligible Japanese resistance, and seized Lashio in early March.

The chief battle took place in central Burma. Slim figured out Kimura's plan, and with great fanfare, he dispatched forces to cross the Irrawaddy River while sending several divisions quietly to the south to outflank the Japanese, cut their line of communications and retreat, and possibly take the entire Japanese force defending central Burma. Advancing on a 140-mile front, the British captured Meiktila on March 4. They took Mandalay two weeks later, while repulsing a simultaneous Japanese counterattack against Meiktila.

Slim sought to gain Rangoon while the roads and rice paddies were still sunbaked, dry, and hard. On May 3, a combined amphibious, land, and airborne attack recaptured the capital city, and the fighting largely came to an end. Most Japanese troops fled to neighboring Thailand.

Charles M. Dobbs and Spencer C. Tucker

See also

China, Role in War; China–Burma–India (CBI) Theater; Churchill, Sir Winston Leonard Spencer; Collaboration; Great Britain, Air Force; Great Britain, Army; Japan, Air Force; Japan, Army; Japan, Navy; Resistance

References

Allen, Louis. *Burma: The Longest War, 1941–1945.* New York: St. Martin's Press, 1984.

Astor, Gerald. *The Jungle War: Mavericks, Marauders, and Madmen in the China–Burma–India Theater of World War II.* New York: John Wiley, 2004.

Bayly, Christopher, and Tim Harper. *Forgotten Armies: The Fall of British Asia, 1941–1945.* Cambridge, MA: Belknap Press of Harvard University, 2005.

Bidwell, Shelford. *The Chindit War: Stilwell, Wingate, and the Campaign in Burma, 1944.* New York: Macmillan, 1979.

Brower, Charles F. *The Joint Chiefs of Staff and Strategy in the Pacific War, 1943–1945.* New York: Palgrave Macmillan, 2012.

Callahan, Raymond A. *Burma, 1942–1945.* London: Davis-Poynton, 1978.

Daugherty, Leo J., III. *The Allied Resupply Effort in the China–Burma–India Theater during World War II.* Jefferson, NC: McFarland, 2008.

Goodall, Felicity. *Exodus Burma: The British Escape through the Jungles of Death 1942.* Stroud: History Press, 2011.

Lunt, James D. *"A Hell of a Licking": The Retreat from Burma, 1941–1942.* London: Collins, 1986.

McLynn, Frank. *The Burma Campaign: Disaster into Triumph, 1942–45.* New Haven, CT: Yale University Press, 2011.

Prefer, Nathan N. *Vinegar Joe's War: Stilwell's Campaigns for Burma.* Novato, CA: Presidio, 2000.

Redding, Tony. *War in the Wilderness: The Chindits in Burma 1943–1944.* Reprint ed. Stroud: The History Press, 2011.

Warren, Alan. *Burma 1942: The Road from Rangoon to Mandalay.* New York: Continuum, 2012.

Webster, Donovan. *The Burma Road: The Epic Story of the China–Burma–India Theater in World War II.* New York: Farrar, Straus and Giroux, 2003.

Y'Blood, William T. *Air Commandos against Japan: Allied Special Operations in World War II Burma.* Annapolis, MD: Naval Institute Press, 2008.

Canada, Role in War

Arguably the greatest contributor, militarily and economically, among the "small" Allied powers in World War II, Canada put 10 percent of its population—slightly more than 1 million men and women—into uniform and provided the fourth-largest output of war matériel.

Canada entered the war superficially united, but French Canadian support was lukewarm, and the specter of overseas conscription, which had been so divisive in World War I, loomed. Since Canada's military contribution could not be decisive, conscription remained a political issue, and its potential for wrecking national unity could not be overestimated.

Prewar isolationism had left Canada virtually disarmed, but when Canadian leaders declared war a week after Britain did (a pointed display of their country's status as a completely self-governing dominion), they were confident that a military effort on the scale of World War I would be unnecessary. This time, Ottawa promised to match commitments to resources and make the economic sinews of war, not expeditionary forces, its priority. Predictably, this "limited liabilities" policy did not survive the defeat of France. Thereafter, for Canada, it would be total war.

On the economic front, after some faltering steps, the results were magnificent. Underutilized capacity, the country's bane during the Great Depression, aided the government in its task of mobilizing the war economy. Coming up with the staggering sums to pay for it all proved an equal challenge. American neutrality—and Britain's precarious economic and financial position—greatly complicated Ottawa's task, a situation finally resolved by the Hyde Park agreement signed with the United States in April 1941. By 1944, the gross national product (GNP) had more than doubled, with 50 percent of that figure being war production. Although foodstuff and vital raw materials such as nickel and aluminum dominated Canada's wartime exports to the United States and Britain, the production of armaments—including close to 1 million motor vehicles—was also very significant. Sound management and the advantages of virtual economic integration with the United States ensured that Canada, alone among the Allies, avoided having to seek Lend-Lease assistance; it even launched its own generous Mutual Assistance Program, with Britain being the chief beneficiary.

Given these very significant contributions to the common cause, Canadian officials aspired to play a role in Allied decision making. Canada more than earned its appointment to the Combined Food and Production and Resources Boards in 1943, but when it came to grand military strategy, vague hopes of "sitting at the table" went unfulfilled. Gracefully, if somewhat reluctantly, Ottawa accepted its status as a junior partner.

From the outset, Prime Minister Mackenzie King's focus had been to help Britain, an approach the great majority of Canadians embraced. Doing so necessitated close cooperation—especially economic cooperation—with the United States. The presumption that Canada could serve as a linchpin between Washington and London was a Canadian conceit, although certainly, a neutral United States could materially assist Britain by helping Canada. Once the United States entered the war, however, direct engagement with the British rendered Canada's erstwhile diplomatic role superfluous. For reasons of mutual benefit, Canadian–American ties deepened steadily. As leading Canadian historian J. L. Granatstein has aptly concluded, "Britain's weakness forced Canada into the arms of the United States," but it generally went willingly and certainly profitably. With a war to win, few Canadians worried about the long-term implications of this shift in regard to their sovereignty.

In military terms, Canada boasted the fourth-largest air force and third-largest navy among the Allies by 1945, as well as an expeditionary force of nearly six divisions. In keeping with the country's "Atlanticist" orientation, Ottawa committed virtually the entire force to Europe. It is scarcely an exaggeration to say the Pacific war, save for some panic after Pearl Harbor, hardly touched the Canadian consciousness.

Nationalism dictated that the government follow a "Canadianization" policy whereby the armed forces would, as far as possible, fight in recognizable national units under national command. At the same time, the English Canadian majority's undiminished emotional attachment to Britain, not to mention practical considerations, guaranteed that these forces would operate under overall British command and fight in British campaigns—in other words, the military-political relationship formalized in 1917 and 1918 would continue. Unfortunately, Canadianization would prove a mixed blessing. On the one hand, it satisfied (and encouraged) national pride and unquestionably aided the voluntary enlistment system. On the other, the limited availability of experienced Canadian commanders—and, particularly in the Royal Canadian Navy (RCN) and Royal Canadian Air Force (RCAF), the inability of domestic industry to produce technically sophisticated armaments in a timely fashion—exacerbated the enormous growing pains experienced by the rapidly expanding armed forces. Moreover, until mid-1943, nationalism also dictated that the army not be split up, a decision that denied the army necessary combat experience.

Canada's military role was that of willing subordinate. Building armed forces in wartime guarantees a steep learning curve, and Canada's experience in the war bears this out. In 1939, the Canadian regular forces numbered 10,000. At peak strength in 1944, 780,000 Canadians were in uniform: 80,000 in the RCN, 210,000 in the RCAF, and the remainder in the army. The achievements of the army in Italy, Normandy, the Scheldt, and the liberation of Holland; of the RCAF in the administration of the British Commonwealth Air Training Plan as well as participation in 6 Group and throughout RAF Bomber Command; and of the RCN in convoy operations in the Battle of the Atlantic, all materially contributed to the Allied victory, at a cost of 42,000 Canadian dead.

Canada's role in the war, both militarily and economically, was far more significant than non-Canadians have recognized over the years. That said, the major impact of Canadian participation was on Canada itself. The war rebuilt the Canadian economy, witnessed the implementation of overdue socioeconomic reforms, and greatly strengthened the sense of nationhood and national self-confidence. Isolationism gave way to internationalism, and the country emerged from the conflict well placed to do more than its share in the immediate postwar years to rebuild and defend Western Europe.

Patrick H. Brennan

See also

Atlantic, Battle of the; Casualties; Churchill, Sir Winston Leonard Spencer; Western European Theater of Operations

References

Bercuson, David J. *Maple Leaf against the Axis: Canada's Second World War.* Toronto, Canada: Stoddart, 1995.

Bouchery, Jean. *The Canadian Soldier in World War II: From D-Day to VE-Day.* Paris: Histoire and Collections, 2007.

Bourrie, Mark. *The Fog of War: Censorship of Canada's Media in World War II.* Vancouver: Douglas and McIntyre, 2012.

Douglas, W.A.B., and Brereton Greenhous. *Out of the Shadows: Canada in the Second World War.* New York: Oxford University Press, 1977.

Granatstein, J. L. *Canada's War: The Politics of the Mackenzie King Government, 1939–45.* Toronto, Canada: Oxford University Press, 1975.

Granatstein, J. L. *How Britain's Weakness Forced Canada into the Arms of the United States.* Toronto, Canada: University of Toronto Press, 1989.

Jackson, Ashley. *The British Empire in World War II.* New York: Hambledon Continuum, 2006.

Keshen, Jeffrey A. *Saints, Sinners, and Soldiers: Canada's Second World War.* Vancouver: University of British Columbia Press, 2004.

Sarantakes, Nicholas Evan. *Allies against the Rising Sun: The United States, the British Nations, and the Defeat of Imperial Japan.* Lawrence, KS: University Press of Kansas, 2009.

Smith, Denis. *Diplomacy of Fear: Canada and the Cold War, 1941–1948.* Toronto, Canada: University of Toronto Press, 1988.

Stacey, C. P., and Barbara M. Wilson. *The Half-Million: The Canadians in Britain, 1939–1946.* Toronto, Canada: University of Toronto Press, 1987.

Casualties

World War II exacted a heavy toll on the combatant nations and the world community as a whole. Although figures vary widely based on the source employed, perhaps 50 million servicemen and civilians were killed in the course of the conflict. World War II is thus the most destructive war in human history (see Table 1).

Table 1 Casualty Figures for World War II

Allied Powers	Battle Deaths	Wounded	Missing in Action	Civilian Dead
Australia	23,365	39,803	32,393	—
Belgium	7,760	14,000	—	76,000
Canada	37,476	53,174	10,888	—
China	1,324,516	1,762,006	115,248	1,000,000
Denmark	4,339	—	—	1,800
France	213,324	400,000	—	350,000
Great Britain	397,762	348,403	90,188	92,673
Greece	73,700	47,000	—	325,000
India	24,338	64,354	91,243	—
Netherlands	6,238	2,860	—	200,000
New Zealand	10,033	19,314	10,582	—
Norway	4,780	—	—	7,000
Poland	320,000	530,000	420,760	3,000,000
South Africa	6,840	14,363	16,430	—
Soviet Union	8,668,400	14,685,593	4,559,000	14,012,000
United States	292,129	670,846	139,709	6,000
Axis Powers				
Bulgaria	10,000	21,878	—	10,000
Finland	79,047	50,000	—	11,000
Germany	2,049,872	4,879,875	1,902,704	410,000
Hungary	147,435	89,000	170,000	285,000
Italy	259,732	77,494	350,000	146,000
Japan	1,506,000	500,000	810,000	500,000
Romania	300,000	—	100,000	200,000

Note: Dashes indicate figure is unknown.

Sources: Data from Bullock, Alan. *Hitler and Stalin: Parallel Lives.* New York: Alfred A. Knopf, 1992; Dupuy, Richard Ernest. *World War II: A Compact History.* New York: Hawthorn Books, 1969; Keegan, John. *The Second World War.* New York: Penguin, 1989; Keegan, John, ed. *The Times Atlas of the Second World War.* New York: Harper and Row, 1989; Krivosheev, G. F. *Soviet Casualties and Combat Losses in the Twentieth Century.* London: Greenhill Books, 1993; and Sorge, Martin K. *The Other Price of Hitler's War: German Military and Civilian Losses Resulting from World War II.* New York: Greenwood, 1986.

In terms of combat losses for the principal Allied powers, the Soviet Union had 8,668,400 military personnel killed. The majority of these were in the army, as the Soviets bore the brunt of the fighting on land against Germany. By the end of the war, the Chinese had 1,324,516 soldiers killed, a number of whom became casualties as early as the

1937 Japanese invasion. The United States, Great Britain, and France suffered far fewer losses, although in relative terms, given their smaller populations, the impact was still high. Of these powers, Great Britain's armed forces had 397,762 men killed. This figure includes losses incurred by imperial and Commonwealth forces: Canada sustained 37,476 deaths, India 24,338, Australia 23,365, New Zealand 10,033, and South Africa 6,840. The United States suffered 292,129 battle deaths, and the French lost 213,324 servicemen. The latter figure includes Free French forces.

Smaller Allied powers also lost heavily in comparison to their populations. Poland had 320,000 killed, and Greece lost 73,700. The Netherlands lost 6,238 servicemen. Belgium's armed forces lost 7,760 men. The dead of Norway totaled 4,780, and Denmark's losses were 4,339, a figure that includes merchant sailors in the service of other Allied navies.

The principal Axis powers had significantly fewer casualties than did the Soviet Union, but their populations were also much smaller. Germany, which waged a two-front war, suffered the most, with 2,049,872 dead. Japan sustained 1,506,000 deaths, and Italy lost 259,732 men. This number includes some 17,500 men killed in battle after that nation declared itself a cobelligerent of the Allies.

The other Axis powers endured heavy losses as well. Romania suffered greatly with 300,000 deaths; most of these incurred while the country was an Axis power but a small number being deaths suffered after it joined the Allies late in the war. Hungary lost 147,435 men, and Finland's dead numbered 79,047 soldiers, sailors, and airmen. Bulgaria, initially an Axis power, suffered 10,000 deaths, with some of these individuals being in the service of the Allies late in the war.

Civilian deaths greatly increased the human toll, as the age of total warfare embraced the civilian sector, too. Including battle deaths, total Soviet deaths in the war may have reached 27 million. Germany was second in terms of civilian losses. Most of these were the result of Allied bombing raids, which claimed the lives of some 410,000 civilians. Air attacks on the home fronts of other nations also carried a heavy cost. In Japan, about 500,000 people lost their lives, whereas Great Britain suffered 92,673 deaths.

Adding to civilian figures were atrocities committed against civilians. Chief among these was the Holocaust, the German campaign to exterminate Europe's Jewish population. The Holocaust claimed an estimated 6 million Jews. Half of this number were Polish citizens, and some 1.2 million came from the Soviet Union. Hungary's figure for Jewish deaths was 450,000, and Romania's total reached 300,000. The Baltic states lost 228,000 of their citizens. Germany itself sent 210,000 of its own people to their deaths.

The aftermath of World War II claimed additional victims. Some of these losses were the result of efforts by the Soviet Union and other Eastern and Central European governments to drive out their German minorities. Perhaps 2 million of the 14 million ethnic Germans who had been living in Eastern Europe died in the course of this expulsion. The final legacy of the war was an estimated 11 million people displaced by the conflict, some of whom perished from simple lack of food or shelter.

In addition to the death totals, large numbers of people were wounded, many of them seriously. These casualties, too, imposed a heavy financial toll on all combatant states after the war. Finally, it should be noted that death tolls in the war would have been much higher save for new miracle drugs and blood plasma.

Eric W. Osborne

See also

Eastern Front; Holocaust, The; Prisoners of War (POWs)

References

Keegan, John. *The Second World War.* New York: Penguin, 1989.

Krivosheev, G. F. *Soviet Casualties and Combat Losses in the Twentieth Century.* London: Greenhill Books, 1993.

Sorge, Martin K. *The Other Price of Hitler's War: German Military and Civilian Losses Resulting from World War II.* New York: Greenwood, 1986.

Central Pacific Campaign

The U.S. Navy's overarching strategy for defeating the Japanese by making a thrust through the Central Pacific had its roots in a long-standing concept for a maritime war with Japan. War Plan Orange dated to 1898, and though modified many times, the basic scheme remained consistent. Plan Orange called for marshaling the main battle fleet in the eastern Pacific, then steaming to the Philippines, where a decisive Mahanian-style battle fleet engagement would occur. Simultaneously, the navy would relieve the beleaguered Philippine army garrison. Faced with catastrophic defeat and total American command of the sea, Japan would presumably surrender.

The successful Japanese strike on Pearl Harbor completely disrupted Plan Orange and the Central Pacific thrust. With all Pacific Fleet battleships sunk or damaged and only five aircraft carriers available in the Pacific, the navy was in no condition to execute Plan Orange, defeat the Imperial Japanese Navy in a decisive battle for command of the sea, or even reinforce or evacuate the Philippine defenders. Consequently, for almost two years, the navy engaged in peripheral operations against the Japanese defensive perimeter, supporting the Marines and the army in the Solomon Islands and New Guinea and repelling Japanese main strike forces at the Battles of the Coral Sea and Midway.

By mid-1943, with Essex-class fleet carriers coming on line from the "two ocean" Naval Expansion Act of 1940 and fast battleships of the North Carolina and South Dakota classes for antiaircraft support and shore bombardment, the commander in chief of the Pacific Fleet, Admiral Chester Nimitz, stood ready to launch the Central Pacific assault against the Japanese Empire.

The dual-pronged Pacific strategy that emerged in 1943 represented a compromise between the services. The ABC Conference (between Britain, Canada, and the United States in March 1941) established Pacific operational areas, which the Joint Chiefs of Staff reconfirmed in March 1942. The agreement gave the navy operational control over the Central and South Pacific areas; the army had responsibility for the southwest Pacific. The army area commander, General Douglas MacArthur, advocated an advance up the New Guinea coast along the New Guinea–Mindanao axis to isolate the Japanese base at Rabaul

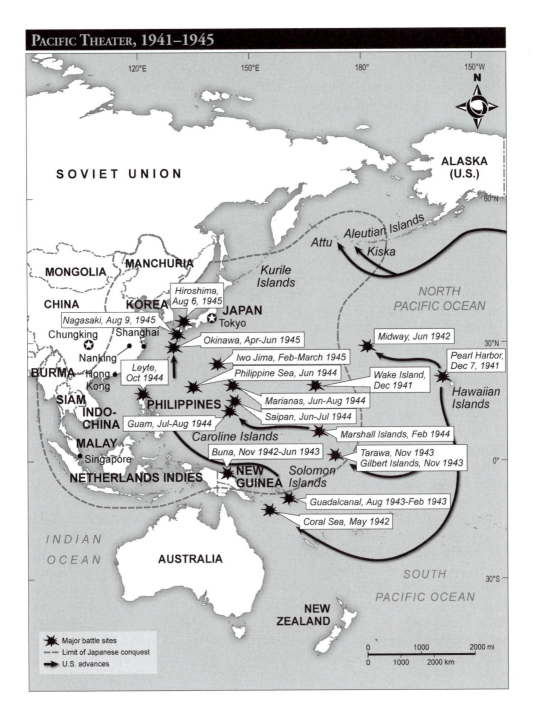

PACIFIC THEATER, 1941–1945

Major battle sites
Limit of Japanese conquest
U.S. advances

and drive to the Philippines. The navy, meanwhile, pressed for a Central Pacific thrust. In March 1943, the Joint Chiefs agreed on a compromise plan whereby both services would advance along their preferred routes while simultaneously supporting each other. The results of this dual-pronged strategy formed from compromise were devastating for Imperial Japan.

To face two simultaneous threats, the Japanese, unable to concentrate against a single-threat axis, had to stretch their air, naval, and ground forces perilously thin. By adopting a "leap-frogging" operational mode in both the Central and southwest Pacific, U.S. forces could attack strategic points, such as islands with airfields, while simply bypassing and isolating large Japanese garrisons, such as Truk and Rabaul. These latter then withered on the vine.

Another component of the Central Pacific strategy was the submarine offensive against Japanese shipping. This offensive further reduced Japan's capability to reinforce and sustain isolated garrisons as U.S. forces advanced key island by key island, beginning with Operation GALVANIC against the Gilbert Islands in November 1943. In the interwar years, the Marine Corps had made great strides in amphibious operations, and Guadalcanal had been a useful test of amphibious doctrine. Nimitz and his chief of staff, Vice Admiral Raymond Spruance, had originally conceived of the first thrust going against the Marshall Islands; however, the Gilberts were closer to Hawaii and within range of land-based air cover.

The Central Pacific thrust offered a number of advantages. The many islands and atolls provided a target-rich environment that prevented the Japanese from determining the precise route of advance and forced them to defend all points. The size of the islands and atolls discouraged the establishment of large garrisons. The long distances between islands mitigated mutual support, and American carrier airpower inhibited supply and reinforcement. Further, the line of communications from Pearl Harbor and the mainland United States would be shorter than that to the southwest Pacific. The Central Pacific also offered a more healthful climate than the jungles of New Guinea. And an advance through the Central Pacific would cut off and isolate Japanese forces in the South Pacific.

There were, of course, some disadvantages to a Central Pacific thrust. These included the requirement for overwhelming naval and air superiority, which could not be achieved until late 1943 and necessitated the defeat of the main Japanese battle fleet (which occurred in the Battle of Midway). The U.S. plan would also rely on successful amphibious operations, which had not been totally proven.

Operation GALVANIC commenced in late autumn 1943 with landings on Tarawa Atoll (the primary objective being Betio, with its airfield) and Makin Atoll. The joint army, navy, and marine force employed overpowering numbers, with more than 200 ships and 35,000 troops under Rear Admiral Richmond K. Turner, commander of V Amphibious Force. Task Forces 52 and 53 assaulted the atolls on November 20, 1943. Six fleet carriers and five light carriers, escorted by six battleships, provided overwhelming firepower, naval gunfire support, and air cover. Additionally, several hundred army, navy, and marine aircraft participated from the base at Ellice Island. Despite Japanese air attacks from the Marshalls, the air threat proved negligible. On Tarawa, strong fortifications, bunkers, hidden obstacles, and barbed wire slowed the advance—a prelude to future Japanese defensive schemes—and with orders to fight to the last man, the garrison staunchly resisted. Very few Japanese survived, another indicator of the bitter struggle unfolding in the Central Pacific Campaign. U.S. forces suffered a 17 percent casualty rate and encountered other problems as well, including faulty beach and surf intelligence, the inability of landing craft to negotiate shallow atoll waters, inadequate landing craft, too little advance shore bombardment, and poor communications. The Gilberts experience provided many valuable lessons for the U.S. Navy and Marines on how to conduct future operations.

The Marshall Islands were next. Despite a dearth of transports, Operation FLINTLOCK finally commenced on January 31, 1944. Eniwetok and Kwajalein (the world's largest coral atoll) succumbed to overwhelming force and the pounding from Vice Admiral Marc Mitscher's Fast Carrier Task Force 58. The Americans had learned from the Gilberts experience, and casualties among the assaulting forces were much lighter. With the capture of the Marshalls by March, 10 weeks ahead of the established timetable, the navy bypassed several heavily fortified Japanese-held islands and turned its attention to the Mariana Archipelago.

The assault on the Marianas, Operation FORAGER, aimed at taking Guam, Saipan, and Tinian Islands. From these bases, the Japanese home islands would be within striking distance of the B-29 Superfortress heavy bombers. The assault on Saipan commenced on June 13, 1944, with landings on June 16. Determined to halt the advance by interdicting the supporting naval forces, Vice Admiral Ozawa Jisaburo mounted an assault on the Americans in the Battle of the Philippine Sea. However, the assault, which commenced on June 19, turned into disaster as the better-trained and better-equipped U.S. Navy pilots decimated the inexperienced Japanese airmen in what came to be called the "great Marianas turkey shoot." Ozawa lost 325 of 375 attacking aircraft; Japanese naval airpower disappeared in a day, never to play any significant role in the war thereafter except in desperate suicide attacks in the last months.

Saipan was taken by July 13. The Marines landed on Tinian on July 24 and secured it on August 2. Guam, the last of the major islands, was struck on July 21 and was finally declared secured on August 10.

With the loss of the Marianas, the Japanese defensive perimeter had been decisively breached. U.S. strategic bombing of the Japanese home islands now began in earnest and ended in the atomic bomb attacks launched from Tinian a year later. From the Marianas, the two prongs of the Pacific strategy came together again with the invasion of the Philippines in October 1944.

Tenacious Japanese defenders and their fortifications did cause heavy American casualties, and the difficulties inherent in staging such massive invasion efforts presented formidable challenges to U.S. operations. Nonetheless, the Central Pacific Campaign succeeded decisively. The Imperial Japanese Navy's hitherto deadly air arm had been utterly destroyed, and the stage was set for the final Allied thrust through the Philippines, Iwo Jima, and Okinawa and on toward the Japanese home islands.

Stanley D. M. Carpenter

See also

Japan, Navy; MacArthur, Douglas; Midway, Battle of; Nimitz, Chester William; Pearl Harbor, Attack on; Southeast Pacific Theater; Southwest Pacific Theater; United States, Marine Corps; United States, Navy

References

Bresnahan, Jim, ed. *Refighting the Pacific War: An Alternative History of World War II*. Annapolis, MD: Naval Institute Press, 2011.

Brower, Charles F. *The Joint Chiefs of Staff and Strategy in the Pacific War, 1943–1945*. New York: Palgrave Macmillan, 2012.

Dull, Paul S. *A Battle History of the Imperial Japanese Navy, 1941–45*. Annapolis, MD: Naval Institute Press, 1978.

Frank, Richard B. *Downfall: The End of the Japanese Imperial Empire*. New York: Random House, 1999.

Harries, Meirion, and Susie Harries. *Soldiers of the Sun: The Rise and Fall of the Imperial Japanese Army*. New York: Random House, 1991.

Johnson, William Bruce. *The Pacific Campaign in World War II*. New York: Routledge, 2006.

Miller, Edward S. *War Plan Orange: The U.S. Strategy to Defeat Japan, 1897–1945*. Annapolis, MD: Naval Institute Press, 1991.

Morison, Samuel Eliot. *History of United States Naval Operations in World War II*. Vol. 8, *New Guinea and the Marianas, March 1944–August 1944*. Boston, MA: Little, Brown, 1948.

Spector, Ronald H. *Eagle against the Sun: The American War with Japan*. New York: Free Press, 1985.

Van de Vat, Dan. *The Pacific Campaign: The U.S.–Japanese Naval War, 1941–1945*. New York: Touchstone, 1991.

Williford, Glen M. *Racing the Sunrise: The Reinforcement of America's Pacific Outposts, 1941–1942*. Annapolis, MD: Naval Institute Press, 2010.

China, Role in War

China, one of the four major Allied powers of World War II, fought Japan alone for four years and throughout the war tied down more than a million Japanese troops. The war strengthened the position of the Chinese Communists and helped to precipitate the eventual downfall of the governing Nationalist Party—the Guomindang, or GMD (Kuomintang, or KMT)—of President Jiang Jieshi (Chiang Kai-shek).

For China, war began in July 1937, when long-standing hostilities with Japan, provoked by the latter country's effective annexation of Manchuria in 1931 and a continuing series of territorial, economic, and political incursions in other areas, caused a small skirmish near the Lugouqiao (Lukouch'iao) Marco Polo Bridge, close to Beijing (Peking) in Hebei (Hopeh) Province, to escalate into full-scale warfare. The Chinese invariably called the conflict "the War of Resistance against Japanese Aggression." Until December 1941, when China formally declared war on Japan and thereby aligned itself with the Western Allies after the Japanese attack on Pearl Harbor, Japan dismissively referred to the Chinese conflict as the "China Incident"; after that date, it became part of the "Greater East Asia War."

For much of the 1930s, the Chinese Nationalist government effectively acquiesced in Japanese demands. Although President Jiang believed that war with Japan would probably become inevitable in time, he sought to defer this until, with the help of German military advisers, he had successfully modernized China's armed forces. In the early 1930s, his first priority was to eliminate the GMD's major political rival—the Chinese Communist Party (CCP) led by the charismatic and innovative Mao Zedong (Mao Tse-tung), against whose forces Jiang mounted annual campaigns every year from 1930 to 1935. Only after December 1936—when another leading Chinese politician, the Manchurian warlord Zhang Xueliang (Chang Hsüeh-liang), captured Jiang and made his release conditional on the formation of a united Nationalist-Communist anti-Japanese front—did Jiang reluctantly and temporarily renounce his deeply rooted anti-Communist hostility.

The two camps never trusted each other, and political factionalism within the GMD also continued throughout the war, hampering Jiang's freedom of action and his ability to wage effective warfare against Japanese forces. Communist and GMD forces remained essentially separate, mounting independent operations. From late 1938 onward, the GMD government, headed by Jiang and based in Chongqing (Chungking) in Sichuan (Szechwan) Province, controlled southwest China. The Communists held sway over northwest China from their base in Yan'an (Yenan) in Shaanxi (Shensi) province.

In its early stages, China's war with Japan was one of rapid movement and military disaster. In late July 1937, Japanese troops took over the entire Beijing-Tianjin (Tientsin) area of north China. They inflicted a series of major defeats on Jiang's military, wiping out most of his modernized units and, over the following 18 months, successively took Shanghai and Nanjing (Nanking), Guangzhou (Canton), and Wuhan, China's provisional capital after Nanjing fell. Chinese troops had occasional triumphs—notably, the April 1938 Battle of Taierzhuang (Hsieh Chan T'ai-Erh-Chuang)—but these were rarely followed up. Japanese leaders assumed Jiang would sue for peace before the end of 1938, but to their frustration, he refused to do so.

Jiang adopted a strategy of "trading space for time," based on the assumption that by retreating, the Chinese could force the Japanese to overextend themselves, making them vulnerable to a lengthy war of attrition. This prediction proved substantially correct, as by 1940, Japanese forces were bogged down in an inconclusive war in mainland China, occupying vast tracts of territory without fully controlling them. Even so, and despite the scorched-earth policy Jiang followed, the regions he ceded to Japanese rule—from March 1940 exercised through the puppet regime of renegade Chinese politician Wang Jingwei (Wang Ching-wei)—included most of China's leading cities, its major industrial areas, and its most fertile and densely populated agricultural regions. Jiang's early, dogged resistance to Japanese invasion won him great national prestige, but his subsequent protracted abandonment of most of northern and eastern China to Japanese occupation eventually damaged his standing and weakened his authority.

From 1931 onward, Jiang sought assistance against Japan from Western powers and the League of Nations, but effectual aid was rarely forthcoming. The league restricted itself to nonrecognition of Manzhouguo (Manchukuo) and moral condemnation of Japan's policies, together with the imposition of limited economic sanctions on Japan—restrictions that only some of its member states observed. In 1938, the U.S. government extended limited economic assistance to China, making a loan against its tung oil supplies.

By the late 1930s, the growing demands of Germany and Italy in Europe preoccupied most Western nations, and the Sino-Japanese War remained a distant sideshow, albeit one with implications for the European powers' colonial positions in Asia. In the summer of 1940, the German conquest of most of Western Europe brought Japanese demands that Britain, France, and the Netherlands forbid the sale or transit of war supplies to China through their Asian colonies; France's Vichy government was also forced to open air bases in Indochina to Japanese warplanes. In the autumn of 1940, Japan formally joined Germany and Italy in the Tripartite Alliance of the Axis powers. These actions brought additional U.S. economic and military assistance for China, including the dispatch of American warplanes, and in 1941, President Franklin D. Roosevelt drastically tightened economic sanctions on Japan and repeatedly demanded the withdrawal of Japanese troops from China.

When Japan attacked American forces at Pearl Harbor on December 7, 1941, simultaneously declaring war on Great Britain and swiftly annexing British, Dutch, and American territories in East and Southeast Asia, China finally formally declared war on Japan. Jiang was named supreme commander of the Allied China Theater, receiving substantial amounts of military aid under the American Lend-Lease program. Even so—and despite his Western-educated wife's skillful dissemination in the United States of an image of China as a heroic, democratic, and modernizing state—Jiang's relations with other Allied leaders were poor.

Jiang's single-minded focus on Chinese interests, regardless of the impact on the broader Allied coalition, annoyed Roosevelt and British prime minister Winston Churchill. Nonetheless, it sometimes paid dividends. At the 1943 Cairo Conference,

The First American Volunteer Group (AVG) of the Chinese Air Force, commanded by Chiang Kai-shek's American military adviser Claire Lee Chennault, recruited American volunteer pilots to fight against the Japanese in China in 1941–1942. Here, a Chinese soldier guards a line of American P-40 fighter planes, painted with the distinctive shark-face emblem of the Flying Tigers, at an airfield in China, probably in 1942. (National Archives)

Allied leaders agreed that China should regain all territories annexed by Japan since 1895. Jiang also sought to end foreign extraterritorial privileges and concessions in China and, less successfully, to regain the British colony of Hong Kong. And at the autumn of 1944 Dumbarton Oaks meeting, China was one of the five great powers awarded permanent Security Council seats in the new United Nations. At the February 1945 Yalta Conference, however, Roosevelt, Churchill, and Soviet leader Josef Stalin agreed (in Jiang's absence) that, in return for joining the war against Japan from which it had remained aloof, the Soviet Union should regain the special rights tsarist Russia had exercised in Manchuria before 1905.

The continuing Chinese inability or reluctance to mount an aggressive campaign against the Japanese occupiers irritated British and American officials, especially U.S. Lieutenant General Joseph W. Stilwell, American commander of the China–Burma–India Theater and Jiang's chief of staff. Stilwell hoped to modernize the Chinese army and lead it in such a venture—an undertaking Jiang opposed as impractical, probably motivated in part by fears that this would weaken his own control of the Chinese military and his postwar position vis-à-vis the Chinese Communists. Over Jiang's opposition, Stilwell also sought to supply weapons to all anti-Japanese forces in China, including the Communists. Ultimately, at Jiang's insistence, Roosevelt withdrew Stilwell in 1944. Many Allied officials and journalists also deplored the pervasive corruption of the Nationalist regime that Jiang, though personally honest, tolerated.

Such shortcomings among the Nationalists enhanced the image of the Chinese Communists. Since 1937, they had supposedly been Jiang's partners against Japan, even though both the Nationalists and Communists believed that civil war was ultimately inevitable and sought to strengthen themselves for the anticipated confrontation. The Communists' Eighth Route Army, created in 1937, and the New Fourth Army built up by Lin Biao (Lin Piao) fought largely behind Japanese lines in central China and the northern Hebei and Shaanxi (Shensi) provinces, working closely with local guerrilla and partisan forces and building up bases that would potentially enhance the postwar Communist position. Communist forces adopted this strategy after their defeat in the "Hundred Regiments" Campaign of August to November 1940, in which Japanese rail and road networks in north China were attacked. CCP–GMD cooperation largely ceased after the 1941 New Fourth Army Incident, when Nationalist troops attacked and defeated that unit in the lower Chanjiang (Yangtze) Valley.

Despite the Chinese Communists' undoubted ruthlessness, their reputation far surpassed that of the Guomindang government. Idealistic young students and intellectuals flocked to join the Communists. Their selfless dedication and austere lifestyle and the charm and ability of their top leaders, especially Zhou Enlai (Chou En-lai), later China's premier, impressed Western journalists and officials who visited their Yan'an base, including the young diplomats of the 1944 U.S. "Dixie Mission." Nonetheless, despite their disillusionment with GMD leaders, senior American officials never endorsed the Chinese Communists.

When the war ended in August 1945, Japanese troops were still in occupation throughout China. In Manchuria, despite objections from Jiang, Soviet forces turned over to Communist Chinese units arms and equipment captured from the Japanese. American leaders, especially Ambassador Patrick J. Hurley in late 1945, were concerned about

Communist inroads in China and sought to strengthen Jiang's regime, to promote reform, and to encourage GMD–CCP reconciliation and the formation of a coalition government in which Communists would have limited influence. Between December 1945 and January 1947, the former U.S. Army chief of staff, General George C. Marshall, was in China endeavoring to secure an accommodation between the two sides. In January 1946, he arranged a temporary cease-fire, but it was broken later that spring when, as Soviet forces withdrew, GMD forces attacked Chinese Communist troops in Manchuria. No further agreement acceptable to both sides could be brokered, and civil war continued until the Communists secured military victory. The GMD government retreated to the island of Taiwan, and on October 1, 1949, Mao proclaimed the new People's Republic of China. From then onward, China would play a major role in the Cold War that succeeded and grew out of World War II.

Priscilla Roberts

See also

Burma Theater; China–Burma–India (CBI) Theater; Churchill, Sir Winston Leonard Spencer; Collaboration; Japan, Army; Marshall, George Catlett; Resistance; Roosevelt, Franklin D.; Stalin, Josef; Yalta Conference

References

Boyle, J. H. *China and Japan at War, 1937–1945: The Politics of Collaboration.* Stanford, CA: Stanford University Press, 1972.

Duus, Peter, Ramon H. Myers, and Mark R. Peattie, eds. *The Japanese Informal Empire in China, 1895–1945.* Princeton, NJ: Princeton University Press, 1990.

Eastman, Lloyd E. *Seeds of Destruction: Nationalist China in War and Revolution, 1937–1945.* Stanford, CA: Stanford University Press, 1984.

Eastman, Lloyd E., ed. *The Nationalist Era in China, 1927–1949.* Cambridge, MA: Harvard University Press, 1991.

Fenby, Jonathan. *Generalissimo: Chiang Kai-shek and the China He Lost.* Darby, PA: Diane Publishing, 2005.

Fenby, Jonathan. *Modern China: The Fall and Rise of a Great Power, 1850 to the Present.* New York: Ecco, 2008.

Ford, Daniel. *Flying Tigers: Claire Chennault and His American Volunteers, 1941–1942.* Rev ed. New York and Washington, DC: HarperCollins and Smithsonian Institution Press, 2007.

Heiferman, Ronald Ian. *The Cairo Conference of 1943: Roosevelt, Churchill, Chiang Kai-shek and Madame Chiang.* Jefferson, NC: McFarland, 2011.

Lary, Diana. *The Chinese People at War: Human Suffering and Social Transformation, 1937–1945.* New York: Cambridge University Press, 2010.

Li, Laura Tyson. *Madame Chiang Kai-shek: China's Eternal First Lady.* New York: Atlantic Monthly Press, 2006.

Morley, J. W., ed. *The China Quagmire: Japan's Expansion on the Asian Continent, 1933–1941.* New York: Columbia University Press, 1983.

Pakula, Hannah. *The Last Empress: Madame Chiang Kai-shek and the Birth of Modern China.* New York: Simon and Schuster, 2009.

Peattie, Mark, Edward Drea, and Hans van de Ven, eds. *The Battle for China: Essays on the Military History of the Sino-Japanese War of 1937–1945*. Stanford, CA: Stanford University Press, 2010.

Schaller, Michael. *The U.S. Crusade in China, 1938–1945*. New York: Columbia University Press, 1979.

Spence, Jonathan. *The Search for Modern China*. 2nd ed. New York: Norton, 1999.

Taylor, Jay. *The Generalissimo: Chiang Kai-shek and the Struggle for Modern China*. Cambridge, MA: Belknap Press of Harvard University, 2009.

Tuchman, Barbara. *Stilwell and the American Experience in China, 1911–1945*. New York: Macmillan, 1970.

Van der Ven, Hans J. *War and Nationalism in China, 1925–1945*. New York: Routledge-Curzon, 2003.

China–Burma–India (CBI) Theater

China–Burma–India (CBI) Theater, a general geographic reference for the immersion of East Asia, Southeast Asia, and South Asia in the war against Japan, also refers to an Allied military command structure in the Pacific Theater that was established early in the war. At the December 1941 ARCADIA Conference in Quebec, British prime minister Winston Churchill and U.S. president Franklin D. Roosevelt agreed to set up the American–British–Dutch–Australian Command (ABDA) under General Sir Archibald Wavell in India. Separate from but nominally equal to the ABDA was the China Theater under Generalissimo Jiang Jieshi (Chiang Kai-shek) as supreme commander, in recognition of China's role in fighting Japan since at least the start of the Sino-Japanese War in 1937. Lieutenant General Joseph Stilwell, who had more experience in China than any other senior U.S. Army officer and spoke Chinese fluently, became the senior Allied officer in the region. His two titles were "commanding general of the United States Army Forces in the Chinese Theater of Operations, Burma, and India" and "chief of staff to the Supreme Commander of the Chinese Theater" (Jiang Jieshi). The chain of command was confusing because American forces in China came under the authority of Wavell's ABDA Command. Wavell also commanded forces in Burma, whereas Stilwell was to have direct command of Chinese forces committed to Burma (initially, three armies of up to 100,000 men). From the beginning, Stilwell and Jiang did not get along, and Stilwell was repeatedly handicapped by Jiang's interference in military matters.

In February, following the loss of most of the Netherlands East Indies, the ABDA Command was done away with. From that point forward, the Pacific became an American responsibility, with the British assuming authority from Singapore to Suez. Jiang continued to control the China Theater, and Wavell, headquartered in India, had authority over India and Burma. At the same time, Stilwell formed a new headquarters, the American Armed Forces: China, Burma, and India. The command included the small prewar U.S. military advisory group and Major General Claire Chennault's American Volunteer Group (AVG, known as the Flying Tigers), later a part of Tenth Army Air Force.

This command structure continued until the August 1943 Quebec Conference, when Churchill and Roosevelt agreed on the establishment of the more integrated South-East

Asia Command (SEAC), with British Admiral Lord Louis Mountbatten as commander and Stilwell as his deputy. Operations in Burma were separated from those in India, now under command of General Claude Auchinleck, commander in chief there since June 1943.

Designed to improve Allied military operations in the region, the new command structure did not achieve that end. Conflicts and different goals remained, with Jiang being the chief problem in Allied cooperation. But the British and Americans also had different priorities. The British were mainly concerned with the defense of India and preventing the Japanese military from exerting an influence on growing Indian nationalism. London saw defeating the Japanese in Burma as the chief means to bring about that end, rather than as a means to channel supplies to China. British military efforts in Burma would thus ebb and flow. The United States was primarily interested in building up China's military strength, and Burma would be a chief route for these supplies to reach China; indeed, President Roosevelt saw China taking its rightful place as a major world power at war's end. U.S. military planners also saw China as a potential location for heavy bombers to be used in the strategic bombing of Japan. These conflicting views were exacerbated by the personalities involved. Stilwell continued to feud with Jiang, and he also held that the British were more interested in defending their Asian empire than in fighting Japan.

A Chinese machine gun crew aim their weapon in a gun pit in the Burmese jungle during World War II. (Library of Congress)

Stilwell wanted to recover Burma, and he worked hard to improve the fighting ability of those Chinese army units he could influence. The only way to deliver substantial military heavy equipment to China—which was essential if its fighting ability was to improve dramatically—was by way of Burma, and so construction of the so-called Ledo Road there became imperative. In the meantime, the United States undertook a massive logistical air supply operation to China from bases in India over "the Hump" of the Himalaya Mountains, the highest in the world. The ubiquitous C-47 (DC-3) aircraft was the workhorse for much of this campaign.

Construction of the 478-mile-long Ledo Road to connect the old Burma Road from Ledo, India, to Bhama, Burma, took 25 months. The new road ran through jungles, over mountains, and across 10 rivers. U.S. Army Brigadier General Lewis A. Pick had charge of this vast project, one of the major engineering accomplishments of the war.

Meanwhile, Jiang refused to yield operational command of the growing Chinese military establishment to General Stilwell. Jiang saw the Chinese forces as much as a means to defeat the Communists in China after the war as to destroy the Japanese forces in the current conflict. Stilwell fervently believed that, properly trained and equipped, Chinese soldiers could be the equal of any in the world, but all of his efforts to eradicate corruption, weed out ineffective leaders, and end political interference in the Chinese military were rebuffed by Jiang. The Chinese Nationalist leader repeatedly promised reforms but delivered only sufficient compliance to keep up the flow of U.S. military aid.

General Chennault and airpower advocates believed that Japan might be bombed into submission from bases in eastern China. Stilwell dismissed such views and pointed out that the Japanese could simply carry out an offensive to wipe out the bases. Nonetheless, the first production B-29 Superfortresses were sent to China from India, and an ambitious base-construction program was undertaken. Although a few air bombing missions were carried out, the Japanese responded by mounting a great ground offensive, the ICHI-GŌ Campaign, in mid-1944, during which all the bases were captured without significant Chinese ground resistance. The B-29s were shifted from CBI to the Marianas in the Central Pacific. Roosevelt now applied heavy pressure on Jiang to carry out the reforms advocated by Stilwell and place an American general, preferably Stilwell, in command of the Chinese army. Frustrated by its inability to turn China into a major theater of war, the United States increasingly used its massive naval strength to invest in the highly productive "leap-frogging" strategy of securing important islands as stepping stones toward Japan across the Central Pacific. As a result, China was more and more marginalized and downgraded to a minor theater of war, chiefly important for its role in tying down a million Japanese troops.

Stilwell, now at wit's end, reached an impasse with Jiang and was recalled to Washington in October 1944. He was replaced by U.S. Army Major General Albert Wedemeyer, a far more tractable individual bent on getting along with Jiang. The demands for reforms in the Chinese military came to an end. In effect, CBI ended in October 1944 when it was divided into two spheres of command, India-Burma and China. Stilwell's deputy, General Daniel L. Sultan, became the commander of U.S. forces in India-Burma and directed the Allied military effort in northern Burma.

The CBI featured unique air, guerrilla, and logistical operations. Among innovative military and air tactics originating in the CBI was the establishment of Long-Range

Penetration Groups, more popularly known as Wingate's Chindits and Merrill's Marauders. Utilizing air assets, British and U.S. commanders projected ground troops far behind Japanese lines, their communication and supply provided by air. Here and elsewhere, guerrilla operations were developed and intelligence and insurgency operations carried out. William Donovan and the Office of Strategic Services were active in the theater.

Finally, the CBI was a major scene of postwar confrontation. Early in the war, Japan had conquered and overrun much of China and most of the European and U.S. colonies in the Pacific. The arrival of Japanese forces in Indochina was a great blow to French influence, and the defeat of the British at Singapore had an even more powerful impact on British prestige. President Roosevelt envisioned the end of colonization after the war, but with the arrival of the Soviet threat, new U.S. President Harry S. Truman was less sympathetic. Although the Philippines, India, Burma, and some other states gained independence just after the war, the process of decolonization was actually delayed in some areas, resulting in costly wars in the Netherlands East Indies and French Indochina. As for China, American efforts by Roosevelt's inept ambassador to China, Patrick J. Hurley, to mediate between the Chinese Nationalists and Communists came to naught; that vast country soon disintegrated into civil war. The United States, which had already committed to Jiang, found itself unable to adopt a neutral stance and paid the price in influence when the civil war ended in a Communist victory in 1949.

Eugene L. Rasor and Spencer C. Tucker

See also

Burma Theater; China, Role in War; Churchill, Sir Winston Leonard Spencer; Collaboration; Japan, Air Force; Japan, Army; Japan, Navy; Resistance; Roosevelt, Franklin D.; Stalin, Josef; Truman, Harry S.

References

Astor, Gerald. *The Jungle War: Mavericks, Marauders, and Madmen in the China–Burma–India Theater of World War II*. New York: John Wiley, 2004.

Bayly, Christopher, and Tim Harper. *Forgotten Armies: The Fall of British Asia, 1941–1945*. Cambridge, MA: Belknap Press of Harvard University, 2005.

Brower, Charles F. *The Joint Chiefs of Staff and Strategy in the Pacific War, 1943–1945*. New York: Palgrave Macmillan, 2012.

Daugherty, Leo J., III. *The Allied Resupply Effort in the China–Burma–India Theater during World War II*. Jefferson, NC: McFarland, 2008.

Levine, Alan J. *The Pacific War: Japan versus the Allies*. Westport, CT: Praeger, 1995.

Plating, John D. *The Hump: America's Strategy for Keeping China in World War II*. College Station, TX: Texas A & M University Press, 2011.

Rasor, Eugene L. *The China–Burma–India Campaign, 1931–1949: Historiography and Annotated Bibliography*. Westport, CT: Greenwood Press, 1998.

Romanus, Charles P., and Riley Sunderland. *United States Army in World War II: China–Burma–India Theater*. 3 vols. Washington, DC: U.S. Government Printing Office, 1952–1958.

Sarantakes, Nicholas Evan. *Allies against the Rising Sun: The United States, the British Nations, and the Defeat of Imperial Japan*. Lawrence, KS: University Press of Kansas, 2009.

Schaller, Michael. *The U.S. Crusade in China, 1938–1945.* New York: Columbia University Press, 1979.

Spector, Ronald H. *Eagle against the Sun: The American War with Japan.* New York: Free Press, 1984.

Thorne, Christopher G. *The Approach of War, 1938–1939.* New York: St. Martin's Press, 1967.

Thorne, Christopher G. *Allies of a Kind: The United States, Britain, and the War against Japan, 1941–1945.* New York: Oxford University Press, 1978.

Thorne, Christopher G. *The Issue of War: States, Societies, and the Far Eastern Conflict of 1941–1945.* New York: Oxford University Press, 1985.

Tuchman, Barbara. *Stilwell and the American Experience in China, 1911–1945.* New York: Macmillan, 1970.

Webster, Donovan. *The Burma Road: The Epic Story of the China–Burma–India Theater in World War II.* New York: Farrar, Straus and Giroux, 2003.

Churchill, Sir Winston Leonard Spencer (1874–1965)

Sir Winston Leonard Spencer Churchill was British political leader, cabinet minister, and prime minister and minister of defense, from 1940 to 1945. Born at Blenheim Palace, Oxfordshire, on November 30, 1874, Churchill was the eldest son of Lord Randolph Churchill, third son of the duke of Marlborough, and a rising Conservative politician, and his wife, Jennie Jerome, an American heiress. Educated at Harrow and the Royal Military Academy, Sandhurst, from 1895 to 1899, Churchill held a commission in the British army. He visited Cuba on leave and saw active service on the Afghan frontier and in the Sudan, where he took part in the Battle of Omdurman. Captured by South African forces in 1899 while reporting on the Boer War as a journalist, he made a dramatic escape from Pretoria and went to Durban, winning early popular fame.

Churchill emulated his father—who attained the position of chancellor of the exchequer before resignation, illness, and premature death cut short his political career—by entering politics in 1900 as a Unionist member of Parliament. In 1904, his party's partial conversion to protectionism caused him to join the Liberals, who made him president of the Board of Trade (1908–1910) and home secretary (1910–1911) after they returned to power.

As first lord of the Admiralty (1911–1915), Churchill enthusiastically backed the campaign of First Sea Lord John "Jackie" Fisher to modernize the British navy with faster battleships and more efficient administration. One of the few initial cabinet supporters of British intervention in World War I, Churchill soon took the blame for the disastrous 1915 Dardanelles expedition against Turkey, which prompted his resignation. He spent the six months up to May 1916 on active service on the Western Front but regained high political office in July 1917, when Prime Minister David Lloyd George made him minister of munitions in his coalition government.

In December 1918, Churchill moved to the War Office, where he unsuccessfully advocated forceful Allied action against Russia, in the hope of eliminating that country's new

Bolshevik government. In late 1920, he became colonial secretary. Two years after Lloyd George's 1922 defeat, Churchill returned to the Conservatives, who made him chancellor of the exchequer in November 1924, a post he held for five years. By 1928, Churchill believed that the postwar peace settlement represented only a truce between wars, a view forcefully set forth in his book *The Aftermath* (1928). When Labour won the 1929 election, Churchill lost office, but he soon began campaigning eloquently for a major British rearmament initiative, especially the massive enhancement of British airpower, to enable the country to face a revived Italian or German military threat. From 1932 onward, he sounded this theme eloquently in Parliament, but Conservative leaders remained unsympathetic to his pleas. Throughout the 1930s, although Churchill held no cabinet position, he nonetheless continued to campaign for rearmament. He also became perhaps the most visible and vocal critic of the appeasement policies of the successive governments of Prime Ministers Stanley Baldwin and Neville Chamberlain, who effectively tolerated German rearmament, Chancellor Adolf Hitler's deliberate contravention of the provisions of the Treaty of Versailles, and Germany's and Italy's territorial demands on their neighbors.

When Britain declared war on Germany in September 1939, Churchill resumed his old position as first lord of the Admiralty. Despite the German attacks on the British aircraft carrier *Courageous* and the battleship *Royal Oak*, as well as the responsibility he himself bore for the Allied disaster in Norway during April and May 1940, he succeeded Chamberlain as prime minister on May 10, 1940, the day Germany launched an invasion of France and the Low Countries. Over the next three months, repeated disasters afflicted Britain, as German troops rapidly overran the Low Countries and France, forcing the British Expeditionary Force to withdraw in disarray that June from the Dunkerque beaches of northern France, abandoning most of its equipment. Throughout the summer of 1940, during the Battle of Britain, German airplanes fiercely attacked British air bases, an apparent prelude to a full-scale cross-Channel invasion.

Churchill responded vigorously to crisis. Although he was 65, he still possessed abundant and unflagging energy; his vitality was fueled by his habit of an afternoon siesta, after which he normally worked until two or three the next morning. His fondness for sometimes fanciful and questionable strategic plans often exasperated his closest advisers, as did his attachment to romantic individual ventures—such as those launched by the Special Operations Executive intelligence agency, whose creation he backed enthusiastically. Even so, Churchill was an outstanding war leader. On taking office, he delivered a series of rousing and eloquent speeches, affirming Britain's determination to continue fighting even without allies and voicing his conviction of ultimate triumph. Churchill also followed a demanding schedule of morale-boosting personal visits to British cities, factories, bomb targets, and military installations, which he continued throughout the war.

Besides rallying the British people to endure military defeat in France and the bombing campaign Germany soon launched against Britain's industrial cities, Churchill's speeches, which caught the international imagination, were designed to convince the political leaders and people of the United States—the only quarter from which Britain might anticipate effective assistance—of his country's commitment to the war. U.S. president Franklin D. Roosevelt responded by negotiating the "destroyers-for-bases" deal of August 1940, whereby the United States transferred 50 World War I–vintage destroyers to Britain in exchange for naval basing rights in British Caribbean Islands and North America.

In a versatile career that spanned four decades, Winston
Churchill, shown here as prime minister around 1941, was
a war correspondent, soldier, writer, and politician. Something of a maverick, in the 1930s he held no government
position and was known for his unrelenting opposition to
Adolf Hitler's Germany and calls for British rearmament.
Once Churchill became British prime minister in May
1940, after the loss of Norway, he proved an inspiring war
leader, whose stirring speeches came to symbolize Britain's
determination to continue the war despite the collapse of
Western Europe. (Library of Congress)

Since the war began, Britain had purchased war supplies in the United States on
a "cash-and-carry" basis. By December 1940, British resources were running low, and
Churchill addressed a letter to Roosevelt, who had just won reelection, requesting that he
provide more extensive U.S. aid to Britain. Roosevelt responded by devising the Lease-
Lend Act that was passed by Congress the following spring, which authorized the president to provide assistance to countries at war whose endeavors enhanced U.S. national
security. In August 1941, Churchill and Roosevelt met for the first time at sea, in Placentia Bay off the Newfoundland coast, and agreed to endorse a common set of liberal war
aims—the Atlantic Charter—and to coordinate their two countries' military strategies.

Churchill also agreed to allow British scientists to pool their expertise in nuclear physics with their American counterparts in the MANHATTAN Project, a largely U.S.-financed effort to build an atomic bomb; the project reached fruition in the summer of 1945.

Churchill was relieved by Japan's December 1941 attack on the American naval base of Pearl Harbor, Hawaii, and the subsequent German and Italian declarations of war on the United States because these actions finally brought the United States fully into the war and, from his perspective, guaranteed an ultimate Allied victory. In the interim, as 1942 progressed, he needed all his talents to sustain British resolution through various disasters, including Japan's conquest of Hong Kong, Malaya, Singapore, and Burma and British defeats in North Africa.

After Germany invaded the USSR in June 1941, Churchill also welcomed the Soviet Union as an ally, though his relations with Soviet leader Josef Stalin were never as close as those with Roosevelt. Churchill made repeated visits to the United States and met Roosevelt at other venues. In addition, all three leaders gathered at major international summit conferences at Tehran in November 1943 and Yalta in February 1945, and Churchill also met Stalin separately on several occasions. He traveled abroad more than any of the other Allied leaders, often at substantial personal risk.

Stalin resented the Anglo-American failure to open a second front in Europe until June 1944, a decision due in considerable part to Churchill's fear that, if Britain and the United States launched an invasion of western Europe too soon, the campaign would degenerate into bloody trench warfare resembling that between 1914 and 1918. Meeting Roosevelt in May 1943 in Washington, he finally succumbed to American pressure to open the second front the following summer. Churchill also resented intensifying U.S. pressure for the phasing out of British colonial rule, a prospect made increasingly probable by Britain's growing international weakness.

As the war proceeded and Soviet forces began to push back German troops, Churchill feared that the Soviet Union would dominate postwar Eastern Europe. Soviet support for Communist guerrillas in occupied countries and for the Soviet-backed Lublin government in Poland reinforced his apprehensions. In October 1944, he negotiated an informal agreement with Stalin whereby the two leaders delineated their countries' respective spheres of influence in Eastern Europe. At the February 1945 Yalta Conference, Churchill and Roosevelt both acquiesced in effective Soviet domination of most of that region. The three leaders also agreed to divide Germany into three separate occupation zones, to be administered by their occupying military forces but ultimately to be reunited as one state. In April 1945, Churchill unavailingly urged American military commanders to disregard their existing understandings with Soviet forces and take Berlin, the symbolically important German capital. Despite the creation of the United Nations in 1945, Churchill hoped that close Anglo-American understanding would be the bedrock of the international world order, a perspective intensified by his continuing fears of Germany.

In July 1945, the British electorate voted Churchill out of office while he was attending a meeting at Potsdam, replacing his administration with a reformist Labour government. Churchill was still, however, honored as "the greatest living Englishman" and the war's most towering figure. He used his prestige to rally American elite and public opinion in favor of taking a stronger line against Soviet expansionism in Europe and elsewhere, a position he advanced to enormous publicity in his famous March 1946 "Iron Curtain" speech at Fulton, Missouri. Churchill's six best-selling volumes of memoirs, *The Second World War*, presented a somewhat roseate view of Anglo-American wartime cooperation, and they were carefully designed to promote the continuing alliance between the two countries, which had become his most cherished objective. From 1951 to 1955, Churchill served again as Conservative prime minister. Declining health eventually forced him to resign from office. Churchill died in London on January 24, 1965. For many, his death marked the symbolic final passing of Great Britain's imperial age. Churchill received the first state funeral for any British commoner since the death of the duke of Wellington over a century before. An idiosyncratic political maverick whose pre-1939 record was, at best, mixed, Churchill rose to the occasion to become the greatest British war leader since the earl of Chatham in the 18th century.

Priscilla Roberts

See also

Atlantic, Battle of the; Great Britain, Air Force; Great Britain, Army; Great Britain, Navy; Hitler, Adolf; Roosevelt, Franklin D.; Stalin, Josef; Western European Theater of Operations; Yalta Conference

References

Berthon, Simon, and Joanna Potts. *Warlords: An Extraordinary Re-Creation of World War II through the Eyes and Minds of Hitler, Roosevelt, Churchill, and Stalin.* New York: Da Capo Press, 2006.

Costigliola, Frank. *Roosevelt's Lost Alliances: How Personal Politics Helped Start the Cold War.* Princeton, NJ: Princeton University Press, 2011.

Fenby, Jonathan. *Alliance: The Inside Story of How Roosevelt, Churchill and Stalin Won One War and Began Another.* San Francisco, CA: MacAdam/Cage, 2007.

Gilbert, Martin S. *Winston S. Churchill.* 8 vols. New York: Random House, 1966–1988.

Hastings, Max. *Winston's War: Churchill, 1940–1945.* New York: Knopf, 2010.

Jablonsky, David. *Churchill and Hitler: Essays on the Political-Military Direction of Total War.* Portland, OR: Cass, 1994.

Jenkins, Roy. *Churchill.* London: Macmillan, 2001.

Johnson, Paul. *Churchill.* New York: Viking, 2009.

Kimball, Warren F., ed. *Churchill and Roosevelt: The Complete Correspondence.* Princeton, NJ: Princeton University Press, 1984.

Larres, Klaus. *Churchill's Cold War: The Politics of Personal Diplomacy.* New Haven, CT: Yale University Press, 2002.

Lukacs, John. *Churchill: Visionary, Statesman, Historian.* New Haven, CT: Yale University Press, 2002.

Ramsden, John. *Man of the Century: Winston Churchill and His Legend since 1945.* New York: Harper Collins, 2002.

Reynolds, David. *In Command of History: Churchill Fighting and Writing the Second World War.* New York: Random House, 2005.

Roberts, Andrew. *Masters and Commanders: How Four Titans Won the War in the West.* New York: Harper, 2009.

Stafford, David. *Roosevelt and Churchill: Men of Secrets.* London: Little, Brown, 1999.

Toye, Richard. *Churchill's Empire: The World that Made Him and the World He Made.* New York: Henry Holt, 2010.

Weinberg, Gerhard L. *Visions of Victory: The Hopes of Eight World War II Leaders.* Cambridge: Cambridge University Press, 2005.

Collaboration

Literally "cooperation" or "unity of effort" but interpreted during World War II to mean working actively with the enemy, implying treasonable activity. The issue is a complex one, for collaboration could run from selling the occupier agricultural produce to rounding up Jews and actively assisting in the prosecution of military activities. Collaboration could be military, political, economic, social, or cultural. In any case, such activities implied treason (in varying degree, of course) on the part of the collaborator. One point that must be made, however, is that one side's "collaborator" was the other side's "ally," "loyalist," or "assistant." Collaboration with enemy occupying forces occurred on both sides during the war.

WESTERN AND NORTHERN EUROPE

France presents a complicated picture. Following their defeat of France, the Germans dictated armistice terms that saw them occupy about two-thirds of the country to the north and west. The French were allowed to establish an "independent" government in the remainder of the country, with its capital at Vichy. The term "collaboration" was actually first used in the course of a meeting between Vichy head of state Marshal Henri Philippe Pétain and German leader Adolf Hitler at Montoire-sur-Loire on October 24, 1940. Pétain and his supporters concluded that Germany had won the war and that, for the foreseeable future, that nation would dominate the Continent. The marshal therefore informed the French people that he accepted "in principle" the idea of "collaboration" with Germany.

Despite Pétain's pronouncement, the French population was bitterly divided, and a small minority at first rallied to the Resistance led by young Brigadier General Charles de Gaulle in London (he had been condemned to death in absentia by the Vichy government as a traitor). Germany had very direct sources of pressure on Vichy, including heavy "administration costs" that amounted to more than 60 percent of French national income, control over traffic across the armistice demarcation line, possession of a million French prisoners of war (POWs), and exploitation of the press.

Following the Allied invasion of French North Africa, the Germans occupied the remainder of France. While de Gaulle established his position in North Africa and the French Empire in general, Vichy premier Pierre Laval became increasingly open about collaborating with Germany within continental France, including active participation in the rounding up and deportation of Jews and the hunting down of partisans by the Milice, the 30,000-man-strong Vichy militia force. Meanwhile, as the fortunes of war shifted, de Gaulle's influence in France grew.

Certainly, a large number of French men and women collaborated with the Nazi regime, and many made sizable fortunes in the process. In addition, little was done after the war to punish such war profiteers. The carefully nurtured myth in postwar France of a nation of resisters was totally false, although thousands of French men and women did risk their all for the Allied cause.

Occupation arrangements varied in other western European countries. Belgium experienced a rather harsh German military rule, whereas the Netherlands and Norway had civil administrations, and Denmark was able to retain sovereignty until August 1943. After the war, the Belgian government punished, in varying degree, some 53,000 men and women adjudged to have collaborated with the German occupiers.

Vidkun Quisling of Norway was one of the most notorious collaborators, his name becoming synonymous with the term *traitor*. In February 1942, Quisling became minister president of Norway, but his effort to Nazify his country was ardently resisted by most of the population. Anton Mussert was his Dutch counterpart and founder of the Netherlands Nazi Party. The party membership was 30,000 at the start of the war, increasing to a peak of 50,000.

EASTERN EUROPE

Although Poles prided themselves after the war on offering little collaboration with the hated German and Soviet occupiers, collaboration did take place in their country. In the General Government set up by the Germans, units of Polish police operated under German command, as did Jewish police in the ghettos established by the Germans. Even during the Holocaust, the Germans discovered those individuals who would collaborate in the concentration camps—the Kapos, or trusties, who worked for the German guards in the Sonderkommando. When Soviet forces invaded eastern Poland, they mobilized large numbers of Poles to fight for them against Germany; many Poles regarded these soldiers as collaborators.

In the rest of Central and Eastern Europe, experiences varied. Bulgaria, nominally an Axis power, hardly participated in the war. Its government did send troops to occupy Thrace and Macedonia in Greece, but it steadfastly rejected Hitler's demands that it dispatch troops to the Eastern Front. Hungary and Romania both supplied troops for the German invasion of the Soviet Union, suffering heavy losses in the process. They also actively participated in rounding up Jews to be sent to the extermination camps. In both Greece and Yugoslavia, there was active resistance to the Germans, although the government of newly independent Croatia, carved from Yugoslavia, was highly supportive of Berlin and its policies.

THE SOVIET UNION

Many inhabitants of the eastern portions of the Soviet Union, such as the Baltic states and Ukraine, openly welcomed the German army as their liberator and collaborated fully with it, until they discovered that German occupation policies were even more repressive than Soviet rule had been. In 1943 alone, as Soviet troops moved westward, the Soviet secret police, or NKVD, arrested more than 931,000 people for questioning. Hundreds of thousands of Soviet minorities—most notably the Crimean Tartars but also Turks and Chechens, among others—were simply deported en masse to the eastern USSR as a consequence of their wartime collaboration with the Germans. General Andrei Vlasov, a Hero of the Soviet Union, agreed to head the German-sponsored Russian Liberation Army, although Hitler refused to allow it any real function. Hundreds of thousands of Soviet prisoners worked in the German army in nonmilitary roles, as cooks, drivers, and the like. Much of their motivation came from the simple desire to stay alive, as millions of Soviet soldiers perished from starvation in German POW camps.

One tragic episode following the war resulted from the decision by the Western powers to hand over to the USSR millions of Soviet citizens, many of whom had lived in the West for decades and had played no wartime collaborative role. Nonetheless, they were shipped off to work at hard labor in the gulags.

FAR EAST

In the Far East, Japan's occupation of its conquered territories was generally quite harsh. Paradoxically, as the war dragged on, Japan encouraged independence from colonial rule in some areas, especially in those lands that had been European or U.S. colonies. A notable example of the latter was the Netherlands East Indies, where indigenous peoples were treated comparatively well, in contrast to Europeans, and where the postwar independence movement was effectively encouraged. There as elsewhere, there was considerable popular support for Tokyo's efforts to eliminate the influence of the European colonial masters. One component of the Japanese theme of a "Greater East Asia Co-prosperity Sphere" was to grant independence to Asian states. But the phrase *Asia for the Asians* actually meant that Asian peoples were to be subordinate to Japan.

In French Indochina, the Japanese allowed the French colonial administration to remain in place for purposes of expediency, for Indochina could thus be held with fewer Japanese troops. In March 1945, however, with the war almost certainly lost for Japan, the French plotted to liberate Indochina themselves. The Japanese then took control and granted Vietnam its "independence." The Vietminh, diehard Vietnamese nationalists led by Ho Chi Minh, rejected collaboration, fought both the French and the Japanese, and appealed to Washington for support.

Much to the surprise of the Japanese, most Filipinos remained loyal to the United States. But under heavy Japanese pressure, the Philippine government did accept the principle of collaboration and even declared war on the United States. Following the liberation of the islands, however, few Filipino collaborators were punished, and the Philippines received independence. Burma had its share of collaborators. A number of Burmese regarded the Japanese as liberators, and the Burmese Independence Army actively fought on their side.

Throughout its long occupation of much of China, Japan sought collaborators. Wang Jingwei (Wang Ching-wei), a founding father of the Nationalist Party, grew disillusioned with Nationalist leader Jiang Jieshi (Chiang Kai-shek) and his failure to make peace with the Japanese. In March 1940, the Japanese installed Wang as head of the puppet Reorganized Nationalist Government in Nanjing (Nanking). However, Wang's hopes of presenting himself as a credible alternative to Jiang were dashed on the rocks of Japanese military domination. Wang died in Japan in November 1944 while undergoing medical treatment.

After the Allied victories in Europe and the Pacific in the spring of 1945, collaborators were variously punished. Many individuals were simply executed on the spot by soldiers and civilians. In France, women who had fraternized with the Germans had their heads shaved, among other indignities. Some key political leaders, such as Quisling, were tried and executed. In France, the aged Marshal Pétain was tried and sentenced to death, but de Gaulle remitted that sentence in recognition of his World War I services, and the marshal spent the remainder of his life in prison.

Arthur I. Cyr and Spencer C. Tucker

See also

China, Role in War; China–Burma–India (CBI) Theater; Churchill, Sir Winston Leonard Spencer; de Gaulle, Charles; Eastern Front; France, Role in War; Hitler, Adolf; Holocaust, The; Poland, Role in War; Prisoners of War (POWs); Resistance

References

Bennett, Rab. *Under the Shadow of the Swastika—The Moral Dilemmas of Resistance and Collaboration in Hitler's Europe.* New York: New York University Press, 1999.

Brody, J. Kenneth. *The Trial of Pierre Laval: Defining Treason, Collaboration, and Patriotism in World War II France.* New Brunswick, NJ: Transaction Books, 2010.

Davies, Peter. *Dangerous Liaisons: Collaboration and World War Two.* New York: Longman, 2004.

Davies, Peter. *France and the Second World War: Occupation, Collaboration, and Resistance.* New York: Routledge, 2000.

Ehrlich, Blake. *Resistance: France, 1940–1945.* Boston, MA, and Toronto, Canada: Little, Brown, 1965.

Glass, Charles. *Americans in Paris: Life and Death under Nazi Occupation.* New York: Viking Penguin, 2010.

Jackson, Julian. *France: The Dark Years, 1940–1944.* New York: Oxford University Press, 2001.

Littlejohn, David. *The Patriotic Traitors: The History of Collaboration in German-Occupied Europe, 1940–45.* Garden City, NY: Doubleday, 1972.

Müller, Rolf-Dieter, and Gerd R. Ueberschär. *Hitler's War in the East, 1941–1945: A Critical Assessment.* Providence, RI: Berghahn Books, 1997.

Munoz, Antonio J., and Oleg V. Romanko. *Hitler's White Russians: Collaboration, Extermination and Anti-Partisan Warfare in Byelorussia, 1941–1944.* Bayside, NY: Europa Books, 2003.

Riding, Alan. *And the Show Went On: Cultural Life in Nazi-Occupied Paris.* New York: Alfred A. Knopf, 2010.

Snow, Philip. *The Fall of Hong Kong: Britain, China, and the Japanese Occupation.* New Haven, CT: Yale University Press, 2003.

Spotts, Frederick. *The Shameful Peace: How French Artists and Intellectuals Survived the Nazi Occupation.* New Haven, CT: Yale University Press, 2009.

Steinberg, David. *Philippine Collaboration in World War II.* Ann Arbor, MI: University of Michigan Press, 1967.

Tomasevich, Jozo. *War and Revolution in Yugoslavia, 1941–1945: Occupation and Collaboration.* Stanford, CA: Stanford University Press, 2002.

Vinen, Richard. *The Unfree French: Life under the Occupation.* New Haven, CT: Yale University Press, 2006.

Combat Fatigue

Combat fatigue—also known as battle fatigue, war neurosis, exhaustion, or shell shock—is a variable group of symptoms including excessive fatigue, an exaggerated startle response, tremors, violence, nightmares, delusions, hallucinations, withdrawal, and catatonia. Herodotus described combat-induced mental illness in the Athenian army during the Battle of Marathon in 490 BC, but the diagnosis was relatively infrequent prior to the 20th century. The Russians established the first military psychiatric service during the Russo-Japanese War. The problem became widespread in World War I, during which it was termed *shell shock* under the mistaken theory that explosive concussions caused small brain hemorrhages leading to cerebral dysfunction. By World War II, it was widely understood that the symptoms were psychiatric in nature, were similar to traumatic neuroses seen in the civilian population, and were not caused by identifiable anatomical brain damage.

In spite of an early British emphasis on battlefield psychiatry and an American attempt to exclude men with psychiatric illness from military service, mental illness remained a major cause of combat disability, with about 30 percent of Allied combat zone casualties being psychiatric. Although physicians in World War I had learned that treatment close to the front lines made it possible to return a number of psychiatrically disabled soldiers to combat, the lesson was forgotten. Early in World War II, patients with combat fatigue were routinely evacuated to rehabilitation hospitals, and most were discharged. As manpower became scarce, more of these men were placed in pioneer or labor details in the rear area, but few returned to combat.

Captain Frederick R. Hanson, an American neurologist and neurosurgeon who had joined the Canadian army early in the war and participated in the landing at Dieppe, transferred to the U.S. Army and developed what became a successful and widely employed treatment for what the British now termed *exhaustion* or *combat fatigue*. The essential parts of the regimen included sedation, brief periods of rest, and treatment in a facility close to the front, where the patients and staff continued to wear combat clothing. Hanson realized that treating these patients as if they were mentally ill and physically separating them from their units made it unlikely that they would return to duty. Using his treatment protocols, the British and American armies were able to return 70 to 80 percent of combat fatigue victims to their units, and only 15 to 20 percent of patients requiring evacuation to the zone of the interior were psychiatric.

Shortly after the Italian invasion, the U.S. Army established the post of division psychiatrist, and Hanson produced a manual for internists so nonpsychiatrists could use his methods. As the war went on, Allied military psychiatrists became convinced that no soldier was immune from combat fatigue. They hypothesized that any man subject to continuous combat for a long enough time would become nonfunctional and estimated that 200 days of constant action was about the maximum a soldier could be expected to tolerate. The British adopted a system of unit rotation to give their men regular periods of rest and were able to stretch the tolerable period to close to 400 days, but the Americans, except in the U.S. Army Air Forces, adopted a more haphazard approach of rotating individuals with the longest periods of service rather than entire units. It was not until later wars that regular unit rotation became standard.

Military physicians, mindful of the heavy clinical and financial burden of long-term psychiatric illness after World War I, correctly warned that the true cost of combat fatigue would not become evident until after the soldiers returned to civilian life.

Jack McCallum

See also

Casualties; Great Britain, Air Force; Great Britain, Army; United States, Army; United States, Army Air Force

References

Cowdrey, Albert E. *Fighting for Life: American Military Medicine in World War II.* New York: Free Press, 1994.

Slight, David. "Psychiatry and the War." In *Medicine and the War*, edited by William H. Taliaferro, 150–171. Chicago, IL: University of Chicago Press, 1944.

Withuis, Jolande, and Annette Mooij, eds. *The Politics of War Trauma: The Aftermath of World War II in Eleven European Countries.* Amsterdam: Amsterdam University Press, 2011.

de Gaulle, Charles (1890–1970)

Charles de Gaulle was a French Army general, leader of Free French Forces, and the president of France. Born on November 22, 1890, in Lille, de Gaulle demonstrated from an early age a keen interest in the military. He graduated from the French Military Academy of Saint-Cyr in 1913 and was commissioned a lieutenant in the army.

De Gaulle's first posting was with Colonel Henri P. Pétain's 33rd Infantry Regiment. During World War I, de Gaulle was promoted to captain, and he demonstrated a high degree of leadership and courage. Wounded twice, he was captured by the Germans at Verdun in March 1916 after being wounded a third time. Later he received the Legion of Honor for this action. Despite five escape attempts, he remained a prisoner of war until the end of the war.

After the war, de Gaulle returned to teach history at Saint-Cyr, and in 1920 he was part of the French military mission to Poland. He returned to France to study and teach at the École de Guerre. De Gaulle then served as an aide to French army commander Marshal Pétain, but the two had a falling-out, apparently because Pétain wanted de Gaulle to ghostwrite his memoirs. De Gaulle also became an important proponent of the new theories of high-speed warfare centered on tanks. In his 1934 book *Vers l'armée de métier* (published in English as *The Army of the Future*), de Gaulle proposed formation of six completely mechanized and motorized divisions with their own organic artillery and air support. Another book, *Le fil de l'epée* (*The Edge of the Sword*), revealed much about de Gaulle's concept of leadership and his belief that a true leader should follow his conscience regardless of the circumstances.

Promoted to major and then to lieutenant colonel, de Gaulle served in the Rhineland occupation forces, in the Middle East, and on the National Defense Council. Although he was advanced to colonel in 1937 and had important political friends such as future premiere Paul Reynaud, de Gaulle's views placed him very much on the outside of the military establishment.

When World War II began, de Gaulle commanded a tank brigade. His warnings about the German use of tanks in Poland fell on deaf ears in the French High Command. De Gaulle commanded the 4th French Tank Division in the 1940 Battle for France. Although the division was still in formation, he secured one of the few French successes of that campaign. Promoted to brigadier general on June 1, 1940, five days later de Gaulle was appointed undersecretary of defense in the Reynaud government. De Gaulle urged

Charles de Gaulle was the most senior French military officer to reject the terms of the armistice that France concluded with Germany in June 1940. Escaping to Britain, he became the leader of the Free French forces in exile, exhorting his compatriots to carry on the fight against Germany. Shown here around 1942, by 1944 he headed what amounted to a French government in exile. From 1959 to 1969, de Gaulle served as president of the Fifth French Republic. (Library of Congress)

Reynaud to fight on, even in a redoubt in the Brittany Peninsula or removing the armed forces to North Africa. De Gaulle's resolve won the admiration of British prime minister Winston Churchill.

De Gaulle and Jean Monnet visited London and suggested to Churchill a plan for an indissoluble Anglo-French union that the French government had rejected. Returning to Bordeaux from the mission to London, de Gaulle learned that the defeatists had won and France would sue for peace. On June 17, he departed France on a British aircraft bound for England. The next day, this youngest general in the French army appealed to his countrymen over the British Broadcasting Corporation (BBC) to continue the fight against Germany. From this point forward, de Gaulle was the most prominent figure in the French Resistance. With Churchill's support and because no prominent French politicians had escaped abroad, de Gaulle then set up a French government-in-exile in London and began organizing armed forces to fight for the liberation of his country. The Pétain government at Vichy declared de Gaulle a traitor and condemned him to death in absentia.

Initially, de Gaulle's position was at best tenuous. Most French citizens did not recognize his legitimacy, and relations with the British and Americans were at times difficult. De Gaulle insisted on being treated as head of state of a major power, whereas American leaders, especially President Franklin D. Roosevelt, and even Churchill persisted in treating him as an auxiliary and often did not consult with him at all on major decisions.

The British attack on the French fleet at Mers-el-Kébir further undermined de Gaulle's credibility. Relations with the United States were not helped by a Free French effort to secure Saint-Pierre and Miquelon off Canada. The United States recognized the Vichy government and continued to pursue a two-France policy even after the United States entered the war in December 1941.

Over time, de Gaulle solidified his position as leader of the Resistance in France. Bitter over British moves in Syria and Lebanon and not informed in advance of the U.S.–British invasion of French North Africa, de Gaulle established his headquarters in Algiers in 1943, where he beat back a British–French effort to replace him with General Henri Giraud. His agent, Jean Moulin, secured the fusion of Resistance groups within France. The French Resistance rendered invaluable service to the British and Americans in the June 1944 Normandy Invasion, and French forces actually liberated Paris that August.

De Gaulle then returned to Paris and established a provisional government there. Full U.S. diplomatic recognition came only with the creation of the new government. De Gaulle secured for France an occupation zone in Germany and a key role in postwar Europe. But with the return of peace the former political parties reappeared, and hopes for a fresh beginning faded. De Gaulle's calls for a new constitutional arrangement with a strong presidency were rejected, and he resigned in January 1946 to write his memoirs.

A revolt among European settlers and the French Army in Algeria, who feared a sellout there to the Algerian nationalists, brought de Gaulle back to power in 1958. A new constitution tailor-made for de Gaulle established the Fifth Republic. De Gaulle's preservation of democracy was his greatest service to his country, but he also brought an end to the Algerian War, and he worked out a close entente with Konrad Adenauer's Federal Republic of Germany. De Gaulle was also controversial, removing France from the North Atlantic Treaty Organization's military command, creating an independent nuclear strike force, encouraging Quebec to secede from Canada, and lecturing the United States on a wide variety of issues. He remained president until 1969, when he again resigned to write a new set of memoirs. Unquestionably France's greatest 20th-century statesman, Charles de Gaulle died at his estate of Colombey-les-Deux-Églises on November 9, 1970.

Thomas Lansford and Spencer C. Tucker

See also
Churchill, Sir Winston Leonard Spencer; France, Role in War; North Africa Campaign; Resistance; Roosevelt, Franklin D.; Western European Theater of Operations

References

Berthon, Simon. *Allies at War: The Bitter Rivalry among Churchill, Roosevelt, and de Gaulle.* New York: Carroll and Graf, 2001.

Cook, Don. *Charles de Gaulle, a Biography.* New York: G. P. Putnam's Sons, 1983.

De Gaulle, Charles. *The Complete War Memoirs of Charles de Gaulle.* Translated by Jonathan Griffin and Richard Howard. New York: Simon and Schuster, 1969.

Fenby, Jonathan. *The General: Charles de Gaulle and the France He Saved.* New York: Simon and Schuster, 2010.

Kersaudy, François. *Churchill and de Gaulle.* New York: Atheneum, 1982.

Lacouture, Jean. *De Gaulle: The Rebel, 1890–1944.* Translated by Patrick O'Brian. New York: W. W. Norton, 1990.

Lacouture, Jean. *De Gaulle: The Ruler, 1945–1970.* Translated by Patrick O'Brian. New York: W. W. Norton, 1992.

Weinberg, Gerhard L. *Visions of Victory: The Hopes of Eight World War II Leaders.* Cambridge: Cambridge University Press, 2005.

Williams, Charles. *The Last Great Frenchman: A Life of General de Gaulle.* New York: Wiley, 1995.

Eastern Front

On June 22, 1941, German forces invaded the Soviet Union in Operation BARBAROSSA. The two states then became locked in a death struggle raging on a front of more than 1,800 miles, involving millions of men and thousands of tanks, artillery pieces, and aircraft and resulting in the deaths of many millions of combatants and civilians.

In the fall of 1940, following the Luftwaffe's failure to drive the Royal Air Force from the skies over Britain, Adolf Hitler ordered plans drawn up for an invasion of the Soviet Union. He postulated a quick, three-month-long campaign. "You have only to kick in the door," he told Field Marshal Karl Gerd von Rundstedt, "and the whole rotten structure will come tumbling down." Defeat the Soviet Union, he reasoned, and Britain would have to sue for peace.

Overconfidence marked German planning. The Germans had little accurate intelligence on the Soviet Union, including few adequate maps. They also had little concern for the impact on the fighting of winter weather and little understanding of the influence of the great distances and how these would render blitzkrieg, at least as it was practiced in Poland in 1939 and against France and the Low Countries in 1940, wholly impractical.

German resources were certainly inadequate for the task that lay ahead, and in the Soviet Union, Hitler's strategic overreach at last caught up with him. On June 22, 1941, the German army deployed 205 divisions, but 60 of these were in garrison or fighting elsewhere: 38 in France, 12 in Norway, 1 in Denmark, 7 in the Balkans, and 2 in North Africa. This left just 145 divisions available for operations in the East. The Germans invaded the Soviet Union with 102 infantry divisions, 14 motorized divisions, 1 cavalry division, and 19 armored divisions. In addition, they deployed 9 divisions to maintain lines of communication as the invasion progressed. There was virtually no strategic reserve. Finland, Romania, and Hungary supplied perhaps 705,000 men in 37 divisions.

The disparity in military hardware was even more striking. The Luftwaffe, still waging operations against Britain and also supporting the Afrika Korps (Africa Corps) in North Africa, was forced to keep 1,150 combat aircraft in these theaters, leaving only 2,770 combat aircraft available for use against the Soviet Union. By contrast, the Soviets had 18,570 aircraft, 8,154 of which were initially in the west. The bulk of these were tactical aircraft. Germany had some 6,000 tanks, the Soviets 23,140 (10,394 in the west), and even in 1941, the Soviets possessed some of the best tanks of the war. Their T-34 was the top tank in the world in 1941.

An invading German soldier, part of Operation BARBAROSSA, hurls a hand grenade while his comrade aims his rifle at adversaries in Russia in 1941. The fighting between Germans and Soviets on the Eastern Front was often harrowing, degenerating at times into a war of attrition. (National Archives)

The German invasion plan called for three axes of advance. Field Marshal Gerd von Rundstedt's Army Group South of four armies (one Romanian) and one panzer group would drive on Kiev and the Dnieper in order to destroy Soviet armies between the Pripet Marshes and the Black Sea. Field Marshal Fedor von Bock's Army Group Center of two armies and two panzer groups was to strike east, taking Smolensk and Moscow. Field Marshal Wilhelm Ritter von Leeb's Army Group North of two armies and one panzer group would thrust north, capture Leningrad, and pin the Soviet forces there against the Baltic Sea. Finland would act in concert with the Germans, reentering the war to reoccupy the Karelian Isthmus and threatening Leningrad from the north. Farther north, German Colonel General Nikolaus von Falkenhorst's Norway Army would carry out an offensive against Murmansk in order to sever its supply route to Leningrad.

Hitler had intended to invade in May, but circumstances caused him to put off the attack until late June. In the spring of 1941, German forces invaded Yugoslavia, went to the rescue of Italian troops in Greece, and drove British forces from Crete. In the process, Hitler secured his southern flank against the possibility of Allied air strikes during the German invasion of the Soviet Union. Historians have argued about the impact of this on delaying the invasion of the Soviet Union. In any case, rainy weather and appalling road conditions in the western USSR imposed delay. The tanks required firm, dry ground.

The invasion began at 3:00 a.m. on June 22, 1941, the longest day of the year, with only two hours of total darkness. The Germans and their allies moved into the Soviet Union along a 2,000-mile front and achieved complete surprise. The bulk of the Red Army's

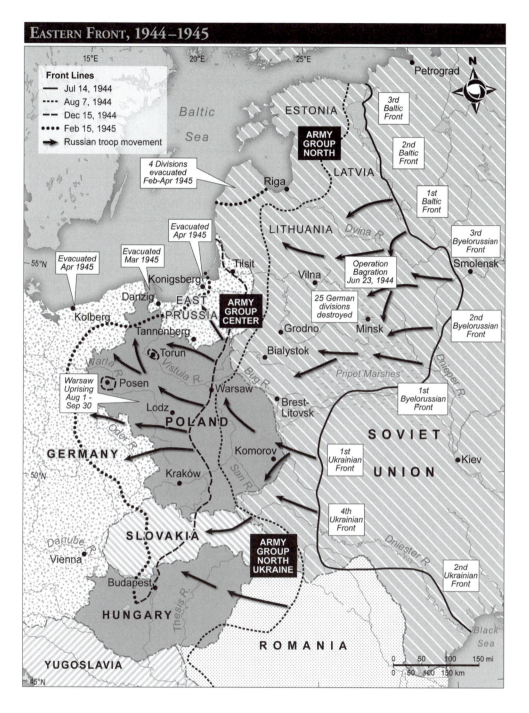

EASTERN FRONT, 1944–1945

Front Lines
— Jul 14, 1944
···· Aug 7, 1944
– – Dec 15, 1944
•••• Feb 15, 1945
→ Russian troop movement

Baltic Sea

Petrograd

ESTONIA

3rd Baltic Front

2nd Baltic Front

ARMY GROUP NORTH

LATVIA

1st Baltic Front

4 Divisions evacuated Feb–Apr 1945

Riga

LITHUANIA

Dvina R.

3rd Byelorussian Front

Smolensk

Evacuated Apr 1945

Vilna

Operation Bagration Jun 23, 1944

Evacuated Mar 1945

Tilsit

Evacuated Apr 1945

Konigsberg

Danzig

Kolberg

EAST PRUSSIA

ARMY GROUP CENTER

25 German divisions destroyed

2nd Byelorussian Front

Grodno

Minsk

Tannenberg

Warta R.

Torun

Vistula R.

Bug R.

Bialystok

Pripet Marshes

Dnieper R.

Warsaw Uprising Aug 1 – Sep 30

Posen

Warsaw

Brest-Litovsk

1st Byelorussian Front

Lodz

POLAND

SOVIET

GERMANY

Oder R.

Komorov

1st Ukrainian Front

Kiev

Kraków

San R.

UNION

4th Ukrainian Front

SLOVAKIA

ARMY GROUP NORTH UKRAINE

Dniester R.

Danube R.

Vienna

Budapest

Thesis R.

2nd Ukrainian Front

HUNGARY

Black Sea

ROMANIA

0   50   100   150 mi
0   50   100   150 km

YUGOSLAVIA

western forces were in forward positions, where they were cut off and surrounded. On the first day alone, 1,200 Soviet aircraft were destroyed, most of them on the ground. Within two days, 2,000 Soviet aircraft had been lost. Within five days, the Germans had captured or destroyed 2,500 Soviet tanks. And within three weeks, the Soviets had lost 3,500 tanks, 6,000 aircraft, and 2 million men, including a significant percentage of the officer corps.

Army Group North broke through frontier defenses, wheeled left to trap and destroy many Soviet divisions against the Baltic, and appeared to have an open route to Leningrad. Meanwhile, Army Group Center, with the bulk of German tanks, attacked north of the Pripet Marshes, completed two huge encirclements, and destroyed vast amounts of Soviet war matériel while taking hundreds of thousands of prisoners. But unexpectedly strong Soviet defenses slowed the advance of Army Group South to Kiev, the Crimea, and the Caucasus.

This development revealed a great problem in German invasion planning. The chief of the General Staff, Colonel General Franz Halder, and many senior generals wanted to concentrate German resources in the center for a drive on Moscow, with supporting movements to the north and south. A thrust there would mean a shorter front, and its advocates believed that Moscow was so important that Soviet dictator Josef Stalin would commit many troops to its defense and thus make it easier for the German army to locate and destroy the remaining Soviet military formations before the onset of winter. But Hitler was fixated on taking Leningrad and, more important, the vast resources of the Ukraine. The compromise solution was to make a decision after the pause in August to refit and rest.

German military intelligence, meanwhile, underestimated Soviet military strength. In December 1940, it had estimated 150 Soviet divisions in the western USSR; by June 1941, that estimate had grown to 175; and now, in late summer, German intelligence concluded that the Soviets still had 250 divisions, despite huge losses in the fighting. Moreover, Soviet soldiers did not give up when surrounded. Nazi racism and German violence made them realize that capture meant death, and so, many Soviet troops fought to the last bullet and attempted to break free rather than surrender. And the vast distances and onset of a severe winter posed tremendous logistical challenges for German army planners because their army had only a small mechanized/motorized force and largely relied on human and animal muscle power. While leaders at home prepared for the Soviet collapse, troops on the front lines gained a grudging respect for their Soviet adversaries.

In August, the Germans paused, and Hitler ordered the tank units of Army Group Center to help with the attack on Leningrad and to complete the encirclement of Soviet forces defending Kiev. Finally, in October, Army Group Center began Operation TYPHOON, the attack on Moscow. By November, it had come close to success, but few tanks were still operational. There was little fuel, and the men lacked winter clothing in one of the coldest Soviet winters of the 20th century.

During the fall campaigning, Stalin prepared to defend Moscow. While troops defended a series of lines on the way to the capital, Moscow's citizens were organized to construct antitank ditches and concentric defenses. Secure in the information that Japan would not take advantage of Soviet weakness and intended to move into South Asia, the Red Army brought divisions from Asia and, having studied German tactics, prepared a counterblow against Army Group Center. On December 5, 1941, the Soviet attack began, stunning the tired, cold, and hungry German troops. Some German generals wanted to retreat all the way to the preinvasion borders, but Hitler insisted that the troops remain in place, and his resoluteness and the limited capacity of Soviet logistics helped stem the Soviet winter offensive. Then came the spring thaw and a temporary lull in the fighting.

The relative force ratio had changed in a year of fighting. A summer, fall, and winter had weakened the German army to the point that it no longer had the striking power it possessed a year before. Meanwhile, the Red Army, encouraged by its winter victories, was preparing to take the offensive in 1942.

Hitler believed that the Soviet state could not afford another year of manpower losses like those in 1941. He believed that if German forces could drive a wedge between the Dnieper and Don Rivers, using the Volga River as a shoulder, they could interrupt Soviet supplies moving up that great and broad transit way and fight their way to Soviet oil resources in the Caucasus region and the Caspian Sea. The German army's High Command estimated that it would need 80 new divisions to replace losses and to provide the striking power for a summer offensive, but Germany could only supply 55 divisions. Hitler promised 80 divisions and obtained troop contributions from reluctant Romanian, Hungarian, and Italian allies, but it was unclear how these troops would perform in the desperate fighting conditions of the Eastern Front. To meet the requirements for mechanized equipment, the German army refitted Czech tanks taken in 1938 and French tanks seized in 1940. Consequently, the German supply system had to carry spare parts for literally hundreds of truck models and tens of tank models, greatly complicating logistics. The Soviets had no such problems. Finally, the panzer units had to move fast enough to fight around defenders and once again surround and capture huge numbers of Soviet troops. Otherwise, the Germans would have to travel as much as 1,200 miles from the offensive's jumping-off point to reach the most productive oil-producing area around Baku.

The Soviets struck first. The Red Army launched an attack in the southern front that coincidentally exposed its flank to Germans massed for the drive to the southeast. Stalin initially refused to end the attack, and losses were heavy. The German summer offensive that finally began in late June 1942 never captured vast numbers of Soviet soldiers as in 1941. Moreover, Hitler kept reassigning units and thereby violating the principles of mass and economy of force. He sent key elements of the Eighteenth Army on the Crimean Peninsula north to Leningrad; he routed and rerouted the Fourth Panzer Army; and by September, when it was clear that Germany could not achieve its overarching goal of seizing the Soviet oil fields, he ordered the Sixth Army to batter its way against three defending armies into Stalingrad.

The desperate battle for control of Stalingrad, a major industrial city on the Volga, captured the world's imagination. Stalin was as determined to hold his namesake city as Hitler was to take it. The fighting was a block-by-block, house-by-house, and room-by-room affair, with the Soviets sometimes defending from across the river. As Lieutenant General Vasily I. Chuikov's Sixty-Second Army held, the Soviets prepared a massive counterstroke, building up armies of troops and many tanks and artillery pieces against the weakly defended flanks held by Romanian and Hungarian troops. On November 19, in Operation URANUS, the Soviets attacked and quickly broke through. Within days, the Soviet pincers met at Kalach, and more than 300,000 German troops were trapped. The German commander, Field Marshal Friedrich Paulus, did not attempt to break out, and Field Marshal Erich von Manstein failed to break through and relieve Sixth Army. With only three divisions, Manstein managed to get within 35 miles of the trapped Sixth Army but could move no farther. German troops held on until the end of January, when 90,000 survivors marched off into captivity. The long battle did at least provide time for the Germans to extricate forces that had penetrated deep into the Caucasus.

The Soviets then followed this great victory with a winter offensive, but eventually, their goals outran their logistical capacity, and there was the typical pause forced by the spring thaw in 1943. As summer approached, Hitler approved a plan to pinch off a huge bulge in German lines north of Kharkov near Kursk, destroy Soviet armies trapped there, and restore the balance on the Eastern Front.

The Germans postponed the attack on the Kursk salient, Operation CITADEL, again and again to May, June, and eventually, early July. Hitler wanted more of the new models of heavy German tanks, especially the Tiger, but as Germany delayed, the Soviets acted, bringing up reinforcements and constructing extensive, deep defenses, including wide belts of minefields, that were up to 60 miles deep. They also positioned reserve armies on the shoulders of the bulge and additional tanks and artillery behind them. Finally, on July 5, the long-awaited attack began. Although German units made little progress in the north, the attacking force from the south bludgeoned its way forward. But on July 10, British and American forces invaded Sicily, clearly threatening to drive Italy from the war. This invasion forced Hitler to end the offensive at Kursk—the greatest tank battle in history.

Within a few weeks, the Soviets began their late summer offensive in the south, which they followed up with a winter offensive that drove German forces out of eastern Ukraine and trapped German troops on the Crimea. As the spring mud in 1944 brought the usual pause in operations, the German lines stretched from near Leningrad in the north, and along the southern edge of Army Group Center, the lines curved inward. The Soviets achieved a great tactical surprise, as they fooled the Germans into expecting a summer attack against positions in the Ukraine. The Soviets then repositioned their tanks and artillery and prepared for a massive offensive against Army Group Center in Operation BAGRATION, which would coincide with the Allied invasion of France. On July 20, 1944, the Soviets struck, and within weeks, they had largely destroyed Army Group Center. The Soviets followed this up with attacks to end the siege of Leningrad and to expel German troops from all Soviet territory. Pausing in the center before Warsaw—which allowed the Germans to destroy the Polish underground army that had joined the fighting—Soviet forces moved into the Balkans, as Romania and Bulgaria desperately sought to avoid Soviet vengeance.

The end was drawing near, and the Soviets continued to advance. One axis aimed at Berlin while the other struck through Hungary. By January 1945, the Soviets had secured most of East Prussia, and in the south, they were at the gates of Budapest. In April, they brought up supplies and reserve troops for the final drive into Germany proper. The Germans conducted a desperate defense of Berlin, using old men and young boys, and the Soviets took huge casualties as Marshal Georgiĭ Zhukov and Colonel General Ivan Konev fought for the honor of liberating the city. In late April, Soviet and American troops met at Torgau on the Elbe, and several days later, Soviet forces occupied Berlin while Hitler committed suicide in his underground bunker. Finally, on May 7, 1945, Germany signed a surrender document that went into effect on all fronts the next day. The Eastern Front had absorbed the lion's share of German military resources from 1941 onward, and the

Soviet ability to stave off defeat and then achieve victory there was critical to the war's outcome.

Charles M. Dobbs and Spencer C. Tucker

See also

Balkans Theater; Collaboration; Eisenhower, Dwight D.; Finland, Role in War; Germany, Air Force; Germany, Army; Hitler, Adolf; Northeast Europe Theater; Poland, Role in War; Resistance; Soviet Union, Air Force; Soviet Union, Army; Stalin, Josef; Zhukov, Georgiĭ Konstantinovich

References

Barros, James, and Richard Gregor. *Double Deception: Stalin, Hitler, and the Invasion of Russia*. DeKalb, IL: Northern Illinois Press, 1995.

Beevor, Antony. *The Fall of Berlin 1945*. New York: Viking, 2002.

Bellamy, Chris. *Absolute War: Soviet Russia in the Second World War*. New York: Knopf, 2007.

Bidermann, G. H. *In Deadly Combat: A German Soldier's Memoir of the Eastern Front*. Translated and edited by Derek S. Zumbro. Lawrence, KS: University Press of Kansas, 2000.

Clark, Alan. *Barbarossa: The Russian–German Conflict, 1941–45*. New York: William Morrow, 1965.

Dallas, Gregor. *1945: The War That Never Ended*. New Haven, CT: Yale University Press, 2005.

Erickson, John. *Stalin's War with Germany*. 2 vols. London: Weidenfeld and Nicolson, 1975–1983.

Fritz, Stephen. *Ostkrieg: Hitler's War of Extermination in the East*. Lexington, KY: University Press of Kentucky, 2011.

Glantz, David M. *The Battle for Leningrad, 1941–1944*. Lawrence, KS: University Press of Kansas, 2002.

Glantz, David M. *Colossus Reborn: The Red Army at War, 1941–1943*. Lawrence, KS: University Press of Kansas, 2005.

Glantz, David M. *Operation Barbarossa: Hitler's Invasion of Russia*. Stroud: The History Press, 2011.

Glantz, David M. *Stumbling Colossus: The Red Army on the Eve of World War*. Lawrence, KS: University Press of Kansas, 1998.

Glantz, David M., and Jonathan M. House. *When Titans Clashed: How the Red Army Stopped Hitler*. Lawrence, KS: University Press of Kansas, 1995.

Hastings, Max. *Armageddon: The Battle for Germany, 1944–1945*. New York: Alfred A. Knopf, 2004.

Hoyt, Edwin P. *Stalin's War: Tragedy and Triumph, 1941–1945*. New York: Cooper Square Press, 2003.

Mawdsley, Evan. *Thunder in the East: The Nazi–Soviet War 1941–1945*. New York: Bloomsbury, 2005.

Mosier, John. *Deathride: Hitler vs. Stalin—The Eastern Front, 1941–1945*. New York: Simon and Schuster, 2010.

Müller, Rolf-Dieter, and Gerd R. Ueberschär. *Hitler's War in the East, 1941–1945: A Critical Assessment.* Providence, RI: Berghahn Books, 1997.

Munoz, Antonio J., and Oleg V. Romanko. *Hitler's White Russians: Collaboration, Extermination and Anti-Partisan Warfare in Byelorussia, 1941–1944.* Bayside, NY: Europa Books, 2003.

Nagorski, Andrew. *The Greatest Battle: Stalin, Hitler, and the Desperate Struggle for Moscow that Changed the Course of World War II.* New York: Simon and Schuster, 2007.

Pleshakov, Constantine. *Stalin's Folly: The Tragic First Ten Days of World War II on the Eastern Front.* Boston, MA: Houghton Mifflin, 2005.

Raack, R. C. *Stalin's Drive to the West, 1938–1945: The Origins of the Cold War.* Stanford, CA: Stanford University Press, 1995.

Slepyan, Kenneth. *Stalin's Guerrillas: Soviet Partisans in World War II.* Lawrence, KS: University Press of Kansas, 2006.

Snyder, Timothy. *Bloodlands: Europe between Hitler and Stalin.* New York: Basic Books, 2010.

Tooze, Adam. *The Wages of Destruction: The Making and Breaking of the Nazi Economy.* New York: Viking, 2007.

Ziemke, Earl Frederick. *Stalingrad to Berlin: The German Defeat in the East.* New York: Dorset Press, 1986.

Eisenhower, Dwight D. (1890–1969)

Dwight David "Ike" Eisenhower was a U.S. Army general, supreme commander of Allied Expeditionary Forces, and commanding general of European Theater of Operations (ETO). Born in Denison, Texas, on October 14, 1890, Eisenhower grew up in Abilene, Kansas. Graduating from the U.S. Military Academy in 1915 as a member of the "class the stars fell on," he was commissioned a second lieutenant of infantry. His first posting after West Point was Fort Sam Houston, Texas.

Eisenhower commanded the fledgling tank corps training center at Camp Colt outside Gettysburg, Pennsylvania, during World War I. Following service in Panama, he graduated first in his class at the Command and General Staff School, Fort Leavenworth, Kansas, in 1926. He also graduated from the Army War College in 1928. During the interwar period, Eisenhower served under a number of the army's finest officers, including Generals Fox Conner, John J. Pershing, and Douglas A. MacArthur. Following his return from the Philippines in 1939, he served successively as chief of staff of the 3rd Infantry Division, IX Corps, and Third Army, where he was promoted to temporary brigadier general in October 1941 and captured Army Chief of Staff General George C. Marshall's attention for his contributions to Third Army's "victory" in the Texas–Louisiana war maneuvers of 1941.

Summoned to the War Department in the aftermath of the Japanese attack on Pearl Harbor, Eisenhower headed the War Plans Division and then the Operations Division of the General Staff before being promoted to major general in April 1942. Marshall then appointed Eisenhower commanding general of the ETO, in June 1942. Promotion to lieutenant general followed in July 1942. His appointment was met with great skepticism from senior British military officers because of his lack of command experience.

Eisenhower commanded Allied forces in Operation TORCH in November 1942 (the invasion of northwest Africa) and in Operation HUSKY in July 1943 (the invasion of Sicily). In the interim, he was promoted to full general in February 1943. The efficient operation of his headquarters—Allied Forces Headquarters—became a model of Allied harmony and led to increased responsibilities in the Mediterranean Theater of Operations. In September 1943, his forces invaded the Italian mainland. Eisenhower's generalship during this phase of the war has long been subject to controversy, but his adept management of diverse personalities and his emphasis on Allied harmony led to his appointment as supreme commander, Allied Expeditionary Forces for the invasion of northwest Europe.

As commander of Operation OVERLORD, the Normandy Invasion on June 6, 1944, Eisenhower headed the largest Allied force in history. Following the expansion of the lodgment area, he took direct command of the land battle on September 1, 1944. As the Allied forces advanced along a broad front toward the German border, he frequently encountered opposition from senior Allied generals over command arrangements and logistical support. He displayed increasing brilliance as a coalition commander, but his operational

Supreme Allied Commander Dwight D. Eisenhower at his headquarters in the European theater of operations in February 1945. Eisenhower's success in planning and launching the Allied D-Day invasion and coordinating the Anglo-American offensives against Germany eventually won him the presidency of the United States. (National Archives)

decisions remained controversial. His support of British Field Marshal Bernard L. Montgomery's abortive Operation MARKET-GARDEN is evidence of his unflinching emphasis on Allied harmony in the campaign in northwest Europe. In mid-December 1944, Eisenhower was promoted to general of the army as his forces stood poised to strike into the heartland of Germany.

When Adolf Hitler launched the Ardennes counteroffensive on December 16, 1944, it was Eisenhower, among senior Allied commanders, who first recognized the scope and intensity of Germany's attack. Marshaling forces to stem the German advance, he defeated Hitler's last offensive in the west. By March 1945, his armies had crossed the Rhine River and encircled the Ruhr industrial area of Germany. As Soviet armies stood on the outskirts of Berlin, Eisenhower decided to seek the destruction of Germany's armed forces throughout southern Germany and not to launch a direct attack toward the German capital. On May 7, 1945, the mission of the Allied Expeditionary Forces was fulfilled as he accepted the unconditional surrender of Germany's armed forces.

Following the war, Eisenhower succeeded General Marshall as army chief of staff. In February 1948, he retired from the military and assumed the presidency of Columbia University, before being recalled to active field duty by President Harry S. Truman in 1950 to become supreme Allied commander, Europe, in the newly formed North Atlantic Treaty Organization (NATO). In 1952, Eisenhower resigned from active military service and accepted the Republican Party's nomination for president. Elected by a wide majority in 1952 and again in 1956, he stressed nuclear over conventional forces, supported expanded U.S. military commitments overseas, and warned of the dangers of a military–industrial complex. He left office in 1961 as one of this nation's most popular chief executives, his two administrations marked by unheralded peace and prosperity. In 1961, Eisenhower retired to his farm in Gettysburg, Pennsylvania. He died in Washington, DC, on March 28, 1969.

Cole C. Kingseed

See also

Bradley, Omar Nelson; Hitler, Adolf; Italy Campaign; MacArthur, Douglas; Marshall, George Catlett; Montgomery, Sir Bernard Law; North Africa Campaign; Patton, George Smith, Jr.; Roosevelt, Franklin D.; United States, Army; Western European Theater of Operations

References

Ambrose, Stephen E. *Eisenhower: Soldier, General of the Army, President-Elect.* New York: Simon and Schuster, 1983.

Chandler, Alfred D., et al., eds. *The Papers of Dwight David Eisenhower: The War Years.* Vols. 1–4. Baltimore, MD: Johns Hopkins University Press, 1970.

D'Este, Carlo. *Eisenhower: A Soldier's Life.* New York: Henry Holt, 2002.

Eisenhower, David. *Eisenhower at War, 1943–1945.* New York: Random House, 1986.

Eisenhower, Dwight D. *Crusade in Europe.* New York: Doubleday, 1948.

Jordan, Jonathan W. *Brothers, Rivals, Victors: Eisenhower, Patton, Bradley and the Partnership that Drove the Allied Conquest in Europe.* New York: New American Library, 2011.

Perret, Geoffrey. *Eisenhower*. New York: Random House, 1999.

Perry, Mark. *Partners in Command: George Marshall and Dwight Eisenhower in War and Peace*. New York: Penguin Press, 2007.

Smith, Jean Edward. *Eisenhower in War and Peace*. New York: Random House, 2012.

Weintraub, Stanley. *15 Stars: Eisenhower, MacArthur, Marshall: Three Generals Who Saved the American Century*. New York: Basic Books, 2007.

Finland, Role in War

Finland numbered some 3.6 million people in September 1939. The country had secured its independence from Russia in 1917, but the Finns had to fight to maintain it. Concerned about the growth of German military power, in the late 1930s Soviet dictator Josef Stalin applied pressure on Finland for territory in the Karelian Isthmus and for the naval base of Hango on the Gulf of Finland to provide protection for Leningrad, the Soviet Union's second-largest city. In return, Stalin was prepared to yield more territory than he sought, but it was far to the north. The Finnish leadership, believing the Soviets were bluffing, rejected the demands. The Soviet Union invaded Finland in November 1939, and the first Soviet–Finnish War (known as the Winter War) lasted until March 1940. The governments of both Great Britain and France discussed the possibility of military intervention, in large part to cut Germany off from Swedish iron ore, but both Norway and Sweden denied transit rights to the Allies. Commander of Finnish armed forces Marshal Carl Mannerheim led a spirited Finnish defense. However, the Finns were overwhelmed by sheer weight of Russian numbers and military hardware. On March 12, 1940, the Finns signed the Treaty of Moscow. By the terms of the treaty, which went into effect at noon the next day, Finland lost one-tenth of its territory, including the entire Karelian Isthmus. The country then had to absorb 400,000 refugees, as virtually all the Finns moved out of the surrendered territory rather than live under Soviet rule.

New Soviet pressure angered the Finns, who signed a secret transit agreement with Germany in August 1940 allowing German troops to pass through Finland to northern Norway. Discussions began between the German and Finnish staffs regarding Operation BARBAROSSA, the German invasion of the Soviet Union, but the Germans never told the Finns details of the plan until the invasion was about to commence. The Germans began arms shipments to Finland in 1941, particularly artillery and antitank weapons. By June 1941, the Finnish government of President Risto Ryti committed to the plan but resisted a formal alliance with Germany, maintaining that the Finns were merely fighting a defensive war against Soviet aggression and were a cobelligerent. Indeed, the Finns managed to evade every request for such an alliance throughout the war.

Finland never defined war aims for this second Soviet–Finnish War, the Continuation War. Halting offensive military operations 50 to 90 miles beyond the 1939 borders (the additional territory taken for defensive reasons) was the clearest statement of its aims. Carl Mannerheim, commander of Finnish armed forces, hoped that by limiting its advance into Soviet territory, Finland might retain its friendship with the United States and Great Britain. The Finnish government endeavored to convey the impression that Finland had been drawn into the conflict, although this was hard to accomplish with German troops in Finland before the commencement of BARBAROSSA, with naval cooperation between Finland and Germany, and with the German air force flying in Finnish air space and refueling at Finnish airfields. Britain warned Finland at the end of September to advance only to the 1939 frontiers and declared war on Finland on December 6, 1941, the same day Finland halted its advance into Soviet territory.

The front with the Soviet Union was stable from May 1942 until June 1944, when the Soviets launched a powerful offensive with vastly superior manpower and firepower. The Ribbentrop–Ryti agreement between the German foreign minister, Joachim von Ribbentrop, and Ryti was signed in late June 1944, promising that Finland would not seek a separate peace in exchange for weapons. Finland had earlier in the year rejected peace terms from the Soviet Union because of their harshness and because Finland hoped that an Allied invasion of Germany would cause the Red Army to race to Berlin. By July, the Red Army was doing exactly that; President Ryti resigned, and Mannerheim assumed office. Mannerheim repudiated Ryti's agreement and negotiated a cease-fire with the Soviet Union. As part of the cease-fire, concluded on September 19, 1944, Finland had to expel or intern all German troops on its soil. This went peacefully until the Germans tried to seize Suursaari Island, which led to bitter fighting there and in Lapland in northern Finland. Although the campaign was virtually over at the end of November 1944 (the date established by the cease-fire agreement for Finnish demobilization), the last German troops did not depart Finland until April 1945.

The cease-fire and later armistice with the Soviet Union reaffirmed the 1940 borders, accepted Soviet reparations demands for raw materials and machinery, and limited the Finnish military in numbers and types of weapons. Finland lost nearly 92,000 dead (including 2,700 civilians) during World War II. The Soviet Union did not occupy Finland, and Finland's political institutions were left intact—the only eastern enemy of the Soviet Union so treated.

Britton W. MacDonald

See also

Casualties; Eastern Front; Germany, Air Force; Germany, Army; Hitler, Adolf; Northeast Europe Theater; Soviet Union, Air Force; Soviet Union, Army; Soviet Union, Navy; Stalin, Josef

References

Clements, Jonathan. *Mannerheim: President, Soldier, Spy.* London: Haus Publishing, 2012.

Erfurth, Waldemar. *The Last Finnish War.* Washington, DC: University Publications of America, 1979.

Irincheev, Bair. *The War of the White Death: Finland against the Soviet Union 1939–40.* Barnsley: Pen and Sword, 2011.

Kinnunen, Tiina, and Ville Kivimäki, eds. *Finland in World War II.* Leiden: Brill, 2011.

Kirby, D. G. *Finland in the Twentieth Century.* Minneapolis, MN: University of Minnesota Press, 1979.

Lunde, Henrik O. *Finland's War of Choice: The Troubled German–Finnish Coalition in World War II*. Havertown, PA: Casemate Publishing, 2011.

Mannerheim, Carl. *The Memoirs of Marshal Mannerheim*. London: Cassell, 1953.

Tillotson, H. M. *Finland at Peace and War, 1918–1993*. Wilby: Michael Russell, 1993.

Trotter, William R. *A Frozen Hell: The Russo-Finnish Winter War of 1939–1940*. Chapel Hill, NC: Algonquin Books, 1991.

Warner, Oliver. *Marshal Mannerheim and the Finns*. London: Weidenfield and Nicolson, 1967.

France, Role in War

On September 3, 1939, for the second time in a generation, France found itself at war with Germany. In sharp contrast to August 1914, this time the mood in the Third Republic was one of somber resignation. Although France was among the victors in World War I, it had been devastated by the war, with 1,385,300 dead and 4,329,200 wounded (690,000 permanently disabled). One-quarter of all French males of military age lay dead. Much of the fighting had been on French soil, and large stretches of northeastern France had been scarred by the fighting. Buildings and railroads would have to be rebuilt and farms put back in cultivation. The costs were staggering, and finances remained a major problem for French governments of the 1920s. Political instability caused by frequent changes of cabinet and the lack of a strong executive were other major problems.

Denied the genuine national security in terms of protection from Germany that it had sought in the Paris Peace Conference following World War I, France played a Cassandra role in the 1920s and 1930s, warning of the German threat and finding little support in this from Great Britain and the United States, its World War I allies. When the German government defaulted on reparations, French troops occupied the Ruhr in 1923. Although this action forced the German government to live up to its treaty obligations and French troops then departed, the financial cost of the operation was high, and it brought condemnation of France from Britain and the United States. It also brought the Left to power in France in 1924.

The Ruhr occupation was the last such independent French action before World War II. Thereafter, France followed Britain's lead regarding Germany in return for a guarantee of Britain's support in the event of a German invasion. Successive British governments, however, refused to commit themselves to collective security arrangements regarding Eastern Europe that might have prevented war. Meanwhile, German leader Adolf Hitler tore up the Treaty of Versailles and the Locarno Pacts, the latter of which Germany had voluntarily signed. In 1936, Hitler sent German troops into the Rhineland. The French army was then regarded as the world's most powerful military force, and France might have acted unilaterally and halted this step, which could have meant the end of Hitler. When the British refused to support military intervention, though, French leaders took this as an excuse to do nothing.

In September 1938, France and Britain permitted Hitler to seize the Sudetenland from Czechoslovakia, a French military ally. In March 1939, Hitler secured the whole of

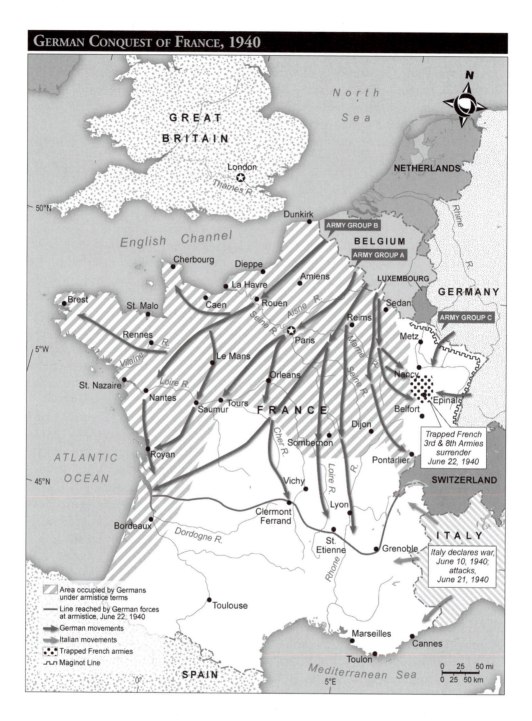

GERMAN CONQUEST OF FRANCE, 1940

Czechoslovakia, prompting Britain, in the worst possible circumstances, to extend a guarantee to Poland—Germany's next target and already a French ally—that Britain would defend it against attack. Following the German invasion of Poland on September 1, 1939, the French government joined Great Britain in declaring war two days later.

The Popular Front that had come to power in France in 1936 had launched a major disarmament program, but on the eve of war France had begun to rearm. It made substantial outlays in arms expenditures and sharp increases in weapons, especially tanks, of which the French army had more than the German army. Time was vital if France (and Britain) were to catch up with German rearmament. The most glaring French military weaknesses, even by May 1940, were in modern aircraft and in antiaircraft guns.

Both London and Paris were confident of military victory, but both governments and their military establishments embarked on the war in leisurely fashion. While the French called up reservists and retrieved artillery from storage, the German army rolled over Poland. The French army carried out only a halfhearted offensive in the Rhineland. Had the offensive been on a larger scale and more forcefully prosecuted, it would have carried to the Rhine. Britain was even slower to mobilize and dispatch the British Expeditionary Force (BEF) to the Continent. France and Britain expected to blockade Germany and use their control of the seas to secure the means to match the Germans in terms of their military establishment, especially in numbers and quality of aircraft. The seven months of inactivity after the German conquest of Poland—known as the *Sitzkrieg* or Phony War— seemed to suggest that time was on the side of the Allies.

Meanwhile, there was sharp dissension on the French home front. From 1935 to 1939, the French Communist Party had been at the forefront of the antifascist crusade and urged rearmament. The German–Soviet Non-Aggression Pact of August 1939, however, converted the French Communists overnight into advocates of neutrality. The government of Premier Édouard Daladier then unwisely moved against the French Communist Party, outlawing it and interning many of its leaders, including those in the National Assembly. Communist agitation against the war continued, however, helping to produce doubt and defeatism, particularly among industrial workers conscripted into the army. This led to the myth that a fifth column had been responsible for the French military defeat in 1940. Dissatisfaction over the lack of aggressive military activity also led to a cabinet crisis and change of premier in March 1940; Paul Reynaud replaced Daladier. The new premier projected energy and optimism, but politics forced Reynaud to keep Daladier as minister of war, and the continuing rivalry between the two men handicapped the war effort.

The Phony War ended on April 9, 1940, when German forces invaded Denmark and Norway. The French joined the British in sending troops to Norway, but these troops could not halt the German conquest and were withdrawn on the opening of the Battle for France. Then, on May 10, 1940, German forces invaded the Low Countries and France. The French Maginot Line, built at great cost beginning in 1929, served its intended purpose of channeling the German invasion to the north through Belgium. However, several elements led to disaster: the failure of France and Britain to work out detailed plans with Belgium (which had declared its neutrality and was fearful that cooperation with the Allies would be the excuse for a German invasion), serious flaws in the Allied command structure, inept French senior military leadership, the inability of the Allies to understand the changed tempo of battlefield conditions that represented the German blitzkrieg, and the misuse of superior armor assets.

British and French military deficiencies, especially in the air, were soon all too evident. Too late, the French attempted major command changes. Only a month after the start of the campaign, on June 10, 1940, the French government abandoned Paris for Bordeaux. To spare the city destruction by the German Luftwaffe, the government declared Paris an open city; four days later German troops moved in. On June 16, at Bordeaux, Reynaud suggested that the government and its armed forces move to French territory in North Africa and continue the fight from there. His vice premier, 84-year-old Marshal Henri Philippe Pétain, opposed this step, as did the new commander of the French army, 73-year-old General Maxime Weygand. Both men considered the war lost and sought to end fighting that they believed could only lead to additional lives lost for no gain. When a majority of the cabinet voted to ask the Germans for terms, Reynaud resigned on June 16.

Ironically, Reynaud had brought Pétain, hero of the World War I Battle of Verdun, into the government on May 18 to stiffen French resolve following initial Allied setbacks in the campaign for France. On June 16, Pétain became premier and immediately opened negotiations with Germany to end the fighting. The Germans delayed to improve conditions, but the French government signed an armistice with Germany on June 22 and with Italy on June 24. Fighting ceased on the battlefields of France on June 25. The campaign had lasted but six weeks. Never before in its military history had France been as broken militarily and psychologically.

The armistice of June 25, 1940, divided France into occupied and unoccupied zones. A pass was necessary for French citizens who desired to move between the two. German forces occupied three-fifths of the country, including northern and western France and the entire Atlantic coast. France had to pay "administrative costs" to the Germans at the absurdly high sum of 20 million reichsmarks a day, calculated at a greatly inflated rate of exchange of 20 francs per reichsmark. This amounted to some 60 percent of French national income. Save for a few units to maintain order, all French military formations were disarmed and demobilized. Ships of the French navy were to assemble in designated ports and be demobilized. The armistice also called for all German prisoners of war to be immediately released, whereas Germany would retain until the end of the war the 1.5 million French prisoners it had captured. France was also forced to surrender German refugees on French territory.

A new French government was then established at Vichy in central France under Pétain to administer the remaining two-fifths of metropolitan France, which included the Mediterranean coast. Vichy France was left with control of its colonies, although Japan sent in troops and established de facto authority over French Indochina during 1940 and 1941. France then played a schizophrenic role until the end of the war. Most French, convinced that for the indefinite future Germany would rule Europe and disgusted with the infighting and weak leadership that had characterized the Third Republic, rallied to the Vichy regime and its calls for a conservative revolution. Meanwhile, young Brigadier General Charles de Gaulle, the only figure of some consequence to escape abroad following the defeat, sought to rally the French to the then-dim hope of eventual victory. He called on French people in Britain or those who could reach there, as well as the French Empire, to join him in continuing the fight. De Gaulle's Free French, soon recognized by the British government, slowly grew in numbers and support as the war wore on and as Germany failed to defeat Britain and suffered rebuff in its invasion of the Soviet Union. The Resistance was an amalgamation of several diverse groups that finally coalesced in May 1943 as the Conseil National de la Résistance (CNR, National Resistance Council), headed by

French Marshal and Vichy leader Philippe Petain (1856–1951, left) and Nazi leader Adolf Hitler (1889–1945, right) share the famous "handshake at Montoire" on October 24, 1940, while interpreter Colonel Schmidt watches. Pétain thereby announces officially that Vichy France is prepared to collaborate with the German Reich. (AP/Wide World Photos)

Jean Moulin. Its military arm was the Forces Françaises de l'Interieur (FFI, French Forces of the Interior).

Although some French men and women were active in the Resistance, most of the population simply tried to endure the German occupation. Many actively collaborated with the German occupiers for financial gain, and a few fervently supported the Nazi policies opposing Communism and persecuting the Jews. The Vichy government organized a force known as the Milice to combat growing numbers of FFI.

British prime minister Winston Churchill's government recognized de Gaulle's government as the legitimate representative of France, but Churchill also created strong Anglophobia in France by his decision to move to secure the French fleet, most notably at Mers-el-Kébir, where fighting occurred with considerable loss of French life. This affair still rankles the French today, as the French government had promised that it would not let the Germans seize the fleet and ultimately scuttled its main fleet to honor that pledge, even after the events of Mers-el-Kébir.

U.S. president Franklin D. Roosevelt strongly distrusted de Gaulle, and the United States maintained diplomatic relations with Vichy until the Allied invasion of North

Africa—Operation TORCH—in November 1942. French resistance to the Allied landings and devious dealings by Vichy representatives ended Allied attempts to negotiate with Pétain's government.

De Gaulle's Free French Forces greatly expanded after the Allied invasion of North Africa. Rearmed and reequipped by the United States, a French Expeditionary Corps of five divisions was sent to Italy in late 1943, and it made a major contribution to the Allied military efforts there. What became the French First Army landed in southern France in August 1944 as part of Operation DRAGOON. Its 10 divisions fought through France into Germany and Austria. Meanwhile, Allied forces had come ashore in Normandy, and the French Resistance played a key role in isolating the beachheads and preventing German resupply. Everywhere, French men and women assisted the Allied armies. Paris was liberated on August 25, the 2nd French Armored Division leading the Allied units into the city to join with those fighting the Germans and saving the city's honor.

De Gaulle soon established his government in Paris, and French troops continued with the liberation of French territory. Following the war, nearly 40,000 French citizens were imprisoned for collaboration, including Marshal Pétain and his vice premier, Pierre Laval. Both men were sentenced to death, although de Gaulle commuted Pétain's sentence to life imprisonment in recognition of his World War I service. At least 10,000 people were executed for collaborating with the Nazis. Collaboration was and still is a highly sensitive topic in postwar France.

The high hopes and idealism of the Resistance were soon dashed. Although an overwhelming 96 percent of Frenchmen voting in an October 1945 referendum rejected the constitutional structure of the Third Republic, sharp political divisions ensured that the Fourth Republic that followed it was virtually a carbon copy of the Third. Not until 1958, when the Fourth Republic was overthrown and de Gaulle returned to power, would France have a constitution that ensured a strong executive. Despite de Gaulle's wartime promises of a new relationship with the colonies, the government in Paris pursued a shortsighted policy of trying to hold on to its major colonies, believing that only with its empire could France still be counted as a great power. Such grandiose and outdated notions led to disastrous wars in Indochina and later in Algeria, ultimately toppling the Fourth Republic.

Dana Lombardy, T. P. Schweider, and Spencer C. Tucker

See also

Africa; Bradley, Omar Nelson; Casualties; Churchill, Sir Winston Leonard Spencer; Collaboration; de Gaulle, Charles; Eisenhower, Dwight D.; Germany, Air Force; Germany, Army; Great Britain, Air Force; Great Britain, Army; Great Britain, Navy; Hitler, Adolf; Holocaust, The; Montgomery, Sir Bernard Law; Mussolini, Benito; North Africa Campaign; Patton, George Smith, Jr.; Poland, Role in War; Prisoners of War (POWs); Resistance; Rommel, Erwin Johannes Eugen; United States, Army; United States, Army Air Force; United States, Navy; Western European Theater of Operations

References

Black, Jeremy. *Avoiding Armageddon: From the Great War to the Fall of France, 1918–1940.* New York: Continuum, 2012.

Burrin, Philippe. *France under the Germans: Cooperation and Compromise.* Translated by Janet Lloyd. New York: New Press, 1996.

Christofferson, Thomas R., and Michael S. Christofferson. *France during World War II: From Defeat to Liberation.* New York: Fordham University Press, 2006.

Dank, Milton. *The French against the French.* New York: J. B. Lippincott, 1974.

Horne, Alistair. *To Lose a Battle: France 1940.* Boston, MA: Little, Brown, 1969.

Jackson, Julian. *The Fall of France: The Nazi Invasion of 1940.* New York: Oxford University Press, 2003.

Jackson, Julian. *France: The Dark Years, 1940–1944.* New York: Oxford University Press, 2001.

Kiesling, Eugenia C. *Arming against Hitler: France and the Limits of Military Planning.* Lawrence, KS: University Press of Kansas, 1996.

Maiolo, Joseph. *Cry Havoc: How the Arms Race Drove the World to War, 1931–1941.* London: John Murray, 2010.

Marrus, Michael R., and Robert O. Paxton. *Vichy France and the Jews.* New York: Basic Books, 1981.

May, Ernest R. *Strange Victory: Hitler's Conquest of France.* New York: Hill and Wang, 2000.

Ousby, Ian. *Occupation: The Ordeal of France, 1940–1944.* New York: St. Martin's Press, 1997.

Paxton, Robert O. *Vichy France: Old Guard and New Order, 1940–1944.* New York: Alfred A. Knopf, 1972.

Shirer, William L. *The Collapse of the Third Republic: An Inquiry into the Fall of France in 1940.* New York: Simon and Schuster, 1969.

Vinen, Richard. *The Unfree French: Life under the Occupation.* New Haven, CT: Yale University Press, 2006.

Warner, Geoffrey. *Pierre Laval and the Eclipse of France, 1931–1945.* New York: Macmillan, 1968.

Germany, Air Force

The German air force, the Luftwaffe, existed officially for barely a decade, but during that time it was the pride of Nazi Germany. Before the war, the Luftwaffe was useful in coercing concessions from other countries. It was the world's most powerful air force in 1939, and once World War II began, it became an essential element of the blitzkrieg—the "lightning war." The Luftwaffe was, however, basically a tactical force, and it came apart under the strain of the German invasion of the Soviet Union.

The Treaty of Versailles after World War I denied Germany an air force. Nonetheless, the Germans continued experimenting with aviation, and the military developed air doctrine and training programs, monitored technological developments, and built an industrial infrastructure for civilian aviation. At the same time, the German military established clandestine air facilities in the Soviet Union to build and test aircraft and train personnel. When Adolf Hitler came to power in January 1933, he pushed development of aviation and in 1935 openly began building an air force. The western Allies were reluctant to use force to halt this development, which was a direct violation of German treaty obligations.

Unlike the army and navy, the Luftwaffe was purely a Nazi creation and became the primary focus of Hitler's rearmament program. Hitler selected Hermann Göring, a World War I ace pilot, as minister of aviation and commander in chief of the Luftwaffe. Hitler was also much impressed with theories, notably those of Italian Giulio Douhet, that future wars could be won by air forces alone.

In 1936, Hitler sent the Kondor Legion, essentially a Luftwaffe outfit, to fight in the Spanish Civil War. Here the Germans gained invaluable experience in testing aircraft, tactical concepts, and experimenting with strategic bombing (as at Guernica). Hitler's boasts about German air power, although many of them were empty, helped face down the French and British in his March 1936 remilitarization of the Rhineland and in the 1938 crisis over Czechoslovakia.

As with so many other agencies in the Reich, the Luftwaffe suffered from organizational weaknesses and overlap at the top. Göring, one of Hitler's inner circle from the early days, was Hitler's designated successor, and Hitler allowed him to run the Luftwaffe without any real interference. The Reich Air Ministry consisted of the office of state secretary for air Erhard Milch; it supervised aviation matters apart from operations. Milch was also inspector general of the Luftwaffe. In addition there was Luftwaffe chief of staff Hans Jeschonnek. Until his suicide in 1943, Jeschonnek headed the air force's organization,

Two German Dornier 217 planes pass over the burning bombing targets of the Breckton Gas Works at Silvertown, a suburb in southeast London, during the Battle of Britain in autumn 1940. (AP/Wide World Photos)

operations, intelligence, training, quartermaster, and signal branches. Milch and Jeschonnek did not get along. Jeschonnek only had access to Göring on operational matters and had no control over personnel, which Göring made his own province. Ernst Udet, chief of the Technical Office and World War I ace, proved an incompetent administrator. Udet reported to Milch, who took over Udet's office after Udet's 1941 suicide. Too late, in May 1944, the administrative structure was streamlined with the creation of the Oberkommando der Luftwaffe (Air Force high command, OKL). Also in 1944, Albert Speer's Armaments Ministry gained control of all German aircraft production, and Milch's ministry was abolished.

The Luftwaffe, the newest of the military services, was the least professional and suffered the most from promotions not based on merit. Göring surrounded himself with advisers whose principal qualifications were that they were Nazis, as opposed to experienced aviation military officers. Many times they either offered poor advice or, not wishing to anger him, agreed with whatever ideas he developed. Increasingly, Göring, who held numerous offices in the Reich, largely abandoned his command of the Luftwaffe, intervening only in fits and starts and often with disastrous results, as during the 1940 Battle of Britain. During the war, the Luftwaffe was also the agency least conscious of communications security.

The Luftwaffe controlled all air services but had little interest in naval aviation. Airborne troops were Luftwaffe personnel, and the air force also had charge of antiaircraft artillery. Eventually the Luftwaffe even fielded 22 ground divisions, including the Hermann Göring Armored Division. The Luftwaffe itself was organized into Luftflotten (air fleets), constituted so as to perform a variety of roles and consisting of a wide variety of aircraft types. At the beginning of the war, Germany had four Luftflotten, and during the course of the conflict three more were added. The next operational division was the Fleigerkorps (flier corps), and below that was the Fleigerdivision (flier division). These last two each contained several Geschwader (squadrons) that were designated as to types (including fighters, bombers, night fighters, training, and so on). Each division controlled three to four Gruppen (groups) comprising three or four Staffein (squadrons). In September 1939, the Luftwaffe had 302 Staffein.

At that point, Germany's chief advantage was in the air, for at the start of hostilities the Luftwaffe was certainly the world's most powerful air force. In September 1939, Göring commanded more than 3,600 frontline aircraft. The death in 1936 of strategic bomber proponent General Walther Wever, however, had brought a shift in emphasis to tactical air power. This remained the case throughout the war. Although Germany developed four-engine bomber prototypes, these were never placed in production. It could be argued, however, that a tactical air force was the best use of Germany's limited resources.

The German air force was essentially built to support ground operations. It suited ideally the new blitzkrieg tactics, and the Junkers Ju-87 Stuka dive-bomber was a highly accurate form of "flying artillery." Impressed by U.S. Marine Corps experiments with precision dive-bombing, the Germans embraced this technique; indeed, all German bombers had to be capable of dive-bombing. This entailed considerable aircraft structural change with attendant production delays and a decrease in bomb-carrying capacity. The flying weight of the Junkers Ju-88 twin-engine bomber went from 6 to 12 tons, sharply reducing both its speed and its bomb-carrying capacity. Nonetheless, the Germans developed some exceptional aircraft. In addition to the Stuka, they had a superb air-superiority fighter in the Messerschmitt Bf-109, certainly one of the best all-around aircraft of the war. And before the end of the war, the Germans had introduced the Messerschmitt Me-262, the world's first operational jet aircraft. But Hitler also wasted considerable resources on the development of terror or "vengeance" weaponry, the V-1 and V-2.

The Luftwaffe played key roles in the German victories over Poland in 1939 and over France and the Low Countries in 1940. Its limitations first became evident during the Battle of Britain, when Göring attempted to wage a strategic bombing campaign with a tactical air force. Germany's defeat in this battle was its first setback of the war. The Luftwaffe was also impressive in the fighting against the Soviet Union, at least until the Battle of Stalingrad. But in the fighting on the Eastern Front, the superb combined-arms instrument that had been the German military to that point began to come unhinged. By the fall of 1941, Germany was overextended, and the Luftwaffe's small airlift capacity of Junkers Ju-52 trimotor transports was unable to fulfill all the missions required of it. Although Germany increased its aircraft production during the war, as the conflict continued, and under relentless Allied bombing, it suffered from lack of aviation fuel. This was the key factor in the defeat of the Luftwaffe, rather than inferior or too few aircraft.

By 1944, the Luftwaffe was feeling the effects of the Allied bomber offensive. In the first half of the year, pilot losses were averaging 20 percent a month, and the scarcity of fuel forced the routine grounding of aircraft not only for operations but also for training.

In a period when replacement aircrews were desperately needed, flight time for trainees had been reduced to less than half that for their Allied counterparts. This in turn led to increasing numbers of accidents. By the time of the June 1944 Normandy invasion, the much-vaunted Luftwaffe had been largely silenced.

Pamela Feltus and Spencer C. Tucker

See also

Balkans Theater; Eastern Front; Hitler, Adolf; Northeast Europe Theater; Western European Theater of Operations

References

Bishop, Chris. *Luftwaffe Squadrons, 1939–45*. London: Amber Books, 2006.

Caldwell, Donald R., and Richard R. Muller. *The Luftwaffe over Germany: Defense of the Reich*. Barnsley: Greenhill Books, 2007.

Cooper, Mathew. *The German Air Force, 1922–1945: Anatomy of a Failure*. London: Jane's, 1981.

Corum, James S. *The Luftwaffe: Creating the Operational Air War, 1918–1940*. Lawrence, KS: University Press of Kansas, 1997.

Hallion, Richard. *Strike from the Sky: The History of Battlefield Air Attack, 1911–1945*. Washington, DC: Smithsonian Institution Press, 1989.

Hayward, Joel S. *Stopped at Stalingrad: The Luftwaffe and Hitler's Defeat in the East, 1942–1943*. Lawrence, KS: University Press of Kansas, 1998.

Mason, Herbert Malloy. *The Rise of the Luftwaffe*. New York: Ballantine, 1973.

McNab, Chris. *The German Luftwaffe in World War II*. London: Amber Books, 2009.

Overy, Richard J. *The Air War 1939–1945*. Washington, DC: Potomac Books, 2005.

Uziel, Daniel. *Arming the Luftwaffe: The German Aviation Industry in World War II*. Jefferson, NC: McFarland, 2011.

Germany, Army

At the tactical level of warfare, the German army—the Reichsheer—of World War II may well have been the best ground force in the history of warfare to that time. On the strategic level, the Germans had major blind spots that go a long way toward explaining why they lost two world wars despite having the best army in the field. At the middle level of warfare—that of operations—historians continue to argue about the German army. One school holds that the German doctrine of blitzkrieg was the most sophisticated example of the operational art to that time. The other school argues that what passed for operational art in the German army was little more than tactics on a grand scale.

The Reichsheer of World War II (the Wehrmacht was the entire German military, not just the army) grew out of the 100,000-man Reichswehr that was allowed to Germany following World War I under the terms of the Treaty of Versailles. On October 1, 1934, Adolf Hitler ordered the threefold secret expansion of the Reichswehr. Conscription was reintroduced in March 1935, establishing a further increased objective base strength of 38 divisions and approximately 600,000 troops. By 1939, the two main components of the

German army were the field army (Feldheer) and the replacement army (Ersatzheer). The field army had more than 2 million soldiers and was organized into 120 divisions—99 infantry, 9 panzer, 6 motorized, 1 cavalry, 3 mountain, and 2 parachute. The replacement army consisted of a force of approximately 100,000 men in training or transit. From 1942 onward, the numbers of replacements became progressively insufficient to keep frontline units up to authorized strength levels.

The infantry division was the primary tactical element of the German army. In 1940, the standard German infantry division had 17,200 troops, 942 motor vehicles, and 5,375 horses. By 1944, there were 226 infantry divisions, but their size had shrunk to 12,352 troops, 615 motor vehicles, and 4,656 horses. Despite its reputation as the master of mechanized and mobile warfare, the German army relied heavily on horses right up until the end of the war. Almost all field artillery in the infantry divisions was horse-drawn. The German divisions were organized according to a triangular structure, with (1) three infantry regiments of three battalions of three companies each; (2) a divisional artillery command with a field artillery regiment of three battalions of three batteries each, a heavy artillery battalion, and an observation battalion; (3) reconnaissance, engineer, signals, and antitank battalions; and (4) the divisional (supply) trains. Each division also generally had an antiaircraft battalion attached to it from the Luftwaffe.

After Greece defeated Italian forces in Albania in late 1940, German forces came to Italy's rescue. German panzer units move southward through Greece in April 1941, despite heavy spring rains and muddy roads. (Library of Congress)

The Germans did, however, field various forms of motorized or mechanized units. By 1941, they had a total of 10 motorized infantry divisions and light infantry divisions. Later in the war, these units were redesignated as panzergrenadier divisions. Germany ultimately fielded 22 of these units. They were organized along the general lines of the infantry divisions, but they had more motor vehicles and an organic tank regiment. In 1940, the standard motorized or light division had 14,000 troops, 3,370 motor vehicles, 158 tanks, and more than 1,500 horses. The 1944 panzergrenadier division had 13,833 soldiers, 2,637 motor vehicles, 48 tanks, and more than 1,400 horses.

The Germans had several specialized divisions. Mountain divisions were essentially smaller and lighter versions of the infantry division. Germany had 3 mountain divisions in 1940 and 13 in 1944. Fortress divisions and security divisions were divisions in name only; they could not be seriously equated with other divisions in the army's order of battle. The fortress divisions were little more than stationary garrisons, seldom larger than a regiment in strength. The security divisions were used to secure rear-area lines of communication and to conduct antipartisan operations on the Eastern Front. In a last act of desperation late in the war, Germany created Volksgrenadier (people's grenadier) divisions for defense of the Reich itself. Heavily manned by old men and young boys with almost no military training, these units were armed with a high proportion of automatic and antitank weapons. Because of the weapons' high firepower and the fact that the units were defending their home ground, these units sometimes gave a surprisingly good account of themselves.

The Germans began the war with one cavalry (horse) division, which fought in the Poland Campaign in 1939. By 1944, Germany actually had four such divisions, all operating on the Eastern Front. Late in the war, Germany fielded its single artillery division, which was based on the Soviet model. The Red Army, which had hundreds of thousands of artillery pieces, fielded almost 100 artillery divisions. But for the Germans, who were chronically short of artillery throughout the war, fielding an artillery division was an almost pointless exercise. The Germans did not have sufficient artillery to equip their infantry and panzer divisions, let alone form more artillery divisions.

Organizationally, all German parachute divisions were part of the Luftwaffe, but operationally they fought under army command. The Germans had 2 parachute divisions in 1940 and 11 in 1944. After the near-disaster on Crete, German parachute divisions never again jumped in combat. They spent the remainder of the war fighting as light infantry, but their traditional paratrooper élan remained, and they were fierce opponents, especially in Italy. The German air force also fielded land divisions that operated under army command. The formation of these air force field units was another desperate measure. As attrition ground down the Luftwaffe's aircraft, especially on the Eastern Front, excess personnel were hastily grouped into these field divisions. Often, the new ground soldiers had little or no infantry training. Germany had 19 such divisions in 1944.

The panzer division was the mailed striking fist of the German army. The first three panzer divisions were raised as completely new units in the fall of 1935, but they were not fully operational until September 1937. Thereafter, new panzer divisions were created by converting infantry or other divisions. There were 9 panzer divisions by 1939 and 26 by 1944. From 1941, the panzer divisions were in action almost constantly and continually subject to being ground down by attrition. A panzer division in 1940 had some

14,000 troops, 1,800 motor vehicles, and 337 horses. The standard panzer division had 324 tanks, and a variation known as a light panzer division had 219 tanks. By 1944, the typical panzer division had 13,700 troops, but the number of motor vehicles had decreased to 48, whereas the number of horses had increased to almost 1,700. On paper, at least, a 1944 panzer division had 150 tanks; in the last year of the war, however, many panzer divisions could only field a handful of tanks.

The Waffen-Schutzstaffel (Waffen-SS) was separate from the army and even from the Wehrmacht. However, it was essentially the Nazi Party's army, and it fielded combat divisions that fought under army command and control, much like the Luftwaffe's field and parachute divisions. By 1944, there were 7 SS panzer divisions and 11 panzergrenadier divisions. The organization of the Waffen-SS divisions was similar to the organization of their Wehrmacht counterparts, but because of their unquestioning loyalty to Hitler they were often better equipped.

The echelon of command above the division was the corps, which consisted of two or more divisions and additional corps support troops and artillery. The two basic types of corps were the army corps, consisting primarily of infantry divisions, and the panzer corps, consisting primarily of panzer divisions. The XCI Armeecorps was the highest-numbered corps. The next-higher echelon of command was the field army, comprising two or more corps. Field armies normally were designated by numbers, but in a few instances they were designated by a name. Field armies also had their own pools of combat assets such as artillery and separate heavy tank battalions. The German army's largest operational unit was the army group (Heeresgruppe), which controlled several field armies or corps directly. The army group was also responsible for providing support to all units in its area, as well as for the rear-area lines of communication and logistical services. Army groups were designated by their locations, by their commander's name, or by a letter.

The Germans had several elite units designated only by their name. Grossdeutschland (greater Germany)—also called "the bodyguard of the German people"—was first formed in 1938 as a ceremonial battalion. By 1939, it had expanded to the size of a regiment, and by 1942 it was an oversized division. At the end of the war, Panzerarmee Grossdeutschland commanded five divisions under two corps. The Panzer Lehr Division, which was the most powerful German armored division in Western Europe at the time of the Allied landings in Normandy, was formed in the winter of 1943–1944 with instructors and troops from the German armored school. The Infantrie-Lehr Regiment was an elite unit formed from instructors and infantry-school troops. In 1944, Hitler personally ordered the Infantrie-Lehr to Anzio to block the Allied landings there.

Command and control in the German army suffered from a confused structure at the very top, which only compounded the German weaknesses at the strategic and operational levels. Three different high-command headquarters were seldom in agreement and often in competition. The Oberkommando das Heeres (army high command, OKH), the Oberkommando der Wehrmacht (armed forces high command, OKW), and the supreme commander (Hitler) and his staff often issued conflicting orders to the same units. In theory, OKH ran the war in the Soviet Union, and the OKW ran the war everywhere else. Hitler's Führerhauptquartier (Führer headquarters) issued all the key strategic orders.

Despite the popular stereotypes, reinforced by countless Hollywood movies and television programs, the common German soldier of World War II was anything but stupid and unimaginative, and his officers and noncommissioned officers (NCOs) were neither machinelike nor inflexible autocrats. Rather, the German army encouraged initiative among its subordinate leaders and stressed flexibility and creativity to a degree far greater than any other army prior to 1945. This was the key to its tactical excellence. German combat orders, rather than dictating detailed and rigid timelines and specific instructions on how to accomplish missions, tended to be short and as broad as possible. The principle under which the German command system operated was called *Auftragstaktik*, which can only very loosely be translated into English as "mission orders." For *Auftragstaktik* to work, a subordinate leader had to understand the intent of his higher commander at least two echelons up. That meant that the subordinate had the right to ask his superior why something was being done, and the superior was obligated to explain. Such a practice was virtually unheard of in almost all the other armies of World War II.

Despite superb organization and tactical tools at the lower levels, the confused high-command structure and Germany's incoherent strategy doomed the German army over the long run. Hitler did a great deal personally to subvert solid military command and control. He distrusted his generals, and for the most part they distrusted him. During the early years of the war, 1939 and 1940, Hitler was the beneficiary of outrageously good luck and inept opponents. This only served to reinforce his belief in what he thought was his divinely inspired military genius. When the commander in chief of the German army, General Walther von Brauchitsch, retired for medical reasons in late 1941, Hitler—the former World War I lance corporal—assumed direct command of the army. By that time, however, Hitler had led Germany once again into its worst strategic nightmare, a two-front war.

The German army also suffered from several internal and external handicaps that were beyond its ability to control. Germany was chronically short of virtually every vital resource necessary for modern warfare. A panzer division in 1940 still had more than 300 horses, and four years later that number had risen to 1,700. Roughly only 10 percent of the army was ever motorized. In 1940, OKH planners estimated that it would require at least 210 divisions to execute the invasions of France and the Low Countries while simultaneously garrisoning Poland and Norway. At the time, they were 20 divisions short. The chronic shortages of manpower and motorized transport only worsened as the war progressed. The situation did not improve even after German industry was mobilized in 1944. By then, of course, it was far too late.

David T. Zabecki

See also

Balkans Theater; Eastern Front; Italy Campaign; North Africa Campaign; Northeast Europe Theater; Rommel, Erwin Johannes Eugen; Western European Theater of Operations

References

Citino, Robert M. *Death of the Wehrmacht: The German Campaigns of 1942*. Lawrence, KS: University Press of Kansas, 2007.

Citino, Robert M. *The Path to Blitzkrieg: Doctrine and Training in the German Army, 1920–1939*. Boulder, CO: Lynne Rienner, 1999.

Citino, Robert M. *The Wehrmacht Retreats: Fighting a Lost War, 1943*. Lawrence, KS: University Press of Kansas, 2012.

Corum, James. *The Roots of Blitzkrieg: Hans von Seeckt and German Military Reform*. Lawrence, KS: University Press of Kansas, 1992.

Creveld, Martin van. *Fighting Power: German and U.S. Army Performance, 1939–1945*. Westport, CT: Greenwood Press, 1982.

Fritz, Stephen G. *Frontsoldaten: The German Soldier in World War II*. Lexington, KY: University Press of Kentucky, 1997.

Helber, Helmut, and David M. Glantz, eds. *Hitler and His Generals: Military Conferences, 1942–1943*. Translated by Roland Winter, Krista Smith, and Mary Beth Friedrich. New York: Enigma, 2003.

Her Majesty's Stationery Office. *German Order of Battle 1944*. Reprinted 1994.

Maiolo, Joseph. *Cry Havoc: How the Arms Race Drove the World to War, 1931–1941*. London: John Murray, 2010.

Mercatante, Steven D. *Why Germany Nearly Won: A New History of World War II in Europe*. Westport, CT: Praeger, 2012.

Mosier, John. *The Blitzkrieg Myth: How Hitler and the Allies Misread the Strategic Realities of World War II*. New York: HarperCollins, 2003.

Mosier, John. *Cross of Iron: The Rise and Fall of the German War Machine, 1918–1945*. New York: Henry Holt, 2006.

Overy, Richard. *The Dictators: Hitler's Germany, Stalin's Russia*. New York: Norton, 2005.

Rosinski, Herbert. *The German Army*. New York: Praeger, 1966.

Stone, David. *Shattered Genius: The Decline and Fall of the German General Staff in World War II*. Havertown, PA: Casemate Publishers, 2012.

Tooze, Adam. *The Wages of Destruction: The Making and Breaking of the Nazi Economy*. New York: Viking, 2007.

U.S. War Department. *TM-E 30–451 Handbook on German Military Forces*. Baton Rouge, LA: Louisiana State University Press, 1990.

Wallach, Jeduha L. *The Dogma of the Battle of Annihilation: The Theories of Clausewitz and Schlieffen and Their Impact on the German Conduct of Two World Wars*. Westport, CT: Greenwood Press, 1986.

Zabecki, David T., and Bruce Condell, eds. *On the German Art of War: Truppenführung*. Boulder, CO: Lynne Rienner, 2001.

Germany, Navy

Under Adolf Hitler, Germany embarked on a program to rebuild its navy on a global scale. The German navy (Kriegsmarine) began this major effort after the signing of the Anglo-German Naval Treaty in June 1935. The goal was creation of a balanced fleet that would serve as the core of a future blue-water navy dominated by battleships. This Z Plan envisioned a powerful fleet that would one day challenge Britain and the United States for world naval mastery.

In 1938, Hitler's aggressive foreign policy forced the navy to consider the possibility of a future naval war against Great Britain. The navy's commander, Grand Admiral Erich

The German pocket battleship *Admiral Graf Spee*, once the pride of the German Navy, is seen on December 17, 1939, as it sinks near Montevideo, Uruguay, following the violent explosion that sent her to the bottom of the sea. Her commander, Captain Hans Langsdorff, scuttled the *Graf Spee*, avoiding internment and a further fight with British warships. (AP/Wide World Photos)

Raeder, designed a strategy to attack the British sea-lanes. His proposal to build ships more suited to a commerce war, including additional U-boats, was rejected by Hitler, who was intent on building a battleship-dominated navy that would serve as an instrument of political and military force commensurate with a world power. Shortages of resources contributed to delays in naval construction, and Raeder's blind confidence in the Führer's diplomatic successes and promises that war would not come before 1942 or 1943 found the navy unprepared for war in September 1939.

At the beginning of the war, the German navy consisted of 79,000 men, 2 battleships, 3 pocket battleships (small, fast, strongly constructed battleships), 1 heavy cruiser, 6 light cruisers, and 33 destroyers and torpedo boats. Fewer than half of the 57 U-boats available were suitable for Atlantic operations. In spite of Raeder's initial pessimism that the navy could only "die gallantly," thereby creating the foundations for a future fleet, he intended to carry out an aggressive naval strategy that would attack British sea communications on a global basis using his concept of diversion and concentration in operational areas of his own choosing and timing. Raeder persistently argued with Hitler that only total economic warfare against England could have a decisive impact.

Hitler's restrictions on naval operations, particularly on the U-boats, frustrated Raeder's attempts to seize the initiative and achieve early successes. In late 1939, concerned that the British were planning to invade Norway, Raeder instigated planning for the successful German occupation of Norway and Denmark (Operation WESERÜBUNG). This April 1940 operation was for the navy its "feat of arms"—justifying its contribution to the war effort and future existence. Although the navy did secure important port facilities for surface raiders and U-boats in Norway as well as the shipping route for iron ore from Sweden, it also suffered substantial losses in the operation in the form of 3 cruisers and 10 destroyers. In June, with the defeat of France, the navy acquired additional ports on the Atlantic and Bay of Biscay for surface ships and submarines. But the navy now had to also protect an extended coastline from occupied France to Scandinavia. From 1940 to 1943, Germany also sent to sea 9 armed auxiliary cruisers.

Raeder's intent to prove the worth of the surface fleet, in particular the battleships, led him to demand of his commanders that they take risks yet avoid unnecessary combat that could lead to losses. Two fleet commanders lost their jobs when they failed to exhibit the necessary aggressiveness. The scuttling of the pocket battleship *Graf Spee* in December 1939 and Hitler's displeasure over this loss further reinforced the inherent contradictions in Raeder's orders to strike boldly but avoid damage to the navy's own ships. With new battleships *Bismarck* and *Tirpitz* joining the fleet, Raeder envisioned a new phase of the Atlantic surface battle, with task forces that would engage Allied convoys protected by capital ships. In an effort to prove the value of the battleships, Raeder pressed the *Bismarck* into service before the other battleships were available for action. Her loss in May 1941 represented the end of the surface war in the Atlantic and Hitler's increasing interference in the use of Germany's remaining capital ships.

Unable to achieve the conditions for a cross-Channel invasion (Operation SEA LION) in September 1940, Raeder tried to divert Hitler from his plans to attack the Soviet Union. Raeder advocated an alternative strategy in the Mediterranean to defeat Britain first, especially given the growing cooperation between that nation and the United States. After the Japanese attack on Pearl Harbor, Raeder saw an opportunity to link up with the Japanese in the Indian Ocean and use the French African colonies and the Atlantic islands of Portugal and Spain to expand the bases for a long-term war against the Anglo-American naval forces in the Atlantic. These plans never materialized, as the war against the Soviet Union faltered and Germany was forced to come to the aid of Italy and secure its southern flank in the Balkans.

Nervous about British threats to Norway and Allied support to the Soviets in the north, Hitler ordered that the two battleships in Brest—the *Gneisenau* and *Scharnhorst*—and the heavy cruiser *Prinz Eugen* be either moved to Norway or scrapped. The "Channel dash" in February 1942 was a tactical success but a strategic defeat for the navy. With the fleet relegated to Norway as a "fleet-in-being," the U-boat arm, under the command of Admiral Karl Dönitz, continued its role as the navy's primary weapon. The lack of Luftwaffe support, though, continued to seriously hamper all operations. The navy never resolved the issue of whether the U-boat war was a "tonnage" war or a commerce war in which U-boats attacked targets that had the greatest potential for a decisive impact. Dönitz continued to argue that all resources should go to the U-boat war and disagreed with the diversion of U-boats to other theaters such as the Mediterranean or to the defense of Norway.

In late December 1942, the failure of the *Hipper* and *Lützow* to close with a weakly defended convoy in the Barents Sea (Operation RAINBOW) led an angry Hitler to attack Raeder and the surface fleet. Raeder resigned, and Dönitz succeeded him. Although Dönitz was determined to prosecute the submarine war ruthlessly, as with the surface fleet, the defeat of the U-boats in May 1943 resulted from Allied technology and successes in codebreaking that reflected the shortcomings in the naval leadership and military structure of the Third Reich. As the military situation of Germany deteriorated, the navy provided support to the army, particularly in the Baltic, where it conducted a massive and highly successful evacuation effort of troops and civilians.

In sharp contrast to the navy's collapse after World War I, the German navy during World War II enforced strict discipline until the end. In April 1945, Hitler named a loyal Dönitz as his heir and successor.

Keith W. Bird

See also

Atlantic, Battle of the; Great Britain, Navy; Signals Intelligence; Southeast Pacific Theater; United States, Navy

References

Blair, Clay. *Hitler's U-Boat War.* 2 vols. New York: Random House, 1996, 1998.

Howarth, Stephen, and Derek Law, eds. *The Battle of the Atlantic, 1939–1945.* London and Annapolis, MD: Greenhill Books and Naval Institute Press, 1994.

Militärgeschtliches Forschungsamt. *Das Deutsche Reich und der Zweite Weltkrieg* (Germany and the Second World War). Translated by Dean S. McMurrey, Edwald Osers, and Louise Wilmott. 7 vols. Oxford: Clarendon Press, 1990–2001.

O'Hara, Vincent P. *Struggle for the Middle Sea: The Great Navies at War in the Mediterranean Theater, 1940–1945.* Annapolis, MD: Naval Institute Press, 2009.

O'Hara, Vincent P., W. David Dickson, and Richard Worth, eds. *On Seas Contested: The Seven Great Navies of the Second World War.* Annapolis, MD: Naval Institute Press, 2010.

Philbin, Tobias R., III. *The Lure of Neptune: German–Soviet Naval Collaboration and Ambitions, 1919–1941.* Columbia, SC: University of South Carolina Press, 1994.

Salewski, Michael. *Die Deutsche Seekriegsleitung 1935–1945* [The German Maritime Warfare Command 1935–1945]. 3 vols. Munich: Bernard and Graefe, 1970–1975.

Thomas, Charles. *The German Navy in the Nazi Era.* Annapolis, MD: Naval Institute Press, 1990.

Great Britain, Air Force

The future of the Royal Air Force (RAF) appeared bleak at the end of World War I. With extensive personnel and aircraft drawdowns, the RAF's existence as an independent service remained in doubt until the appointment of General Sir Hugh Trenchard as chief of the Air Staff in January 1919. As dogged as he was visionary, Trenchard proved the viability of the third service, and by the mid-1920s he secured the RAF's future. In search of a mission, the RAF turned to imperial policing, especially in Somaliland, Aden, Palestine, India, and Iraq, where it proved highly successful.

Still, growth in force size was slow due to economic difficulties and an ever-shrinking defense budget. Of the 52 squadrons approved in 1923, only 42 had been established by 1934. In 1935, the transition to monoplane designs began, a process resulting in the most successful British fighter aircraft of the early war years—the Hawker Hurricane designed by Sydney Camm, which entered service in 1937; and the Supermarine Spitfire, designed by R. J. Mitchell, which appeared in 1938. In 1936, future manpower needs were addressed with the establishment of an RAF Volunteer Reserve. By January 1939, the total RAF establishment consisted of 135 squadrons.

Despite advancements in fighter types as defense against strategic bombers, the prevailing attitude throughout European air services reflected the airpower theories of such visionaries as Brigadier General Billy Mitchell in the United States and Giulio Douhet in Italy, both of whom argued the primacy of the bomber. To overcome the loss of strategic mobility, a difficulty that was suffered by the armies of the Western Front in World War I, Britain embraced the concept of strategic bombing. This concept was based on the theory that long-range bombing would inevitably undercut an opponent's will and civilian morale, as well as cripple his economic ability to wage war.

The beginning of World War II in September 1939 found the RAF considerably better prepared than it had been only four years earlier. The Bomber Command order of battle included 54 squadrons equipped with Bristol Blenheims, Vickers Wellingtons, Armstrong Whitleys, and Handley Page Hampdens. The critical weakness lay in the mismatch between air strategy and the instruments of war available in 1939. The RAF had no heavy bomber capable of delivering the crippling physical and economic blows necessary for strategic bombing success. Not until the Handley Page Halifax heavy bomber entered service in late 1940 did Bomber Command possess a heavy bomber that could carry the air war deep into enemy territory.

Fighter Command entered the war considerably better prepared in terms of equipment capability. The 35 home-based fighter squadrons with first-line Hurricanes and Spitfires were enhanced by a series of coastal radar stations known as Chain Home. Though relatively primitive, the radar network soon proved robust and difficult for the German Luftwaffe to destroy. Thus with a total of 1,466 aircraft, of which roughly 1,000 were first-line, the RAF faced Reichsmarshall Hermann Göring's Luftwaffe.

The first months of the war can best be described as a sparring match characterized mainly by frustrated attempts by the RAF to attack German navy warships. In France, Air Chief Marshal Sir Hugh Dowding, commander in chief of Fighter Command, insisted on sending only those squadrons for the Advanced Air Striking Force (AASF) that were equipped with older, less robust aircraft such as the Gloster Gladiator. He feared losing first-rate aircraft and stripping home defense of fighting capability. Despite Dowding's conservatism, the RAF lost nearly 1,000 aircraft in the Battle of France, half of them fighters.

The Luftwaffe had high hopes of quickly dispatching the undermanned and outgunned RAF when as a precursor to invasion it launched Operation SEA LION, Germany's main air offensive against Britain, on August 8, 1940. However, Dowding's pre-war innovations soon showed their worth. Fighter Command employed the group or area command-and-control system, in which each group was subdivided into sectors encompassing forward and primary airfields. Initially, groups 11 and 12 covered the country; they were later further divided into four groups. Within each sector and group, an operations room controlled activities; the whole enterprise was coordinated at Fighter Command Headquarters. Connected by telephone to the Chain Home system and the

Observer Corps, the command-and-control system allowed for a reaction to a raid in a matter of minutes with an appropriate number of aircraft being vectored to target. The system allowed Fighter Command to husband resources, identify incoming raids, scramble appropriate units, vector aircraft to target, and essentially ambush incoming German raids. This combination of the Chain Home system, coordinated sector control, and superior air frames—all due in large measure to the pre-war efforts of Dowding—proved to be the decisive factors that led the United Kingdom to win the Battle of Britain.

In the first phase of the Battle of Britain, the Germans sought to draw the RAF into the air and destroy its fighting strength by attrition. By late August, that strategy had failed, and the Germans turned to destroying British airfields south of the Thames. This far more dangerous threat to RAF viability took a great toll of RAF men and machines by early September. Dowding estimated that three more weeks of such assaults would destroy Fighter Command's ability to mount any viable defense. Then, on the night of August 24, German bombers were dispatched to strike an oil storage depot near London. Their navigation was faulty, and they dropped their bombs on London. Churchill immediately ordered the bombing of Berlin on the night of August 25. One hundred and three British aircraft took off that night for Germany, 89 of them for Berlin. Only 29 bombers actually reached Berlin because of clouds and poor navigation equipment. The raid was certainly not a success, but it led Adolf Hitler to order a concentration on London. The Luftwaffe's primary target became the destruction of London rather than the vastly more important RAF airfields and production facilities. The shift to bombing London on September 7 allowed Fighter Command to repair airfields and facilities. For the next several months, British cities suffered through an almost nightly bombing campaign dubbed the Blitz, a failed strategy to attack civilian morale. Although the Chain Home radar network did not operate especially well at night, improved radar and night fighters, including the Beaufighter, proved capable of challenging German night bombing, and German losses mounted. In early autumn 1940, Hitler canceled SEA LION, and by May 1941 the air assault abated. Of the more than 3,000 pilots who flew in the RAF in the Battle of Britain as Winston Churchill's "few," some 500 died in combat.

In the initial stages of the war, the RAF had been loath to attack German industrial targets, despite the doctrine of strategic bombing. During the battles for France and Britain, Bomber Command had been reduced to attacking German shipping and invasion force transport. Some successful raids against Luftwaffe airfields occurred with good results. The turning point for the strategic air campaign occurred on the night of September 23, 1940, when 84 bombers attacked Berlin. Although bomb damage and RAF losses were minimal, the RAF practice of night bombing first industrial (especially oil) and infrastructure targets and later civilian targets had commenced. In 1942, the Avro Lancaster heavy bomber arrived in numbers. Having a range of more than 1,600 miles and capable of carrying 22,000 lb of bombs, the Lancaster was Britain's mainstay heavy bomber of World War II, and it enabled Bomber Command to carry the air war deep into Germany. The Lancaster Mark II, which appeared in 1943, had a range of 2,250 miles and could carry 14,000 lb of bombs. However, night navigation and target identification proved highly problematic. With no visual reference aids at night, bomber crews relied on Pathfinders. First fielded in August 1942, Pathfinder aircraft flew ahead of the formations, identified targets, and dropped color-coded marker flares. As the

Firebombs are loaded into a Royal Air Force bomber before an attack on industrial Germany in 1942. Heavy British and American bombing raids against German targets continued, with ever growing intensity, well into 1945, reducing large areas of many German cities to rubble. (Library of Congress)

war progressed, electronic navigation improved, including the relatively primitive radio set known as "Gee," followed by the more-sophisticated blind-bombing device called "Trinity." The latter was a precursor to the advanced "Oboe" system, which employed a ground-distance-measuring station. The H2S system provided a radar display indicating prominent geographic features such as rivers, coastline, and urban structures, thus providing the hitherto missing navigational landmarks.

Night-bombing accuracy always suffered compared with the daylight assaults carried out by the B-17s and B-24s of the U.S. Army Air Forces (USAAF) Eighth Air Force beginning in 1943. To counter the night bombing, the Luftwaffe developed efficient night fighters and relied on massed antiaircraft artillery. When the Blitz ended, Bomber Command increased the intensity of night strategic bombing. In a night raid on Hamburg on May 8, 1941, 300 bombers dropped several new 4,000 lb bombs.

On February 22, 1942, Air Chief Marshal Sir Arthur Harris took charge of Bomber Command. An energetic and enthusiastic advocate of terror bombing, Harris resolved to bludgeon Germany into submission. Night bombing of industrial targets increased immediately. To underscore the new attitude (and the advantage of the Lancasters with improved electronic navigation and targeting gear), Harris ordered the first thousand-bomber raid, which struck the German city of Köln (Cologne) on

May 30, 1942. Simultaneously, the newly fielded and capable De Havilland Mosquito quickly established itself as an extraordinary melding of mission capabilities, including reconnaissance, bomber, fighter-bomber, and night fighter. Under Harris, British strategic night bombing increased in intensity, capability, and destructive force for the next three years.

Italy's entry into the war on June 10, 1940, found the RAF in the Middle East and Mediterranean dispersed over 4 million square miles of mainly desolate and hostile terrain. Its 300 first-line aircraft were organized into 29 operational squadrons. Most of the aircraft represented previous generations of fighters. Whereas this was suitable for imperial policing against tribesmen and ill-organized rebels, the Italian and later the German air forces presented a difficult problem. The Italians could send up to 1,200 additional aircraft from Sicily and Italy to augment the 500 already in Africa. With imperial strategic interests threatened, notably the tenuous India/Far East supply line through the Suez Canal, Britain embarked on rapid air and troop reinforcement. Because few aircraft could make the journey completely by air, a scheme was developed for shipping aircraft by sea to the Gold Coast; the planes then made a difficult flight across Africa to Egypt. Gradually, the Desert Air Force established air superiority in North Africa and aided Field Marshal Archibald Wavell's advance through Libya. Additionally, Malta, a linchpin of British Mediterranean power, was heavily reinforced; the island and its RAF garrison withstood furious, concerted Axis air assaults.

With the injection into North Africa in February 1941 of German ground forces supported by the Luftwaffe, the air advantage temporarily swung back to the Axis. As more Hurricanes, Spitfires, and American-made Curtiss Kittyhawks arrived, the Desert Air Force slowly overwhelmed the Axis air forces. By the time of the Battle of El Alamein at the end of October 1942, RAF aircraft outnumbered Axis aircraft by 1,200 to 690. Because it had more aircraft and was reinforced by top-of-the-line fighters and because many of its pilots were veterans of the Battle of Britain, the RAF gained air superiority and contributed heavily to the eventual Allied North African victory.

The war effort of the RAF Coastal Command is often overlooked, yet it played a tremendous part in subduing the submarine threat and keeping the sea lifeline open. In the early months, before Germany could mount a credible U-boat threat, the RAF concentrated maritime defense efforts against enemy commerce raiders. With only 19 home-based squadrons operating outdated aircraft, Coastal Command could do little more than close-in coastal patrol. As equipment and numbers improved, particularly with the arrival of the Short Sunderland and the American B-24 Liberator, Coastal Command's reach extended to practically the entire world. By late 1940, Coastal Command aircraft had begun mine-laying operations and raids on the coast of France and in the North Sea.

By 1941, the German submarine threat intensified, and Coastal Command took up the challenges of shipping protection in the approaches and submarine hunting. The most dangerous area lay in a reconnaissance gap halfway across the Atlantic that land-based aircraft could not reach. In this area, U-boats inflicted great casualties until the wide-scale employment of the Liberator, which operated from bases in Scotland, Iceland, and Canada and closed the gap in aerial coverage. Additionally, a new airborne radar, the ASV, improved air-dropped depth charges, and the organization of antisubmarine warfare (ASW) forces into hunter-killer groups of combined air and ship units all contributed to the growing effectiveness of ASW air operations. By late 1943, the Battle of the Atlantic had been won, and Coastal Command had played a major role in that victory. Of German U-boat losses in the Atlantic, 55 percent are believed to have been the result of air attack (although many of these losses were to aircraft flown from escort carriers). A further 19 percent of U-boat losses were the result of combined aircraft-warship actions.

In short, the RAF grew from a relatively small force wedded to strategic bombing and imperial policing in the early 1930s to a highly capable multimission force by the end of the war. Aircraft design advanced measurably with attendant gains in effectiveness and lethality. By 1943, the RAF deployed thousands of aircraft to every theater of operations and simply wore down the enemy through superior technology and weight of numbers. Advances in technology—particularly bomber navigation, targeting, and ASW radar—far outstripped Axis technological development, giving Britain's RAF not only a decisive quantitative advantage, but also a qualitative advantage by 1943.

In many respects, the RAF had established itself by 1945 as a coequal partner with the Royal Navy in defense of the British Empire and home islands. Certainly, the RAF consumed a huge portion of Britain's war economy, and its role and sacrifice in the war cannot be discounted. Fighter Command saved the nation in 1940, and Coastal Command challenged and eventually helped nullify the U-boat maritime trade threat. Although the effectiveness and morality of the strategic bombing offensive may be debated, its destruction of key German industrial targets, notably those of oil production and transportation, contributed significantly to the eventual Allied victory.

From an initial manning of 175,692 personnel (RAF and Women's Auxiliary Air Force [WAAF]) on September 1, 1939, the RAF reached a peak of 1,079,835 personnel of all ranks, branches, and nationalities (including Allied personnel serving in the RAF and Imperial/Dominion forces) by May 1, 1945. Of that number, 193,313 served as aircrew. The RAF had 9,200 aircraft of all types in all theaters in an operational status as of May 1, 1945. The cost was high. Relative to all other British services and branches, the RAF suffered the greatest personnel losses. From 1939 to 1945, the RAF lost 70,253 personnel, killed or missing. Bomber Command flew 372,650 sorties, losing 8,617 aircraft and 47,268 men— killed in combat or taken prisoner—and a further 8,305 were killed in training accidents. Deaths from other causes cost Bomber Command ground crews and WAAFs a further 1,570 deaths. Fighter Command lost 3,690 aircrew killed in action and 1,215 seriously wounded.

Stanley D. M. Carpenter

See also
Atlantic, Battle of the; Casualties; Churchill, Sir Winston Leonard Spencer; North Africa Campaign; Western European Theater of Operations

References

Dean, Sir Maurice. *The Royal Air Force and Two World Wars*. London: Cassell, 1979.
Goulter, Christina J. M. *A Forgotten Offensive: Royal Air Force Coastal Command's Anti-Shipping Campaign, 1940–1945*. London: Frank Cass, 1995.

Hough, Richard, and Denis Richards. *The Battle of Britain: The Greatest Air Battle of World War II.* New York: W. W. Norton, 1989.

James, T.C.G. *The Battle of Britain.* New York: Routledge, 2000.

James, T.C.G. *The Growth of Fighter Command, 1936–1940.* New York: Routledge, 2001.

Mason, Francis K. *The British Fighter Since 1912.* Annapolis, MD: Naval Institute Press, 1992.

Middlebrook, Martin, and Chris Everitt. *The Bomber Command Diaries: An Operational Reference Book, 1939–1945.* Sittingbourne: Ian Allan Publishing, 2011.

Overy, Richard J. *The Air War 1939–1945.* Washington, DC: Potomac Books, 2005.

Probert, Henry. *The Forgotten Air Force: The Royal Air Force in the War against Japan 1941–1945.* Washington, DC: Brassey's, 1995.

Rawlings, John D. R. *The History of the Royal Air Force.* New York: Crescent Books, 1984.

Robertson, Scot. *The Development of RAF Strategic Bombing Doctrine, 1919–1939.* Westport, CT: Praeger, 1995.

Saunders, Hilary St. George. *Per Ardua: The Rise of British Air Power, 1911–1939.* London: Oxford University Press, 1945.

Terraine, John. *The Right of the Line: The Royal Air Force in the European War, 1939–1945.* Ware, Hertfordshire: Wordsworth Editions Limited, 1997.

Great Britain, Army

For many of the British army's commanding officers who had served as infantry subalterns during World War I 20 years earlier, the events of September and October 1939 must have conjured up a powerful sense of déjà vu. Then, as in 1914, a small expeditionary force of two corps assembled to take up position on the left of the French line in Flanders, awaiting the inevitable German advance across the Belgian plain. Decades-old plans for entrenchment and the tactics of a static war of attrition were dusted off and reissued. However familiar the first months of World War II may have been to these veterans of Arras and Ypres, their army's war was to take a dramatically unexpected turn less than a year later when the British Expeditionary Force (BEF) was ignominiously ejected from the European mainland after just a few weeks of sharp, mobile combat. They were not to return for another four years. Of the seven army-strength formations raised by Britain during the period 1939–1945, only one, the 2nd, was to fight in northwest Europe again. The bulk of Britain's land operations were conducted far from its old World War I trench lines—in the Western Desert of North Africa, Sicily and Italy, the Balkan Peninsula, Norway, Malaysia, Burma, and the northeast frontier of India. Such a fast-paced global struggle required a very different kind of army from that of World War I, with much greater technical specialization and more attention paid to the thorny problems of supply, communications, and control.

Although many key aspects of army life, such as the centuries-old regimental system, were carried forward mostly unaltered into World War II, the British army of 1939–1945 was to a large degree a hurriedly reinvented institution. This ad hoc metamorphosis was a necessary reaction to the new conditions of warfare, for which the interwar years had inadequately prepared the army's leaders and structures. After the demobilization that followed the 1918 armistice, the British army had quickly returned to its traditional role as a small imperial security force made up of long-service regulars, the part-time home reserve of the Territorial Army (TA), and a variegated auxiliary of colonial troops overseas. The problems of policing such trouble spots of the Empire as Palestine and India were far removed from the new theories of mechanized breakthrough warfare being discussed by forward-thinking military strategists in Europe, and the army languished in its attachment to the bayonet and the quick-firing rifleman—important for crowd control in overseas colonies, but less useful on the modern battlefield.

There were, in spite of this, significant attempts to bring the army up to date. Captain B. H. Liddell Hart's revised infantry manual stressed the "expanding torrent" tactics of mobility and exploitation, and Colonel J.F.C. Fuller called for fresh thinking on tank warfare. The Experimental Mechanized Force established briefly in the late 1920s was the world's first prototype for the armored division. But a combination of Treasury parsimony and knee-jerk opposition from the "Colonel Blimps" who dominated the army's upper echelons prevented any profound reform until the eve of war, when—prompted by the dynamic but ill-fated Minister of War Leslie Hore-Belisha—the government finally accepted the need for rearmament funding and a peacetime conscription bill. The doubling in size of the Territorial Army in March 1939 and passage of the National Service Act a month later provided for hundreds of thousands of new recruits, but in the short term these developments only added to the administrative confusion of a force hurriedly trying to reequip for a new continental commitment in alliance with France.

At the outbreak of war, the army's manpower stood at 897,000, the regulars and TAs having merged by government decree. Five regular infantry divisions were available in the United Kingdom for transportation to France. Two infantry divisions were deployed in Palestine suppressing the Arab revolt; the Western Desert Force (WDF) in Egypt had a fledgling armored division (another was forming in the UK, and would eventually join the BEF); and the remainder of the Empire was garrisoned either by individual battalions of regulars, units from the 300,000-strong Indian army, or indigenous militia like the King's African Rifles (KAR) in Kenya and Uganda. From these modest beginnings, the government of Prime Minister Neville Chamberlain proposed to recruit an army of 55 divisions (32 British, the remainder Indian and Dominion) for what it suggested would be at least a three-year war. There was as yet little clear plan as to where these divisions would be employed, or when.

Political control of the armed forces was exercised during hostilities through the War Cabinet, a subset of the full cabinet that liaised with the Chiefs of Staff Committee (COS) representing the uniformed heads of the army, Royal Navy, and Royal Air Force (RAF). The chief of the Imperial General Staff (CIGS) was the army's representative on the COS and, after the appointment of General Sir Alan Brooke in 1941, its permanent chairman. The CIGS had a vice-chief responsible for operations, plans, intelligence, and training and a deputy chief in charge of general organization. With the adjutant general (personnel), quartermaster general (logistics), and master general of ordnance, these men collectively made up the Army Council, which was chaired by the secretary of state for war. The

War Office retained nominal ministerial responsibility for the army. However, Winston Churchill, appointed prime minister and minister of defence in May 1940, preferred to deal with the uniformed chiefs directly, and so Whitehall was relegated to a purely administrative function.

Operational control in the United Kingdom was vested in General Headquarters (GHQ) Home Forces, and the country was divided into a series of command districts: South Eastern, Southern, Western, Northern, Scottish, Eastern, London, and Northern Ireland. Various overseas GHQs were established in the Middle East, East Africa, Persia, and Iraq and in other theaters according to the vagaries of war; the commander in chief of the Indian army held sway across the Indian subcontinent. In 1939 and 1940, there was an unsuccessful attempt to create a viable Anglo-French Supreme War Council, but as the multinational character of the war developed with the entry of the United States in December 1941, command of British forces was increasingly delegated to pan-Allied authorities such as the Combined Chiefs of Staff at the strategic level and Supreme Headquarters, Allied Expeditionary Forces (SHAEF) and South-East Asia Command (SEAC) at the operational level.

The spiritual core of the army remained the 5 guard and 64 line infantry regiments that performed a unique administrative, but nontactical, function. Following the pattern established in World War I, the army expanded not by creating new regiments but by adding battalions to existing regiments, some of which traced their origins to the 17th century. The heart of the regiment was an organizational depot located at the home barracks, while its component field battalions served scattered across the world in various brigade formations. It was uncommon for two or more of the same regiment's battalions to serve closely together at the front.

Regimental tradition was a powerful reinforcement of esprit de corps, particularly as most regiments had a regional recruitment base. But as the war progressed and manpower became scarcer, the territorial associations of each regiment were weakened, with a corresponding loss of group identity. The remainder of the army was similarly divided into administrative units with regimental or corps-level designations but no tactical roles. The Royal Armoured Corps was a composite of the old cavalry regiments, now mechanized, and the Royal Tank Regiment. The Royal Corps of Signals handled communications for the entire army down to individual battalion levels, where company signalers took over. Some of the services, such as the Royal Artillery and the Royal Engineers, had traditions and battle honors every bit as distinguished as those of the infantry; others, such as the Reconnaissance Corps, were newly created and short-lived. The most important noncombat services were the Royal Army Service Corps, which carried supplies to troops in the field; the Royal Army Ordnance Corps (RAOC), responsible for the procurement and maintenance of equipment; and the Royal Army Medical Corps, which handled the sick and wounded.

The greater emphasis in World War II on technical and logistical matters caused a much larger proportion of manpower to be allocated to the "tail" (as opposed to the "teeth") of the army than was the case during World War I. Some support formations became so unwieldy that they gave birth to spin-off services of their own, such as the Royal Electrical and Mechanical Engineers, which was formed from the RAOC in 1942. Other notable services handled pay, military policing, spiritual affairs (the Royal Army Chaplains), intelligence, catering, physical training, and education—the last being accused by many conservative officers of foisting socialist ideology onto the rankers, precipitating the Labour Party's 1945 election victory! Eventually a General Service Corps was created to process incoming recruits and provide basic training and ultimate service allocation. The all-women's Auxiliary Territorial Service played an increasingly critical role in support of the regulars, as did the Queen Alexandra's Imperial Nursing Service and the First Aid Nursing Yeomanry on the medical front.

Tactically, each late-war British army was divided into four corps, each with two infantry divisions and one armored division. An infantry division of 18,000 men consisted of three brigades of three battalions apiece, an independent machine-gun battalion, three Royal Artillery (RA) field regiments, and an antitank and antiaircraft regiment, plus the usual supporting attachments of signalers, engineers, and so on. Tank brigades were often temporarily attached to infantry divisions on an as-needed basis. The full-strength infantry battalion had four rifle companies of three platoons apiece, a headquarters company, and a support company. The structure of armored divisions changed markedly throughout the war as experiments to find the best mixture of tanks to other services evolved. In 1939, there were two armored brigades per division, each of three regiments, with a motorized infantry battalion, field artillery regiment, and accompanying support units. By D-Day, this had changed to a single armored brigade of three tank regiments (78 tanks per regiment) plus a fully mechanized infantry battalion in armored personnel carriers, a motorized infantry brigade in trucks, an armored reconnaissance regiment, one or two RA field regiments, and a plethora of antitank, antiaircraft, and other support formations, for a total of 343 armored vehicles at full strength.

Two forces existing out of the standard army structure, special services and the Home Guard, deserve mention. The special services or "Commando" brigades were created after the Battle of France as Britain's only way of directly striking back at the Germans on the European continent. Although their hit-and-run tactics were of limited utility in the absence of an Allied second front, they played an important propaganda role in the testing years before Operation OVERLORD and later became a useful auxiliary to the conventional armies fighting in France and the Low Countries. Certain theaters of war spawned their own commando-like units, such as the Special Air Service (SAS) in the Western Desert and Orde Wingate's Chindits in Burma. The Parachute Regiment, which by the end of the war was two divisions strong, was originally a part of special services. The Home Guard, formed by a call for underage and overage volunteers after Dunkerque, was originally intended as a last-ditch militia in the event of a German invasion of the British Isles. As the threat of attack receded, the Home Guard's function adapted to take over security and antiaircraft duties in the home islands from the regular army and to act as a training service for those about to be conscripted. At its peak in 1943, there were 1.7 million Home Guardsmen in 1,100 battalions.

By the end of the war, more than 3.5 million men and women had served in the regular forces, with the peak of 2.9 million reached in 1945. Eleven armored, 34 infantry, and 2 airborne divisions had been created. Other Imperial forces had expanded at an even greater rate: the Indian army was more than 2.5 million men strong by V-J Day. Despite its early muddles and campaign disasters, the army had matured to become one of the world's preeminent fighting forces and a signal contributor to the ultimate Allied victory. It had accomplished this with casualties of 264,443 killed, 41,327 missing, and 277,077 wounded.

Alan Allport

See also

Casualties; Churchill, Sir Winston Leonard Spencer; Italy Campaign; Montgomery, Sir Bernard Law; North Africa Campaign; Northeast Europe Theater; Western European Theater of Operations

References

Brayley, Martin, and Mike Chappell. *The British Army, 1939–1945*. London: Osprey, 2001.

Crang, Jeremy. *The British Army and the People's War, 1939–1945*. Manchester: Manchester University Press, 2000.

Fraser, David. *And We Shall Shock Them: The British Army in the Second World War*. London: Hodder and Stoughton, 1983.

French, David. *Raising Churchill's Army: The British Army and the War against Germany, 1919–1945*. Oxford: Oxford University Press, 2000.

Graham, Dominick. *Against Odds: Reflections on the Experiences of the British Army, 1914–45*. New York: St. Martin's Press, 1999.

Maiolo, Joseph. *Cry Havoc: How the Arms Race Drove the World to War, 1931–1941*. London: John Murray, 2010.

Place, Timothy. *Military Training in the British Army, 1940–1944: From Dunkirk to D-Day*. London: Frank Cass, 2000.

Great Britain, Navy

The somewhat disappointing performance of the Royal Navy during World War I led to considerable improvements in many tactical and operational areas by 1939. Despite the treaty limitations of the interwar years, the Royal Navy had reemerged as the world's dominant naval force by 1939. (The U.S. Navy did not embark on a massive rebuilding program until the Two Ocean Navy Act of 1940, and it became the larger naval and maritime force only by 1944.) Significant improvements in tactical and operational doctrine occurred in the 1920s and 1930s, especially in surface action and night-fighting techniques. In contrast to the lack of offensive-mindedness with concomitant reluctance to risk assets that characterized the Royal Navy in World War I, the Royal Navy of 1939 was imbued with a reinvigorated offensive spirit.

Weaknesses did hamper operations, notably the poor state of naval aviation, particularly when compared with naval aviation in the United States and Japan. Of the seven aircraft carriers in service at the start of 1939, only the *Ark Royal* (laid down in 1935) could be considered a modern carrier. Four of the other six had been modified earlier from battleship or battle cruiser hulls. The five new fleet carriers under construction would not begin operational service until well into 1940.

Despite the lessons of antisubmarine warfare (ASW) learned by 1918 and the need to protect merchant shipping and convoys, the Royal Navy had relatively poor commerce protection capabilities in 1939. Warship design had primarily emphasized coastal protection and submarine hunting, resulting in the short-range corvette ship type, which first came into service in 1939, and small escort destroyers. Although these ships had long-endurance capabilities, they proved unsuitable for open-ocean convoy escort primarily because of their size. Open-ocean convoy protection had been neglected, especially in training programs, and larger destroyers capable of trans-Atlantic convoy protection were in short supply. Despite the drawbacks, Britain managed to improve ASW capability and assets fairly quickly in response to the German U-boat threat. Although the smaller corvettes proved minimally effective for long-range mid-ocean operations, their successor—the larger, more seaworthy frigate, particularly the River-class dating from the 1940 building program—proved especially effective for convoy escort after 1942.

The initial German threat came from a three-part German offensive against commerce (*Handelskreig*) based on submarines, mines, and surface raiders. The Royal Navy quickly and effectively addressed each threat, although significant casualties did occur. Germany began the war with not many more submarines than it had at the start of World War I—just 51 operational U-boats, about half of them coastal vessels. The organization of British convoys in the Western Approaches, combined with the Straits of Dover mine barrage, resulted in nine U-boats sunk by the end of 1939.

Although some vessels were lost to German mines, the navy reduced this menace with new technology, including degaussing against magnetic mines. Surface raiders threatened British commerce, particularly in the remote waters of the Indian Ocean and South Atlantic. Although Germans raiders such as the *Atlantis* and pocket battleship *Graf Spee* provided some tense moments early in the war, by late 1941 most surface raiders had been hunted down and sunk.

In April 1940, Germany attacked Norway, primarily to secure its northern flank and the vital iron ore trade with Sweden. The British navy opposed the German landings, but a daring run of 10 German destroyers into Narvik subdued the Norwegian defenses. The combination of the entire German surface fleet with German land-based air power quickly resulted in the occupation of Norway. Reacting to the German moves, a Royal Navy force of destroyers attacked the Germans at Narvik, but it suffered heavy losses. A follow-on attack three days later by a large force based around the battleship *Warspite* devastated the Germans, which severely hampered future enemy surface operations. Ultimately, though, the Royal Navy could not prevent German victory, especially in the face of effective enemy airpower. Additionally, the German fast battleships *Scharnhorst* and *Gneisenau* sank the fleet carrier *Glorious*.

The fall of France and loss of French ports heralded a realignment of Royal Navy forces, because prior to World War I, Britain had relied on France for the bulk of Mediterranean sea power. With the appearance of a hostile Vichy government, though, the navy established Force H based at Gibraltar under Vice Admiral Sir James Somerville and charged with controlling the western Mediterranean. Force H carried out a distasteful duty in the bombardment of the French Fleet at Mers-el-Kébir in July 1940. Force H also played a central role in the destruction of the German battleship *Bismarck* in

Two Royal Navy aircraft carriers, two battleships, and a destroyer, December 17, 1942, part of the covering force for the Allied invasion of North Africa. The ships were ready to engage the Italian Navy should it attempt to interfere. Note the *Supermarine Seafire* aircraft (the naval counterpart of the *Spitfire*) aboard the carrier in the foreground. (AP/Wide World Photos)

May 1941, as well as in hunting down and destroying the Atlantic commerce raiders. But the loss of France allowed Germany to base long-range U-boats in Bay of Biscay ports such as Brest and Lorient. The toll on British and Imperial shipping dramatically increased by autumn 1940 as Adolf Hitler declared (on August 17, 1940) a total blockade of the British Isles.

By the autumn of 1941, the tide in the commerce war had turned in favor of Britain. Escort ships provided by the United States (50 World War I–era destroyers) and the increasing number of Royal Canadian Navy destroyers, improved detection equipment including radar; high-frequency direction-finding sets and Antisubmarine Detection Investigation Committee (ASDIC or sonar), implementation of a cohesive and effective enemy submarine tracking system based on radio intercepts and code-breaking, and better cooperation with RAF Coastal Command all contributed to the reduction of the German submarine threat and effectiveness. Additionally, Germany's loss of the *Bismarck* and the relatively ineffective German effort to use heavy surface units to interdict the convoys to the northern Soviet Union across the Arctic above Norway all helped to lessen the threat to British maritime commerce by the middle of 1943. The Soviet convoys began receiving more robust escort following the destruction of the ill-fated PQ17 convoy in the summer of 1942. This enhanced escort included greater destroyer strength and escort carriers.

The destruction of the battleship *Scharnhorst* off the Norwegian North Cape in December 1943 by a British battleship and cruiser force essentially ended the German surface threat to British and Allied maritime shipping.

Finally, despite a high number of U-boats operating in the Atlantic by March 1943 (up to 70 at any given time), the increasing skill of Allied submarine hunters and the closing of the "Black Hole" area south of Greenland, where air cover had not been previously available, meant a diminishing submarine threat and higher losses in U-boats. Escort carriers provided air cover while long-range maritime patrol aircraft (primarily modified B-24 Liberator bombers) made U-boat operations less effective. Additionally, hunter-killer escort groups attached to vulnerable convoys mauled the Germans.

In the Mediterranean, Italy's entry into the war in May 1940 required reinforcement of the theater naval forces under Admiral Sir Andrew Cunningham. With some modernized older battleships and the new carrier *Illustrious*, Cunningham defeated the Italians in fleet engagements at Calabria in July 1940 and Cape Matapan in March 1941 and raided the Italian anchorage at Taranto in November 1941 with naval aircraft. Cunningham stressed the improvement of antiaircraft protection, which paid off as the naval war in the Mediterranean increasingly devolved into attacks on shipping and naval vessels by Axis aircraft.

Faced with substantial damage to their supply convoys by British destroyers and submarines, the Germans dispatched U-boats to the Mediterranean in October 1941, resulting in the sinking of the battleship *Barham* and the carrier *Ark Royal*. At the fleet anchorage in Alexandria, the battleships *Queen Elizabeth* and *Valiant* were sunk at their moorings by Italian *Maiale* human torpedoes.

Faced with the loss of capital ships and the threat of enemy aircraft and submarine attack, British resources in the Mediterranean were stretched dangerously thin. Malta, the linchpin of Britain's efforts to hold the Mediterranean, came under horrendous air attack. Convoys to resupply and reinforce the island suffered substantial casualties, among them the aircraft carrier *Eagle*.

The entry of the United States into the war in December 1941 had a profound impact on the Mediterranean Theater. Operation TORCH, the Allied landings in North Africa in November 1942, resulted in the eventual destruction of Axis forces in North Africa. Reinforced and reconstituted, the Mediterranean Fleet conducted an ambitious and destructive assault on Italian shipping throughout 1942 and 1943 that crippled enemy resupply efforts. Cunningham admonished his sailors and airmen to "sink, burn and destroy: let nothing pass." By the end of 1942, Britain had again established maritime supremacy in the Mediterranean, despite substantial losses.

In the Pacific Theater, Japan entered the war against Britain concurrent with the assault on the United States. Quickly overrunning Hong Kong, the Japanese army forced the capitulation of Singapore, Britain's "Gibraltar of the Pacific." Faced with the loss of basing facilities, the Royal Navy withdrew from Southeast Asian waters, particularly after the loss of the battleship *Prince of Wales* and battle cruiser *Repulse* to air attack in December 1941 (Force Z under Admiral Sir Tom Phillips). The admiral's disregard of the air threat coupled with woefully inadequate antiaircraft protection (the navy had only two modern destroyers) greatly aided the land-based Japanese aviators, who easily sank both capital ships.

Following the crippling of the U.S. Pacific Fleet at Pearl Harbor, Japan's main striking force—Vice Admiral Nagumo Chūichi's First Air Fleet—wreaked havoc on the remnants of British sea power in the Indian Ocean in the spring of 1942. In carrier-based air attacks against British surface units, the veteran Japanese naval aviators sank detached portions of Admiral Sir James Somerville's forces based in Ceylon, including two cruisers and the carrier *Hermes*. However, Somerville avoided a general action and preserved his force as the Japanese withdrew to support their thrust into New Guinea and the Solomon Islands. Naval action in the Pacific Theater after May 1942 involved mainly U.S. and Australian naval units, but, with the defeat of Germany in May 1945, the Royal Navy again engaged Japan with substantial forces.

Under Admiral Sir Bruce Fraser, the Pacific Fleet of four carriers (later joined by two additional decks) and two battleships with substantial escort destroyers and cruisers arrived in the Pacific in March 1945, where they joined the Americans in the assault on the Japanese home islands and Okinawa. Equipped with the U.S. Hellcat and Corsair fighters, Royal Naval aviators did great destruction to the Japanese. American aircraft proved greatly superior to earlier British Seafire (modified from the Spitfire), Martlet, Fulmar, and Sea Hurricane models. The heavily armored British carrier decks proved worthwhile as a defense against Japanese suicide kamikaze aircraft (the lightly armored American carriers suffered more extensive damage).

From strategic and operational viewpoints, the Royal Navy performed exceptionally well in the war. Although losses were heavy (1,525 warships of all types, including 224 major surface units of which 5 were battleships or battle cruisers and 5 were fleet carriers; and 50,000 personnel dead), the aggressiveness and risk-taking nature of senior and individual ship commanding officers overcame the tenacious and highly competent Axis opponents. In the Atlantic, the Axis commerce warfare offensive failed to starve the country into submission or impede the arrival of overwhelming U.S. forces and personnel. In the Mediterranean, the Royal Navy kept British and Imperial ground and air forces supplied and reinforced while simultaneously strangling the Axis supply lines to North Africa. In the Pacific, despite initial defeats by the Japanese, British sea power returned late in the conflict and helped the U.S. Navy carry the fight to the Japanese home islands. As it had not done in the previous war, the navy at all levels showed exceptional ability to adapt rapidly to technological and methodical innovations and advances in doctrine, organization, and training. To man the new ships of more than 900 major combatants and the supporting shore establishment (training, research, logistics, support, and administration), by war's end Royal Naval personnel had increased from the prewar 129,000 to 863,500, which included 72,000 women in the Women's Royal Naval Service (WRNS). In short, the navy vindicated itself following the disappointments of World War I. British sea power both kept Britain in the fight until the United States arrived in force and subsequently provided the domination needed to attack the Axis powers at all vulnerable points with little interference.

Stanley D. M. Carpenter

See also

Atlantic, Battle of the; Churchill, Sir Winston Leonard Spencer; North Africa Campaign; Northeast Europe Theater; Southwest Pacific Theater; Western European Theater of Operations

References

Barnett, Correlli. *Engage the Enemy More Closely: The Royal Navy in the Second World War.* New York: W. W. Norton, 1991.

Gray, Edwyn. *Operation Pacific: The Royal Navy's War against Japan, 1941–1945.* London: Cooper, 1990.

Jackson, Robert. *The Royal Navy in World War II.* Annapolis, MD: Naval Institute Press, 1997.

Lavery, Brian. *Churchill's Navy: The Ships, Men and Organization, 1939–1945.* Annapolis, MD: Naval Institute Press, 2006.

Levy, James P. *The Royal Navy's Home Fleet in World War II.* New York: Palgrave Macmillan, 2004.

Llewellyn-Jones, Malcolm, ed. *The Royal Navy and the Mediterranean Convoys: A Naval Staff History.* New York: Routledge, 2007.

O'Hara, Vincent P. *Struggle for the Middle Sea: The Great Navies at War in the Mediterranean Theater, 1940–1945.* Annapolis, MD: Naval Institute Press, 2009.

O'Hara, Vincent P., W. David Dickson, and Richard Worth, eds. *On Seas Contested: The Seven Great Navies of the Second World War.* Annapolis, MD: Naval Institute Press, 2010.

Roskill, Stephen W. *The War at Sea, 1939–1945.* 4 vols. London: Her Majesty's Stationery Office, 1954–1961.

Roskill, Stephen W. *White Ensign: The British Navy at War, 1939–1945.* Annapolis, MD: Naval Institute Press, 1960.

Titterton, G. A. *The Royal Navy and the Mediterranean.* Vols. 1–2. London: Whitehall History in association with Frank Cass, 2002.

Greece, Role in War

The nation of Greece, with a population of some 7.3 million people in 1940, was drawn into World War II by Italy's invasion from Albania. Greek dictator General Ioannis Metaxas had sought to maintain his nation's neutrality, but that policy ended when an Italian invasion began a Balkan campaign that drew in Britain as well as Germany and other Axis powers. The result of these developments was Axis control of the Balkans until the last months of the war. Greece suffered horribly in the war and continued to suffer in the years immediately afterward in a costly civil war from 1946 to 1949.

In October 1940, without informing his ally Adolf Hitler in advance, Italian dictator Benito Mussolini launched an invasion from Albania. Having superiority in both numbers and military hardware, Mussolini confidently expected to complete the conquest before winter set in. The Greeks, however, resisted valiantly. They not only held the Italians but went on the offensive and drove them back, while the British bombed Albania and neutralized the Italian navy. Mussolini's invasion of Greece turned into a disaster from which neither he nor his regime recovered. Determined to shore up his southern flank before he began an invasion of the Soviet Union, Hitler stepped in. Metaxas died at the end of January 1941, and in April the Führer sent the German army against both Greece and Yugoslavia, quickly overwhelming both. Neither the courage and will of the Greeks nor British army reinforcements sufficed to withstand the Luftwaffe and the panzers.

A Greek gun crew at work in 1940 during the campaign in Albania. In October 1940, Italy attempted to invade Greece by way of Albania. After a bitter battle, Greek troops overcame the Albanians, marking the first Allied victory of the war. (Library of Congress)

The Axis occupation of Greece involved German, Italian, and Bulgarian troops and lasted three years. It was a dark period in the history of a nation that had undergone much suffering since Roman times. The Germans set up a puppet government and insisted that the Greeks pay the full cost of the occupation, which resulted in catastrophic inflation. The Germans also requisitioned resources and supplies, with no concern for the fate of a population that, even in the best of times, was obliged to import most of its food. Famine and disease decimated Greece and killed perhaps 100,000 people in the winter of 1941–1942 alone. The suffering was such that British prime minister Winston Churchill agreed—under pressure from the Greek government in exile and the United States—to partially lift the blockade so the International Red Cross might bring in food supplies. Greeks living in Western Thrace and Eastern Macedonia also had to undergo forced Bulgarianization. The flourishing Jewish community in Salonika was devastated in the Holocaust; fewer than 10,000 of an estimated 70,000 Greek Jews survived the war. The Greek underground fought back with sabotage and ambush and tied down 120,000 Axis troops. In reprisal, the Germans and Italians burned whole villages and executed large numbers of Greek hostages for every Axis soldier slain.

Greek king George II and his ministers went into exile in Egypt with the retreating British forces in 1941. Almost immediately, Greek resistance groups formed. Of the various resistance movements that had appeared during the German occupation, the largest was the National Liberation Front (EAM), with the National People's Liberation Army as its military wing. Relations were poor between EAM and the National Republican Greek League. Indeed, actual fighting broke out between the two groups in the winter of 1943–1944, although a truce was arranged in February 1944. As in Yugoslavia, the communist-dominated EAM apparently enjoyed wider support than the nationalist underground. When the Germans pulled out of Greece, EAM held the vast majority of the country. Greek society was fractured into three factions: the monarchists, the republicans, and the communists.

At approximately the same time, in October 1944, Churchill journeyed to Moscow to meet with Soviet leader Josef Stalin. Churchill struck a bargain with Stalin concerning predominance in various Balkan states, under the terms of which Britain was to have 90 percent predominance in Greece. The Greek communists, who had carried the brunt of resistance against the Axis and now controlled the majority of territory, understandably resented this imperial arrangement struck in Moscow and were unwilling to submit to it.

When the Nazis withdrew, George Papandreou, a left-of-center statesman, headed a government of national unity. Fearing the communist underground, however, he requested British troops, who began arriving early in October 1944. When the British called on the guerrilla forces to disarm and disband, EAM quit the cabinet, called a general strike, and held protest demonstrations. In this serious situation, Churchill took the impetuous decision to fly with Foreign Secretary Anthony Eden to Athens on Christmas Day 1944. Though the government and EAM reached accord early in 1945, it quickly broke down. EAM members took to the hills with their weapons.

In the first Greek elections, held in 1946, the Royalist People's Party was victorious, and a Royalist ministry took office. A September 1946 plebiscite resulted in a majority vote for the king's return. King George II, who was unpopular in Greece, died the following April and was succeeded by his son Paul, who reigned until 1964.

By the end of 1946, communist rebels were ready to attempt a comeback, assisted by the communist governments of Yugoslavia, Bulgaria, and Albania. (Ironically, Tito's support for the civil war in defiance of Stalin was one reason Yugoslavia was subsequently expelled from the international communist movement.) The communists came close to winning in Greece, but Greece was saved as a Western bastion because the British were determined that the nation—with its strategic control of the eastern Mediterranean—not become communist. But in February 1947, deep in its own economic problems, Britain informed a shocked Washington that it could no longer bear the burden of supporting Greece. U.S. president Harry S. Truman agreed to take over the responsibility, and in March 1947, he announced the Truman Doctrine of aid to free nations threatened by internal or external aggression. This policy received the enthusiastic support of the U.S. Congress and an appropriation of $400 million for both Greece and Turkey. Ultimately, the United States contributed about $750 million for the final three years of guerrilla warfare.

Gradually, General Alexander Papagos, Greek commander in chief, dismissed incompetent officers and created a military force sufficient to turn the military tide. Another important factor was that Marshal Tito (Josip Broz) needed to concentrate on resisting Soviet pressures, cutting off many of the supplies for the rebel cause. By the end of 1949,

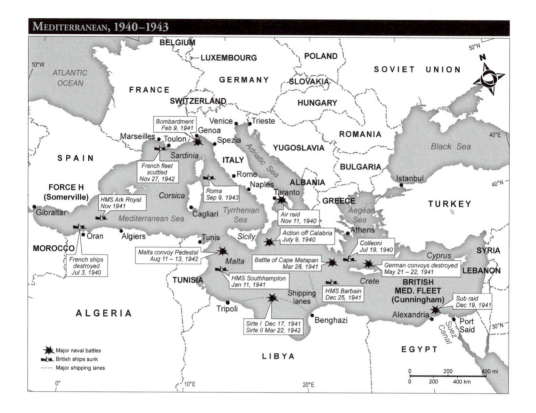

the communists had been defeated and Greece saved for the West. The cost of the civil war to Greece was as great as the cost from the tormented years of World War II and the Nazi occupation. As with so many civil wars, the struggle had been waged without quarter on either side. Thousands of hostages had been taken and simply disappeared. A million Greeks had been uprooted and displaced by the fighting. Casualties may have been as high as half a million people—all of them Greeks killed by Greeks. After the war, the purges and reprisals continued for some time. Unfortunately for Greece, further upheaval fanned by other nations and dictatorship lay ahead before true democracy could be achieved.

Spencer C. Tucker

See also

Balkans Theater; Casualties; Churchill, Sir Winston Leonard Spencer; Collaboration; Germany, Air Force; Germany, Army; Great Britain, Air Force; Great Britain, Army; Great Britain, Navy; Hitler, Adolf; Italy, Air Force; Italy, Army; Mussolini, Benito; Resistance

References

Allen, Susan Heuck. *Classical Spies: American Archaeologists with the OSS in World War II Greece.* Ann Arbor, MI: University of Michigan Press, 2011.

Beevor, Antony. *Crete: The Battle and the Resistance.* London: John Murray, 1991.

Blytas, George C. *The First Victory: Greece in the Second World War.* Westcliff-on-Sea: Cosmos Publishing, 2009.

Drez, Ronald J. *Heroes Fight Like Greeks: The Greek Resistance against the Axis Powers in World War II*. Colorado Springs, CO: Ghost Road Press, 2009.

Hondros, John L. *Occupation and Resistance: The Greek Agony*. New York: Pella Publishing, 1983.

Mazower, M. *Inside Hitler's Greece: The Experience of Occupation, 1941–1944*. New Haven, CT: Yale University Press, 1993.

Papastratis, Procopis. *British Policy towards Greece during the Second World War, 1941–1944*. Cambridge: Cambridge University Press, 1984.

Sadler, John. *Operation Mercury: The Battle for Crete, 1941*. Mechanicsburg, PA: Stackpole Books, 2008.

Smith, Peter. *War in the Aegean: The Campaign for the Eastern Mediterranean in World War II*. Mechanicsburg, PA: Stackpole Books, 2008.

Woodhouse, C. M. *The Struggle for Greece, 1941–1949*. London: Hart-Davis, MacGibbon, 1976.

Hiroshima and Nagasaki, Bombing of (August 6 and 9, 1945)

The U.S. bombing of the Japanese city of Hiroshima was the first use of the atomic bomb. On July 25, 1945, commander of United States Strategic Air Forces general Carl Spaatz received orders to use the 509th Composite Group, Twentieth Air Force, to deliver a "special bomb" attack on selected target cities in Japan, specifically Hiroshima, Kokura, Niigata, or Nagasaki. Following rejection of conditions promulgated by the Potsdam Proclamation on July 26, a declaration threatening Japan with total destruction if unconditional surrender was not accepted, President Harry S. Truman authorized use of the special bomb.

Assembled in secrecy and loaded on the Boeing B-29 Superfortress *Enola Gay*, the bomb consisted of a core of uranium isotope 235 shielded by several hundred pounds of lead, encased in explosives designed to condense the uranium and initiate a fission reaction. Nicknamed "Little Boy," the bomb possessed a force equivalent to 12,500 tons of TNT (12.5 kilotons).

The *Enola Gay*, commanded by Colonel Paul Tibbets, departed Tinian at 2:45 a.m. on August 6. Two B-29s assigned as scientific and photographic observers followed, and the three aircraft rendezvoused over Iwo Jima for the run over Japan. Captain William Parsons of the U.S. Navy completed the bomb's arming in the air shortly after 6:30 a.m. The flight to Japan was uneventful, and Tibbets was informed at 7:47 a.m. by weather planes over the targets that Hiroshima was clear for bombing. Japan's eighth largest city (it had about 245,000 residents in August 1945), Hiroshima was an important port on southern Honshu and headquarters of the Japanese Second Army.

The *Enola Gay* arrived over the city at an altitude of 31,600 feet and dropped the bomb at 8:15:17 a.m. local time. After a descent of nearly 6 miles, the bomb detonated 43 seconds later at some 1,890 feet over a clinic and about 800 feet from the aiming point, Aioi Bridge. The initial fireball expanded to 110 yards in diameter, generating heat in excess of 300,000 degrees Centigrade, with core temperatures more than 50 million degrees Centigrade. At the clinic directly beneath the explosion, the temperature was several thousand degrees. The immediate concussion destroyed almost everything within 2 miles of ground zero. The resultant mushroom cloud rose to 50,000 feet and was observed by B-29s more than 360 miles away. After 15 minutes, the atmosphere dropped radioactive "black rain," adding to the death and destruction.

Hiroshima's Industrial Promotion Hall, one of the few buildings left standing after the dropping of the atomic bomb on August 6, 1945, that killed 100,000 people outright. Today the building is part of the Hiroshima Peace Memorial, designated a UNESCO World Heritage Site in 1996. (Library of Congress)

Four square miles of Hiroshima's heart disappeared in seconds, including 62,000 buildings. More than 71,000 Japanese died, another 20,000 were wounded, and 171,000 were left homeless. Some estimates place the number of killed at more than 200,000. About one-third of those killed instantly were soldiers. Most elements of the Japanese Second General Army were at physical training on the grounds of Hiroshima Castle when the bomb exploded. Barely 900 yards from the explosion's epicenter, the castle and its residents were vaporized. Also killed was one American prisoner of war in the exercise area. All died in less than a second. Radiation sickness began the next day and added to the death toll over several years.

Following three observation circuits over Hiroshima, the *Enola Gay* and its escorts turned for Tinian, touching down at 2:58 p.m. The bombing mission, 12 hours and 13 minutes long covering 2,960 miles, changed the nature of warfare but did not end the war. Truman released a statement on August 7 describing the weapon and calling on Japan to surrender, but his message was ignored by most Japanese leaders as propaganda. Following the Japanese refusal to surrender, Twentieth Air Force headquarters on Guam issued Field Order 17 on August 8, directing that, on the following day, the second atomic bomb on Tinian Island be dropped on another Japanese city. Kokura was designated as the primary target, and Nagasaki, a city of some 230,000 persons, was the alternate.

At 3:49 a.m. on August 9, Boeing B-29 Superfortress bomber *Bockscar* (sometimes written as *Bock's Car*), commanded by Major Charles Sweeney, departed Tinian. It was followed by a second B-29 as scientific observer and a third as photographic observer. The *Bockscar* carried a plutonium nuclear-fission bomb nicknamed "Fat Man" that was 10 feet 8 inches long and 5 feet in diameter, with a payload greater than that of the Hiroshima bomb. The plutonium 238 isotope core consisted of two melon-shaped hemispheres surrounded by a ring of explosive charges designed to drive the sections together, achieving "critical mass" and a chain reaction releasing 22 kilotons of energy in one-millionth of a second.

Sweeney flew to Kokura but found it overcast and circled for 10 minutes. Despite the clouds, bombardier Kermit Beahan believed they could bomb visually. Sweeney, concerned about a faulty valve that limited fuel, decided to divert to Nagasaki, which was also partly obscured by clouds. Beahan believed he could bomb by radar, but a break in the clouds allowed him to bomb visually, using the Mitsubishi shipyards as his aiming point.

The *Bockscar* released the bomb from 31,000 feet at 11:02 a.m. local time. The bomb detonated 53 seconds later, approximately 1,500 feet over the city, destroying everything within a 1,000 yard radius. An intense blue-white explosion pushed up a pillar of fire 10,000 feet, followed by a mushroom cloud to 60,000 feet.

Although the bomb missed its intended aiming point by 8,500 feet, it leveled one-third of the city. Called the "Red Circle of Death," the fire and blast area within the Urakami Valley section destroyed more than 18,000 homes and killed 74,000 people. Another 75,000 were injured, and many later died from wounds or complications. Blast forces traveling in excess of 9,000 mph damaged buildings 3 miles away, and the concussion was felt 40 miles from the epicenter. "Ashes of Death" from the mushroom cloud spread radiation poisoning, killing all who were not killed outright within 1,000 yards of the epicenter. The bomb might have killed thousands more, but it detonated away from the city center in a heavy industrial area, vaporizing three of Nagasaki's largest war factories but "minimizing" deaths.

Sweeney made one complete circle of the city to determine damage and then left after fuel concerns and heavy smoke made other circuits futile. Critically low on fuel, he flew to Okinawa, landing at Yontan Field about 12:30 p.m., his gas tanks virtually empty. After refueling, *Bockscar* flew to Tinian, arriving there at 10:30 p.m. local time after a 20-hour flight.

Included in the instrument bundle dropped from the observation plane was a letter addressed to Japanese physicist Professor F. Sagane that urged immediate surrender and threatened continued atomic destruction of Japanese cities. Written by three American physicists, the letter was a bluff, as no other atomic bombs were then ready. Nonetheless, the second atomic attack, coupled with the August 8 declaration of war by the Soviet Union, provided Japanese emperor Hirohito with the excuse to end the war.

Mark E. Van Rhyn

See also

Atomic Bomb, Decision to Employ; Truman, Harry S.; United States, Army Air Force

References

Chinnock, Frank W. *Nagasaki: The Forgotten Bomb.* New York: World Publishing, 1969.

Ham, Paul. *Hiroshima Nagasaki.* New York: HarperCollins, 2011.

Hogan, Michael J., ed. *Hiroshima in History and Memory*. Cambridge: Cambridge University Press, 1996.

Ishikawa, Eisei. *Hiroshima and Nagasaki: The Physical, Medical, and Social Effects of the Atomic Bombings*. Translated by David L. Swain. New York: Basic Books, 1981.

Maddox, Robert James. *Weapons for Victory: The Hiroshima Decision Fifty Years Later*. Columbia, MO: University of Missouri Press, 1995.

Nobile, Philip. *Judgment at the Smithsonian: The Bombing of Hiroshima and Nagasaki*. New York: Marlowe and Company, 1995.

Pacific War Research Society. *The Day Man Lost: Hiroshima, August 6, 1945*. Tokyo: Kodansha International Ltd., 1972.

Sherwin, Martin J. *A World Destroyed: Hiroshima and Its Legacies*. 3rd ed. Stanford, CA: Stanford University Press, 2000.

Thomas, Gordon, and Max Morgan-Witts. *Enola Gay*. New York: Stein and Day, 1977.

Weller, George. *First into Nagasaki: The Censored Eyewitness Dispatches on Post-Atomic Japan and Its Prisoners of War*. Edited by Anthony Weller. New York: Crown Books, 2006.

Hitler, Adolf (1889–1945)

Adolf Hitler was the leader (*Führer*) of Germany. Born on April 20, 1889, in Braunau am Inn, Austria, Hitler had a troubled childhood. He was educated at primary school and Realschule in Linz, but he dropped out at age 16. Hitler aspired to become an artist, and on the death of his mother Klara in 1907 (his father Alois had died in 1903), he moved to Vienna. He attempted to enroll at the Viennese Academy of Fine Arts but was unsuccessful. Hitler lived in flophouses and made some money selling small paintings of Vienna scenes to frame shops. It was in Vienna that Hitler acquired his hatred of Jews, who had assimilated into Vienna society, together with an aversion to internationalism, capitalism, and socialism. He developed an intense sense of nationalism and expressed pride in being of German descent.

Probably to avoid compulsory military service, Hitler left Austria in May 1913 and settled in the south German state of Bavaria. On the outbreak of World War I, he enlisted in the Bavarian army and served in it with distinction. Here he found the sense of purpose he had always previously lacked. He saw extensive military action, was wounded, and served in the dangerous position of *Meldegänger* (runner). Temporarily blinded in a British gas attack, Hitler ended the war in a military hospital. He had risen to the rank of lance corporal and won the Iron Cross First Class, an unusual distinction for someone of his rank.

After the war, Hitler returned to Munich and worked for the military, reporting to it on political groups, and he then became involved in politics full time. In the summer of 1919, Hitler joined the Deutsche Arbeiterpartei (German Worker's Party), later known as the Nationalsozialistische Deutsche Arbeiterpartei (NSDAP, National Socialist Party or Nazi party). His oratorical skills soon made him one of its leaders. Disgruntled by Germany's loss in the war, Hitler became the voice of the dispossessed and angry. He blamed Germany's defeat on the "November criminals"—the communists, the Jews, and the Weimar Republic.

Taking a cue from Benito Mussolini's march on Rome the previous year, on November 8, 1923, Hitler and his followers attempted to seize power in Bavaria as a step toward controlling all of Germany. This Beer Hall Putsch was put down by the authorities with some bloodshed. Hitler was then arrested and brought to trial for attempting to overthrow the state. He used his trial to become a national political figure in Germany. Sentenced to prison, he served only nine months (1923–1924). While at the Landsberg Fortress, he dictated his stream-of-consciousness memoir, *Mein Kampf* (My Struggle). Later, when he was in power, royalties on sales of the book and his images made him immensely wealthy, a fact he deliberately concealed from the German people.

Hitler formed few female attachments during his life. He was involved with his niece, Geli Raubal, who committed suicide in 1931, and later with Eva Braun, his mistress whom he hid from the public. Deeply distrustful of people, Hitler was a vegetarian who loved animals and especially doted on his dogs. He was also a severe hypochondriac, suffering from myriad real and imagined illnesses.

Hitler restructured the NSDAP, and by 1928 the party had emerged as a political force in Germany, winning representation in the Reichstag. In April 1932, Hitler ran against Field Marshal Paul von Hindenburg for the presidency of Germany. Hitler railed against the Weimar Republic for the Treaty of Versailles at the end of World War I, the catastrophic inflation of 1923, the threat posed by the communists, and the effects of the Great Depression. Hindenburg won, but Hitler received 13 million votes in

The Nazi Party, led by Adolf Hitler, attracted many former German soldiers who had fought in World War I. Economic crises, especially the Great Depression that began in 1929, boosted the appeal of its authoritarian message of national unity and regeneration to other Germans. Besides manipulating the prevailing climate of fear and anger within Germany to gain political power, Hitler and his followers also made shrewd use of mass political spectacle. This 1928 Nazi Party rally in the Bavarian city of Nuremberg, headquarters of the Nazi movement, was one of many such well-choreographed, high-profile events, designed to attract followers and intimidate opponents. (National Archives)

a completely free election, and by June 1932 the Nazis were the largest political party in the Reichstag.

On January 30, 1933, Hindenburg appointed Hitler chancellor. Hitler quickly acted against any political adversaries. Fresh elections under Nazi auspices gave the Nazis in coalition with the Nationalists a majority in the Reichstag. An Enabling Act of March 1933 gave Hitler dictatorial powers. On the death of Hindenburg in August 1934, Hitler amalgamated the office of president and took control of the armed forces. In the "Night of the Long Knives" of July 1934, Hitler purged the party and also removed several political opponents. Hitler also reorganized Germany administratively, dissolving political parties and labor unions and making Germany a one-party state. Nazi Germany became a totalitarian state that Hitler, now known as the *Führer*, ruled alone.

Resistance to the Nazis was crushed, and many dissidents were sent to concentration camps. The ubiquitous Gestapo kept tabs on the population, but the state was not characterized solely by repression by any means. In the first several years, Hitler was carried forward on a wave of disillusionment with the Weimar Republic, and a plebiscite showed that a solid majority of Germans approved of his actions.

Almost immediately after assuming political power, Hitler initiated actions against the Jews. They were turned into a race of "untouchables" within their own state, unable to pursue certain careers and a public life. The Nuremberg Laws of 1935 defined as Jewish anyone with one Jewish grandparent. That a terrible fate would be their lot was clear in Hitler's remarks that war in Europe would lead to the "extinction of the Jewish race in Europe."

In 1934, Hitler took Germany out of the League of Nations and the Geneva Disarmament Conference. Germans were put back to work; and rearmament, albeit at first secret (it was announced openly in 1935), was begun. Hitler's most daring gamble was in March 1936, when he marched German troops into the Rhineland and remilitarized it. In November 1937, he announced plans to his top advisers and generals for an aggressive foreign policy and war, and in March 1938 he began his march of conquest with the *Anschluss* (annexation) of Austria. That fall, he secured the Sudetenland of Czechoslovakia, and in March 1939, he took over the remainder of Czechoslovakia. Poland was the next pressure point. To secure his eastern flank, in August 1939 Hitler concluded a nonaggression pact with the Soviet Union. On September 1, 1939, German forces invaded Poland, touching off World War II.

Applying new tactics of close cooperation between air and ground elements centered in a war of movement that came to be known as the blitzkrieg (lightning war), the German military enjoyed early success on the battlefield. Poland was taken within one month. When Britain and France, which had gone to war with Germany on the invasion of Poland, rejected peace on a forgive-and-forget basis, Hitler invaded the west. Norway and Denmark were taken beginning in April 1940. France and Benelux fell in May and June. Hitler's first rebuff came in the July–October 1940 Battle of Britain, when the Luftwaffe failed to drive the Royal Air Force from the skies, a necessary precursor to a sea invasion. After next securing his southern flank in the Balkans by invading and conquering Greece and Yugoslavia in April 1941, Hitler invaded the Soviet Union that June. When the United States entered the war against Japan in December 1941, Hitler declared war on the United States.

Increasingly, Germany suffered the consequences of strategic overreach: German troops not only had to garrison much of Europe, but they also were sent to North Africa. Hitler's constant meddling in military matters, his changes of plans, and his divide-and-rule concept of administration all worked to the detriment of Germany's cause. On Hitler's express orders, millions of people, mainly Jews, were rounded up and systematically slaughtered.

From mid-January 1945, Hitler took up residence in Berlin. He refused negotiation to the end, preferring to see Germany destroyed. Hitler married Eva Braun on April 29, 1945, and—rather than be taken by the Russians, who were then closing in on Berlin—he committed suicide in the bunker of the Chancellery on April 30, 1945.

Wendy A. Maier Sarti

See also

Eastern Front; Germany, Air Force; Germany, Army; Germany, Navy; Holocaust, The; Mussolini, Benito; Northeast Europe Theater; Western European Theater of Operations

References

Barros, James, and Richard Gregor. *Double Deception: Stalin, Hitler, and the Invasion of Russia*. DeKalb, IL: Northern Illinois Press, 1995.

Bullock, Alan. *Hitler: A Study in Tyranny*. New York: Harper, 1952.

Bullock, Alan. *Hitler and Stalin: Parallel Lives*. New York: Alfred A. Knopf, 1992.

Burleigh, Michael. *The Third Reich: A New History*. New York: Hill and Wang, 2000.

Evans, Richard J. *The Coming of the Third Reich*. New York: Penguin, 2004.

Evans, Richard J. *The Third Reich in Power*. New York: Penguin, 2006.

Evans, Richard J. *The Third Reich at War: How the Nazis Led Germany from Conquest to Disaster*. New York: Penguin, 2009.

Fest, Joachim C. *Hitler*. Translated by Richard and Clara Winston. New York: Harcourt Brace Jovanovich, 1974.

Flood, Charles Bracelen. *Hitler: The Path to Power*. Boston, MA: Houghton Mifflin, 1989.

Gordon, Sarah. *Hitler, Germans, and the Jewish Question*. Princeton, NJ: Princeton University Press, 1988.

Hitler, Adolf. *Hitler's Second Book: The Unpublished Sequel to Mein Kampf*. Edited by Gerhard L. Weinberg. Translated by Krista Smith. New York: Enigma Books, 2006.

Hitler, Adolf. *Mein Kampf*. Translated by Ralph Manheim. New York: Houghton Mifflin, 1999.

Jones, J. Sydney. *Hitler in Vienna, 1907–1913: Clues to the Future*. New York: Stein and Day, 1983.

Kershaw, Ian. *Hitler*. 2 vols. New York: W. W. Norton, 1999–2000.

Lukacs, John. *Hitler and Stalin: June 1941*. New Haven, CT: Yale University Press, 2006.

Mosier, John. *Deathride: Hitler vs. Stalin—The Eastern Front, 1941–1945*. New York: Simon and Schuster, 2010.

Overy, Richard. *The Dictators: Hitler's Germany, Stalin's Russia*. New York: Norton, 2005.

Stolfi, R.H.S. *Hitler: Beyond Evil and Tyranny*. Amherst, NY: Prometheus Books, 2011.

Todd, Allen. *The European Dictatorships: Hitler, Stalin, Mussolini.* Cambridge: Cambridge University Press, 2002.

Weinberg, Gerhard L. *Visions of Victory: The Hopes of Eight World War II Leaders.* Cambridge: Cambridge University Press, 2005.

Wilson, A. N. *Hitler.* New York: Basic Books, 2012.

Holocaust, The

The Holocaust was the Nazi effort to exterminate the Jews of Europe during World War II. Historians have developed several interpretations of the Holocaust. While some see it as the last, most horrible manifestation of historical anti-Semitism, others view it as the outcome of factors inherent in Western civilization, such as economic rationalization, technocracy, and the eugenics movement. The "intentionalists" see Adolf Hitler as the crucial factor in the Holocaust, determined on the destruction of the Jews from the beginning. A straight line supposedly runs from his earliest anti-Semitic comments through World War II and his final testament of April 1945. On the other hand, the "functionalists" see the persecution of the Jews as a slowly developing process, exhibiting no overall plan. Not until after the beginning of World War II, when the Nazis found themselves in control of well over 3,000,000 Jews, did the full implementation of the Holocaust occur. Attempts have been made to reconcile these positions, for example, emphasizing the fusion of anti-Semitism with bureaucratic techniques of extermination.

The French Revolution of 1789 saw the beginning of the process of emancipation of the European Jews and their increasing assimilation into European society. At the same time, traditional Christian anti-Judaism gave way to modern racial anti-Semitism, fostered by hyper-nationalism, social Darwinism, and pseudo-racial "science." Anti-Semites made the Jews the scapegoat for all the supposed ills of the modern world, including capitalism, socialism, and the press.

Anti-Semitism was a pan-European movement, as is exemplified by the Dreyfus Affair in France. Indeed, Eastern Europe (especially Russia) was the scene of violent pogroms and ritual murder trials into the 20th century. In about 1900, agents of the tsarist secret police, the Okrana, wrote the *Protocols of the Elders of Zion*, a forgery proclaiming a Jewish conspiracy to dominate the world.

By 1900, Jews in Germany numbered about 600,000 of a population of 60 million. Jews were prominent in such areas as banking, journalism, and medicine. Some 85 percent were assimilationists and enthusiastically supported Germany during World War I. Nonetheless, Germany's defeat in World War I and the accompanying economic turmoil of the early 1920s allowed extremist right-wing groups such as the National Socialist German Workers Party, led by Adolf Hitler, to spread. These groups held Jews responsible for everything from betraying Germany on the home front during World War I to causing the evils of urban life. Whether it stemmed from his Vienna years, as portrayed in *Mein Kampf,* or developed essentially after his entry into politics at the end of World War I, Hitler's obsessive, pathological anti-Semitism, its identification with Bolshevism, and a crude social Darwinism became the core of his and Nazism's ideology.

Hitler's overall role and guilt in fostering the persecution of the Jews is clear. After 1934, however, he gradually withdrew from domestic politics, fostering power struggles among various party agencies. In this atmosphere, his lieutenants attempted to anticipate his wishes—a process that led to increasingly radical anti-Jewish measures.

The Nazis' assumption of power in 1933 led to increased random attacks on Jews. The Nazis did not appear to have a coordinated plan to deal with the "Jewish question." Indeed, the years 1933 to 1938 saw a tension between party radicals such as Joseph Goebbels and Julius Streicher and moderates such as Foreign Minister Konstantin von Neurath and Economics Minister Hjalmar Schacht, who feared that anti-Semitic actions would damage Germany's international position and economic recovery. Some level of anti-Semitism was common among many Germans, but there is little evidence that most Germans were imbued with an eliminationist anti-Semitism, ready to murder Jews once they were given the opportunity.

The opening of the Nazi attack included a one-day unsuccessful boycott of Jewish stores on April 1, 1933, and the April 7 Law for the Restoration of the Professional Civil Service, which dismissed non-Aryans from government service. Although the boycott was unpopular with large sections of the public and the civil service law included exemptions such as World War I veterans, these actions began a gradual process that by 1939 would lead to the exclusion of Jews from German life.

On July 14, 1933, the Law for the Prevention of Genetically Diseased Offspring was promulgated, which by 1937 led to the sterilization of some 200,000 people. Although the Nazi eugenics program was not aimed specifically at Jews, and indeed was influenced by the general European and American eugenics movement, it ran on a parallel track with the anti-Jewish legislation. By World War II, the two tracks would merge in a program of euthanasia and mass murder.

In September 1935, the so-called Nuremberg Laws were passed by a special session of the Reichstag convened during the Nazi Party rally of that month. The laws were drawn up in great haste during the rally itself, indicative of the unsystematic nature of Nazi policy concerning the Jews during the 1930s. Jews became subjects, not citizens; it became illegal for Jews to marry or have extramarital relations with non-Jews. On November 14, a supplementary law was enacted, defining a "full Jew" (having three or four Jewish grandparents) and the categories of first-degree and second-degree *Mischling* (mixed race).

In 1938, there was another major escalation of anti-Jewish persecution. In Austria, after the *Anschluss* in March, a wave of humiliations, beatings, and murders occurred that were worse than anything else seen so far in Germany. The Nazis quickly set up agencies to forcibly expropriate Jewish businesses and expedite emigration, the latter effort led by Adolf Eichmann, Zionist expert of the Sicherheitsdienst (SD, Security Service). Some scholars see this sequence of violence, expropriation, and emigration as a model for how the Nazis would later attempt to handle the "Jewish question," with emigration replaced by something far worse.

During the spring and summer of 1938, violent attacks on Jews in Germany increased, culminating in the pogrom of November 9–10. In retaliation for the murder of the third secretary of the German Embassy in Paris, Ernst von Rath, by Jewish youth Herschel Grynspan, Jews were attacked all over Germany, businesses were vandalized, and synagogues were burned. The streets were so covered with glass they appeared to be made of crystal, hence the term "crystal night" to describe the event. Party, police, and governmental offices all were complicit in the pogrom. Estimates hold that some 91 Jews died, 30,000 were arrested, and a like number were sent to concentration camps. A total of 267 synagogues were burned, and 7,500 businesses were vandalized. The Jews received no insurance payments and in fact were fined more than a billion reichsmarks.

The period from November 1938 to the outbreak of World War II saw the removal of Jews from virtually all aspects of German society. During a Reichstag speech in January 1939, Hitler made his infamous threat that if international Jewry succeeded in starting another world war, the result would not be its victory but "the annihilation of the Jewish race in Europe."

By the time the war broke out, more than half of German and Austrian Jews had departed Germany, the official policy of which still promoted emigration. Emigrants were subject to expropriation and payment of flight taxes. Few countries were willing to increase their quota of Jewish immigrants, however. International conferences such as that held in Évian, France, in July 1938 proved fruitless.

After their conquest of Poland in the fall of 1939, the Nazis found themselves in control of some 2 million Jews. Another million were in the Soviet sphere of occupation. Nazi treatment of Poles and Jews, considered inferior races, was brutal. Western Poland was annexed to Germany, and the eastern part was transformed into the General Government under Nazi lawyer Hans Frank. To facilitate the implementation of Nazi policies, head of the Schutzstaffel (SS) Heinrich Himmler on September 27 amalgamated all police and security services in the Reichssicherheitshauptamt (RSHA, Reich Security Main Office) under Reinhard Heydrich.

On September 21, Heydrich issued instructions to *Einsatzgruppen* (mobile strike forces) leaders in which he distinguished between the "final aim" of Jewish policy and the steps leading to it. Jews were to be moved from the countryside and concentrated in cities near rail lines, implying the ghettoization of Polish Jews. Each ghetto was to elect a Jewish Council (*Judenrat*) that would be responsible for carrying out Nazi orders. In October, Jews were expelled from the annexed area of Poland, called the Warthegau, into the General Government. In addition, Frank ordered that all Jews must perform compulsory labor and wear a Star of David on the right sleeve of their clothing.

Despite the mention of the "final aim" and the brutality of these measures, most scholars do not believe the Nazis had yet adopted the idea of mass extermination. Their main goals during 1940 were either fostering emigration by Jews or deporting them to a colony in Africa or the Near East.

The first major ghetto was established in Lodz in February 1940. The Warsaw ghetto, the largest, was established in October 1940. Ghettos were in older sections of cities, with inadequate living space, housing, and food. They were surrounded by walls and barbed wire, and attempts to leave were punished by death. Disease and starvation were common. Jewish Councils had their own police forces, which were themselves brutal in enforcing Nazi orders. The Nazi film *The Eternal Jew* (1940) cynically portrayed these conditions as normal Jewish living habits.

Despite the terrible conditions, Jews secretly practiced their religion, educated their children, and maintained cultural activities. In Warsaw, the historian Emmanuel

Ringelblum started the Oneg Shabbat ("in celebration of the Sabbath"), a secret organization that chronicled life in the ghetto. Its records, partly recovered after the war, are an invaluable picture of ghetto life.

In a speech to senior army officers on March 30, 1941, preceding the invasion of the Soviet Union (Operation BARBAROSSA), Hitler maintained that, in contrast to war in the west, the war against the Soviet Union would be a war of annihilation, a brutal campaign to subjugate inferior Slavs and to exterminate Jewish-Bolshevism. Hitler's BARBAROSSA Decree of May 13, 1941, and the Commissar Order of June 6, 1941, as well as orders issued by various generals, called for liquidation of the Bolshevik leadership without trial, reprisals against whole villages for partisan actions, and the freeing of military personnel from prosecution for crimes against civilians. These orders would pave the way for military complicity in war crimes against Russian soldiers and civilians and against the Jews.

After the German invasion of the Soviet Union on June 22, 1941, four *Einsatzgruppen*, each numbering 600–1,000 men, swept through the conquered territories in the wake of the invading armies, shooting Communist Party functionaries and especially male Jews. The *Einsatzgruppen* were drawn primarily from various security and SS units. The German army provided no obstacles to their actions and in some cases actively cooperated with them. After their numbers were augmented in August, the *Einsatzgruppen* rapidly expanded their killing of Jews, including women and children. Between June and August the *Einsatzgruppen* killed approximately 50,000 Jews; in the next four months some 500,000 would perish. On October 29 and 30 at Babi Yar near Kiev, some 33,000 Jews were shot, and their bodies were dumped in a ravine. Hitler had undoubtedly given the overall approval to widen the killing in August, and he regularly received reports of *Einsatzgruppen* activities.

Collaborators throughout Eastern Europe actively aided—and in some cases, outdid—the Nazis. For example, the German invasion of Lithuania was accompanied by horrendous butchery of Lithuanians against Lithuanians. Germany's Romanian allies actively murdered Jews. On October 22, the Romanian military headquarters in Odessa was blown up and 60 lives were lost. In reprisal, Romanian army units massacred 19,000 Jews and locked another 20,000 in warehouses in a nearby village, which were then set on fire and machine-gunned. Babi Yar and Odessa were perhaps the two worst massacres of the war.

Although no written order has come to light and although Hitler confined himself to murderous ranting about the Jews, there can be no doubt that the Holocaust proceeded with Hitler's express knowledge and desire. Scholars are divided, however, about when exactly the "final solution" was put into effect. Some authorities place the decision as early as the spring of 1941 during the planning for Operation BARBAROSSA, and others argue that there was a gradual escalation of measures throughout the summer and fall of 1941. Hitler's final decision may have come on December 12, 1941, in a talk to party leaders at the Reich Chancellery, one day after his declaration of war on the United States. Hitler now saw the events he had described in his speech of January 30, 1939, as coming to pass: the Jews had started a world war, and now they would perish.

On January 20, 1942, the much-postponed Wannsee Conference held for the purpose of coordinating activities by various agencies with regard to the "final solution" took place. Chaired by Reinhard Heydrich, it included major SS and government agency representatives. Europe's Jewish population was set at an exaggerated figure of 11 million. The

Jews—even those not under Nazi control—were to be "evacuated" to the east. This "final solution to the Jewish question" would be implemented first in the General Government. Hitler's hatred of the Jews, the realization that the war against the Soviet Union would not be over quickly, the huge number of Jews in Eastern Europe augmented by deportations from the west, and killing actions initiated by local commanders all combined to replace deportation with systematic mass murder.

Since execution by shooting was too inefficient and was stressful for the shooters, the Nazis began gassing victims. The model for mass murder came from the euthanasia program, which had been ordered by Hitler on September 1, 1939, and which officially ended in August 1941 after strong protests from German churches. Known as the T-4 program (named after its headquarters at Tiergartenstrasse 4 in Berlin), it had been responsible for killing some 5,000 children and 70,000 to 80,000 adults, at first by injection and then by carbon monoxide. Several T-4 staff members were transferred to the extermination program of Eastern Europe.

In December 1941, Chelmno, near Lodz in the Warthegau, was the first extermination center to begin operation. Between March and July 1942, in connection with Operation REINHARD (the plan to kill the Jews of the General Government), three more death camps were set up: Belzec, Sobibor, and Treblinka. Deportations to these camps from Polish ghettos took place throughout 1942 and into the fall of 1943.

As Jews were rounded up, they were told they were being resettled to labor camps in the east. When the Jews arrived in the camps, their belongings were confiscated and they were then forced to undress and to move down a ramp ("the tube") into gas chambers falsely labeled as showers. The Jews were then killed with gas fed into the chamber. Special units of Jewish prisoners called *Sonderkommandos* removed the dead from the gas chambers, collected their possessions, and then buried the corpses in mass graves. Eventually, the *Sonderkommandos* too were killed. Jews from all over occupied Europe, as well as Roma (gypsies), were killed in these camps. Authorities estimate the approximate death toll at 1.9 million.

Majdanek (near Lublin in the General Government) and Auschwitz (in a section of southern Poland annexed to Germany) operated as concentration, extermination, and forced-labor camps. Exterminations in gas chambers began in Majdanek in the fall of 1942 and greatly increased in November 1943, when the Nazis launched Operation HARVEST FESTIVAL to kill off the remaining Jews in the General Government. By the time Soviet forces overran Majdanek in July 1944, some 360,000 people had died.

Auschwitz I was set up as a concentration camp in May 1940. Here the Nazis brutally murdered thousands at the "Black Wall" and carried on gruesome pseudoscientific medical experiments, including sterilization, castration, and hypothermia. Auschwitz II or Auschwitz-Birkenau was essentially an extermination camp. It began operations on September 3, 1941, when 900 Soviet prisoners of war died after being gassed with Zyklon B, crystallized hydrogen cyanide. By 1943, four large gas chambers or crematoria were at work as Jews from all over Europe were brought to Auschwitz. Work to expand the facility continued essentially until the summer of 1944. During the spring and summer of 1944, more than 400,000 Hungarian Jews were deported to Auschwitz and gassed. A conservative estimate puts the overall death toll here at 1.1 million Jews, 75,000 Poles, 21,000 Roma, and 15,000 Soviet prisoners of war.

Slave laborers in a barrack at Buchenwald concentration camp, near Weimar, Germany, on April 16, 1945. On April 11, 1945, the U.S. 3rd Army assumed control of the camp, finding many prisoners dead from starvation and scientific experiments. (National Archives)

Prisoners destined for the camps were packed into unheated and unventilated cattle cars with no food and perhaps one bucket for a toilet. Many died before reaching the camp. Upon arrival, prisoners underwent "selection": those unfit for work were immediately sent to the gas chambers, which were disguised as showers. *Sonderkommandos* cleaned the gas chambers, cremated the corpses, and collected valuables.

In the fall of 1941, I.G. Farben decided to build a Buna (synthetic rubber) plant at Auschwitz to exploit cheap slave labor. The so-called Auschwitz III expanded into a 40-square-mile area with numerous subcamps. Periodic selections singled out weak and sick workers for extermination.

Numerous survivors, including Elie Wiesel and Primo Levi, have described the brutal Auschwitz camp regime, which was intended to dehumanize its victims. "*Kapos*"—usually incarcerated criminals—enforced order. Hunger was all-pervasive. Finally, on January 27, 1945, Soviet forces liberated the few remaining prisoners in Auschwitz. Some 60,000 had been forced on death marches to camps in Germany. Many died on the marches or before the German camps were liberated.

Between 1942 and early 1945, the Nazis extended the Holocaust to occupied western, central, and southern Europe. Numerous government agencies including the RSHA, the Transport Ministry, and the Foreign Office lent their assistance. Adolf Eichmann, head of RSHA Jewish Affairs and Evacuation Affairs (coded IV-B-4), coordinated the deportations. The European rail system was taken over and used to move Jews east to the killing sites.

In many places, the Nazis were assisted by collaborationist authorities, but elsewhere, such as in Denmark and in Italian-held areas, they were actively resisted by local officials. The result was that thousands of Jews went into hiding or were assisted in escaping the Nazi dragnet. Although exact numbers will never be known, it is estimated that 3.5 million to 4 million people died in the six death camps. When victims of pogroms, the *Einsatzgruppen*, and those who died of overwork, starvation, and disease are added, the Holocaust claimed some 6 million lives.

Resistance was made difficult by numerous factors—the impossibility of believing the reality of what was happening, the hostility of local populations, the difficulty of obtaining weapons, the deception of the Nazis, and the decision of Jewish councils to obey Nazi demands in hopes of saving the lives of the remnant Jewish population that worked in defense industries.

Most Jews who were rounded up for execution or transport to a camp went without resistance. In some cases, however, open rebellion broke out. The most famous example is the Warsaw Rising, beginning on April 19, 1943, in which 700 to 1,000 resistance fighters in the Warsaw ghetto held off several thousand heavily armed German and Baltic auxiliaries under SS-Brigadeführer Joseph (Jürgen) Stroop for almost four weeks. Revolts in Treblinka in August 1943 and in Sobibor in October 1943 led to the closing of these camps. On October 7, 1944, the *Sonderkommando* at Auschwitz revolted, killing several SS men and blowing up one of the crematoria. All were killed in the ensuing escape attempt. In several cases, Jews were able to escape the ghettos and either join or form their own partisan groups that fought against the Nazis.

Allied officials were clearly aware of the Holocaust by late 1942, but like the Jews themselves, they had difficulty believing what they were hearing. In addition, anti-Semitism was still strong in many countries. American State Department official Breckinridge Long worked actively to keep Jewish refugees out of the United States. In the Allied countries, winning the war was the first priority. American Jewish organizations were hesitant to make waves or press President Franklin D. Roosevelt for fear of stirring up even more anti-Semitism. In a still-controversial decision, the Allies refused to bomb the Auschwitz camp or the rail lines leading to it. Not until early 1944 did Roosevelt create the War Refugee Board, after the Treasury Department had exposed the State Department's duplicity.

Some governments or individual diplomats resisted the Nazis. The Danish people ensured the rescue of more than 95 percent of Danish Jews. The Bulgarian government refused to give over its native Jews, although it handed over Jews in occupied territories. The Italian fascist government refused cooperation with the Nazis, and Franco's government allowed Jewish refugees to travel through Spain. Diplomats defied their orders by issuing visas to Jews. The Swede Raoul Wallenberg and other diplomats in Budapest rescued thousands of Jews in the summer and fall of 1944 by issuing false papers and setting up safe havens. Citizens from France to Poland sheltered Jews, in some cases for years, at tremendous risk to themselves. In 1940, Chiune Sugihara, a minor diplomat in the Japanese consulate in Kaunas, Lithuania, quietly defied his government's orders and issued illegal visas to more than 2,000 Jewish families.

In the case of the churches, it was more often individuals than institutions that did rescue work. Numerous Protestant, Eastern Orthodox, and Catholic clergy and laymen intervened to help Jews, whereas others remained silent or backed Nazi actions. Controversy still surrounds the role of Pope Pius XII, who never publicly condemned the Holocaust, even when the Jews of Rome were being rounded up in October 1943.

As the Nazi empire crumbled in late 1944 and early 1945, Himmler and others carried out increasingly desperate negotiations, attempting to trade Jewish lives for ransom. As the Soviet army moved westward, hasty attempts were made to dismantle camps and burn victims' bodies. Prisoners were forced on death marches back to camps within Germany. By May 1945, the last of the camps had been overrun. Some 50,000 prisoners were liberated, but many were so sick and emaciated they died soon after. In his political testament of April 29, 1945, Hitler blamed the war on the Jews and called on Germans to continue the struggle against international Jewry.

The pre–World War II Jewish population of Europe had been approximately 9 million. At the end of the war, 3 million remained. In Poland, some 45,000 survived out of a prewar population of 3 million, many of whom were Hasidic Jews. In the words of the sect's founder, Israel Ba'al Shem Tov: "In forgetfulness is the root of exile. In remembrance the seed of redemption."

Donald E. Thomas Jr.

See also

Casualties; Collaboration; Eastern Front; Greece, Role in War; Hitler, Adolf; Poland, Role in War; Resistance; Roosevelt, Franklin D.; Western European Theater of Operations

References

Bartov, Omer, ed. *The Holocaust: Origins, Implementations, Aftermath*. London and New York: Routledge, 2000.

Bergen, Doris L. *War and Genocide: A Concise History of the Holocaust*. Lanham, MD: Rowman and Littlefield, 2009.

Breitman, Richard. *The Architect of Genocide: Himmler and the Final Solution*. New York: Alfred A. Knopf, 1991.

Breitman, Richard. *Official Secrets: What the Nazis Planned, What the British and Americans Knew*. New York: Hill and Wang, 1998.

Evans, Richard J. *Lying about Hitler: History, Holocaust, and the David Irving Trial*. New York: Basic Books, 2002.

Friedlaender, Saul. *Nazi Germany and the Jews*. Vol. 1, *The Years of Persecution, 1933–1939*. New York: HarperCollins, 1997.

Friedlaender, Saul. *Nazi Germany and the Jews*. Vol. 2, *The Years of Extermination, 1939–1945*. New York: HarperCollins, 2008.

Fritz, Stephen G. *Ostkrieg: Hitler's War of Extermination in the East*. Lexington, KY: University Press of Kentucky, 2011.

Goldhagen, Daniel Jonah. *Hitler's Willing Executioners: Ordinary Germans and the Holocaust.* New York: Alfred A. Knopf, 1996.

Hilberg, Raul. *The Destruction of the European Jews.* 3rd ed. New Haven, CT: Yale University Press, 2002.

Kershaw, Ian. *Hitler.* 2 vols. New York: W. W. Norton, 1998 and 2000.

Kershaw, Ian. *Hitler, the Germans, and the Final Solution.* New Haven, CT: Yale University Press, 2008.

Lanzman, Claude. *Shoah: An Oral History of the Holocaust.* New York: Pantheon, 1985.

Laqueur, Walter, ed. *The Holocaust Encyclopedia.* New Haven, CT: Yale University Press, 2001.

Mayer, Arno J. *Why Did the Heavens Not Darken? The "Final Solution" in History.* New York: Pantheon, 1988.

Shermer, Michael, and Alex Grobman. *Denying History: Who Says the Holocaust Never Happened and Why Do They Say It?* Revised and updated ed. Berkeley, CA: University of California Press, 2000.

Snyder, Timothy. *Bloodlands: Europe between Hitler and Stalin.* New York: Basic Books, 2010.

United States Holocaust Memorial Museum. *Historical Atlas of the Holocaust.* New York: MacMillan, 1996.

Wistrich, Robert S. *Hitler and the Holocaust.* New York: Modern Library, 2003.

Italy, Air Force

In the period between World Wars I and II, the Royal Italian Air Force (Regia Aeronautica) was regarded as one of the most advanced in the world, winning 96 international aviation awards. In 1939, Italy also had the third-largest European commercial air fleet, behind only Germany and the United Kingdom. Moreover, with the possible exception of Japan, Italy had more interwar combat experience than any other nation, from the suppression of the Senussi in Libya to the Italo-Ethiopian War and culminating in the Spanish Civil War, where the Italians contributed more aircraft than did Germany. Between 1935 and 1939, Italy expended 1,500 aircraft in combat, and an additional 925 planes were exported. The Royal Italian Air Force was also the most Fascist of the three services and the favorite of Italian dictator Benito Mussolini and the Fascist Party.

Yet in World War II, the Italian air force was found wanting. When Italy entered the war in June 1940, its air force had almost 1,000 front-line aircraft, backed by about 2,000 second- and third-line aircraft. But these figures were deceptive. Italy had a few high-performance planes—those that had set a number of aviation records—but most of the aircraft were, in fact, obsolete.

The chief of staff and undersecretary of the Regia Aeronautica, General Giuseppe Valle, commanded the air force. Italy was organized into three air zones, with several regional commands and army-air cooperation units and land- and sea-based naval reconnaissance units. The air force retained control of all pilots, and coordination between the three military branches was poor at best. The lack of a coherent air philosophy and an effective building program compounded the problem.

General Valle was relieved of his command on October 31, 1939, charged with responsibility for the poor state of the air force when it was mobilized at the beginning of the war. He was placed on trial, and although he was later freed, the public mistakenly held him responsible for the state of unpreparedness. General Francesco Pricolo commanded the air force from October 31, 1939 to November 14, 1941, when he was, in turn, replaced by General Rino Corso Fougier until July 26, 1943.

Italy joined the war in June 1940 and only fought in the Battle for France for several weeks, after which it received some French aircraft. Later, Mussolini insisted on sending aircraft to Belgium to assist in the Battle of Britain. The Germans thought the planes would be far more useful in North Africa. They proved hopelessly inadequate in the skies over Britain and had to be withdrawn. In 1941, Italy sent a more effective air contingent to fight in the Soviet Union.

In the Mediterranean Theater, the Italian air force was invoked in air strikes against Malta, targeted on British merchant ships and naval units operating near Italy. It also conducted raids against Gibraltar and Palestine and even as far afield as the Persian Gulf. However, the Italians soon learned that aircraft that had been successful against stationary merchant ships docked in harbors during the Spanish Civil War were ineffective in high-altitude bombing attacks against warships. Indeed, early in the war, the aircraft occasionally attacked Italian warships by mistake, although recognition improved as the war unfolded. But not until March 1941 did the air force place liaison officers on board warships at sea.

The Italian air force was more successful in fighting in the Balkans, against Greece and Yugoslavia. It also fought in the Western Desert from 1940 to 1943, as well as in Ethiopia. When fielding modern machines—the later models with German engines—the air force was effective. But despite the fact that the Italian air force had operated in Libya since 1911, its aircraft still lacked dust filters on the eve of war, and its tactics were reminiscent of World War I acrobatics.

With the exception of three fighters embarked on two battleships late in the war, the only sea-based air effort (apart from ship-launched reconnaissance aircraft) involved the crash conversion of two passenger ships into aircraft carriers. Neither was completed by the armistice. The failure to develop aircraft carriers seriously affected Italian naval operations in the war, largely because of the short range of Italy's land-based fighters.

On the whole, Italy's aviation industry was badly organized and inefficient, producing a wide variety of aircraft types in small numbers. The various companies involved resisted manufacturing each other's more successful designs, and the almost artisan production methods resulted in production times that were more than 50 percent longer than for comparable German aircraft. The Italian air force largely depended on radial engines, but these low-powered machines seldom exceeded 1,000 hp. Adoption of the bulkier but much more powerful German-designed Daimler-Benz in-line engine helped solve that problem.

The fact that the CR-42, a wood-and-canvas biplane fighter with nonretractable landing gear, was still in production in 1944 (and a serious candidate for the Daimler-Benz engine) reveals the sad state of Italian aircraft production. Italian fighters were almost all underarmed, due to financial considerations and poorly designed, weak wings. Radios were not installed in all aircraft until 1942; fuel was stored in thinly lined, leaking tanks; most airfields were dirt runways; and pilots were slow to adapt to closed canopies. On any given day, operational efficiency was rarely higher than 70 percent. Ground-support aircraft, based on precepts developed by General Amadeo Mecozzi, were so poorly designed that early in the war, Italy simply retired its ground-attack planes and purchased 159 Ju-87 Stuka dive-bombers from Germany.

One area in which the Italian air force excelled was the torpedo bomber. Although use of this plane was hindered by interservice rivalry before the war, the torpedo bomber was deployed to units by late 1940. German air units later successfully emulated Italian torpedo-bombing tactics and purchased torpedoes from Italy. Yet the Italians chose simply to adapt a three-engine SM-79 level bomber for torpedo bombing rather than design a true torpedo bomber.

Although Italy formally embraced the concept of strategic bombing developed by General Giulio Douhet, it did not practice it. Ironically, Douhet had more influence on British and U.S. air policies than at home. Italy did produce a partially successful four-engine bomber, the P-108, but only in small numbers. With the armistice in September 1943, there were two Italian air forces: one for the Fascist state in the north and another, utilizing many different Allied aircraft, that fought for the Allied government in the south.

Jack Greene

See also

Balkans Theater; Greece, Role in War; Italy Campaign; Mussolini, Benito; North Africa Campaign; Western European Theater of Operations

References

Arena, Nino. *La Regia Aeronautica, 1939–1943*. 4 vols. Rome: Uffico Storico, 1982–1986.

Dunning, Chris. *Courage Alone: The Italian Air Force, 1940–1943*. Aldershot: Hikoki Publications, 1998.

Dunning, Chris. *Regia Aeronautica: The Italian Air Force 1923–1945—An Operational History*. Sittingbourne: Classic Publications, 2010.

Gooch, John. *Mussolini and His Generals: The Armed Forces and Fascist Foreign Policy, 1922–1940*. New York: Cambridge University Press, 2007.

Greene, Jack, and Alessandro Massignani. *The Naval War in the Mediterranean, 1940–1943*. London: Chatham Publishing, 1998.

Overy, Richard J. *The Air War 1939–1945*. Washington, DC: Potomac Books, 2005.

Rastelli, Achille. *La portaerei italiana* [The Italian Aircraft Carrier]. Milan: Mursia, 2001.

Shores, Christopher. *Regia Aeronautica*. 2 vols. Carrolton, TX: Squadron/Signal Publications, 1976.

Italy, Army

When Italy entered World War II on June 10, 1940, the Regio Esercito (Royal Army) had 1,630,000 men under arms. This figure would rise during the war to 2,563,000. King Victor Emmanuel III was nominal commander in chief, with the title of *comandante supremo delle Forse Armato dello Stato* (supreme commander of the Royal Army of the Kingdom of Italy), but Italian dictator Benito Mussolini exercised actual command.

Contrary to popular misconceptions, some units of the army fought well in World War II, but the army itself was basically a light infantry force lacking in equipment and poorly prepared for a modern European war. In 1940, it numbered 73 divisions—43 infantry; 5 Alpine; 3 light; 2 motorized; 3 armored; 12 "self-transportable," with a regiment of truck-drawn artillery; 3 militia; and 2 Libyan. Many military formations were under-strength, and much of the army's equipment was obsolete at best. Morale was not always optimal, for many Italians thought their nation was on the wrong side in the war. The men were often indifferently led, as many officer appointments were made on the basis of party loyalty rather than ability.

An Italian infantry division was composed of two infantry regiments, an artillery regiment, an engineer company, and occasionally an attached Blackshirt (Voluntary Militia for National Security, or MVSN) legion. The "binary" division had only about 10,000 men at full strength. The royal infantry regiments pledged allegiance to the king, but the highly motivated Blackshirt legions, which numbered about 1,300 men each, swore loyalty to Mussolini. Many regular army officers deeply resented the inclusion of Blackshirt regiments in the army. In 1940, the equivalent of four MVSN divisions were destroyed in fighting in North Africa. Eventually, "M battalions" made of Blackshirts fought in the Soviet Union and in Yugoslavia. They also manned antiaircraft artillery batteries throughout the Italian Empire.

In 1940, the Italian army had more than 8,000 artillery pieces, which were classified as divisional (field), corps (medium), and army (heavy). Much of the artillery was left over from World War I, and some guns were modernized World War I prizes, such as pieces manufactured at Skoda. In 1940, Italy had more than 1,200 tanks, but most were only two-man light "tankettes." Many of the larger models were too thinly armored to stop armor-piercing bullets, let alone stand up to northern European armor.

On June 20, 1940, Mussolini entered the war by attacking France in the western Alps with 32 divisions. The Italians did poorly, being largely held at bay by 5 French divisions. When the leaders in Paris surrendered on June 24, the Italians took a small portion of southeastern France. The French admitted to having 37 soldiers killed in the campaign; Italian losses were 631.

On October 28, 1940, on short notice, Mussolini sent Italian troops into Greece from Albania. The invasion involved fewer than 100,000 Italian troops, and by late November, the Greek army had driven the Italian army back into Albania, where both forces suffered heavily in a bloody stalemate during the winter. Hitler came to the rescue of his ally on April 6, 1941, when German forces invaded Greece and conquered it in a few short weeks. Italian forces, chiefly the Second Army, also participated in the invasion and conquest of Yugoslavia that same month.

Italy's subsequent occupation of portions of Yugoslavia, France, Corsica, and Greece tied down numerous divisions. Resistance efforts created an ever growing list of casualties. During their occupation of Yugoslavia, the Italians raised a number of units usually organized on religious lines—Catholic, Orthodox Christian, and Muslim—from men seeking to fight the Partisans.

After Hitler invaded the Soviet Union in June 1941, Mussolini eagerly offered Italian forces. Eventually, Italy sent more than 250,000 men to the Soviet Front. Most of the Italian Eighth Army was lost in the Battle of Stalingrad. Included in Italian forces operating mainly in the Ukraine was a Croatian legion raised in Croatia. The Italians also helped organize a small Cossack anticommunist volunteer group. If the units sent to the Soviet Union had been added to forces in North Africa, they might well have affected the outcome of the struggle there.

Italy made a major military effort in North Africa in order to fulfill Mussolini's dream of establishing a great Italian empire. Before the war, Italy had colonized Libya, Eritrea, Somalia, and Ethiopia (Abyssinia). Italian forces there were, however, underequipped and undergunned compared with the British forces they had to fight.

Amedeo Umberto di Savoia, the duke of Aosta, commanded forces in Italian East Africa (Somalia, Ethiopia, and Eritrea). Of his 256,000 men, 182,000 were "indigenous" levies. European colonists, including some Blackshirt troops, formed part of the units under the duke's command. Fighting there began in early July 1940 when the Italians captured a number of small British posts, but they halted their offensive in the Sudan when intelligence estimates magnified the actual British forces arrayed against them.

On August 4, the Italians invaded British Somaliland from Ethiopia. They were able to overwhelm the small British forces defending that colony. The British withdrew to Aden, and their losses were only one-tenth those of the Italians. During the 1940–1941 winter, the British built up their resources, and beginning on January 19, 1941, they went on the offensive. By the end of 1941, the British had secured control of Italian East Africa.

In North Africa, Field Marshal Rodolfo Graziani commanded some 236,000 Italian troops. After the defeat of France, Italian forces were shifted to eastern Libya to face the British in Egypt. Major General Richard O'Connor, the British commander in Egypt, had only 31,000 men—largely from the 4th Indian Division and the 7th Armoured Division, later reinforced by the 6th Australian Division. Graziani appeared to be in a position to overwhelm the outnumbered British; however, his troops were short of heavy artillery, tanks, and antitank and antiaircraft weapons, as well as transport and logistical support. A shortage of radios often reduced communications to relaying information by messenger.

On September 13, 1940, Graziani, pressed to act prematurely by Mussolini, launched an offensive against the British. The Italians fared badly, and by December, the British had penetrated the Italian chain of forts that were protecting the Libyan border but set too far apart to be mutually supporting. Many Italian units fought effectively but to no avail. By January 1941, the British had taken some 100,000 Italian prisoners.

In February 1941, General Erwin Rommel arrived in Libya with his Afrika Korps (Africa Corps). Although smaller in number than the Italian force and officially under Italian control, the Afrika Korps quickly became the dominant partner. The Germans were far better equipped and more effectively organized and led. By contrast, the Italians lacked mobility, adequate staffing, and an effective system of command and control.

The Italians fought back and forth across northern Africa until they were finally defeated at Tunis in May 1943. A major factor in the Axis defeat was Britain's control of Malta, which enhanced the British ability to intercept by sea and air supplies destined for Axis troops in North Africa. British communications intelligence, notably ULTRA intercepts, also played a role in the Allied victory.

In July 1943, the British and the Americans invaded Sicily, held by 190,000 Italians and 40,000 Germans. The performance of Italian units varied widely. The newly formed and indifferently equipped coastal divisions, composed of middle-aged home guards, often surrendered without a fight. Certain defeat in Sicily led the Fascist Grand Council to strip Mussolini of power in July. Marshal Pietro Badoglio then formed a new government, and on September 3, he signed a secret armistice with the Allies, to go into effect five days later. The Germans, well aware of Italian efforts to switch sides, immediately implemented plans to take control of Italy. When the Germans occupied Rome on September 10, King Victor Emmanuel III and Badoglio fled south and made Brindisi the new seat of government. Meanwhile, German troops arrested and disarmed Italian army units. More than 600,000 Italians were deported to labor camps in Germany.

German commando units rescued Mussolini on September 12, 1943, and set up the Italian Social Republic (RSI), with its capital at Salo in the north. Many Fascists joined the new RSI army. New units and those from the former Italian army that remained loyal to fascism were formed into various bodies. The first of these was the Esercito Nazionale Repubblicano (ENR, National Republican Army), arranged into four divisions composed of formations newly raised by officers still loyal to Mussolini and mixed with some autonomous older units. Many thousands were recruited into the ENR divisions from among Italian soldiers interned by the Germans. These formations were usually trained in Germany and then deployed to Italy. Most of their fighting was against partisans.

The Guardia Nazionale Repubblicano (GNR, National Republican Guard) replaced the old Blackshirts. Basically a policing unit, it ultimately numbered 80,000 men. It was assigned to local security duties and fighting the partisans. Some GNR units in occupied France and Yugoslavia continued occupation duties in cooperation with the Germans.

As the struggle with the partisans intensified, all able-bodied Fascists were organized into a new militia, the Brigate Nere (Black Brigades). Formed in June 1944 as an armed branch of the RSI's new Fascist Party, this militia eventually numbered some 30,000 men. Composed of fanatical Fascists, it engaged in a no-holds-barred struggle with the partisans. The members of the Black Brigades were motivated by the belief that they would be killed in the event of a Fascist defeat.

The "x" MAS (Decima Mas) unit was an autonomous force organized by Prince Julio Valerio Borghese. Composed of 25,000 volunteers, it gained a reputation for effective and hard fighting against the partisans, primarily Tito's Yugoslav Partisans in Istria. It also included a women's unit. In addition, the Germans recruited Italian volunteers into the Waffen-SS. These units had both Italian and German names and usually were commanded by German officers. They performed well on the Anzio Front and against partisans.

In the south of Italy, the newly reorganized government led by King Victor Emmanuel III and Badoglio established an "army of the south," with the status of a cobelligerent force. It was organized as the Corpo Italiano di Liberazione (CIL, Italian Liberation Corps). Composed of old Italian Royal Army men and units, to which new recruits were added, the CIL was formed into six weak divisions, known as "combat groups." With the transfer of some Allied units to participate in the Riviera landings in France, four of these divisions were brought into the line and saw combat. They fought well and sustained casualties of 1,868 dead and 5,187 wounded. Many Italians also served with the Allied forces in support units, handling transportation and ammunition and other supplies. Some of these units were muleteers working in the rugged mountain tracks. Partisan forces also fought in the north, behind German lines. As the war drew to a close, thousands joined partisan groups in order to sanitize their pasts or ensure their futures.

The Italian army suffered substantial casualties in the war. The total of those in the army who died fighting the Allies, in German reprisals following the armistice with the Allies, and in fighting the Germans probably exceeded 300,000 men. In addition, an unknown but large number were wounded, and some 600,000 were taken as prisoners.

A.J.L. Waskey

See also

Balkans Theater; Casualties; Eastern Front; Greece, Role in War; Italy Campaign; Mussolini, Benito; North Africa Campaign; Western European Theater of Operations

References

Cloutier, Patrick. *Regio Esercito: The Royal Italian Army in Mussolini's Wars, 1935–1943*. N.p.: Lulu.com, 2007.

Gooch, John. *Mussolini and His Generals: The Armed Forces and Fascist Foreign Policy, 1922–1940*. New York: Cambridge University Press, 2007.

Hamilton, Hope. *Sacrifice on the Steppe: The Italian Alpine Corps in the Stalingrad Campaign, 1942–1943*. Havertown, PA: Casemate Publishing, 2011.

Jowett, Philip S. *The Italian Army, 1940–1945: Africa, 1940–1943*. Oxford: Osprey Publishing, 2000.

Jowett, Philip S. *The Italian Army, 1940–1945: Europe, 1940–1943*. Oxford: Osprey Publishing, 2000.

Jowett, Philip S. *The Italian Army, 1940–1945: Italy, 1943–1945*. Oxford: Osprey Publishing, 2001.

Lamb, Richard. *War in Italy, 1943–1945*. New York: St. Martin's Press, 1993.

Madeja, W. Victor. *Italian Army Order of Battle, 1940–1944*. Allentown, PA: Game Marketing, 1990.

Nafziger, George F. *The Italian Order of Battle in WW II: An Organizational History of the Divisions and Independent Brigades of the Italian Army*. 3 vols. West Chester, OH: Nafziger Collections, 1996.

Tyre, Rex. *Mussolini's Soldiers*. Osceola, WI: Motorbooks International, 1995.

Tyre, Rex. *Mussolini's Afrika Korps: The Italian Army in North Africa, 1940–1943*. Bayside, NY: Axis Europa Magazine, 1996.

Italy Campaign (1943–1945)

At the American–British Casablanca Conference in January 1943, with a cross-Channel invasion of France no longer an option for that year, British prime minister Winston Churchill and U.S. president Franklin D. Roosevelt and their military staffs agreed to follow the Axis defeat in North Africa with an invasion of Sicily. Several weeks later, the Americans also agreed to a subsequent invasion of the Italian Peninsula. This campaign would allow the Allies to retain the strategic initiative, expand their control in the Mediterranean, open a second front on the mainland of Europe to relieve pressure on the Soviets, and provide air bases closer to strategic bombing targets in Austria, Romania, and parts of Germany.

In a month-long campaign commencing on July 10, 1943, in their largest amphibious assault in the war to date, Allied troops defeated Axis forces in Sicily. The Allied conquest of Sicily had a profound effect in Italy, where, faced with growing unrest and the reluctance of Italian forces to oppose the Allies, the Fascist Grand Council launched a coup d'état that overthrew Italian dictator Benito Mussolini and installed a new government led by Marshal Pietro Badoglio. Secret negotiations between the Allies and the new Italian government for an armistice began immediately but soon became bogged down by the Allied insistence on unconditional surrender. A "short military armistice" was eventually signed, on September 3. Meanwhile, however, Adolf Hitler used the interlude to move another 16 German divisions to Italy, including the crack 1st SS Panzer Division from the Soviet Union.

The Germans then occupied the entire country and took control of most of the Italian army. Much of the Italian fleet escaped to Malta. On September 12, 1943, German commandos led by Schutzstaffel (SS) Standartenführer Otto Skorzeny rescued Mussolini from captivity in the mountains at Gran Sasso in a daring airborne raid. Hitler then installed Mussolini as head of the Italian Social Republic (RSI) in northern Italy.

The strategic logic for continuing the Allied campaign in the Mediterranean appeared obvious to the British Chiefs of Staff, who saw an invasion of Italy as an opportunity to accomplish several goals: to continue the ground war against Germany utilizing experienced troops who would otherwise remain idle for a year; to draw Axis troops away from France and the Soviet Union; and possibly to create opportunities elsewhere in the eastern Mediterranean. The U.S. Joint Chiefs of Staff, however, were far less convinced and believed that Allied efforts should be directed to the cross-Channel invasion of France, now sanctioned for the spring of 1944. They were also skeptical of British motives, fearing that the postwar preservation of colonial interests was a high priority for Britain—a goal they vehemently opposed. A final decision to invade the Italian mainland was not made until the Trident Conference in Washington in May 1943, but there was no strategic plan other than to continue the existing operations. The Americans were reluctant to commit to a new Italian campaign, and there was no new, large-scale amphibious landing in northern Italy. Any such operation would have been beyond the range of Allied fighter aircraft, and it is an open question whether that type of operation and an airborne raid to capture Rome would have brought the campaign to a rapid conclusion.

The Allied invasion plan envisaged a pincer movement across the Straits of Messina by General Sir Harold Alexander's 15th Army Group, with the first objective being the vital southern Italian port of Naples. In Operation BAYTOWN, Lieutenant General Bernard Montgomery's Eighth Army crossed from Sicily to Reggio di Calabria on September 3, followed by the British 1st Airborne Division, which landed by sea at Taranto six days later. The main assault, by 165,000 troops of the Anglo-U.S. Fifth Army under Lieutenant General Mark W. Clark, went ashore at Salerno in Operation AVALANCHE, 35 miles south of Naples, on September 9. Salerno was chosen chiefly because it was the farthest point in the north for which air support could be provided from Sicily. The Allies hoped that, once ashore, their invading forces would somehow find a way to open the road to Rome before the end of the year.

German field marshal Albert Kesselring had convinced Hitler that Italy could be easily defended because of its ideal terrain. The central mountainous spine of the Apennines rises above 10,000 feet and has lateral spurs that run east and west toward the coast, between which are deep valleys containing wide rivers flowing rapidly to the sea. The north-south roads were confined to 20-mile-wide strips adjacent to the Adriatic and Tyrrhenian coasts, where the bridges that carried them were dominated by natural strong points.

Kesselring formed the six divisions in the south of Italy into the Tenth Army under General Heinrich von Vietinghoff, but he had anticipated a landing at Salerno and stationed the 16th Panzer Division in the area. At Salerno, Fifth Army attacked with two corps abreast: the U.S. VI Corps and the British X Corps. Initial resistance was light, but the Germans reinforced by September 11 and, despite their weakness, launched a counteroffensive that almost split Fifth Army between the two invading corps. By September 15, the beachhead was secure, in large part because of an overwhelming weight of firepower in the form of accurate naval gunfire and massive air support and because more reserves were landed. Fifth Army then began an advance on Naples, 30 miles away. Montgomery, disappointed that he had only been assigned a secondary role, was needlessly cautious in his advance—so much so that a group of dismayed war correspondents drove themselves through German-occupied territory to contact Fifth Army more than a day before Montgomery's advanced units managed to do so on September 16.

Two days later, Kesselring ordered a fighting withdrawal to the first of the series of mountainous, fortified defensive lines, from which the Germans planned to defend the approaches to Rome. On October 1, Fifth Army captured Naples while Eighth Army advanced up the Adriatic coast and captured the airfields at Foggia; there, the Allies installed the U.S. Fifteenth Air Force to launch strategic bombing raids against the Reich. By early October, the two Allied armies had formed a continuous, 120-mile line across the peninsula running along the Volturno and Biferno Rivers. But in the previous three weeks, Fifth Army alone had taken 12,000 casualties.

Henceforth, the campaign in Italy became a slow, remorseless, and grinding battle of attrition, and as the rain and snow turned the battlefield into a muddy quagmire, the appalling struggles resembled World War I battles. Kesselring had fortified a series of defensive lines, known collectively as the Winter Line, between Gaeta and Pescara. The western end based on the Garigliano and Rapido Rivers, known as the Gustav Line, was particularly strong and hinged on the great fortress of the Benedictine Abbey at Monte Cassino.

On October 12, the Allies began the Volturno River Campaign, with the objective of seizing the approaches to Rome. Their plan was too ambitious, given the Germans' skill at defending the mountainous terrain. Between the Volturno and Rome lay 120 miles of rugged country. Fifth Army's VI Corps successfully attacked across the line of the Volturno River, and X Corps seized two crossings. To exploit the success, General Clark ordered an advance across the entire Fifth Army front. Particularly in the VI Corps area, poor roads, demolished bridges, and the difficulties of bringing supplies forward combined with German resistance to slow the advance. Meanwhile, in a series of bitterly contested actions, Eighth Army crossed the Trigno River and advanced to the Sangro River. By November 15, however, the Germans had stopped the advance along the Winter Line, a position that extended along the Garigliano River to Mount Camino, the Mignano gap, the mountains to the northeast, and the Sangro River to the Adriatic Sea.

The Winter Line Campaign, lasting from November 15, 1943, to January 15, 1944, marked the failure of the Allied plan for a major winter offensive. Eighth Army was to break through on the Adriatic coast and then swing left behind the Germans, at which time Fifth Army would advance. When the two came within supporting distance, Fifth Army would launch an amphibious operation south of Rome. Although its efforts to break into the German position were initially successful, Eighth Army fell victim as much

A German shell explodes in the sea in 1944, as the Germans try to prevent Allied supply ships from reaching the beach at Anzio, in Italy. Known as one of the largest and most troubled Allied attacks during the course of World War II, Anzio was the site of a massive British and U.S. amphibious assault on German troops situated in this small port on the west coast of Italy. (Getty Images/Hulton Archive)

to weather as to the German defense. In early December, the Sangro River, vital to Eighth Army communications, rose 8 feet, and bridges were under water or washed away.

By mid-December, it was clear that the efforts to break through the German defenses were futile. Meanwhile, Fifth Army successfully cleared the heights dominating the Mignano gap after much hard fighting, but it was stopped at the Rapido River. Allied forces had reached the defensive position of the Gustav Line, which generally ran along the Garigliano, Rapido, and Sangro Rivers. One of the key points was the town of Cassino on the Rapido. However, four successive attacks by Fifth Army failed to make any significant headway. The winter campaign had degenerated into a situation in which two separate armies were attempting to penetrate the Gustav Line.

In four months, the Allies had slogged just 70 miles from Salerno and were still 80 miles from Rome. Fifth Army alone had incurred 40,000 casualties, far exceeding German losses, and a further 50,000 men were sick; meanwhile, six experienced divisions were withdrawn for the cross-Channel invasion of France, Operation OVERLORD. The supreme Allied commander of the European Theater of Operations and U.S. forces in Europe, General Dwight D. Eisenhower, and Montgomery also departed to lead the cross-Channel invasion. In recognition of British predominance in Italy, General Maitland "Jumbo" Wilson was appointed to head the Mediterranean Command, and Lieutenant General Oliver Leese became commander of Eighth Army.

Kesselring, who was appointed commander of Army Group C on November 21, now had 15 (albeit weakened) divisions in Tenth Army vigorously holding the Gustav Line. On January 22, 1944, in an attempt to unhinge this force, the Allies launched another amphibious landing, Operation SHINGLE, at Anzio, 30 miles south of Rome. The U.S. VI Corps, under Major General John Lucas, achieved complete surprise and safely landed 70,000 troops within a week, but it failed to exploit the advantage. Churchill later wrote, "I had hoped that we were hurling a wild cat on to the shore, but all we got was a stranded whale."

Kesselring hastily improvised eight divisions into Fourteenth Army, commanded by General Eberhard von Mackensen. This force resolutely counterattacked at Anzio, employing "Goliath" remote-controlled, explosive-filled miniature tanks for the first time in the war. The beachhead was saved only by the excellent tactical use of intelligence in one of ULTRA's most important triumphs. Major General Lucian K. Truscott replaced Lucas, but for three months, he could do no more than hold the defensive ring. Meanwhile, Allied forces to the south were unable to break through the Gustav Line. Losses were heavy on both sides as the Allies battered against the line. VI Corps held on at Anzio but was unable to break out of the beachhead. A stalemate persisted until spring.

On January 17, V Corps launched an attack on the Gustav Line but was forced to call it off within a month, after the badly exhausted troops had advanced just 7 miles, at a cost of 17,000 casualties. The New Zealand Corps then attempted a direct assault on Monte Cassino, preceded by the questionable bombing by 145 B-17 Flying Fortresses that destroyed the famous monastery. The 1st Parachute Division troops defending the heights were some of the German army's finest, and they did not flinch. They now took up positions in the ruined monastery. A third attack by New Zealand and Indian infantry, using even heavier air and artillery bombardments, also failed to break through, not least because the rubble created an impregnable defensive position.

On May 11, the Allies launched a fourth attack, Operation DIADEM, in which General Alexander coordinated Fifth and Eighth Armies as an army group for the first time. The aim was to destroy the German armies. In an astonishing feat of arms, Polish and Free French troops seized Monte Cassino, and XIII Corps broke the Gustav Line in a set-piece battle. Moreover, Kesselring, who had been duped into expecting another amphibious landing farther north, was slow to send reinforcements southward.

Alexander was alerted to the German movements through ULTRA intelligence, and when victory seemed complete, he ordered the Anzio breakout on May 23. He planned for the U.S. VI Corps to strike directly inland to encircle the German Tenth Army. Rome would thus be ripe for the taking, but more important, the Germans would be unable to form any organized defenses in the rest of Italy, enabling the rapid occupation of the country right up to the Alps. However, Clark, perhaps the most egocentric Allied commander in the war, was enticed by the glory of capturing Rome and altered the direction of his thrust toward the city. Fifth Army linked up with VI Corps on May 25 and made the triumphant march into Rome on June 4, but the spectacle of the first capture of an Axis capital was eclipsed by the Allied invasion of France two days later.

Clark's change of objective from Alexander's intent enabled Kesselring to withdraw to the Pisa-Rimini Line, 150 miles north of Rome. This line was the first of the next series of defense lines across the peninsula that were known collectively as the Gothic Line, which he reached in August. Alexander still hoped to make for Vienna, but the Italian Campaign had assumed a definite secondary status to the invasion of France. Six divisions were withdrawn in the summer, and when the autumn rains and mud forced operations to be suspended at the end of the year, another seven divisions were withdrawn.

A prolonged Allied tactical air-interdiction program during the autumn and winter of 1944 effectively closed the Brenner Pass and created an acute German fuel shortage that drastically reduced the mobility of Army Group C in northern Italy (commanded by Vietinghoff after Kesselring was severely injured in a road accident in October). Although the Germans still had more than half a million men in the field, the Allies had been invigorated in both spirit and outlook by substantial reinforcements, including the Brazilian Expeditionary Force, and an abundant array of new weapons.

On April 9, after the ground had dried, Alexander launched his spring offensive, with Eighth Army attacking through the Argenta Gap. Fifth Army struck on April 15, and just 10 days later, both Allied armies met at Finale nell'Emilia, after having surrounded and eliminated the last German forces. The Allies then advanced rapidly northward, the Americans entering Milan on April 29 and the British reaching Trieste on May 2. Fifth Army continued to advance into Austria, linking with the U.S. Seventh Army in the Brenner Pass on May 6.

The isolated and hopeless position of German and RSI forces led Schutzstaffel (SS) General Karl Wolff, military governor and head of the SS in northern Italy, to initiate background negotiations for a separate surrender as early as February 1945. The talks, facilitated by Allen Dulles, head of the U.S. Office of Strategic Services in Switzerland, held much promise, although they were complicated and took place in an atmosphere of mutual suspicion and mistrust. Wolff wished to avoid senseless destruction and loss of life and to repel the spread of communism; he also hoped to ingratiate himself with the West in case war crimes trials were held in the future. From the Allied perspective, Wolff offered the prospect of preventing the creation of a Nazi redoubt in the Alps. The head of the SS, Heinrich Himmler, halted the talks in April, forestalling their conclusion before the Allied spring offensive, but by April 23, Wolff and Vietinghoff decided to disregard orders from Berlin. Wolff ordered the SS not to resist the Italian partisans on April 25, and an unconditional surrender was signed four days later, to be effective on May 2, six days before the German surrender in the West.

The Italian Campaign gave the Allies useful victories in the interval between the reconquest of the Mediterranean and the reconquest of northwest Europe. In a theater of increasingly secondary importance, Kesselring's position was merely a defensive one, and the best the Allies could claim was that they kept 22 enemy divisions from fighting in another theater. Allied casualties came to 188,746 for Fifth Army and 123,254 for Eighth Army, whereas German casualties were about 434,646 men. The Italian Campaign did, however, afford the Allies experience in amphibious operations and the stresses of coalition warfare, all of which proved invaluable during the invasion of France.

Philip L. Bolté and Paul H. Collier

See also

Churchill, Sir Winston Leonard Spencer; Eisenhower, Dwight D.; Hitler, Adolf; Italy, Air Force; Italy, Army; Italy, Navy; Montgomery, Sir Bernard Law; Mussolini, Benito

References

Atkinson, Rick. *The Day of Battle: The War in Sicily and Italy, 1943–1944*. New York: Henry Holt, 2007.

Carver, Michael. *The War in Italy, 1939–1945*. London: Macmillan, 2001.

D'Este, Carlo. *World War II in the Mediterranean, 1942–1945*. Chapel Hill, NC: Algonquin Press, 1990.

Gooch, John. *Italy and the Second World War*. London: Cass, 2001.

Gooderson, Ian. *A Hard Way to Make a War: The Allied Campaign in Italy in the Second World War*. London: Conway, 2008.

Graham, Dominick, and Shefford Bidwell. *Tug of War: The Battle for Italy, 1943–45*. London: Hodder and Stoughton, 1986.

Higgins, Trumbull. *Soft Underbelly: The Anglo-American Controversy over the Italian Campaign, 1939–1945*. New York: Macmillan, 1968.

Howard, Michael. *The Mediterranean Strategy in the Second World War*. London: Greenhill, 1968.

Lamb, Richard. *War in Italy, 1943–1945: A Brutal Story*. New York: St. Martin's Press, 1993.

Starr, Chester G., ed. *From Salerno to the Alps*. Nashville, TN: Battery Press, 1986.

Strawson, John. *Italian Campaign*. London: Secker and Warburg, 1987.

Italy, Navy

In the interwar period, the Royal Italian Navy (Regia Marina) had been designed to fight the French navy in surface naval battles reminiscent of the 1916 Battle of Jutland. On the eve of World War II, the navy began transforming itself, albeit unsuccessfully, into an "oceanic" navy that would not be confined by the British-controlled Mediterranean choke points of Gibraltar and the Suez. In the unlikely event that funding and resources were made available, the Italian navy by 1942 would include 9 battleships, 3 aircraft carriers, 36 cruisers (including 12 small Capitani Romani class, of which 3 were completed before the armistice), and 84 oceangoing submarines. The navy had 5.4 officers for every 100 sailors (France had 7.5 and Britain 9.2 officers per 100 sailors), and many of the sailors were volunteers.

On the eve of Italy's June 10, 1940, entry into the war, the navy was consuming about 33 percent of the annual military budget, placing it well behind the army but ahead of the air force. The core of the navy was built around the new 30-knot, massive, Littorio-class battleships armed with 9–15 inch guns. Two were being completed when war was declared, and a third was added during the war. Italy also had two small, older, and completely rebuilt and speedy World War I–era battleships ready for sea and two others that were almost ready. Although they were the weakest Axis battleships of the war, they were more powerful than any cruiser.

Italy also had 7 heavy cruisers, 12 light cruisers (adding 3 during the war), 59 destroyers (adding 10), 62 large torpedo boats (adding 17), and 113 submarines (adding 32). Various escorts, raiders, MAS-style patrol torpedo (PT) boats, and successful war-built corvettes—the 700 ton Gabbiano class, of which 28 were completed before the armistice—rounded out the major fleet units.

Although it was a substantial force on paper, the Italian navy suffered from fundamental problems. Italy lagged in several key areas of naval technology. One area was sonar, which was just beginning to be introduced at the start of the war. Also, in the disastrous March 1941 Battle of Matapan, the Italians discovered to their dismay that the Allies had deployed radar on their warships. The Italians did not deploy their first warship radar until a year later, in March 1942. Ironically, Italy's scientific community had been working on radar in the mid-1930s, but the Italian government did not fully support its efforts. Of ULTRA intercepts, the Italians knew nothing, although they assumed the Germans were letting the Allies know about Italian operations, and the Germans assumed the Italians were doing the same.

Italian ship armor plate was inferior as judged by Allied standards. Italian heavy ships relied on long-range gunnery, but guns in cruiser and destroyer turrets were mounted too close to each other, thus interfering in the flight of shells, a problem compounded by an immoderate 1 percent weight tolerance for shells. This resulted in excessive salvo spreads, as opposed to the much tighter British salvos.

The Italians sought to avoid night fighting by their heavy ships, and the navy lacked flashless night charges for ships with 8-inch or larger guns, an error not rectified until 1942. The navy dropped night-fighting training for large ships in the 1930s, precisely when the British navy was adopting such tactics for its heavy ships, including battleships. Italian losses in night surface actions during the war would be heavy and almost completely one-sided.

Italy also experienced problems with its submarines. There were three classes of submarines. The large oceangoing submarines were part of the new oceanic navy. Many were based out of Bordeaux, France. In 189 patrols, they sank more than 500,000 tons of Allied ships, with another 200,000 tons damaged. They also conducted mostly ineffective runs to Japan for key war supplies, and they operated in the Indian Ocean and Red Sea. Medium and small submarines hunted closer to home. In the Mediterranean Sea, these classes conducted 1,553 patrols with dismal results when contrasted to the successes tallied by far fewer German submarines dispatched to that theater. This outcome was, in part, due to the Italian doctrine that called for submarines to submerge during daytime and wait for a target to come within range. The Italians eschewed attacks on the surface in wolf packs at night. Their torpedoes were reliable but had smaller warheads than those of most other nations, thus causing less damage. Despite its long coastline and its colonies, Italy had only 25,000 mines in 1939, and the most dated of these were from World War I.

In the 1920s, the Italians experimented with the snorkel, a tube to the surface that allowed submarines to secure air while submerged, but they ultimately dropped its development as a dead end. Their submarines also suffered from slow submerging speeds—they were two or three times slower than German boats. Italy also had to rebuild many of its submarines during the war because their large sails (the superstructure where the surface bridge and periscope were located) were easily picked up by radar. Italian periscopes were too short, and the Mediterranean itself was a much clearer sea than the Atlantic, which made it easier for Allied pilots to locate submerged submarines.

Italy also failed to develop the aircraft carrier. Italian dictator Benito Mussolini and the navy High Command believed that the country's long coastline and the many Italian islands and bases in the central Mediterranean rendered aircraft carriers unnecessary. But the slow communication and response between the Italian navy and air force, fueled by interservice rivalries, meant that too few planes arrived too late too often; early in the war, Italian planes actually attacked Italian ships several times. High-level bombing of warships under way also proved to be ineffective. Mussolini changed his mind about the aircraft carrier, and during the war, he twice intervened personally to secure the conversion of two passenger ships to carriers, although neither was completed before the end of the war.

Italy also failed to develop torpedo bombers before the war, in large part because of interservice jealousy. The air force, with only limited funds, opposed development of torpedo bombers, preferring to use the money for high-altitude bombers. So although the Italian navy developed a torpedo for air launch, it was not until the war was several months old that the air force carried out its first torpedo attack. In the course of the war, the Italians achieved several successes with these airplanes.

The most innovative naval arm was the "x" MAS (Decima Mas). This unit was made up of (1) midget submarines; (2) underwater swimmers trained in sabotage; (3) surface speedboats filled with explosives and piloted by crewmen who jumped off shortly before the vessels hit their targets; and (4) the slow-moving torpedo, or SLC, which was ridden by two men under water into enemy harbors. The most successful of these weapons was the SLC, directly developed from a World War I weapon that was employed against Austria-Hungary with good results; it was usually launched from a submarine. The most spectacular success for the SLCs occurred on December 18, 1941, when three of them entered Alexandria harbor and crippled the British battleships *Queen Elizabeth* and *Valiant*. With the exception of the midget submarines, the naval High Command ignored these weapons until 1935 and then only grudgingly supported junior officers involved in innovative development. A more forceful development program begun after World War I might well have made an important difference in World War II.

In spite of these limitations, the fuel-strapped Italian navy fought bravely during the war and transported to Africa 85 percent of the supplies and 92 percent of the troops that left port. In numerous battles above, on, and below the seas, the navy sank many Allied warships and forced the British to maintain a powerful naval force at both ends of the Mediterranean. In September 1943, when Italy switched sides in the war, the bulk of the Italian fleet joined the Allies.

Italian naval losses before the armistice consisted of 1 battleship, 11 cruisers, 44 destroyers, 41 large torpedo boats, 33 MAS-style PT boats, 86 submarines, and 178 other vessels. After the armistice, Italy lost 1 battleship, 4 destroyers, 5 large torpedo boats, 25 MAS boats, 3 submarines, and 23 other vessels. Mussolini's Italian Social Republic, organized in north Italy, seized some Italian warships, and most of these were subsequently sunk; the most important was the heavy cruiser *Bolzano*. Total wartime personnel losses for the Italian navy came to 28,837, with 4,177 of this number occurring after the armistice. Up to the armistice, Italy also lost 2,018,616 tons of merchant shipping.

Jack Greene

See also
Italy Campaign; Mussolini, Benito; North Africa Campaign

References

Bragadin, Marc'Antonio. *The Italian Navy in World War II.* Annapolis, MD: Naval Institute Press, 1957.

Cernuschi, Enrico. *Le navi da guerra italiane, 1940–1945.* Parma: Ermanno Albertelli Editore, 2003.

Giorgerini, Giorgio. *La guerra italiana sul mare: La marina tra vittoria e sconfitta, 1940–1943.* Milan: Mondadori, 2001.

Gooch, John. *Mussolini and His Generals: The Armed Forces and Fascist Foreign Policy, 1922–1940.* New York: Cambridge University Press, 2007.

Greene, Jack, and Alessando Massignani. *The Naval War in the Mediterranean, 1940–1943.* London: Chatham Publishing, 1998.

Knox, MacGregor. *Hitler's Italian Allies: Royal Armed Forces, Fascist Regime, and the War of 1940–1943.* Cambridge: Cambridge University Press, 2000.

O'Hara, Vincent P. *Struggle for the Middle Sea: The Great Navies at War in the Mediterranean Theater, 1940–1945.* Annapolis, MD: Naval Institute Press, 2009.

O'Hara, Vincent P., and Enrico Cernuschi. *Dark Navy: The Italian Regia Marina and the Armistice of 8 September 1943.* Ann Arbor, MI: Nimble Books, 2009.

O'Hara, Vincent P., W. David Dickson, and Richard Worth, eds. *On Seas Contested: The Seven Great Navies of the Second World War.* Annapolis, MD: Naval Institute Press, 2010.

Sadkovich, James J. *The Italian Navy in World War II.* Westport, CT: Greenwood Press, 1994.

Japan, Air Force

Japan did not possess an independent air force during World War II. Instead, the army and navy each had their own air service. Each had different hypothetical enemies in the interwar period: the army planned to fight against the Soviet Union, and the navy expected to fight the United States and Britain in the western Pacific Ocean. As a consequence, each service developed its own air arm tailored to meet its particular needs.

Unfortunately for the Japanese war effort, neither service cooperated with the other. Army and navy aircraft employed different electrical systems; when the Japanese developed an Identification, Friend or Foe (IFF) capability, army operators on Iwo Jima in 1944 could not identify Japanese navy aircraft as friendly. Further, aircraft factories were divided between those areas that made army planes and those producing naval aircraft, and each kept design developments secret from the other. There was no exchange of data. The navy's Zero fighter was superior to the army's Hayabusa, but the navy did not want to share the Zero with the army. If the army had adopted the Zero, the number of Japanese fighter aircraft produced during the war would have been greatly increased. There was little standardization between the Zero and Hayabusa, even in small screw parts.

Japan also failed to develop heavy bombers comparable to those of Britain and the United States. Not until January 1944 did the army and navy agree to develop a joint, 6-engine heavy bomber, dubbed the "Fugaku," but this project came too late and had to be abandoned. Finally, each service also concealed its weaknesses from the other; thus, it was 1945 before army leaders discovered how catastrophic the 1942 Battle of Midway had been for the Japanese naval air arm.

At the beginning of the Pacific war in December 1941, the Japanese army possessed 4,800 aircraft. Most army fighters were of the obsolescent Nakajima Ki-27 Type 97 ("Abdul" in the Allied recognition system). The army had only 50 first-class fighters—the Nakajima Ki-43 Hayabusa ("Oscar"), which made its debut over Malaya in December 1941. The Ki-43 gradually became the army's most numerous fighter; 5,751 were built during the war. Later, the army introduced new fighters: the Nakajima Ki-44 Shoki ("Tojo"), with initial deliveries in September 1942; the Kawasaki Ki-61 Hien ("Tony"), in August 1942; and the Nakajima Ki-84 Hayate ("Frank"), in April 1944. The best of Japan's wartime army fighters to reach mass production, the Ki-84 was superior to the North American P-51 Mustang and Republic P-47 Thunderbolt in certain respects. The

Japanese army had no heavy bombers or dive-bombers and only three medium types: the Mitsubishi Ki-21 Type 97 ("Gwen"), the Nakajima Ki-49 Donryu ("Helen"), and the Mitsubishi Ki-67 Hiryu ("Peggy").

As of December 1941, the Imperial Japanese Navy air arm, which played a major role in the early battles in the Pacific, possessed 3,000 airplanes, 1,300 of which were with the fleet in 1941. Most numerous of its aircraft was the excellent, highly maneuverable Mitsubishi A6M Zero fighter ("Zeke"). Others included the Nakajima B5N Type 97 torpedo-bomber and light bomber ("Kate"); the Aichi D3A Type 99 carrier dive-bomber ("Val"); and two twin-engine, land-based medium bombers, the Mitsubishi G3M ("Nell") and the G4M Type 1 ("Betty"). Zero fighters took part in every major Japanese operation of the war. In the first six months of the war, the Zero was superior to any Allied fighter aircraft. Japan produced a total of 10,370 Zeros during World War II. As new Allied aircraft were introduced, the Japanese navy developed new aircraft, such as the Kawanishi NIK2-J Shiden ("George") and the Nakajima B6N Tenzan ("Jill").

In the Sino-Japanese War and the first stage of the Pacific war, the Japanese air forces met with considerable success. They dominated the skies over China and instituted strategic bombing of Chinese cities in 1938. The Japanese naval air arm was undoubtedly the best in the world, and Japanese pilots were among the best trained. In 1941, first-line Japanese pilots had 500 to 800 flying hours, and 50 percent of army pilots and 10 percent of navy pilots had combat experience against China and/or the Soviet Union.

On December 7, 1941, the naval air arm executed the attack on Pearl Harbor, conclusively demonstrating the supremacy of airpower in modern naval warfare and establishing the effective combination of carriers and aircraft. A few days later, navy land-based aircraft sank the British battleship *Prince of Wales* and the battle cruiser *Repulse* off Malaya. For the first time, a self-defending battleship under way had been sunk by aircraft, which showed that in the future, ships would require air protection. However, in 1942, Japanese air forces suffered heavy losses in the Battles of Midway and Guadalcanal. These battles spelled the ruin of the fine Japanese naval air arm and revealed the serious flaw of an inadequate pilot-replacement system; much of the trained naval air arm was lost in the battle and could not be replaced. The army also sustained heavy aircraft and pilot losses over New Guinea in 1943, and navy air squadrons were badly hurt at Truk and the Caroline Islands from February to April 1944.

The Battle of the Philippine Sea ("the great Marianas turkey shoot") in June 1944 and the Battle of Leyte Gulf in October 1944 finished off the Japanese naval air arm as an effective fighting force. The army and navy delivered new planes, such as the Hayate and Tenzan, but shortages of adequately trained pilots and fuel negated any advantage. By 1944, Japan was so short of aviation fuel that it could scarcely train its pilots; Japanese aviators had only about 120 hours of flying time before combat.

Japan produced some excellent, highly maneuverable aircraft during the war, but they tended to be lightly armored and caught fire easily. The Zero fighter was essentially unarmored, and Allied pilots dubbed the G4M Type 1 ("Betty") bomber "the flying cigarette lighter" because it so readily caught fire. Japanese aircraft simply could not sustain heavy damage. The planes also tended to be more lightly armed than their U.S. counterparts. When the Boeing B-29s began the strategic bombing of Japan, Japanese fighters had difficulty shooting them down. The Japanese planes also lacked airborne radar.

At the end of World War II, in a desperate effort to halt the inexorable progress of U.S. forces toward Japan, young Japanese kamikaze (literally, "divine wind") pilots flew suicide missions against U.S. naval vessels. On May 11, 1945, two kamikaze dive bombers hit the USS *Bunker Hill* within 30 seconds of each other, leaving 372 American sailors dead and 264 wounded. (National Archives)

As Japan faced overwhelming Allied forces by late 1944, the military instituted kamikaze suicide attacks. Such strikes were ordered by Vice Admiral Ōnishi Takijirō during the Battle of Leyte Gulf, and they reached culmination in the Battle of Okinawa between April and June 1945. The kamikaze strike proved highly effective: the U.S. Navy sustained greater personnel losses from these attacks during the Battle of Okinawa than in all its previous wars combined. Yet even this new tactic could not turn the tide for Japan.

In the period between 1940 and 1945, the United States produced 297,199 aircraft; during the same period, Japan produced 74,656. In the Pacific war, the Japanese army lost 15,920 planes and the Japanese navy 27,190.

Kotani Ken

See also

China–Burma–India (CBI) Theater; Japan, Army; Japan, Navy; Midway, Battle of; Pearl Harbor, Attack on; Southeast Pacific Theater; Southwest Pacific Theater; United States, Army Air Force

References

Edwards, Peter J. *The Rise and Fall of the Japanese Imperial Naval Air Service.* Barnsley: Pen and Sword, 2010.

Hata, Ikuhito, Yazuho Izawa, and Christopher Shores. *Japanese Army Air Force Fighter Units and Their Aces: 1932–1945.* Rev. ed. Toronto: Grub Street Books, 2011.

Hata, Ikuhito, Yazuho Izawa, and Christopher Shores. *Japanese Naval Air Force Fighter Units and Their Aces: 1932–1945.* Rev. ed. Toronto: Grub Street Books, 2011.

Marder, A. J. *Old Friends, New Enemies.* Oxford: Clarendon Press, 1981.

Overy, Richard J. *The Air War 1939–1945.* Washington, DC: Potomac Books, 2005.

Peattie, Mark R. *Sunburst: The Rise of Japanese Naval Air Power, 1909–1941.* Annapolis, MD: Naval Institute Press, 2002.

Roberts, J. B. *Japanese Aircraft of the Pacific War.* London: G. P. Putnam, 1979.

Treadwell, Terry C. *The Setting of the Rising Sun: Japanese Military Aviation 1877–1945.* Amberley, 2011.

Japan, Army

The Imperial Japanese Army (Dai Nippon Teikoku Rikugun) defies easy or simple recounting, in no small measure because Japanese official histories of World War II begin in September 1931 with the start of the Manchurian Campaign. Thus, any account of the Japanese army and the war really has to cover a 14-year period and to be divided into two very separate parts. One of these parts concerns its campaigns both on the ground and in the air because the Rikugun, as with the navy, had its own air force. Also, the Rikugun was involved in two wars, one in East Asia and the other in the Pacific and Southeast Asia, that were largely separate from one another, and both contained a number of campaigns that again were very largely separate from one another. Thus, the war in East Asia divides into the campaign in Manchuria, 1931–1932; the Sino-Japanese War, 1937–1944; and the final phase of the war, after December 1944, which saw major Japanese withdrawals throughout southern China and then defeat at Soviet hands in August 1945 in northern China and Manchuria. This accounting leaves unlisted the period of Japanese encroachment in northern China and Inner Mongolia between 1932 and 1936, in which time the power of the Chinese Nationalist Party—the Guomindang, or GMD (Kuomintang, or KMT)—was neutralized in these areas, as well as the four-phase China war of 1927 to 1945.

The other part concerns the process by which the Rikugun came to dominate the political process in Japan and, in effect, to control the Japanese state. This was the most important single dimension of Rikugun activity because of its results and implications, but the process by which the army came to dominate the Japanese state was, in turn, the product of developments that reached back into the 1920s and beyond, at least to the Russian and Chinese Civil Wars. In the course of these two conflicts, Japanese military formations found themselves undertaking operations without direct control and guidance from superior authority in Tokyo. This situation bred a habit of independent action, which over time came to be identified with the belief that action could and would not be repudiated by Tokyo. The first real example of this came in 1928, when Japanese military personnel from the Guandong (Kwantung) Army, the garrison force in Manchuria, murdered the local warlord, but the Army Ministry blocked all moves to have those responsible tried by courts-martial, on the grounds that such proceedings would be damaging to the army's prestige. The cabinet gave way, and having surrendered on such a crucial matter, it had no real basis on which to oppose deliberate insubordination when events revealed powerful support within Japan for the Guandong Army's action in 1931 and 1932 in overrunning Manchuria.

The Manchurian episode was crucial to the process whereby the Imperial Army in effect came to control the state. Officers of the Guandong Army staged the Mukden (Shenyang) Incident in Liaoning on September 18, 1931, and what followed amounted to a coup inside Mukden by the Guandong Army. After an emergency cabinet meeting in Tokyo, the Japanese government announced that it was committed to a policy of nonaggression within Manchuria, but the Army Ministry declared that it would not consult the cabinet about future policy but would be bound by the Guandong Army's decisions. The cabinet immediately denied the Guandong Army's request for three divisions and ordered the Korean command not to provide reinforcements for that army, whereupon the Korean command did just that on September 21. The government found itself confronted by a fait accompli and outmaneuvered at every turn by a military that played the card of public opinion against any attempt to halt proceedings inside Manchuria. The government fell in December; then, on May 15, 1932, the new premier, Inukai Tsuyoshi, was assassinated by a group of naval officers and army cadets.

This event marked the beginning of the military's domination of the political process within Japan because in its aftermath, the Rikugun would only nominate an army minister if a party leader did not head the government. After the May 15 incident, governments could only be formed with the assent of the military and only if they were prepared to accede to the military's demands. When Hirota Kōki became prime minister in July 1936 in the wake of the army mutiny on February 26, 1936, he found that the army minister had effective veto power over all appointments. In practice, the army could refuse to appoint an army minister or use the threat of resignation in order to ensure compliance with its will. There was to be no basic change in such arrangements until Japan was overwhelmed by national defeat.

In terms of the major military commitments in this 14-year period, the Manchurian Campaign was of minor importance. There was no serious, sustained, or coherent resistance within Manchuria, set up by the Japanese as a puppet state known as Manzhouguo (Manchukuo, and after 1934 Manzhoudiguo [Manchoutikuo], the Manzhou [Manchu] Empire). The Sino-Japanese War, which began in 1937, was another matter. The ease with which Japanese forces overran northern China after July 1937 was testimony to the extent of Japanese success over the previous five years, but the real point was that the Rikugun found itself involved in a protracted war it had not sought and that tied down its resources. As in 1932, the Japanese navy instigated fighting in Shanghai in Jiangsu (Kiangsu) Province, and again, the army had to be deployed there to rescue its sister service: it could only do so by extensive mobilization and escalation of a crisis it would have preferred to have resolved through threat, intimidation, and a series of piecemeal Chinese surrenders, rather than war. The war and the Japanese military effort quickly widened.

There were some defeats along the way, the most notable being in front of Tai'erzhuang (Tai'erh-Chuang) on April 6–7, 1938. The next day, Imperial General Headquarters formally sanctioned an escalation of the war by ordering the capture of Xuzhou (Hsuchow), Jiangsu Province. This move enabled the Japanese military to link what had been two very separate efforts, in northern and central China, and then to develop the offensive that would result in the capture of the Wuhan cities of Hubei (Hupeh) Province in October.

The period after 1938 was notable for two developments, namely, the rice raids that began in Hubei Province in late 1940 and then the opening of the "Three All"—"Kill All, Burn All, Destroy All"—campaigns in Communist-held/infected areas in northern China. In the course of this and subsequent Japanese operations, the population of Communist base areas was reduced from an estimated 44 million to 25 million by a policy of mass deportations, murder, and deliberate starvation. The Communists were neutralized as a threat, with no major guerrilla activity in northern China for the remainder of the war, but as in all matters Japanese in this war, success was an illusion. By 1938, if not before, the Japanese army, with a million troops in China, found itself learning again the truth of the Clausewitzian dictum that it is easy to conquer but hard to occupy. The reason for this was the adoption by the GMD regime in China of a policy of protracted resistance that precluded negotiations. The Japanese countered with a strategic bombing offensive, but this did not bring the GMD leadership to surrender. Perhaps the only point of real interest in these campaigns was the first attempt by any armed force to use airpower to kill a head of state. On August 30, 1941, army bombers attacked a villa in Chongqing (Chungking) in Sichuan (Szechwan), where Jiang Jieshi (Chiang Kai-shek) was known to be taking part in staff talks.

These efforts ran concurrently with defeats at Soviet hands. Japanese commitments in China dictated a cautious policy in Manchuria and Inner Mongolia, but in 1938 and 1939, several small and two major clashes occurred between Japanese and Soviet forces. The first major clash took place between July 11 and August 10, 1938, in the area around Zhanggufeng (Chang-ku-feng) where Manchuria, Korea, and the Maritime Provinces met; the second occurred between May and September 1939 in the area between the Halha River and Nomonhan. In both cases, single Japanese divisions attempted to clear Soviet forces from their territorial holdings, but in the first action, the Japanese were checked, and in the second, they were subjected to attack by an enemy possessing overwhelming numerical superiority in aircraft, tanks, and artillery. Beginning on August 20, the Soviets undertook an offensive that literally shredded the Komatsubara Force and then totally destroyed one infantry regiment on the banks of the Halha. By mid-September, the Japanese had brought three fresh divisions to Nomonhan, but by this stage, both sides had very little interest in continuing the battle, and a local truce was arranged: the Zhanggufeng and Nomonhan disputes were resolved in June 1940.

The defeat at Nomonhan coincided with the 1939 German-Soviet Non-Aggression Pact, and Germany's act, together with the Anglo-French declaration of war on Germany, caused Japan to adopt a cautious policy and wait on events. The German victory in northwest Europe in the spring of 1940 was immediately followed by a change of government.

On July 21, Prince Konoe Fumimaro replaced the more circumspect Yonai Mitsumasa as prime minister. The two services' precondition for allowing Konoe to form a government was his prior acceptance of their demands for a treaty with Germany and Italy, additional credits for the army, a nonaggression treaty with the Soviet Union, and the adoption of a forward strategy in Southeast Asia.

In the China theater, however, the international situation offered the army the means to isolate the Chinese Nationalist regime by intimidating the British and French colonial authorities in Southeast Asia. The German attack on the Soviet Union in June 1941 and the U.S. embargo of various goods, which was drastically extended that July, placed Japan in a situation in which a choice had to be made. At the navy's insistence, Japan's leaders decided to move into Southeast Asia to ensure access to raw materials. Without these assets, Japanese leaders believed their nation could not survive as a great power, even if this move meant war with the United States.

The army's role in such a war would be to provide garrisons in the islands that were to mark the defensive perimeter on which the Americans would be fought to a standstill. The navy's belief was that the fleet and land-based aircraft would be able to meet the Americans more or less on the basis of equality and thereafter fight them to exhaustion. A stalemate would then force the United States to reach some kind of negotiated settlement. Although this has been overlooked, the role of the army in the Pacific war was therefore very limited in one sense, and even in the initial phase, during which Southeast Asia was overrun, the commitment of the Imperial Army remained modest. The campaigns in Burma, Malaya, the Netherlands East Indies, and the Philippines involved only 11 Japanese divisions, the equivalent of a single army, and after these conquests were completed, no single campaign, whether in the southwest, central, or north Pacific, involved a corps equivalent or more in the field until that in the Philippines in 1944 and 1945. Admittedly, the defeats Japan incurred in eastern New Guinea (March 1942 to December 1943) and thereafter along the northern coast of the island (December 1943 to May 1944) and in the central and upper Solomons (February to November 1943) did involve more than a corps equivalent, but these were a series of local defeats largely separated from one another. Probably no single reverse, even that on Guadalcanal (August 1942 to February 1943) at the very beginning of second-phase operations, involved more than two divisions.

The only defeat of corps-sized proportions incurred by the Rikugun prior to the Philippines Campaign was in northeast India at Imphal and Kohima in the 1943–1944 campaigning season, the so-called March on Delhi, launched from Burma, that went disastrously wrong. The origins of this defeat lay in the ease with which the Japanese, with just one division, had frustrated a corps-sized British offensive in the Arakan in 1943, a campaign in which the Japanese outthought and outfought British forces with ease and one that bears comparison with the original campaigns of Japanese conquest in Southeast Asia.

In these 1941–1942 campaigns, the Japanese had no military margin of superiority, but they outfought individual enemies that were defensively dispersed and subjected to successive amphibious assaults by Japanese forces enjoying local air and naval superiority. The campaigns, conducted across a frontage of more than 3,000 miles, were characterized by economy of effort and even an almost aesthetic quality, as successive landings penetrated to the depth of Allied defenses.

Thereafter, the problem for Japan and the Rikugun was threefold. First, once they were no longer taking the initiative in the Pacific, Japanese garrisons were subjected to an overwhelming attack by massively superior Allied assets. No force could sustain itself against such an attack, and no resistance, however protracted and effective in terms of tying down U.S. military assets, could alter a pattern of defeat that brought American forces astride Japanese lines of communication to the south and took the war to the home islands. Second, the Rikugun deployed formations to the Pacific primarily at the expense of garrison forces in Manchuria and China, where these formations were not easily replaced. By 1944, ammunition shortages precluded Rikugun live-fire training. By August 1945, the class of 1945 was basically untrained, and the 1944 class was little better. The army, which had numbered some 24 divisions in the mid-1920s and 51 divisions in December 1941, raised 3 armored and 107 infantry divisions for service overseas; 1 tank and 55 infantry divisions remained in the home islands.

Despite these numbers, the quality of the army was declining because Japan quite simply lacked adequate industrial capacity to meet the requirements of total war. Japanese output in 1944 was equivalent to 4 percent of the American production of mortars, 4.7 percent of tanks, 8 percent of antiaircraft ammunition, perhaps 10 percent of all ordnance, and 6.5 percent of small-arms ammunition. With minimum capability, the divisions in the home islands in 1945 were singularly ill-prepared to resist assault landings.

The Japanese army never, as it happened, experienced defeat in the home islands, but it faced defeat repeatedly on the continental mainland. The year 1945 saw Japanese forces defeated throughout Burma (with the exception of Tenasserim) and, in August, also throughout Manchuria, northern China, and Korea, as well as on Sakhalin and in the Kuriles, when Soviet forces put together a masterly short campaign. The Japanese forces numbered some 750,000 troops, but of these, some 300,000 were Manchurians suited only to garrison duties. The Japanese troops were mustered in 17 infantry divisions, equipped with 1,155 tanks, 5,360 artillery pieces, and 1,800 aircraft, but these were utterly routed by an enemy force consisting of 1 tank and 11 infantry armies. Seeking to consolidate what they held and to allow removal of formations to more important theaters, the Japanese had already begun major withdrawals within China, ending the period of Japanese successes that had begun in the spring of 1944 when Japan undertook a series of offensives throughout southern China. The Japanese conduct of these operations resembled their previous efforts in terms of brutality.

In July 1945, the Japanese army had 26 infantry divisions in China and another 7 in Korea, but even so, its position was hopeless. The extent of failure can be gauged by the fact that Japan managed to conjure into existence an alliance that included the world's most populous country; the greatest empire; the greatest industrial, naval, and air power; and the greatest military power. However unintentional, this was a formidable achievement, but it went in tandem with fundamental failure by the army leadership to comprehend the nature of the war in which it was involved. Drawing on its own highly selective interpretation of Japanese history and hobbled by the fact that, never having been defeated, it could not understand defeat, the army was dominated by an ethos that stressed a castelike reverence for rank and was strictly hierarchical. A very formal organization, it had no real capacity for flexibility and initiative at the lower levels. Its broad distaste for political and economic liberalism coexisted with its belief in what it deemed traditional

Japanese martial values—specifically, its willingness to die in order to fight. The war was to prove, however, that sacrifice could not confound superior enemy matériel.

H. P. Willmott

See also

Burma Theater; Central Pacific Campaign; China, Role in War; China–Burma–India (CBI) Theater; Collaboration; Resistance; Southeast Pacific Theater; Southwest Pacific Theater; Tōjō Hideki

References

Cook, Haruko Taya, and Theodore F. Cook. *Japan at War: An Oral History.* New York: New Press, 1992.

Coox, Alvin. *Kogun: The Japanese Army in the Pacific War.* Quantico, VA: Marine Corps Association, 1959.

Crowley, James. *Japan's Quest for Autonomy: National Security and Foreign Policy, 1930–1938.* Princeton, NJ: Princeton University Press, 1966.

Dower, John. *Japan in Peace and War.* New York: New Press, 1993.

Drea, Edward J. *In the Service of the Emperor: Essays on the Imperial Japanese Army.* Lincoln, NE: University of Nebraska Press, 1998.

Drea, Edward J. *Japan's Imperial Army: Its Rise and Fall, 1853–1945.* Lawrence, KS: University Press of Kansas, 2009.

Duus, Peter, Ramon H. Myers, and Mark R. Peattie, eds. *The Japanese Wartime Empire, 1931–1945.* Princeton, NJ: Princeton University Press, 1931–1945.

Harries, Meirion, and Susie Harries. *Soldiers of the Sun: The Rise and Fall of the Imperial Japanese Army.* New York: Random House, 1991.

Kotani, Ken. *Japanese Intelligence in World War II.* Oxford: Osprey, 2009.

Maiolo, Joseph. *Cry Havoc: How the Arms Race Drove the World to War, 1931–1941.* London: John Murray, 2010.

Myers, Ramon H., and Mark R. Peattie, eds. *The Japanese Colonial Empire, 1895–1945.* Princeton, NJ: Princeton University Press, 1984.

Japan, Navy

By the 1920s, the Nippon Teikoku Kaigun (Imperial Japanese Navy, or IJN), which dated only from the late 1860s, ranked as the third-largest navy in the world. By then, it had fought three wars, and at the Battle of Tsushima in May 1905, it won one of the most comprehensive and annihilating victories ever recorded in naval warfare. The IJN was to fight two more wars, one in the western Pacific, directed against China, and the other throughout the Pacific, eastern and Southeast Asia, and the Indian Ocean. The latter resulted in utter and total national defeat and the destruction of the Kaigun as a service.

From 1907 onward, IJN leaders identified the United States as the enemy against which preparations had to be made. Yet the Kaigun faced a basic and insoluble problem, namely, Japan's acceptance of the limitation of its navy to three-fifths those of the United States and Great Britain, as agreed at the 1921–1922 Washington Naval Conference. This stance resulted from the conviction of Minister of the Navy Admiral Kato Tomosaburo that the only thing worse for Japan than an unrestricted naval construction race with the United States would be war against that country. Kato believed an unrestricted naval race could only bring the remorseless and irreversible erosion of Japan's position relative to the United States, and Japan therefore had to seek security through peaceful cooperation and diplomatic arrangements rather than through international rivalry and conquest. Kato and others viewed the navy as a deterrent and, in the event of war, a defense; however, they also believed Japan's best interests would be served not by confrontation and conflict with the United States but by arrangements that limited American naval construction relative to Japan and so provided the basis of future American recognition and acceptance of Japan's regional position. The problem was that events unfolded in a manner that forced the IJN into planning for a war that, by its own calculations, it was certain to lose.

The basis of this position was twofold. First, the Kaigun found itself obliged to fight not one but two wars. It would have to confront an American enemy that would seek battle and undertake major amphibious undertakings across the western Pacific to bring the war to Japanese home waters. It would also be obliged to fight a maritime war to defend Japanese shipping and seaborne trade. Losing either would result in Japan's full-scale

The Japanese battleship *Yamato*—shown here in trials in 1941—and its sister ship *Musashi* were the largest battleships ever built. In a last-ditch Japanese effort to stop the American invasion of the island of Okinawa, on April 6, 1945, the Japanese navy dispatched the *Yamato*, plus one cruiser and eight destroyers, on a one-way mission to protect Okinawa, with instructions to fight on until destroyed. Allied codebreakers immediately deciphered these orders. The following day, U.S. bombers and torpedo bombers attacked the *Yamato*. Hit by at least 11 torpedoes and 6 bombs, the *Yamato* exploded and sank, losing 2,055 of its 2,332-man crew. The four surviving Japanese destroyers returned to Japan. (Naval Historical Center)

defeat, no matter whether its navy lost a naval war that left the merchant fleet intact and undiminished or whether Japan was defeated in a maritime war that left its fleet's naval forces unreduced. In the event, Japan and the Kaigun suffered a double defeat, both naval and mercantile.

In a very obvious sense, the maritime defeat was one that could have been predicted. Four Shimushu- or Type A-class escort warships were ordered under the 1937 naval estimates, but none was begun before November 1938, to be completed between June 1940 and March 1941. In December 1941, these four ships were the only purpose-built escorts in service with the IJN, and they all lacked underwater detection gear (sonar).

Quite simply, Japanese industry did not have the capacity to build and service both warships and merchantmen, nor to build both fleet units and escorts (see Table 1). Japan's limited industrial capacity forced it to choose between warships and merchantmen, between building and refitting. Moreover, the Kaigun had no real understanding of trade defense and the principles of convoy. Not until November 1943 did the navy institute general convoy, and lacking sufficient escorts and integrated air defense, this practice merely concentrated targets rather than protecting shipping.

Herein, too, lay the basis of Japan's naval defeat in the Pacific. In order to fight and defeat the American attempt to carry the war across the Pacific, the Kaigun developed the *zengen sakusen* (all-out battle strategy), a concept that envisaged the conduct of the decisive battle in five phases. Submarines gathered off the Hawaiian Islands would provide timely reports of U.S. fleet movements, and with top surface speeds of 24 knots, they were to inflict a series of nighttime attacks on U.S. formations. It was anticipated that they would suffer accumulated losses of one-tenth of strength in this phase and the same in the next, when Japanese shore-based aircraft, especially built for superior range and strike capability, would engage American formations. The enemy would then be subjected to night attack by massed destroyer formations, Japanese battle cruisers and cruisers being used to blast aside escorts: the Japanese anticipated massed scissors attacks using as many as 120 Long Lance torpedoes in a single effort. Thereafter, with U.S. formations losing their cohesion and organization, Japanese carriers would join the battle, employed in separate divisions rather than concentrated, in order to neutralize their opposite numbers. Finally, Japanese battleships would engage the American battle line, in what Japanese planners expected to be the decisive battle. In the 1930s, when these ideas were formulated, the Japanese expected the main battle would take place around the Marianas.

The Kaigun organized its formations and building and refitting programs accordingly. Destroyers featured torpedo armaments, and battleships and cruisers emphasized armament, speed, and armor rather than range. The Yamato-class battleships, at their full displacement of 71,659 tons, carried a main armament of 9–18.1 inch guns, an armored belt of 16 inches, and turrets with a maximum of 25.6 inches of armor; they had a top speed of 27.7 knots and a range of 8,600 nautical miles at 19 knots or 4,100 nautical miles at 27 knots. These ships were deliberately conceived as bigger and more formidably armed and protected than any American battleship able to use the Panama Canal. The Japanese quest for qualitative superiority extended through the other classes of warships. As part of this process, the Kaigun developed the famous Long Lance torpedo; land-based and carrier-based aircraft such as the A6M Zero-sen and long-range Betty bomber; and long-range submarines, one type equipped with seaplanes in order to extend scouting range:

Table 1 Wartime Commissioning/Completion of Major Units by the Japanese and U.S. Navies

	CV	CVL	CVE	BB	CB	CA	CL	DD	Esc/DE	CD/PF	SS
December 1941											
Imperial Japanese Navy	—	—	—	—	—	—	—	—	—	—	—
U.S. Navy	—	—	—	—	—	—	1	2	—	—	2
1942											
Imperial Japanese Navy	2	2	2	2	—	—	1	10	—	—	20
U.S. Navy	1	—	11	4	—	—	8	84	—	—	34
1943											
Imperial Japanese Navy	—	1	2	—	—	—	3	12	18	—	36
U.S. Navy	6	9	24	2	—	4	7	126	234	65	56
1944											
Imperial Japanese Navy	5	1	—	—	—	—	3	7	20	72	35
U.S. Navy	7	—	33	2	2	1	11	78	181	8	80
January–September 1945											
Imperial Japanese Navy	—	—	—	—	—	—	—	3	20	39	20
U.S. Navy	4	—	9	—	—	8	6	61	5	—	31
Wartime totals											
Imperial Japanese Navy	7	4	4	2	—	—	7	32	58	111	116
U.S. Navy	18	9	77	8	2	13	33	349	420	73	203

Note: The drawing of direct comparisons between different types of warships, specifically escorts, is somewhat difficult. Counted under the heading "Esc" in the Japanese listings are named escorts and patrol boats; under the heading "CD" are the *kaiboken*, or coastal defense ships. These types were not the direct equivalents of U.S. destroyer escorts and frigates, respectively, but diversity precludes these types of American and Japanese ships being compared with anything but one another. U.S. figures exclude Lend-Lease vessels.

Dashes = zero	CL = light cruiser
CV = fleet carrier	DD = destroyer
CVL = light carrier	Esc = escort
CVE = escort carrier	DE = destroyer escort
BB = batttleship	CD = coastal defense ship
CB = battle cruiser	PF = frigate
CA = heavy cruiser	SS = submarine

individually and collectively, these were qualitatively unequaled in 1941 and 1942, and in terms of night-fighting capability in 1941, the Kaigun undoubtedly had no peer.

Despite these apparent advantages, the Japanese naval battle plan represented an inversion of the reality of what was required. By December 1941, the Kaigun had basically secured parity in the Pacific with the United States, with warships, carrier air groups and aircraft, and a pool of trained manpower that were qualitatively probably the best in the world. The problem, however, was that Japan and its armed services lacked the means to fortify the islands of the central and western Pacific. The perimeter along which the Japanese planned to fight the Americans to a standstill largely consisted of gaps. Japan had neither the shipping nor the base organizations needed to transform the island groups into the air bases that were essential to the fleet. The latter, moreover, could not be guaranteed to be permanently ready to meet any American move, which would, by definition, be made with a strength and at a time that all but ensured American victory. Individual Japanese bases or even several bases within a group or neighboring groups could be overwhelmed by an enemy free to take the initiative and choose when to mount offensive operations, a second flaw within the *zengen sakusen* concept. By 1942, the Kaigun was only prepared to fight the battle it intended to win, and it could only win the battle it intended to fight. Instead, of course, the battle it was called on to fight was not the one for which it had prepared.

The IJN, moreover, faced not one enemy but two. It opened hostilities with a total strength of 10 battleships; 6 fleet and 3 light fleet carriers and 1 escort carrier; 18 heavy and 20 light cruisers; 111 destroyers; and 71 submarines. A token of its future problems lay in the fact that only 1 fleet unit, a destroyer, was not in service on December 6, 1941. But even when it went to war, the Kaigun faced a prewar U.S. Navy that, between May 1942 and November 1943, fought it to a standstill. After that date, the Kaigun faced a wartime U.S. Navy, virtually every ship of which had entered service after Pearl Harbor. The Japanese shipbuilding effort from 1942 to 1944, though substantial, was simply overwhelmed by a truly remarkable American industrial achievement: 18 U.S. fleet carriers to 7 for Japan, 9 light fleet carriers to 4, 77 escort carriers to 4, 8 battleships to 2, 13 heavy and 33 light cruisers to 4 light cruisers, 349 destroyers and 420 destroyer escorts to 90, and 203 submarines to 116. U.S. superiority was not simply numerical: radio, radar, and diversity of weaponry were all areas in which the Kaigun could not match its U.S. enemy but was systematically outclassed as the war entered its second and third years.

During 1943 and 1944, the Americans acquired such overwhelming numerical superiority that the Kaigun was denied not merely any chance of victory but even any means of effective response. Between December 26, 1943, and October 24, 1944, Japanese warships and aircraft destroyed no American fleet units, if U.S. submarines are excluded. The simple truth was not just that the Japanese were prepared to die in order to fight but also that the only way the Japanese could fight was to die.

Events in 1945 conspired to demonstrate the singular ineffectiveness of such a course of action, as Japanese losses between July 1944 and August 1945 reflected both this dilemma and the wider national defeat. In the war overall, the Kaigun lost 1,028 warships of 2,310,704 tons, of which 631 warships of 1,348,492 tons were destroyed in the last 13 months of the war (see Table 2). The wartime losses incurred by the merchant fleet—not the service auxiliaries—told the same story, totaling 1,181.5 merchantmen (there

Table 2 The State of Japanese Shipping, 1941–1945 (in tons)

Year	Tonnage Built	Captured and Salvaged	Total Acquisitions	Tonnage Lost	Net Loss in Year	Shipping Available on		Tonnage Afloat	Tonnage Laid up	Percent Laid up
						March 31, 1942	6,150,000	5,375,000	775,000	12.61
1942	266,000	566,000	832,000	1,065,000	−233,000	December 31, 1942	5,942,000			
						March 31, 1943	5,733,000	4,833,000	900,000	15.70
1943	769,000	109,000	878,000	1,821,000	−943,000	December 31, 1943	4,999,000			
						March 31, 1944	4,352,000	3,527,000	825,000	18.96
1944	1,699,000	36,000	1,735,000	3,892,000	−2,157,000	December 31, 1944	2,842,000			
						March 31, 1945	2,465,000	1,659,000	806,000	32.70
1945	559,000	6,000	565,000	1,782,000	−1,217,000	August 15, 1945	1,625,000	948,000	677,000	41.66

Note: The figures presented in this table are based on my own calculations. These, however, are not complete and differ in virtually every detail from figures generally given in Western histories, the sources of which are normally American and date from the period immediately after the end of the war. The figures here have been taken from such a source. I would advise that a certain caution be exercised with respect to the detail of these figures and calculations and would note that Japanese merchant-shipping losses in this table include ships of unknown ownership and one Thai ship but not foreign ships under charter. These caveats noted, I vouch for the general accuracy of the figures and the conclusions that have been drawn from them.

were navy, army, and civilian ships and, occasionally, shared ships, which are here calculated as one half a ship) of 3,389,202 tons, of which 811 vessels of 2,077,249 tons were lost in this same final period, after the Battle of the Philippine Sea. Losses of this order were both the cause and the result of defeat, in practice reducing the Kaigun to no more than an ever less effective coastal defense force.

By August 1945, Japan had been pushed to the edge of final, total, and comprehensive defeat, losing all semblance of strategic mobility. Its industry was in end-run production; its people would have died by the millions from disease and starvation had the war lasted into the spring of 1946. To all intents and purposes, the Kaigun had by then ceased to exist, as American carrier air groups flew combat air patrol over Japanese airfields. A remarkable American achievement, unparalleled in 400 years, had reduced the Kaigun to impotent irrelevance. States, especially great powers, are rarely defeated by naval power, but in this case, the Kaigun had been entirely powerless to prevent such an outcome.

H. P. Willmott

See also
Central Pacific Campaign; Midway, Battle of; Southeast Pacific Theater; Southwest Pacific Theater; Yamamoto Isoroku

References

Agawa, Hiroyuki. *The Reluctant Admiral: Yamamoto and the Imperial Navy*. Translated by John Bester. Tokyo: Kodansha, 1979.

Asada, Sadao. *From Mahan to Pearl Harbor: American Strategic Theory and the Rise of the Imperial Japanese Navy*. Annapolis, MD: Naval Institute Press, 2006.

Dull, Paul S. *A Battle History of the Imperial Japanese Navy, 1941–45*. Annapolis, MD: Naval Institute Press, 1978.

Evans, David C., and Mark R. Peattie. *Kaigun: Strategy, Tactics & Technology in the Imperial Japanese Navy, 1887–1941*. Annapolis, MD: Naval Institute Press, 1997.

Ford, Douglas. *The Elusive Enemy: U.S. Naval Intelligence and the Imperial Japanese Fleet*. Annapolis, MD: Naval Institute Press, 2011.

Hastings, Max. *Retribution: The Battle for Japan, 1944–45*. New York: Alfred A. Knopf, 2008.

Howarth. Stephen. *The Fighting Ships of the Rising Sun: The Drama of the Imperial Japanese Navy, 1895–1945*. New York: Atheneum, 1983.

Ike Nobutaka, ed. and trans. *Japan's Decision for War: Records of the 1941 Policy Conferences*. Stanford, CA: Stanford University Press, 1967.

Kotani, Ken. *Japanese Intelligence in World War II*. Oxford: Osprey, 2009.

Nomura Minoru. *Tenno, Fushiminomiya to Nihonkaigun* (Emperor Hirohito, Prince Fushimi and the Imperial Japanese Navy). Tokyo: Bungeishunju, 1988.

O'Hara, Vincent P., W. David Dickson, and Richard Worth, eds. *On Seas Contested: The Seven Great Navies of the Second World War*. Annapolis, MD: Naval Institute Press, 2010.

Peattie, Mark R. *Sunburst: The Rise of Japanese Naval Air Power, 1909–1941.* Annapolis, MD: Naval Institute Press, 2001.

Pelz, Stephen E. *Race to Pearl Harbor: The Failure of the Second London Naval Conference and the Onset of World War II.* Cambridge, MA: Harvard University Press, 1974.

Prados, John. *Combined Fleet Decoded: The Secret History of American Intelligence and the Japanese Navy in World War II.* Annapolis, MD: Naval Institute Press, 2001.

Latin America and the War

After World War II began in Europe, representatives of the United States and Latin American nations convened in Panama in September 1939 and issued a "general declaration of neutrality," indicating that it was the intention of all the American republics to remain neutral in the European conflict. In the event that the United States and Latin America were drawn into the, U.S. strategic planners did not envision an important military role for the armed forces of Latin America, beyond defense of their own countries. However, the United States did want the Latin American nations to furnish bases for U.S. operations, to increase the flow of strategic materials, and to take action to curb Axis subversive and intelligence activities.

The United States engaged in negotiations with the Latin American nations concerning closer military cooperation and the acquisition of bases. Washington signed a series of bilateral "staff agreements" promising military aid in return for the Latin American nations' promise to call for assistance if attacked, to combat subversive activities, to exchange intelligence, and to permit the transit of U.S. forces going to the aid of another Latin American country. In response to the request for bases, Latin American leaders expressed concerns about jurisdiction and access. The United States responded by offering to provide financing and technical assistance for bases, with the host country retaining jurisdiction and administration. Moreover, the bases would be open not only to the United States but also to all other Latin American nations. The United States signed staff agreements with every Latin American nation except Argentina and base agreements with 16 countries.

The U.S. Lend-Lease Act, which went into effect in March 1941, authorized the president to lend, lease, or sell military items to any country whose defense was deemed vital to the defense of the United States. In April, Roosevelt certified that Latin America came under the provisions of the act, and in October 1941, the U.S. Congress approved funding for Latin America. Washington eventually provided $475 million in Lend-Lease aid to Latin America, with some $348 million of that amount going to Brazil.

When the United States officially entered the war in December 1941, all of the Latin American nations made some positive response. Nine countries declared war on the Axis powers in December 1941: Costa Rica, Cuba, the Dominican Republic, El Salvador, Guatemala, Haiti, Honduras, Nicaragua, and Panama. Colombia and Mexico broke diplomatic relations with the Axis powers. Brazil, Ecuador, Paraguay, and Peru declared their solidarity with the United States, and the remaining countries granted the United States nonbelligerent status, giving it greater freedom of action within their national territories.

A meeting of the American republics called by the United States and Chile convened in Rio de Janeiro on January 15, 1942. Washington was not seeking a joint declaration of war because of the military demands that would result. Instead, it supported a joint declaration calling for a break in relations with the Axis powers. The conference approved a resolution that "recommended" a break in diplomatic relations as well as in commercial and financial connections. Those countries that had not already broken diplomatic relations quickly did so, except for Argentina and Chile. The conference also established the Inter-American Defense Board, made up of military and naval representatives from each country to coordinate hemispheric defense.

The fact that the consultative conference was held in Rio de Janeiro indicated the special role that the United States assigned to Brazil. U.S. planners believed that the most likely scenario for an Axis attack on the Western Hemisphere was a German assault launched from Africa against Brazil's northeastern "bulge." The United States wanted to send U.S. troops to defend the bulge, but the Brazilians were unwilling to accept U.S. ground forces and wanted U.S. arms instead. Both sides eventually accepted a trade-off between U.S. troops and arms for the Brazilians. Brazil received a large increase in military aid in return for permitting unrestricted U.S. air operations in the Brazilian northeast and even the stationing of U.S. troops. In August 1942, Brazil declared war on the Axis after German submarines attacked Brazilian shipping. Brazil also became the only Latin American country to provide a major military force for combat. (Mexico provided one fighter squadron.) With the United States furnishing training, supplies, and transport, the Brazilian Expeditionary Corps of approximately 25,000 men participated in the 1944–1945 Italian Campaign.

The United States recognized early on that it had to address the economic as well as the military consequences of war. Even in the summer of 1940, Washington planners were already thinking in terms of a "hemispheric economic policy" that called for much closer economic relations with Latin America. Strategic metals were of particular interest to the United States; in November 1940, the U.S. government contracted to purchase virtually the entire Latin American production of copper and tin. The United States also developed a blacklist of firms and individuals operating in Latin America who were considered pro-Axis or anti–United States. U.S. firms were prohibited from dealing with anyone or any firm on this "Proclaimed List of Certain Blocked Nationals," and Franklin D. Roosevelt's administration attempted, with considerable success, to persuade Latin American governments to enforce this blacklist. The United States also dramatically increased its lending to Latin America, mainly to finance the purchase of U.S. products.

The U.S. entry into the war led to even greater efforts at economic cooperation between the United States and Latin America. As mentioned, the Rio Conference in January 1942 approved a resolution recommending a break in commercial and financial relations with the Axis powers. The conference also called for a complete economic mobilization of the American republics to provide an adequate supply of both military and civilian goods. U.S. purchases of Latin American commodities continued to be at the center of U.S.–Latin American economic relations. Washington stepped up its purchases of strategic metals, reaching agreements with 12 Latin American nations to buy metals. Cut off from its principal source of natural rubber in Asia, the United States also entered into contracts with 16 Latin American nations to promote the production of rubber. In addition, actions were taken to improve transportation within the hemisphere. An inter-American technical commission was established to improve maritime transportation, and the United States tried to improve land transportation by reviving construction on the Inter-American Highway, concentrating on the Central American section of the road. Axis-connected firms operating airlines in Bolivia, Brazil, Colombia, Ecuador, and Peru were forced out of business and were replaced by U.S. firms or locally controlled operations. The United States even provided aircraft for local airlines in Brazil and Chile. The net effect of all of these actions was to create an even greater economic interdependence between the United States and Latin America. From 1941 to 1945, the United States purchased more than 50 percent of Latin America's exports and provided more than 60 percent of its imports.

Wartime themes and postwar plans came together at the Chapultepec Conference in Mexico City in February and March 1945. The Latin American nations were concerned that the United States might relegate the inter-American system to a lesser role once it had served its wartime purposes. They also hoped that the United States would facilitate the transition to a peacetime economy and would aid in Latin America's postwar development. When the United States finally agreed to the Chapultepec Conference, it sent an impressive delegation, including the new secretary of state, Edward Stettinius, who was returning from the Yalta Conference. The Latin American nations wanted to put the inter-American system on a more formal basis, but the United States delayed action until the next regular inter-American conference. Latin American demands for a strengthening of the inter-American security system led to the Act of Chapultepec, which classified an attack against any American state as an attack against all American states and required consultation on the measures to be taken in response, including the use of force. Although the act applied only for the duration of the war, it was to be incorporated in a permanent treaty once the war concluded. On the question of economic relations, the United States agreed to aid in the transition to a peacetime economy by gradually reducing its purchases of strategic raw materials; it also indicated, in general terms, its support for economic development in Latin America but did not commit itself to any specific programs of assistance.

The warm glow of the Chapultepec Conference soon faded. The meeting scheduled for Rio in October 1945 to place the Act of Chapultepec into treaty form was postponed, and there were repeated delays in holding the technical conference to deal with inter-American economic problems. The war had put the Latin American nations in the role of principal supporters of the inter-American system at the very time that the United States was shifting its emphasis to global organization. Latin America wanted to enlist U.S. support in dealing with its growing social and economic problems; the United States, however, was preparing for another struggle: the Cold War with the Soviet Union.

Don M. Coerver

See also
Italy Campaign; Roosevelt, Franklin D.; Southeast Pacific Theater

References

Bethell, Leslie, and Ian Roxborough, eds. *Latin America between the Second World War and the Cold War: Crisis and Containment, 1944–1948*. Cambridge: Cambridge University Press, 1992.

Friedman, Max Paul. *Nazis and Good Neighbors: The United States Campaign against the Germans of Latin America in World War II*. New York: Cambridge University Press, 2003.

Hilton, Stanley E. *Hitler's Secret War in South America, 1939–1945: German Military Espionage and Allied Counterespionage in Brazil*. Baton Rouge, LA: Louisiana State University Press, 1981.

Humphreys, R. A. *Latin America and the Second World War*. Vol. 1, *1939–1942*. London: Athlone Press, 1981.

Humphreys, R. A. *Latin America and the Second World War*. Vol. 2, *1942–1945*. London: Athlone Press, 1982.

Leonard, Thomas M., and John F. Bratzel, eds. *Latin America during World War II*. Lanham, MD: Rowman and Littlefield, 2006.

McCann, Frank D., Jr. *The Brazilian–American Alliance, 1937–1945*. Princeton, NJ: Princeton University Press, 1973.

Newton, Ronald C. *The "Nazi Menace" in Argentina, 1931–1947*. Stanford, CA: Stanford University Press, 1992.

Paz, María Emilia. *Strategy, Security, and Spies: Mexico and the U.S. as Allies in World War II*. University Park, PA: Pennsylvania State University Press, 1997.

Schoonover, Thomas D. *Hitler's Man in Havana: Heinz Luning and Nazi Espionage in Latin America*. Lexington, KY: University Press of Kentucky, 2008.

MacArthur, Douglas (1880–1964)

Douglas MacArthur was a U.S. Army general and, during World War II, supreme commander of Allied forces in the southwest Pacific. Born on January 26, 1880, in Little Rock, Arkansas, the son of General Arthur MacArthur, Douglas MacArthur graduated from the U.S. Military Academy in 1903 with highest honors and as first captain. Following service in the Philippines and Japan, he became an aide to President Theodore Roosevelt (1906–1907). He took part in the 1914 occupation of Veracruz, Mexico, where he was nominated for the Medal of Honor, and served on the General Staff (1913–1917).

After the United States entered World War I in April 1917, MacArthur went to France as chief of staff of the 42nd Infantry Division. Promoted to temporary brigadier general, he fought with the division in the Second Battle of the Marne. MacArthur then led the 8th Infantry Brigade in the Saint-Mihiel and Meuse-Argonne Offensives. He commanded the 42nd Division at the end of the war.

Following occupation duty in Germany, MacArthur returned to the United States as superintendent of West Point (1919–1922), where he carried out much-needed reforms. He again served in the Philippines and claimed that his extensive service there gave him special insight into the "Oriental mind." MacArthur was then chief of staff of the army (1930–1935), his reputation suffering in the 1932 Bonus Army Incident when he employed force to oust a protest by World War I veterans in Washington, DC. In 1935, MacArthur returned to the Philippines as adviser to the Philippine government in establishing an army capable of resisting a Japanese invasion. He retired from the U.S. Army in 1937 and became field marshal of Philippine forces.

Recalled to active service with the U.S. Army in July 1941, MacArthur received command of all U.S. forces in the Far East. Believing his forces could defend the islands, he scrapped the original, sound plan to withdraw into the Bataan Peninsula. His refusal to allow Major General Lewis Brereton to launch an immediate retaliatory strike against the Japanese on Formosa (Taiwan) following the attack on Pearl Harbor meant that most of his air force was caught and destroyed on the ground.

Although the Japanese force invading the Philippines was composed of only 57,000 men, half that of MacArthur's own numbers, many of the general's men were poorly trained (some were recent inductees), and they were thinly spread. The Japanese had little difficulty taking Manila and much of the island of Luzon. MacArthur then ordered his forces

General Douglas MacArthur commanded U.S. forces in the Philippine Islands when the United States entered World War II in December 1941. By spring 1942, Japanese military units had overrun most of the Philippines. MacArthur escaped by submarine to Australia. He subsequently commanded Allied forces in the southwest Pacific, and then headed the Allied occupation of Japan. (Library of Congress)

to follow the original plan for withdrawing into the Bataan Peninsula. Unfortunately, the bases there were not ready, and the retreating troops had to abandon precious stocks of supplies and ammunition in the process. Over the next months, MacArthur spent most of his time on Corregidor. Rather than see him become a prisoner of the Japanese, President Franklin D. Roosevelt ordered MacArthur to Australia on February 22, 1942, where he became supreme commander of Allied forces in the southwest Pacific. MacArthur was also awarded the Medal of Honor, an honor that many defenders of Bataan and Corregidor believed was undeserved. Officials in Washington were also miffed by MacArthur's acceptance of a $500,000 payment from his friend Manuel Quezon, the Philippine president.

From Australia, MacArthur initially developed a deliberate strategy to return to the Philippines. The slow pace of the Allied advance led Washington to insist on a leapfrogging approach that would bypass strongly held Japanese islands and positions, such as Rabaul on New Britain Island and Truk. In the spring of 1944, MacArthur's troops invaded New Guinea and isolated Rabaul. By September, they had taken Morotai and the rest of New Guinea.

In a meeting with Roosevelt in Hawaii in July 1944, Admiral Chester Nimitz, who commanded forces in the Central Pacific, proposed moving against Formosa, whereas MacArthur sought to retake the Philippines. The goal of both approaches was to deny Japanese forces access to supplies in the south. The upshot was that Roosevelt agreed MacArthur would be allowed to retake the Philippines, and Nimitz shifted his resources against Okinawa.

MacArthur commanded ground forces in the liberation of the Philippines. In October, U.S. troops landed on Leyte. They then secured Luzon between January and March 1945, followed by the southern Philippines. An invasion of Japan proved unnecessary, and MacArthur, one of those promoted to the new rank of General of the Army, presided over the formal Japanese surrender ceremony on the battleship *Missouri* in Tokyo Bay on September 2 in his capacity as supreme commander of the Allied powers.

President Harry S. Truman then named MacArthur commander of Allied occupation forces in Japan. In this position, the general in effect governed Japan as a benevolent despot, presiding over the institution of a new democratic constitution and domestic reforms. On the beginning of the Korean War in June 1950, Truman appointed MacArthur commander of the UN forces sent there to prevent a North Korean victory. During the perilous UN withdrawal into the Pusan Perimeter, MacArthur husbanded his resources, and in September 1950, he launched a brilliant (but also lucky) invasion at Inchon that cut North Korean supply lines to the south. He then oversaw the United Nations Command (UNC) invasion of North Korea, but his faulty troop dispositions and his disdain for possible Chinese intervention nearly led to disaster. His increasingly public disagreement with Truman over the course of the war—which the administration in Washington sought to limit and MacArthur wanted to widen by attacking China proper—led to his removal from command in April 1951.

MacArthur returned to the United States a national hero. He then retired from the military, accepting the position of chairman of the board of Remington Rand Corporation. His attempt to run for the presidency as a Republican in 1952 quickly collapsed, and the nomination and office went to another general, whom MacArthur held in great disdain—Dwight D. Eisenhower. MacArthur died in Washington, DC, on April 5, 1964.

T. Jason Soderstrum and Spencer C. Tucker

See also

Australia, Role in War; Central Pacific Campaign; Eisenhower, Dwight D.; Japan, Air Force; Japan, Army; Japan, Navy; Nimitz, Chester William; Roosevelt, Franklin D.; Southeast Pacific Theater; Southwest Pacific Theater; Truman, Harry S.; United States, Army; United States, Army Air Force; United States, Marine Corps; United States, Navy

References

Brower, Charles F. *The Joint Chiefs of Staff and Strategy in the Pacific War, 1943–1945*. New York: Palgrave Macmillan, 2012.

Buhite, Russell D. *Douglas MacArthur: Statecraft and Stagecraft in America's Far Eastern Policy*. Lanham, MD: Rowman and Littlefield, 2008.

Frank, Richard B. *MacArthur*. New York: Palgrave Macmillan, 2009.

Harvey, Robert. *American Shogun: A Tale of Two Cultures*. New York: Overlook, 2006.

James, D. Clayton. *The Years of MacArthur*. 3 vols. Boston, MA: Houghton Mifflin, 1970–1985.

Manchester, William Raymond. *American Caesar: Douglas MacArthur, 1880–1964*. Boston, MA: Little, Brown, 1978.

Perret, Geoffrey. *Old Soldiers Never Die: The Life of Douglas MacArthur*. Holbrook, MA: Adams Media, 1996.

Schaller, Michael. *Douglas MacArthur: The Far Eastern General.* New York: Oxford University Press, 1989.

Weintraub, Stanley. *15 Stars: Eisenhower, MacArthur, Marshall: Three Generals Who Saved the American Century.* New York: Basic Books, 2007.

Yockelson, Michael. *MacArthur: America's General.* Nashville, TN: Thomas Nelson, 2011.

Marshall, George Catlett (1880–1959)

George Catlett Marshall was a U.S. Army general, chief of staff of the army, secretary of state, and secretary of defense. If not America's greatest soldier, General of the Army George Marshall was one of the nation's most capable military leaders and certainly one of the most influential figures of the 20th century. Born in Uniontown, Pennsylvania, on December 31, 1880, Marshall graduated from the Virginia Military Institute in 1901. Commissioned in the infantry in 1902, he then held a variety of assignments, including in the Philippines. He attended the Infantry and Cavalry School, Fort Leavenworth, in 1907 and was an instructor at the Staff College between 1907 and 1908.

After the United States entered World War I, Marshall went to France with the American Expeditionary Forces as training officer to the 1st Division in June 1917. Promoted to lieutenant colonel in 1918, he became chief of operations of the U.S. First Army, winning

The highly efficient General George C. Marshall was chief of staff of the U.S. Army during World War II. Known as the "Organizer of Victory" and promoted to general of the armies in 1944, Marshall oversaw the creation and successful employment of the largest military force in U.S. history. His greatest regret was that he did not command in person the Allied force that invaded Western Europe in June 1944. (Library of Congress)

admiration for his logistical skills in directing the repositioning of hundreds of thousands of men quickly across the battlefront for the Meuse-Argonne Offensive. After working on occupation plans for Germany, Marshall became aide to General John J. Pershing, who was named chief of staff of the army in 1921.

Beginning in 1924, Marshall spent three years in Tianjin (Tientsin), China, with the 15th Infantry Regiment, then five years as assistant commandant in charge of instruction at the Infantry School, Fort Benning, Georgia, where he helped to train numerous future U.S. generals. He won promotion to colonel in 1932, holding assorted command posts in the continental United States. He was promoted to brigadier general in 1936.

In 1938, Marshall became head of the War Plans Division in Washington, then deputy chief of staff with promotion to major general that July. President Franklin D. Roosevelt advanced Marshall over many more senior officers to appoint him chief of staff of the army as a temporary general on September 1, 1939, the day that German armies invaded Poland. As war began in Europe, Marshall worked to revitalize the American defense establishment. Assisted by pro-Allied civilians such as Secretary of War Henry L. Stimson, he instituted and lobbied for programs to recruit and train new troops; expedite munitions production; assist Great Britain, China, and the Soviet Union in resisting the Axis powers; and coordinate British and American strategy. After the United States entered the war in December 1941, Marshall presided over an increase in U.S. armed forces from a mere 200,000 to a wartime maximum of 8 million men and women. For this, he became known as the "Organizer of Victory."

Marshall was a strong supporter of opening a second front in Europe, a campaign ultimately deferred until June 1944. Between 1941 and 1945, he attended all the major wartime strategic conferences, including those at Placentia Bay, Washington, Quebec, Cairo, Tehran, Malta, Yalta, and Potsdam. Marshall was the first to be promoted to the newly authorized five-star rank of General of the Army in December 1944. Perhaps his greatest disappointment was that he did not exercise field command, especially command of the European invasion forces. Roosevelt and the other wartime chiefs wanted him to remain in Washington, and Marshall bowed to their wishes. He was a major supporter of the Army Air Forces, and in 1945, he advocated use of the atomic bomb against Japan.

On the urging of President Harry S. Truman, Marshall agreed to serve as special envoy to China (1945–1947). As secretary of state (1947–1949), he advanced the Marshall Plan to rebuild Europe, and he then served as president of the American Red Cross (1949–1950). Truman persuaded him to return to government service as secretary of defense in September 1950. In that capacity, Marshall worked to repair relations with the other agencies of government that had become frayed under his predecessor and to build up the U.S. military to meet the needs of the Korean War and commitments in Europe, while at the same time maintaining an adequate reserve. Marshall opposed General Douglas MacArthur's efforts for a widened war with China and supported Truman in his decisions to fight a "limited war" and to remove MacArthur as commander of UN forces.

Marshall resigned in September 1951, ending 50 years of dedicated government service. Awarded the Nobel Peace Prize in 1953 for the Marshall Plan, he was the first soldier so honored. He died in Washington, DC, on October 16, 1959.

Spencer C. Tucker

See also

Atomic Bomb, Decision to Employ; Bradley, Omar Nelson; Churchill, Sir Winston Leonard Spencer; Italy Campaign; MacArthur, Douglas; North Africa Campaign; Roosevelt, Franklin D.; United States, Army; Western European Theater of Operations

References

Brower, Charles F., ed. *George C. Marshall: Servant of the American Nation*. New York: Palgrave Macmillan, 2011.

Brower, Charles F. *The Joint Chiefs of Staff and Strategy in the Pacific War, 1943–1945*. New York: Palgrave Macmillan, 2012.

Cray, Ed. *General of the Army: George C. Marshall, Soldier and Statesman*. New York: W. W. Norton, 1990.

Marshall, George C. *The Papers of George Catlett Marshall*, edited by Larry I. Bland. 5 vols. to date. Baltimore, MD: Johns Hopkins University Press, 1981–.

Perry, Mark. *Partners in Command: George Marshall and Dwight Eisenhower in War and Peace*. New York: Penguin Press, 2007.

Pogue, Forrest C. *George C. Marshall*. 4 vols. New York: Viking, 1963–1987.

Roberts, Andrew. *Masters and Commanders: How Four Titans Won the War in the West*. New York: Harper, 2009.

Stoler, Mark A. *George C. Marshall: Soldier-Statesman of the American Century*. Boston, MA: Twayne Publishers, 1989.

Stoler, Mark A. *Allies and Adversaries: The Joint Chiefs of Staff, the Grand Alliance, and U.S. Strategy in World War II*. Chapel Hill, NC: University of North Carolina Press, 2000.

Taaffe, Stephen R. *Marshall and His Generals: U.S. Army Commanders in World War II*. Lawrence, KS: University Press of Kansas, 2011.

Weintraub, Stanley. *15 Stars: Eisenhower, MacArthur, Marshall: Three Generals Who Saved the American Century*. New York: Basic Books, 2007.

Midway, Battle of (June 3–6, 1942)

The Battle of Midway was a decisive naval engagement of World War II that turned the tide of the war in the Pacific. Beginning in January 1942, the Japanese attempted to extend their defensive perimeter by seizing bases in Papua and New Guinea and in the Solomon Islands, which would be used to support future operations against New Caledonia, Fiji, and Samoa. By early March, they had taken the entire north coast of Papua and New Guinea and begun preparations for an amphibious invasion of Port Moresby. On May 7–8, these events resulted in the Battle of the Coral Sea when the Japanese invasion force encountered an American carrier force. In the first naval battle in which neither fleet sighted the other, the aircraft carrier *Lexington* was sunk and the carrier *Yorktown* was heavily damaged. However, the Japanese had their light carrier *Shoho* sunk, and the loss of its air cover caused the invasion force to turn back. At the same time, the Americans damaged the carrier *Shokaku*. The Americans were able to repair the *Yorktown* in time for the

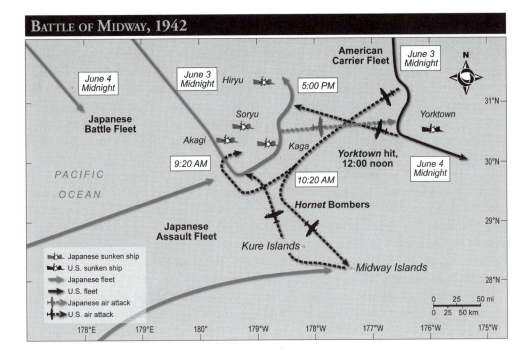

next battle, whereas *Shokaku* could not be readied for that second and decisive fight. The second carrier, *Zuikaku*, also did not participate due to a shortage of aircraft. Thus, on balance, the Battle of the Coral Sea was a strategic U.S. victory.

A second battle soon developed after the Japanese turned their focus on the strategic island of Midway. Despite the setback at Coral Sea, the Japanese continued with their plans to seize Midway Island and bases in the Aleutians. Admiral Yamamoto Isoroku, commander in chief of the Combined Fleet, convinced the Imperial General Staff that the capture of Midway would allow Japan to pursue its Asian policies behind an impregnable eastern shield of defenses in the Central Pacific. The capture of Midway would serve as a dramatic response to the April 1942 U.S. raid on Tokyo. It would also deprive the United States of a forward base for submarines, and it would be a stepping stone to the capture of Hawaii. Most importantly, perhaps, it would draw out the U.S. aircraft carriers, giving the Japanese the opportunity to destroy them.

Admiral Yamamoto sent out the bulk of the Japanese fleet. For the operation, he would use some 200 ships—almost the entire Japanese navy—including 8 carriers, 11 battleships, 22 cruisers, 65 destroyers, 21 submarines, and more than 600 aircraft. His plan called for diversionary attacks on the Aleutian Islands both to distract the Americans from Japanese landings on Midway and to allow the Japanese to crush the U.S. reaction force between their forces to the north and at Midway. The Aleutian operation would also secure the islands of Attu and Kiska, placing forces astride a possible U.S. invasion route to Japan.

Yamamoto correctly assumed that the U.S. Pacific Fleet commander, Admiral Chester W. Nimitz, would have to respond to a landing on Midway. When the Pacific Fleet arrived in the area, Japanese carrier and battleship task forces, waiting unseen to the west of the Midway strike force, would fall on and destroy the unsuspecting Americans. Yamamoto believed that the *Yorktown* had been sunk in the Coral Sea fight and that the *Enterprise* and *Hornet* were not likely to be in the Midway area when the strike force attacked the island. He was not correct. This miscalculation was one of several breakdowns in Japanese intelligence and communication that contributed to the eventual American victory.

For the Aleutians, Yamamoto committed an invasion force of 2,400 men in three escorted transports, a support group of two heavy cruisers and two light carriers, and a covering force of four older battleships. The battle began in the Aleutians with air strikes on June 3, followed by landings three days later. The Aleutian phase of the operation went well for the Japanese. Carrier aircraft inflicted heavy damage on the U.S. base at Dutch Harbor, and the Japanese then made unopposed landings on Kiska and Attu. They kept this toehold on continental U.S. territory until mid-1943.

Despite the Japanese success in the Aleutians, the action there proved to be superfluous to the coming battle at Midway. U.S. intelligence had broken the Japanese naval code, putting the basic outlines of the Midway plan into American hands and thus allowing the Americans to disregard the attacks on the Aleutians in favor of concentrating on Midway. The Pacific Fleet was ready with three fleet aircraft carriers, including the *Yorktown*. She had been hastily repaired at Pearl Harbor to allow operations in only 2 days instead of an estimated 90 and was sent back to sea with an air group formed of planes from other carriers. She sailed just in advance of a picket line of Japanese submarines that Yamamoto hoped would intercept ships departing Pearl Harbor. The U.S. ships were concentrated in an ambush position some 350 miles northeast of Midway, awaiting the westward advance of Yamamoto's armada.

On June 3, American naval reconnaissance planes sighted, at a distance of 600 miles, the Japanese armada of some 185 ships advancing on Midway. The battle began when Boeing B-17 Flying Fortress bombers from Midway Island struck without effect at the Japanese carrier strike force, about 220 miles southwest of the U.S. fleet. That same night, four Consolidated patrol bombers (PBYs) from Midway staged a torpedo attack and damaged an oiler, although she was able to regain her place in the formation.

Early on June 4, Nagumo sent 108 Japanese planes from the strike force to attack and bomb Midway, while the Japanese carriers again escaped damage from U.S. land-based planes. However, as the morning progressed, the Japanese carriers were soon overwhelmed by the logistics of almost simultaneously sending a second wave of bombers to finish off the Midway runways, zigzagging to avoid the bombs of attacking aircraft, and rearming to launch planes to sink the now sighted U.S. naval forces. American fighters and bombers, sent from Midway airfields, and aircraft from three U.S. carriers attacked the Japanese fleet. But three successive waves of U.S. torpedo bombers were virtually wiped out during their attacks on the carriers from 9:30 to 10:24 a.m.: Japanese fighters and antiaircraft guns shot down 47 of 51 planes. The Japanese now believed that they had won the battle.

The U.S. aircraft carrier *Yorktown* (CV-5), shown here shortly after three Japanese bombs struck it on June 4, 1942, during the Battle of Midway. At first it seemed that the ship could be saved, but eventually it was sunk by torpedoes from the Japanese submarine I-168. (Naval Historical Center)

The Japanese First Air Fleet commander, Nagumo Chūichi, had ordered planes returning from strikes on Midway to rearm with torpedoes to strike the American ships. But as this effort was in progress at about 10:30 a.m., 37 dive-bombers from the carrier *Enterprise* at last located the Japanese carriers in their most vulnerable state, while their decks were cluttered with armed aircraft, ordnance, and fuel. The Japanese fighters in the air were also down low, having dealt with the torpedo bomber attacks. Within the span of a few minutes, three of the four Japanese carriers—the *Soryu*, *Kaga*, and *Akagi*—were in flames and sinking. Planes from the only intact Japanese carrier, the *Hiryu*, now struck back, heavily damaging the *Yorktown*. In late afternoon, the *Hiryu* too was hit and badly damaged. The Japanese abandoned her the next day.

During the battle between the U.S. and Japanese naval forces, the two fleets neither saw each other nor exchanged gunfire; all contact was made by Japanese carrier-based planes and American land- and carrier-based aircraft. Yamamoto's first reaction on learning of the loss of three of his carriers was to bring up his battleships and recall the two light carriers from the Aleutians in hopes of fighting a more conventional sea battle. But the loss of the *Hiryu* and Nagumo's gloomy reports led him to call off the attack on Midway. Yamamoto still hoped to trap the Americans by drawing them westward into his heavy ships, but the U.S. task force commander, Rear Admiral Raymond Spruance, refused to play his game and reported to Nimitz that he was unwilling to risk a night encounter with superior Japanese forces. By the night of June 6, the Battle of Midway was over. It had been costly for Japan. In the battle itself, the Japanese had lost 4 fleet aircraft carriers and 332 aircraft, most of which went down with the carriers. The Japanese also had a heavy cruiser sunk and another badly damaged. Three destroyers and a fleet oiler were damaged as well, and a battleship was slightly damaged. The Americans lost the aircraft carrier *Yorktown*, 1 destroyer, and 147 aircraft (38 of these being shore based).

The Japanese navy was still a formidable fighting force, but once it lost the four fleet carriers and their well-trained aircrews and maintenance personnel, the continued Japanese preponderance in battleships and cruisers counted for little. The subsequent Japanese defeat in the protracted fight for Guadalcanal was due principally to a lack of air assets. It can be reasonably stated that the Battle of Midway was indeed the turning point of the long struggle in the Pacific Theater.

James H. Willbanks

See also

Central Pacific Campaign; Japan, Navy; Nimitz, Chester William; Pearl Harbor, Attack on; Signals Intelligence; Southeast Pacific Theater; Southwest Pacific Theater; United States, Navy; Yamamoto Isoroku

References

Bresnahan, Jim, ed. *Refighting the Pacific War: An Alternative History of World War II*. Annapolis, MD: Naval Institute Press, 2011.

Carlson, Elliott. *Joe Rochefort's War: The Odyssey of the Codebreaker Who Outwitted Yamamoto at Midway*. Annapolis, MD: Naval Institute Press, 2011.

Fuchida, Mitsuo, and Okumiya Masatake. *Midway: The Battle That Doomed Japan—The Japanese Navy's Story*. Annapolis, MD: Naval Institute Press, 1955.

Isom, Dallas Woodbury. *Midway Inquest: Why the Japanese Lost the Battle of Midway*. Bloomington, IN: Indiana University Press, 2007.

Lord, Walter. *Incredible Victory*. New York: Harper and Row, 1967.

Lundstrom, John B. *First Team: Pacific Naval Air Combat from Pearl Harbor to Midway*. Annapolis, MD: Naval Institute Press, 1984.

Morison, Samuel Eliot. *History of United States Naval Operations in World War II*. Vol. 4, *Coral Sea, Midway, and Submarine Actions, May 1942–August 1942*. Boston, MA: Little, Brown, 1949.

Parshall, Jonathan, and Anthony Tully. *Shattered Sword: The Untold Story of the Battle of Midway*. Washington, DC: Potomac Books, 2005.

Prange, Gordon W. *Miracle at Midway*. New York: McGraw-Hill, 1982.

Smith, Peter C. *Dauntless Victory: Fresh Perspectives on America's Seminal Naval Victory of World War II*. Barnsley: Pen and Sword, 2007.

Symonds, Craig. *The Battle of Midway*. New York: Oxford University Press, 2011.

Toll, Ian W. *Pacific Crucible: War at Sea in the Pacific, 1941–1942*. New York: Norton, 2011.

Montgomery, Sir Bernard Law (First Viscount Montgomery of Alamein) (1887–1976)

Sir Bernard Law Montgomery was a British army field marshal who was instrumental in the planning and execution of key engagements in North Africa and Europe. Whether considered a latter-day Marlborough or Wellington or "the most overrated general of World War II," Montgomery remains the most controversial senior Allied commander of World War II. Montgomery was born in Kennington, London, on November 17, 1887. His father became the Anglican bishop of Tasmania, but the family returned to Britain when Montgomery was 13. He attended Saint Paul's day school, Hammersmith, and entered the Royal Military Academy, Sandhurst, in 1907. The next year, Montgomery was commissioned into the Royal Warwickshire Regiment. Montgomery served in India, and in World War I, he fought on the Western Front and was wounded in the First Battle of Ypres in 1914. He was then posted to a training assignment in England but returned to the front to fight as a major in the 1916 Battle of the Somme. Montgomery ended the war as a division staff officer. Following occupation duty in Germany after the war, he graduated from the Staff College at Camberley in 1921 and returned there as an instructor five years later. In 1929, Montgomery rewrote the infantry training manual. He then served in the Middle East, commanded a regiment, and was chief instructor at the Quetta Staff College from 1934 to 1937. Between 1937 and 1938, he commanded 1st Brigade. He then took charge of the 3rd Infantry Division, which he led in France as part of the British Expeditionary Force after the start of World War II. He distinguished himself in the British retreat to Dunkerque in May and June 1940, and in July, he took charge of V Corps in Britain, protecting the English south coast.

In April 1941, Montgomery assumed command of XII Corps, which held the crucial Kent area in England. Montgomery established himself as a thorough professional soldier and had no time or patience for the amateur traditions observed by many of his colleagues. Playwright George Bernard Shaw called him "that intensely compacted hank of steel wire." He was also very much the maverick.

Montgomery helped plan the disastrous Dieppe raid of August 1942 but left to command the First Army in the planned Allied invasion of North Africa. On August 13, following the death of General W.H.E. Gott, he took command of Eighth Army in Egypt, repulsing Field Marshal Erwin Rommel's attack at Alam Halfa between August and September 1942.

Montgomery rebuilt Eighth Army's morale. Known for his concern for his men's welfare, he was also deliberate as a commander. In the Battle of El Alamein in October and November 1942, his superior forces defeated and drove west German and Italian forces under Rommel. His less-than-rapid advance allowed the bulk of the Axis forces to escape. Montgomery was made a full general that November.

Following the Axis surrender in the Battle of Tunis of May 1943, Montgomery played an active role in planning Operation HUSKY, the invasion of Sicily, and he led Eighth Army in the invasions of both Sicily in July and Italy in September. He returned to Britain to assist in planning Operation OVERLORD, the Allied invasion of Normandy, then temporarily commanded its land forces in the landing until General Dwight Eisenhower moved his headquarters to France in September.

General Bernard Law Montgomery commands British forces at El Alamein in November 1942. Montgomery's defeat of German general Erwin Rommel at El Alamein proved to be a turning point for the Allies. It was the first British defeat of German troops in the field during World War II. Montgomery subsequently commanded the British military forces that took part in the June 1944 Allied invasion of Western Europe. (National Archives)

Promoted to field marshal in September 1944, Montgomery commanded the British 21st Army Group. He sought to finish the war by the end of the year with a daring invasion of Germany across the Rhine at Arnhem in Operation MARKET-GARDEN, a surprise from the conservative Montgomery. The plan, however, failed that same month. Montgomery's forces defended the north shoulder in the German Ardennes Offensive (the Battle of the Bulge) in December. At a later press conference, "Monty" gave the impression that he had saved the day for the Americans in the Ardennes, necessitating a statement by British prime minister Winston Churchill that the battle had basically been an American show. Montgomery then directed the drive into northern Germany.

Following the war, Montgomery commanded British occupation troops in Germany between May 1945 and June 1946. From 1946 to 1948, he was chief of the Imperial General Staff. He next served as chairman of the Western European commanders in chief from 1948 to 1951 and commander of North Atlantic Treaty Organization (NATO) forces in Europe and deputy supreme commander between 1951 and 1958. He retired in September 1958. A prolific writer, he personally drafted his memoirs that same year. Montgomery died at Isington Mill, Hampshire, England, on March 24, 1976.

Colin F. Baxter and Spencer C. Tucker

See also

Churchill, Sir Winston Leonard Spencer; Eisenhower, Dwight D.; Great Britain, Army; Italy Campaign; North Africa Campaign; Rommel, Erwin Johannes Eugen; Western European Theater of Operations

References

Baxter, Colin F. *Field Marshal Bernard Law Montgomery, 1887–1976*. Westport, CT: Greenwood Press, 1999.

Brighton, Terry. *Patton, Montgomery, & Rommel: Masters of Battle*. New York: Crown Books, 2009.

Chalfont, Alun. *Montgomery of Alamein*. New York: Atheneum, 1976.

Hamilton, Nigel. *Monty*. 3 vols. New York: McGraw-Hill, 1981–1986.

Horne, Alistair, with David Montgomery. *Monty: The Lonely Leader, 1944–1945*. New York: HarperCollins, 1994.

Lewin, Ronald. *Montgomery as a Military Commander*. New York: Stein and Day, 1972.

Montgomery, Bernard L. *The Memoirs of Field-Marshal the Viscount Montgomery of Alamein, K G*. London: Collins, 1958.

Mussolini, Benito (1883–1945)

Benito Amilcare Andrea Mussolini was Italian dictator from 1922 to 1943. Born in Predappio, near Forli in Romagna, Italy, on July 29, 1883, to a blacksmith Socialist father and a schoolteacher mother, Benito Mussolini was named after the Mexican revolutionary and president Benito Juárez. He attended local schools and earned a teaching diploma in 1901. His mother wanted him to be a schoolteacher, but Mussolini found the profession too boring.

As an adolescent, Mussolini had joined the revolutionary or syndicalist branch of the Italian Socialist Party. He found that he enjoyed the role of agitator, fomenting strikes and establishing unions. At age 19, he fled to Switzerland to avoid compulsory military service. He stayed there for three years, doing odd jobs and living on money sent by his mother. He intermittently attended some university classes and served time in jail. An amnesty caused Mussolini to return to Italy and perform his military service. He then edited a socialist newspaper, *La Lotta di Classe* (The Class Struggle), at Forli and was secretary of the local Socialist Party at Forli. His opposition to war with the Ottoman Empire in 1911 and 1912 earned him national prominence. He was now one of the leaders of the left wing of the Italian Socialist Party. In 1913, he became editor of the Socialist daily *Avanti* (Forward), published in Milan.

On the outbreak of World War I, however, Mussolini abruptly modified his socialism by embracing Italian nationalism and urging intervention on the Allied side. This interventionist position caused his expulsion from the Socialist Party. Mussolini then founded a French-financed daily, *Il Popolo d'Italia* (The People of Italy). In October 1914, he also founded the prowar group Fasci Rivoluzionario d'Azione Internazionalista (Revolutionary Fasci for International Action) to bring about intervention in the war. In December of that year, the group became the Fasci di Azione Rivoluzionaria (Fasci for Revolutionary Action). The word *fascio* recalled the bundle of sticks carried by the lictors of ancient Rome, representing state power; one stick might be broken, but fastened together, the sticks were unbreakable. Mussolini liked to call up ancient glories, and this bundle of sticks later became the emblem of Fascist Italy. His belief that the proletariat should unite and create a formidable organization before seizing power was the germ of the Italian Fascist movement. Following Italy's entry into the war on the Allied side in May 1915, Mussolini was called up for the army and served until 1917 on the Austrian front, reaching the rank of corporal. He was wounded slightly and discharged.

On the return of peace, the Socialist Party resumed its agitation. Mussolini's reaction to this was to organize ex-soldiers in the Fascio di Combattimento (Combat Bands) in March 1919. Mussolini carefully built the Fascist organization, paying special attention to the Blackshirt squads, militia supported with financial contributions (not always voluntary) from businessmen and landlords. Distinguished by their black shirts and Roman salute, the Blackshirts were clashing with Socialists and Communist groups by the summer of 1919. Mussolini's policy was to meet every act of violence with greater violence, and between 1921 and 1922, a veritable civil war with the Socialists raged through the length of Italy.

The Fascist political program was little more than devotion to their leader ("Il Duce"), Italian nationalism, "law and order," and opposition to communism. After they came to power, the Fascists claimed they had saved Italy from communism. There is, however, little support for that in fact. Certainly, Mussolini did exploit middle- and upper-class fears of socialism and communism.

In the 1921 elections, the Fascists gained less than 10 percent of the vote, but the size of the organization (300,000 members by the end of September 1922) made force—or the threat of it—a possible route to power. By September 1922, Mussolini was openly demanding that he be named premier. In late October, some 10,000 of his followers converged on Rome. During this March on Rome, Mussolini remained safe in Milan until he was informed that it had succeeded, a fact carefully concealed by Fascist historians.

When King Victor Emmanuel III refused to authorize martial law, Premier Luigi Facta resigned, and on October 29, 1922, the king called Mussolini as premier. It was all quite legal—or almost so. On November 25, threatened with new elections held under Fascist supervision, Parliament conceded Mussolini full powers for 1 year; he held them for 20.

A new election law and the trampling of the rights of the opposition in 1924 gave the Fascists 374 of 535 seats. Mussolini then proceeded to disband the opposition parties and secure complete power as Il Duce. He alone made the decisions, and he was not only head of state but also foreign minister, chief of the armed service branches, minister of the interior, and minister of the colonies. This concentration of authority produced chaos rather than efficiency. Restoring the economy also proved elusive. The only real domestic achievements of his regime were advances in literacy (Fascist education was more formative than informative) and the 1929 accord with the Vatican (the Lateran Treaty).

Fascist politician Benito Mussolini became prime minister of Italy in 1922, a position he soon transformed into a personal dictatorship. Known as *Il Duce* (The Leader) from the mid-1920s onward, he stressed military glory and looked back to the Roman Empire, deliberately appealing to nationalist forces within Italy. An eloquent orator, Mussolini enjoyed using grandiloquent, bombastic rhetoric in carefully staged public appearances. (Library of Congress)

Mussolini's dominant motivations were his personal vanity and desire for adulation; not surprisingly, flattery was a key factor in his undoing. He became captivated by his own myth of the invincible leader and came to believe his own propaganda that only he could make the right decisions and that his intuition was always correct. Serious study and discussion were not Mussolini's style. He rushed to rapid decisions, often with unfortunate results. He also changed his mind frequently and precipitously, and he was totally inept as a war leader. He ordered military campaigns begun on short notice, with no thought of the need for detailed planning. The hallmarks of the Italian state and military under Mussolini were administrative confusion and incompetence.

Mussolini pursued an aggressive foreign policy, beginning with the Italian bombardment of the Greek island of Corfu in 1923. Alienation from the West over Italy's 1935 invasion of Abyssinia (Ethiopia) and support of the Fascist side in the 1936–1939 Spanish Civil War led to a rapprochement with Adolf Hitler's Germany.

This Rome–Berlin Axis became a formal alliance in 1939. The year before, Mussolini had allowed Hitler to annex Austria; four years previously, he had helped uphold Austrian independence against an attempted Nazi coup. He was also a prime mover behind the agreement at Munich in September 1938 that led to the dismemberment of Czechoslovakia. In April 1939, Mussolini ordered the invasion of Albania.

When the general European war began in September 1939, Mussolini, fearful that Germany would not win, declared Italy's nonbelligerency. With Germany about to defeat

France and being anxious to join in the spoils, he declared war on France on June 10, 1940, and sent Italian divisions into southeastern France and into Egypt from Libya, with little military success. He also insisted on sending obsolete Italian aircraft to participate in the Battle of Britain. In October 1940, without consulting with Hitler, he ordered Italian forces to invade Greece from Albania. The Greeks promptly drove the Italian forces out, leading Hitler to come to the rescue of his hard-pressed ally in the spring of 1941. Mussolini also sent Italian forces to assist the Germans in their invasion of the Soviet Union, a step that was particularly unpopular in Italy.

Following Allied victory in North Africa and the successful Allied invasion of Sicily, the Fascist Grand Council voted to depose Mussolini on July 25, 1943. Hitler ordered him rescued by German commandos, and Mussolini was then installed as nominal leader of a puppet state in northern Italy, under complete German control. In September 1943, Italy switched sides in the war. As the end of the war approached, Mussolini and his mistress, Clara Petacci, attempted to flee northern Italy with a German convoy in April 1945. Partisans captured them on April 28 and shot both that same day. Their bodies and those of other members of Mussolini's government were taken to Milan and strung up there, upside down, in the great square, the Piazzale Loreto. Mussolini's body was later rescued and buried in the family mausoleum.

Mussolini never accepted responsibility for his failures but blamed others, when he alone was responsible. He claimed the Italian people were not worthy of him. He may have been the least brutal of the major dictators of World War II, but he was bad enough. To the end, his chief motivation was personal power rather than the good of the Italian people.

Annette Richardson and Spencer C. Tucker

See also

Balkans Theater; Greece, Role in War; Hitler, Adolf; Italy, Air Force; Italy, Army; Italy Campaign; Italy, Navy; North Africa Campaign; Western European Theater of Operations

References

Blinkhorn, Martin. *Mussolini and Fascist Italy.* 3rd ed. London: Routledge, 2006.

Bosworth, R.J.B. *The Italian Dictatorship: Problems and Perspectives in the Interpretation of Mussolini and Fascism.* London: Arnold, 1998.

Bosworth, R.J.B. *Mussolini.* Rev. ed. New York: Bloomsbury, 2011.

Bosworth, R.J.B. *Mussolini's Italy: Life Under the Fascist Dictatorship, 1915–1945.* New York: Penguin, 2006.

Collier, Richard. *Duce! The Rise and Fall of Benito Mussolini.* London: Collins, 1971.

Corvaja, Santi. *Hitler and Mussolini: The Secret Meetings.* Translated by Robert L. Miller. New York: Enigma Books, 2008.

Gooch, John. *Mussolini and His Generals: The Armed Forces and Fascist Foreign Policy, 1922–1940.* New York: Cambridge University Press, 2007.

Hibbert, Christopher. *Benito Mussolini: The Rise and Fall of Il Duce.* Harmondsworth: Penguin, 1975.

Joseph, Frank. *Mussolini's War: Fascist Italy's Military Struggles from Africa and Western Europe to the Mediterranean and Soviet Union 1935–45.* Solihull: Helion Press, 2010.

Mack Smith, Denis. *Mussolini's Roman Empire*. New York: Viking, 1976.

Mack Smith, Denis. *Mussolini*. London: Weidenfeld and Nicolson, 1981.

Mallett, Robert. *Mussolini and the Origins of the Second World War, 1933–1940*. New York: Palgrave Macmillan, 2003.

Morgan, Philip. *The Fall of Mussolini: Italy, the Italians, and the Second World War*. New York: Oxford University Press, 2007.

Mussolini, Benito. *My Rise and Fall*. New York: Da Capo Press, 1998.

O'Brien, Paul. *Mussolini in the First World War: The Journalist, the Soldier, the Fascist*. New York: Berg, 2004.

Strang, G. Bruce. *On the Fiery March: Mussolini Prepares for War*. Westport, CT: Praeger, 2003.

Todd, Allen. *The European Dictatorships: Hitler, Stalin, Mussolini*. Cambridge: Cambridge University Press, 2002.

Weinberg, Gerhard L. *Visions of Victory: The Hopes of Eight World War II Leaders*. Cambridge: Cambridge University Press, 2005.

Nimitz, Chester William (1885–1966)

Chester William Nimitz was a U.S. Navy Admiral of the Fleet and commander of the Pacific Fleet. Born far from the sea on February 24, 1885, in Fredericksburg, Texas, Chester Nimitz graduated from the U.S. Naval Academy in 1905. He then served with the U.S. Asiatic Fleet, steadily advancing in rank and position. Promoted to lieutenant in 1910, he assumed command of the submarine *Skipjack* in 1912. He then studied diesel engine construction in Europe and supervised construction of the U.S. Navy's first diesel ship engine. On U.S. entry into World War I in April 1917, Lieutenant Commander Nimitz served as chief of staff to the commander of submarines in the Atlantic Fleet (1917–1919).

Following the war, Nimitz was appointed to the Navy Department staff in Washington, and in 1920 he transferred to Pearl Harbor to oversee construction of a new submarine base there. Over the next 20 years, he served in a wide variety of submarine billets as well as aboard battleships and destroyers. He also spent several tours in Washington and helped establish the first Naval Reserve Officer Training Corps programs in American universities. He won promotion to rear admiral in 1938.

When Japan attacked Pearl Harbor in 1941, Nimitz was chief of the Bureau of Navigation. On December 31, 1941, on the recommendation of navy secretary Frank Knox, President Franklin D. Roosevelt promoted Nimitz to full admiral and appointed him commander of the U.S. Pacific Fleet, replacing Admiral Husband E. Kimmel at Pearl Harbor. Although a single U.S. command in the Pacific would have been far more advantageous, General Douglas MacArthur would not agree to serve under a naval officer. As a result, two commands emerged. As commander in chief, Pacific Ocean Area, Nimitz directed all U.S. military forces in the Central Pacific and provided support to MacArthur and his Southwest Pacific forces.

Although the Allies made the war against Japan secondary to their Europe First strategy, Nimitz did not delay his plans to halt Japanese expansion, retake Japan's gains, and push the war to the Japanese homeland. Using information provided by American codebreakers about Japanese plans, Nimitz halted the Japanese invasion of Port Moresby in the Battle of the Coral Sea in May 1942 and the Japanese effort to take Midway that June. The latter battle transferred the initiative to the Americans. Nimitz and MacArthur cooperated in a series of island-hopping campaigns that progressed closer and closer to the Japanese mainland. Nimitz's forces took the Gilbert Islands in November 1943, the Marshall

Admiral of the Fleet Chester W. Nimitz, shown here in 1944, commanded the U.S. Pacific Fleet from December 31, 1941, until the Japanese surrender. Although the defeat of Germany was the top Allied priority, from 1942 onward Nimitz pursued an aggressive strategy toward Japan. His June 1942 victory at the Battle of Midway gave U.S. forces the initiative in the Pacific, an advantage they never subsequently lost. (Naval Historical Society)

Islands in February 1944, and the Mariana Islands in August 1944. In October, he joined MacArthur's forces to retake the Philippines. Nimitz's accomplishments were recognized in December 1944 by his promotion to the newly established five-star rank of Admiral of the Fleet. In early 1945, Nimitz directed the offensives against Guam, Iwo Jima, and Okinawa. His forces were preparing to invade Japan when the Japanese surrendered. On September 2, Nimitz signed the formal Japanese surrender aboard the battleship *Missouri* in Tokyo Bay.

Nimitz returned to Washington in October and assumed the post of chief of naval operations. For the next two years, he supervised the postwar demobilization of men and ships and provided input into the development of nuclear-powered submarines. Nimitz retired in December 1947. In the following years, he briefly served as adviser to the secretary of the navy and for two years he was the United Nations commissioner for Kashmir. Nimitz died on February 20, 1966, near San Francisco, California.

James H. Willbanks

See also

Central Pacific Campaign; MacArthur, Douglas; Midway, Battle of; Pearl Harbor, Attack on; Roosevelt, Franklin D.; Signals Intelligence; Southeast Pacific Theater; Southwest Pacific Theater; United States, Marine Corps; United States, Navy

References

Borneman, Walter. *The Admirals: Nimitz, Halsey, Leahy, and King—The Five-Star Admirals Who Won the War at Sea.* Boston, MA: Little, Brown, 2012.

Brink, Randall. *Nimitz: The Man and His Wars.* New York: Penguin, 2000.

Driskell, Frank A., and Dede W. Casad. *Chester W. Nimitz, Admiral of the Hills.* Austin, TX: Eakin Press, 1983.

Harris, Brayton. *Admiral Nimitz: The Commander of the Pacific Ocean Theater.* New York: Palgrave Macmillan, 2012.

Hoyt, Edwin P. *How They Won the War in the Pacific: Nimitz and His Admirals.* New York: Weybright and Talley, 1970.

Morison, Samuel Eliot. *History of U.S. Naval Operations in World War II.* 15 vols. Boston, MA: Little, Brown, 1947–1962.

Potter, Elmer B. *Nimitz.* Annapolis, MD: Naval Institute Press, 1976.

Potter, Elmer B. "Fleet Admiral Chester William Nimitz." In *Men of War: Great Naval Leaders of World War II*, edited by Stephen Howarth, 129–157. New York: St. Martin's Press, 1992.

Tuohy, William. *America's Fighting Admirals: Winning the War at Sea in World War II.* St. Paul, MN: Zenith Press, 2007.

North Africa Campaign (1940–1943)

The campaign in North Africa was fought over control of the Suez Canal. Great Britain depended on the canal for access to Middle Eastern oil and raw materials from Asia. The Suez Canal and the Mediterranean also formed the primary lifeline to Britain's overseas dominions. The ground campaign in North Africa and the naval campaign for the Mediterranean, therefore, were two sides of the same strategic coin.

The fight to control North Africa began in October 1935 when Italy invaded Ethiopia (Abyssinia). Britain, meanwhile, stationed a significant military force in Egypt to protect the Suez Canal. Britain and France also agreed to divide the responsibility for maintaining naval control of the Mediterranean, with the main British base in Egypt at Alexandria.

Italy was the unknown variable in the Mediterranean strategic equation. A neutral Italy would mean that British access to the vital sea-lanes would remain reasonably secure. However, operating from its main base at Taranto in southern Italy and supported by Italian air force bases in Sicily and Sardinia, the seemingly powerful Italian navy had the potential to close off the Mediterranean. When Germany invaded France in June 1940, Italian dictator Benito Mussolini could not resist the opportunity to grab his share of the spoils. On June 10, Italy declared war on Great Britain and France.

The British and Italian armies initially faced each other across the Libyan-Egyptian border in an area known as the Western Desert. Italian Marshal Rodolfo Graziani had some 250,000 ground troops in Libya, and General Sir Archibald Wavell, British commander in chief of the Middle East, had only 100,000 soldiers to defend Egypt, Sudan, and Palestine. The British army, however, was far better organized, trained, equipped, and led.

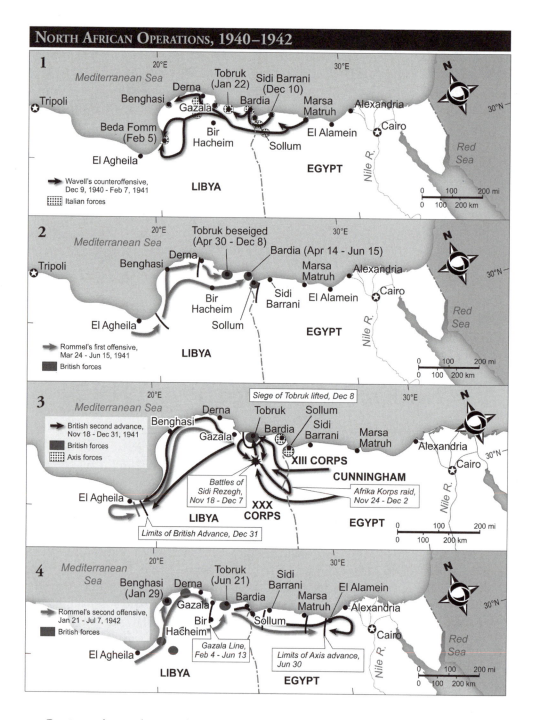

NORTH AFRICAN OPERATIONS, 1940–1942

1
Mediterranean Sea

Tripoli · Benghasi · Derna · Tobruk (Jan 22) · Sidi Barrani (Dec 10) · Marsa Matruh · Alexandria · Cairo

Gazala · Bardia · Bir Hacheim · Sollum · El Alamein

Beda Fomm (Feb 5) · El Agheila

EGYPT · LIBYA · Nile R. · Red Sea

→ Wavell's counteroffensive, Dec 9, 1940 - Feb 7, 1941
▦ Italian forces

0 100 200 mi
0 100 200 km

2
Mediterranean Sea

Tripoli · Benghasi · Derna · Tobruk besieged (Apr 30 - Dec 8) · Bardia (Apr 14 - Jun 15) · Marsa Matruh · Alexandria · Cairo

Bir Hacheim · Sidi Barrani · El Alamein · Sollum

El Agheila · LIBYA · EGYPT · Nile R. · Red Sea

→ Rommel's first offensive, Mar 24 - Jun 15, 1941
■ British forces

0 100 200 mi
0 100 200 km

3
Mediterranean Sea

Siege of Tobruk lifted, Dec 8

Benghasi · Derna · Tobruk · Sollum · Sidi Barrani · Marsa Matruh · Alexandria · Cairo

Gazala · Bardia · XIII CORPS · CUNNINGHAM

→ British second advance, Nov 18 - Dec 31, 1941
■ British forces
▦ Axis forces

El Agheila

Battles of Sidi Rezegh, Nov 18 - Dec 7

Afrika Korps raid, Nov 24 - Dec 2

XXX CORPS · LIBYA · EGYPT · Nile R.

Limits of British Advance, Dec 31

0 100 200 mi
0 100 200 km

4
Mediterranean Sea

Benghasi (Jan 29) · Derna · Tobruk (Jun 21) · Sidi Barrani · El Alamein

Gazala · Bardia · Marsa Matruh · Alexandria

Bir Hacheim · Sollum · Cairo

El Agheila · LIBYA · EGYPT · Nile R. · Red Sea

→ Rommel's second offensive, Jan 21 - Jul 7, 1942
■ British forces

Gazala Line, Feb 4 - Jun 13

Limits of Axis advance, Jun 30

0 100 200 mi
0 100 200 km

Graziani reluctantly moved into Egypt on September 13, 1940, halting at Sidi Barrani just short of the British main positions at Mersa Matrûh. The Battle of Britain was then reaching its climax, and the beleaguered British were facing a possible German invasion. By October 1940, however, the threat from Operation SEA LION had eased, and the British began to reinforce Wavell. Through December, 126,000 more Commonwealth troops arrived in Egypt from Britain, Australia, New Zealand, and India. On December 9, the Western Desert Force, commanded by General Sir Richard O'Connor, attacked at Sidi Barrani.

The British drove the Italian Tenth Army from Egypt and achieved a major victory on January 3, 1941, at Bardia, just inside Libya. Driving deeper into Cyrenaica (eastern Libya), the British captured the vital port of Tobruk on January 22. Continuing forward, O'Connor trapped the Italian Tenth Army at Beda Fomm on February 7, 1941. In just two months, two British divisions advanced 500 miles, destroyed 10 Italian divisions, and captured 130,000 prisoners. The British suffered only 555 dead and some 1,400 wounded.

Shortly after the British successes in North Africa, Prime Minister Winston Churchill decided on February 22 to send British troops to Greece. Most of those forces were withdrawn from Cyrenaica, leaving Wavell with only five brigades in Libya. But just a few weeks earlier, German leader Adolf Hitler had decided to reinforce the Italians in North Africa with German forces. On January 8, the Luftwaffe's Fliegerkorps X started operating from bases in Sicily against Allied shipping headed for Benghazi in Libya. The British forward units in Libya were forced to resupply through Tobruk, more than 450 miles away. Two German divisions and two additional Italian divisions were sent to Libya from Italy. On February 12, Lieutenant General Erwin Rommel took command of the German divisions. In short order, Rommel's force grew into the three-division-strong Deutsches Afrika Korps.

Rommel probed El Agheila on March 24 and continued driving rapidly to the east, despite Hitler's orders to maintain an overall defensive posture. The Germans surrounded Tobruk on April 10 but were unable to take the fortress by a coup de main. Rommel left a siege force of mostly Italian units and continued his drive toward the Egyptian border. But the Tobruk garrison held out for 240 days and tied down vital Axis manpower in Rommel's rear area. Rommel's main force, meanwhile, reached Sollum on the Egyptian border on April 14, and the Germans occupied the key terrain of the Halfaya Pass.

Churchill pushed for an immediate counteroffensive, but Wavell wanted to gain control of the Halfaya Pass first. On May 15, the British launched Operation BREVITY under the command of Brigadier William Gott. Rommel skillfully parried the thrust and then counterattacked. By May 27, the Germans recaptured the Halfaya Pass, but they then began to run out of supplies and had to halt. They dug in and reinforced their positions, using the 88-mm antiaircraft guns in an antitank role. The British came to call the heavily fortified and fiercely defended pass "Hellfire Pass."

Churchill continued to pressure Wavell for action. Operation BATTLEAXE began on June 15 with a frontal attack through the Halfaya Pass toward Sollum. The German 88-mm antiaircraft guns stopped the British armor, and the Germans then counterattacked. The British lost 91 tanks, and Operation BATTLEAXE was over by June 17. Churchill relieved Wavell four days later and replaced him the following month with General Sir Claude Auchinleck. General Sir Alan Cunningham (the brother of Admiral Andrew Cunningham) took command of the Western Desert Force, which had been redesignated the British Eighth Army.

Rommel's force in North Africa slipped to near bottom priority for logistical sustainment after Germany attacked the Soviet Union in June 1941. By November 1941,

Rommel had 414 tanks, 320 aircraft, and 9 divisions (three German), 4 of which were tied down in the siege of Tobruk. The British had some 700 tanks, 1,000 aircraft, and 8 (larger) divisions. Operation CRUSADER opened on November 18 with British XIII Corps advancing on the Halfaya Pass and XXX Corps attempting to sweep around Rommel's southern flank to reach Tobruk. Following a string of fierce tank battles on November 22 and 23, Rommel drove deep into the British rear with two panzer divisions and the Ariete Armored Division in an attempt to relieve the Axis forces at Halfaya and simultaneously to cut off the Eighth Army.

As the British tank losses rose, Cunningham wanted to halt the operation. Auchinleck relieved Cunningham and replaced him with Major General Neil Ritchie. The British finally broke through to Tobruk on November 29. Overwhelmed by attrition to his forces, Rommel began to withdraw on December 7. The Germans retreated back across Cyrenaica, reaching El Agheila on January 6, 1942. Operation CRUSADER was a victory for the British, but they were unable to exploit it because of a lack of reinforcements.

Rommel launched his second offensive on January 21, 1942. Within days he drove the British back almost 300 miles, halting on February 4 between Gazala and Bir Hacheim. Both sides then concentrated on building up their strength for the next four months. Rommel resumed operations on May 26 with Operation VENEZIA, his attack against the Gazala Line. Both forces were roughly equal in strength, but Ritchie's armored units were widely dispersed, whereas Rommel kept his concentrated. Rommel swept his armor around the Free French Brigade at Bir Hacheim on the southern end of the line and turned north, cutting across the Allied rear. A secondary attack in the north by Axis forces pinned down the Allied forces there.

By May 28, the Axis armored units behind the Allied lines were in trouble. Rommel had lost more than one-third of his tanks, and the rest were short of fuel and ammunition. On May 29, the Italian Trieste Division managed to clear a path through the center of the Gazala Line, and that opening became a lifeline to Rommel's panzers. On May 30, Rommel consolidated his remaining armor in a defensive position that came to be called "the Cauldron."

On June 5 and 6 Rommel successfully beat back Ritchie's series of piecemeal counterattacks against the Cauldron. On June 10 and 11, the Axis finally drove the Free French from Bir Hacheim, and on June 11, Rommel's panzers broke out of the Cauldron. The Eighth Army once more started falling back to the Egyptian border. On June 15, German tanks reached the coast, and Rommel shifted his attention to Tobruk, which fell on June 21. Along with the vital port, the Axis forces captured 2,000 tons of much-needed fuel and 2,000 wheeled vehicles.

The British fell back to Mersa Matrûh about 100 miles inside Egypt. Rommel, now promoted to field marshal for his victory at Gazala, pursued. Auchinleck relieved Ritchie and personally assumed command of the Eighth Army. Rommel had only 60 operational tanks, but he still attacked at Mersa Matrûh on June 26 and routed four British divisions in three days of fighting. The British fell back again another 120 miles to the east to the vicinity of El Alamein, less than 100 miles from Alexandria.

Auchinleck was determined to hold near El Alamein. Although under constant pressure from Rommel's forces, Auchinleck improvised a fluid defensive line anchored on Ruweisat Ridge a few miles south of the El Alamein perimeter. Rommel attacked on

July 1, intending to sweep around El Alamein, but Auchinleck skillfully battled Rommel to a standstill over the course of three weeks of fighting. Auchinleck then launched a major counterattack on July 21–22 but made no progress. Exhausted, both sides paused to regroup.

Despite the fact that the British had finally halted Rommel's advance, Churchill relieved Auchinleck in early August and replaced him with General Sir Harold Alexander as commander in chief of the Middle East. Sir William Gott was promoted to general and placed in command of the Eighth Army. On August 7, while flying to Cairo to take up his appointment, Gott was killed when a German fighter attacked his airplane. Churchill then selected Lieutenant General Bernard L. Montgomery to succeed Gott in command of the Eighth Army.

On August 31, 1942, Rommel launched what he believed would be the final attack to carry the Axis forces to the Nile. Montgomery, however, had made extensive preparations around El Alamein, based on a plan developed by Auchinleck. Montgomery also had the advantage of knowing Rommel's plan through ULTRA intercepts. Rommel intended to sweep around to the south of Ruweisat Ridge and cut off El Alamein from the rear. However, the British had laid extensive minefields and had heavily fortified Alam Halfa Ridge behind and southeast of El Alamein. Rommel's attack ran short of fuel and stalled by September 3. Montgomery counterattacked immediately but halted as soon as the Axis forces were pushed back to their starting positions. Taken together, the battles of Ruweisat Ridge and Alam Halfa were the real operational turning point of the war in North Africa.

Montgomery used the time after Alam Halfa to plan carefully a set-piece counterattack from El Alamein. Rommel, meanwhile, returned to Germany on sick leave. When Montgomery finally launched the attack, the British had an overall force superiority ratio of three to one. Rommel immediately returned from Germany when the battle of El Alamein started on October 23, 1942. The Allies tried for five days to break through the Axis positions and took 10,000 casualties in the process. On October 31, Montgomery renewed the attack with strong support from the Royal Air Force. Critically short of fuel and ammunition, Rommel was forced to disengage on November 3. The following day, the 1,400-mile Axis withdrawal to Tunisia began.

For the next three months, Montgomery followed rather than aggressively pursued Rommel and the Axis forces across the northern coast of Africa. Rommel reached the Tunisian border at the end of January 1943. By the time he got there, however, another Allied force was waiting for him.

On November 8, 1942, four days after Rommel began his long withdrawal, the British and Americans initiated Operation TORCH, the invasion of Northwest Africa. U.S. Lieutenant General Dwight D. Eisenhower had overall command. In a coordinated series of landings, the Western Task Force under Major General George S. Patton Jr. landed on the Atlantic coast near Casablanca; the Center Task Force under Major General Lloyd Fredendall landed just inside the Mediterranean around Oran; and the Eastern Task Force under Major General Charles Ryder landed near Algiers. Although all the landing sites were in Vichy French territory, the ultimate objectives of the operation were the Tunisian city of Tunis and the port and airfield complex at Bizerte.

The Germans reacted by sending troops from Sicily to Tunisia on November 9. From the moment the Allies landed, the campaign in Northwest Africa and the race for Tunis

German field marshal Erwin Rommel with his troops at El Alamein, Egypt, in November 1942. The charismatic Rommel's defeat at the hands of British commander Bernard Law Montgomery marked the end of Axis success in North Africa and the beginning of a series of Allied victories. (Library of Congress)

were a logistical battle. The side that could mass forces more quickly would win. For the Germans, control of the Tunis complex was critical to prevent Rommel from being trapped between Montgomery in the east and the newly formed British First Army in the west. On November 28, the Allies reached Tebourba, only 12 miles from Tunis, but an Axis counterattack drove them back 20 miles in seven days. In January 1943, the winter rains and resulting mud brought mechanized operations to a halt in northern Tunisia. The Axis side had temporarily won the race.

Waiting for better weather in the spring, the Allies continued to build up their forces. Lieutenant General Sir Kenneth Anderson's British First Army was organized into three corps—the British V Corps, the U.S. II Corps, and the French XIX Corps. The Axis forces in northern Tunisia now consisted of Colonel General Jürgen von Arnim's Fifth Panzer Army. Once Rommel's Panzerarmee Afrika crossed into southern Tunisia, it occupied positions in the old French fortifications of the Mareth Line. Rommel's 10 divisions were well below half strength, with a total of only 78,000 troops and 129 tanks. Before he had to face Montgomery, rapidly closing from the rear, Rommel intended to eliminate the threat of the British First Army to his north. On February 14, the Germans launched the first leg of a two-pronged offensive, with von Arnim's forces attacking through the Faid Pass for Sidi Bou Zid. The following day, Rommel in the south attacked toward Gafsa. The bulk of Rommel's forces, however, remained along the Mareth Line. By February 18, the Kasserine

Pass was in Axis hands, and the U.S. Army had suffered its first major defeat at the hands of the Germans. Rommel tried to advance north through the Kasserine Pass on February 19, but he did not get the support he expected from von Arnim. Hampered by a divided German command structure and the rapidly massing Allied reinforcements, the attack stalled.

The Allies recaptured Kasserine Pass on February 25. Rommel returned to the Mareth Line and prepared to face Montgomery. When the Eighth Army reached Tunisia, the Allies reorganized their command structure along the lines agreed to at the Casablanca Conference. General Eisenhower became the Supreme Commander of all Allied forces in the Mediterranean west of Tripoli. Alexander became Eisenhower's deputy and simultaneously commander of the 18th Army Group, which controlled the First and Eighth Armies, and the now separate U.S. II Corps commanded by Patton. On February 24, the Axis powers also realigned their command structure, with Rommel becoming the commander of Armeegruppe Afrika, which included the Afrika Korps, von Arnim's Fifth Panzer Army, and the Italian First Army under General Giovanni Messe. For the first time, the Axis powers had a unified command structure in Africa.

Montgomery's units crossed into Tunisia on February 4, reaching Medenine on February 16. Hoping to catch the British off balance, Rommel on March 6 attacked south from the Mareth Line. Warned by ULTRA, Montgomery was ready. Immediately following the failure of the Medenine attack, Rommel returned to Germany on sick leave. Von Arnim assumed overall Axis command, and Messe took command in south Tunisia. On March 20, Montgomery attempted a night penetration of the center of Mareth Line. That attack failed, and on March 23 he shifted the weight of his main attack around the southwestern flank of the line through the Matmata Hills. By March 26, the British broke through the Tebaga Gap, forcing the Italian First Army and the remainder of the Afrika Korps back to the north. Under continuous pressure from the Eighth Army on one side and U.S. II Corps on the other, the Axis forces withdrew north to Enfidaville.

On April 7, 1942, the Allied First and Eighth Armies linked up, squeezing the Axis forces into a tight pocket. On the east coast, the Eighth Army took Gabes on April 6; Sfax on April 10; Sousse on April 12; and Enfidaville on April 21. In the north, the U.S. II Corps, now under Lieutenant General Omar N. Bradley, took Mateur on May 3 and Bizerte on May 7. Montgomery's 7th Armoured Division also captured Tunis on May 7. The remaining Axis forces in Tunisia were caught in two pockets, one between Bizerte and Tunis and the other on isolated Cape Bon.

Von Arnim surrendered his forces on May 12, and Messe surrendered his on May 13. The Royal Navy, waiting in strength offshore, made sure that few Germans or Italians escaped to Sicily by sea. Axis losses in Tunisia alone totaled 40,000 dead or wounded, 240,000 prisoners, 250 tanks, 2,330 aircraft, and 232 vessels. British and American casualties were 33,000 and 18,558, respectively. For the entire North African Campaign, the British suffered 220,000 casualties. Total Axis losses came to 620,000, which included the loss of three field armies. The losses were large for what amounted to a secondary theater for both sides.

David T. Zabecki

See also

Africa; Bradley, Omar Nelson; Churchill, Sir Winston Leonard Spencer; Eisenhower, Dwight D.; Germany, Air Force; Germany, Army; Germany, Navy; Great Britain, Army;

Great Britain, Navy; Hitler, Adolf; Italy, Air Force; Italy, Army; Montgomery, Sir Bernard Law; Mussolini, Benito; Patton, George Smith, Jr.; Rommel, Erwin Johannes Eugen; Signals Intelligence

References

Atkinson, Rick. *An Army at Dawn: The War in North Africa, 1942–1943.* New York: Henry Holt, 2002.

Barnett, Correlli. *The Desert Generals.* New York: Viking Press, 1961.

Gordon, John W. *The Other Desert War: British Special Forces in North Africa, 1940–1943.* Westport, CT: Greenwood, 1987.

Greene, Jack, and Alessandro Massignani. *Rommel's North African Campaign.* Conshocken, PA: Combined Publishing, 1999.

Howe, George. *United States Army in World War II: The Mediterranean Theater of Operations: Northwest Africa: Seizing the Initiative in the West.* Washington, DC: Center of Military History, Department of the Army, 1957.

Kitchen, Martin. *Rommel's Desert War: Waging World War II in North Africa, 1941–1943.* New York: Cambridge University Press, 2009.

Liddell Hart, Basil H., ed. *The Rommel Papers.* New York: Harcourt, Brace, 1953.

Moorehead, Alan. *The March to Tunis: The North African War, 1940–1943.* New York: Harper and Row, 1967.

Pitt, Barrie. *The Year of Alamein, 1942.* New York: Paragon House, 1990.

United Kingdom, National Archives. *Special Forces in the Desert War, 1940–1943.* Kew: National Archives Press, 2001.

Northeast Europe Theater

In August 1939, the Soviet Union and Germany concluded a nonaggression pact that allowed Adolf Hitler to begin his invasion of Poland without fear of Soviet intervention. In return, the Soviets acquired territory in the Baltic states and eastern Poland. With the defeat of France in June 1940, Soviet troops occupied the Baltic states of Lithuania, Latvia, and Estonia and then incorporated them into the Soviet Union.

World War II operations in northeastern Europe may be divided into three stages: the Russo-Finnish War of 1939–1940; the German invasion and conquest of Denmark and Norway in the spring of 1940; and the struggle in the Baltics, Finland, and northwestern Russia between the Soviet Union on the one side and Finland and Germany on the other from June 1941 until fall of 1944. Sweden remained officially neutral during the war.

Soviet leader Josef Stalin initiated the Russo-Finnish War (also known as the Winter War) when Finnish leaders refused his demands for the Karelian Isthmus and bases. Although Stalin offered more territory than he demanded (albeit in the far north), Finnish leaders believed the Soviets were bluffing. On November 30, 1939, five Soviet armies crossed the border. The main attack came in the southeast from the Leningrad area in the direction of Finland's second-largest city, Viipuri (Vyborg).

The unprepared Soviet forces were soon halted by deep snow and woods, but also by the fierce and stubborn Finnish resistance. A major share of blame for the failure of the

Soviets to win the war quickly rested with Stalin, who had refused to take Finland seriously. Stalin personally intervened to reject the plan advanced by chief of staff Marshal Boris M. Shaposhnikov that entailed a careful buildup and employment of the best Soviet troops, even those from the Far East. Many of the Soviet units were poorly trained scratch formations. Worse, the Soviet troops were unprepared for winter fighting.

By January 1940, Soviet troops had moved deep into Finnish territory in the north. In the southwest, however, the Finns halted the main Soviet thrust at the so-called Mannerheim Line. After the Soviets regrouped and brought up reinforcements, it was only a matter of time before Finland was defeated. At the beginning of February, the Red Army began another determined attack, managing to achieve a breakthrough after two weeks. Finland surrendered on March 12, 1940.

Under the peace terms, Finland was forced to surrender more territory than Stalin had originally demanded, including eastern Karelia and large areas in the northeast as well as a naval base at Petsamo. Although Finland lost 25,000 men killed and a comparable number of wounded, the Soviets lost perhaps 250,000 killed and a comparable number of wounded. One consequence of the war was that it convinced Hitler that his armed forces could defeat the Soviet Union easily.

Hitler believed that the Allies intended to occupy Norway, and he was determined to beat them there. Securing Norway would guarantee the Germans access to vital Swedish iron ore, which in the winter came from the Norwegian port of Narvik. The many fjords along the Norwegian coast would also provide bases for German submarines and surface raiders into the North Atlantic, as well as airfields from which the Luftwaffe might attack Britain. Acquiring Denmark would mean additional foodstuff, especially dairy products, for the Reich.

The German assault on Norway and Denmark began on April 9, 1940. With virtually no military means to defend itself, Denmark succumbed in less than a day. The occupation of Norway, spearheaded by air attacks, saw the first real employment of paratroopers near Oslo and the port city of Stavanger. At the same time, German amphibious landings took place at Narvik, Trondheim, Bergen, Kristiansand, and Oslo. Allied forces landed in Norway beginning on April 15. While British troops in the south had to be evacuated after two weeks, a combined Norwegian, British, French, and Polish force gained a foothold in the north, taking Narvik on May 28. The Germans sent reinforcements to the north to recapture it. This, combined with the German invasion of France, forced the Allied expeditionary force to withdraw on June 8. Norway capitulated two days later.

The Norwegian Campaign brought immense gains to Germany, but it also badly damaged the German surface navy. Germany lost 3 cruisers and 10 destroyers, half of the navy total. Hitler had secured additional food production for the Reich and protection for his northern flank on the Baltic. Most important, the Kriegsmarine had locations for naval bases nearer to the Allied Atlantic convoy routes. From these bases, it would launch attacks into the North Atlantic and later the Allied PQ Arctic convoys bound for the Soviet Union.

Both Norway and Denmark were under occupation until the German capitulation. The Germans established a puppet state in Norway headed by home-grown Nazi Vidkun Quisling, whose name became synonymous with "traitor." King Haakon VII escaped abroad on June 7, and after the Allies evacuated Narvik, he set up a government-in-exile

During the Norwegian Campaign of 1940, British and German naval forces clashed at the Battle of Narvik, on April 10 and 13, 1940. The Germans paid a heavy price for invading Norway, but ultimately considered their losses acceptable, because their occupation of Norway provided northern bases for the German submarine fleet. These, in turn, helped Germany to attack and destroy Allied shipping during the lengthy Battle of the Atlantic. (Library of Congress)

in Britain. Most of the country's 4.7 million tons of merchant shipping now passed into Allied hands, an invaluable addition. In 1941, 40 percent of foreign tonnage destined for English seaports was Norwegian. By the end of the war, Hitler had some 400,000 men and major artillery assets in Norway, providing security and protecting it against invasion although it was a serious drain on stretched German resources.

Operation BARBAROSSA, the attack on Soviet Russia, began in the early hours of June 22, 1941. Army Group North's 4th Panzer Group and Sixteenth Army advanced through Lithuania, Latvia, and Estonia toward the Russian border. At the northern end of the line, German troops were aided by Finnish forces. Finland rejoined the war against the Soviet Union as a cobelligerent. In the so-called Continuation War, 16 revamped Finnish divisions recaptured the territory lost earlier to the Soviet Union. The Finns refused, however, to shell Leningrad. In the winter of 1941, when Soviet lines were stretched to the breaking point, a determined Finnish assault would undoubtedly have given the Germans Leningrad, with uncertain consequences for the war in the east.

The Finns had originally planned to unite their troops with German Army Group North around Leningrad. On September 1, they reached the former Finnish-Soviet border. Mannerheim now essentially went over to defensive operations. Soviet resistance stiffened, and after capturing Petrosawodsk and Medweschjegorsk on the western and northern shore of Lake Onega, the Finns established a defensive position slightly inside Soviet territory in December 1941.

To the south, German forces in Operation BARBAROSSA had come close enough to Leningrad by September 1 to start shelling the city. A week later, Leningrad had been cut off from the last land connection, and Hitler decided to starve the city into capitulation. Food supplies ran out after a month, and in November, 11,000 people died. Even though the Soviets managed to supply the city via the frozen Lake Ladoga in winter, up to 20,000 people died each day of starvation, exhaustion, and disease. Attempts to relieve the city between August 19 and the end of September 1942 were defeated by the German Eighteenth Army. On January 11, 1943, the Soviets managed to establish a small corridor south of Lake Ladoga through which they could also deliver supplies. The siege ended in January 1944 after 900 days. Other than that, the northern sector of the Eastern Front saw only limited action between fall 1941 and January 1944.

Pressed by the Soviet Leningrad, Wolchow, and 2nd Baltic Fronts, German Army Group North then withdrew from the Leningrad area in January 1944 and fled toward the Baltic coast. By the end of April, the Soviets had recaptured most of their pre-June territory in the Baltics. As Army Group Center also had fallen back, Army Group North was now certain to be cut off. The 3rd Belorussian Front, the northern front of the Soviet drive on Army Group Center, took Vilnius on July 13.

In July and August, the Red Army's three Baltic fronts occupied the eastern parts of Latvia and Lithuania. German army defensive positions fell in succession. Tallinn (Reval) fell on September 22 and the Germans fled to the islands of Dagö and Ösel. The Red Army captured Riga on October 15. Already at the end of September, the whole of Army Group North was trapped in Courland, where it remained until the end of the war, although the German navy carried out perhaps its most brilliant operation of the war, evacuating many troops and German civilians by sea.

By October 1944, Soviet forces had advanced into Eastern Prussia, and fighting now took place inside Germany. After stopping at Memel, the 1st Baltic and the 2nd and 3rd Belorussian Fronts advanced on Königsberg (Kaliningrad) and the coast, trapping German troops and civilians against the Baltic Sea for the remainder of the war. Those who could not be evacuated surrendered on May 9, 1945, with the rest of the German army.

In June 1944, the Soviet Karelian and Leningrad Fronts began an invasion of Finland on both flanks of the Lake Ladoga. West of the lake, they overwhelmed defenses at the Mannerheim Line. Vyborg was taken on July 20. To the north and east, even though they failed to achieve a breakthrough, the Soviets forced the Finns to retreat and took the Murmansk Railway. In northern Finland the Soviet Fourteenth Army threw back German forces at Liza, supported by a large amphibious landing near Petsamo.

In accordance with the September 19, 1944, armistice ending Finnish participation in the war, Finland had to help eject German forces from its soil, since Hitler refused to extract them. By the end of the month, the Germans had withdrawn completely into Norway. In late January 1945, the Soviets reached the coast west of Danzig and the mouth of the Vistula River. By the end of the month, the Soviets had passed Posen (Poznan). By early February, the Red Army had reached the Oder within 40 miles of

Berlin, surrounding large German troop concentrations at Posen and Breslau. Neither side gave quarter in the bitter fighting, and as they advanced, Soviet troops took their revenge on the Germans with as many as 3 million civilian casualties, as well as looting and rape.

Thomas J. Weiler and Spencer C. Tucker

See also

Casualties; Collaboration; Eastern Front; Finland, Role in War; Germany, Air Force; Germany, Army; Germany, Navy; Hitler, Adolf; Soviet Union, Air Force; Soviet Union, Army; Soviet Union, Navy; Stalin, Josef

References

Claasen, Adam R. A. *Hitler's Northern War: The Luftwaffe's Ill-Fated Campaign, 1940–1945*. Lawrence, KS: University Press of Kansas, 2001.

Haupt, Werner. *The Wehrmacht in Russia 1941–1945*. Lancaster, PA: Schiffer Publishing, 2000.

Irincheev, Bair. *The War of the White Death: Finland against the Soviet Union 1939–40*. Barnsley: Pen and Sword, 2011.

Kersaudy, François. *Norway 1940*. New York: St. Martin's Press, 1991.

Lunde, Henrik O. *Finland's War of Choice: The Troubled German–Finnish Coalition in World War II*. Havertown, PA: Casemate Publishing, 2011.

Lunde, Henrik O. *Hitler's Pre-Emptive War: The Battle for Norway, 1940*. Haverford, PA: Casemate Publishing, 2010.

Mann, Chris, and Chester Jörgensen. *Hitler's Arctic War: The German Campaigns in Norway, Finland, and the USSR, 1940–1945*. New York: St. Martin's Press, 2003.

Newton, Steven H. *Retreat from Leningrad: Army Group North 1944–1945*. Lancaster, PA: Schiffer Military History Book, 1995.

Trotter, William R. *A Frozen Hell: The Russo-Finnish Winter War of 1939–1940*. Chapel Hill, NC: Algonquin Books, 1991.

Patton, George Smith, Jr. (1885–1945)

George Smith Patton Jr. was a U.S. Army general and commander of the Third Army in the European Theater of Operations. Born on November 11, 1885, in San Gabriel, California, George Patton Jr. attended the Virginia Military Institute for a year before graduating from the U.S. Military Academy in 1909. An accomplished horseman, he competed in the 1912 Stockholm Olympic Games. He also participated in the 1916–1917 Punitive Expedition into Mexico.

On U.S. entry into World War I, Patton was deployed to France as an aide to American Expeditionary Forces (AEF) commander General John J. Pershing, but he was later transferred to the Tank Corps and, as a temporary major, he commanded the first U.S. Army tank school at Langres, France. He then commanded the 304th Tank Brigade as a temporary lieutenant colonel. Wounded in the Saint-Mihiel Offensive, he was promoted to temporary colonel and took part in the Meuse-Argonne Offensive.

After the war, Patton remained an ardent champion of tank warfare. He graduated from the Cavalry School in 1923, the Command and General Staff School in 1924, and the Army War College in 1932. Returning to armor, Patton was promoted to temporary brigadier general in October 1940 and to temporary major general in April 1941, when he took command of the newly formed 2nd Armored Division. Popularly known as "Old Blood and Guts" for his colorful speeches to inspire the men, Patton commanded I Corps and the Desert Training Center, where he prepared U.S. forces for the invasion of North Africa.

In November 1942, Patton commanded the Western Task Force in the landing at Casablanca, Morocco, as part of Operation TORCH. Following the U.S. defeat in the Battle of the Kasserine Pass, he won promotion to lieutenant general and assumed command of II Corps in March 1943. He quickly restored order and morale and took the offensive against the Axis forces.

In April, Patton received command of the Seventh Army for the invasion of Sicily in July 1943. He used a series of costly flanking maneuvers along the northern coast of the island to reach Messina ahead of the British Eighth Army on the eastern side. Patton, however, ran afoul of the press and his superiors when he struck two soldiers who suffered from battle fatigue.

Relieved of his command, Patton was then used as a Trojan horse to disguise the location of the attack of Operation OVERLORD, the cross-Channel invasion of France. The

George S. Patton Jr. was one of the most controversial generals in American history. Flamboyant, swaggering, and toting a pair of pearl-handled pistols, he was known equally for battlefield successes and outlandish behavior. His German opponents in World War II considered him the best U.S. general. (Library of Congress)

Germans assumed that Patton would command any such invasion, but he actually remained in Britain in command of Third Army, the fictional 1st U.S. Army Group, in a successful ruse to trick the Germans into believing the invasion would occur in the Pas de Calais area.

Following the Normandy Invasion, Patton was at last unleashed in August when his Third Army arrived in France and spearheaded a breakout at Saint-Lô and campaigned brilliantly across northern France. Moving swiftly, his forces swung wide and then headed east, although he was frustrated by the refusal of General Omar Bradley and Supreme Commander General Dwight D. Eisenhower to recognize the importance of sealing the Falaise–Argentan Gap. Patton's forces crossed the Meuse River in late August to confront German defenses at Metz, where the Germans held the Americans until December. During the German Ardennes Offensive (Battle of the Bulge), Patton executed a brilliant repositioning movement and came to the relief of the hard-pressed American forces at Bastogne.

By the end of January, Patton began another offensive, piercing the Siegfried Line between Saarlautern and Saint Vith. On March 22, the Third Army crossed the Rhine at Oppenheim. Patton continued his drive into Germany and eventually crossed into Czechoslovakia. By the end of the war, his men had covered more ground (600 miles) and liberated more territory (nearly 82,000 square miles) than any other Allied force.

Promoted to temporary general, Patton became military governor of Bavaria. He soon found himself in trouble again for remarks in which he criticized denazification and argued that the Soviet Union was the real enemy. Relieved of his post, he assumed command of the Fifteenth Army, slated to write the official U.S. Army history of the war. Patton suffered a broken neck in an automobile accident near Mannheim and died at Heidelberg on December 21, 1945.

T. Jason Soderstrum and Spencer C. Tucker

See also

Bradley, Omar Nelson; Eisenhower, Dwight D.; Italy Campaign; Montgomery, Sir Bernard Law; North Africa Campaign; United States, Army; Western European Theater of Operations

References

Blumenson, Martin, ed. *The Patton Papers*. 2 vols. Boston, MA: Houghton Mifflin, 1972–1974.

Blumenson, Martin. *Patton: The Man behind the Legend, 1885–1945*. New York: William Morrow, 1985.

D'Este, Carlo. *Patton: A Genius for War*. New York: HarperCollins, 1995.

Hirshson, Stanley P. *General Patton: A Soldier's Life*. New York: HarperCollins, 2002.

Hogg, Ian V. *The Biography of General George S. Patton*. London: Hamlyn, 1982.

Jordan, Jonathan W. *Brothers, Rivals, Victors: Eisenhower, Patton, Bradley and the Partnership that Drove the Allied Conquest in Europe*. New York: New American Library, 2011.

Rickard, John Nelson. *Advance and Destroy: Patton as Commander in the Bulge*. Lexington, KY: University Press of Kentucky, 2011.

Yeide, Harry. *Fighting Patton: George S. Patton Jr. through the Eyes of His Enemies*. Minneapolis, MN: Zenith Books, 2011.

Pearl Harbor, Attack on (December 7, 1941)

Japanese military action against the U.S. naval base at Pearl Harbor, the Hawaiian Islands, which caused America to enter the war. By early 1941, tensions between Japan and the United States had reached breaking point. Japan's invasion of China beginning in 1937 and its occupation of French Indochina in 1940 and 1941 had led President Franklin D. Roosevelt to embargo scrap metal and oil and to freeze Japanese assets in the United States. The Japanese particularly resented the embargo on oil, characterizing it as "an unfriendly act." Japan had no oil of its own and had limited stockpiles. Without oil, the Japanese would have to withdraw from China. An army-dominated government in Tokyo now sought to take advantage of British, French, and Dutch weakness in Asia to push its own plans to secure hegemony and resources. Japan was determined to seize this opportunity, even if that meant war with the United States. The United States misread Tokyo's resolve, believing that it could force Japan to back down.

Both sides visualized the same scenario for war in the Pacific. The Japanese would seize U.S. and European possessions in the Far East, forcing the U.S. Navy to fight its way across the Pacific to relieve them. Somewhere in the Far East, a great naval battle would occur to decide Pacific hegemony. In March 1940, commander of the Combined Fleet

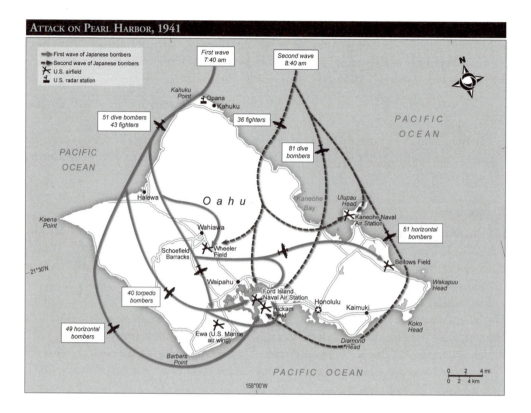

ATTACK ON PEARL HARBOR, 1941

First wave of Japanese bombers
Second wave of Japanese bombers
U.S. airfield
U.S. radar station

Admiral Yamamoto Isoroku scrapped the original plan—which called for using submarines and cruisers and destroyers with the Long Lance torpedo and savaging the U.S. battle fleet as it worked its way west—in favor of a preemptive strike against the U.S. fleet, which Roosevelt had shifted from San Diego to Pearl Harbor on the island of Oahu. Yamamoto believed that such an attack, destroying the U.S. carriers and battleships, would buy time for Japan to build its defensive ring. Yamamoto also misread American psychology when he believed that such an attack might demoralize the American people and force Washington to negotiate a settlement that would give Japan hegemony in the western Pacific. With both sides edging toward war, U.S. Pacific Fleet commander Admiral Husband E. Kimmel and army Lieutenant General Walter C. Short made their dispositions for the defense of Oahu. Both men requested additional resources from Washington, but the United States was only then rearming, and little additional assistance was forthcoming.

The Japanese, meanwhile, trained extensively for the Pearl Harbor attack. They fitted their torpedoes with fins so that they could be dropped from aircraft in the shallow water of Pearl Harbor, and they also planned to use large armor-piercing shells to be dropped as bombs from high-flying aircraft. No deck armor would be able to withstand them.

Following the expiration of a self-imposed deadline for securing an agreement with the United States, Tokyo ordered the attack to go forward. On November 16, 1941, Japanese submarines departed for Pearl Harbor, and 10 days later the First Air Fleet, commanded by Vice Admiral Nagumo Chūichi, sortied. This attack force was centered on six aircraft carriers: the *Akagi, Hiryu, Kaga, Shokaku, Soryu,* and *Zuikaku.* They carried 423 aircraft, 360 of which were to participate in the attack. Accompanying the carriers were 2 battleships, 3 cruisers, 9 destroyers, and 2 tankers.

Surprise was essential if the attack was to be successful. The Japanese maintained radio silence, and Washington knew only that the fleet had sailed. A "war warning" had been issued to military commanders in the Pacific, but few American leaders thought the Japanese would dare attack Pearl Harbor. Nagumo planned to approach from the northwest and move in as close as possible before launching his aircraft, and then recover them farther out, forcing any U.S. air reaction force to fly two long legs.

Nagumo ordered the planes to launch beginning at 6:00 a.m. at a point about 275 miles from Pearl Harbor. Two events should have made a difference to the Americans but did not. Before the launch, American picket ships off the harbor entrance detected one Japanese midget submarine. Then they sank another. There were five Japanese midget submarines in the operation. Carried to the area by mother submarines, they were to enter the harbor and then wait for the air attack. Probably only one succeeded.

At 7:50 a.m., the first wave of Japanese aircraft began its attack on the ships at Pearl Harbor and air stations at Ewa, Ford Island, Hickam, Kaneohe, and Wheeler. Most U.S.

In the aftermath of the Japanese attack on Pearl Harbor, December 7, 1941, rescuers pull a seaman from the water as the 31,800 USS *West Virginia* burns in the background. (Library of Congress)

planes were destroyed on the ground. They were easy targets as Short, to avoid sabotage by the many Japanese on the island, had ordered the planes bunched together and ammunition stored separately. The attack achieved great success. Over some 140 minutes, the Japanese sank 4 of the 8 U.S. battleships in the Pacific and badly damaged the rest. Seven smaller ships were also sunk, and 4 were badly damaged. A total of 188 U.S. aircraft were destroyed, and 63 were badly damaged. The attack also killed 2,280 people and wounded 1,109. The attack cost the Japanese only 29 aircraft and fewer than 100 aircrew dead.

The chief drawbacks in the attack from the Japanese point of view were that the U.S. carriers were away from Pearl Harbor on maneuvers and could not be struck. The Japanese failed to hit the oil tank storage areas, without which the fleet could not remain at Pearl Harbor. Nor had they targeted the dockyard repair facilities. Nagumo had won a smashing victory but was unwilling to risk his ships. The task force recovered its aircraft and departed.

Yamamoto's preemptive strike was a brilliant tactical success. The Japanese could carry out their plans in the South Pacific without fear of significant U.S. naval intervention. However, the Pearl Harbor attack also solidly united American opinion behind a war that ultimately led to Japan's defeat.

T. Jason Soderstrum and Spencer C. Tucker

See also

Japan, Air Force; Japan, Navy; Roosevelt, Franklin D.; United States, Navy; Yamamoto Isoroku

References

Clausen, Henry C. *Pearl Harbor: Final Judgment.* New York: Crown, 1992.

Gillon, Steven M. *Pearl Harbor: FDR Leads the Nation into War.* New York: Basic Books, 2011.

Miller, Edward S. *Bankrupting the Enemy: The U.S. Financial Siege of Japan before Pearl Harbor.* Annapolis, MD: Naval Institute Press, 2007.

Prange, Gordon W., with Donald M. Goldstein and Katherine V. Dillon. *At Dawn We Slept: The Untold Story of Pearl Harbor.* New York: Harper and Row, 1975.

Russell, Henry Dozier. *Pearl Harbor Story.* Macon, GA: Mercer University Press, 2001.

Satterfield, Archie. *The Day the War Began.* New York: Praeger, 1992.

Shirley, Craig. *December 1941: 31 Days that Changed America and Saved the World.* Nashville, TN: Thomas Nelson, 2011.

Toland, John. *Infamy: Pearl Harbor and Its Aftermath.* Garden City, NY: Doubleday, 1982.

Toll, Ian W. *Pacific Crucible: War at Sea in the Pacific, 1941–1942.* New York: Norton, 2011.

Weintraub, Stanley. *Long Day's Journey into War: December 7, 1941.* New York: Dutton, 1991.

Poland, Role in War

Poland was the first nation to fight the Germans in World War II. The Poles would fight the Germans longer than anyone else, and they fought them on all fronts. On September 1, 1939, 1.8 million German troops moved into Poland from three directions. The Germans had more than 2,600 tanks to only 180 for the Poles and more than 2,000

A German motorized detachment moves through the remains of a Polish town during the Blitzkrieg of September 1939, when German forces invaded Poland, beginning World War II. (Library of Congress)

combat aircraft for only 420 Polish planes. Furthermore, the Polish armed forces were only about one-third mobilized by the time the attack came. Britain and France had pressured Poland not to mobilize earlier to avoid presenting Germany with the provocation of aggressive behavior.

Britain and France declared war on Germany on September 3. Under the security guarantees that had been given to Poland, that nation was supposed to fight a defensive campaign for only two weeks, at which time the Allies would counterattack from the west. That Allied offensive never occurred. By September 14, the Germans had surrounded Warsaw. Three days later, Soviet forces invaded Poland from the east. The last Polish forces surrendered on October 5.

There are many myths about Germany's so-called blitzkrieg campaign against Poland. The Polish air force was not destroyed on the ground on the first day of the war, and Polish horse cavalry units never mounted wave after wave of suicidal attacks against the German panzers. Nor was the campaign a walkover. The Poles held out for twice as long as they were expected to. In six weeks of fighting, the Germans suffered 50,000 casualties and lost 697 aircraft and 993 armored vehicles.

Under a secret clause of the German–Soviet Non-Aggression Pact of August 1939, Germany and the Soviet Union participated in a fourth modern partition of Poland. The Soviets absorbed the eastern part of the country, including the great cultural centers of Lwow and Wilno. In the Soviet zone, 1.5 million Poles were deported to labor camps in Siberia. In a deliberate effort to exterminate the Polish intelligentsia and leadership classes,

Soviet authorities transported thousands of captured Polish officers, including many reservists from universities and industry, to the Katyń Forest of eastern Poland and other locations, where they were executed and buried in anonymous mass graves.

Of the territory they occupied, the Germans annexed Pomerania, Posnania, and Silesia in the west. What was left became the General Government, under the harsh rule of Hans Frank. The Germans than began a campaign to liquidate the Jews of Poland and grind down the rest of the Poles. The Polish Jews were first herded into ghettos while the Germans built more than 2,000 concentration camps in Poland, including the industrial-scale death centers at Auschwitz, Birkenau, and Treblinka.

Several Poles, including many in the armed forces, managed to escape from the country before the Germans and Soviets tightened their viselike grip on it. Poles who escaped established a government-in-exile in London, with Wfladysflaw Raczkiewicz as president and General Wfladysflaw Sikorski as prime minister. In Poland, meanwhile, the Polish Resistance established the Armia Krajowa (AK, Home Army), which became the largest underground movement in Europe with 400,000 fighters.

Outside of Poland, the Polish army, air force, and navy reorganized themselves in Britain and continued the war. The Britain-based Polish army eventually fielded a corps in Western Europe. After Germany attacked the Soviet Union in June 1941, the Soviets released several thousand Polish prisoners of war to establish another corps under General Wfladysflaw Anders. The Polish II Corps was allowed to leave the Soviet Union by way of Persia and Egypt, and it eventually fought with distinction in North Africa and Italy.

Prior to the start of the war, Polish intelligence had managed to duplicate a German Enigma cipher machine. They turned over copies to both the French and British in July 1939, which was the starting point of the Allies' spectacular success with radio-derived communications intelligence. Later in the war, the intelligence service of the AK recovered a German V-2 rocket that had crashed in the Bug River after a test flight and sent the key components to London.

In 1943, the Soviets formed their own division of Polish troops to fight on the Eastern Front. That unit would eventually grow to field-army strength. But when the Germans discovered, later that year, the bodies of the Polish officers executed at the Katyń Forest and broadcast this news to the world, it opened a rift in Polish–Soviet relations that remained until the end of the Cold War.

As the Red Army slowly pushed the Germans from the Soviet Union and back to the west, the USSR's postwar intentions for Eastern Europe began to unfold. At the Allied Tehran Conference, British and U.S. leaders agreed to Soviet leader Josef Stalin's demands that the Soviet Union be allowed to keep the Polish territory taken in September 1939—in effect, the old Curzon Line established by the Allied governments in the peace settlement following World War I. After the war, Poland was partly compensated for its territorial losses in the east with a strip of German land in the west to the line of the Oder and Neisse Rivers. In July 1944, after the city of Lublin was liberated, the Soviets established their own Polish government, a direct rival to the one in London, which was now led by Stanislaw Mikoflajczyk.

By August 1, 1944, the Red Army reached the right bank of the Vistula River opposite Warsaw. Armia Krajowa units in the city rose up against the Germans, anticipating Soviet support against the common enemy. The Soviets did nothing. Not only did they not help the AK, they refused landing rights on Soviet-controlled airfields for any Allied aircraft that might attempt aerial supply missions. The Poles fought on alone, street by street and house by house for 63 days, and in the end the Wehrmacht and the Waffen-Schutzstaffel (Waffen-SS) destroyed virtually the entire city. When the Germans finally withdrew from what was left of Warsaw, the Soviets moved across the river. The destruction of Warsaw eliminated the remaining political and military institutions in Poland still loyal to the London government and paved the way for a complete Soviet takeover. The final blows to a free Poland were delivered by the victorious Allies at the Yalta Conference. World War II ended, but Poland remained under the Soviet yoke until the very end of the Cold War more than 40 years later.

Poland suffered as heavily as any nation in the war, losing an estimated 38 percent of its national assets. The country lost 22 percent of its population—some 500,000 military personnel and 6 million civilians. Roughly half the Poles who died between 1939 and 1945 were Jews. Most of the approximately 5.4 million victims died in concentration camps and ghettos or by starvation, epidemic, or other causes resulting from the brutal occupation. One million of the survivors were war orphans, and another half million were invalids.

David T. Zabecki

See also

Casualties; Collaboration; Germany, Air Force; Germany, Army; Holocaust, The; Prisoners of War (POWs); Resistance; Signals Intelligence; Soviet Union, Air Force; Soviet Union, Army; Stalin, Josef; Yalta Conference

References

Coutouvidis, John, and Jaime Reynolds. *Poland, 1939–1947.* New York: Holmes and Meier, 1986.

Davies, Norman. *Rising '44: The Battle for Warsaw.* New York: Viking, 2004.

Fritz, Stephen G. *Ostkrieg: Hitler's War of Extermination in the East.* Lexington, KY: University Press of Kentucky, 2011.

Koskodan, Kenneth K. *No Greater Ally: The Untold Story of Poland's Forces in World War II.* Oxford: Osprey Publishing, 2009.

Lane, A. T. *Victims of Stalin and Hitler: The Exodus of Poles and Balts to Britain.* New York: Palgrave Macmillan, 2004.

Lukas, Richard C. *Forgotten Holocaust: The Poles under German Occupation, 1939–1944.* Lexington, KY: University Press of Kentucky, 1986.

Paul, Allen. *Katyń: Stalin's Massacre and the Triumph of Truth.* DeKalb, IL: Northern Illinois University Press, 2010.

Prazmowska, Anita J. *Britain and Poland 1939–1943: The Betrayed Ally.* New York: Cambridge University Press, 1995.

Rossino, Alexander B. *Hitler Strikes Poland: Blitzkrieg, Ideology, and Atrocity.* Lawrence, KS: University Press of Kansas, 2003.

Snyder, Timothy. *Bloodlands: Europe between Hitler and Stalin.* New York: Basic Books, 2010.

Terry, Sarah Meiklejohn. *Poland's Place in Europe: General Sikorski and the Origin of the Oder-Neisse Line, 1939–1943.* Princeton, NJ: Princeton University Press, 1992.

Prisoners of War (POWs)

In 1929, the Geneva Convention Relative to the Treatment of Prisoners of War (POWs) replaced the Hague Convention of 1907 regarding protection of POWs. The Hague Convention had dealt primarily with the means of war (for example, it prohibited the use of exploding bullets), whereas the Geneva Convention dealt exclusively with the protection of victims of war. It held that POWs should be considered on a par with the detaining power's garrison troops as far as rations, living space, clothing, and access to medical care were concerned. It also addressed such issues as permissible work and punishment and access to letters and packages. Forty powers signed the convention, but the Soviet Union did not, meaning that prisoners taken by its forces were not subject to Geneva Convention protection. Although the Japanese delegates at Geneva signed the POWs convention, the Tokyo government never ratified it. Its military leaders assumed no Japanese would be taken prisoner and that the convention would thus be applied unilaterally. Cultural attitudes also played an important role, and authorized punishments for POWs were much milder than those the Japanese meted out to their own soldiers. Although in 1942 the Japanese government pledged to live up to the spirit of the convention, its treatment of Allied POWs during the war clearly ran counter to its assurance.

EUROPE, EASTERN FRONT

On September 1, 1939, German forces invaded Poland; two days later Britain and France declared war on Germany, igniting World War II. Two weeks later, Soviet forces invaded eastern Poland in accordance with the secret provisions of the August 1939 German–Soviet Non-Aggression Pact. In 1940, Soviet authorities executed perhaps 15,000 Polish officers in the Katyń Forest of eastern Poland. Prisoners taken by the Germans were sent to slave-labor camps. The Poles thus did not benefit from the Geneva Convention.

In June 1941, German forces invaded the Soviet Union. In response to inquiries by the U.S. government, Moscow had stated that the Soviet Union would observe the Hague Convention of 1907 regarding land warfare, the Geneva Protocol of 1925 regarding chemical and bacteriological warfare, and the Geneva Convention of 1929 regarding care for the wounded and sick of warring armies. However, the Soviets said they would observe the agreements on POWs only as "they were observed by the Germans."

The German government was as obstinate on the issue as the Soviets, and the cost was ultimately very high for the POWs captured in the fighting. Both German and Soviet POWs suffered conditions that were approached only by treatment accorded to prisoners of the Japanese. Of some 5.7 million Soviet soldiers taken prisoner by the Germans, at least 3.3 million died in captivity, a mortality rate of 57 percent. This compares with a mortality rate of only 3.5 to 5.1 percent for British and American POWs in German hands.

Many Soviet prisoners taken early in the fighting were simply starved to death. According to Adolf Hitler's notorious Commissar Order, political officers were to be shot on capture. Jewish soldiers taken prisoner were handed over to the Schutzstaffel (SS) to be executed. Conditions were horrendous for the others. The Germans marched the prisoners long distances to the rear, and there were no prepared lodging or sanitary facilities and little food for them when they reached the camp locations. As a result, POWs died by the hundreds of thousands. The leaders of the Reich regarded the prisoners as subhuman and treated them accordingly. Of 3.2 million Soviet soldiers taken prisoner by December 1941, 2 million were dead by February 1942.

As the German advance came to a halt and it became impossible to demobilize German soldiers, the Reich's leaders sought to make more effective use of the Soviet POWs by putting them to work in difficult conditions in road building, mining, and agriculture. Not until mid-1944, however, did food rations for Soviet POWs approach those of other Allied POWs in German captivity. So difficult was it for Soviet POWs that at least a quarter million volunteered to serve as auxiliaries to the German army, working as cooks, drivers, and the like, in an effort to simply stay alive. Tens of thousands of others also agreed to serve in a German-sponsored Russian Liberation Army led by former Soviet Lieutenant General Andrei A. Vlasov. Hitler, however, refused it any combat role and it became simply a means to encourage desertions.

The plight of Soviet POWs in German hands did not end with the defeat of Germany. Soviet leader Josef Stalin's infamous Order 270 of August 1941 had branded as traitors all Red Army personnel who allowed themselves to be taken prisoner, regardless of circumstances. It also ordered rations cut off to their families. Of some 1.8 million Soviet POWs repatriated at the end of the war, at least 150,000 were sentenced to long prison terms of forced labor for having "aided the enemy."

On the other side, about a third of the nearly 3 million German and Austrian soldiers taken by the Soviets in the war died in captivity. Of some 91,000 Germans taken prisoner in the Battle of Stalingrad, fewer than 5,000 survived Soviet captivity. Death rates were comparable for the 2 million Axis soldiers taken prisoner by the Soviets.

The only difference in German and Soviet treatment of POWs was that, for the Germans, it was systematic government policy to work the prisoners to death, whereas POWs in Soviet hands fell victim to the general inefficiency and indifference of the Soviet POW camp system (GUPVI), lack of resources in a country ravaged by war, and individual acts of reprisal. Rising numbers of German POWs after 1942 simply overwhelmed available Soviet means to care for them. The Soviet Union did not begin major repatriation of its POWs until 1947, and the last of them were not released until 1956.

WESTERN EUROPE

During World War II in Europe and North Africa, the Axis powers captured some 8.5 to 9 million enemy soldiers, of whom 6 million—the vast majority—were Soviets. In turn, the Allies took some 8.25 million Axis soldiers captive, 3.4 million of whom surrendered with the end of hostilities on the Western Front.

Few problems were reported for prisoners held by the Italian government. Experiences for POWs held by the Germans varied according to their citizenship. Treatment was decidedly better for western Europeans and North Americans than for those from eastern or southern Europe. The Germans did not expend scarce resources on the prisoners, however. Thus, in consequence of the high number of parcels sent to western Allied POWs, the German government decided to cut food rations to U.S. and British Commonwealth POWs by one-third, forcing these Allied governments to subsidize German Geneva Convention obligations. The

Germans did, however, employ many of their French and Belgian POWs in labor activities (such as the armaments industry) that directly benefited the German war effort.

The Germans organized their POW camps quite methodically. Internally, the camps were run by the prisoners. Generally there was an SAO—Senior Allied Officer or Senior American Officer, depending on the mix of prisoners. Officers were segregated from enlisted men. *Stalags* were camps that held enlisted personnel as well as noncommissioned officers. *Oflags* were camps with only officers and some noncommissioned officers. In stalags, there was generally a "man of confidence" who was usually elected by his fellow POWs, although on occasion he was appointed by the Germans.

Camps usually contained more than one compound, and prisoners were segregated among the compounds by uniform, not by claimed citizenship. Hence, U.S. personnel who flew with the RAF and were captured in RAF uniform were considered to be British and housed with British flyers. Compounds held French, Russian, British, Commonwealth, and various other nationalities. Some camps held only one nationality; some held many different nationalities.

There were also POW camps located in areas that held concentration camps. Auschwitz, which is known for being an extermination center, was actually a complex of camps comprising more than just the extermination center. French, Soviet, and other nationalities of POWs were held there. Two exceptions to the generally satisfactory German treatment of western POWs came in Hitler's Commando Order of October 1942, which allowed the killing out-of-hand of Allied commandoes, and Berga, a Buchenwald subcamp that held 352 U.S. "Jewish" POWs. Of that number, only 70 were actually Jewish, but the others were chosen by the Germans because they "appeared" Jewish. Prisoners were regularly beaten and starved, and several were murdered.

There have been unsubstantiated charges in recent years of British and U.S. mistreatment of German POWs in the months immediately following the end of the war in Europe. There is, however, no proof of this nor of any widespread mistreatment of Axis POWs by British and U.S. authorities during the war itself.

FAR EAST

Japanese cultural attitudes played an overwhelming role in Japanese treatment of its POWs. The Japanese believed that soldiers should die in battle rather than surrender and that those who allowed themselves to be taken prisoner had dishonored themselves. Japanese treatment of POWs was atrocious. Prisoners were subject to torture, starvation, beatings, and denial of medical care. Most were required to perform slave labor, from building railroads to working in coal mines and factories, all of which were forbidden by the Geneva Convention. Mistreatment was rampant, as were disease and starvation, not only among military prisoners but with civilian internees. Nor would the Japanese allow humanitarian aid to reach the prisoners.

The generally accepted figure for Allied POWs in Japanese hands is 320,000: 140,000 Europeans and North Americans and 180,000 Chinese, Filipino, Indian, and other Asian troops. Most of Japan's prisoners were taken in the Japanese successes of late 1941 and early 1942, especially in the Netherlands East Indies. Although the Japanese soon released many of the nonwhite prisoners, they held their white captives until the surrender in 1945.

The Japanese captured some 25,600 U.S. prisoners. Of these, 8,288 died, a rate of 35.6 percent. This was appreciably higher than the rate for all prisoners who died in Japanese hands: 37,800 or 26.9 percent. Part of this disparity was the result of the many American and Filipino POWs who died in the Bataan Death March. Prisoners of the Japanese received no medical care and little food, and they were seldom allowed to contact their families. Many of the prisoners were transferred from the Philippines and other places to Japan or Manchuria to prison camps. Sent by ship, the prisoners were entombed below decks with little or no access to fresh air or water. Many hundreds of men died of the conditions in these "Hell Ships," but the exact total is unknown. Several of the ships, unmarked by the Japanese as transporting POWs, were sunk by Allied planes or submarines. In addition, many POWs who ended up in Manchuria were subjected to the horrors of biological warfare and vivisection experiments carried out by the infamous Japanese Unit 731.

Japanese military codes forbade surrender, and in consequence, the western Allies took very few Japanese prisoners. On Iwo Jima, U.S. Marines took fewer than 300 prisoners from the 21,000-man Japanese garrison, and only about 7,400 of nearly 115,000 Japanese soldiers on Okinawa surrendered. It is also true that once Allied soldiers learned of the barbaric treatment accorded by the Japanese to their prisoners, there was a tendency to decline to take prisoners, although this was never official policy.

Some 633,000 Japanese personnel were taken prisoner in Southeast Asia, and most of them surrendered to the British at the end of the war. Many of these were held well after the war and worked as laborers without pay. Only in October 1947 were Japanese released from Singapore. Some Japanese POWs were also rearmed and forced to serve with Dutch forces in the Netherlands East Indies in violation of international law, and nearly 1,000 died.

It is unclear how many Japanese were taken prisoner by the Soviet Union, which entered the war in the Pacific on August 9, 1945. The Soviets claimed to have captured 594,000 Japanese and claimed that upward of 71,000 of these were immediately freed. Japanese scholars, however, insist that the number was much higher. Sent to Siberia, the Japanese worked there for several years before they were released. Because of the dishonor associated with being captured, few Japanese ex-POWs have left memoirs of their experiences. The record of Americans and Europeans held by the Japanese is, however, well documented.

NORTH AMERICA

When the United States entered World War II, little thought had been given to the establishment of POW facilities. In March 1942, President Franklin D. Roosevelt authorized the evacuation of Japanese Americans from "military areas," especially on the West Coast of the United States. Ultimately some 120,000 Japanese Americans were affected. Although they were not called prisoners of war, they were interned in camps in Wyoming, California, Colorado, Arizona, Idaho, and Arkansas.

Following the Axis defeat in North Africa, large numbers of German and Italian POWs were brought to camps in the United States. Ultimately, some 425,000 Axis prisoners of war were held in the United States. By the end of the war, the United States had established 141 permanent base camps and 319 branch camps, each holding an average of about 2,500 prisoners. Given the labor shortage in the United States because of the demands of the war, many of the POWs went to work, but they were paid for their labor according to rank.

Officers were not required to work, although several did accept supervisory positions. Contractors who hired the POWs paid the U.S. government some $22 million for their services, so that the program was nearly self-sufficient. By the end of the war, of 370,000 POWs in the United States, nearly 200,000 were employed in nonmilitary jobs, most of them in agriculture. Conditions in the U.S. camps were generally excellent. The major problem came from die-hard Nazi fellow prisoners, who had to be segregated in special camps.

Following the war, several thousand U.S.-held POWs were turned over to France and Britain to work in mines and help clear bombed roads and cities. Most of these POWs were repatriated to Germany in late 1947 and early 1948, embittered over their postwar treatment.

Spencer C. Tucker and Patricia Wadley

See also

Casualties; Collaboration; Eastern Front; Hitler, Adolf; Holocaust, The; Japan, Army; Roosevelt, Franklin D.

References

Beattie, Edward J., Jr. *Diary of a Kriegie.* New York: Thomas Y. Crowell, 1946.

Daws, Gavin. *Prisoners of the Japanese: POWs of World War II in the Pacific.* New York: William Morrow, 1994.

Durand, Arthur A. *Stalag Luft III: The Secret Story.* Baton Rouge, LA: Louisiana State University Press, 1988.

Foy, David A. *For You the War Is Over: American Prisoners of War in Nazi Germany.* New York: Stein and Day, 1984.

Fritz, Stephen G. *Ostkrieg: Hitler's War of Extermination in the East.* Lexington, KY: University Press of Kentucky, 2011.

Gillies, Midge. *The Barbed Wire University: The Real Lives of Prisoners of War in the Second World War.* London: Aurum Press, 2012.

Hirschfeld, Gerhard, ed. *The Politics of Genocide: Jewish and Soviet Prisoners of War in Nazi Germany.* Boston, MA: Allen and Unwin, 1986.

Hubbard, Preston John. *Apocalypse Undone: My Survival of Japanese Imprisonment during World War II.* Nashville, TN: Vanderbilt University Press, 1990.

Keefer, Louis E. *Italian Prisoners of War in America, 1942–1946: Captives or Allies?* Westport, CT: Greenwood Press, 1992.

Knox, Donald. *Death March: The Survivors of Bataan.* New York: Harcourt Brace Jovanovich, 1981.

Kochan, Miriam. *Prisoners of England.* London: Macmillan Press, 1980.

Krammer, Arnold. *Nazi Prisoners of War in America.* New York: Stein and Day, 1979.

MacKenzie, S. P. "The Treatment of Prisoners of War in World War II." *Journal of Modern History* 66 (1994): 487–520.

Snyder, Timothy. *Bloodlands: Europe between Hitler and Stalin.* New York: Basic Books, 2010.

Thompson, Kyle. *A Thousand Cups of Rice: Surviving the Death Railway.* Austin, TX: Easkin Press, 1994.

Vance, Jonathan F., ed. *Encyclopedia of Prisoners of War and Internment.* Santa Barbara, CA: ABC-CLIO, 2000.

Resistance

Defined here as the act of opposing a foreign occupying power, resistance has existed since the beginning of warfare and conquest. There have always been citizens of an occupied nation who refused to accept the military verdict and attempted to continue the fight against the victor, sometimes with success. During World War II, there was some degree of resistance in every Axis-occupied country, not only to the military conquest but also to Axis ideology. The degree varied sharply, depending on the nation and circumstances.

The word *resistance*, in the sense of actions taken, encompasses everything from noncooperation to civil disobedience, conducting intelligence activities, committing sabotage and assassinations, running escape lines, and even carrying out hit-and-run raids against small enemy units. *Resistance* can also mean an organization or a particular movement, such as the maquis in France. Resistance may be undertaken by individuals or by groups of people organized to work clandestinely against an oppressor. To the occupied people, those who engage in such activities are resisters and are often held up as heroes. To the occupying power, they are bandits, criminals, and even terrorists.

To exacerbate the confusion, most nations have created myths concerning their resistance activities. As a consequence, we will never know, even approximately, the numbers of people actually involved in such activities. After the war, for quite understandable reasons, the governments of many countries, including France, sought to magnify the numbers of citizens involved in resistance work and their contribution to victory.

Resistance movements during World War II were sharply fragmented along national lines, and there were even bitter rivalries within groups of resisters in individual nations that often led to bloodshed. These rivalries were the result of deep ideological and religious differences, long-standing ethnic feuds, fiefdoms, and petty jealousies among the leaders themselves. In Czechoslovakia, Defense of the Nation and the Falcon Organization vied with one another. In the Netherlands, various religious and political groups emerged, but they did not work together until September 1944. In France, resisters were markedly divided at first: not until May 1943 was the National Council of the Resistance (CNR) formed, uniting all major French resistance groups. In Greece, infighting among the National Popular Liberation Army (ELAS), the National Republican Greek League (EDES), and the Communist National Liberation Front (EAM) led to a civil war after World War II had ended. In Albania, royalist Zogists fought a prorepublican group of resisters.

The Yugoslavia Resistance was polarized between the royalist Chetniks under the leadership of Dragoljub "Draza" Mikahlović and Communist Partisans led by Josip Broz (better known as Tito). The Chetniks were promonarchy and conservative, whereas the Partisans were antimonarchy and sought a postwar communist state. The Chetniks were also reluctant to embark on the types of operations that would bring reprisals against the civilian population, such as direct attacks on German troops. The Partisans felt no such compunction. Inside the Soviet Union, many resisters sought not only freedom from the Germans but also freedom from Soviet control as well.

Often, Allied agents who parachuted into an occupied state had difficulty sorting out all these rivalries and making the appropriate determinations as to where Allied financial and military assistance should be directed. Throughout the occupied countries, the communist resistance groups, although they were late to take the field (until the German invasion of the Soviet Union in June 1941, Josef Stalin advocated close ties with Nazi Germany), tended to be highly effective because they were better trained and organized; with strong ideological motivation, they had no reservations about the use of force.

Geography impacted resistance activities and determined the levels of action and participation. Mountainous, forested, or swampy terrain favored the guerrilla. It was thus easier to conduct resistance activities in Norway, Yugoslavia, Albania, and Greece, all countries with many hills, forests, and caves. In Asia, jungles often worked to the advantage of the resistance forces as well.

Resistance took many forms and was both passive and active. Passive resistance was generally nonconfrontational and a method of coping and asserting one's patriotism. Passive resistance involved many people in occupied Europe and in Asia. It encompassed a wide range of activities and might include nothing more than reading an illegal newspaper, selling or buying goods on the black market, or not handing in materials decreed necessary for the Axis war machine. It might also mean secretly listening to church sermons, praying for a royal family or leaders in exile, listening to broadcasts from the British Broadcasting Corporation (BBC), leaving a public place when a German entered it, or other such actions. At the highest levels, passive resistance might include balking at anti-Jewish legislation or not handing over individuals sought by the occupier and seeking to evade the occupying power's exactions.

Active resistance included intelligence gathering; acting as couriers or radio operators; disseminating information or Allied propaganda, through such means as underground newspapers; printing false identification papers and ration cards; rescuing downed Allied pilots and assisting them to neutral nations; committing acts of sabotage; freeing prisoners; hiding Jews; and even carrying out assassinations of individuals and conducting military actions against small numbers of occupying troops. Active resistance was far more dangerous and often life-threatening, both to the individual involved and to his or her family. For that reason, those who engaged in it were always a minority. Considerable courage as well as clairvoyance were required for a Frenchman to see, in 1940, that Germany might indeed lose the war, let alone for him to be willing to risk all toward that end.

The British Special Operations Executive (SOE), established by Prime Minister Winston Churchill in 1940, helped finance and train agents from the nations of Axis-occupied countries to carry out active resistance activities. Its U.S. counterpart, the Office of Strategic Services (OSS), conducted similar activities. The SOE and OSS enjoyed some successes, but they also experienced a number of failures leading to the deaths of agents. The most dramatic failure resulted from ENGLANDSPIEL, an elaborate German counterintelligence operation in the Netherlands that ended in the deaths of many Allied agents. Resisters had to exercise constant vigilance—and not only against the occupying forces. The governments of their own countries, working with the occupiers, often sent out forces (such as the Milice in France) to hunt them down.

One notable resistance success was the February 1943 strike executed by British-trained Norwegian resisters against the hydroelectric plant at Vermork, Norway. This raid and the subsequent sinking of a ferry delayed German production of the heavy water essential for the production of an atomic bomb.

The Poles, who suffered terribly at the hands of their German and Soviet occupiers during the war, immediately established active resistance operations. They provided immensely useful intelligence on the German development of V weapons, and they created the secret Home Army. Jews in the Warsaw ghetto employed active resistance as well, rising up against the Germans and providing a heroic example of courage against impossible odds.

The French maquis also fought the Germans. Resistance activities mounted from the Vercors Plateau in the Alps of eastern France provoked a strong reaction in the form of 20,000 German troops who, in June 1944, decimated the Vercors maquis and mounted savage reprisals against the civilian population. The Germans carried out ferocious reprisals elsewhere as well. Often, they executed innocent civilian villagers or hostages at the rate of 20 or more for each of their own slain. Reprisals were especially fierce after British-trained Czech commandos assassinated the Reich protector of Bohemia and Moravia, Reinhard Heydrich. His death led the Germans to kill most of the inhabitants of Lidice and level the town. Communities in other parts of Europe endured a similar fate.

Resistance activities sharply increased as the Axis powers suffered military reversals, especially when it became clear that they would lose the war. Resisters had to be constantly on guard and regularly change their modus operandi. They also had to contend with double agents, of whom there were a substantial number. French Resistance leader Jean Moulin, the head of the National Resistance Council (CNR), for example, was betrayed to the Gestapo by an informant.

The effectiveness of resistance activities during the war is difficult to gauge. Such activities may not have greatly hastened the end of the war, but they did affect events in that the occupiers were forced to divert many troops from the fighting fronts to occupation duties and to hunting down the resistance forces. Resistance in all its forms was a vindication of national identity and pride and a statement for freedom. Unfortunately for resistance leaders in many countries, their bright and idealistic hopes that the war would bring new political structures were, for the most part, left unfulfilled. In most nations, these individuals were thanked politely and then shown the door, as the old elites soon reestablished themselves in power.

Some resistance groups, of course, fought not only against the Axis powers but also against colonial forces. Thus, in Vietnam, the Vietminh led by Ho Chi Minh fought both the Japanese and the French. As a consequence, the resistance continued in a number of countries after World War II ended, utilizing the methods and weapons supplied to fight the Japanese. Such was the case in Vietnam, in the Philippines, and even in the Soviet Union.

Annette Richardson and Spencer C. Tucker

See also

Balkans Theater; China, Role in War; Churchill, Sir Winston Leonard Spencer; Collaboration; de Gaulle, Charles; Eastern Front; France, Role in War; Greece, Role in War; Poland, Role in War

References

Bennett, Rab. *Under the Shadow of the Swastika: The Moral Dilemma of Resistance and Collaboration in Hitler's Europe.* New York: New York University Press, 1999.

Davies, Peter. *France and the Second World War: Occupation, Collaboration, and Resistance.* New York: Routledge, 2000.

Foot, Michael D. *SOE in France: An Account of the Work of the British Special Operations Executive in France, 1940–1944.* London: Her Majesty's Stationery Office, 1966.

Fritz, Stephen G. *Ostkrieg: Hitler's War of Extermination in the East.* Lexington, KY: University Press of Kentucky, 2011.

Gluckstein, Donny. *A People's History of the Second World War: Resistance Versus Empire.* London: Pluto Press, 2012.

Haestrup, Jorgen. *European Resistance Movements, 1939–1945: A Complete History.* Westport, CT: Praeger, 1981.

Levine, Allan. *Fugitives of the Forest: The Heroic Story of Jewish Resistance and Survival during the Second World War.* Guilford, CT: Lyons Press, 2008.

Lucas, Peter. *The OSS in World War II Albania: Covert Operations and Collaboration with Communist Partisans.* Jefferson, SC: McFarland, 2007.

Mazower, Mark. *Hitler's Empire: How the Nazis Ruled Europe.* New York: Penguin, 2008.

Mazower, Mark. *Inside Hitler's Greece: The Experience of Occupation, 1941–1944.* New Haven, CT: Yale University Press, 1993.

Michel, Henri. *The Shadow War: Resistance in Europe, 1939–1945.* London: Andre Deutsch, 1972.

Mountfield, David. *The Partisans.* London: Hamlin Publishing Group, 1979.

Müller, Rolf-Dieter, and Gerd R. Ueberschär. *Hitler's War in the East, 1941–1945: A Critical Assessment.* Providence, RI: Berghahn Books, 1997.

Schoenbrun, David. *Soldiers of the Night: The Story of the French Resistance.* New York: E. P. Dutton, 1980.

Semelin, Jacques. *Unarmed against Hitler: Civilian Resistance in Europe, 1939–1943.* Translated by Suzan Husserl-Kapit. Westport, CT: Praeger, 1993.

Shepherd, Ben, and Juliet Pattinson, eds. *War in a Twilight World: Partisan and Anti-Partisan Warfare in Eastern Europe, 1939–45.* New York: Palgrave Macmillan, 2010.

Slepyan, Kenneth. *Stalin's Guerrillas: Soviet Partisans in World War II.* Lawrence, KS: University Press of Kansas, 2006.

Snow, Philip. *The Fall of Hong Kong: Britain, China, and the Japanese Occupation.* New Haven, CT: Yale University Press, 2003.

Snyder, Timothy. *Bloodlands: Europe between Hitler and Stalin.* New York: Basic Books, 2010.

Tomasevich, Jozo. *War and Revolution in Yugoslavia, 1941–1945: Occupation and Collaboration.* Stanford, CA: Stanford University Press, 2002.

Rommel, Erwin Johannes Eugen (1891–1944)

Erwin Johannes Eugen Rommel was a German army general and commander of the Afrika Korps (Africa Corps). Born in Heidenheim, Württemberg, Germany, on November 15, 1891, Rommel joined the German army in 1910 with the 124th (6th Württemberg) Infantry Regiment as an officer cadet. He then attended the officers' training school at Danzig (present-day Gdansk, Poland) and was commissioned in January 1912.

During World War I, Rommel was wounded while fighting in France in September 1914. On his recovery, he won renown in service on the Italian and Romanian fronts. He fought at Mount Cosna and at Caporetto. In the latter battle, he and his men took 9,000 Italian troops prisoner and captured 81 guns. Promoted to captain, he was also awarded the Pour le Mérite.

Rommel remained in the Reichswehr after the war and took charge of security at Friedrichshaven in 1919. In January 1921, he was posted to Stuttgart, where he commanded an infantry regiment, and then he was assigned to Dresden in 1929, where he was

Charismatic German field marshal Erwin Rommel, who won renown as the legendary "Desert Fox," was one of the most masterful tacticians of World War II, admired even by his enemies. Unlike German forces on the Eastern front, troops under Rommel's command in Western Europe and North Africa did not have a record of major atrocities against civilians and prisoners of war. Their restraint further burnished Rommel's reputation as a genuinely admirable German war hero. (Library of Congress)

an instructor at the Infantry School until 1933. There, he wrote *Infantry Attacks*, a textbook on infantry tactics. In 1935, Rommel received command of a battalion of the 17th Infantry Regiment. He taught briefly at the War Academy (in 1938) and then had charge of Adolf Hitler's army security detachment.

In 1940, Rommel assumed command of the 7th Panzer Division and led it in spectacular fashion in the invasion of France. Promoted to Generalleutnant (U.S. equiv. major general) in February 1941, he received command of German forces in Libya (the Afrika Korps). An aggressive, bold commander who led from the front, he employed daring attacks and was tenacious in battle. His skill as a field commander earned him the sobriquet "Desert Fox." Promoted to General der Panzertruppen (U.S. equiv. lieutenant general) in July 1941 and colonel general in January 1942, he was elevated to field marshal in June 1942.

Denied sufficient resources to achieve victory, Rommel was defeated in the October 1942 Battle of El Alamein, but he conducted a skillful withdrawal west into Tunisia. After returning to Germany for reasons of health and recuperation, he was assigned as commander of Army Group B with responsibility for northern Italy. In November 1943, he became inspector general of coastal defense in France and worked to strengthen the so-called Atlantic Wall.

On January 1, 1944, Rommel became head of Army Group B in France, subordinated to the German commander in chief, West Field Marshal Rudolf Gerd von Rundstedt. Based on his experiences in North Africa, Rommel believed that if an Allied invasion was to be stopped, it would have to be at the beaches. Rundstedt and Hitler, however, envisioned a cordon on the shoreline and large, mobile German forces inland that would destroy the Allies once they landed. Rommel correctly believed that Allied air and naval supremacy would render that outcome impossible.

Rommel did what he could to improve the coastal defense against an Allied invasion. When the invasion occurred, he was in Germany trying to secure two more panzer divisions and additional artillery. In meetings with Hitler, he went so far as to ask the German dictator why he thought the war could still be won. On July 17, 1944, he was badly wounded in an air attack by three Royal Air Force (RAF) fighters that caught his staff car on the road.

Rommel, not a fanatic Nazi, grew despondent over Hitler's estrangement from reality but failed in his efforts to convince the German leader that the war was lost. When he was approached about participating in a plot to overthrow the Führer, he refused to join in, but he also failed to inform the authorities. In the aftermath of the unsuccessful attempt on Hitler's life, he was given the choice of a trial for treason or suicide. He chose the latter. Rommel died on October 14, 1944, near Ulm, and was accorded a full military funeral.

Annette Richardson

See also

Germany, Army; Hitler, Adolf; Montgomery, Sir Bernard Law; North Africa Campaign; Signals Intelligence; Western European Theater of Operations

References

Battistelli, Pier. *Erwin Rommel*. Oxford: Osprey Publishing, 2010.

Douglas-Home, Charles. *Rommel*. New York: Saturday Review Press, 1973.

Fraser, David. *Knight's Cross: A Life of Field Marshal Erwin Rommel.* New York: Harper Collins, 1994.

Heckmann, Wolf. *Rommel's War in Africa.* Translated by Stephen Seago. Garden City, NY: Doubleday, 1981.

Lemay, Benoît. *Rommel: Germany's Flawed Champion.* Haverford, PA: Casemate Publishers, 2012.

Lewin, Ronald. *Rommel as Military Commander.* London: Batsford, 1968.

Messenger, Charles. *Rommel: Leadership Lessons from the Desert Fox.* New York: Palgrave Macmillan, 2009.

Mitcham, Samuel W., Jr. *Rommel's Desert War: The Life and Death of the Afrika Korps.* Mechanicsburg, PA: Stackpole Books, 2008.

Rutherford, Ward. *The Biography of Field Marshal Erwin Rommel.* London: Hamlyn, 1981.

Young, Desmond. *Rommel.* London: Collins, 1967.

Roosevelt, Franklin D. (1882–1945)

Franklin Delano Roosevelt, a Democratic U.S. politician, was president from 1933 to 1945. Born on January 30, 1882, at his family's Hyde Park estate in Dutchess County, New York, Roosevelt was educated at home until age 14. He then attended Groton Preparatory School, Harvard University, and Columbia University Law School. In 1905, Roosevelt married his distant cousin Eleanor Roosevelt, President Theodore Roosevelt's niece.

After passing the bar examination, Roosevelt joined the law firm of Carter, Ledyard and Milburn. In 1910, he won a seat in the New York Senate, where he served two terms and was a strong advocate of progressive reform. In 1913, he was appointed assistant secretary of the navy, and he worked diligently and effectively in that post. A strong advocate of intervention of the Allied side and military preparedness, he helped prepare the navy for its role in World War I.

In 1920, Roosevelt ran unsuccessfully as the vice presidential candidate of the Democratic Party on the ticket headed by James M. Cox. During the campaign, he advocated U.S. entry into the League of Nations. In 1921, Roosevelt was stricken with polio. Although his suffering was acute and left him permanently disabled, he remained intensely interested in politics. In 1924, he attended the Democratic Convention and nominated Alfred E. Smith, governor of New York, for president. Four years later, Roosevelt was elected governor of New York. His efforts in seeking relief for suffering New Yorkers following the stock market crash in 1929 led to his reelection in 1930.

In November 1932, Roosevelt was elected president of the United States on the Democratic ticket, triumphing over incumbent President Herbert Hoover. He promised the American people a "New Deal," and he told Americans that "the only thing we have to fear is fear itself." He launched an extensive legislative program designed to alleviate suffering, reform the economy, and bring about recovery. The American people welcomed Roosevelt's programs, and in 1936, they overwhelmingly reelected him to office.

With the beginning of World War II in Europe in September 1939, Roosevelt increasingly turned his attention to foreign affairs and military preparedness. On September 8,

From the time World War II began in Europe in September 1939, Franklin D. Roosevelt, president of the United States from 1932 to 1945, positioned his country firmly in the Allied camp. The United States formally entered the war against Germany, Italy, and Japan in December 1941, after the Japanese attack on Pearl Harbor. The United States' military and economic strength proved crucial in bringing an Allied victory, as American industrial and agricultural production met the wartime needs of both the United States and its allies. Roosevelt died of a stroke in April 1945, shortly before Allied forces defeated first Germany and then Japan. (Library of Congress)

1939, he proclaimed a limited national emergency, which allowed expansion of the army from 135,000 men to 227,000. Believing that the security of the United States demanded the defeat of the Axis powers and sensing that Adolf Hitler was a mortal threat to the world, Roosevelt gradually moved the United States from its isolationist stance. Later in September, he called on Congress to amend the Neutrality Act, which it did the next month, allowing the Allies to purchase arms in the United States on a cash-and-carry basis. Following the defeat of France in 1940, Roosevelt pledged to support Britain in every manner short of declaring war. In September, he concluded an agreement with Britain whereby that country would receive 50 World War I–vintage destroyers in return for granting the United States rights to bases located in British territory in the Western Hemisphere. He also initiated a major rearmament program in the United States and secured passage of the Selective Service Act, the first peacetime draft in the nation's history.

By early 1941, Roosevelt and British prime minister Winston Churchill were coordinating their nations' policies toward the Axis powers. In the spring of 1941, Roosevelt ordered U.S. destroyers to provide protection as far as Iceland for the North Atlantic convoys bound for Britain. In March 1941, on his urging, Congress passed the Lend-Lease Act that extended U.S. aid to countries fighting the Axis powers.

Roosevelt also began pressuring Japan to leave China, which the Japanese had invaded in 1937. When Japanese troops occupied southern Indochina in the spring of 1941, he embargoed scrap metal and oil shipments to Japan. Roosevelt also ordered the Pacific Fleet from San Diego to Honolulu, Hawaii, in order to intimidate Japan, but the embargo caused Japanese leaders to opt for war with the United States. On December 7, 1941, Japanese aircraft attacked the U.S. Pacific Fleet at Pearl Harbor, Hawaii. The following day, Roosevelt called for a declaration of war on Japan, referring to the Japanese attack as "a date which will live in infamy." No solid evidence exists to substantiate persistent allegations that the president set up the fleet at Pearl Harbor in order to bring about the U.S. entry in the war.

From 1941 to 1945, Roosevelt skillfully guided the United States through the war and worked to ensure a secure postwar world. During the course of the war, the United States fielded not only a navy larger than all the other navies of the world combined but also the largest air force and the most mobile, most heavily mechanized, and best-armed army in world history. It also provided the machines of war, raw materials, and food that enabled other nations to continue fighting the Axis powers. In these circumstances, full economic recovery occurred in the United States.

In 1944, Roosevelt ran successfully for an unprecedented fourth presidential term against Republican candidate Thomas Dewey. In February 1945, he met Churchill and Soviet dictator Josef Stalin at Yalta in the Crimea. The Yalta Conference built on decisions already reached at the prior Tehran Conference and was an effort to secure a stable postwar world. Roosevelt gambled that, with his considerable charm, he could convince Stalin that he had nothing to fear from the United States and that Britain, the Soviet Union, China, and the United States could cooperate to secure a peaceful postwar world. Although accused of making unnecessary concessions to the Soviet Union at Yalta, Roosevelt really had little choice but to do so, as the Red Army already occupied much of Eastern Europe and the U.S. military wished to induce the Soviets to enter the war against Japan.

At Yalta, Roosevelt was already ill, and shortly afterward, he sought rest at his summer home in Warm Springs, Georgia. He died there of a massive cerebral hemorrhage on April 12, 1945.

Kathleen Hitt and Spencer C. Tucker

See also
Churchill, Sir Winston Leonard Spencer; Eisenhower, Dwight D.; Marshall, George Catlett; Pearl Harbor, Attack on; Stalin, Josef; United States, Navy; Yalta Conference

References

Beschloss, Michael. *The Conquerors: Roosevelt, Truman and the Destruction of Hitler's Germany, 1941–1945.* New York: Simon and Schuster, 2002.

Black, Conrad. *Franklin Delano Roosevelt: Champion of Freedom.* New York: PublicAffairs, 2003.

Brands, H. W. *Traitor to His Class: The Privileged Life and Radical Presidency of Franklin Delano Roosevelt.* New York: Doubleday, 2008.

Burns, James MacGregor, and Susan Dunn. *The Three Roosevelts.* New York: Grove Atlantic, 2001.

Collier, Peter, and David Horowitz. *The Roosevelts: An American Saga.* New York: Touchstone, 1995.

Costigliola, Frank. *Roosevelt's Lost Alliances: How Personal Politics Helped Start the Cold War.* Princeton, NJ: Princeton University Press, 2011.

Dallek, Robert. *Franklin D. Roosevelt and American Foreign Policy, 1932–1945.* New York: Oxford University Press, 1995.

Davis, Kenneth S. *FDR: Into the Storm, 1937–1940—A History.* New York: Random House, 1993.

Davis, Kenneth S. *FDR: The War President, 1940–1943—A History.* New York: Random House, 2000.

Edmonds, Robin. *The Big Three: Churchill, Roosevelt and Stalin in War and Peace.* New York: Norton, 1991.

Fenby, Jonathan. *Alliance: The Inside Story of How Roosevelt, Churchill and Stalin Won One War and Began Another.* San Francisco, CA: MacAdam/Cage, 2007.

Freidel, Frank. *Roosevelt: A Rendezvous with Destiny.* Boston, MA: Little, Brown, 1990.

Gillon, Steven M. *Pearl Harbor: FDR Leads the Nation into War.* New York: Basic Books, 2011.

Goodwin, Doris Kearns. *No Ordinary Time: Franklin and Eleanor Roosevelt—The Home Front in World War II.* New York: Simon and Schuster, 1994.

Hamby, Alonzo L. *For the Survival of Democracy: Franklin Roosevelt and the World Crisis of the 1930s.* New York: Simon and Schuster, 2004.

Larrabee, Eric. *Commander in Chief: Franklin Delano Roosevelt—His Lieutenants and Their War.* New York: Simon and Schuster, 1987.

Meacham, Jon. *Franklin and Winston: An Intimate Portrait of an Epic Friendship.* New York: Random House, 2003.

Persico, Joseph E. *Roosevelt's Centurions: FDR and the Commanders He Led to Victory in World War II.* New York: Random House, 2012.

Roberts, Andrew. *Masters and Commanders: How Four Titans Won the War in the West.* New York: Harper, 2009.

Smith, Jean Edward. *FDR.* New York: Random House, 2007.

Stafford, David. *Roosevelt and Churchill: Men of Secrets.* New York: Overlook, 2000.

Weinberg, Gerhard L. *Visions of Victory: The Hopes of Eight World War II Leaders.* Cambridge: Cambridge University Press, 2005.

Signals Intelligence (SIGINT)

The collection and analysis of electromagnetic emissions that provide insight into an enemy's technological capabilities. The broader category of signals intelligence (known today as SIGINT) includes both communications intelligence (COMINT) and electronic intelligence (ELINT). COMINT includes the monitoring of radio and telephone traffic, the decryption of coded messages, and analysis of message content. ELINT is the collection and analysis of electromagnetic emissions such as telemetry and radar signals. This essay deals with COMINT.

SIGINT played a key role in World War II. In the 1920s, the knowledge that cryptanalysis had achieved important results in several countries during World War I led to the development of new and improved cipher methods and especially new cipher machines. These were produced not only for diplomatic and military communications, but for use in business. American Edward Hugh Hebern had been working since 1917 to develop a rotor-driven machine, but he secured a U.S. patent only in 1924.

Also in 1917, German Arthur Scherbius experimented with a similar machine; he secured a German patent on February 23, 1918. He was followed in October 1919 by Dutch inventor Hugo Alexander Koch and Swede Arvid Gerhard Damm. In 1923, Scherbius purchased the Koch patents and produced a new rotor-driven cipher machine known as "Enigma." Scherbius demonstrated the Enigma machine in 1923 at Bern and in 1924 at the World Postal Congress at Stockholm. He developed several versions of the Enigma; the commercial version, Enigma-D, was purchased by several countries, including the Netherlands, Sweden, Switzerland, Czechoslovakia, the United States, Great Britain, and Japan.

The Enigma influenced production of cipher machines in other countries for military uses. In Sweden, engineer Boris Hagelin began his improved machine series; in Great Britain, "Type X" was an improved Enigma. In Japan, a special version was constructed, and experiments led to the "97-shiki-O-bun In-ji-ki" for high-level diplomatic communications (later identified by the Americans with the code name "Purple"). During the Spanish Civil War, the Nationalist side and their allied Italians employed Enigma-D machines, and the Italians also used their Enigma version known as "Alfa." The Poles developed their own cipher machine, "Lacida," and the Czechs experimented with a version driven by compressed air rather than electricity. Hagelin successfully marketed his machines in Sweden and France, later with the Italian navy, and finally in the United States, where 140,000 copies of his M-209 machine were built.

The Germans relied heavily on the Enigma machine for military communications during the war. Only in 1975, with the publication of Frederick Winterbotham's book *The Ultra Secret*, did it become generally known that Allied cryptanalysts had unlocked the secrets of the Enigma machine and that Allied intelligence had been able to read the most secret German military and diplomatic communications, although not in real time. Winterbotham's book was only the first in a flood of publications about Allied code-breaking. These included work published by the Poles, who in 1932 and 1933 had been the first to crack the secrets of the Enigma; the French, who had delivered to the Poles cipher materials secured from a German agent; the British, who established at Bletchley Park a decryption center; and the Americans, who also came into this operation and worked to break the Japanese codes.

The concentration on Enigma obscured the fact that there was not one Enigma machine, but rather several versions. Moreover, Bletchley Park could break only some of the cipher key nets of Enigma, depending on the number of signals sent in the daily settings of the various key nets. Concentration on Enigma also led to neglect of the many other machine- or hand-cipher systems of other nations, which were tackled by the cryptanalysts of many countries with mixed success.

The German defeat of Poland in September 1939 came so rapidly that Polish cryptanalysts had virtually no impact on that campaign. Evacuated by way of Romania to France, however, they joined the French Deuxième Bureau (intelligence service), which

The ability of the British and Americans to decipher a wide variety of German and Japanese military codes and the messages they transmitted gave the Allies vital advantages in anticipating and outwitting moves by the Axis powers on land and sea. Although tens of thousands of British and American personnel were employed in World War II codebreaking, the Allied capture of German Enigma cipher machines, such as this one, was kept secret not just during World War II but for several decades afterward. (National Cryptologic Museum/National Security Agency)

was operating in close conjunction with the British. But Allied efforts against the German Enigma key nets only had limited success at first and did not greatly influence Allied operations until mid-1940. With the defeat of France, that nation's cryptanalysts went to the unoccupied southern zone. From there, some Poles went on to Algeria and then joined the British at Bletchley Park.

On the Axis side, the German naval decryption service, the xB-Dienst, enjoyed considerable success in breaking the hand-cipher systems of the Royal Navy, which at this time did not use machines but rather super-enciphered codebooks. This fact enabled German warships in most cases to evade superior British forces. It also provided the Germans with information about Allied convoys.

In May 1940, Bletchley Park at last was able, with only short delays, to decrypt the main operational Enigma key net of the German Luftwaffe. This was aided by the introduction of the first "bombes"—devices developed by mathematicians Alan Turing and Gordon Welchman to determine the daily settings of the German machines. These intercepts, now known by the intelligence code name of ULTRA, influenced the Battle of Britain, as daily reports by the German air groups revealed their strengths and intended operations. Using this information, Britain's "home chain" radar, and a system of coast watchers, the British could use fewer fighter aircraft with maximum efficiency, sending fighters aloft at the right time to intercept incoming German bombers.

But Bletchley Park could not then break the Enigma key nets of the German army. Of special importance at the time was breaking the German navy key nets, especially those used by the U-boats. The German Enigma machine was known to the British from a replica the Poles had constructed and delivered to France and Britain in August 1939, but the problem was the wiring of the cipher-rotors. Only five of these were known; but the German navy used eight, and these had to be identified, together with information about the cipher settings, which changed daily. This was only accomplished in May and June 1941.

Despite decoding delays, the Allies were able to read German radio signals and thus had the means to destroy their surface supply organization in the Atlantic. This in turn forced the Germans to cancel commerce raiding operations by their large surface combatants. Also, from early August 1941, it became possible to decrypt U-boat radio traffic, which made it possible for the Allies to reroute their Atlantic convoys around the German U-boat dispositions. This prevented the sinking of perhaps 300 merchant ships in the second half of 1941.

Not all German officials had confidence in the security of the ciphers. Admiral Karl Dönitz tried several times after mid-1941 to improve the system. He introduced a code for the grid map positions and a separate cipher key net for the Atlantic U-boats. Then, on February 1, 1942, Dönitz ordered the introduction of an improved cipher machine known as "M-4" that had a divided "Umkehrwalze B" reflective rotor and an additional, fourth, rotor, the so-called "Greek Beta." This change produced an 11-month blackout at Bletchley Park in reading German U-boat traffic. At the same time, xB-Dienst was able—partially in 1942 and more so in 1943—to decrypt the Anglo-American super-enciphered codebook "Naval Cipher No. 3" used for communication with the convoys. Although there were decoding delays, the decryption led to excellent results for the U-boats in the North Atlantic until early spring 1943.

On October 30, 1942, in the Mediterranean, a German U-boat was forced to surface, and a specially trained British boarding party was able to salvage important cipher materials, especially the "weather short signal book." This was used to find "cribs," the cipher/clear text compromises that aided in determining daily settings of the MC4 machine. Thus, from mid-December 1942, Bletchley Park could once again send to the submarine tracking room of the Admiralty the dispositions of the German U-boat Wolf Packs in order to reroute convoys. But there were now so many Wolf Packs that new tactics had to be found to avoid repetition of the heavy losses incurred in mid-March, when the Germans introduced a new weather short signal book, producing a new blackout. By concentrating the available bombes to U-boat traffic, Bletchley Park was again able after only 10 days to break the U-boat cipher. Coupled with this, the Allies committed additional antisubmarine forces, very-long-range aircraft, hunter-killer groups of destroyers and the first escort carriers, radar in escort ships and lightweight radar in aircraft, high-frequency direction finders, and Leigh lights. The turning point came in late May 1943, when Dönitz redeployed his submarines from the North Atlantic convoy routes to the Central Atlantic and to distant operational areas. At the same time, Bletchley Park decrypted the orders, enabling the British to relocate their air groups from the convoy routes to Britain over to a strong offensive against U-boat routes in and out of the Bay of Biscay.

In June 1943, the British realized that the Germans had decrypted their signals, and the Admiralty changed to a new super-enciphered code, Naval Cipher No. 5, which led to a blackout for xB-Dienst. On July 1, the Germans introduced a new "Greek rotor C/Gamma," but this led to only a short interruption in decryption at Bletchley Park because of the introduction of a new high-speed bombe. Development of high-speed bombes in the United States led to the transfer in November 1943 of decryption work on the U-boat cipher to the U.S. decryption organization Op-20G, while Bletchley Park concentrated on the German Enigma ciphers of the German air force and the army, both of which had substantially increased the number of their key nets.

Bletchley Park's first break into the German army ciphers had come as the Germans prepared to invade the Soviet Union in June 1941. This provided information about German deployment of forces to Poland and preparation of trains specifically to transport prisoners of war, clear proof that the deployments were not simply an effort to blackmail the Soviet Union. During the invasion itself, Bletchley Park was able to intercept and read a great many German signals. Because the British did not trust the security of the Soviet code and cipher systems, decryptions from the German forces on the Eastern Front were transmitted to Moscow in a special secure cipher and only under cover stories. It is as yet unknown if the Soviets were aware from their spies in Britain, including Kim Philby and especially John Cairncross at Bletchley Park, of the source of the information and, if so, whether Soviet leader Josef Stalin trusted it. Also, while the German army, navy, and air force decryption services were able to read Soviet codes and some ciphers and use the information thus obtained in operations, we also do not know how extensively and when the Soviets could decrypt German signals.

Signals intelligence was of great importance in the Mediterranean Theater. When Italy entered the war on June 10, 1940, the Allies could read many of the Italian codes and ciphers. In addition, some ciphers were captured from Italian submarines forced to surface. But the Italians soon changed many of their systems, and decryption fell off sharply as a result. Then, in February 1941, Bletchley Park cracked the German air force cipher "Light Blue" and the Italian version of the Enigma known as "Alfa," used for radio communication between Rome and the Dodecanese Islands. These successes had important consequences, most notably in defeating the Italian navy at the Battle of Cape Matapan in March 1941.

In May 1941, decryption of the German signals provided excellent intelligence concerning German plans to invade Crete, but the British defense of the island failed because the German air force controlled the skies and because the intercepts included misleading information about a German seaborne invasion. As it transpired, this was not a significant German effort, but it led the British to shift defensive assets to the north away from the airfields, where the main German assault occurred. The Battle of Crete revealed both the advantages and disadvantages of SIGINT regarding enemy intentions.

From June 1941, Bletchley Park's decryption of the Italian Hagelin naval cipher machine "C-38m" used in communications between Supermarina in Rome and Tripoli had important consequences for resupply of Axis forces in the western desert. Axis shipping losses increased dramatically in the second half of 1941 and 1942, when it became possible to vector Allied submarines and surface warship strike groups from Malta to intercept Italian convoys between Sicily and the Tunisian coast and Tripoli. The British always tried first to send reconnaissance aircraft to report the target so the signals they sent prevented the Italians from recognizing the true source of the information.

Decrypted signals had to be used judiciously. Thus Afrika Korps commander General Erwin Rommel exaggerated the evils of his supply situation in order to gain additional support, causing British prime minister Winston Churchill twice to order his commanders in the field to begin offensives that then failed in Rommel's counterattacks. Rommel also learned much about British force strengths in Egypt because the U.S. military attaché in Cairo used a code broken by the Italians for his reports. Allied commanders also made different use of SIGINT results in operations extending from El Alamein to Tunisia and during the landing operations at Sicily, Salerno, and Anzio. Revelations of the ULTRA secret in 1975 did force a reconsideration of the military reputations of several Allied commanders, including Field Marshal Bernard Montgomery.

In connection with the preparation of the Normandy Invasion, the Allies in Operation FORTITUDE successfully used radio deception to convince the Germans of the presence in southeast England of a U.S. Army group commanded by Lieutenant General George S. Patton Jr., a force that in fact did not exist. This false information led Adolf Hitler to believe that the Normandy Invasion was a feint and that the Allies planned to make their major cross-Channel attack in the Pas de Calais area. Hitler thus held back his panzer divisions of the Fifteenth Army from Normandy until too late and then sent them piecemeal into action.

The western Allies also succeeded in the decryption of the German army teleprinter cipher machine used for communications between the highest levels from the army High Command and field armies. This was made possible by development of the first electronic precursor of the later computers, the "Colossus" machine, which became operational in the spring of 1944. It proved important in halting the German counterattack against the breakthrough at Argentan and led to the encirclement of strong German forces at Falaise. But Allied reliance on ULTRA intelligence, as the German decryptions were known, meant the German Ardennes Offensive (Battle of the Bulge) of late December 1944 took the Allies unawares, as the Germans had observed strict radio silence and used only secure land lines for communication.

Other belligerents and also neutral powers employed SIGINT during the war. The Finns cracked many Soviet codes, and the Swedish mathematician Arne Beurling broke into the German naval teleprinter Siemens T-52 cipher machine. German teleprinter lines running through Swedish territory were tapped there. Swedish intelligence officers, who favored the Allied side, delivered information to the British naval attaché at Stockholm. Thus the Admiralty learned of the German plan to attack convoy PQ 17 in July 1942 with large surface ships, destroyers, submarines, and aircraft, whereupon British First Sea Lord Admiral of the Fleet Sir Dudley Pound ordered the convoy to scatter without waiting for the report of the departure of the German Task Forces. This led to catastrophe for the convoy, as German aircraft and U-boats sank two-thirds of its merchant ships. The rising number of cipher key nets employed by the Germans also overstretched Bletchley Park capacities. Thus even by mid-1942, of about 50 key nets then in use, Bletchley Park could only decrypt about 30, and these with varying time delays and gaps.

SIGINT also had great influence in the Far East Theater. In September 1940, American cryptanalysts under the leadership of William Friedman broke the Japanese diplomatic Purple cipher. (Recently it has been revealed that both the Germans and Soviets were also able to break Purple.) Thus, during negotiations with Japanese in 1941, the U.S. State Department not only knew the documents the Japanese diplomats would present but also their specific negotiating instructions. Purple intercepts provided clear evidence in late 1941 that the Japanese had decided to break off negotiations. But the diplomatic communications gave no hints of Japanese military plans, and the Japanese army codes were still difficult to decrypt. The Japanese navy's super-enciphered codes, especially JN.25— an earlier version of which had been broken—could not be read after changes in the codebooks and super-enciphering tables. Thus U.S. military and naval leaders had to depend on traffic analysis and direction finding, which did provide clear evidence, supported by optical observations, of the deployment of Japanese forces for attacks against the Philippines, Malaya, and the Netherlands East Indies. There was, however, no direct indication of an attack against Pearl Harbor, which thus came as a great surprise.

Breaking the new version of JN.25 and other Japanese codes took time, because reconstructing the tables and codebook was always difficult after changes. In 1942, by clever evaluation of vague indications, Commander Joseph J. Rochefort concluded that the Japanese planned first to invade New Guinea and then to strike at Midway. This conclusion enabled Pacific Fleet Commander Admiral Chester Nimitz to counter the Japanese moves, leading to the Battles of the Coral Sea and Midway.

During the struggle for the Solomon Islands in late 1942 and 1943, U.S. cryptanalysts learned to decrypt the Japanese codes more quickly, and by 1944 they could in most cases provide timely decryptions of Japanese signals in support of strategic operations. Of special importance was the success in breaking the so-called "Maru" cipher for Japanese logistical support to the islands they held in the Pacific. This allowed U.S. submarines to be directed with considerable accuracy to intercept positions, which in turn produced rising losses in the already thinly stretched Japanese merchant ship capacity and in Japanese warships. SIGINT closely supported General Douglas MacArthur's Southwest Pacific Forces from New Guinea to the Philippines and the Central Pacific Forces under Admiral Nimitz against the Marshall, Caroline, and Mariana Islands and finally against Iwo Jima and Okinawa.

In the Indian Ocean area, British cryptanalysts were able to break Japanese army and air force codes. On the other side, the Japanese had only limited success in decryption operations. In consequence, they employed mainly traffic analysis and direction finding for their military and naval operations.

There is no doubt that SIGINT was of great importance to all belligerents in the war. It is also true that the Allies were much more effective in its use. SIGINT alone did not win the war for the Allies, but undoubtedly it significantly shortened the length of the conflict.

Jürgen Rohwer

See also

Churchill, Sir Winston Leonard Spencer; Hitler, Adolf; MacArthur, Douglas; Midway, Battle of; Montgomery, Sir Bernard Law; Nimitz, Chester William; North Africa Campaign; Patton, George Smith, Jr.; Pearl Harbor, Attack on; Rommel, Erwin Johannes Eugen

References

Alvarez, David. *Allied and Axis Signals Intelligence in World War II*. London: Frank Cass, 1999.

Bauer, Friedrich L. *Decrypted Secrets. Methods and Maxims of Cryptology*. New York: Springer, 1997.

Beesly, Patrick. *Very Special Intelligence: The Story of the Admiralty's Operational Intelligence Centre, 1939–1945*. London: Greenhill Books, 2000.

Bertrand, Gustave. *Enigma: ou la plus grande enigme de la guerre 1939–1945* [Enigma: Or the Greatest Enigma of the War 1939–1945]. Paris: Plon, 1973.

Boyd, Carl. *Hitler's Japanese Confidant: General Oshima Hiroshi and Magic Intelligence, 1941–1945*. Lawrence, KS: University Press of Kansas, 1993.

Briggs, Asa. *Secret Days: Codebreaking in Bletchley Park*. Barnsley: Pen and Sword Press, 2011.

Budiansky, Stephen. *Battle of Wits: The Complete Story of Codebreaking in World War II*. New York: Free Press, 2002.

Carlson, Elliott. *Joe Rochefort's War: The Odyssey of the Codebreaker Who Outwitted Yamamoto at Midway*. Annapolis, MD: Naval Institute Press, 2011.

Drea, Edward J. *MacArthur's Ultra: Codebreaking and the War against Japan, 1942–1945*. Lawrence, KS: University Press of Kansas, 1992.

Hinsley, F. H., et al. *British Intelligence in the Second World War*. 5 vols. London: Her Majesty's Stationery Office, 1979–1990.

Kreis, John F. *Piercing the Fog: Intelligence and Army Air Forces Operations in World War II*. Honolulu, HI: University Press of the Pacific, 2004.

Lewin, Ronald. *The Other Ultra: Codes, Ciphers and the Defeat of Japan*. London: Hutchinson, 1982.

Prados, John. *Combined Fleet Decoded: The Secret History of American Intelligence and the Japanese Navy in World War II*. Annapolis, MD: Naval Institute Press, 2001.

Rohwer, Jürgen, and Eberhard Jäckel, eds. *Die Funkaufklärung und ihre Rolle im Zweiten Weltkrieg* [Codebreaking and Its Role in World War II]. Stuttgart: Motorbuch Verlag, 1979.

Welchman, Gordon. *The Hut Six Story: Breaking the Enigma Codes*. New York: McGraw-Hill, 1982.

Winton, John. *Ultra in the Pacific: How Breaking Japanese Codes and Ciphers Affected Naval Operations against Japan, 1941–1945*. London: Leo Cooper, 1993.

Southeast Pacific Theater

The U.S. Navy's strategy for the defeat of Japan by a thrust through the Central Pacific depended on control of the southeastern Pacific, particularly the Panama Canal region through which all shipping destined for the Central, South, and Southwest Pacific Theaters transited. In this regard, the Imperial Japanese Navy squandered a huge potential strategic advantage in not challenging the United States in these waters using their large and capable submarine force. But Japanese doctrine called for submarines to operate in direct fleet support or as scouting forces. The Japanese never adopted the more aggressive commerce raiding and interdiction roles for their submarines that were used with great success by both Germany and the United States in the Atlantic and the western Pacific. In this regard, once the anticipated threat to the Panama Canal failed to materialize, the United States dedicated little by way of naval protection to shipping in the region.

The March 1941 ABC Conference of Britain, Canada, and the United States established Pacific operational areas that the Joint Chiefs of Staff reconfirmed in March 1942. The agreement gave the navy operational control over the central, southern, northern, and southeastern Pacific areas of operation; the army was responsible for the southwest Pacific. Further, the Pacific Military Council determined in March 1943 that all of the Pacific should be under the "strategic command" of Admiral Chester Nimitz, commander in chief, Pacific, although General Douglas MacArthur held overall command of the southwest Pacific. The actual boundaries had been established earlier in Joint Chiefs of Staff directives of April 4, 1942, to MacArthur and Nimitz that outlined the southeastern Pacific as everything east of a line drawn from the Mexico-Guatemala border to the mid-Pacific near Clipperton Island and then southward to the South Pole. To patrol this vast ocean area, Rear Admiral John F. Shafroth commanded a tiny force of three older light cruisers and several destroyers. As events played out, however, Shafroth's force proved more than sufficient, given the lack of Japanese activity.

Concern between the Pearl Harbor attack and the Midway victory over the security of the Panama Canal did not reflect in the naval defenses initially allotted to the region. To protect not only the canal itself but also transiting shipping, the U.S. Army had capable forces, but only in the 10-mile-wide Panama Canal Zone. The various Latin American countries offered little in terms of genuine security, even after Mexico and Colombia declared war on the Axis powers in 1943. The navy provided only minimal resources for

Rear Admiral Clifford E. Van Hook's Panama Canal Force, consisting of the elderly destroyers *Borie*, *Barry*, *Tattnall*, and *Goff* along with the gunboat *Erie*, 2 patrol craft, 2 small converted motor yachts, and 24 Catalina maritime patrol aircraft. Although a few Japanese submarines entered the area as part of the June 1942 Japanese naval offensive against Midway and the Aleutian Islands, they did no damage. However, German U-boats did tremendous destruction to shipping on the Caribbean side of the canal, including two sinkings just outside the eastern entrance. But, again, the Japanese threat, which might have included carrier strikes, a possibility envisioned in war plans prior to December 1941 (Rainbow 5), never materialized on the Pacific side. Nor did the large 5,200-ton Japanese submarines of the I-400 class carrying 3 bomber-seaplanes (fielded in late 1944 and clearly designed for operations against the U.S. west coast and the Panama Canal) ever deploy to the region as anticipated.

Despite the ultimate lack of a credible Japanese threat to American shipping in the southeastern Pacific, a fact not realized until later in the war, naval commanders in 1942 assigned whatever escort assets were available to open-ocean vessels, particularly troop convoys transiting to the Central and Southwest Pacific Theaters and Pearl Harbor. In late January 1942, Shafroth's light cruisers *Trenton* and *Concord* and some destroyers escorted 2 large convoys from the canal through to Bora Bora with 4,500 men assigned to the construction of a new naval fueling station. At about the same time, the carrier *Lexington* and its assigned force escorted an 8-ship convoy carrying 20,000 troops through the southeastern Pacific (2 for Christmas Island, 2 for Canton Island, and 4 for New Caledonia).

In retrospect, the failure of the Imperial Japanese Navy to harass Allied shipping or to attempt even limited interdiction operations in the southeastern Pacific represented a tremendous missed strategic opportunity. Although such a southeastern Pacific campaign would likely not have changed the eventual outcome of the war, it certainly would have mitigated Allied pressure in other Pacific areas of operation and complicated thrusts against the Japanese defensive perimeter.

Stanley D. M. Carpenter

See also

Central Pacific Campaign; Germany, Navy; Japan, Navy; Latin America and the War; MacArthur, Douglas; Nimitz, Chester William; Southwest Pacific Theater; United States, Navy

References

Brower, Charles F. *The Joint Chiefs of Staff and Strategy in the Pacific War, 1943–1945*. New York: Palgrave Macmillan, 2012.

Dull, Paul S. *A Battle History of the Imperial Japanese Navy, 1941–45*. Annapolis, MD: Naval Institute Press, 1978.

Johnson, William Bruce. *The Pacific Campaign in World War II*. New York: Routledge, 2006.

Morison, Samuel Eliot. *History of United States Naval Operations in World War II*. Vol. 3, *The Rising Sun in the Pacific*. Boston, MA: Little, Brown, 1948.

Morison, Samuel Eliot. *The Two-Ocean War: A Short History of the United States Navy in the Second World War*. Boston, MA: Little, Brown, 1963.

Van der Vat, Dan. *The Pacific Campaign: The U.S.–Japanese Naval War 1941–1945.* New York: Touchstone, 1991.

Williford, Glen M. *Racing the Sunrise: The Reinforcement of America's Pacific Outposts, 1941–1942.* Annapolis, MD: Naval Institute Press, 2010.

Southwest Pacific Theater

Geographical area known to the Japanese as the Southern Resource Area and also the Southeast Area and to the Allies as the Southwest Pacific Area (SWPA). Major land areas in this theater were the Philippine Islands, the Netherlands East Indies, New Guinea, Australia, the Bismarck Archipelago, and the Solomon Islands. In August 1942, the boundary was redrawn to exclude Guadalcanal and certain others of the Solomon Islands.

Japan entered the SWPA in a quest for oil. Oil powered Japan's economy and its armed forces, and the U.S. embargo of oil had helped trigger the Japanese decision to go to war against the United States. Dependent on foreign oil imports and rapidly using up its stocks, Japan needed to secure oil, the absence of which would paralyze Japanese industry within a year and immobilize the fleet within two years. Oil resources in the Netherlands East Indies, Japanese leaders believed, would make Japan self-sufficient in that vital commodity.

Japanese Southern Army headquarters in Saigon in French Indochina supervised army operations from the Philippines south. Navy leaders, meanwhile, decided that U.S. airfields and fleet bases could not be tolerated on the flank of this advance. Japanese Lieutenant General Homma Masaharu's Fourteenth Army with two divisions invaded the Philippines beginning on December 8, 1941. U.S. resistance officially ended on May 7, 1942. Meanwhile, Lieutenant General Imamura Hitoshi's Sixteenth Army with three divisions invaded the Netherlands East Indies beginning on December 20. Dutch resistance there ceased on March 8.

The Japanese had only a marginal shipping capacity during the war. By May 1942, the Japanese were securing oil from the conquests, but the fleet was only using about 42 percent of its merchant tanker capacity. Iron, manganese, chrome, and copper awaited exploitation in the Philippines. The Japanese desperately needed bauxite from the Netherlands East Indies for aircraft aluminum. Nickel was available from the Celebes. Local Japanese commanders were inefficient at developing these resources, and what materials the Japanese did extract from Borneo, Java, and Sumatra encountered shipping bottlenecks.

As the Japanese pushed south, their navy engaged in several actions. The Battle of the Java Sea largely destroyed the American–British–Dutch–Australian (ABDA) fleet. The United States won a small victory against Japanese transports in the Battle of Makassar Strait. There was also a fight at Badung Strait, and the Allied cruisers *Houston* and *Perth* were destroyed in the Battle of Sunda Strait. The short-lived ABDA Command collapsed in early March 1942, and the Japanese breached the Malay Barrier.

The startling successes of their initial campaigns encouraged the Japanese navy leadership to propose that five divisions invade Australia. Shipping and logistics, however, posed insurmountable problems as Japan, already short of shipping capacity, had lost 700,000 tons of shipping—nearly 12 percent of total capacity—sunk or severely damaged in the first four months of war. The Japanese army had never considered operating in the SWPA and had not planned how to campaign over such a large area and with such extended lines of communications. Japanese army planners estimated that to capture Australia would require 12 divisions and 1.5 million tons of shipping. The Japanese did not have the military assets and resources for such an operation. Australia was simply one continent too far.

Rather than invade Australia, Imperial General Headquarters in Tokyo ordered six of the divisions that had participated in the southern operations back to the Japanese home islands, China, and Manchuria. Planners redirected their logistical effort to the northwest and west when they should have been building bases—especially air bases—and establishing and supplying garrisons in the south.

On March 30, 1942, the U.S. Joint Chiefs of Staff established the Southwest Pacific Area. General Douglas MacArthur received command. It succeeded the ABDA area formed on January 15 as well as the Australia–New Zealand Area (ANZAC) established at the end of January. The first priority was to strengthen lines of communications to Australia and to build up logistics and airpower. The air war here would be primarily land-based.

Japan landed troops on New Guinea in February and March 1942. Japan sought Port Moresby on the south coast as an air base, part of its campaign to cut the lines of communications to Australia and to deny the port as a base for Allied counterattacks. In the May 1942 Battle of the Coral Sea, the U.S. Navy deflected the Japanese seaborne invasion attempt. The Japanese then attempted to seize Port Moresby by land, crossing over the Owen Stanley Mountains. Australian forces fought a delaying action south toward Port Moresby that weakened the Japanese and ultimately halted this thrust. The Australians then drove the Japanese back to New Guinea's north coast. A Japanese landing at Milne Bay failed, boosting Allied morale.

On July 2, 1942, the U.S. Joint Chiefs of Staff ordered MacArthur to begin an offensive to clear the Japanese from New Guinea. This effort was limited by the availability of forces and because the Americans' army and navy were both constrained by the priority given to Europe. The long fight for Buna concluded in late January 1943. The Australians and Americans executed shore-to-shore and ship-to-shore operations up New Guinea's coast. Rabaul on New Britain was initially a target, but the Americans chose to bypass that major Japanese bastion, cutting it off from outside resupply.

Although progress was slow, the Allies kept the initiative, imposed a tremendous drain on Japanese resources, and prevented the Japanese from consolidating their conquests. Weather, disease, and inhospitable terrain inflicted heavy losses on all combatants in this theater, but especially on the Japanese. Particularly devastating to the Japanese was the loss of so many of their air assets, and the destruction of Japanese transports in the Battle of the Bismarck Sea gave Japan a stark warning of the precariousness of its position.

The Americans launched almost every operation so as to extend their air umbrella and logistics closer to the Philippines. The strategy of island-hopping, which made use of growing U.S. Navy strength in the theater, allowed U.S. forces to advance, yet bypass strong Japanese ground forces. Allied shipping constraints and a shortage of service troops were greater impediments to the advance than shortfalls in combat troops.

The SWPA was the location of one of two major U.S. offensives (comprising mainly land-based air and ground forces) aimed at Japan. The second location was the Central

Pacific, in which the U.S. offensives comprised mainly carrier air and sea power. The Japanese had insufficient assets to meet both offensives and were often off balance as they tried to maneuver against the two. The Japanese were simultaneously heavily committed in Burma and China and had to maintain major forces in Manchuria as a check on potential action by the Soviet Union.

The American SWPA and Central Pacific offensives indirectly supported each other early in the campaigns and then directly supported one another as they converged at the Luzon-Formosa-China coast area. The speed, flexibility, and mass of the two Allied thrusts neutralized the defender's traditional advantage of interior lines of communications. Coordination between the U.S. Army and Navy of current and future operations was critically important.

The Japanese regarded campaigns in New Guinea as a means to delay their enemies, reduce enemies' resources, and gain time to reorganize for a counteroffensive. Rather than weakening the Allies, however, the campaigns here became a drain on Japanese manpower, ships, and aircraft. Allied airpower cleared Japanese from the air and sea. Nowhere did the Japanese stop the advance, nor could they sustain the attrition that went with it.

The vast majority of Japanese troop and logistics shipping occurred in SWPA waters. Oil moved north through these waters, and U.S. submarines attacked the vital

Curtiss SB2C-3 "Helldiver" aircraft bank over a U.S. carrier in mid-January 1945 before landing, following strikes on Japanese shipping in the China Sea. (Naval Historical Center)

Malaya/Netherlands East Indies–Japan line of communications. Japan lost half its cargo-carrying capacity in 1944 to air and submarine attacks. Critical oil and raw materials required for war production in the home islands were sent to the ocean bottom.

The Battle of the Philippine Sea in June 1944 largely destroyed what remained of Japanese naval aviation. Japanese navy leaders then developed plans for a decisive battle, depending on the avenue of the U.S. advance. When the Americans invaded the Philippines in October, the Japanese immediately initiated their plan, which resulted in the Battle of Leyte Gulf—the greatest naval battle, in terms of ships and numbers of men engaged, in history. In the ensuing battle, the U.S. Navy all but destroyed the Japanese navy as an organized fighting force.

The inability of Japan to transport men and supplies to Leyte and its similar difficulties in supplying and reinforcing Luzon hastened Japan's defeat in the Philippines. The U.S. conquest of the Philippines enabled U.S. airpower there to sever the seaborne supply lines between the Japanese home islands and its Southern Resource Area. U.S. Navy forces swept into the South China Sea in January 1945 and severed Japanese lines of communications with Indochina. The American conquest of the Philippines, the ability of carrier task forces to go wherever they pleased, and the strangulation wrought by the submarine fleet completely isolated the Southern Resource Area.

Large Japanese ground forces remained in Indochina and in the Netherlands East Indies, but they could play no role in the defense of the home islands, nor could raw materials reach the home islands. This fact made MacArthur's use of Australian forces in Borneo in mid-1945 all the more questionable. It was a campaign with little strategic value.

The last operations in the SWPA were American preparations for the invasion of Japan. The Philippines provided staging areas for 18 U.S. Army divisions, large numbers of aircraft, logistics organizations, and hundreds of ships. With Japan's surrender in August, operations in the SWPA came to an end. The conclusion of hostilities did not bring peace, however, as wars in which indigenous peoples sought independence from their colonial occupiers soon began.

John W. Whitman

See also

Australia, Role in War; Central Pacific Campaign; Japan, Air Force; Japan, Army; Japan, Navy; MacArthur, Douglas; Southeast Pacific Theater; United States, Army; United States, Army Air Force; United States, Marine Corps; United States, Navy

References

Bergerud, Eric. *Touched with Fire: The Land Campaign in the South Pacific.* New York: Penguin Books, 1996.

Bergerud, Eric. *Fire in the Sky. The Air War in the South Pacific.* Boulder, CO: Westview Press, 2000.

Brower, Charles F. *The Joint Chiefs of Staff and Strategy in the Pacific War, 1943–1945.* New York: Palgrave Macmillan, 2012.

Craven, Wesley F., and James E. Cate, eds. *The Army Air Forces in World War II.* Vols. 1, 4, 5. Chicago, IL: University of Chicago Press, 1948–1958.

Hattori Takushiro. *The Complete History of the Greater East Asia War.* 4 vols. Translated by Headquarters, 500th Military Intelligence Service Group. Tokyo: Masu Publishing, 1953.

Johnson, William Bruce. *The Pacific Campaign in World War II.* New York: Routledge, 2006.

Morison, Samuel Eliot. *History of United States Naval Operations in World War II.* Vols. 3–6, 8, 12–13. Edison, NJ: Castle Books, 2001.

Morton, Louis. *United States Army in World War II. The War in the Pacific. Strategy and Command: The First Two Years.* Washington, DC: U.S. Army Center of Military History, 1989.

Sarantakes, Nicholas Evan. *Allies against the Rising Sun: The United States, the British Nations, and the Defeat of Imperial Japan.* Lawrence, KS: University Press of Kansas, 2009.

Williford, Glen M. *Racing the Sunrise: The Reinforcement of America's Pacific Outposts, 1941–1942.* Annapolis, MD: Naval Institute Press, 2010.

Soviet Union, Air Force

As part of the reorganization of the Soviet armed forces in 1923, air squadrons were retained under the control of the ground commanders to which they were attached. However, administratively they came under the control of a Chief Directorate of the Air Force of the Red Army. In 1925, the Soviets created a General Staff of the Air Force. Systematic numbering of squadrons began in 1926, and their formation was standardized as five squadrons—each divided into three sections—for an air brigade. As armed force doctrine evolved, operational control of all air units was placed under the Chief Directorate of the Air Force in 1928.

Nikolai Polikarpov produced fighters such as the I-5 by 1924, and Andrei Tupolev created the first Soviet bomber designs, such as the ANT-4, in 1927. Development stalled during the Great Purges in the late 1930s, when the government ordered the imprisonment of some 450 aircraft designers and engineers, although most were allowed to continue their work from confinement. During the 1936–1939 Spanish Civil War, the Soviet Union supplied both I-15 and I-16 aircraft and pilots and instructors to the Republican side. However, these aircraft were outclassed by the German Messerschmitt Bf-109 fighter. From October 1936 to December 1938, the Soviet Union sent 1,409 aircraft to Spain, of which 1,176 were destroyed. Nevertheless, by January 1937, 17 Soviet pilots had been decorated as Heroes of the Soviet Union.

The Spanish experience spurred a Soviet response to develop aircraft specifically for ground-attack and close-support duties. Representative of this effort were the Yak-1, MiG-1, and LaGG-3, which entered service in 1939 and 1940. These three designs were later improved. Alexander Yakovlev's Yak-1 was powered by a 1,100 hp engine and had a top speed of 360 mph. It was armed with a 20 mm cannon and two 7.62 mm machine guns. The virtue of this fighter was its simple construction and reliability. The Yak-1 could complete a 360 degree turn in 17 seconds. It enjoyed one of the highest productions of any aircraft of the war; a total of 30,000 were manufactured. Artem Mikoyan and Mikhail Gurievitch combined to produce the 1,350 hp MiG-1, which had a maximum speed of

In 1941, two soldiers load bombs onto a Red Army aircraft, which is covered with camouflage netting. Air power soon became vital to the Soviet ability to strike back at Germany. Between June 1941 and December 1944, Soviet factories produced 97,000 military aircraft, and Allied Lend-Lease aid provided an additional 18,865. (Library of Congress)

380 mph. However, the MiG-1 was best suited to an interceptor role at high altitude. The LaGG-3 was the collaboration of Semyon Lavochkin, Vladimir Gorbunov, and Mikhail Gudkov. The LaGG-3, built entirely of wood, had armament, engine, and speed comparable to that of the Yak-1. However, the LaGG-3 had a tendency to spin during sharp turns.

Another reorganization of the Soviet air force took place in July 1940, with a view toward concentrating air assets. The 20 to 30 plane squadrons were amalgamated into 60-plane regiments. Between 3 and 5 regiments made up an air division, each of which supported a ground army. By February 1941, although 106 new air regiments had been authorized, only 19 had actually been formed. Moreover, by the date of the German invasion on June 22, 1941, only 20 percent of Soviet air force units had been fitted with the new Yak, MiG, and LaGG models. In April 1942, Lieutenant General Alexander Novikov took command of the Red Army Air Force. In May, he ordered that all Soviet airpower—heretofore apportioned sporadically among the ground armies and employed without concentration—should be unified. These remnants of surviving post–German invasion Soviet airpower were gathered to become the First Air Army.

The initial success of Germany's invasion of the Soviet Union owed much to the German Luftwaffe, which destroyed many Soviet air force aircraft on the ground. In only the first two days, 2,500 Soviet planes had been destroyed and the Germans had achieved air superiority. Another factor contributing to the demise of the Soviet air force was poor tactics; Soviet bombers attempted to attack without fighter protection. When threatened,

Soviet bombers formed a tight wedge pattern, while threatened Soviet fighters maneuvered into a defensive circle. At the beginning of the campaign against Germany—and frustrated by their lack of tactical training and having to fly outclassed aircraft—many Soviet pilots resorted to attempting to ram German aircraft during engagements.

As the German offensive into the Soviet Union continued, the Soviets organized an evacuation eastward of much of their industry, including more than half of the aircraft factories. As a result, production fell off dramatically in the second half of 1941. By June 1942, however, 1,000 aircraft per month were once again being produced in factories that had been relocated east of the Urals. Moreover, the refabricated aviation plants began to produce upgraded aircraft models such as the MiG-3, which had an increased combat radius, and an up-gunned version of the Yak-1 with 12.7 mm cannon and a 1,260 hp engine. LaGG production was decreased in favor of a new product that was the creation of Sergei Ilyushin. His Il-2 Shturmovik began to reach the front lines in mid-July 1942. The impetus behind the design was the creation of a "flying tank": an aircraft with the ability to operate at altitudes of 50 to 500 feet and survive enemy ground fire while supporting Soviet forces by destroying German tanks. A design revision, Il-2m3, began delivery in November 1942. It added protection from German fighters. The new Shturmovik was a two-seater; the gunner faced rearward and manned a 12.7 mm machine gun. The pilot now controlled two 23 mm cannon and either a 1,300 lb bomb load or 880 lbs of bombs and 8 rockets. The Il-2 proved so successful that, at 35,000 units, it was the highest-production aircraft of the war, indeed of all time. Soviet leader Josef Stalin personally prioritized its production, reportedly remarking, "The Il-2 is as necessary to our armies as air or bread!" The Germans dubbed the Il-2 Der Schwarze Tod (the black death).

Soviet pilots revised and developed new principles of engagement, following the practices of their top aces such as Alexander Pokryshkin. His formula was "altitude-speed-maneuver-fire." From a higher altitude, a pilot had the opportunity to select his target and maneuver with speed into an advantageous position for attack. Squadron formations gave way to the "loose pair" of two aircraft operating together, either covering the other (attacking) aircraft. This tactic was first used during the late 1941 Battle of Moscow and resulted in Luftwaffe losses of 1,400 aircraft between October and December 1941. The six Soviet air regiments taking part in the defense of the capital were given the honorific "Guards" designation. From November 15 to December 5, Soviet pilots flew 15,840 sorties, compared with only 3,500 for the Luftwaffe.

The new air doctrine also stipulated that bombers have fighter escorts: 4 bombers with 10 fighters and 16–24 bombers protected by a group of 20 fighters. The fighters were organized into groups. Each group consisted of 3–4 pairs totaling 6–8 fighters. Normally, 4 groups would constantly patrol a sector of the combat area. When fighters escorted ground-attack aircraft, the fighters divided into an escort group and an assault group. The escort group remained with the ground-attack aircraft but flew 300 to 1,000 feet higher to engage enemy fighters. The assault group flew 1,500 to 3,000 feet above the escort group and usually a half mile ahead to scout for enemy patrols and act as an advance guard to prevent enemy fighters from closing on the escort group.

Soviet aircraft production continued to climb during the war. From June 1941 to December 1944, the Soviets produced some 97,000 aircraft. During the war, the Soviet air force also benefited greatly from Lend-Lease deliveries of British and U.S. aircraft. The

Soviets received 2,097 P-40 Tomahawks, 1,329 Supermarine Spitfires, 4,746 Bell Airacobras, 2,400 Bell Kingcobras, and several transports and bombers. Lend-Lease provided a total of 18,865 aircraft.

By 1945, the Red Army Air Force numbered 17 air armies, each composed of 2 fighter divisions, 2 fighter-bomber divisions, a night-bomber regiment, a reconnaissance squadron, and a liaison squadron. These air armies were held in reserve and tasked to support ground operations on a case-by-case basis. They were under the command of air officers who coordinated efforts with ground commanders. General Novikov also established an air reserve that could be moved around to achieve local air superiority. By 1945, 40 percent of Soviet air strength was held in a reserve capacity. In October 1942, Lavochkin produced the La-5 aircraft. Its 1,600 hp engine propelled the aircraft 30 mph faster than the Messerschmitt Bf-109F. Simultaneously, Yakovlev produced the Yak-9, which increased the Yak-1's combat radius and was armed with either a 20 mm or a 37 mm cannon and a 12.7 mm synchronized machine gun.

The Soviets had also organized a long-range aviation force in March 1942. The core of this was the Petlyakov Pe-8 four-engine bomber. But, throughout the war, Soviet emphasis, as with the Luftwaffe, was on ground-support aviation.

All major Soviet campaigns after the Battle of Moscow had substantial air involvement. One-quarter of Soviet airpower was concentrated in the area of Stalingrad by mid-November 1942 for the planned counteroffensive. In the Battle of Kursk in July 1943, the Soviets deployed 1,300 aircraft. During the Battle of Berlin in April 1945, Soviet aircraft were flying a daily average of 15,000 sorties.

The Soviets also organized foreign-piloted air formations, several of which distinguished themselves in combat. These included Regiment Normandie of French pilots, 1st Polish Warsaw Fighter Regiment, 2nd Krakow Night Bomber Regiment, 3rd Polish Ground Attack Regiment, and the Czechoslovak Fighter Regiment. Also noteworthy is the organization of a 400-woman-strong 588th Night Bomber Regiment, the pilots of which were known by the Germans as the "night witches." During the course of the war, these women flew some 24,000 sorties. Lidiia Litviak was the first woman pilot to shoot down an enemy aircraft in daytime combat.

The Red Army Air Force, much of which was destroyed early in the German invasion of the Soviet Union in June 1941, grew dramatically in size during the war. It certainly played an important role in the Soviet victory in World War II on the Eastern Front, especially—as its name indicates—in ground-support aviation.

Neville Panthaki

See also
Eastern Front; Germany, Air Force; Northeast Europe Theater

References

Boyd, Alexander. *The Soviet Air Force since 1918.* London: Macdonald and Jane's, 1973.

Cottam, Kazimiera Janina, ed. *Women in Air War: The Eastern Front of World War II.* Rev. ed. Nepean, Canada: New Military Publishers, 1997.

Cottam, Kazimiera Janina. *Women and Resistance: Selected Biographies of Soviet Women Soldiers.* Nepean, Canada: New Military Publishers, 1998.

Jackson, R. *The Red Falcons: The Soviet Air Force in Action, 1919–1969.* Brighton: Clifton House, 1970.

Miller, R. *The Soviet Air Force at War.* Translated by Leland Fetzer. Alexandria, VA: Time-Life Books, 1983.

Myles, Bruce. *Night Witches: The Untold Story of Women in Combat.* Chicago, IL: Academy Chicago Press, 1990.

Nedialkov, Dimitar. *In the Skies of Nomonhan: Japan versus Russia May–September 1939.* Reprint ed. Manchester: Crecy Publishing, 2011.

Noggle, Anne. *A Dance with Death: Soviet Airwomen in World War II.* College Station, TX: Texas A & M University Press, 1994.

Overy, Richard J. *The Air War 1939–1945.* Washington, DC: Potomac Books, 2005.

Pennington, Reina. *Wings, Women, and War: Soviet Airwomen in World War II Combat.* Lawrence, KS: University Press of Kansas, 2001.

Von Hardesty, and Ilya Grinberg. *Red Phoenix Rising: The Soviet Air Force in World War II.* Lawrence, KS: University Press of Kansas, 2012,

Wagner, Ray, ed. *The Soviet Air Force in WWII. The Official History.* Originally Published by the Ministry of Defense of the USSR. Garden City, NY: Doubleday, 1973.

Soviet Union, Army

Russia's defeat in World War I gave strong impetus to Soviet dictator Josef Stalin's industrialization campaign of the 1930s. His emphasis on technological progress, articulated in a speech on February 4, 1931, also implied the need for improvements in military technology to enable the Soviet Union to catch up with the western powers. Soviet Commissar of War Kliment Voroshilov claimed that a future war would be "a war of factories." The Japanese takeover of all Manchuria in the same year provided a compelling reason for Soviet rearmament.

Stalinist repression, however, had sharply affected the military leadership. Perhaps 40 million people were "repressed" during the Stalin era; half that number died. The so-called Great Terror that did away with the old-guard Bolshevik leadership also struck down senior military officers. Among the executed were 3 of 5 marshals, 13 of 15 army commanders, 8 of 9 fleet admirals and admirals grade I, 50 of 57 corps commanders, and 154 of 186 divisional commanders. Undoubtedly, the purges claimed the most aggressive and outspoken officers, and their loss was keenly felt, especially during the German invasion of the Soviet Union in June 1941. Among those killed was Marshal Mikhail Tukhachevsky, who had foreseen in his "Problems Concerning the Defence of the USSR" of 1936 the German operational concept for an invasion of the Soviet Union and had developed a counter to it. Although it enjoyed modern weapons at the beginning of the war, the Red Army remained committed to the concept that wars were won not by training and technology but by the masses and ideology.

Despite the purges, the Soviet military under Stalin had a strong influence on military-economic policy as it pushed for an armament-in-depth that implied not only state investment in stocks of weapons but support for civilian heavy industry. On the eve of World War II, aircraft, tank, and armament plants were concentrated in the western parts of the

Soviet Red Army soldiers in 1941. In Russia, World War II was known as the Great Patriotic War. The battles of 1941–1945 between German and Soviet forces on the Eastern Front were the greatest military confrontation in history, in which more than 10 million Soviet soldiers, 5 million Axis troops, and 14 to 17 million Soviet civilians died. For decades, the losses and suffering of World War II dominated the collective memory of the Soviet people. (Library of Congress)

Soviet Union. Although some efforts were made during the period before the German invasion of June 1941 to relocate military and general industrial production to the less vulnerable area east of the Ural Mountains, advocates of such a policy were often branded as "defeatists." The German invasion of the western Soviet territories was in fact an economic near-disaster, depriving the Red Army of much of its military industrial base.

The alliance between the Soviet Union and Germany of August 23, 1939, brought advantages to each side. It allowed Adolf Hitler to attack Poland secure in the fact that he would not have to wage war with the Soviet Union, and it bought time for Stalin to rebuild the Red Army, which he himself had so weakened in the Great Purges. The pact between Germany and the Soviet Union also yielded great economic advantages to the German war machine in the form of Soviet raw materials and the activities of the USSR as a purchasing agent for Germany abroad. It brought far less advantage to the Soviet Union, although it did secure time for Stalin to rebuild his military, and the Red Army also benefited from establishment of a joint tank training center at Kazan and an air base at Lipetsk. Germany also provided some finished machinery and a few weapons of war. But the German and Soviet division of Poland that flowed from the pact also meant the end of a buffer between the two states and the presence of a common military border.

Stalin was shocked at the speed with which Germany defeated France in 1940. Given the punishment that little Finland had inflicted on the Soviet Union in the Winter War of 1939–1940, it is no wonder that Stalin doubted the ability of the Red Army to stand up to the German military. The Soviet leadership counted on a stalemated struggle similar to that of the Western Front in World War I, or at least a war of several years. Critical to a prolonged struggle that would give the Soviet Union a chance to win was denying the Germans eastern Ukraine, which was the reason why so much Soviet armor was positioned forward in June 1941. Stalin quickly acted on the fall of France to cash in any remaining chips under the pact of August 1939, annexing the Baltic states and taking Bessarabia and northern Bukovina from Romania.

The success of the German tank divisions in France also led Stalin to reverse his decision in the fall of 1939 to eliminate the five Soviet tank corps. A decree of July 6, 1940, ordered the creation of nine new Red Army mechanized corps, and, in February and March 1941, other decrees called for an additional 20 formations.

The invasion of the Soviet Union began early on the morning of June 22, 1941. Stalin was determined not to be tricked into a war with Germany. Not only did the Soviet Union provide no provocation, but it continued to make deliveries of goods under the German–Soviet Non-Aggression Pact even as the invasion was in progress. Stalin rejected calls by his generals in the weeks and days before the attack to put Soviet forces in the border areas on alert. Even when he was informed that German troops were invading and firing on Soviet positions, Stalin refused for hours to allow an order to return fire; he claimed that Hitler must not be aware of what was going on.

On paper, the Red Army seemed in an excellent position to resist a German attack. It had some 5.37 million men under arms, and in the two weeks after the invasion another 5 million were called to the colors. It also enjoyed superiority over its attacker in major areas of military equipment. Germany had some 6,000 tanks, the Soviets 23,140 (10,394 of them in the west). Much of this equipment was also of high caliber. By 1941, the Soviets possessed some of the best tanks of the war. Their BT-series and T-26 were superior in armor, firepower, and maneuverability to the German light PzKpfw I and II and could destroy any German tank. Similarly, the Soviet T-34 medium tank and KV-1 heavy tank were superior to the PzKpfw III and IV, and indeed to any German tank in June 1941. Soviet units also enjoyed superiority in numbers of certain weapons. Thus a fully equipped Soviet tank division was to have 375 tanks; a German panzer division had only between 135 and 208. A fully equipped Soviet rifle division had 1,304 machine guns, whereas a German infantry division possessed only 486.

Although Soviet formations in the west were not fully equipped when Operation BARBAROSSA occurred, they should have been able to repel the German attack. Nonetheless, the Red Army sustained staggering losses early in the invasion. The bulk of Soviet forces in the western areas were in forward positions, where they were easily cut off and surrounded. On the first day alone, 1,200 Soviet aircraft were destroyed, most of them on the ground. Within two days, 2,000 Soviet aircraft had been lost. Within five days, the Germans had captured or destroyed 2,500 Soviet tanks. Within three weeks, the Soviets had lost 3,500 tanks, 6,000 aircraft, and 2 million men, including a significant percentage of the officer corps.

For more than a week, Stalin remained incommunicado, stunned by his failure and hiding from his people. Not until July 3 did he address the nation. Others were made the scapegoats for Stalin's own failures. General Dimitri G. Pavlov, commander of the sector that had borne the brunt of the German attack, had pleaded with Stalin a week before the German onslaught to be allowed to establish rearward defensive positions. He and eight other generals and political officials were tried and shot.

In the first months of the invasion, Stalin consistently ignored sound military advice from his generals, with disastrous results. His orders that the army stand and fight merely meant that larger portions of it were surrounded and destroyed. German armored pincers took Minsk in mid-July, along with 290,000 prisoners, 2,500 tanks, and 1,400 guns. Smolensk followed a week later with 100,000 prisoners, 2,000 tanks, and 1,900 guns. During August and September, instead of letting his armies escape a German panzer pincer on Kiev, Stalin ordered the city held. German infantry then sealed off Kiev. It fell on September 19 and with it most of five Soviet armies: 665,000 prisoners and vast quantities of weapons.

Fortunately for the Soviet Union, the campaign was sufficiently prolonged for Stalin to grow as a war leader. He absorbed specialist knowledge, and, if lacking in imagination, by the end of the war had grown into a highly effective military strategist. He was also famed, and feared, for his frequent and often abrupt interference in the conduct of operations. Front commanders reported to him daily and received orders directly from him. On August 8, Stalin took over the position of supreme commander in chief. There were frequent changes in the top professional leadership of the General Staff (Glavnokomand). At first, Georgiï K. Zhukov was commanding general; from the end of July 1941, it was Boris M. Shaposhnikov; from May 1942 it was Aleksandr M. Vasilevskii; and from February 1945 to March 1946 it was Alexi I. Antonov. Officers who had been imprisoned under the purges were now released to take command. Prominent among some 4,000 so freed was colonel, later marshal of the Soviet Union, Konstantin K. Rokossovsky, who had undergone extensive torture.

Supply remained a serious problem for the army. Early in August 1941, a Main Directorate of the Red Army was established under the General Staff that was responsible for supplying the army. Arms shortages were especially acute in the winter of 1941–1942. By December 1941, only 39 percent of aircraft production goals had been met, and artillery shell production was no more than 20 to 30 percent of targets.

The rapid conversion of Soviet industry to military purposes and the relocation of entire factories east of the Urals both registered considerable results in 1942, when 59 percent of industrial production was devoted to arms manufacture, compared with only 30 percent before 1940. The military share of the state budget on the army also increased dramatically. The General Staff and government concentrated the Soviet Union's entire productive capacity on the war effort, and achievements were dramatic. During 1942, Germany produced 9,200 tanks, but the Soviet Union built 24,089; only the United States, with 24,997, built more. Superior military production to that of Germany was a major factor in the Soviet military victory in the war. In 1944, thanks in large part to the organizing genius of Albert Speer, Germany managed to produce 22,100 tanks, but the Soviet Union kept ahead, with 28,963. Artillery production also grew, from 42,300 guns in 1941 to 127,000 in 1942. Other weapons systems underwent similar production increases.

The vast distances in the Soviet Union and the primitive transportation helped to break down the German blitzkrieg, which had prospered on the short distances of Poland and France. Weather also helped to save the Red Army. Hitler believed that the Red Army could be defeated in a short campaign of only six weeks, and the German army was ill-prepared to deal with the Russian winter and temperatures of –5 degrees Fahrenheit. Eventually, temperatures in the winter of 1941–1942 plunged to –60 degrees Fahrenheit. Soviet forces were able to fight in those conditions, but the German army was unprepared.

Hitler also miscalculated Soviet manpower resources. In 1941, some 22 million Soviet citizens had experienced some degree of military training. Before the invasion, the Germans had estimated Soviet strength in the west at about 155 divisions: 100 infantry, 25 cavalry, and the equivalent of 30 mechanized. This was not far off the mark; actual Soviet strength was 177 divisional equivalents, but this included air force and border troops, and Soviet divisions were smaller than their German counterparts. By mid-August, the Germans had met and defeated the Soviet force they had expected, but by then another 160 Soviet divisions had appeared. By the summer of 1942, despite near-catastrophic losses, the Soviet field army numbered 5,534,000 officers and men.

The bulk of Soviet soldiers were poorly trained. The low educational level of the population hampered creation of technically effective combat units. The numerous nationalities and languages of the Soviet Union also worked against an efficient, cohesive military establishment. Women proved invaluable in the war effort; some 10 percent of Soviet military personnel and 15 percent of partisan forces were female, many of them serving in combat roles. Women went to the front as pilots, navigators, mechanics, and political officers. In sharp contrast to other armies in the war, there were all-women ground units, including the 1st Independent Volunteer Women's Rifle Brigade and the 1st Independent Women's Reserve Rifle Regiment. Women were also heavily involved in partisan activities in the western portions of the Soviet Union occupied by the Germans.

Improving circumstances enabled the Red Army to take the offensive in November 1942. The winter campaign of 1942–1943 broke the German stranglehold on Leningrad and drove Axis forces west. Stalingrad, Rostov, and Kursk were all liberated. When the Germans began Operation CITADEL in the summer of 1943, the Red Army halted the German drive in the great Battle of Kursk. That summer and fall, the Red Army resumed the advance, and from this point the Soviets maintained the initiative for the remainder of the war. On a 1,200-mile front, Soviet forces destroyed more than 200 Axis divisions and more than 14,000 aircraft. During this period, partisan activity complemented the combat actions of the regular Soviet forces, tying down large numbers of German troops in maintaining lines of communication stretching all the way back to Germany. In the newly liberated regions, industrial enterprises were set up that increased steadily growing military production. Soviet forces also received improved arms: the machine pistol (PPS), a new heavy machine gun, the 76 mm artillery piece, a 57 mm antitank gun, a new 152 mm howitzer, and 120 mm and 160 mm mortars. Furthermore, production was increased of the magnificent T-34 tank with its 76 mm gun, and new KV-85 and IS heavy tanks were introduced.

A large amount of U.S. Lend-Lease aid was certainly important to the Red Army's war effort. The Soviet Union received 375,000 American trucks, 50,000 jeeps, and

12,000 railroad cars. These greatly enhanced the mobility of the Red Army and allowed it to carry out sustained offensive operations. The United States also supplied sufficient food to provide one-half pound per Russian soldier a day.

If lacking in flair, many Soviet soldiers fought hard during the war with a dogged persistence, even in hopeless situations. Nonetheless, a staggering 5.25 million Soviet soldiers were taken prisoner during the war. Desertion rates remained high, in part because of the brutal conditions. One source estimates that the Soviet Union executed 157,000 people during the war on charges of cowardice or desertion.

Soviet military casualties continued to be high, in part because of the costly Soviet practice of attacking without tanks, holding the armor back until a breakthrough was achieved. The Soviets lost more men in the battle for Berlin alone at the end of the war than the United States lost during the war in all theaters combined.

By the end of 1944, the Red Army had almost completely liberated Soviet territory. In January 1945, the Red Army began its offensive against Berlin. The East Prussian Campaign and the Vistula-Oder Operation were the most important strategic operations for the Red Army in the war. In the spring of 1945, the Red Army mounted simultaneous operations on a vast front extending from the Baltic to the Carpathians. On April 25, troops of the First Ukrainian Front met the First American Army in Torgau at the Elbe, symbolizing the end of Nazi Germany. By the end of the fighting in Europe, despite its horrific losses during the conflict, the Red Army had 6 million men under arms, double the number for the German army.

Three months after the conclusion of fighting in Europe, the Soviet Union declared war on Japan. On August 9, Soviet forces mounted a large, rapid, and highly successful invasion of Manchuria. Lasting only a week, this bold operation was conducted in difficult terrain against what were considered some of Japan's best troops and ended with Soviet control of Manchuria.

Eva-Maria Stolberg and Spencer C. Tucker

See also

Casualties; Eastern Front; Northeast Europe Theater; Poland, Role in War; Prisoners of War (POWs); Stalin, Josef; Zhukov, Georgiĭ Konstantinovich

References

Bellamy, Chris. *Absolute War: Soviet Russia in the Second World War.* New York: Alfred A. Knopf, 2007.

Bialer, Seweryn. *Stalin and His Generals: Soviet Military Memoirs of World War II.* New York: Pegasus, 1969.

Dubb, Walter S., Jr. *The Soviet Economy and the Red Army, 1930–1945.* Westport, CT: Praeger, 1995.

Erickson, John. *The Road to Berlin: Stalin's War with Germany.* New York: Harper and Row, 1983.

Erickson, John. *The Road to Stalingrad: Stalin's War with Germany.* New York: Harper and Row, 1975.

Erickson, John. *The Soviet High Command: A Military-Political History, 1918–1941.* Portland, OR: Frank Cass, 2001.

Glantz, David M. *The Battle for Leningrad, 1941–1944*. Lawrence, KS: University Press of Kansas, 2002.

Glantz, David M. *Colossus Reborn: The Red Army at War, 1941–1943*. Lawrence, KS: University Press of Kansas, 2005.

Glantz, David M. *Operation Barbarossa: Hitler's Invasion of Russia*. Stroud: The History Press, 2011.

Glantz, David M. *Stumbling Colossus: The Red Army on the Eve of World War*. Lawrence, KS: University Press of Kansas, 1998.

Glantz, David M., and Jonathan M. House. *When Titans Clashed: How the Red Army Stopped Hitler*. Lawrence, KS: University Press of Kansas, 1995.

Goldman, Stuart D. *Nomonhan, 1939: The Red Army's Victory that Shaped World War II*. Annapolis, MD: Naval Institute Press, 2012.

Gorodetsky, Gabriel. *Grand Delusion: Stalin and the German Invasion of Russia*. New Haven, CT: Yale University Press, 1999.

Harrison, Mark. *Soviet Planning in Peace and War, 1938–1945*. Cambridge: Cambridge University Press, 1985.

Merridale, Catherine. *Ivan's War: Life and Death in the Red Army, 1939–1945*. New York: Henry Holt, 2006.

Overy, Richard. *Russia's War: A History of the Soviet War Effort: 1941–1945*. London: TV Books, 1998.

Reese, Roger R. *Red Commanders: A Social History of the Soviet Army Officer Corps, 1918–1991*. Lawrence, KS: University Press of Kansas, 2005.

Reese, Roger R. *Why Stalin's Soldiers Fought: The Red Army's Military Effectiveness in World War II*. Lawrence, KS: University Press of Kansas, 2011.

Shtemenko, Sergei M. *The Soviet General Staff at War 1941–1945*. Moscow: Progress Publishers, 1970.

Soviet Union, Navy

When World War II began in September 1939, the Soviet navy was in the process of implementing great changes. In late 1935, Soviet leader Josef Stalin had switched from the strategic concept of a small war at sea and planned to build a large oceangoing fleet. In August 1939, the Naval Staff had finalized a building plan for the next 10 years for 15 battleships, 16 battle cruisers, 2 light aircraft carriers, 28 cruisers, 36 destroyer-leaders, 163 destroyers, 442 submarines, and many smaller vessels. Of the new ships, only 1 cruiser, 4 leaders, 13 destroyers, and 158 submarines had been completed by the time the war began. In addition to these, the Soviet navy had available only 3 old battleships, 5 cruisers, 17 destroyers, and 7 submarines.

During the November 1939–March 1940 war against Finland, the Baltic Fleet carried out shore bombardment and submarine operations against supply traffic to Finland. The fleet sank only a few Finnish ships, at the cost of one submarine lost. The end of the war, however, pushed the Soviet borders forward in the Arctic by inclusion of the entire "Fisherman's Peninsula" and in the Baltic in the Karelian sector. These territorial acquisitions and Hanko at the entrance of the Gulf of Finland as a new naval base greatly improved the defenses of Leningrad, the Soviet Union's second-largest city.

A nonaggression pact with Germany brought further territorial gains for the Soviet Union. In the summer of 1940, acting under its secret provisions, the USSR incorporated the Baltic states, further improving the base situation for the Soviet Baltic Fleet. In the Black Sea, Soviet territorial gains in Bessarabia created an additional buffer for Odessa and allowed the establishment of a Danube Flotilla.

The rising danger of war with Germany forced the Soviet navy in October 1940 to scale down its naval building program. Although Soviet intelligence agencies received many reports about German preparations for an attack, and British and U.S. leaders also sent warnings based on their intelligence reports, Stalin refused to believe Adolf Hitler would attack the Soviet Union before he concluded the war in the west by subduing Britain. He even forbade preparations for a preventative counterattack into the German deployments, which his General Staff had proposed. The German attack of June 22, 1941, therefore, caused great disorder and led to heavy Soviet losses, especially in the army and air force, but also to the Baltic and Black Sea fleets.

The program to build an oceangoing fleet had to be scrapped, as well. By that time, 4 cruisers, 7 destroyer-leaders, 30 destroyers, and 204 submarines had been commissioned, and the Soviets had added a further 4 submarines from the Estonian and Latvian fleets to their own forces. Ships in the Far East yards would be completed, whereas the bigger ships in the western yards were laid up for completion after the war. Of the ships partly completed, only 3 battleships, 2 battle cruisers, 10 cruisers, 2 destroyer-leaders, 42 destroyers, and 91 submarines would be launched.

The Baltic Fleet—now comprising 2 old battleships, 3 cruisers, 2 destroyer-leaders, 19 destroyers, and 70 submarines—had to defend the entrances to the Bay of Riga and the Gulf of Finland by laying mine barrages. At the same time, the Germans and the Finns (the Finns had reentered the war as a cobelligerent of Germany) tried to blockade the Baltic fleet by laying mines. The German attack forced the Soviets to abandon its Baltic bases and the Finnish harbor at Hanko, incurring great losses in the process. The German "Juminda barrage" of mines was particularly effective, augmented as it was by air attacks against Soviet ships in the enclosed harbor fortress at Kronstadt and at Leningrad. In 1941, the Leningrad shipyards managed to complete 7 destroyers and 5 submarines, but the Soviet Union lost 1 battleship, 15 destroyers, and 28 submarines in mine and air attacks, with many more vessels damaged.

From 1942 until October 1944, the Baltic fleet was confined to the innermost part of the Gulf of Finland by German and Finnish mine barrages. Only the submarines could even try to break out into the open. This tactic met with some success in 1942, when the Soviets launched 31 submarine operations; 22 of these breached the mine barriers and reached the Baltic, where they sank 25 ships. Twelve submarines, however, were lost in these actions. In 1943, all attempts to break through the barriers failed, and 4 more submarines were lost. Only after the Finnish truce of October 1944 did Soviet submarines again try to reach the Baltic Sea. By the end of the war, the remaining 22 submarines managed to sink 35 ships, including the liners *Wilhelm Gustloff*, *General Steuben*, and *Goya*. The *Wilhelm Gustloff* was the largest German ship ever sunk by a Soviet submarine; some 9,300 people lost their lives. In the case of the *General Steuben*, of 4,000 people aboard

A fast patrol boat of the Soviet sea fleet maneuvers at high speed near Sevastopol during an attack on an enemy submarine on July 13, 1942. The Black Sea fleet played a vital and heroic part in the epic defense of Sevastopol, shelling and blasting enemy coastal emplacements, landing parties of marines to harass the enemy rear, and gaining valuable information from scouts shot ashore through submarine torpedo tubes. (AP/Wide World Photos)

(including 2,000 German military wounded), only 300 survived; and in the *Goya* only 183 survived of some 7,000 passengers and crew. Most of those perishing in these German ships were refugees from East Prussia and the Baltic states. Baltic fleet vessels, operating in conjunction with aircraft, also supported the operations of the Red Army in late 1944 and early 1945. They carried out landing operations in the Gulf of Finland and on the Baltic Islands, and they also attacked German naval forces in the area.

In June 1941, the Black Sea Fleet consisted of 1 old battleship, 6 cruisers, 3 destroyer-leaders, 13 destroyers, and 44 submarines. The German invasion of the Ukraine that month forced the fleet to first support and then evacuate the cities captured by German and Romanian forces in operations beginning in the Danubian estuaries and lasting through mid-1942. Nikolaev, which contained the chief Soviet building yards, had to be evacuated that August. The cruisers, leaders, and destroyers already launched there were towed to Caucasian ports, and the remaining ships were destroyed before the German forces occupied the city.

Between August and October, German and Romanian forces surrounded Odessa by land, and Soviet forces there had to be supported by the fleet, which then evacuated the city successfully. For six months, the Soviet main base at Sevastopol also had to be supplied and supported by naval operations that involved nearly all available naval forces.

In December 1941, the fleet undertook a great amphibious operation against German forces occupying the Kerch Peninsula in an attempt to relieve the defenders at Sevastopol. By May 1942, however, the Germans had annihilated the Soviet ground forces, and only remnants could be successfully evacuated. During and to the very end of the final German attack on Sevastopol, Soviet surface ships and submarines attempted to supply the fortress and evacuate the wounded. During these operations, which lasted through mid-July 1942, the Black Sea Fleet lost 1 cruiser, 2 destroyer-leaders, 9 destroyers, and 12 submarines. Five of the submarines were lost during operations to interdict Axis sea traffic on the west coast of the Black Sea, an area heavily mined by both the Germans and Romanians.

From August 1942 until September 1943, the Black Sea Fleet concerned itself primarily with the supply of harbors on the Caucasian coast that were endangered by the continuing German offensive. This allowed the Red Army to hold Taupse, and naval landing operations coordinated with submarine and motor torpedo boat attacks assisted in the Soviet offensive on the Kuban Peninsula as well. Here Soviet forces successfully interrupted sea traffic between Romania and Crimea. The attacks against German sea traffic along the west coast, however, were largely a failure.

The battle for the Crimea began in October 1943 and lasted until May 1944. The Black Sea Fleet again tried to disrupt sea traffic from Konstanta to Sevastopol with submarines, light surface forces, and air attacks. On Stalin's order, the larger ships were kept out of these operations. After a short pause, in August 1944 the Red Army began its offensive into Romania. Once Romania capitulated, Bulgaria was occupied, and the Germans were forced to scuttle the remainder of their naval forces in the Black Sea—effectively ending naval combat in that theater. Between July 1942 and the end of Black Sea naval operations, the Black Sea Fleet lost 1 destroyer-leader, 2 destroyers, and 14 submarines. A few small submarines were transferred via inland waterways from the Arctic and by rail from the Pacific to augment the fleet there, but they arrived too late to participate in operations against German–Romanian shipping.

The Soviet Northern Fleet began the war with 8 destroyers and 15 submarines. Its first task was to support the Red Army in halting the German offensive toward Murmansk. The submarines were then sent to attack German supply traffic along the Norwegian coast from the Lofoten Islands to Kirkenes, although they met only limited initial success. A few British submarines sent to Murmansk for some months achieved slightly better results. The Northern Fleet was soon augmented by the transfer of 8 submarines along interior waterways from the Baltic in 1941. A further 5 submarines came from the Pacific in 1942 and 1943, and 12 new submarines arrived from the Caspian during that time as well. The fleet carried out operations throughout the war, inflicting some losses on German shipping and losing 25 submarines, mainly to mine barrages and antisubmarine forces. The fleet also supported Allied convoys over the final portion of the route to Murmansk with destroyers—including 3 sent from the Pacific Fleet via the northern sea route—and naval aircraft. The main defense burden for these convoys, however, fell to the British Home Fleet. In the later years of the war, British and American surface ships and submarines assisted in defending the northern sea route as well. Overall, the Northern Fleet suffered minimal losses beyond the submarines; only 3 destroyers and some escort vessels and auxiliaries were damaged or sunk.

The Soviet Pacific Fleet served as a reservoir of personnel and for the training of naval crews for most of the war. However, the Pacific Fleet transferred a few destroyers to the Northern Fleet, along with some submarines. In the last month of the war, strengthened by Lend-Lease deliveries of U.S. ships, the Pacific Fleet took part in the war against Japan, conducting landing operations on the east coast of Korea, Sakhalin Island, and in the Kurile Islands. Lend-Lease played a vital role in securing the route along the Aleutian Islands to Kamchatka and Soviet bases in the Far East, especially Vladivostok. This proved to be a much safer route than either Murmansk or Arkhangelsk for Allied supplies to reach the Soviet Union, not least because of the Soviet–Japanese nonaggression pact of March 1941. The fleet lost only 5 submarines through accidents during these operations, though 2 were eventually recovered. One more submarine, which was en route to the Northern Fleet, was lost to a Japanese submarine attack just off the west coast of the United States. A submarine also went down in the final days of the war, sunk in all likelihood by a Japanese mine.

Outside of these major theater operations, the Soviet navy also used river flotillas. The first flotilla operations came on the Pripjet River in September 1939 against the Poles. Other operations followed: on the Danube and the Dnieper in 1941; on the Volga in 1942; and on the Danube again in 1944 and 1945. Flotillas carried out operations on Lake Ladoga and Lake Onega from 1941 to 1944, and they assisted the Red Army in its operations on smaller seas, rivers, and lakes.

Jürgen Rohwer

See also

Atlantic, Battle of the; Eastern Front; Finland, Role in War; Germany, Navy; Great Britain, Navy; Stalin, Josef

References

Achkasov, V. I., and N. B. Pavlovich. *Soviet Naval Operations in the Great Patriotic War, 1941–1945.* Annapolis, MD: Naval Institute Press, 1981.

Herrick, Robert W. *Soviet Naval Strategy: Fifty Years of Theory and Practice.* Annapolis, MD: Naval Institute Press, 1968.

Meister, Jürg. *Soviet Warships of the Second World War.* London: MacDonald and Jane's, 1977.

O'Hara, Vincent P., W. David Dickson, and Richard Worth, eds. *On Seas Contested: The Seven Great Navies of the Second World War.* Annapolis, MD: Naval Institute Press, 2010.

Philbin, Tobias R., III. *The Lure of Neptune: German–Soviet Naval Collaboration and Ambitions, 1919–1941.* Columbia, SC: University of South Carolina Press, 1994.

Rohwer, Jürgen, and Gerhard Hümmelchen. *Chronology of the War at Sea 1939–1945.* London: Greenhill Books, 1992.

Rohwer, Jürgen, and Mikhail S. Monakov. *Stalin's Ocean-Going Fleet: Soviet Naval Strategy and Shipbuilding Programs, 1935–1953.* London: Frank Cass, 2001.

Strekhnin, Yuriy Fedorovich. *Commandos from the Sea: Soviet Naval Spetsnaz in World War II.* Translated by James F. Gebhardt. Annapolis, MD: Naval Institute Press, 1996.

Stalin, Josef (Iosif Vissarionovich Dzhugashvili) (1879–1953)

Josef Stalin was general secretary of the Central Committee of the Communist Party, supreme commander of the Soviet armed forces, marshal of the Soviet Union, and Soviet dictator. Stalin was indisputably one of the most powerful rulers in history, as well as one of the greatest murderers.

Born Iosif Vissarionovich Dzhugashvili in the Georgian town of Gori on December 21, 1879, Stalin was the only child of his parents to survive infancy. His parents were semiliterate peasants, the descendants of serfs; his father worked as a cobbler and his mother as a washerwoman and domestic. Soso, the common Georgian nickname for Iosef, Iosif, or Josef, was admitted to the four-year elementary ecclesiastical school in Gori in September 1888 and graduated (six years later) in July 1894. His mother wished a career in the priesthood for him, so in September 1894, he entered the Tiflis theological seminary on a free scholarship.

Stalin's "official" biographies obscure more than they reveal, and they differ for the most part on the cause of Soso's exit from the seminary in 1899. Some say he was expelled for revolutionary activity, and others claim that he quit, but it was at seminary that Dzhugashvili was introduced to Russian socialism and Marxism. His career as a low-level party functionary began in 1901 and included "expropriations" (robbery) and counterfeiting in support of the Russian Social Democratic Labor Party (RSDLP). Arrested, he was tried, convicted, and exiled to Siberia in 1903 under the pseudonym Koba.

Koba escaped from exile in 1904, and the next year he joined the Bolshevik faction of the RSDLP (Georgia being a stronghold of the Menshevik faction), which was led by Vladimir Lenin. By 1907, he was recognized as an outstanding Bolshevik propagandist—particularly on the nationalities question—in the Caucasus. By 1912, he was sponsored by Lenin to membership in the Bolshevik-controlled RSDLP Central Committee at the Prague conference where the final split between the Bolsheviks and Mensheviks took place. Stalin (steel), as he was then known, was freed from Siberian exile by the Russian Revolution of March 1917. He returned to Petrograd and became editor of the party newspaper *Pravda*. His seniority on the Central Committee allowed him to assume leadership of the Bolsheviks until Lenin's return to Petrograd from Switzerland in April 1917. Stalin seems to have played little role in the Bolshevik seizure of power in October 1917.

Stalin's supposed expertise on the nationalities question led to his appointment as commissar of nationalities in the new Bolshevik government. Throughout the Civil War period, the real government of Russia was the Bolshevik Politburo of five men: Lenin, Leon Trotsky, Lev Kamenev, Nikolai Bukharin, and Stalin. To Stalin fell the day-to-day management of the party, which gave him considerable power. In 1922, his power base was expanded when he was appointed general secretary of the Central Committee, whereby de facto control of the Politburo accrued to him.

Following Lenin's incapacitation by stroke in 1923 and his death on January 21, 1924, over time Stalin was able to parlay his base of power into control of the organs of Soviet governance. By 1929, his accumulation of power was complete and unchallengeable. In the 1930s, he began to purge "old Bolsheviks"—his former adversaries—in his quest to maintain and strengthen his hold on power.

Josef Stalin, secretary general of the Soviet Communist Party and supreme commander of the Soviet armed forces in World War II, dominated the Soviet Union from 1929 until his death in 1953. He led his country through terrible suffering and near defeat in 1941 and 1942 to ultimate triumph over Germany. Deeply suspicious of all threats to his own dictatorial position within Russia, as Soviet ruler Stalin brutally eliminated politicians, military officers, and millions of ordinary Russians whose loyalty to himself he considered questionable. (Library of Congress)

Periodic purges were not unprecedented after the Bolshevik seizure of power. Most were directed at subordinate officials and low-ranking party members, who bore the brunt of policy failures. The Great Purges, conducted on Stalin's orders, were characterized by their focus on party and state elites, the use of mass terror, and dramatic public "show trials" and "confessions" by the accused.

Beginning in 1936, in a series of show trials held in Moscow, numerous leading Communists and old Bolsheviks were tried; they confessed and were executed or sentenced to hard labor. At the same time, millions of ordinary Soviet citizens simply disappeared in what became known as the "deep comb-out." Eventually some 8 million people were arrested, 1 million of whom were executed; the remainder were sent to the gulags. In 1937, after the destruction of his former adversaries, Stalin began to eliminate potential threats to his power with the purge of Red Army leaders. Eventually, 40 to 50 percent of the senior officer corps disappeared. Not all were executed or died in the gulags; many survived and were rehabilitated in World War II. Others left in the army found the previously closed path to military prominence open.

Simultaneously, Stalin reversed Lenin's New Economic Policy, which had introduced a degree of capitalism in order to revive the economy, purged the middle-class peasants who had emerged under that policy (the Kulaks), and carried out the collectivization of agriculture. Reliable casualty figures for the collectivization drive are unavailable, but if one includes the famine fatalities, the number of those who died may exceed 10 million people—a figure that, for whatever it may be worth, Stalin gave to Winston Churchill in Moscow in August 1942. Russian writer Nikolai Tolstoi has put the number who died in the gulags under Stalin at 12 million people. These numbers compare with a total of 15,000 executions in the last 50 years of the tsars. In terms of the sheer number of victims, the Soviet Union under Stalin unquestionably outdistanced Hitler's Germany.

In addition to pushing the collectivization of agriculture, Stalin also implemented a series of five-year plans that set quotas for growth in all areas of the economy. Much of this effort was devoted to the exploitation of Soviet natural resources and development of heavy industry. The last of these plans prior to World War II also emphasized armaments production. Although growth was uneven, considerable progress was registered, much of which came at the expense of the living standards of the Soviet people.

In the 1930s, German ambitions alarmed Stalin, who grew interested in collective security. He instructed People's Commissar for Foreign Affairs Maksim Litvinov to pursue an internationalist course. In 1934, the USSR joined the League of Nations. Stalin also secured defensive pacts with other nations, including France. In the late 1930s, many western leaders still distrusted the Soviet Union; thus, even though the Kremlin was willing to enter into arrangements with the west against Germany and Japan, no effective coalition was forged, and events during the decade took a course that largely ignored the Soviet Union. Unsentimental in such matters, in August 1939 Stalin arranged a nonaggression pact with Germany that allowed Adolf Hitler to invade Poland without fear of war with the Soviets. Stalin hoped, thereby, to gain time to strengthen his own military. He also gained territory in eastern Poland and the Baltic states. When Finnish leaders rejected his demands, Stalin ordered Soviet forces to invade Finland in November 1939, in order to secure territory and bases against a potential German attack.

Stalin discounted numerous western warnings in the winter and spring of 1941 that Germany was preparing to attack the Soviet Union, viewing these as efforts by the Allied powers and the United States to trick the USSR into war with Germany. In consequence, Soviet forces were largely unprepared for Operation BARBAROSSA, the German invasion of June 22, 1941. Soviet military units were not even immediately authorized to return fire.

For nearly two weeks after the German attack, Stalin remained incommunicado, but he finally reappeared to proclaim the "Great Patriotic War" and rally his people and the Red Army to the defense of the "motherland." During the course of the fighting on the Eastern Front, Stalin grew dramatically as a military commander. All important strategic and operational decisions—and some not so important—required his personal approval as supreme commander. He also absorbed specialist military knowledge, although he held no strategic dogmas or pet operational blueprints. For the most part, Stalin allowed his generals to formulate their own views and develop their own plans following his general ideas, based on well-founded knowledge of the situation. If Stalin bears great responsibility for the early defeats suffered by the Soviet Union in the first two years of the war, he must also be credited for Soviet successes in its last two years.

Besides rallying the Soviet people and armed forces with speeches and rhetoric, Stalin demonstrated his own readiness to stand firm against the German onslaught. On October 15, 1941, the Germans having driven to within 50 miles of Moscow, the Soviet government and diplomatic community were evacuated to Kuibyshev on the Volga. This caused panic among the Muscovites, who believed they had been abandoned. The announcement on October 17 that Stalin was in the Kremlin restored relative calm to the city. Stalin remained in the Kremlin, directing strategic operations throughout the siege of Moscow and, with rare exceptions, for the remainder of the war.

During the war, Stalin had a clear picture of his postwar objectives. As the western powers had used the new eastern European states after World War I to isolate Communist Russia and contain Bolshevism, so Stalin planned to use the same states—under Soviet control as satellites—to exclude western influences from his own empire. At no time in the war after June 1941 was less than three-quarters of the German army committed on the Eastern Front. Stalin used this fact, delays by the western Allies in opening a true second front, and the great suffering of the Soviet Union (up to 27 million dead in the war) to secure massive amounts of Lend-Lease aid. He also used the actual occupation of eastern and much of central Europe by the Red Army to secure major concessions from the west at Tehran, Yalta, and Potsdam, thereby ushering in the Soviet empire.

Stalin continued to rule the Soviet Union with an iron fist almost until the day of his death. He died on March 5, 1953, a month after suffering a stroke, at Kuntsevo near Moscow.

Arthur T. Frame and Spencer C. Tucker

See also

Balkans Theater; Churchill, Sir Winston Leonard Spencer; Eastern Front; Finland, Role in War; Hitler, Adolf; Northeast Europe Theater; Poland, Role in War; Roosevelt, Franklin D.; Soviet Union, Air Force; Soviet Union, Army; Soviet Union, Navy; Yalta Conference; Zhukov, Georgii Konstantinovich

References

Barros, James, and Richard Gregor. *Double Deception: Stalin, Hitler, and the Invasion of Russia.* DeKalb, IL: Northern Illinois Press, 1995.

Berthon, Simon, and Joanna Potts. *Warlords: An Extraordinary Re-Creation of World War II through the Eyes and Minds of Hitler, Roosevelt, Churchill, and Stalin.* New York: Da Capo Press, 2006.

Bullock, Alan. *Hitler and Stalin: Parallel Lives.* New York: Alfred A. Knopf, 1992.

Conquest, Robert. *Stalin: Breaker of Nations.* New York: Penguin, 1991.

Deutscher, Isaac. *Stalin: A Political Biography.* New York: Oxford University Press, 1969.

Fenby, Jonathan. *Alliance: The Inside Story of How Roosevelt, Churchill and Stalin Won One War and Began Another.* San Francisco, CA: MacAdam/Cage, 2007.

Figes, Orlando. *The Whisperers: Private Life in Stalin's Russia.* New York: Metropolitan Books, 2007.

Gorodetsky, Gabriel. *Grand Delusion: Stalin and the German Invasion of Russia.* New Haven, CT: Yale University Press, 1999.

Hasegawa, Tsuyoshi. *Racing the Enemy: Stalin, Truman, and the Surrender of Japan.* Cambridge, MA: Belknap Press of Harvard University, 2005.

Lukacs, John. *Hitler and Stalin: June 1941.* New Haven, CT: Yale University Press, 2006.

Mawdsley, Evan. *The Stalin Years: The Soviet Union 1929–1953*. Manchester: Manchester University Press, 2003.

McNeal, Robert H. *Stalin: Man and Ruler*. New York: New York University Press, 1988.

Montefiore, Simon Sebag. *Stalin: The Court of the Red Tsar*. New York: Alfred A. Knopf, 2004.

Montefiore, Simon Sebag. *Young Stalin*. New York: Alfred A. Knopf, 2007.

Mosier, John. *Deathride: Hitler vs. Stalin—The Eastern Front, 1941–1945*. New York: Simon and Schuster, 2010.

Murphy, David E. *What Stalin Knew: The Enigma of Barbarossa*. New Haven, CT: Yale University Press, 2005.

Overy, Richard. *The Dictators: Hitler's Germany, Stalin's Russia*. New York: Norton, 2005.

Pleshakov, Constantine. *Stalin's Folly: The Tragic First Ten Days of World War II on the Eastern Front*. Boston, MA: Houghton Mifflin, 2005.

Raack, R. C. *Stalin's Drive to the West, 1938–1945: The Origins of the Cold War*. Stanford, CA: Stanford University Press, 1995.

Service, Robert. *Stalin: A Biography*. Cambridge, MA: Belknap Press of Harvard University, 2005.

Snyder, Timothy. *Bloodlands: Europe between Hitler and Stalin*. New York: Basic Books, 2010.

Suvorov, Viktor. *The Chief Culprit: Stalin's Grand Design to Start World War II*. Annapolis, MD: Naval Institute Press, 2008.

Todd, Allen. *The European Dictatorships: Hitler, Stalin, Mussolini*. Cambridge: Cambridge University Press, 2002.

Tucker, Robert C. *Stalin as Revolutionary 1879–1929*. New York: W. W. Norton, 1973.

Tucker, Robert C. *Stalin in Power: The Revolution from Above, 1928–1941*. New York: Norton, 1990.

Ulam, Adam B. *Stalin: The Man and His Era*. 4th ed. Boston, MA: Beacon Press, 2001.

Volkogonov, Dimitrii. *Stalin: Triumph and Tragedy*. Translated and edited by Harold Shukman. New York: Grove Weidenfeld, 1991.

Weeks, Albert L. *Stalin's Other War: Soviet Grand Strategy, 1939–1941*. Lanham, MD: Rowman and Littlefield, 2002.

Weinberg, Gerhard L. *Visions of Victory: The Hopes of Eight World War II Leaders*. Cambridge: Cambridge University Press, 2005.

Tōjō Hideki (1884–1948)

Tōjō Hideki was a Japanese army general and prime minister from 1941 to 1944. Born in Tokyo on December 30, 1884, Tōjō graduated from the Military Academy in 1905. A career staff officer, he served as an attaché in Europe in the early 1920s. During the early 1930s, he associated himself with the Control Faction, an influential clique within the Japanese military that favored military cooperation with the civil bureaucracy and large corporations to expand Japanese influence in China. The failure of a coup attempt by the rival Imperial Way Faction in February 1936 paved the way for the Control Faction's domination of the army and eventually of Japan itself.

Because of his position as one of the Control Faction leaders, Tōjō's career in the late 1930s prospered. In 1938, he was recalled to Tokyo from Manzhouguo (Manchukuo), where he had been serving on the staff of the Guandong (Kwantung) Army, to take up an appointment as a vice minister of the army. In 1940, he became army minister in the cabinet of Konoe Fumimaro. An ardent militarist determined to advance Japanese power by force of arms, Tōjō was a keen supporter of the Axis alliance with Nazi Germany and expansion of the war in China.

Following the collapse of the Konoe cabinet in October 1941, Tōjō, still an active army officer, was appointed prime minister in an atmosphere of escalating tension with the United States. As prime minister, he did nothing to alleviate those tensions but rather prepared Japan for a war that he considered inevitable. On December 7, 1941, Japan initiated hostilities in the Pacific with its attack on Pearl Harbor.

Following an early succession of victories in Southeast Asia and the Pacific during 1941 and 1942, it became increasingly apparent that Tōjō and other Japanese leaders had grossly underestimated the political will and resources of the United States and its allies. In view of Japan's growing matériel inferiority, Tōjō attempted to centralize and coordinate the war effort by taking personal control of key posts in the cabinet and in the army in 1943 and 1944. These actions, however, aroused opposition among members of powerful civil and military circles who resented Tōjō's intrusions. He also made a vain attempt to cultivate closer relations with Japan's Asian neighbors by convening the Greater East Asia Conference in November 1943. But the conference, which was attended by Japanese-sponsored puppet rulers from China and Southeast Asia, merely produced a vague declaration of Asian solidarity.

General Tōjō Hideki, an army officer and militant nationalist, supported Japanese expansion in China and elsewhere in Asia. He became prime minister of Japan on October 17, 1941, and in this position he sanctioned the December 7, 1941, attack on Pearl Harbor. Forced out of power in July 1944, as the Japanese military situation deteriorated, after Japan's defeat Tōjō unsuccessfully attempted suicide. Put on trial for war crimes in 1948 before the International Military Tribunal for the Far East in Tokyo, Tōjō was convicted and hanged. (Library of Congress)

Under increasing pressure from his military and political rivals, who held him responsible for Japan's mounting defeats, Tōjō resigned in July 1944 after the fall of Saipan. Koiso Kuniaki became the new prime minister. Following Japan's surrender on August 15, 1945, Tōjō was tried and convicted of war crimes. He was hanged in Tokyo on December 23, 1948.

John M. Jennings

See also
Collaboration; Japan, Army; Pearl Harbor, Attack on

References

Bond, Brian. *British and Japanese Military Leadership in the Far Eastern War, 1941–1945*. London: Frank Cass, 2004.

Browne, Courtney. *Tōjō: The Last Banzai*. New York: Holt, Rinehart and Winston, 1967.

Butow, Robert. *Tōjō and the Coming of the War*. Princeton, NJ: Princeton University Press, 1961.

Hoyt, Edwin P. *Warlord: Tōjō against the World*. Lanham, MD: Scarborough House, 1993.

Maga, Tim. *Judgment at Tokyo: The Japanese War Crimes Trials*. Lexington, KY: University of Kentucky Press, 2001.

Totani, Yuma. *The Tokyo War Crimes Trial: The Pursuit of Justice in the Wake of World War II*. Cambridge, MA: Harvard University Press, 2008.

Weinberg, Gerhard L. *Visions of Victory: The Hopes of Eight World War II Leaders.* Cambridge: Cambridge University Press, 2005.

Truman, Harry S. (1884–1972)

Harry Truman was a U.S. political leader and president from 1945 to January 1953. Born in Lamar, Missouri, on May 8, 1884, Truman grew up on the family farm in Grandview. Poor eyesight kept him from the U.S. Naval Academy and the U.S. Military Academy. Truman never formally attended college, but he read for the bar at night at the Kansas City School of Law. He enlisted in the National Guard as a young man and served in combat in France during World War I as a field artillery battery commander.

Following the war, Truman entered politics, and with the backing of "Boss" Tom Pendergast, he was elected a judge in the court of Jackson County, Missouri. He served in that post from 1926 to 1934, when he was elected to the U.S. Senate from Missouri. Truman remained active as a reserve officer, rising to the rank of colonel and only retiring from the Army Reserve after he left the presidency. He was reelected to the Senate in 1940, but he remained relatively obscure until his service as chairman of the Committee to Investigate the National Defense Program, when he helped eliminate millions of dollars of waste in defense contracting. His efforts contributed significantly to the efficiency of the U.S. defense industry on the eve of the U.S. entry into World War II and thereafter.

President Franklin D. Roosevelt selected Truman as his running mate in 1944, and Truman was sworn in as vice president in January 1945. Roosevelt did not share with Truman his thinking on many significant war-related issues, and Truman was thus poorly prepared to become president when Roosevelt died suddenly on April 12, 1945. Yet despite his almost blind start, Truman made some bold moves virtually immediately. He supported the San Francisco Conference of Nations that established the United Nations, and he mustered popular and bipartisan support for that fledgling organization, with the intention of altering the nation's traditionally isolationist outlook in favor of a postwar internationalist foreign policy.

When the Germans surrendered only 26 days after he assumed office, Truman appointed General Dwight D. Eisenhower to head the American occupation zone in Germany, and he supported a vigorous program of denazification and war crimes prosecution. He opposed, however, the draconian Morgenthau Plan, the goal of which was to convert Germany into an agricultural state. Attending the July 1945 Potsdam Conference, Truman worked with Soviet dictator Josef Stalin and new British prime minister Clement Attlee to build on the agreements that had been reached by Stalin, Roosevelt, and British prime minister Winston Churchill at Yalta. Truman also decided to employ the atomic bomb against Japan, a decision he later said he never regretted or agonized about.

As it became increasingly clear that the Soviet Union was systematically acting contrary to the Yalta and Potsdam agreements, Truman concluded that a strong Anglo-American stand was the only means of preventing a total Soviet domination of Europe. But rapid American demobilization had reduced U.S. military strength in Europe to 391,000 men by 1946, whereas the Soviets still had 2.8 million troops under arms. Truman used U.S. economic power and the country's momentary nuclear monopoly to blunt the Soviet

Harry S. Truman, a Democrat from Missouri, became president of the United States on April 12, 1945, following the death of Franklin D. Roosevelt. As president, Truman oversaw the final months of World War II and made the decision to drop the atomic bomb. His presidency saw the development of the Cold War divisions between the Soviet Union and the United States that would endure until the late 1980s. (Library of Congress)

aspirations in postwar Europe. He also effectively blocked the Soviets from assuming any role in the occupation of Japan.

Truman was wary of Soviet conventional military power in Europe, but he also tried to maintain the wartime alliance that he considered essential to the viability of the United Nations. When Soviet intentions finally became crystal clear—first with the 1948 Communist coup in Czechoslovakia and then with the Berlin Blockade—the defining Cold War American policy of containment solidified with three landmark decisions: the spring 1947 Truman Doctrine, which provided $400 million in economic aid to enable Greece and Turkey to resist internal and external Communist threats; the $12 billion Marshall Plan, which boosted the economic recovery of Western Europe, enabling the entire region to withstand Soviet pressure; and the establishment in April 1949 of the North Atlantic Treaty Organization (NATO), a security pact including the United States and most West European nations under the terms of which all signatories pledged themselves to go to war to defend any member that came under external attack.

Truman decided on an airlift as the answer to a Soviet blockade of Berlin, demonstrating U.S. resolve to block the spread of communism in Western Europe. In May 1949, when it became clear that the Soviets had no intention of allowing all of Germany's four occupation zones to reunite under a democratically elected government, Truman supported the establishment of the Federal Republic of Germany, formed from the three western occupation zones. The Soviets retaliated almost immediately by establishing the German Democratic Republic in the east. In what he described as his most difficult decision while in office, Truman authorized the employment of U.S. forces in Korea in June 1950, within a week of the North Korean invasion of South Korea. Truman's decision to remove General Douglas MacArthur as U.S. and UN commander in Korea and the negative American public reaction to this, together with the stalemate in the war there, led Truman not to run for reelection in 1952. He left office in January 1953. Truman died in Kansas City, Missouri, on December 26, 1972.

David T. Zabecki

See also

Atomic Bomb, Decision to Employ; Churchill, Sir Winston Leonard Spencer; Eisenhower, Dwight D.; MacArthur, Douglas; Marshall, George Catlett; Roosevelt, Franklin D.; Stalin, Josef

References

Beschloss, Michael R. *The Conquerors: Roosevelt, Truman, and the Destruction of Hitler's Germany, 1941–1945.* New York: Simon and Schuster, 2002.

Hamby, Alonzo S. *Man of the People: A Life of Harry S. Truman.* New York: Oxford University Press, 1995.

Hasegawa, Tsuyoshi. *Racing the Enemy: Stalin, Truman, and the Surrender of Japan.* Cambridge, MA: Belknap Press of Harvard University, 2005.

McCoy, Donald R. *The Presidency of Harry S. Truman.* Lawrence, KS: University Press of Kansas, 1984.

McCullough, David. *Truman.* New York: Simon and Schuster, 1992.

Miscamble, Wilson D. *The Most Controversial Decision: Truman, the Atomic Bombs, and the Defeat of Japan.* Cambridge: Cambridge University Press, 2011.

Moskin, J. Robert. *Mr. Truman's War: The Final Victories of World War II and the Birth of the Postwar World.* New York: Random House, 1996.

Sand, Gregory W. *Defending the West: The Truman-Churchill Correspondence, 1945–1960.* Westport, CT: Praeger, 2004.

Truman, Harry S. *Memoirs.* 2 vols. Garden City, NY: Doubleday, 1955–1956.

United States, Army

When World War II began in Europe, the U.S. Army ranked 19th in the world in size; with only 190,000 men, it was just after that of Portugal. On September 1, 1939, as the war started in Europe, President Franklin D. Roosevelt named General George C. Marshall to be army chief of staff. Junior to some 60 other general officers when appointed, Marshall proved to be a brilliant choice. A superb organizer and staff officer, he came to be known as the "Organizer of Victory."

In September 1940, Congress passed the Selective Training and Service Act (the Burke-Wadsworth Act), the nation's first peacetime draft. The measure provided for the registration of all males between the ages of 21 and 35 and the induction into the armed forces of 800,000 draftees. Securing men was relatively easy, but training them and mobilizing U.S. military production would take time, and much of the new U.S. weaponry was going to Great Britain to keep that nation in the war. Marshall's draftees trained with broomsticks for rifles and logs representing artillery pieces. Trucks bore signs with the word tank.

As World War II began, the United States deployed a citizen army, mainly volunteers and draftees. Only two Regular Army divisions in 1940 were sufficiently equipped to be considered real divisions. In any case, most of the army's Regulars were soon scattered to assist in training. At the height of the war, Regulars made up only 3.5 percent of the Army Ground Forces, 2.6 percent of the Army Service Forces, and 1.3 percent of the Army Air Forces. The vast majority of the officers—54 for every 1,000 enlisted men—were National Guardsmen, Reservists, or newly commissioned. Ultimately, 59 percent of army officers were drawn from the ranks.

By December 7, 1941, the army was training 16 Regular Army divisions in the continental United States, along with 18 National Guard divisions, and 2 Army of the United States divisions (composed of Regulars, federalized Guardsmen, and Reservists). There were also the Regular Army's Philippine Division and 12 Philippine army divisions, all of which were destroyed in fighting there early in 1942.

U.S. forces were initially poorly equipped and ineffectively trained, and they lacked supporting weaponry such as tanks and antitank and antiaircraft guns. Ammunition was also scarce. All this changed when the United States fully mobilized for war. By 1944, U.S. steel production was about half the world total. This statistic translated into large numbers of aircraft and ships but also 86,333 tanks, 650,000 Willys jeeps, and 12,573,000 rifles and carbines. The army had so many vehicles that it could have placed every man and woman in the service in them at the same time and had room left over.

Marshall stressed firepower and maneuver. To him, this meant not only that tanks would play a prominent role but also that the entire army would be mechanized and motorized to a degree beyond that of any other military in the world. This emphasis would also enable the army to make effective use of the "triangular" concept, worked out while he was deputy commander of the Infantry School at Fort Benning, Georgia, between 1927 and 1932. The army went from large, foot-bound, 2-brigade (4-regiment) infantry divisions of 22,000 men to highly mobile, 3-regiment, 15,245-man (14,037 in January 1945) divisions. This triangular concept extended to the lowest level. One maneuver unit would fix an enemy formation in place while another turned its flank and the third maneuver unit remained in reserve.

In July 1941, President Roosevelt called for an estimate of the forces required to defeat "potential enemies." Tasked with this assignment, Major Albert C. Wedemeyer estimated that by the end of 1943, Germany and its allies might field 400 divisions. Conventional wisdom held that attacking forces needed a 2-to-1 ratio to overcome defenders, and Wedemeyer thus set the requirement at 800 divisions. Leaving out the Soviet Union, which he believed might not be able to withstand the German onslaught, he calculated that other allies could provide 100 divisions, which meant the United States would have to raise 700. Counting support troops, this would mean a total U.S. military of 28 million men. But the U.S. population was only 135 million people, and industrial production requirements, which experts believed would limit any military to a maximum of 10 percent of the overall population, meant that the armed forces could comprise no more than 13.5 million men. Of this total, the army would get 8.8 million—2.05 million in the air forces and 6.75 million in the ground forces. The latter were to be formed into 5 armies, 3 purely offensive task forces and 2 defensive ones. Wedemeyer postulated 215 maneuver divisions—61 armored, 61 mechanized, 54 infantry, 4 cavalry, 10 mountain, and 7 airborne. He thought that with overwhelming air superiority, firepower, and heavy armored components as well as a high degree of mechanization and motorization, such numbers would suffice. Transporting a force of this size to Europe would require 1,000 ships, and building these alone would take two years, as would raising, equipping, and training the troops.

As it evolved, the U.S. Army fell far short of Wedemeyer's figure. Instead, the so-called 90-division gamble was instituted. Actually, the U.S. Army of World War II numbered only 89 divisions—66 infantry, 1 (dismounted) cavalry, 16 armored, 5 airborne, and 1 mountain. Only 2 divisions did not enter sustained combat, and only 1 failed in combat.

In early 1943, Marshall reorganized the army into three major components: the Army Ground Forces, the Army Service Forces, and the Army Air Forces. In personnel, the army grew to 8,157,386 men and women by April 1945, of whom 1,831,091 served in the 16 Army Air Forces. Many of the army's best soldiers were not in the infantry, however. The Army Air Forces and specialist branches, such as rangers and paratroops, and the service staffs were permitted to skim off too high a proportion of the best-educated and fittest recruits. The infantry rifle companies were, however, called on to fight the Wehrmacht, the most skilled army of modern times.

The army worked on developing new high-firepower weapons. These included remodeled Browning automatic rifles; the Browning air-cooled, lightweight .30 caliber machine gun; the Mark II .50 caliber machine gun (which remains in use); and the superb M1 Garand infantry rifle with an 8-round clip. The M1, designed by John C. Garand and adopted by the army in 1936, fired 40 rounds a minute in the hands of the average rifleman, but an expert could get off 100 rounds in the same time frame. It had 40 percent less recoil than the Springfield '03 it replaced and had only 72 parts, compared to 92 for the Springfield. The Garand could be entirely broken down using only one tool, a .30 caliber round. There was also the lightweight (5 lb) M1 Carbine, which was issued to officers instead of a handgun. Later, the army introduced the M3 submachine gun, most of the parts of which were stamped out. This weapon was capable of a rate of fire of 450 rounds per minute.

The artillery developed new techniques to minimize the time necessary for all guns in a battery to fire on a target and to coordinate the fire of several batteries so that their shells rained down on one spot simultaneously (the "time on target," or TOT, technique). The 105 mm howitzer and the 155 mm "Long Tom" artillery pieces provided the U.S. Army with remarkably effective firepower. Self-propelled guns also enabled the artillery to keep up with the fast-moving armored and mechanized formations.

The army was not so efficient in other areas. Congress had abolished the Tank Corps in 1920 and relegated tanks to the infantry. Not until 1931 did the cavalry, which still employed horses, receive light "tankettes," known as "combat cars." The U.S. Armored Force came into being only in July 1940 after the defeat of France, but its M-3 Grant, designed hurriedly in 1940, was obsolescent before it was built. Even the M-4 Sherman medium tank, the main U.S. and British tank of the war, had trouble matching up with some of the more powerful German tanks. The army had no heavy tank in the field until the M-26 Pershing arrived in Europe in January 1945 because its armor commanders, notably Lieutenant General George S. Patton Jr., believed that tanks should not fight other tanks. Between 1944 and 1945, the 3rd Armored Division alone had 648 Shermans completely destroyed in combat and another 700 knocked out of action, repaired, and put back into operation—a loss rate of 580 percent. The U.S. lost 6,000 tanks in Europe in World War II, whereas the German army never had more than 1,500 tanks operable at any one time.

Despite shortcomings, the U.S. Army had greater firepower than any other army in the world. It was not only the quality and quantity of military equipment and supplies produced but also the speed with which new weapons came on-line. The bazooka antitank weapon, for example, went from development to production of 5,000 units in only 30 days.

The U.S. way of waging war, then and now, is to use machines if possible to do the killing and to minimize American loss of life. The army carried a strong indirect fire punch, including massive air forces and substantial quantities of field artillery. For Operation COBRA, the Normandy breakout in July 1944, VII Corps disposed of 43 battalions of field artillery. In December 1944 in Europe alone, the army fired more than 3 million rounds of 105 mm ammunition. Artillerymen were able to shift and mass fire on a target on a scale never before seen. The time-on-target technique was a devastating weapon. Air-ground coordination vastly exceeded that of other combatants. Joint and combined operations typified the army's campaigns.

Europe was the U.S. Army's principal theater. It was accorded a priority over the Pacific, which affected all fighting and supply efforts. Seventy-seven percent of army divisions, a total of 68, went to Europe, and there were more than 3 million army personnel in Europe and the Mediterranean by April 1945. The Pacific absorbed only 23 percent of all army divisions (21). But despite the priority of Europe, the Pacific Theater claimed half or more of the army forces for the first two years of the war. Only in October 1943 were there more divisions in Europe than in the Pacific; 1.8 million army personnel served in the Pacific by the end of the war.

Although green U.S. Army divisions experienced some problems at first, notably in the Battle of Kasserine Pass in February 1943, they also showed a great ability to learn from their mistakes and adapt. As the army gained experience in the late summer of 1944, its units were arguably better, man for man, than the highly touted Germans. Average

American soldiers of the 289th Infantry Regiment march along a snow-covered road on their way to cut off the St. Vith-Houffalize road in Belgium in January 1945. (National Archives)

U.S. infantry divisions could defeat average German divisions and could even match elite German divisions. They were significantly better than Japanese divisions, whose tactics had deteriorated to digging in and dying in place.

Army doctrine and tactics were also basically sound and flexible. The Germans and Japanese were impressed at how quickly the Americans adapted and how rapidly they replaced unsuccessful tactics with effective ones. Communications, engineering, and medical services were the best in the world. Only at the senior command level in Europe did the army show some debatable weaknesses, with a desire to execute the safe rather than the risky course of action—for instance, the broad-front strategy. Yet even that "cautious" approach presented the Germans with crisis piled on crisis, unsustainable attrition, and too much pressure everywhere to allow recovery.

European combat, especially long, multiple-month campaigns, cut heavily into available army manpower. In Europe, 81 percent of all casualties occurred in the divisions, and they were heavily concentrated in the infantry. Units might lose 30 percent of their men in a week, yet they stayed in the line and continued to fight. The 9th Division, for instance, sustained 17,974 casualties in a four-month period, yet it fought on.

The army did not replace combat losses efficiently or in the necessary quantities, despite training 1.1 million men as replacements and despite a peak strength of

99,288 Women's Army Corps personnel to replace men for battle. There were too few divisions to allow frequent rotation off the line for rest and training. Units were usually short of personnel, and replacements from the United States could hardly replace battle casualties, let alone nonbattle losses. A flow of replacements from the United States was mandatory. But that system did not always work well. Regardless, the personnel system did keep the divisions fighting for extended periods of time. Units learned how to receive, train, and integrate replacements.

The manpower situation was different in the Pacific. Campaigns were usually relatively short in duration and limited in space, with obvious exceptions such as those on New Guinea and Luzon. Battalions and regiments were the key maneuver units, not divisions and corps as in Europe. And in the Pacific, infantry losses were far higher than expected. During the entirety of the war, the U.S. Army sustained in action 937,259 total casualties—killed, wounded, taken prisoner, and missing (234,874 dead).

The U.S. Army had come a long way since 1939. By 1945, it was the best-armed, most-mobile, best-equipped, best-supplied, most-educated, and highest-paid army in history.

John W. Whitman and Spencer C. Tucker

See also

Bradley, Omar Nelson; Burma Theater; Casualties; China-Burma-India (CBI) Theater; Combat Fatigue; Eisenhower, Dwight D.; Italy Campaign; MacArthur, Douglas; Marshall, George Catlett; North Africa Campaign; Patton, George Smith, Jr.; Prisoners of War (POWs); Signals Intelligence; Southwest Pacific Theater; United States, Army Air Force; United States, Marine Corps; United States, Navy; Western European Theater of Operations

References

Huston, James A. *The Sinews of War: Army Logistics, 1775–1953.* Washington, DC: Center of Military History, U.S. Army, 1988.

Mansoor, Peter R. *The GI Offensive in Europe: The Triumph of American Infantry Divisions, 1941–1945.* Lawrence, KS: University Press of Kansas, 1999.

Murray, Williamson, and Allan R. Millett. *A War to Be Won: Fighting the Second World War.* Cambridge, MA: Belknap Press of Harvard University, 2000.

Perret, Geoffrey. *There's a War to Be Won: The United States Army in World War II.* New York: Random House, 1991.

U.S. Army. *United States Army in World War II.* 78 vols. Washington, DC: Center of Military History, U.S. Army, 1947–1998.

Weigley, Russell F. *Eisenhower's Lieutenants: The Campaigns of France and Germany, 1944–1945.* Bloomington, IN: Indiana University Press, 1981.

Wilson, John B. *Maneuver and Firepower: The Evolution of Divisions and Separate Brigades.* Washington, DC: Center of Military History, U.S. Army, 1998.

United States, Army Air Force

World War II witnessed a dramatic change in the scope and use of airpower by the U.S. military. Prior to and during World War II, there was no independent air force. Instead, the army controlled the employment of airpower over land, and the navy had charge of it over water. Since World War I, airpower advocates such as Brigadier General William Mitchell had argued for an independent air force. (And for his outspoken criticism of the military leadership, a tribunal court-martialed Mitchell in 1926.) Whatever its status, the pre–World War II Army Air Corps remained a relatively small coterie of professionals in which all pilots had to be officers.

By the mid-1930s, Air Corps theory centered around strategic bombing—the use of large bombers to destroy specific industrial targets and thereby cripple an opposing army for lack of essential supplies and win a war without a costly ground assault. Not only was such a campaign relatively inexpensive, it also created an argument for air force independence, since this was a mission unique to airpower. The strategic bombing theory entailed a number of corollary assumptions. First was the belief that the bomber would always reach the target. The aircraft envisioned by army leaders were large, fast, and heavily armed. As a result, there was little development of long-range fighter aircraft prior to the war, since escorts were held to be unnecessary. Another assumption involved the denigration of tactical aviation—aircraft used to support the immediate needs of the battlefield. Leaders believed that by tying aircraft to ground forces, airpower lost its unique advantage along with the justification for independence. These ideals were epitomized by Major General Henry "Hap" Arnold, who became chief of the Army Air Corps in October 1938 and held that post throughout the war.

Whatever theory existed, tight budgets and isolationist views in Congress limited the growth of American aviation between the world wars. In 1939, even with war clearly on the horizon, the American aviation industry delivered only 921 aircraft to the U.S. Army and U.S. Navy. Changes quickly ensued following the German invasion of Poland in September 1939. European governments placed large orders with American aircraft firms. And earlier, in November 1938, President Franklin D. Roosevelt, long concerned about the threat posed by Adolf Hitler's Germany, had privately expressed a desire for an Air Corps of 20,000 aircraft, but publicly, he sought half that number. At the time, the Air Corps only possessed some 1,600 aircraft. Following the fall of France in May 1940, Roosevelt increased his goal to 50,000 aircraft for the army and navy together.

Despite massive orders, the aviation industry mobilized slowly. By 1941, the Air Corps possessed only 5,500 aircraft, and few matched the performance of their European counterparts. Only in heavy bombers, with the Boeing B-17, did American equipment approach that of Europe. In March 1941, Robert Lovett became assistant secretary of war for air, and he immediately set about increasing U.S. production. Output rose from 12,000 aircraft annually to 96,000 by the end of 1944. Manpower also increased dramatically. From 43,000 personnel in 1939, the number of people serving in the Air Corps rose to 300,000 by December 1941. To meet increased manpower requirements, the Air Corps lowered its standards, but it remained much more difficult to enter the Air Corps than other services.

The organization of the corps also changed with expansion. In 1941, the Air Corps gave way to the U.S. Army Air Forces (USAAF), with Arnold as chief; it was coequal with the Army Ground Forces and the Army Service Forces. In return for greater autonomy, Arnold verbally promised Army Chief of Staff General George C. Marshall, himself a strong supporter of airpower, that he would not seek independent status for the air force for the duration of the war.

Individual theaters each had their own numbered air forces, sometimes further divided by primary mission. For example, the First Air Force remained in New York, provided training, and oversaw the defense of the Northeast region of the United States; the Eighth Air Force served in Great Britain and undertook the strategic bombardment of continental Europe; and the Ninth Air Force, which began in the Mediterranean Theater, moved to Britain in 1943 as a tactical air force for the invasion of France. By the end of the war, there were 16 numbered air forces.

In 1941, to utilize airpower properly, the Air War Plans Division wrote AWPD/1 as an annex to the army's comprehensive plan to defeat the Axis powers. AWPD/1 embodied the tenets of strategic bombardment. It called for 1,060 medium bombers, 3,740 heavy bombers, 3,740 very heavy bombers, and 2,000 fighters to destroy 154 specific industrial targets in Germany—primarily aircraft-manufacturing sites, followed by power plants, the transportation network, and synthetic petroleum plants. In six months, the authors argued, Germany would be unable to resist the Allied armies, and civilian morale would

One of 16 Army B-25s takes off in April 1942 from the deck of the USS *Hornet*, deep in the Western Pacific, on its way to take part in the first U.S. air raid on the Japanese home islands. The operation, known as the DOOLITTLE RAID after its commander, Lieutenant Colonel James "Jimmy" Doolittle, was militarily negligible in its impact, but boosted U.S. morale. With insufficient fuel to return to their carriers, all 16 aircraft were crash-landed in Chinese or Soviet territory. (AP/Wide World Photos)

be shattered, making an invasion unnecessary. These attacks were to be carried out in precision daylight strikes.

With the American entrance into the war on December 7, 1941, the USAAF could not immediately launch the kind of offensive action envisioned in AWPD/1. In the Pacific Theater, the Japanese advanced so rapidly that American forces found themselves fighting defensive battles for their very survival. With the American aircraft industry just beginning to gear up, it would take time to deploy the kind of force called for in AWPD/1 to defeat either Japan or Germany.

Major General Carl Spaatz commanded the Eighth Air Force, charged with carrying the air war to Germany. Activated in January 1942, the Eighth did not fly its first mission until July 4, 1942, when American medium bombers joined British aircraft attacking German airfields in the Netherlands. On August 17, 1942, American strategic bombardment began when 12 B-17s attacked the railroad marshaling yard in Rouen, France. That November, the Eighth lost much of its force to the Mediterranean Theater, where Allied troops had invaded North Africa. The North African Campaign provided valuable experience to American airmen. Most important, the Americans learned from the British the value of close cooperation between air and ground forces.

In January 1943, President Roosevelt, British prime minister Winston Churchill, and their respective military staffs met in Casablanca to discuss strategy. Despite British pressure for the USAAF to join the Royal Air Force in its area attacks against German cities at night, the Americans argued for daylight precision strikes, which meant that Germany would be bombed around the clock. From the meeting came a directive for the Combined Bomber Offensive (CBO) that eventually destroyed Germany's industrial base as well as its civilian morale. To accomplish the goals of the CBO, Brigadier General Ira Eaker, the new commander of the Eighth Air Force, oversaw the development of the Pointblank Directive, which called for establishing air supremacy first by using the bomber to attack aircraft-manufacturing plants. To protect themselves from enemy fighters, bombers flew in large box formations that massed defensive firepower. The first large Pointblank raid was against the Schweinfurt ball-bearing works, with a second mission against the Messerschmitt plant at Regensburg. American P-47 fighters had only enough range to escort the bombers to the German border. As a result, the Eighth lost 60 bombers, one-sixth of the attacking force. A second raid in October cost an equal number of bombers during a day referred to as "Black Thursday." The USAAF could not sustain such losses, and American bombers suspended raids deep into Germany until long-range escorts became available. Meanwhile, Arnold questioned the leadership of the Eighth and replaced Eaker, whom he sent to the Mediterranean, with Major General James H. Doolittle. Spaatz returned to England to oversee all American air operations as commander of the U.S. Strategic Air Forces in Europe.

Technical changes improved USAAF performance. By January 1944, external fuel tanks and increased tankage permitted P-47 and P-38 fighters to escort the bombers far into Germany. Finally, P-51 Mustangs began reaching units in Britain; they could escort bombers as far as Berlin.

In February 1944, the Americans launched Operation ARGUMENT, a coordinated attack on the German aircraft industry by both the Eighth Air Force and the Fifteenth Air Force flying from Italy. "Big Week," February 20–25, 1944, witnessed thousands of sorties. The loss rate was only one-sixth that of the previous year, and U.S. fighter escorts began to take a grievous toll on inexperienced German pilots. In the air battles of 1944, the USAAF gained mastery of Europe's skies not directly through bomb damage but rather through the attrition of German pilots. In March 1944, Spaatz began the systematic bombing of Germany's petroleum industry. German fighters had to defend their source of fuel. Attrition among German aircrews could not be replaced, and the lack of fuel meant replacement pilots had greatly reduced training time. By the date of the Allied invasion of France on June 6, 1944, the German air force could not challenge Allied airpower. The appearance of Germany's jet and rocket fighters, the Me-262 and Me-163, created brief consternation within the USAAF, but these aircraft were too few in number and their pilots were too inexperienced to pose a serious threat.

On the other side of the world, the USAAF provided support for General Douglas MacArthur's ground forces in the southwest Pacific. Initially, the Pacific Theater lacked large industrial targets within range; however, heavy bombers did contribute to the ultimate victory. More important were the medium bombers of the Fifth Air Force commanded by Major General George C. Kenney. Operations tended to be directed against Japanese island garrisons and shipping. To meet the low-level operations found in the theater, Kenney modified many B-25 bombers to carry additional machine guns or cannon in the nose. His pilots also practiced bombing from treetop level using fragmentation bombs slowed by parachutes. Finally, to better strike ships, Kenney's bombers attacked from mast height.

The USAAF also flew missions in the China–Burma–India Theater, although operations there were decidedly of secondary importance. Part of the problem involved logistics. The Japanese controlled all of coastal China as well as Burma. To supply China and the American forces there, the USAAF developed an aerial route over the Himalayas, referred to as "the Hump." By July 1944, despite a slow start, the operation was finally delivering sufficient matériel to meet operational needs, although at a very high cost. In China, Major General Claire Chennault led the Fourteenth Air Force in its efforts to push back the Japanese. Always operating at the limits of supply, his forces enjoyed only moderate success.

By 1944, the U.S. Navy's advance through the Central Pacific included the Mariana Islands. These islands provided bases for the Boeing B-29 Superfortresses then entering service. To ensure the proper use of the new bombers, Arnold maintained operational authority over their employment by controlling the Twentieth Air Force directly from Washington. Though the bombers were initially deployed in India and China, the Marianas proved far superior as bases, and all of the bombers eventually flew from there. But initial efforts to strategically bomb Japan did not fare well. The B-29 was unique in that it was the first aircraft to contend with the jet stream, making bombing accuracy more difficult than normal. Not until January 1945, when Major General Curtis LeMay arrived in the Marianas to improve effectiveness, did the B-29s have a vital impact on Japanese industry. Instead of high-altitude, precision strikes against industrial targets, the B-29s switched to low-altitude, night incendiary attacks against cities. The largely wooden structures in Japan became so much kindling. The most destructive of these raids—and probably the single most destructive raid in the history of air warfare—occurred on the night of March 9–10, 1945, when the B-29s set 16 square miles of Tokyo aflame, killing at least 90,000 people. The destruction of cities peaked on August 6, 1945, when the B-29 *Enola Gay* dropped the first atomic bomb on Hiroshima. A second atomic bomb fell on Nagasaki three days later.

The U.S. Army Air Forces fought in every theater of World War II, contributing substantially to the Allied victory. As Germany and Japan surrendered, teams from the United States conducted a survey of the exact impact of the bombing. The U.S. Strategic Bombing Survey (USSBS) concluded that airpower had a notable impact on Germany and Japan, yet bombing itself could not have won the war. Aircraft played an integral part in the Allied war-fighting capabilities, making victory possible. The most effective uses of bombing were the systematic assault on the German petroleum industry late in 1944 and the assault against transportation. In the Pacific, to avoid conflict with the navy, the USSBS assessed the USAAF campaign as part of the overall force applied against Japan. The report concluded that the atomic bombs simply compelled Japan's leaders to accept reality.

By the end of the war, the USAAF had taken delivery of some 158,800 aircraft, including 51,221 bombers and 47,050 fighters. A total of 22,948 aircraft were lost in action. During the conflict, the USAAF flew 2,363,800 combat sorties and dropped 2,057,000 tons of bombs, 75 percent of them on Germany. By March 1945, the USAAF had more than 1,831,000 personnel, representing 22.4 percent of the army's total strength. USAAF personnel casualties over the course of the war came to 115,382, including 40,061 dead. Even without the unqualified endorsement of the USSBS, the USAAF had proved its worth, leading to its independence from the army in 1947.

Rodney Madison

See also

Atomic Bomb, Decision to Employ; Casualties; Central Pacific Campaign; China–Burma–India (CBI) Theater; Churchill, Sir Winston Leonard Spencer; Hiroshima and Nagasaki, Bombing of; Hitler, Adolf; Italy Campaign; MacArthur, Douglas; Marshall, George Catlett; Poland, Role in War; Roosevelt, Franklin D.; Southeast Pacific Theater; Southwest Pacific Theater; Western European Theater of Operations

References

Bergerud, Eric M. *Fire in the Sky: The Air War in the South Pacific*. New York: Basic Books, 1999.

Biddle, Tami Davis. *Rhetoric and Reality in Air Warfare: The Evolution of British and American Ideas about Strategic Bombing, 1941–1945*. Princeton, NJ: Princeton University Press, 2002.

Craven, Wesley Frank, and James Lea Cate, eds. *The Army Air Forces in World War II*. 7 vols. Washington, DC: Office of Air Force History, 1983.

Kreis, John F. *Piercing the Fog: Intelligence and Army Air Forces Operations in World War II*. Honolulu, HI: University Press of the Pacific, 2004.

Nalty, Bernard C., John F. Shiner, and George M. Watson. *With Courage: The U.S. Army Air Forces in World War II*. Washington, DC: Air Force History and Museum Program, 1994.

Overy, Richard J. *The Air War 1939–1945*. Washington, DC: Potomac Books, 2005.

Perret, Geoffrey. *Winged Victory: The Army Air Forces in World War II*. New York: Random House, 1993.

Schaffer, Ronald. *Wings of Judgment: American Bombing in World War II*. New York: Oxford University Press, 1985.

Sherry, Michael S. *The Rise of American Air Power: The Creation of Armageddon*. New Haven, CT: Yale University Press, 1988.

United States, Marine Corps

Founded in 1775 as a shipboard security force for the Continental navy, the Marine Corps struggled to maintain its institutional viability while performing numerous and varied missions around the globe during the first century of its existence. Sustained by its reputation as a rapidly deployable, tenacious combat force, the corps and its civilian proponents argued that the U.S. expansionist policies of the late 19th and early 20th centuries demanded a naval infantry force capable of seizing and defending advanced naval bases. Progressive Marine Corps leaders had begun preparing this new doctrine when World War I interrupted their planning, although the valiant exploits of the corps during this conflict further endeared the service to the American public. Following World War I, the prevalent antimilitarism of the 1920s ushered in a period of military retrenchment, and the resulting scramble for available funds heightened interservice rivalries. The Marine Corps' lack of a clearly defined mission brought tremendous scrutiny on its funding and reductions in its strength that threatened its very existence. A massive public relations campaign featuring the Marine service in policing domestic mail routes and protecting American interests in Latin America and China bolstered the Corps' public image and political clout with Congress, allowing the Marines to withstand meager appropriations and perpetuate the claim of being America's premier fighting force.

In the early 1920s, U.S. military strategists began planning for numerous wartime contingencies, focusing primarily on Japan, the nation's Pacific rival. Recognizing the navy's need to secure advance operating bases on islands west of Hawaii in any war against Japan, the Marine Corps adopted amphibious assault as its raison d'être.

Integrating the newly constituted Fleet Marine Force into the U.S. Navy, the Marines streamlined their bureaucracy and concentrated on preparations for seizing and defending advance bases in the Pacific. The corps assigned personnel to naval intelligence and planning staffs and began educating its officers in the tactics of amphibious operations. Lieutenant Colonel Earl "Pete" Ellis's exhaustive studies of Japanese-held Pacific islands in the early 1920s formed the nucleus of the Marines' amphibious assault doctrine. In 1934, the corps published a more exhaustive guide to amphibious operations, *The Tentative Manual for Landing Operations*, and held a series of fleet landing exercises designed to test its concepts. These exercises were crucial in highlighting the need for detailed logistical planning, speed in ship-to-shore movement, overwhelming fire superiority from air and naval bombardment, and specialized equipment to successfully carry out opposed landings. Although Marine aviation utilized previous experience in Latin America to develop rudimentary close-air support tactics based on dive-bombing (which the German Luftwaffe then adopted), the navy's ambivalence toward developing close-in naval gunfire support techniques and constraints on the procurement of new equipment severely limited the development of U.S. amphibious warfare prior to 1939.

Between 1939 and 1941, as the U.S. military buildup went forward, the Marine Corps tripled in size from some 25,000 to 75,000 men and improved its amphibious capabilities. However, the corps was spread thinly to cover a wide range of duties in garrisons and aboard ships, from Iceland to the Caribbean to Hawaii and numerous smaller islands throughout the Pacific.

On December 7, 1941, Marines aboard battleships at Pearl Harbor and at nearby airfields assisted in defending Hawaii against the Japanese attacks. Elsewhere in the Pacific, isolated Marine garrisons on Guam and in China had little choice but to surrender. Marines on Wake Island and in the Philippines valiantly attempted to resist Japanese invasions, but Wake fell after two weeks of resistance, and the Philippines surrendered in May 1942.

Marines were at the forefront of early U.S. operations against Japan. In the southwest Pacific, the 1st Marine Division carried out assaults in the Solomon Islands in August 1942. The long campaign for Guadalcanal revealed the complexities of conducting amphibious operations under battle conditions, including the need for increased logistical support and a simplified command-and-control structure. Advancing up the Solomons from 1942 to 1944 toward the Japanese fortress at Rabaul, the Marines found themselves engaged in jungle warfare against a determined Japanese foe.

In 1943, encouraged by success in the Solomons, the U.S. Navy and Marine Corps undertook a thrust through the Central Pacific toward the main Japanese islands. The atolls of the Gilbert and Marshall Islands proved a different kind of challenge to the Marines than the jungle warfare of the southwest Pacific. Ineffective fire support, confused communications, and a shortage of proper equipment made the initial assault at Tarawa a bloody and sobering affair.

Employing the lessons learned from Tarawa to refine their amphibious doctrine, the Marines advanced through the key Marshall Islands atolls of Kwajalein, Roi-Namur, and Eniwetok. During the summer of 1944, Marines landed on Saipan, Tinian, and Guam in the Marianas. They also learned how to conduct sustained combat operations on these larger, extensively fortified islands. In the fall of 1944, Marine infantry and aviation forces assisted General Douglas MacArthur's advance on the Philippines. Marines landed on Peleliu in September and suffered heavy casualties in a savage, week-long battle. From September 1944 to April 1945, Marine Corps tactical air support became a vital component of army operations on Leyte and Luzon.

In February 1945, the Marines invaded the island of Iwo Jima in their most spectacular and costly operation of the war. Nearly the entire 21,000-man Japanese garrison died defending the island, while inflicting almost 30,000 casualties on American forces in a 36-day slugfest. During the battle, a journalist snapped a photo of five Marines and one navy corpsman raising a flag on Iwo's Mount Suribachi. This image instantly became an icon of Marine Corps valor and esprit de corps as well as a symbol of American fortitude in World War II. In June 1945, the Marines and the army secured Okinawa, just 360 miles from Japan, after three months of ferocious combat in the hills and caves across the island. After the Japanese surrender in August 1945, the Marines served throughout the Pacific in occupation duties.

In this award-winning photograph, which served as the model for the Marine Corps War Memorial, U.S. troops raise the American flag on Iwo Jima on February 23, 1945. Strategically, the capture of the small island almost a month later was crucial to the United States because it was an ideal site from which to bomb Japan. (National Archives)

World War II was a defining moment for the Marines. Their seemingly prophetic development of amphibious assault doctrine in the interwar period proved invaluable to winning the Pacific campaigns, and their prior planning and experience also aided the army-led invasions of Europe. The corps had grown to twenty times its prewar strength, with approximately 500,000 men in six Marine infantry divisions and four Marine air wings. It had honed its amphibious doctrine, while expanding its aviation and combat support capabilities. Though the corps comprised less than 5 percent of the U.S. military in the war, Marines constituted nearly 10 percent of all American wartime casualties, with 19,733 killed and 67,207 wounded.

Despite continued and often heated interservice clashes between the army, the navy, and the new U.S. Air Force, the Marines' combat performance during World War II further attached the corps to the public, thus ensuring the service would survive demobilization as a separate institution within the navy and an elite component of the U.S. military establishment.

Derek W. Frisby

See also

Casualties; Central Pacific Campaign; Japan, Army; Japan, Navy; MacArthur, Douglas; Nimitz, Chester William; Pearl Harbor, Attack on; Southeast Pacific Theater; Southwest Pacific Theater; United States, Navy

References

Alexander, Joseph. *A Fellowship of Valor: The Battle History of the United States Marines.* New York: HarperCollins, 1997.

Clark, George B. *United States Marine Corps Generals of World War II: A Biographical Dictionary.* Jefferson, NC: McFarland, 2008.

Frank, Benis M., George W. Garand, Frank O. Hough, Douglas T. Kane, Verle E. Ludwig, Bernard C. Nalty, Henry I. Shaw Jr., Truman R. Stroubridge, and Edwin T. Turnbladh. *History of U.S. Marine Corps Operations in World War II.* 5 vols. Washington, DC: Historical Branch, Headquarters, Marine Corps, 1958–1968.

Millett, Allan R. *"Semper Fidelis": A History of the United States Marine Corps.* Rev. ed. New York: Free Press, 1991.

Moskin, J. Robert. *The U.S. Marine Corps Story.* Rev. ed. New York: McGraw-Hill, 1987.

United States, Navy

U.S. naval preparations for war were under way long before the Japanese attack on Pearl Harbor on December 7, 1941. The government was well into the move away from its post–World War I emphasis on naval arms limitation following the outbreak of war between China and Japan in July 1937. On May 7, 1938, Congress passed a naval expansion bill authorizing a 20 percent increase in the overall tonnage of the navy. President Franklin D. Roosevelt and his advisers hoped that this step would deter the Japanese from further expansion in the Pacific that might threaten American interests there. The Japanese, however, continued their actions. The concern of the Roosevelt administration over this failure was heightened by the outbreak of war in Europe in September 1939 and the string of Allied defeats that followed. On June 20, 1940, believing that the United States might soon stand alone in the face of Axis aggression, Congress passed a second naval expansion bill, which called for a two-ocean navy through a 70 percent increase in overall naval tonnage.

Despite the fact that the bulk of the navy was based in the Pacific, the initial deployment of U.S. naval forces in World War II was in the Atlantic theater and took place while the United States was still technically neutral. President Roosevelt aligned the United States with the European Allied powers, and following the fall of France, he sent material aid to Great Britain. The transport of these supplies across the Atlantic via merchant convoys led to the need to protect them against German submarines. By mid-1941, U.S. naval forces were engaged in escorting convoys to Iceland, where they then became Britain's responsibility. This situation led to an escalation of hostilities with the September 1941 German torpedo attack on the escorting destroyer *Greer*. Roosevelt responded with a "shoot on sight" order regarding Axis warships threatening convoys. On October 31, 1941, a German submarine torpedoed and sank the U.S. destroyer *Reuben James*, the first American warship lost in World War II.

Yet war for the United States came not in the Atlantic but in the Pacific. With the Japanese attack on Pearl Harbor, the nation formally joined the Allied side. The U.S. Navy, which by late December was under the direction of the commander in chief of the U.S. Fleet, Admiral Ernest J. King, faced a multiple-theater conflict. In the Atlantic, the war at sea centered on the protection of Allied supply lines to Great Britain. Although the Battle of the Atlantic was fought primarily by British and Canadian forces, the United States contributed through the deployment of convoy escorts largely under the direction of the Atlantic Fleet commander, Admiral Royal E. Ingersoll. In early 1943, the United States assumed responsibility for the protection of convoys in the Central Atlantic. In addition to the destroyer forces deployed for this duty, "hunter-killer groups" based around escort carriers executed search-and-destroy operations against Axis submarines. Through the use of radar and sonar, these forces played an important role in the Allied victory in the critical Battle of the Atlantic. By the close of the war, U.S. naval units had accounted for 25 percent of the 781 German U-boats sunk during the conflict.

In addition to commerce protection, the U.S. Navy also contributed warships to aid the Royal Navy in fleet surface operations in the Atlantic. In March 1942, the United States sent its first naval task force, centered on the aircraft carrier *Wasp*, into the Atlantic. The U.S. Navy provided critical gunfire support and sealift in all the Allied amphibious operations of the war, beginning with Operation TORCH, the Allied invasion of North Africa, and extending through Operation OVERLORD, the Normandy Invasion. As with the U-boat war, the British provided the lion's share of the vessels required for this task.

Initial American involvement in the Mediterranean Theater was the result of Allied disagreement over the strategy to attack the European Axis powers. Although the United States favored an attack on German-held France via the English Channel, to take place in mid-1943, the prevailing British view called for a peripheral attack via the Mediterranean. This attack took the form of the November 1942 Operation TORCH, the amphibious invasion of North Africa. The Royal Navy conducted assaults on the Mediterranean beachheads of northern Africa, and the United States had responsibility for the Atlantic coast. The majority of the naval units covering the landing forces and providing fire support were British, and overall command of the naval force rested with the Royal Navy, but the U.S. Navy employed a task force under Rear Admiral H. Kent Hewitt that included 1 fleet carrier, 3 battleships, and 4 converted escort carriers. Following this operation, U.S. involvement increased through the mid-1943 Allied invasion of Sicily. Hewitt once again commanded an American squadron under the direction of the Royal Navy. This arrangement was repeated in the Allied invasion of mainland Italy.

In the June 1944 Normandy Invasion, of all the Allied gunfire support ships—7 battleships, 23 cruisers, and 80 destroyers—the United States supplied 3 battleships, 3 cruisers, and 31 destroyers. These vessels provided invaluable covering fire for amphibious forces landing on the beaches. The final major Allied landing in the Atlantic theater, Operation DRAGOON—the August 1944 invasion of southern France—was predominantly

Two Coast Guard–manned tank landing ships (LSTs) open their bows in the surf that washes on Leyte Island beach as soldiers build sandbag piers out to their ramps to speed up unloading operations in 1944. The Battle of Leyte Gulf, in October 1944, is known as the largest naval battle in history. (National Archives)

composed of U.S. units and under the command of Admiral Hewitt. The U.S. gunfire support ships included 3 battleships, 3 heavy cruisers, and numerous destroyers.

Although the involvement of the U.S. Navy in both the Atlantic and the Mediterranean was eclipsed by that of the Royal Navy, the chief reason for this was that the United States bore the brunt of the naval war in the Pacific. This effort faced great challenges from the outset, as the U.S. Pacific Fleet, under the command of Admiral Husband E. Kimmel, was gravely wounded by the Japanese attack on Pearl Harbor, which put all of the fleet's battleships out of commission. In any case, the initial American effort in the vast Pacific centered on the U.S. Navy's carriers, which had not been in Pearl Harbor at the time of the attack. The denuded U.S. Pacific Fleet was further weakened following the loss of the British capital ships *Prince of Wales* and *Repulse* on December 10, 1941, and the February 1942 destruction of the American–British–Dutch–Australian (ABDA) Command, a collection of Allied warships. As a result of these blows, the U.S. Navy was, for most of the war, the sole Allied naval force pitted against the Japanese, who seized the U.S. possessions of Wake Island, Guam, and the Philippines.

Amid these disasters, U.S. and British military officials met in early 1942 and resolved that the United States would assume responsibility for the Pacific Theater. American strategists realized that, to defeat Japan, it was necessary to recapture lost American possessions and take Japanese Pacific holdings, thus isolating the Japanese home islands and starving their war machine of supplies. Command of the Pacific was divided into two theaters to achieve this end. The Southwest Pacific was under General Douglas MacArthur, who pursued an advance from Australia through the Netherlands East Indies to the Philippines. The North, Central, and South Pacific areas were assigned to Admiral Chester Nimitz, who succeeded Admiral Kimmel as commander of the U.S. Pacific Fleet. Consequently, Nimitz was in charge of the majority of U.S. naval forces in the Pacific. He pursued War Plan Orange, a prewar strategy that called for an advance toward Japan through the Central Pacific.

These operations, however, could not take place until the country's industrial strength produced more warships to augment the force that remained after Pearl Harbor. War Plan Orange saw the role of submarines as scouts for the U.S. battle line, but after the Japanese attack on Pearl Harbor, the U.S. Navy deployed its submarines with the destruction of Japanese overseas commerce as a key mission. Surface units were charged with preventing further Japanese expansion. While the submarine war unfolded, a critical concern was the threat posed to Australia, which was both a vital naval base and an area to station troops. The need to protect Australia led to the Battle of the Coral Sea in May 1942. This engagement aborted a Japanese landing at Port Moresby in New Guinea. A Japanese attempt to take Midway Island and draw out and destroy the U.S. carriers led to the pivotal Battle of Midway in June 1942. The loss of four of Japan's finest carriers in this battle was a great blow to further Japanese expansion in the Pacific and, in a very real sense, the turning point in the Pacific war.

The U.S. Navy subsequently implemented its plan to defeat Japan. The amphibious operations that ensued were made possible by the tremendous wartime naval production of the United States. By 1944, the U.S. Navy was larger than all other navies of the world combined, and the Pacific Fleet comprised 14 battleships, 15 fleet carriers, 10 escort carriers, 24 cruisers, and hundreds of destroyers and submarines. The Japanese, whose industrial base was much smaller than that of the United States, could not match this production.

One of the keys to Allied victory in the war was the ability of U.S. Navy task forces to operate at great distances across the vast Pacific. To support this effort, the navy created an extensive logistics network. This Service Force Pacific Fleet, known as the "fleet train," included tankers and supply and repair ships moving in the wake of the combat ships. A massive system of reprovisioning and repair, the fleet train markedly reduced the need for combat ships to spend precious time moving to and from their home bases and thus greatly increased the number of combat ships deployed.

In the Central Pacific, the navy lifted army and marine elements to take Japanese-held islands in the Marshall, Caroline, Mariana, and Philippine Islands. In the Battle of Leyte Gulf from October 23 to 26, 1944, the U.S. Navy eliminated the Imperial Japanese Navy (IJN) as a cohesive fighting force and cut the Japanese off from their southern resources area. The Allied conquest of Okinawa in mid-1945 signaled to American amphibious forces the completion of Plan Orange. With the destruction of the IJN and the seizure of bases within striking distance of Japan, the home islands were both isolated and subjected to the strategic bombing of cities and the devastation of coastal trade.

Equally important in the isolation of Japan was the submarine campaign, the most successful *guerre de commerce* (war against trade) in modern history. Of Japan's total of 8 million tons of merchant shipping (at best marginal for meeting Japanese requirements in peacetime), U.S. submarines sank almost 5 million tons, thus crippling Tokyo's ability to supply the home islands, especially with oil.

By the end of World War II, the U.S. Navy had participated in every major theater of the naval war. The cost was high, as the navy lost 36,674 officers and enlisted personnel. In the Battle of Okinawa alone, Japanese kamikaze attacks caused the navy more casualties than it had suffered in all its previous wars combined. Materially, the navy lost 2 battleships, 4 fleet aircraft carriers, 1 light carrier, 6 escort carriers, 12 cruisers, 68 destroyers, and 47 submarines in the course of the war. Nevertheless, the manpower and industrial strength of the United States had not only made good the losses but also augmented the navy to the point that its size in both personnel and ships eclipsed that of all the other naval powers of the world combined. This force was pivotal to the Allied victory in World War II.

Eric W. Osborne

See also

Atlantic, Battle of the; Central Pacific Campaign; Germany, Navy; Great Britain, Navy; Italy, Navy; Italy Campaign; Japan, Navy; MacArthur, Douglas; Midway, Battle of; Nimitz, Chester William; North Africa Campaign; Pearl Harbor, Attack on; Roosevelt, Franklin D.; Southeast Pacific Theater; Southwest Pacific Theater; Western European Theater of Operations

References

Blair, Clay. *Silent Victory: The U.S. Submarine War against Japan.* Philadelphia, PA: Lippincott, 1975.

Borneman, Walter. *The Admirals: Nimitz, Halsey, Leahy, and King—The Five-Star Admirals Who Won the War at Sea.* Boston, MA: Little, Brown, 2012.

Hornfischer, James D. *Neptune's Inferno: The U.S. Navy at Guadalcanal.* New York: Bantam, 2011.

Howarth, Stephen. *To Shining Sea: A History of the United States Navy, 1775–1998.* Norman, OK: University of Oklahoma Press, 1999.

Hoyt, Edwin. *How They Won the War in the Pacific: Nimitz and His Admirals.* New York: Weybright and Talley, 1970.

Lundstrom, John B. *First Team: Pacific Naval Air Combat from Pearl Harbor to Midway.* Annapolis, MD: Naval Institute Press, 1984.

Miller, Edward D. *War Plan Orange: The U.S. Strategy to Defeat Japan, 1897–1945.* Annapolis, MD: Naval Institute Press, 1991.

Miller, Nathan. *The United States Navy: A History.* Annapolis, MD: Naval Institute Press, 1997.

Morison, Samuel Eliot. *History of U.S. Naval Operations in World War II.* 15 vols. Boston, MA: Little, Brown, 1947–1962.

Morison, Samuel Eliot. *The Two-Ocean War: A Short History of the United States Navy in the Second World War.* Boston, MA: Little, Brown, 1963.

O'Hara, Vincent P. *Struggle for the Middle Sea: The Great Navies at War in the Mediterranean Theater, 1940–1945.* Annapolis, MD: Naval Institute Press, 2009.

O'Hara, Vincent P., W. David Dickson, and Richard Worth, eds. *On Seas Contested: The Seven Great Navies of the Second World War.* Annapolis, MD: Naval Institute Press, 2010.

Silverstone, Paul H. *The Navy of World War II.* New York: Routledge, 2007.

Western European Theater of Operations

In accordance with its military pact with the Poles, France was to invade Germany two weeks after a German attack on Poland occurred, thereby forcing the Germans into a two-front war. However, following the German invasion of September 1, 1939, the best the French could manage was a token drive in the Saar region by nine divisions. French forces advanced a maximum of 5 miles on a narrow front. Casualties were negligible, but the French then halted; and when Poland collapsed, they withdrew to the Maginot Line. A more vigorous French thrust would have driven forward to the Rhine, with untold consequences for the course of the war. German forces manning the West Wall had little ammunition, no tanks, and virtually no air support.

But if the French effort in response to the German invasion of Poland was pathetic, Britain's was worse. The Royal Navy did impose a naval blockade on Germany, but the effects of this were far different from those caused by a similar blockade in World War I. This blockade was nullified by Germany's nonaggression pact with the Soviet Union, the secret terms of which promised Germany strategic natural resources. Germany could also secure necessary supplies from Italy, and both countries acted as purchasing agents for Berlin abroad. Two weeks into the war, the British Expeditionary Force (BEF) had not even completed assembling, and London rejected pleas for the Royal Air Force (RAF) bombing raids against Germany that had been agreed to before the war.

Following the German victory over Poland and the rejection by Britain and France of his terms for peace on a "forgive and forget" basis, Adolf Hitler prepared to move west. In late November 1939, he informed his military chiefs that Germany could deal with the Soviet Union only when it was free in the west. He was determined to attack France and Britain "at the earliest moment."

All was then quiet in the west. This period of the war came to be known as the "Sitzkrieg," the "Phony War," or the "Bore War." France carried out a full mobilization, and its forces manned the Maginot Line, but Britain imposed only a partial conscription, and by mid-October, it had only four divisions in France. Hardly any air action took place, with both sides reluctant to unleash the bombing of cities. Bad weather and the pleas of his generals for additional time caused Hitler to postpone the German invasion of France.

The Allies had no intention to take the offensive themselves. The commander of the French army, General Maurice Gamelin, said, "The first one who comes out his shell will be in peril." Meanwhile, First Lord of the Admiralty Winston Churchill developed a scheme to mine the coastal waters of neutral Norway in order to deny Germany access to high-grade Swedish iron ore shipped from the port of Narvik. Allied Scandinavian plans, including discussions of sending troops to aid Finland in its war against the Soviet Union, were soon an open secret. Initially, Hitler had no intention of opening a new front in Northern Europe, for in mid-December, he set January 14, 1940, as the start date for the western offensive, which was then postponed again. In February, however, Hitler concluded that the British intended to move against Norway and that Germany would have to move first. The German invasion of Norway began on April 9, 1940, catching the Allies by complete surprise.

The Germans took Denmark in only one day, but Norway proved more difficult to subdue. The Allies landed troops in the north and occupied Narvik, but mounting aircraft losses, the unsatisfactory situation elsewhere in Norway, and the German invasion of France brought evacuation in early June. The Norwegian Campaign badly hurt the German surface navy; it lost 3 cruisers and 10 destroyers, half of its total, but Hitler secured additional food production for the Reich and protection for his northern flank on the Baltic. Most important, the Kriegsmarine (German navy) secured locations for naval bases nearer to the Allied Atlantic convoy routes. Thus, it could now launch attacks into the North Atlantic and later strike Allied convoys bound for the Soviet Union. But Hitler also suffered the consequences of strategic overreach; by 1944, he had 365,000 of his best troops in Norway, a serious drain on his badly stretched resources.

Hitler's next stroke was the oft-delayed invasion of France and the Low Countries. On January 10, 1940, a German military aircraft was forced to land in Belgium. Its passenger was carrying the operational plans for the German attack in the west. Compromise of this plan led Hitler to abandon it and caused the German invasion to be delayed until May. The old plan would have seen the Germans encountering the best British and French divisions, but the new plan, SICHELSCHNITT (meaning "the cut of the sickle"), shifted the major effort from central Belgium to just north of the Maginot Line. The northern effort would occur first, drawing the Allies into Belgium. Then the major blow would fall to the south, in the hilly and wooded Ardennes. The Germans planned to cross the Meuse River and crack the French lines at Sedan, then swing northwest to the Channel and cut off the best British and French divisions in Belgium.

The campaign for France and the Low Countries began on May 10, 1940. The Allies matched the German invading forces on the ground and outnumbered the Germans in tanks. Their problem lay in tactical employment. The first three French tank divisions did not assemble for training until January 1940, and the majority of French tanks along the eastern frontier were split into isolated packets as infantry support. The Germans dominated the air, a vital factor in their success, and the Allies were sadly deficient in antiaircraft weapons. Other important factors in the outcome of the campaign included appallingly inadequate senior French military leadership, catastrophic failures in French military intelligence, and the lack of adequate reserves to deal with the German breakthrough.

German airborne forces in the north secured vital bridges and also the Belgian bastion of Eben Emael. The Allies followed the German script by pouring their forces into Belgium. On May 13, German forces to the south crossed the Meuse. For all intents and purposes, the struggle for France was over on May 15 when the Germans penetrated the Meuse defenses.

Once the panzer divisions were free, the way was clear to drive to the English Channel and cut off the main Allied armies in Belgium. By May 24, the Germans had captured Boulogne and isolated Calais, forcing the BEF to rely on Dunkerque (Dunkirk) for resupply. Allied forces in Belgium were now cut off from the bulk of the French forces to the south. As British forces withdrew northward to the coast, King Leopold III surrendered his armed forces on May 28, despite promises that his nation would not undertake any such unilateral action. This action opened a gap between the BEF left flank and the sea, into which the Germans now poured, threatening to cut off the BEF entirely. At this point, Hitler, in his first major military blunder of the war, intervened. For five days, he kept the German armored thrust from the south in place, saving the BEF and probably enabling Britain to continue in the war.

During the period between May 27 and June 4, the British carried out an epic evacuation at Dunkerque. In Operation DYNAMO, they evacuated some 365,000 troops, of whom about 225,000 were British. The BEF was forced to abandon virtually all its equipment in France, but it did extract almost all its remaining personnel. In Britain, the evacuation swept away the "phoniness" of the war, but many Britons were oblivious to the fact that, in May 1918, there had been 10 times the number of British divisions in France as in May 1940, that they had left the French in the lurch, or that the French First Army had held the Germans from the beaches and allowed the BEF to escape.

On June 5, after having consolidated, the Germans struck south, cutting through French forces and reaching the Seine River west of Paris four days later. Stunned by these developments and unprepared for improvised action, much of the French army simply disintegrated. On June 13, the government declared Paris an open city to spare it air attack, and the next day, German troops took peaceful possession of the French capital.

On June 12, the new French army commander, General Maxime Weygand, had concluded that the situation was hopeless and so informed the cabinet. Two days earlier, Italian dictator Benito Mussolini, convinced that the war was all but won, had brought his country into the conflict on the German side by invading southeastern France. Thirty-two Italian divisions attacked five French divisions along the Italian border but made little headway.

On June 16, French premier Paul Reynaud was forced to resign, and a majority of the cabinet voted to ask Hitler for terms. The new premier was 84-year-old Marshal Henri Philippe Pétain, a World War I hero who had been brought into the government as deputy premier in order to bolster French resolve but who now favored an immediate armistice. On June 17, the Pétain government opened negotiations with the Germans. Fighting ceased on the battlefields of France on June 25.

France was divided into occupied and unoccupied zones, and its army was reduced to 100,000 officers and men. The navy, almost entirely intact, remained under French control but was to be disarmed in French ports. France also had to pay for the German occupation of three-fifths of its territory.

Paris was included in the German occupation zone, so the new French government established itself at Vichy, in south-central France. The new Vichy France was frankly totalitarian and, to a considerable degree, collaborationist. Pétain and his advisers believed that Germany had won the war and that, at least for the foreseeable future, France would be under German control. It took something akin to clairvoyance in the dark days of June

1940 to foresee a possible Allied victory, but a small number of Frenchmen and Frenchwomen vowed to continue the fight and took the lead in forming resistance groups. In London, on June 18, young Brigadier General Charles de Gaulle, who had been undersecretary of war only a few days before, announced over the British Broadcasting Corporation (BBC) the establishment of the Free French. He soon secured British military assistance and, ultimately, recognition of his government.

Winston Churchill, who had become British prime minister on May 10, feared that the Germans would acquire the French fleet, although the French government had promised London that it would scuttle its ships rather than see them fall into German hands. This pledge was not sufficient for Churchill, who ordered Operation CATAPULT. The British would offer French naval commanders a cruel choice between continuing the fight, disarming in neutral ports, or scuttling their ships. The British rather easily acquired some 130 French vessels of all types, but at Mers-el-Kébir in Algeria, there was fighting in which the British sank a number of French ships and killed nearly 1,300 French seamen. Despite this, the French government honored its pledge more than two years later. In November 1942, the Germans tried to seize the bulk of the French navy—80 ships assembled at Toulon—but the French scuttled 77 of them.

The Germans now dominated the Continent. They were emphatically the senior partner in the German-Italian combination, they were on good terms with Francisco Franco in Spain, and the Soviet Union was benevolently neutral. History seemed to repeat itself, for the Germans now controlled almost exactly the same geographic area as had Napoleon, and in 1940, as in 1807, only Great Britain remained at war with the would-be conqueror.

Britain now awaited a German attack. In early June, there was only one properly equipped and trained division to defend the British Isles. BEF equipment abandoned in France included 600 tanks, 1,000 field guns, 500 antiaircraft guns, a vast number of small arms, and half a million tons of stores and ammunition. The fleet was far to the north, away from the Luftwaffe. If German forces could have landed in Britain in the weeks following Dunkerque, there would have been little means of stopping them. Hitler and his military chiefs, however, were caught off guard by the speed of the French defeat and had no plans for a follow-up invasion of Britain. Not until late July did they begin planning for a descent on England, code-named SEA LION (SEELÖWE).

Following the defeat of France, Hitler had postponed any decision regarding Britain. He hoped and expected that the British people would recognize that Germany had won and agree to a negotiated peace. Some of his generals urged him to strike Britain before it could reorganize and consolidate its strength, but he refused. In early June, RAF Fighter Command had only about a sixth of the number of aircraft that the Germans could send against Britain. Yet when formal orders were issued for SEA LION, German preparations were half-hearted. In any case, command of the air was the necessary prerequisite for any invasion.

Official British dates for the Battle of Britain are July 10 to October 31, 1940. The Germans, however, never achieved their goal of driving the RAF from the skies. Ineffective German leadership, intelligence failures resulting in poor targeting decisions, radar and ULTRA in the hands of the British, the lack of a strategic bomber on the German side, superior British pilot and aircraft replacement, and the German concentration on London all contributed to the German defeat.

Finally, on November 1, with the Luftwaffe sustaining prohibitive losses, the Germans shifted to night bombing—what Londoners called "the Blitz." Heavy bombing continued into May 1941. Although savage and relentless, night area bombing had no strategic result. The German air offensive had failed, in what was the first serious German military setback of the war. In mid-October 1940, Operation SEA LION was officially shelved until the spring, when it was postponed indefinitely.

Hitler failed to recognize the need to maintain the pressure on Britain. He could have intensified aircraft and submarine attacks against shipping to the British Isles, which might have brought an eventual British collapse, but his attention was increasingly drawn eastward to the Soviet Union. The commander of the German navy, Grand Admiral Erich Raeder, and the commander of the air force, Hermann Göring, both believed that the defeat of Britain would leave Germany in a much stronger position vis-à-vis the Soviet Union. Hitler contended that the Soviet Union was preparing to attack Germany and that Britain was holding out only because its leaders hoped that Germany and the Soviet Union would go to war: if he could eliminate the Soviet Union, then Britain would capitulate. Hitler lacked patience and failed to understand the limitations of the blitzkrieg in terms of distance and resupply. He also did not appreciate interdiction or an indirect approach. Finally, Hitler was driven by ideological and political factors. In June 1941, after shoring up his Balkan flank, he sent his armies against the Soviet Union.

In December 1941, the United States joined the conflict as an active participant. Hitler and Mussolini then declared war on the United States, resolving a possible strategic dilemma for President Franklin D. Roosevelt concerning the Allied policy of concentrating first on Germany. Soviet leader Josef Stalin called for an immediate invasion of Western Europe by British and U.S. ground forces, but it would take many months for the vast U.S. industrial base to shift to war production, for armed forces to be raised and trained, and for the Battle of the Atlantic to be won. In 1942, the U.S. contribution to the war in Europe came in the form of strategic bombing, and there was little of that.

The Americans preferred the earliest possible cross-Channel invasion of northern France. Army Chief of Staff General George C. Marshall was a strong supporter of an invasion of northwestern Europe in the fall of 1942. The British were leery, fearful that such a move would lead to a repeat of the situation in northeastern France in World War I. Proof that the Western Allies were not ready to undertake a cross-Channel invasion was provided in Operation JUBILEE, the raid on Dieppe on the coast of Normandy on August 19, 1942. The raid buried the myth that a cross-Channel invasion was feasible in 1942, and it cast grave doubts on the Allied plan for a cross-Channel invasion in 1943.

Roosevelt had promised Stalin that the Western Allies would undertake an invasion by the end of 1942, and he was determined to honor that pledge. He met that commitment with Operation TORCH, the Allied invasion of French North Africa in November 1942. With success there, U.S. military leaders, most notably General Marshall, attempted to secure British approval for a cross-Channel invasion in 1943. Churchill demurred and convinced Roosevelt to pursue operations in the Mediterranean against Italy. The British leader wanted an Allied concentration in the Mediterranean, which he termed the "soft underbelly of Europe." The Americans reluctantly agreed to invasions first of Sicily and then of Italy, but they insisted on the cross-Channel invasion of France for the spring of 1944.

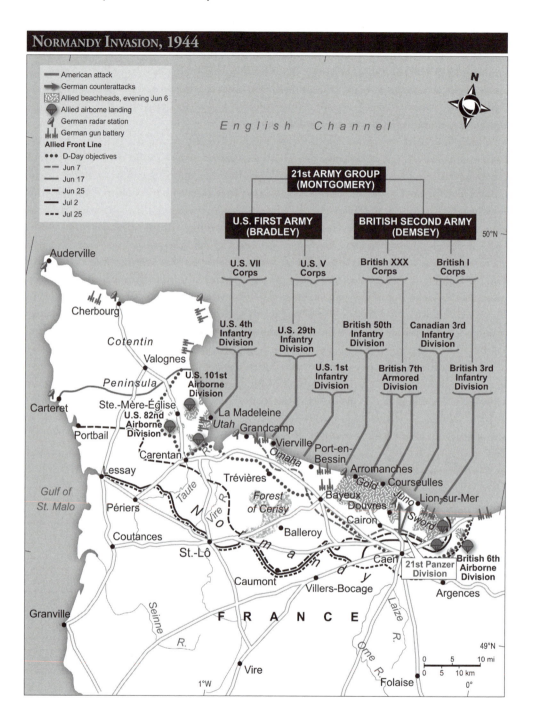

NORMANDY INVASION, 1944

Legend:
- American attack
- German counterattacks
- Allied beachheads, evening Jun 6
- Allied airborne landing
- German radar station
- German gun battery
- **Allied Front Line**
- ••• D-Day objectives
- — — Jun 7
- ——— Jun 17
- – – Jun 25
- ——— Jul 2
- – – – Jul 25

English Channel

21st ARMY GROUP (MONTGOMERY)

U.S. FIRST ARMY (BRADLEY)　　**BRITISH SECOND ARMY (DEMSEY)**

U.S. VII Corps　**U.S. V Corps**　**British XXX Corps**　**British I Corps**

U.S. 4th Infantry Division　**U.S. 29th Infantry Division**　**British 50th Infantry Division**　**Canadian 3rd Infantry Division**

U.S. 1st Infantry Division　**British 7th Armored Division**　**British 3rd Infantry Division**

Auderville
Cherbourg
Cotentin
Valognes
Peninsula
Carteret
Ste.-Mère-Église
U.S. 101st Airborne Division
U.S. 82nd Airborne Division
La Madeleine
Utah Grandcamp
Portbail
Carentan
Vierville
Port-en-Bessin
Omaha
Arromanches
Lessay
Trévières
Courseulles
Gulf of St. Malo
Périers
Forest of Cerisy
Bayeux
Gold
Juno
Lion-sur-Mer
Douvres
Sword
Coutances
Balleroy
Cairon
St.-Lô
Caen
21st Panzer Division
British 6th Airborne Division
Caumont
Villers-Bocage
Argences
Granville
F R A N C E
Seinne R.
Taute
Vire R.
N o r m a n d y
Laize R.
Orne R.
Vire
Folaise

49°N
50°N
0　5　10 mi
0　5　10 km
1°W
0°

The Allies developed precise and elaborate plans for the invasion in Normandy. Prior to the landing, Allied air forces would conduct a massive bombing campaign to isolate the region. The landing itself would be preceded by a night drop of three divisions of paratroops. The next morning, five infantry divisions would go ashore along the 50-mile stretch of coast. Some 10,000 aircraft would secure the skies, while hundreds of ships provided naval support.

Success was probable if the Allies could establish a bridgehead large enough to build up their strength. Once they broke through the German lines, the Allies would have the whole of France for maneuver because their armies were fully mechanized and the bulk of the defending German forces were not. Field Marshal Erwin Rommel, who had charge of the coastal defenses, well understood that the German defense was doomed unless it could destroy the invaders on the beaches. Hitler did not agree and indeed welcomed the invasion as an opportunity to destroy the British and U.S. forces. In Britain, the Allied armies were immune to attack; in France, they could be destroyed. Let them come, he said: "They will get the thrashing of their lives."

The only possibility of German success was to introduce panzer reserves rapidly, but this step was fatally delayed by Allied air superiority and Hitler's failure to immediately commit resources available elsewhere. Operation FORTITUDE, the Allied deception plan, convinced Hitler that the Normandy Invasion was a feint and that the main thrust would come in the Pas de Calais sector.

The Allies put ashore a million men within a month following D-Day, but a great storm severely damaged one of two artificial harbors that had been towed across the Channel. The Germans then turned the French ports into forts, destroying them when they had to surrender. Supply became a major problem and remained so until near the end of the war. The Normandy countryside also proved ideal defensive terrain, and not until the end of July were the Allies able to break out in Operation COBRA (July 25–31), when Lieutenant General Omar Bradley's U.S. First Army forced the German line west of Saint-Lô, with Major General J. Lawton Collins's VII Corps making the main effort. Lieutenant General George S. Patton Jr. arrived in France on July 6, and two days after the start of COBRA, Bradley ordered him to take command of VIII Corps.

On August 1, the U.S. command was reorganized. Bradley moved up to command 12th Army Group, Lieutenant General Courtney Hodges assumed command of the First Army, and Patton's Third Army was activated. In the British zone of operations, General Bernard Montgomery's mostly British Commonwealth 21st Army Group comprised Lieutenant General D. G. Crerar's Canadian First Army and Lieutenant General Miles C. Dempsey's Second British Army. Patton's Third Army scored the greatest success, although the general was fortunate to arrive in command when the static warfare of the previous two months had finally passed into the mobile warfare at which he excelled. The weather was also dry, and the flat terrain of northern France was ideal tank country. Patton took full advantage of the circumstances. He was certainly the outstanding general of the campaign for France. Third Army displayed instant efficiency and soon had parlayed the local breakthrough of COBRA into a theater-wide breakout. After the breakout, Patton's Third Army turned west to clear out the Brittany Peninsula, then turned to the east after taking Brest. In a single month, the Third Army liberated most of France north of the Loire River.

Meanwhile, the Allies launched Operation DRAGOON on the Côte d'Azur near Cannes in southern France. The operation had been planned largely to secure the large French Mediterranean ports for a rapid Allied buildup in France. Originally code-named ANVIL and planned to coincide with D-Day, this effort had to be postponed because of a shortage of landing craft as a consequence of OVERLORD priorities and the British reluctance to divert assets from Italy. On August 15, some 86,000 men went ashore on a 30-mile front 20 miles east of the French naval base of Toulon. German ground forces were thinly spread and inadequate in numbers and resources. Lieutenant General Alexander Patch's Seventh Army ultimately consisted of 10 divisions: 7 U.S. and 3 French. The invaders then pushed up the Rhône River valley. By the time of the linkup with Bradley's 12th Army Group near the Swiss border in the fall of 1944, the southern Allied force had grown into the 6th Army Group of 23 divisions under Lieutenant General Jacob Devers. DRAGOON provided him two large, intact French ports that could be used to help supply the expanding Allied buildup in France.

The Allies now squandered a golden opportunity. Montgomery was making little progress, while Patton and his Third Army swung wide in an enormous enveloping movement that prevented German forces from consolidating along the Seine. Patton's rapid drive made it possible to trap large numbers of two German field armies, including seven panzer divisions, in the so-called Falaise pocket. The destruction of these German forces was within Allied reach, but Eisenhower and Bradley did not grasp the significance of the situation and refused to authorize Patton to span a 15-mile-wide gap between Argentan and Falaise, the former having been assigned as a British objective.

The pocket was finally closed, and 60,000 Germans were killed or captured in the pocket, with substantial amounts of arms and equipment seized; yet some 100,000 Germans escaped. Without Bradley's imposition of a delay, which gave the Germans from August 13 to 18 to extract their forces, the Allies might have captured them all and brought the war to an end in 1944. German forces in France now fought their way homeward under Allied pursuit. Paris was liberated on August 25, a task wisely left to the French. By August 31, Patton's Third Army reached the Meuse at Verdun, and the following day, it gained the Moselle River. In the north, Montgomery drove into Belgium, all the while complaining of shortages of supplies and fuel and pressing for a single thrust under his command into Germany itself.

Between the two Allied spearheads, there was virtually little resistance. Facing Patton's six strong divisions were five weak German divisions with few tanks or antitank guns. Facing the British was the hastily assembled German First Parachute Army, a scratch force of some 18,000 men, boys, and walking wounded. In the sector between Aachen and Metz, the Germans had only eight infantry battalions. On the whole front, the Germans fielded some 100 tanks and 570 aircraft. In tanks and in aircraft, the Allies had a 20-to-1 advantage.

Yet the Allied advance stalled. The supply lines of the Allies were lengthening even as those of the Germans were contracting. The original Allied plan had been to consolidate on the Seine while opening the Brittany ports and establishing a sound logistical base, but that plan had been nullified by their unanticipated rapid advance after the Saint-Lô breakout. Much of the French railroad system had been destroyed by Allied air strikes, and the bulk of the supplies had to move from the Normandy beaches by road to the front. Despite the best efforts of the Allies, supplies were simply insufficient for the broad-front strategy on which Eisenhower insisted. The supply situation was made even worse by the need of essential services for liberated French cities and towns, and there were natural obstacles in the Vosges Mountains, the Ardennes, and the Hürtgen Forest.

By the end of August, the German army had suffered more casualties than at Stalingrad—losing roughly 500,000 soldiers and 1,600 tanks in what was one of the greatest defeats in the history of warfare. One daring thrust through the north, south, or center might have proved decisive. There were two competing schools of Allied operational strategy: the narrow front and the broad front. Montgomery and Patton were the two leading proponents of the narrow front, provided it was for their own forces; Eisenhower wanted the broad front. Eisenhower controlled the flow of supplies and made the ultimate decision. Arguing that there were only sufficient resources for one major thrust, Montgomery pressed Eisenhower to halt Patton's Third Army and concentrate resources behind his troops. He believed he could make a quick end to the war, and he wanted the British to lead the charge and take Berlin. Patton wanted, above all else, to beat Montgomery to that prize.

While this discussion was in progress, Montgomery missed a chance to shorten the war. British tanks took Brussels on September 3 and Antwerp the next day, so rapidly that the Germans were unable to destroy its port facilities. Only the opening of the 45-mile-long Scheldt estuary stood between the Allies and relief of their growing supply difficulties. But Montgomery preferred to concentrate his troops for a thrust across the Rhine into northern Germany and overlooked the enormous logistical implications of Antwerp. The British were well positioned to take the German Fifteenth Army fleeing northeastward up the coast. An advance of less than 10 miles beyond Antwerp would have sealed off the Walcheren and South Beveland Peninsula. But Montgomery halted at Antwerp. Consequently, the Fifteenth Army escaped across the Scheldt at night and then went back into Holland.

Eisenhower now had to decide between concentrating on a narrow front or launching a broad-based attack in which the Allies would attack, regroup, and then attack again. Although Allied headquarters had always known that no major thrust could be made into Germany until Antwerp had been secured as a supply base, Eisenhower allowed Montgomery to ignore opening Antwerp in favor of securing a bridgehead across the Rhine and perhaps ending the war in one bold stroke. Also affecting the plan was pressure to use the airborne divisions that had participated in the Normandy Invasion and were now recuperating in Britain. Unfortunately, Montgomery failed to carry out the detailed staff planning of his earlier campaigns to make the plan work.

The operation was code-named MARKET-GARDEN. MARKET, the airborne segment, involved three paratroop divisions; GARDEN, the ground portion, was centered in the British Second Army. The airborne forces were to secure key bridges over the Maas (Meuse), Waal, and Lek (lower Rhine) Rivers, then Second Army would race up a corridor from Belgium along a 60-mile-long narrow causeway, cross the rivers, and secure Arnhem on the lower Rhine. The plan involved a high degree of risk, but the prize of outflanking the Siegfried Line (called the West Wall by the Germans) and gaining entry into northern Germany seemed worth it.

Factors involved in the failure of the operation included the refusal to modify the hastily developed plan, the lack of coordination with the Dutch underground, and the ignoring of Dutch warnings as well as ULTRA intercepts and late photographic evidence of the presence of two battle-hardened panzer divisions transferred from the Eastern Front and reconstituting around Arnhem. The operation also suffered from insufficient men and logistical support. But the greatest tactical mistake was to drop the British 1st Airborne

Division 7 to 8 miles from Arnhem, allowing German panzers to isolate it. MARKET-GARDEN began on September 17 and ended on September 26. The operation, which Montgomery later termed "90 percent successful," was, in fact, a total failure.

By mid-September, the Allied opportunity had been lost and the Germans had recovered sufficiently to slow the advance almost to a standstill. The task of forcing the Germans from the Scheldt fell chiefly to Lieutenant General Guy Simonds's First Canadian Army. This effort consumed two months of hard fighting. Patton was also held up in a month of bloody fighting before the fortress of Metz. With the onset of bad weather, any chance for the Allies to win the war in 1944 was gone. The Germans not only managed to rebuild their shattered divisions but also transferred new units into the battle, so that they actually enjoyed a manpower advantage over the Allied Expeditionary Forces, although they were numerically inferior in tanks, artillery, and, above all, airpower. Between September and December 1944, the U.S. Army suffered one of its worst defeats in the Battle of the Hürtgen Forest, ideal defensive terrain. The Germans, who were now defending their own homeland, resisted with great tenacity.

Hitler now proposed a final offensive in the west. In September 1944, with the Eastern Front static for several months and the Allied offensive in the west gaining ground, he conceived of a sudden offensive to take the Allies by surprise, break their front, and recapture Antwerp. He hoped at the least to buy three to four months to deal with the advancing Soviets. Western Front commander Field Marshal Karl Gerd von Rundstedt thought the plan was unrealistic, as did other high-ranking officers. But Hitler refused to change his mind, and substantial German forces were transferred from the Eastern Front to the west for what would be the biggest battle fought on the Western Front in World War II and the largest engagement ever fought by the U.S. Army.

On December 16, the Germans launched their Ardennes Offensive. It caught the Western Allies completely by surprise, and bad weather restricted the use of Allied airpower. The German force of 24 divisions pushing against 3 divisions of Hodges's First Army drove a "bulge" 50 miles deep and 70 miles wide into the American defenses, which gave the Battle of the Bulge its name.

Allied resources diverted to the battle and clearing skies that permitted the intervention of Allied aircraft turned the tide. The battle dragged on to mid-January, but before the Germans could switch resources to the east, the Soviets launched their last great offensive. In effect, the Ardennes Offensive hastened the end of the war. Both sides suffered heavily, but the Western Allies quickly made up their losses, whereas the Germans could not. Deaf to all reason, Hitler categorically forbade retreat. Everything that could be of use to the enemy had to be destroyed. The fate of his people was irrelevant, for he concluded that if the Germans were unable to win, then they did not deserve to survive.

On March 7, 1945, U.S. forces captured intact a German bridge across the Rhine at Remagen and immediately put forces across. In the west, the Germans now had fewer than 60 understrength and poorly equipped divisions to oppose 85 well-equipped Allied divisions. With both Patton and Hodges making solid progress, Eisenhower ordered Bradley's 12th Army Group to make the main thrust, pushing through central Germany and ignoring Berlin, on which the Soviets were advancing. Ninth Army would encircle the Ruhr while the remainder of Montgomery's 21st Army Group covered Bradley's drive by moving northeast, cutting off German forces in Denmark and Norway. Lieutenant General Jacob Devers's 6th Army Group, meanwhile, provided right-flank security for Bradley, advancing down the Danube to secure the so-called *Alpenfestung*, or National Redoubt. The Ruhr was encircled on April 1. Seventh Army, in the meantime, took Nuremberg, crossed the Danube, and moved into Austria, joining up in the Brenner Pass with elements of the Fifth Army from Italy. On April 11, the Ninth Army reached the Elbe near Magdeburg. German resistance now rapidly collapsed. Soviet forces took Berlin, and on May 8, Admiral Karl Dönitz, Hitler's successor, surrendered German forces unconditionally. The war in Europe was over.

Spencer C. Tucker

See also

Bradley, Omar Nelson; Churchill, Sir Winston Leonard Spencer; Collaboration; de Gaulle, Charles; Eisenhower, Dwight D.; France, Role in War; Germany, Air Force; Germany, Army; Germany, Navy; Great Britain, Air Force; Great Britain, Army; Great Britain, Navy; Hitler, Adolf; Marshall, George Catlett; Montgomery, Sir Bernard Law; Mussolini, Benito; Northeast Europe Theater; Patton, George Smith, Jr.; Poland, Role in War; Resistance; Rommel, Erwin Johannes Eugen; Roosevelt, Franklin D.; Stalin, Josef; United States, Army; United States, Army Air Force; United States, Navy

References

Breuer, William B. *Storming Hitler's Rhine: The Allied Assault: February–March 1945*. New York: St. Martin's Press, 1985.

Dallas, Gregor. *1945: The War that Never Ended*. New Haven, CT: Yale University Press, 2005.

D'Este, Carlo. *Decision in Normandy*. New York: E. P. Dutton, 1983.

Gelb, Norman. *Dunkirk: The Complete Story of the First Step in the Defeat of Hitler*. New York: William Morrow, 1989.

Hastings, Max. *Armageddon: The Battle for Germany, 1944–1945*. New York: Alfred A. Knopf, 2004.

Hastings, Max. *Overlord: D-Day, June 6, 1944*. New York: Simon and Schuster, 1984.

Kershaw, Ian. *The End: The Defiance and Destruction of Hitler's Germany, 1944–1945*. New York: Penguin, 2011.

MacDonald, Charles B. *A Time for Trumpets: The Untold Story of the Battle of the Bulge*. New York: William Morrow, 1985.

Mosier, John. *The Blitzkrieg Myth: How Hitler and the Allies Misread the Strategic Realities of World War II*. New York: HarperCollins, 2003.

Prados, John. *Normandy Crucible: The Decisive Battle That Shaped World War II in Europe*. New York: New American Library, 2011.

Tooze, Adam. *The Wages of Destruction: The Making and Breaking of the Nazi Economy*. New York: Viking, 2007.

Whitaker, W. Denis, and Shelaugh Whitaker. *Rhineland: The Battle to End the War*. New York: St. Martin's Press, 1989.

Whiting, Charles. *West Wall: The Battle for Hitler's Siegfried Line*. Staplehurst: Spellmount, 1999.

Yalta Conference (February 4–11, 1945)

In January 1944, the Allied Powers' European Advisory Commission on Germany began meeting in London. It was decided that Germany's postwar government would be an Allied control council in Berlin, composed of commanders of the occupying forces of the various powers. But the commission members needed clarification from the Allied leaders on other matters. Between August and October 1944, delegates at the Dumbarton Oaks Conference in Washington worked to draft proposals for a postwar United Nations international organization. They, too, needed to decide several issues. To resolve these and other matters, a second and last meeting of the Big Three—British prime minister Winston Churchill, U.S. president Franklin D. Roosevelt, and Soviet leader Josef Stalin—and their staffs (some 700 people in all) occurred from February 4 to 11, 1945, in the Soviet Union, at Yalta in the Crimea.

The meeting at Yalta (code-named ARGONAUT) was less significant than either its detractors or supporters alleged. Many of the decisions confirmed there had already been taken during the earlier 1943 Tehran Conference and other meetings. At the time, its outcome generated considerable satisfaction. Only with the developing Cold War and the realization that Soviet help had not been necessary in the Pacific war did Yalta become such a fractious issue in U.S. politics, with Republican Party leaders charging that there had been a Democratic Party "giveaway" to the Communists.

The bargaining position of the Western leaders had not appreciably improved since the Tehran Conference. Indeed, they had just suffered the humiliation of the initial German successes in the Ardennes Offensive (Battle of the Bulge). The Red Army, by contrast, had smashed German Army Group Center and was then only 50 miles from Berlin.

Another factor at Yalta was Roosevelt's determination to draw Stalin "out of his shell" and bring the Soviet Union into postwar cooperation with the Western powers. As a result, he continued the conciliatory tactical approach he had employed at the Tehran Conference by making every effort to accommodate the Soviet leader. It did not enhance the Western bargaining position when Roosevelt announced that U.S. troops were unlikely to remain long in Europe. He also continued his practice of distancing himself from Churchill, most notably on colonial issues. Another factor at work was that Roosevelt and the United States had chosen to seek the speediest possible conclusion to the war with the least expenditure of American lives, rather than wage the war for certain geopolitical objectives, as Churchill had preferred.

British prime minister Winston Churchill (left), U.S. president Franklin D. Roosevelt (center), and Soviet leader Josef Stalin (right) met at Yalta, Crimea (present-day Ukraine) on February 4–11, 1945, to discuss military and political strategy for ending World War II. Churchill and Roosevelt were later criticized for granting Stalin major territorial concessions in Eastern Europe and China. In practice, these agreements largely ratified the existing Soviet position in areas that the Soviet military already controlled when the war ended. (Library of Congress)

Stalin, however, knew exactly what he wanted. After World War I, the Western Allies had sought to construct a *cordon sanitaire* (protective barrier) to contain Bolshevism. Stalin's goal was now the reverse—he wanted a belt of east European satellite states to exclude the West. This arrangement was to provide security against another German invasion and to protect a severely wounded Soviet Union, which had suffered the deaths of as many as 27 million citizens and terrible material losses against the West and its influences.

Roosevelt secured Soviet agreement to the Declaration on Liberated Europe. The leaders pledged that the provisional governments of liberated areas would be "representative of all democratic elements" and that there would be "free elections . . . responsive to the will of the people." But events would prove that such lofty phrases were subject to completely different interpretations.

In discussions on Germany, the Big Three agreed to government by an Allied control council. German occupation zones were also set, and at the suggestion of the Western leaders, France was allowed a zone, although Stalin insisted it be carved from territory already assigned to Britain and the United States. The three leaders also agreed on steps to demilitarize Germany, dissolve the National Socialist Party, and punish war criminals. Further, in what would later be regarded as a controversial decision, they agreed that all nationals accused of being "deserters or traitors" were to be returned to their countries of origin.

The Soviets insisted on exacting heavy reparations from Germany for damages inflicted by that nation on the Soviet Union. The Western Allies, remembering the trouble caused by reparations after World War I and fearful they would be subsidizing Soviet exactions, refused to set a specific amount but tentatively agreed to discuss the sum of $20 billion. The Soviet Union was to receive half of any reparations.

Particularly important to Roosevelt was the establishment of a postwar United Nations organization. Well aware of this and not greatly interested in the organization himself, Stalin used it to secure concessions on other matters. The Big Three adopted recommendations from the Dumbarton Oaks Conference that the United Nations be organized on the lines of the old League of Nations, complete with the General Assembly, Security Council, and Secretariat. It also set the composition of the Security Council. Roosevelt agreed that the Soviet Union might have three votes in the General Assembly. The most difficult matter to resolve was that of the veto in the Security Council, although this only became an issue in U.S. politics later, when the Soviet Union exercised that privilege so liberally. The U.S. Senate would not have approved American participation without the veto provision.

Poland was a particularly vexing matter for the two Western leaders, but the Red Army already occupied the country. Regarding boundaries, Stalin demanded and succeeded in establishing the Curzon Line, with slight modifications, as Poland's eastern border. The Allies were more strenuous in objecting to the Oder-Neisse Line as its western boundary, and there was no agreement on this matter at Yalta. Regarding the Polish government, Moscow had, only a month before Yalta, recognized the Lublin Poles as the official government of Poland. Stalin agreed to broaden this puppet government on a "democratic basis," and he pledged to hold "free and unfettered elections as soon as possible on the basis of universal suffrage and secret ballot." The Western Allies secured the same concessions for Yugoslavia, Romania, and Bulgaria.

The most controversial decisions taken at Yalta concerned the Far East. These decisions were kept secret from China. Stalin had already made it clear that the Soviet Union would enter the war against Japan sometime after the defeat of Germany. This matter was, in fact, never in doubt. The problem lay in the timing. Here, Stalin was in the same position enjoyed by the Allies before the invasion of northern France. Tardy Soviet entry into the Pacific war might mean heavy U.S. casualties in an invasion of the Japanese home islands. No one knew whether the atomic bomb would work and, even if it did, whether it would be decisive in bringing about Japan's defeat.

Stalin pledged to enter the war against Japan "two or three months" after the defeat of Germany. In return, the Soviet Union would receive South Sakhalin Island, concessions in the port of Dairen, the return of Port Arthur as a naval base, control over railroads leading to these ports, and the Kurile Islands (which had never been Russian territory). Outer Mongolia would continue to be independent of China, but China would regain sovereignty over Manchuria. In effect, these concessions would replace Japanese imperialism with that of the Soviet Union, but the Western leaders believed they were necessary to secure the timing of the Soviet entry into the Pacific war. In future years, what Americans disliked most about Yalta was that these concessions turned out to be unnecessary.

Spencer C. Tucker

See also

China, Role in War; Churchill, Sir Winston Leonard Spencer; Poland, Role in War; Roosevelt, Franklin D.; Stalin, Josef

References

Dallas, Gregor. *1945: The War That Never Ended*. New Haven, CT: Yale University Press, 2005.

Feis, Herbert. *Churchill–Roosevelt–Stalin: The War They Waged and the Peace They Sought*. Princeton, NJ: Princeton University Press, 1957.

Fischer, Louis. *The Road to Yalta: Soviet Foreign Relations, 1941–1945*. New York: Harper and Row, 1972.

Gardner, Lloyd C. *Spheres of Influence: The Great Powers Partition Europe, from Munich to Yalta*. Chicago, IL: Ivan R. Dee, 1993.

Harbutt, Fraser J. *Yalta 1945: Europe and America at the Crossroads*. New York: Cambridge University Press, 2010.

Mastny, Vojtech. *Russia's Road to the Cold War: Diplomacy, Warfare, and the Politics of Communism, 1941–1945*. New York: Columbia University Press, 1979.

Plokhy, S. M. *Yalta: The Price of Peace*. New York: Viking, 2010.

Reynolds, David. *Summits: Six Meetings That Shaped the Twentieth Century*. New York: Basic Books, 2007.

Snell, John L. *The Meaning of Yalta: Big Three Diplomacy and the New Balance of Power*. Baton Rouge, LA: Louisiana State University Press, 1956.

Stettinius, Edward R., Jr. *Roosevelt and the Russians: The Yalta Conference*. Edited by Walter Johnson. New York: Harold Ober Associates, 1949.

Theoharis, Athan G. *The Yalta Myths: An Issue in U.S. Politics, 1945–1955*. Columbia, MO: University of Missouri Press, 1970.

Thomas, Hugh. *Armed Truce: The Beginnings of the Cold War, 1945–1946*. New York: Atheneum, 1987.

Yamamoto Isoroku (1884–1943)

Yamamoto Isoroku was the Japanese navy admiral who devised the December 1941 attack against U.S. forces at Pearl Harbor. Born in Nagaoka, Honshu, Japan, on April 4, 1884, Yamamoto was the biological son of the former samurai Takano Sadayoshi and the adoptive son of Yamamoto Tatewaki. Educated at the Naval Academy (1901–1904), he fought in the 1904–1905 Russo-Japanese War and took part in the great Japanese naval victory in the Battle of Tsushima. He attended the Naval Staff College in 1915 and 1916.

Admiral Yamamoto Isoroku, a leading Japanese proponent of naval aviation, was the architect of the successful attack on the U.S. naval establishment at Pearl Harbor that precipitated American entry into World War II. His death in an aerial ambush two years later was a major blow to Japanese morale. (Library of Congress)

Initially trained in gunnery, Yamamoto became a leading advocate of naval airpower during the 1920s and 1930s, in part because of his experiences as chief executive officer at Kasumigaura Naval Flight School between 1924 and 1926, when he became a pilot as well. Also significant in forming Yamamoto's perceptions were his two periods as a resident officer in the United States. Between 1919 and 1921, he studied English at Harvard University. Promoted to captain in 1923, he served as naval attaché in Washington, DC, from 1926 to 1928. Yamamoto's time in the United States persuaded him of that country's unlimited economic potential and the relatively low quality of the U.S. Navy.

On returning to Japan from the United States, Yamamoto took command of the aircraft carrier *Akagi* and used her as a platform to test out new concepts in naval aviation. He was a delegate to the 1929–1930 London Naval Conference. He became chief of the navy's technical service in 1930 and was promoted to rear admiral the next year. In this position, he pushed the development of modern aircraft for the navy. In 1933, he took command of the 1st Naval Air Division. Yamamoto headed the Japanese delegation to the 1935–1936 London Naval Conference, where he presented Tokyo's position that it would no longer abide by the 5-to-5-to-3 naval ratio with the United States and Britain. He returned home a hero. Appointed vice minister of the navy in 1936, Yamamoto opposed his government's decision to proceed with construction of the giant Yamato-class battleships, believing they were a waste of precious resources. Unable to overcome the reliance on traditional battleships, Yamamoto nonetheless pushed the construction of aircraft carriers, long-range bombers and flying boats, and the new Zero fighter. His opposition to the increasingly belligerent official position led to his removal from his government post.

Appointed commander in chief of the Combined Fleet in August 1939 and promoted to full admiral in November 1940, Yamamoto opposed Japan's adherence to the Tripartite Pact and the movement toward war with the United States. Although he allegedly remarked privately that he would "run wild" for six months to a year, he had "utterly no confidence" after that. Nonetheless, he rejected the navy's original plan to lie in wait for the U.S. Pacific Fleet in the Far East, after the American ships had been savaged by submarine and torpedo attacks. Instead, Yamamoto devised a preemptive strike against the Pacific Fleet anchorage at Pearl Harbor in the Hawaiian Islands. He hoped that by crippling U.S. naval power at the war's outset, Japan might use the breathing spell that would ensue to conquer the Southern Resource Area and erect an impregnable defensive barrier.

Yamamoto did what he could to prepare his fleet for war, purging ineffective officers and insisting on realistic, rigorous—even dangerous—training, both day and night, so that when war came, the fleet was the best trained in the world, certainly at night fighting. However, he ignored technological advances, such as radar, which Japanese ships did not receive until 1943.

The success of the Pearl Harbor attack on December 7, 1941, enhanced Yamamoto's prestige, which he used to persuade the Naval General Staff to accept his overly complex Midway plan in April 1942. Designed to draw out the remnants of the U.S. Fleet, specifically the carriers absent from Pearl Harbor on December 7, Yamamoto's Midway campaign ended in disaster on June 4 to 6 with the Combined Fleet's loss of four fleet carriers, a blow from which the Japanese navy never recovered.

Although the tide of the Pacific war clearly shifted in favor of the Allies after Midway, U.S. leaders remained wary of Yamamoto's leadership. Accordingly, when U.S. intelligence learned that Yamamoto intended a one-day inspection trip to the northern Solomons in April 1943, the Pacific Fleet commander, Admiral Chester Nimitz, with the approval of President Franklin D. Roosevelt, dispatched aircraft to intercept his plane. On April 18, P-38 fighters shot down Yamamoto's aircraft near Buin in southern Bougainville Island, killing the admiral. His remains were recovered and returned to Tokyo, where he was honored with a state funeral.

Bruce J. DeHart and Spencer C. Tucker

See also

Japan, Navy; Midway, Battle of; Nimitz, Chester William; Pearl Harbor, Attack on; Roosevelt, Franklin D.; Signals Intelligence; United States, Navy

References

Agawa, Hiroyuki. *The Reluctant Admiral: Yamamoto and the Imperial Navy.* Tokyo: Kodansha International, 1979.

Bond, Brian. *British and Japanese Military Leadership in the Far Eastern War, 1941–1945.* London: Frank Cass, 2004.

Davis, Donald A. *Lightning Strike: The Secret Mission to Kill Admiral Yamamoto and Avenge Pearl Harbor.* New York: St. Martin's Press, 2005.

Dull, Paul S. *A Battle History of the Imperial Japanese Navy, 1941–1945.* Annapolis, MD: Naval Institute Press, 1978.

Glines, Carol V. *Attack on Yamamoto.* New York: Crown Books, 1990.

Hall, R. Cargill. *Lightning over Bougainville: The Yamamoto Mission Revisited.* Washington, DC: Smithsonian Institution Press, 1991.

Hoyt, Edwin P. *Yamamoto: The Man Who Planned Pearl Harbor.* New York: McGraw-Hill, 1990.

Potter, John D. *Yamamoto: The Man Who Menaced America.* New York: Viking, 1965.

Prados, John. *Combined Fleet Decoded: The Secret History of American Intelligence and the Japanese Navy in World War II.* Annapolis, MD: Naval Institute Press, 2001.

Prange, Gordon W. *At Dawn We Slept: The Untold Story of Pearl Harbor.* New York: McGraw-Hill, 1981.

Prange, Gordon W., Donald Goldstein, and Kathleen Dillon. *Miracle at Midway.* New York: Penguin, 1982.

Stille, Mark. *Yamamoto Isoroku.* Oxford: Osprey Publishing, 2012.

Ugaki, Matome. *Fading Victory: The Diary of Admiral Matome Ugaki, 1941–1945.* Edited by Donald M. Goldstein and Kathleen V. Dillon. Translated by Masataka Chihaya. Reprint ed. Annapolis, MD: Naval Institute Press, 2008.

Wible, J. T. *The Yamamoto Mission: Sunday, April 18, 1943.* Fredericksburg, TX: Admiral Nimitz Foundation, 1988.

Zhukov, Georgiĭ Konstantinovich (1896–1974)

Georgiĭ Konstantinovich Zhukov was a marshal of the Soviet Union and perhaps better known in the West than any other Soviet military leader of World War II. Born in Strelkovka, Kaluga Province, Russia, on November 19, 1896, Zhukov was the son of peasants, his father a cobbler and his mother a carter. He was apprenticed as a furrier at age 12. Conscripted into the Russian army in 1915, Zhukov served in the cavalry during World War I, rising to noncommissioned officer (NCO) rank. After recovering from wounds received from an enemy mine, he joined the Red Army in 1918.

Zhukov commanded from platoon through squadron in the Russian Civil War, joining the Communist Party in 1919. He took charge of a cavalry regiment in 1922 and a brigade in 1930. In 1932, he received command of a cavalry division; four years later, he led a corps. Zhukov was one of the few senior officers to survive the military purges of 1937. Serving as deputy commander of the Belorussian Military District, he was sent to the Far East in June 1939 to deal with Japan's attempted invasion of Mongolia. By the end of August, he had decisively repulsed the Japanese in the Battle of Khalkin Gol (Nomonhan). In 1940, he was promoted to full general, and near the end of the Russo-Finnish War, he was appointed chief of the General Staff. After the Germans invaded the Soviet Union in June 1941, Zhukov asked to be relieved from that post when Josef Stalin rejected his suggestion that Kiev be abandoned before it was lost to the Germans. Stalin's decision cost the Soviets some 665,000 soldiers captured by the Germans.

During the course of World War II, Zhukov was involved in the planning and execution of nearly every major campaign of the Eastern Front. In October 1941, he replaced Marshal Kliment Voroshilov at Leningrad and galvanized the defense there. Then, as commander of the West Front that same month, he organized the defense of Moscow; in November and December, he launched the counteroffensive that forced the Germans back from Moscow. In the fall of 1942, Zhukov and General Aleksandr Vasilievsky planned the counteroffensive at Stalingrad that trapped German General Friedrich Paulus's Sixth Army. Promoted to marshal of the Soviet Union and appointed deputy supreme commander of the Red Army, he returned to Leningrad in 1943 and lifted the siege there. Then, in July, as special representative for Stavka (the Soviet High Command), again along with Vasilievsky, Zhukov supervised the defense of the Kursk salient and the subsequent offensive that swept across the Ukraine.

Georgiĭ Zhukov, chief of the Soviet army's general staff at the time of the German invasion of Russia during 1941–1942, led the Soviet defense. He later coordinated the Soviet counteroffensives across the Ukraine and Poland, which culminated in 1945 in the successful Soviet invasion of Germany. From May 1945 to April 1946, he was the first military commander and military governor of the Soviet Occupation Zone in Germany. (Library of Congress)

In the summer and autumn of 1944, Zhukov commanded the Belorussian Campaign, which destroyed German Army Group Center and ended the German occupation of Poland and Czechoslovakia. In April 1945, he personally commanded the final assault on Berlin, and he took the official German surrender for the Soviet Union on May 8, 1945, then remained to command Soviet occupation forces in Germany.

In 1946, Zhukov assumed command of all Soviet ground forces, but one year later, he fell victim to Stalin's paranoia and desire to diminish the reputation of potential rivals and was demoted to command the Odessa Military District. After Stalin's death in 1953, Zhukov became deputy minister of defense and then, in 1955, defense minister. During the Nikita Khrushchev years, his fortunes rose and fell but rose again when Khrushchev was deposed in 1964. Zhukov died in Moscow on June 18, 1974.

Arthur T. Frame

See also

Eastern Front; Finland, Role in War; Germany, Army; Northeast Europe Theater; Poland, Role in War; Resistance; Soviet Union, Army; Stalin, Josef

References

Anfilov, Viktor. "Georgy Konstantinovich Zhukov." In *Stalin's Generals*, edited by Harold Shukman, 343–60. New York: Grove Press, 1993.

Axell, Albert. *Marshal Zhukov: The Man Who Beat Hitler*. New York: Longman, 2003.

Chaney, Otto P., Jr. *Zhukov.* Norman, OK: University of Oklahoma Press, 1996.

Colvin, John. *Zhukov: The Conqueror of Berlin.* London: Weidenfeld and Nicolson, 2004.

Coox, Alvin D. *Nomonhan: Japan against Russia, 1939.* Stanford, CA: Stanford University Press, 1985.

Forczyk, Robert. *Georgy Zhukov.* Oxford: Osprey Publishing, 2012.

Fugate, Bryan I., and Lev Dvoretsky. *Thunder on the Dnepr: Zhukov, Stalin, and the Defeat of Hitler's Blitzkrieg.* Novato, CA: Presidio Press, 1997.

Glantz, David M. *Zhukov's Greatest Defeat: The Red Army's Epic Disaster in Operation Mars, 1942.* Lawrence, KS: University Press of Kansas, 1999.

Goldman, Stuart D. *Nomonhan, 1939: The Red Army's Victory that Shaped World War II.* Annapolis, MD: Naval Institute Press, 2012.

Jukes, Geoffrey. *Kursk: The Clash of Armour.* New York: Ballantine Books, 1968.

Le Tissier, Tony. *Zhukov at the Oder: The Decisive Battle for Berlin.* Westport, CT: Praeger, 1996.

Mawdsley, Evan. *Thunder in the East: The Nazi–Soviet War 1941–1945.* New York: Bloomsbury, 2005.

Roberts, Geoffrey. *Stalin's General: The Life of Georgy Zhukov.* New York: Random House, 2012.

Spahr, William J. *Zhukov: The Rise and Fall of a Great Captain.* Novato, CA: Presidio Press, 1993.

Zhukov, Georgiĭ K. *Marshal of the Soviet Union, G. Zhukov: Reminiscences and Reflections.* Translated by Vic Schneierson. 2 vols. Moscow: Progress Publishers, 1985.

Zhukov, Georgiĭ K. *Marshal Zhukov's Greatest Battles.* Edited by Harrison Salisbury. Translated by Theodore Shabad. With new introduction. New York: Cooper Square Press, 2002.

Zhukov, Georgiĭ K. *The Memoirs of Marshal Zhukov.* London: Jonathan Cape, 1971.

Primary Source Documents

The Nazi–Soviet Non-Aggression Pact, Protocols, and Clarifications, August 23, 1939

Non-Aggression Pact between Germany and the Union of Soviet Socialist Republics, 23 August 1939

The Government of the German Reich and the Government of the Union of Soviet Socialist Republics, guided by the desire to strengthen the cause of peace between Germany and the Union of Soviet Socialist Republics, and taking as a basis the fundamental regulations of the Neutrality Agreement concluded in April 1926 between Germany and the Union of Soviet Socialist Republics, have reached the following agreement:

Article 1. The two Contracting Parties bind themselves to refrain from any act of force, any aggressive action and any attack on one another, both singly and also jointly with other Powers.

Article 2. In the event of one of the Contracting Parties becoming the object of warlike action on the part of a third Power, the other Contracting Party shall in no manner support this third Power.

Article 3. The Governments of the two Contracting Parties shall in future remain continuously in touch with one another, by way of consultation, in order to inform one another on questions touching their joint interests.

Article 4. Neither of the two Contracting Parties shall participate in any grouping of Powers which is directed directly or indirectly against the other Party.

Article 5. In the event of disputes or disagreements arising between the Contracting Parties on questions of this or that kind, both Parties would clarify these disputes or

---

On August 23, 1939, Count Joachim von Ribbentrop, the German foreign minister, and V. M. Molotov, his Soviet counterpart, signed a nonaggression pact between their two countries, together with several secret protocols delineating the Soviet and German spheres of influence in Eastern Europe and the Baltic republics, including an understanding on the partitioning of Poland between the two signatory powers. Under the agreement, the Soviet Union also provided appreciable quantities of valuable war supplies to Germany. These agreements were subjected to further clarifications on August 28, 1939, September 28, 1939, and, in one case, also on January 10, 1941. They paved the way for Hitler to invade Poland one week later, the event that, in turn, impelled Great Britain and France to declare war on Germany, the beginning of general war in Europe.

disagreements exclusively by means of friendly exchange of opinion or, if necessary, by arbitration committees.

Article 6. The present Agreement shall be concluded for a period of ten years on the understanding that, insofar as one of the Contracting Parties does not give notice of termination one year before the end of this period, the period of validity of this Agreement shall automatically be regarded as prolonged for a further period of five years.

Article 7. The present Agreement shall be ratified within the shortest possible time. The instruments of ratification shall be exchanged in Berlin. The Agreement takes effect immediately after it has been signed.

Source: U.S. Department of State. *Nazi–Soviet Relations 1939–1941: Documents from the Archives of the German Foreign Office*, edited by Raymond James Sontag and James Stuart Beddie, 76–78, 105–107. Washington, DC: U.S. Government Printing Office, 1948.

Secret Supplementary Protocol on the Border of the Spheres of Interest of Germany and the USSR, signed by V. M. Molotov and Joachim von Ribbentrop, 23 August 1939

In signing the nonaggression pact between Germany and the Union of Soviet Socialist Republics, the undersigned plenipotentiaries of the two sides discussed in strict confidentiality the issue of delimiting the spheres of mutual interest in Eastern Europe. This discussion led to the following result:

1. In the event of territorial-political reorganization of the districts making up the Baltic states (Finland, Estonia, Latvia, Lithuania), the northern border of Lithuania is simultaneously the border of the spheres of interest of Germany and the USSR. The interests of Lithuania with respect to the Vilnius district are recognized by both sides.

2. In the event of territorial-political reorganization of the districts making up the Polish Republic, the border of the spheres of interest of Germany and the USSR will run approximately along the Pisa, Narew, Vistula, and San rivers.

   The question of whether it is in the signatories' mutual interest to preserve the independent Polish State and what the borders of that state will be can be ascertained conclusively only in the course of future political development.

   In any event, both governments will resolve this matter through friendly mutual agreement.

3. Concerning southeastern Europe, the Soviet side emphasizes the interest of the USSR in Bessarabia. The German side declares its complete political disinterest in these areas.

4. This protocol will be held in strict secrecy by both sides.

Source: U.S. Department of State. *Nazi–Soviet Relations 1939–1941: Documents from the Archives of the German Foreign Office*, edited by Raymond James Sontag and James Stuart Beddie, 76–78, 105–107. Washington, DC: U.S. Government Printing Office, 1948.

Clarification of the Secret Supplementary Protocol of 23 August 1939, signed in Moscow by V. M. Molotov and Count F. W. Schulenburg, 28 August 1939

In order to clarify the first paragraph of point 2 of the "Secret Supplementary Protocol" of 23 August 1939, this is to explain that said paragraph is to be read in the following final version, namely:

> "2. In the event of the territorial-political reorganization of the districts making up the Polish State, the border of the spheres of interest of Germany and the USSR will run approximately along the Pisa, Narew, Vistula, and San rivers."

Source: U.S. Department of State. *Nazi–Soviet Relations 1939–1941: Documents from the Archives of the German Foreign Office,* edited by Raymond James Sontag and James Stuart Beddie, 76–78, 105–107. Washington, DC: U.S. Government Printing Office, 1948.

Confidential Protocol Concerning the Possibility of Resettling the Population Residing within the Spheres of Interest of the Governments of the USSR and Germany, signed by V. M. Molotov and Joachim von Ribbentrop, 28 September 1939

The Government of the USSR will not impede German citizens or other persons of German ancestry residing within its spheres of interest should they desire to move to Germany or to German spheres of interest. It agrees that this resettlement will be conducted by persons authorized by the German Government in accordance with responsible local authorities and that in the process the property rights of the resettled persons will not be infringed.

The German Government assumes the same obligation with respect to persons of Ukrainian or Belorussian ancestry residing within its spheres of interest.

Source: U.S. Department of State. *Nazi–Soviet Relations 1939–1941: Documents from the Archives of the German Foreign Office,* edited by Raymond James Sontag and James Stuart Beddie, 76–78, 105–107. Washington, DC: U.S. Government Printing Office, 1948.

Secret Supplementary Protocol on Changing the Soviet–German Agreement of 23 August Concerning the Spheres of Interest of Germany and the USSR, signed by V. M. Molotov and Joachim von Ribbentrop, 28 September 1939

The undersigned plenipotentiaries state the concurrence of the German Government and the Government of the USSR in the following:

Point 1 of the secret supplementary protocol signed on 23 August 1939 is changed so that the territory of the Lithuanian state is included in the sphere of interest of the USSR because, on the other side, Lublin voivodeship and parts of Warsaw voivodeship are included in the sphere of interest of Germany (see map accompanying the Treaty on Friendship and the Border between the USSR and Germany, signed today). As soon as the Government of the USSR takes special measures on Lithuanian territory to protect its interests, the present German-Lithuanian border, with the objective of making it a natural and simple border, will be adjusted so that the Lithuanian territory that lies southwest of the line shown on the map goes to Germany.

It is further stated that economic agreements between Germany and Lithuania now in force must not be broken by the aforementioned measures by the Soviet Union.

Source: U.S. Department of State. *Nazi–Soviet Relations 1939–1941: Documents from the Archives of the German Foreign Office,* edited by Raymond James Sontag and James Stuart Beddie, 76–78, 105–107. Washington, DC: U.S. Government Printing Office, 1948.

Secret Supplementary Protocol on Preventing Polish Agitation on the Territory of the Other Treaty Signatory, signed by V. M. Molotov and Joachim von Ribbentrop, 28 September 1939

The undersigned plenipotentiaries, in concluding the Soviet-German treaty on the border and friendship, have stated their concurrence in the following:

Neither side will permit on their territories any sort of Polish agitation affecting the territory of the other country. They will abort such agitation on their own territories and will inform each other as to effective measures to accomplish this.

Source: U.S. Department of State. *Nazi–Soviet Relations 1939–1941: Documents from the Archives of the German Foreign Office,* edited by Raymond James Sontag and James Stuart Beddie, 76–78, 105–107. Washington, DC: U.S. Government Printing Office, 1948.

Secret Protocol of 10 January 1941, Clarifying the Agreements of August 1939

The Chairman of the Council of People's Commissars of the USSR V. M. Molotov, with the authorization of the Government of the USSR on one side, and German Ambassador Count von der Schulenburg, with the authorization of the Government of Germany on the other side, have concurred on the following:

1. The government of Germany renounces its claims to the part of the territory of Lithuania indicated in the Secret Supplementary Protocol of September 28, 1939, and shown on the map that is attached to this Protocol.
2. The Government of the USSR agrees to compensate the Government of Germany for the territory indicated in point 1 of the present Protocol with a payment to Germany in the amount of 7,500,000 gold dollars, the equivalent of 31,500,000 German marks.

    Payment of the sum of 31.5 million German marks will be made as follows: one-eighth, i.e., 3,937,500 German marks, in deliveries of nonferrous metals over a three-month period beginning from the day of signing of the present Protocol, and the remaining seven-eighths, i.e., 27,562,500 German marks, in gold through deductions from German payments of gold that the German side has to make before February 11, 1941, based on an exchange of letters between the People's Commissar of Foreign Trade of the USSR A. I. Mikoyan and the Chairman of the German Economic Delegation Mr. Schnurre that took place in conjunction with the signing of the "Agreement of January 10, 1941, on Mutual Deliveries of Commodities for the Second Treaty Period according to the Economic Agreement of February 11, 1940, between the USSR and Germany."

3. The present Protocol . . . comes into force immediately upon signing.

Source: U.S. Department of State. *Nazi–Soviet Relations 1939–1941: Documents from the Archives of the German Foreign Office*, edited by Raymond James Sontag and James Stuart Beddie, 76–78, 105–107. Washington, DC: U.S. Government Printing Office, 1948.

Clare Hollingworth on the German Invasion of Poland: Excerpts from *The Three Weeks' War in Poland* (1940)

Since all British correspondents had been expelled from Berlin some days before, I decided to have a look round in German Silesia. Katowice was too quiet for news. I crossed the frontier at Beuthen without trouble. (Though news of my crossing so upset the Polish Foreign Office that the British Embassy were required to vouch for me.) The German frontier town was nearly deserted. It was open to enfilading fire from Polish batteries, and the Germans evidently thought it prudent to evacuate civilians. Those who remained looked depressed and unhappy. I spoke to old acquaintances and found increased trust in Hitler, even among those who had been critical—but, linked with this, a refusal to believe in war.

"It won't come to that, liebes Fraülein, don't you worry. The Führer will get Germany her rights without war this time, just as he did before."

They told me stories of the "atrocities" committed by Poland against her German minority, and asked me if I had seen such things. I had not.

"Ah, you don't see them, but they happen every day. Why do you suppose our people come across the frontier to escape the Poles?" Then I learned an interesting thing. German "refugees" from Poland were not being allowed into the Reich. They were being kept for use on the frontier. We were to hear much of them before the end of the war.

I found a noticeable shortage of supplies in Beuthen. There was no soap for foreigners, while even for Germans it was strictly rationed. Aspirin itself, the German product par excellence, was unobtainable. A friendly butcher showed the meat ration, the weekly allowance for a family with two children; it was enough for three meals, I reckoned, and your

---

On August 30, 1939, Clare Hollingworth, who had begun working for the British newspaper the *Daily Telegraph*, beginning what would become a renowned career as a war correspondent, was staying with friends in Katowice, Poland, on the border with Germany. War was generally considered imminent. She decided to cross the frontier into Germany, borrowing the British Consul's official car for the purpose. During this brief day trip, Hollingworth saw German tanks massed on the border in readiness to attack Poland, and one night later, after she had returned to Katowice, the invasion began. Hollingworth became the first reporter to file a dispatch on the outbreak of the European war. In a book published in 1940 she described at greater length these events and her experiences.

German is no vegetarian. The family's tea ration would have made a good "mash" (as they say in the Midlands) for six English tea-drinkers; and the coffee, which tasted like burnt toast, and *was* burnt maize, could perhaps serve twelve. Oils and fats could be bought with a special permit only. Butter, cream and milk had been unobtainable for five weeks. I found it impossible to get meals in restaurants, and should have gone hungry, had not a waiter, well tipped in the past, produced a partridge from nowhere. What kind of victualling is this, I wondered, on which to begin a major war?

I drove along the fortified frontier road via Hindenburg (which in the nineteen-twenties the townsfolk voted to call "Leninburg") to Gleiwitz, which had become a military town. On the road were parties of motor-cycle despatch-riders, bunched together and riding hard. As we came over the little ridge into the town, sixty-five of them burst past us, each about ten yards behind the other. From the road I could see bodies of troops, and at the roadside hundreds of tanks, armoured cars and field guns stood or moved off toward the frontier. Here and there were screens of canvas or planking, concealing the big guns; they seemed not to be camouflaged against air-attack. I guessed that the German Command was preparing to strike to the north of Katowice and its fortified lines: the advance which was to reach Czestochowa in two days of war.

In the middle of all this I bought odd things—wine, electric torches—and drove back peacefully. Now and then a trooper would spot the Union Jack on my car and give a sudden, astonished gape. As we reached a length of road which lies parallel with the frontier, I looked across a hollow, some wire and tank-barricades, and watched the peasant-women moving about the Polish fields, a few hundred yards away. In the evening I returned to Poland, without trouble, the feverish preparations of the German military uppermost in my mind.

[The next day, Hollingworth learned that in her absence the Polish authorities had uncovered and, so they believed, squelched various plots by German–Polish nationals, activities in which the German Consul was openly implicated, a fact that "showed me again that we stood on the edge of war." She nonetheless retired to bed, but was awoken in the early hours of 1 September 1939.]

Slam! Slam! . . . a noise like doors banging. I woke up. It could not be later than five in the morning. Next, the roar of airplanes and more doors banging. Running to the window I could pick out the planes, riding high, with the guns blowing smoke-rings below them. There was a long flash into the town park, another, another. Incendiary bombs? I wondered. As I opened my door I ran against the friends with whom I was staying, in their dressing-gowns.

"What is all this about?"

"We aren't sure. A big air-raid practice was announced for to-day. Or it may be something more. We are trying to reach Zoltaszek" (my old friend the Chief of Police). Just then the Polish maid appeared.

"Only Mrs. Zoltaszek is at home."

"Then ask her what's going on. Is this an air-raid practice? What does she know?" they pressed the girl. She spoke into the telephone for a moment and then turned, her eyes wide open.

"She . . . she says it's the beginning of war! . . ."

I grabbed the telephone, reached the *Telegraph* correspondent in Warsaw and told him my news. I heard later that he rang straight through to the Polish Foreign Office, who had had no word of the attack. The *Telegraph* was not only the first paper to hear that Poland was at war—it had, too, the odd privilege of informing the Polish Government itself.

I had arranged for a car to come on the first hint of alarm, but it did not arrive. We stood, drank coffee, walked about the rooms and waited; I was alternately cursing my driver and wondering whether the *Telegraph* would produce a Special Edition for my news. The war, as a tragic disaster, was not yet a reality. When my driver came at last, he met my fury with a pitying smile.

"It's only an air-raid practice," he said.

We ran down to the British Consulate, which I knew well. On our way I noticed smiles on the faces turned up to the sky. "Well," they seemed to be saying, "so this is the air-raid practice."

"But of course it's an air-raid practice, Herr Konsul," the Secretary of the Consulate was saying as I arrived. My own reaction, for the moment, was actual fear: fear that I had made the *gaffe* of my life by reporting a non-existent war.

However, official confirmation of the war came soon enough. At once the Secretary—one of the German minority, who had worked at the Consulate since its opening in 1920—burst into tears.

"This is the end of poor Germany," she wept.

Just then my sympathy with "poor Germany" was not all that it might have been.

Everyone at the Consulate was working furiously. Papers were being stuffed into the big, old-fashioned stoves until ashes fluffed under one's feet. The Consul was whipping round by telephone to ensure the departure of those British subjects who remained.

Source: Hollingworth, Clare. *The Three Weeks' War in Poland*, 11–17. London: Duckworth, 1940. Used by permission of Gerald Duckworth & Co. Ltd.

W. H. Auden, "September 1, 1939"

I sit in one of the dives
On Fifty-second Street
Uncertain and afraid
As the clever hopes expire
Of a low dishonest decade:
Waves of anger and fear
Circulate over the bright
And darkened lands of the earth,
Obsessing our private lives;
The unmentionable odour of death
Offends the September night.

Accurate scholarship can
Unearth the whole offence
From Luther until now

As German tanks invaded Poland, the British poet W. H. (Wystan Hugh) Auden (1907–1973) wrote one of his most famous poems. At the beginning of 1939, Auden, together with his long-time friend, the British writer Christopher Isherwood, moved to the United States, where he would base himself for the next 33 years. During the 1930s, Auden, like his Oxford University contemporaries Isherwood and the poets Stephen Spender, Louis MacNeice, and Cecil Day Lewis, had been a prominent figure on the intellectual and literary European left. He had lived in Germany and spoken at public meetings and rallies protesting against the brutal policies of the Fascist powers, both their internal repression of dissent and their attacks on other countries. By late 1938, Auden had become uncomfortable with political activism. His poem treated the coming of war with weary resignation, as a measure that while possibly necessary and inevitable was likely to bring further suffering in its train. It also suggested that the United States would not find it possible for very long to remain in its "euphoric dream" of neutrality. Auden later came to dislike this poem, and during his lifetime refused to allow its republication.

That has driven a culture mad,
Find what occurred at Linz,
What huge imago made
A psychopathic god:
I and the public know
What all schoolchildren learn,
Those to whom evil is done
Do evil in return.

Exiled Thucydides knew
All that a speech can say
About Democracy,
And what dictators do,
The elderly rubbish they talk
To an apathetic grave;
Analysed all in his book,
The enlightenment driven away,
The habit-forming pain,
Mismanagement and grief:
We must suffer them all again.

Into this neutral air
Where blind skyscrapers use
Their full height to proclaim
The strength of Collective Man,
Each language pours its vain
Competitive excuse:
But who can live for long
In an euphoric dream;
Out of the mirror they stare,
Imperialism's face
And the international wrong.

Faces along the bar
Cling to their average day:
The lights must never go out,
The music must always play,
All the conventions conspire
To make this fort assume
The furniture of home;
Lest we should see where we are,
Lost in a haunted wood,
Children afraid of the night
Who have never been happy or good.

The windiest militant trash
Important Persons shout
Is not so crude as our wish:
What mad Nijinsky wrote
About Diaghilev
Is true of the normal heart;
For the error bred in the bone
Of each woman and each man
Craves what it cannot have,
Not universal love
But to be loved alone.

From the conservative dark
Into the ethical life
The dense commuters come,
Repeating their morning vow;
'I will be true to the wife,
I'll concentrate more on my work,'
And helpless governors wake
To resume their compulsory game:
Who can release them now,
Who can reach the dead,
Who can speak for the dumb?

All I have is a voice
To undo the folded lie,
The romantic lie in the brain
Of the sensual man-in-the-street
And the lie of Authority
Whose buildings grope the sky:
There is no such thing as the State
And no one exists alone;
Hunger allows no choice
To the citizen or the police;
We must love one another or die.

Defenseless under the night
Our world in stupor lies;
Yet, dotted everywhere,
Ironic points of light
Flash out wherever the Just
Exchange their messages:
May I, composed like them
Of Eros and of dust,

Beleaguered by the same
Negation and despair,
Show an affirming flame.

Source: Auden, W. H. *Another Time*, 112. London: Faber and Faber, 1940. Copyright © 1939 by W. H. Auden. Reprinted by permission of Curtis Brown, Ltd.

Winston Churchill's Wartime Speeches, May–June 1940

Winston Churchill, "Blood, Toil, Tears, and Sweat": Speech in the British House of Commons, 13 May 1940

On Friday evening last I received from His Majesty the mission to form a new administration . . .

To form an administration of this scale and complexity is a serious undertaking in itself. But we are in the preliminary phase of one of the greatest battles in history. We are in action at many other points—in Norway and in Holland—and we have to be prepared in the Mediterranean. The air battle is continuing, and many preparations have to be made here at home.

In this crisis I think I may be pardoned if I do not address the House at any length today, and I hope that any of my friends and colleagues or former colleagues who are affected by the political reconstruction will make all allowances for any lack of ceremony with which it has been necessary to act.

I say to the House as I said to ministers who have joined this government, I have nothing to offer but blood, toil, tears, and sweat. We have before us an ordeal of the most grievous kind. We have before us many, many months of struggle and suffering.

In May 1940, as German military forces launched a blitzkrieg attack and quickly overran most of Western Europe, Winston Churchill, a veteran politician who had been one of the staunchest advocates of opposition to German expansionism during the 1930s, became British prime minister. Taking power when Great Britain faced an increasingly grim war situation, in his first speech as prime minister Churchill stated that all he could offer the British people was "blood, toil, tears, and sweat." This was the first in a series of dramatic speeches that rallied the country's population at a time of growing peril. The British government had already dispatched an expeditionary force to help France resist the German invasion. By early June, it was clear that the British military had suffered a serious defeat. Britain launched a desperate effort to evacuate its troops from the Dunkerque beaches in France, sending every type of vessel across the Channel to bring its soldiers home. Most of Britain's military equipment was lost in France. Addressing not just his British audience but also the government and people of the United States, the only possible source of outside aid for his country, Churchill promised that his country would fight on and would never surrender.

You ask, what is our policy? I say it is to wage war by land, sea, and air. War with all our might and with all the strength God has given us, and to wage war against a monstrous tyranny never surpassed in the dark and lamentable catalogue of human crime. That is our policy.

You ask, what is our aim? I can answer in one word. It is victory. Victory at all costs—Victory in spite of all terrors—Victory, however long and hard the road may be, for without victory there is no survival . . .

Source: Churchill, Winston S. *The Complete Speeches*, 8 vols., edited by Robert Rhodes James, 6: 6218–6220. New York: Chelsea House Publishers, 1974. Reproduced with permission of Curtis Brown, London on behalf of the Estate of Sir Winston Churchill. Copyright © Winston S. Churchill.

Winston Churchill, "We Shall Never Surrender": Speech in the British House of Commons, 4 June 1940

In a long series of very fierce battles, now on this front, now on that, fighting on three fronts at once, battles fought by two or three divisions against an equal or sometimes larger number of the enemy, and fought very fiercely on old ground so many of us knew so well, our losses in men exceed 30,000 in killed, wounded and missing . . .

In the confusion of departure it is inevitable that many should be cut off. Against this loss of over 30,000 men we may set the far heavier loss certainly inflicted on the enemy, but our losses in material are enormous. We have perhaps lost one-third of the men we lost in the opening days of the battle on March 21, 1918, but we have lost nearly as many guns—nearly 1,000—and all our transport and all the armored vehicles that were with the army of the north.

These losses will impose further delay on the expansion of our military strength. That expansion has not been proceeding as fast as we had hoped. The best of all we had to give has been given to the B.E.F., and although they had not the number of tanks and some articles of equipment which were desirable they were a very well and finely equipped army. They had the first fruits of all our industry had to give. That has gone and now here is further delay.

How long it will be, how long it will last depends upon the exertions which we make on this island. An effort, the like of which has never been seen in our records, is now being made. Work is proceeding night and day, Sundays, and week days. Capital and labour have cast aside their interests, rights and customs and put everything into the common stock. Already the flow of munitions has leaped forward. There is no reason why we should not in a few months overtake the sudden and serious loss that has come upon us without retarding the development of our general program.

The French Army has been weakened, the Belgian Army has been lost and a large part of those fortified lines upon which so much faith was reposed has gone, and many valuable mining districts and factories have passed into the enemy's possession . . .

We must never forget the solid assurances of sea power and those which belong to air power if they can be locally exercised. I have myself full confidence that if all do their duty and if the best arrangements are made, as they are being made, we shall prove ourselves once again able to defend our island home, ride out the storms of war, outlive the menace of tyranny, if necessary for years, if necessary, alone.

At any rate, that is what we are going to try to do. That is the resolve of His Majesty's Government, every man of them. That is the will of Parliament and the nation. The British Empire and the French Republic, linked together in their cause and their need, will defend to the death their native soils, aiding each other like good comrades to the utmost of their strength, even though a large tract of Europe and many old and famous States have fallen or may fall into the grip of the Gestapo and all the odious apparatus of Nazi rule.

We shall not flag nor fail. We shall go on to the end. We shall fight in France and on the seas and oceans; we shall fight with growing confidence and growing strength in the air. We shall defend our island whatever the cost may be; we shall fight on beaches, landing grounds, in fields, in streets and on the hills. We shall never surrender and even if, which I do not for a moment believe, this island or a large part of it were subjugated and starving, then our empire beyond the seas, armed and guarded by the British Fleet, will carry on the struggle until, in God's good time, the New World with all its power and might, sets forth to the liberation and rescue of the Old.

Source: Churchill, Winston S. *The Complete Speeches*, 8 vols., edited by Robert Rhodes James, 6: 6225–6231. New York: Chelsea House Publishers, 1974. Reproduced with permission of Curtis Brown, London on behalf of the Estate of Sir Winston Churchill. Copyright © Winston S. Churchill.

Three-Power (Tripartite) Pact between Germany, Italy, and Japan, Signed at Berlin, September 27, 1940

The governments of Germany, Italy and Japan, considering it as a condition precedent of any lasting peace that all nations of the world be given each its own proper place, have decided to stand by and co-operate with one another in regard to their efforts in greater East Asia and regions of Europe respectively wherein it is their prime purpose to establish and maintain a new order of things calculated to promote the mutual prosperity and welfare of the peoples concerned.

Furthermore, it is the desire of the three governments to extend co-operation to such nations in other spheres of the world as may be inclined to put forth endeavours along lines similar to their own, in order that their ultimate aspirations for world peace may thus be realized.

Accordingly, the governments of Germany, Italy and Japan have agreed as follows:

Article One

Japan recognizes and respects the leadership of Germany and Italy in establishment of a new order in Europe.

Article Two

Germany and Italy recognize and respect the leadership of Japan in the establishment of a new order in greater East Asia.

In September 1940, the governments of Germany, Italy, and Japan formally allied themselves with each other, to establish a "new order" in both Europe and Asia. This alignment effectively linked all the various opponents of the Western democracies, intensifying the ideological aspects of the international conflict.

Article Three

Germany, Italy and Japan agree to co-operate in their efforts on aforesaid lines. They further undertake to assist one another with all political, economic and military means when one of the three contracting powers is attacked by a power at present not involved in the European war or in the Chinese-Japanese conflict.

Article Four

With the view to implementing the present pact, joint technical commissions, members of which are to be appointed by the respective governments of Germany, Italy and Japan will meet without delay.

Article Five

Germany, Italy and Japan affirm that the aforesaid terms do not in any way affect the political status which exists at present as between each of the three contracting powers and Soviet Russia.

Article Six

The present pact shall come into effect immediately upon signature and shall remain in force 10 years from the date of its coming into force. At the proper time before expiration of said term, the high contracting parties shall at the request of any of them enter into negotiations for its renewal.

Source: U.S. Department of State, Publication 1983. *Peace and War: United States Foreign Policy, 1931–1941*, 571–572. Washington, DC: U.S. Government Printing Office, 1943.

German Massacres of Jews: Oral History of Martin Koller

Oral History of Martin Koller

After three weeks' leave, I took a train back to the front. Something happened to me en route that I still think about to this day: my encounter with injustice. At one point, a strange officer came into our compartment. He was amiable and polite, and introduced himself in broken German with a Baltic accent as a lieutenant from Latvia. We talked about all kinds of things, everyday subjects, war and private life. And then he said he'd taken part in shooting Jews somewhere in the Baltic. There had been more than 3,000 of them. They had had to dig their own mass grave "as big as a soccer field." He told me all this with a certain pride.

I was completely at a loss and asked stupid questions like "Is that really true? How was it done? Who led this operation?" And I got a precise answer to each. It was true; anybody could check it; they did it with 12 men armed with machine pistols and one machine gun. The ammunition had been officially provided by the *Wehrmacht,* and a German SS lieutenant, whose name he didn't remember, had been in command. I became confused and started to sweat. This just didn't fit into the whole picture—of me, of my country, of the world, of the war. It was so monstrous that I couldn't grasp it.

Until early 1942, the Nazi regime relied on ad hoc measures, primarily mass killings and other brutal atrocities, to reduce the numbers of Jews in the east. One of the most dramatic of these was the two-day massacre of 33,000 Ukrainian Jews at Babi Yar ravine near Kiev over September 28–29, 1941, but throughout the area under German occupation thousands of smaller-scale episodes occurred. Polish and Russian partisans who offered resistance to German occupation were treated equally harshly. By the end of 1941, between 500,000 and 1,000,000 Jews had died. German leaders nonetheless felt that such uncoordinated measures had hardly dented the problem, and a more systematic strategic approach was essential. Moreover, shooting, the most common method of execution, was somewhat inefficient, and subjected those who wielded the guns to some stress.

Martin Koller, born in 1923, was the son of a Protestant pastor who had fought in World War I at Verdun. His father revered combat soldiers but disliked Hitler and the Nazis. In 1939, Koller, who wanted to learn to fly, applied to join the Luftwaffe. He became a skilled pilot, flying tactical reconnaissance missions on the Eastern Front, where he learned by chance of one massacre of the Jews.

"Can I see your identification?" I asked, and "Do you mind if I note it down?" He didn't mind, and was just as proud of what he had done as I was of the planes I'd shot down. And while I scribbled his strange name down on a cigarette package, my thoughts somersaulted: either what he's told me is true, in which case *I* can't wear a German uniform any longer, or he's lying, in which case *he* can't wear a German uniform any longer. What can, what should I do? My military instinct told me, "Report it!"

I returned to the squadron and was right back in action. I flew and fought as best I could. I didn't think about the Latvian's story. Then my orderly came to collect my laundry. That's when I found the shirt I'd worn on the train. I emptied the pockets, and there was that piece of paper with the address. I finally had to do something. The same night, I wrote a report to the squadron leader.

The commander remained seated behind his desk when I came, still in my flight suit, to report. He pointed to my paper: "What do you want me to do with this?" I shrugged and ventured, "Forward it, of course, Captain."

I had done my duty; now I could forget it. Then I received a message that told me I was to report to Colonel Bauer at Simferopol in the Crimea two days later.

The colonel had my report in hand. With all the stamps and entries on it, it had become an official document.

"I wanted to speak with you," said the colonel, "before I act on this report. Do you understand that?" "No, Colonel," I said stupidly.

He leaned back, took a deep breath, and said, "My dear young friend. . . ." My dear young friend? No superior had ever said that to me before. I felt good.

"What do you think I should do with this?" I sat stiffly on the sofa and didn't know what to do with the question. What does a colonel do with reports? I swallowed and said, "I don't know, Colonel. Maybe forward it?"

The colonel slid closer and put an arm around my shoulder. I smelled his good aftershave and was frozen. "Son," said the colonel with a frown. Son? He was talking like my father, but I liked it. Then he offered me cigarettes. We smoked. The colonel said, "If I pass on this report, you'll be jumping out of the frying pan and into the fire."

Then he nudged me and said, "You know what, son?" I shook my head and looked at him. "If we get out of this alive, we'll go home and clean up that mess. Thousands, believe me, thousands will be with us!"

And the colonel picked up my report, held it over the wastebasket and asked, "So, do you want to jump into the fire, or do you want to be there with the rest of us, for the big clean-up? Can I quash your report?" "Yes, sir, *Herr Oberst*," I said, convinced.

"Thank you, Lieutenant," the colonel said, and dropped my report about the Latvian lieutenant and the execution of the Jews into the wastebasket.

Source: Steinhoff, Johannes, Peter Pechel, and Dennis Showalter, eds. *Voices from the Third Reich: An Oral History*, 344–346. Regnery Publishing, Inc. All rights reserved. Reprinted by special permission of Regnery Publishing Inc., Washington, DC. Copyright © 1989.

Franklin D. Roosevelt, "The Arsenal of Democracy," Fireside Chat on National Security and the Common Cause, 29 December 1940

This is not a fireside chat on war. It is a talk on national security; because the nub of the whole purpose of your President is to keep you now, and your children later, and your grandchildren much later, out of a last-ditch war for the preservation of American independence and all the things that American independence means to you and to me and to ours . . .

Never before since Jamestown and Plymouth Rock has our American civilization been in such danger as now.

For, on September 27, 1940, by an agreement signed in Berlin, three powerful nations, two in Europe and one in Asia, joined themselves together in the threat that if the United States of America interfered with or blocked the expansion program of these three nations—a program aimed at world control—they would unite in ultimate action against the United States.

The Nazi masters of Germany have made it clear that they intend not only to dominate all life and thought in their own country, but also to enslave the whole of Europe, and then to use the resources of Europe to dominate the rest of the world.

It was only three weeks ago their leader stated this: "There are two worlds that stand opposed to each other." And then in defiant reply to his opponents, he said this: "Others are correct when they say: With this world we cannot ever reconcile ourselves. . . . I can beat any other power in the world." So said the leader of the Nazis.

In other words, the Axis not merely admits but proclaims that there can be no ultimate peace between their philosophy of government and our philosophy of government.

In view of the nature of this undeniable threat, it can be asserted, properly and categorically, that the United States has no right or reason to encourage talk of peace, until

---

As 1940 came to an end, Franklin D. Roosevelt responded to Winston Churchill's appeal for assistance with a public "fireside chat" with the American people. He urged that the United States must become the world's "arsenal of democracy," mounting a major rearmament effort of its own while supplying the Allies. His speech laid the groundwork for the Lend-Lease legislation passed early the next year, under which the U.S. government provided massive military assistance to the Allies.

the day shall come when there is a clear intention on the part of the aggressor nations to abandon all thought of dominating or conquering the world.

At this moment, the forces of the states that are leagued against all peoples who live in freedom, are being held away from our shores. The Germans and the Italians are being blocked on the other side of the Atlantic by the British, and by the Greeks, and by thousands of soldiers and sailors who were able to escape from subjugated countries. In Asia, the Japanese are being engaged by the Chinese nation in another great defense.

In the Pacific Ocean is our fleet.

Some of our people like to believe that wars in Europe and in Asia are of no concern to us. But it is a matter of most vital concern to us that European and Asiatic war-makers should not gain control of the oceans which lead to this hemisphere . . .

If Great Britain goes down, the Axis powers will control the continents of Europe, Asia, Africa, Australasia, and the high seas—and they will be in a position to bring enormous military and naval resources against this hemisphere. It is no exaggeration to say that all of us, in all the Americas, would be living at the point of a gun—a gun loaded with explosive bullets, economic as well as military.

We should enter upon a new and terrible era in which the whole world, our hemisphere included, would be run by threats of brute force. To survive in such a world, we would have to convert ourselves permanently into a militaristic power on the basis of war economy.

Some of us like to believe that even if Great Britain falls, we are still safe, because of the broad expanse of the Atlantic and of the Pacific. But the width of those oceans is not what it was in the days of clipper ships. At one point between Africa and Brazil the distance is less than from Washington to Denver, Colorado—five hours for the latest type of bomber. And at the North end of the Pacific Ocean America and Asia almost touch each other.

Even today we have planes that could fly from the British Isles to New England and back again without refueling. And remember that the range of the modern bomber is ever being increased . . .

There are those who say that the Axis powers would never have any desire to attack the Western Hemisphere. That is the same dangerous form of wishful thinking which has destroyed the powers of resistance of so many conquered peoples. The plain facts are that the Nazis have proclaimed, time and again, that all other races are their inferiors and therefore subject to their orders. And most important of all, the vast resources and wealth of this American Hemisphere constitute the most tempting loot in all the round world.

Let us no longer blind ourselves to the undeniable fact that the evil forces which have crushed and undermined and corrupted so many others are already within our own gates. Your Government knows much about them and every day is ferreting them out.

Their secret emissaries are active in our own and in neighboring countries. They seek to stir up suspicion and dissension to cause internal strife. They try to turn capital against labor, and vice versa. They try to reawaken long slumbering racial and religious enmities which should have no place in this country. They are active in every group that promotes intolerance. They exploit for their own ends our natural abhorrence of war. These trouble-breeders have but one purpose. It is to divide our people into hostile groups and to destroy our unity and shatter our will to defend ourselves.

There are also American citizens, many of them in high places, who, unwittingly in most cases, are aiding and abetting the work of these agents. I do not charge these American citizens with being foreign agents. But I do charge them with doing exactly the kind of work that the dictators want done in the United States.

These people not only believe that we can save our own skins by shutting our eyes to the fate of other nations. Some of them go much further than that. They say that we can and should become the friends and even the partners of the Axis powers. Some of them even suggest that we should imitate the methods of the dictatorships. Americans never can and never will do that.

The experience of the past two years has proven beyond doubt that no nation can appease the Nazis. . . . We know now that a nation can have peace with the Nazis only at the price of total surrender . . .

The history of recent years proves that shootings and chains and concentration camps are not simply the transient tools but the very altars of modern dictatorships. They may talk of a "new order" in the world, but what they have in mind is only a revival of the oldest and the worst tyranny. In that there is no liberty, no religion, no hope.

The proposed "new order" is the very opposite of a United States of Europe or a United States of Asia. It is not a Government based upon the consent of the governed. It is not a union of ordinary, self-respecting men and women to protect themselves and their freedom and their dignity from oppression. It is an unholy alliance of power and pelf to dominate and enslave the human race.

The British people and their allies today are conducting an active war against this unholy alliance. Our own future security is greatly dependent on the outcome of that fight. Our ability to "keep out of war" is going to be affected by that outcome.

Thinking in terms of today and tomorrow, I make the direct statement to the American people that there is far less chance of the United States getting into war, if we do all we can now to support the nations defending themselves against attack by the Axis than if we acquiesce in their defeat, submit tamely to an Axis victory, and wait our turn to be the object of attack in another war later on.

If we are to be completely honest with ourselves, we must admit that there is risk in any course we may take. But I deeply believe that the great majority of our people agree that the course that I advocate involves the least risk now and the greatest hope for world peace in the future.

The people of Europe who are defending themselves do not ask us to do their fighting. They ask us for the implements of war, the planes, the tanks, the guns, the freighters which will enable them to fight for their liberty and for our security. Emphatically we must get these weapons to them in sufficient volume and quickly enough, so that we and our children will be saved the agony and suffering of war which others have had to endure.

Let not the defeatists tell us that it is too late. It will never be earlier. Tomorrow will be later than today.

Certain facts are self-evident.

In a military sense Great Britain and the British Empire are today the spearhead of resistance to world conquest. They are putting up a fight which will live forever in the story of human gallantry.

There is no demand for sending an American Expeditionary Force outside our own borders. There is no intention by any member of your Government to send such a force. You can, therefore, nail any talk about sending armies to Europe as deliberate untruth.

Our national policy is not directed toward war. Its sole purpose is to keep war away from our country and our people.

Democracy's fight against world conquest is being greatly aided, and must be more greatly aided, by the rearmament of the United States and by sending every ounce and every ton of munitions and supplies that we can possibly spare to help the defenders who are in the front lines. It is no more unneutral for us to do that than it is for Sweden, Russia and other nations near Germany, to send steel and ore and oil and other war materials into Germany every day in the week.

We are planning our own defense with the utmost urgency; and in its vast scale we must integrate the war needs of Britain and the other free nations which are resisting aggression.

This is not a matter of sentiment or of controversial personal opinion. It is a matter of realistic, practical military policy, based on the advice of our military experts who are in close touch with existing warfare. These military and naval experts and the members of the Congress and the Administration have a single-minded purpose—the defense of the United States . . .

We must be the great arsenal of democracy. For us this is an emergency as serious as war itself. We must apply ourselves to our task with the same resolution, the same sense of urgency, the same spirit of patriotism and sacrifice as we would show were we at war . . .

I believe that the Axis powers are not going to win this war. I base that belief on the latest and best information.

We have no excuse for defeatism. We have every good reason for hope—hope for peace, hope for the defense of our civilization and for the building of a better civilization in the future.

I have the profound conviction that the American people are now determined to put forth a mightier effort than they have ever yet made to increase our production of all the implements of defense, to meet the threat to our democratic faith.

As President of the United States I call for that national effort. I call for it in the name of this nation which we love and honor and which we are privileged and proud to serve. I call upon our people with absolute confidence that our common cause will greatly succeed.

Source: Franklin D. Roosevelt, Speech, "The Arsenal of Democracy," December 29, 1940. Fireside Chat Files: State Department, 1940, Franklin D. Roosevelt Library Digital Archives.

Henry R. Luce, "The American Century," February 1941

There is one fundamental issue which faces America as it faces no other nation. It is an issue peculiar to America and peculiar to America in the 20th Century—now. It is deeper even than the immediate issue of War. If America meets it correctly, then, despite hosts of dangers and difficulties, we can look forward and move forward to a future worthy of men, with peace in our hearts.

If we dodge the issue, we shall flounder for ten or 20 or 30 bitter years in a chartless and meaningless series of disasters . . .

Where are we? We are in the war. All this talk about whether this or that might or might not get us into the war is wasted effort. We are, for a fact, in the war . . .

Furthermore—and this is an extraordinary and profoundly historical fact which deserves to be examined in detail—America and only America can effectively state the war aims of this war . . .

The big, important point to be made here is simply that the complete opportunity of leadership is ours . . .

In the field of national policy, the fundamental trouble with America has been, and is, that whereas their nation became in the 20th Century the most powerful and the most vital nation in the world, nevertheless Americans were unable to accommodate themselves spiritually and practically to their fate. Hence they have failed to play their part as a world power—a failure which has had disastrous consequences for themselves and for all mankind. And the cure is this: to accept wholeheartedly our duty and our opportunity as the most powerful and vital nation in the world and in consequence to exert upon the world the full impact of our influence, for such purposes as we see fit and by such means as we see fit . . .

Consider the 20th Century. It is ours not only in the sense that we happen to live in it but ours also because it is America's first century as a dominant power in the world. So far, this century of ours has been a profound and tragic disappointment. No other century has

---

In February 1941, as the United States moved steadily closer to war with Germany, the leading American magazine publisher Henry R. Luce, the son of a Chinese missionary, wrote an influential essay, "The American Century," envisaging an enormous postwar expansion of his country's international role. Luce's article later came to seem an almost emblematic statement prophesying the rise of the United States to world power from the mid-20th century onward.

been so big with promise for human progress and happiness. And in no one century have so many men and women and children suffered such pain and anguish and bitter death . . .

What can we say about an American Century? It is meaningless merely to say that we reject isolationism and accept the logic of internationalism. What internationalism? . . .

Ours cannot come out of the vision of any one man. It must be the product of the imaginations of many men. It must be a sharing with all peoples of our Bill of Rights, our Declaration of Independence, our Constitution, our magnificent industrial products, our technical skills. It must be an internationalism of the people, by the people and for the people . . .

Once we cease to distract ourselves with lifeless arguments about isolationism, we shall discover that there is already an immense American internationalism. American jazz, Hollywood movies, American slang, American machines and patented products, are in fact the only things that every community in the world, from Zanzibar to Hamburg, recognizes in common. Blindly, unintentionally, accidentally and really in spite of ourselves, we are already a world power in all the trivial ways—in very human ways. But there is a great deal more than that. America is already the intellectual, scientific and artistic capital of the world. Americans—Midwestern Americans—are today the least provincial people in the world. They have traveled the most and they know more about the world than the people of any other country. America's worldwide experience in commerce is also far greater than most of us realize.

Most important of all, we have that indefinable, unmistakable sign of leadership: prestige. And unlike the prestige of Rome or Genghis Khan or 19th Century England, American prestige throughout the world is faith in the good intentions as well as in the ultimate intelligence and ultimate strength of the whole American people. We have lost some of that prestige in the last few years. But most of it is still there.

* * *

No narrow definition can be given to the American internationalism of the 20th Century. It will take shape, as all civilizations take shape, by the living of it, by work and effort, by trial and error, by enterprise and adventure and experience.

And by imagination!

As America enters dynamically upon the world scene, we need most of all to seek and to bring forth a vision of America as a world power which is authentically American and which can inspire us to live and work and fight with vigor and enthusiasm. And as we come now to the great test, it may yet turn out that in all of our trials and tribulations of spirit during the first part of this century we as a people have been painfully apprehending the meaning of our time and now in this moment of testing there may come clear at last the vision which will guide us to the authentic creation of the 20th Century—our Century.

* * *

America as the dynamic center of ever-widening spheres of enterprise, America as the training center of the skillful servants of mankind, America as the Good Samaritan, really believing again that it is more blessed to give than to receive, and America as the powerhouse of the ideals of Freedom and Justice—out of these elements surely can be fashioned a vision of the 20th Century to which we can and will devote ourselves in joy and gladness and vigor and enthusiasm . . .

It is in this spirit that all of us are called, each to his own measure of capacity, and each in the widest horizon of his vision, to create the first great American Century.

Source: Luce, Henry. "The American Century." *Life.* Vol. 10, February 1941. Copyright 1941. The Picture Collection Inc. Used with permission. All rights reserved.

Hitler's Decision to Invade the Soviet Union: Adolf Hitler to Benito Mussolini, June 21, 1941

Duce!

I am writing this letter to you at a moment when months of anxious deliberation and continuous nerve-racking waiting are ending in the hardest decision of my life. I believe—after seeing the latest Russian situation map and after appraisal of numerous other reports—that I cannot take the responsibility for waiting longer, and above all, I believe that there is no other way of obviating this danger—unless it be further waiting, which, however, would necessarily lead to disaster in this or the next year at the latest.

The situation: England has lost this war. With the right of the drowning person, she grasps at every straw which, in her imagination, might serve as a sheet anchor. Nevertheless, some of her hopes are naturally not without a certain logic. England has thus far always conducted her wars with help from the Continent. The destruction of France—in fact, the elimination of all west-European positions—is directing the glances of the British warmongers continually to the place from which they tried to start the war: to Soviet Russia.

Both countries, Soviet Russia and England, are equally interested in a Europe fallen into ruin, rendered prostrate by a long war. Behind these two countries stands the North American Union goading them on and watchfully waiting. Since the liquidation of Poland, there is evident in Soviet Russia a consistent trend, which, even if cleverly and cautiously, is nevertheless reverting firmly to the old Bolshevist tendency to expansion of the Soviet State. The prolongation of the war necessary for this purpose is to be achieved by tying up German forces in the East, so that—particularly in the air—the German Command can no longer vouch for a large-scale attack in the West. I declared to you only recently, Duce, that it was precisely the success of the experiment in Crete that demonstrated how necessary it is to make use of every single airplane in the much greater project against

---

One of Hitler's greatest mistakes was his decision to invade the Soviet Union in June 1941, a war that would bleed Germany white of men and resources. Writing to his fellow dictator, Benito Mussolini, on June 21, 1941, Hitler explained his decision to invade the Soviet Union in terms that made it clear that ultimately he expected victory there. Apparently, he had probably always intended to break the Nazi–Soviet Non-Aggression Pact whenever it seemed convenient to him.

England. It may well happen that in this decisive battle we would win with a superiority of only a few squadrons. I shall not hesitate a moment to undertake such a responsibility if, aside from all other conditions, I at least possess the one certainty that I will not then suddenly be attacked or even threatened from the East. The concentration of Russian forces—I had General Jodl submit the most recent map to your Attaché here, General Maras—is tremendous. Really, all available Russian forces are at our border. Moreover, since the approach of warm weather, work has been proceeding on numerous defenses. If circumstances should give me cause to employ the German air force against England, there is danger that Russia will then begin its strategy of extortion in the South and North, to which I would have to yield in silence, simply from a feeling of air inferiority. It would, above all, not then be possible for me without adequate support from an air force, to attack the Russian fortifications with the divisions stationed in the East. If I do not wish to expose myself to this danger, then perhaps the whole year of 1941 will go by without any change in the general situation. On the contrary, England will be all the less ready for peace, for it will be able to pin its hopes on the Russian partner. Indeed, this hope must naturally even grow with the progress in preparedness of the Russian armed forces. And behind this is the mass delivery of war material from America which they hope to get in 1942.

Aside from this, Duce, it is not even certain whether I shall have this time, for with so gigantic a concentration of forces on both sides—for I also was compelled to place more and more armored units on the eastern border, also to call Finland's and Rumania's attention to the danger—there is the possibility that the shooting will start spontaneously at any moment. A withdrawal on my part would, however, entail a serious loss of prestige for us. This would be particularly unpleasant in its possible effect on Japan. I have, therefore, after constantly racking my brains, finally reached the decision to cut the noose before it can be drawn tight. I believe, Duce, that I am hereby rendering probably the best possible service to our joint conduct of the war this year. For my overall view is now as follows:

1. France is, as ever, not to be trusted. Absolute surety that North Africa will not suddenly desert does not exist.
2. North Africa itself, insofar as your colonies, Duce, are concerned, is probably out of danger until fall. I assume that the British, in their last attack, wanted to relieve Tobruk. I do not believe they will soon be in a position to repeat this.
3. Spain is irresolute and—I am afraid—will take sides only when the outcome of the war is decided.
4. In Syria, French resistance can hardly be maintained permanently either with or without our help.
5. An attack on Egypt before autumn is out of the question altogether. I consider it necessary, however, taking into account the whole situation, to give thought to the development of an operational unit in Tripoli itself which can, if necessary, also be launched against the West. Of course, Duce, the strictest silence must be maintained with regard to these ideas, for otherwise we cannot expect France to continue to grant permission to use its ports for the transportation of arms and munitions.
6. Whether or not America enters the war is a matter of indifference, inasmuch as she supports our opponent with all the power she is able to mobilize.

7. The situation in England itself is bad; the provision of food and raw materials is growing steadily more difficult. The martial spirit to make war, after all, lives only on hopes. These hopes are based solely on two assumptions: Russia and America. We have no chance of eliminating America. But it does lie in our power to exclude Russia. The elimination of Russia means, at the same time, a tremendous relief for Japan in East Asia, and thereby the possibility of a much stronger threat to American activities through Japanese intervention.

I have decided under these circumstances as I already mentioned, to put an end to the hypocritical performance in the Kremlin. I assume, that is to say, I am convinced, that Finland, and likewise Rumania, will forthwith take part in this conflict, which will ultimately free Europe, for the future also, of a great danger. General Maras informed us that you, Duce, wish also to make available at least one corps. If you have that intention, Duce—which I naturally accept with a heart filled with gratitude—the time for carrying it out will still be sufficiently long, for in this immense theater of war the troops cannot be assembled at all points at the same time anyway. You, Duce, can give the decisive aid, however, by strengthening your forces in North Africa, also, if possible, looking from Tripoli toward the West, by proceeding further to build up a group which, though it be small at first, can march into France in case of a French violation of the treaty; and finally, by carrying the air war and, so far as it is possible, the submarine war, in intensified degree, into the Mediterranean.

So far as the security of the territories in the West is concerned, from Norway to and including France, we are strong enough there—so far as army troops are concerned—to meet any eventuality with lightning speed. So far as air war on England is concerned, we shall for a time remain on the defensive—but this does not mean that we might be incapable of countering British attacks on Germany; on the contrary, we shall, if necessary, be in a position to start ruthless bombing attacks on British home territory. Our fighter defense, too, will be adequate. It consists of the best squadrons that we have.

As far as the war in the East is concerned, Duce, it will surely be difficult, but I do not entertain a second's doubt as to its great success. I hope, above all, that it will then be possible for us to secure a common food-supply base in the Ukraine for some time to come, which will furnish us such additional supplies as we may need in the future. I may state at this point, however, that, as far as we can tell now, this year's German harvest promises to be a very good one. It is conceivable that Russia will try to destroy the Rumanian oil region. We have built up a defense that will—or so I think—prevent the worst. Moreover, it is the duty of our armies to eliminate this threat as rapidly as possible.

I waited until this moment, Duce, to send you this information, because the final decision itself will not be made until 7 o'clock tonight. I earnestly beg you, therefore, to refrain, above all, from making any explanation to your Ambassador at Moscow, for there is no absolute guarantee that our coded reports cannot be decoded. I, too, shall wait until the last moment to have my own Ambassador informed of the decisions reached.

The material that I now contemplate publishing gradually, is so exhaustive that the world will have more occasion to wonder at our forbearance than at our decision, except for that part of the world which opposes us on principle and for which, therefore, arguments are of no use.

Whatever may now come, Duce, our situation can become no worse as a result of this step; it can only improve. Even if I should be obliged at the end of this year to leave 60 or 70 divisions in Russia, that is only a fraction of the forces that I am now continually using on the eastern front. Should England nevertheless not draw any conclusions from the hard facts that present themselves, then we can, with our rear secured, apply ourselves with increased strength to the dispatching of our opponent. I can promise you, Duce, that what lies in our German power, will be done.

Any desires, suggestions, and assistance of which you, Duce, wish to inform me in the contingency before us, I would request that you either communicate to me personally or have them agreed upon directly by our military authorities.

In conclusion, let me say one more thing, Duce. Since struggling through to this decision, I again feel spiritually free. The partnership with the Soviet Union, in spite of the complete sincerity of the efforts to bring about a final conciliation, was nevertheless often very irksome to me, for in some way or other it seemed to me to be a break with my whole origin, my concepts, and my former obligations. I am happy now to be relieved of these mental agonies.

Source: U.S. Department of State. *Nazi–Soviet Relations 1939–1941*, 349–353. Documents from the Archives of the German Foreign Office. Washington, DC: U.S. Government Printing Office, 1948.

The Atlantic Charter, August 14, 1941

The President of the United States of America and the Prime Minister, Mr. Churchill, representing His Majesty's Government in the United Kingdom, being met together, deem it right to make known certain common principles in the national policies of their respective countries on which they base their hopes for a better future for the world.

First, their countries seek no aggrandizement, territorial or other;

Second, they desire to see no territorial changes that do not accord with the freely expressed wishes of the peoples concerned;

Third, they respect the right of all peoples to choose the form of government under which they will live; and they wish to see sovereign rights and self-government restored to those who have been forcibly deprived of them;

Fourth, they will endeavor, with due respect for their existing obligations, to further the enjoyment by all States, great or small, victor or vanquished, of access, on equal terms, to the trade and to the raw materials of the world which are needed for their economic prosperity;

Fifth, they desire to bring about the fullest collaboration between all nations in the economic field with the object of securing, for all, improved labor standards, economic advancement and social security;

Sixth, after the final destruction of the Nazi tyranny, they hope to see established a peace which will afford to all nations the means of dwelling in safety within their own boundaries, and which will afford assurance that all the men in all lands may live out their lives in freedom from fear and want;

Seventh, such a peace should enable all men to traverse the high seas and oceans without hindrance;

Eighth, they believe that all of the nations of the world, for realistic as well as spiritual reasons must come to the abandonment of the use of force. Since no future peace can

---

The Atlantic Charter was approved after President Franklin D. Roosevelt and British prime minister Winston Churchill met secretly at sea, at Argentia Harbor, off Placentia Bay on the Newfoundland coast, from August 8 to 11, 1941. It represented the first formal statement of the principles and objectives for which the United States and Great Britain were fighting or preparing to fight.

be maintained if land, sea or air armaments continue to be employed by nations which threaten, or may threaten, aggression outside of their frontiers, they believe, pending the establishment of a wider and permanent system of general security, that the disarmament of such nations is essential. They will likewise aid and encourage all other practicable measures which will lighten for peace-loving peoples the crushing burden of armaments.

Source: U.S. Department of State. *A Decade of American Foreign Policy: Basic Documents, 1941–1949,* 2. Washington, DC: U.S. Government Printing Office, 1950.

Franklin D. Roosevelt, Address to the U.S. Congress, December 8, 1941

Yesterday, December 7, 1941—a date which will live in infamy—the United States of America was suddenly and deliberately attacked by naval and air forces of the Empire of Japan.

The United States was at peace with that Nation and, at the solicitation of Japan, was still in conversation with its Government and its Emperor looking toward the maintenance of peace in the Pacific. Indeed, one hour after Japanese air squadrons had commenced bombing in Oahu, the Japanese Ambassador to the United States and his colleague delivered to the Secretary of State a formal reply to a recent American message. While this reply stated that it seemed useless to continue the existing diplomatic negotiations, it contained no threat or hint of war or armed attack.

It will be recorded that the distance of Hawaii from Japan makes it obvious that the attack was deliberately planned many days or even weeks ago. During the intervening time the Japanese Government has deliberately sought to deceive the United States by false statements and expressions of hope for continued peace.

The attack yesterday on the Hawaiian Islands has caused severe damage to American naval and military forces. Very many American lives have been lost. In addition American ships have been reported torpedoed on the high seas between San Francisco and Honolulu.

Yesterday the Japanese Government also launched an attack against Malaya.

Last night Japanese forces attacked Hong Kong.

Last night Japanese forces attacked Guam.

Last night Japanese forces attacked the Philippine Islands.

Last night the Japanese attacked Wake Island.

On December 8, 1941, in an address which, though short, was one of the most famous speeches he ever delivered, President Franklin D. Roosevelt officially informed Congress of the Japanese attack on Pearl Harbor. Although Japan's behavior put the United States in a de facto state of war, he sought an official declaration of hostilities from Congress. With the exception of one dissenting vote from Congresswoman Jeannette Rankin of Minnesota, both the Senate and the House voted unanimously in favor of his request.

This morning the Japanese attacked Midway Island.

Japan has, therefore, undertaken a surprise offensive extending throughout the Pacific area. The facts of yesterday speak for themselves. The people of the United States have already formed their opinions and well understand the implications to the very life and safety of our Nation.

As Commander in Chief of the Army and Navy I have directed that all measures be taken for our defense.

Always will we remember the character of the onslaught against us.

No matter how long it may take us to overcome this premeditated invasion, the American people in their righteous might will win through to absolute victory. I believe I interpret the will of the Congress and of the people when I assert that we will not only defend ourselves to the uttermost but will make very certain that this form of treachery shall never endanger us again.

Hostilities exist. There is no blinking at the fact that our people, our territory, and our interests are in grave danger.

With confidence in our armed forces—with the unbounded determination of our people—we will gain the inevitable triumph—so help us God.

I ask that the Congress declare that since the unprovoked and dastardly attack by Japan on Sunday, December 7, a state of war has existed between the United States and the Japanese Empire.

Source: U.S. Department of State. *Peace and War: United States Foreign Policy, 1931–1941,* 838–839. Washington, DC: U.S. Government Printing Office, 1943.

The Final Solution: The Wannsee Protocol, January 20, 1942

Top Secret

Minutes of Meeting

This meeting of top German officials with responsibility for Jews under their control was held on 20 January 1942 in Berlin, at Grossen Wannsee, Berlin, No. 56/58. Those present included Gauleiter Dr. Meyer and Reichsamtleiter Dr. Leibbrandt of the Ministry for the Occupied Eastern Territories; Dr. Stuckart, Secretary of State of the Ministry for the Interior; Secretary of State Neumann, Plenipotentiary for the Four Year Plan; Dr. Freisler, Secretary of State of the Ministry of Justice; Dr. Bühler, Secretary of State of the Office of the General Government; Dr. Luther, Under Secretary of State of the Foreign Office; SS-Oberführer Klopfer of the Party Chancellery; Ministerialdirektor Kritzinger of the Reich Chancellery; SS-Gruppenführer Hofmann of the Race and Settlement Main Office; SS-Gruppenführer Müller and SS-Obersturmbannführer Eichmann of the Reich Main Security Office; SS-Oberführer Dr. Schöngarth of the Security Police, Security Department, Commander of the Security Police, Security Department (SD) of the General Government; SS-Sturmbannführer Dr. Lange of the Security Police, Security Department, Commander of the Security Police and the Security Department for the General-District of Latvia, in his capacity as deputy to the Commander of the Security Police and the Security Department for the Reich Commissariat "Eastland" . . .

In January 1942, top German officials met at Wannsee, Berlin, to discuss the best means for exterminating Jews throughout Europe. They listed not only those Jews then resident in Germany and territories occupied by Germany, but also in countries allied with Germany, neutral, or not yet conquered. In their discussion, officials contemplated first the forcible deportation of Jews to territories in the East, their employment in labor camps, where many of them were expected to die of "natural causes," and then a "final solution" to remove the remainder permanently from European life. In all, these discussions envisaged disposing of over 11 million Jews throughout Europe. Where persons of mixed blood were concerned, some latitude might be allowed, especially if combined with forcible sterilization. Effectively, the meeting sanctioned genocide on a massive scale, where possible to be implemented by methods adapted from industrial processes designed to handle large quantities of raw materials or animals.

II.

At the beginning of the discussion Chief of the Security Police and of the SD, SS-Obergruppenführer Heydrich, reported that the Reich Marshal [Hermann Göring] had appointed him delegate for the preparations for the final solution of the Jewish question in Europe and pointed out that this discussion had been called for the purpose of clarifying fundamental questions. The wish of the Reich Marshal to have a draft sent to him concerning organizational, factual and material interests in relation to the final solution of the Jewish question in Europe makes necessary an initial common action of all central offices immediately concerned with these questions in order to bring their general activities into line. The Reichsführer-SS [Heinrich Himmler] and the Chief of the German Police (Chief of the Security Police and the SD) [Reinhard Heydrich] was entrusted with the official central handling of the final solution of the Jewish question without regard to geographic borders. The Chief of the Security Police and the SD then gave a short report of the struggle which has been carried on thus far against this enemy, the essential points being the following:

a)   the expulsion of the Jews from every sphere of life of the German people
b)   the expulsion of the Jews from the living space of the German people

In carrying out these efforts, an increased and planned acceleration of the emigration of the Jews from Reich territory was started, as the only possible present solution.

By order of the Reich Marshal, a Reich Central Office for Jewish Emigration was set up in January 1939 and the Chief of the Security Police and SD was entrusted with the management. Its most important tasks were

a)   to make all necessary arrangements for the preparation for an increased emigration of the Jews
b)   to direct the flow of emigration
c)   to speed the procedure of emigration in each individual case

The aim of all this was to cleanse German living space of Jews in a legal manner.

All the offices realized the drawbacks of such enforced accelerated emigration. For the time being they had, however, tolerated it on account of the lack of other possible solutions of the problem.

The work concerned with emigration was, later on, not only a German problem, but also a problem with which the authorities of the countries to which the flow of emigrants was being directed would have to deal. Financial difficulties, such as the demand by various foreign governments for increasing sums of money to be presented at the time of the landing, the lack of shipping space, increasing restriction of entry permits, or the cancelling of such, increased extraordinarily the difficulties of emigration. In spite of these difficulties, 537,000 Jews were sent out of the country between the takeover of power and the deadline of 31 October 1941. Of these:

• approximately 360,000 were in Germany proper on 30 January 1933
• approximately 147,000 were in Austria (Ostmark) on 15 March 1939
• approximately 30,000 were in the Protectorate of Bohemia and Moravia on 15 March 1939

The Jews themselves, or their Jewish political organizations, financed the emigration. In order to avoid impoverished Jews remaining behind, the principle was followed that wealthy Jews have to finance the emigration of poor Jews; this was arranged by imposing a suitable tax, i.e., an emigration tax, which was used for financial arrangements in connection with the emigration of poor Jews and was imposed according to income.

Apart from the necessary Reichsmark exchange, foreign currency had to be presented at the time of landing. In order to save foreign exchange held by Germany, the foreign Jewish financial organizations were—with the help of Jewish organizations in Germany—made responsible for arranging an adequate amount of foreign currency. Up to 30 October 1941, these foreign Jews donated a total of around 9,500,000 dollars.

In the meantime the Reichsführer-SS and Chief of the German Police had prohibited emigration of Jews due to the dangers of an emigration in wartime and due to the possibilities of the East.

III.

Another possible solution of the problem has now taken the place of emigration, i.e., the evacuation of the Jews to the East, provided that the Führer gives the appropriate approval in advance.

These actions are, however, only to be considered provisional, but practical experience is already being collected which is of the greatest importance in relation to the future final solution of the Jewish question.

Approximately 11 million Jews will be involved in the final solution of the European Jewish question, distributed as follows among the individual countries:

[The document proceeds to list the number of Jews living not only in states such as France, Hungary, and Rumania already currently under German occupation or control, but also in countries at war with Germany including Britain and Russia; allied with it, such as Italy; sympathetic but neutral, such as Spain and Portugal; and simply neutral, including Ireland, Sweden, and Switzerland.]

Under proper guidance, in the course of the final solution the Jews are to be allocated for appropriate labor in the East. Able-bodied Jews, separated according to sex, will be taken in large work columns to these areas for work on roads, in the course of which action doubtless a large portion will be eliminated by natural causes.

The possible final remnant will, since it will undoubtedly consist of the most resistant portion, have to be treated accordingly, because it is the product of natural selection and would, if released, act as a the seed of a new Jewish revival (see the experience of history).

In the course of the practical execution of the final solution, Europe will be combed through from west to east. Germany proper, including the Protectorate of Bohemia and Moravia, will have to be handled first due to the housing problem and additional social and political necessities.

The evacuated Jews will first be sent, group by group, to so-called transit ghettos, from which they will be transported to the East.

SS-Obergruppenführer Heydrich went on to say that an important prerequisite for the evacuation as such is the exact definition of the persons involved.

It is not intended to evacuate Jews over 65 years old, but to send them to an old-age ghetto—Theresienstadt is being considered for this purpose.

In addition to these age groups—of the approximately 280,000 Jews in Germany proper and Austria on 31 October 1941, approximately 30% are over 65 years old— severely wounded veterans and Jews with war decorations (Iron Cross I) will be accepted in the old-age ghettos. With this expedient solution, in one fell swoop many interventions will be prevented.

The beginning of the individual larger evacuation actions will largely depend on military developments. Regarding the handling of the final solution in those European countries occupied and influenced by us, it was proposed that the appropriate expert of the Foreign Office discuss the matter with the responsible official of the Security Police and SD.

In Slovakia and Croatia the matter is no longer so difficult, since the most substantial problems in this respect have already been brought near a solution. In Rumania the government has in the meantime also appointed a commissioner for Jewish affairs. In order to settle the question in Hungary, it will soon be necessary to force an adviser for Jewish questions onto the Hungarian government.

With regard to taking up preparations for dealing with the problem in Italy, SS-Obergruppenführer Heydrich considers it opportune to contact the chief of police with a view to these problems.

In occupied and unoccupied France, the registration of Jews for evacuation will in all probability proceed without great difficulty.

Under Secretary of State Luther calls attention in this matter to the fact that in some countries, such as the Scandinavian states, difficulties will arise if this problem is dealt with thoroughly and that it will therefore be advisable to defer actions in these countries. Besides, in view of the small numbers of Jews affected, this deferral will not cause any substantial limitation.

The Foreign Office sees no great difficulties for southeast and western Europe.

SS-Gruppenführer Hofmann plans to send an expert to Hungary from the Race and Settlement Main Office for general orientation at the time when the Chief of the Security Police and SD takes up the matter there. It was decided to assign this expert from the Race and Settlement Main Office, who will not work actively, as an assistant to the police attaché.

IV.

[Intermarriages between Jews and non-Jews could give rise to problems in defining precisely who qualified as a Jew, and here it was proposed to follow the guidelines given in the earlier Nuremberg Laws of the 1930s, though in many cases exceptions and exemptions for meritorious conduct or the reverse were at least theoretically possible, as were forcible sterilization and the compulsory dissolution of mixed marriages.]

With regard to the issue of the effect of the evacuation of Jews on the economy, State Secretary Neumann stated that Jews who are working in industries vital to the war effort, provided that no replacements are available, cannot be evacuated.

SS-Obergruppenführer Heydrich indicated that these Jews would not be evacuated according to the rules he had approved for carrying out the evacuations then underway.

State Secretary Dr. Bühler stated that the General Government would welcome it if the final solution of this problem could be begun in the General Government, since on the one hand transportation does not play such a large role here nor would problems of labor supply hamper this action. Jews must be removed from the territory of the General Government as quickly as possible, since it is especially here that the Jew as an epidemic carrier represents an extreme danger and on the other hand he is causing permanent chaos in the economic structure of the country through continued black market dealings. Moreover, of the approximately 2.5 million Jews concerned, the majority is unfit for work.

State Secretary Dr. Bühler stated further that the solution to the Jewish question in the General Government is the responsibility of the Chief of the Security Police and the SD and that his efforts would be supported by the officials of the General Government. He had only one request, to solve the Jewish question in this area as quickly as possible.

In conclusion the different types of possible solutions were discussed, during which discussion both Gauleiter Dr. Meyer and State Secretary Dr. Bühler took the position that certain preparatory activities for the final solution should be carried out immediately in the territories in question, in which process alarming the populace must be avoided.

The meeting was closed with the request of the Chief of the Security Police and the SD to the participants that they afford him appropriate support during the carrying out of the tasks involved in the solution.

Source: Minutes of the Wannsee Protocol, January 20, 1942. Available at House of the Wannsee Conference Memorial and Educational Site. http://www.ghwk.de/engl/protengl.htm.

Japanese Fighting Experiences:
From Triumph to Disaster

Wakatsuki Kikuo, aged seventy-one in 1986 and a salaryman, recalls his part in the invasion of Singapore.

I was in the color guard of the 114th Infantry Regiment of the Kiku corps. In the dark of night we left Johor Baharu at the southern tip of the Malay Peninsula to land on Singapore. We crossed over a pontoon bridge amid the rubble of shelling from both sides. After landing, we wandered around the small island of Singapore for a week or so. At the front, heroic hand-to-hand combat was unfolding. First Lieutenant Ran, one year ahead of me in school, was killed. Many others were wounded or dead. I heard that Second Lieutenant Yamamoto was blown up by a bomb in a trench, in a direct hit. He was a graduate of military cadet school who had entered the military the same year as I.

In the Bukit Timah highland, I dug a foxhole for myself with a shovel I carried with me. When I sat down in the foxhole, I could hear the shells from both sides hissing overhead.

Told that the enemy would use poison gas, we tensed up for a while. All infantrymen carried gas masks, but they were never used.

I could see the large shells of our new mortar weapons wobble across the sky.

On the outskirts of Singapore, the enemy was shooting at point-blank range from their stronghold. We flung ourselves on the ground, unable to make a move. I felt more dead than alive. I felt that the hair on my head would turn white overnight. After a long time the assault ended suddenly, so I immediately retreated. Behind me was a cliff, which I crawled down. After that I went to the highland. I heard the word "banzai" here and there. It was the report of the fall of Singapore.

I shed tears of joy, but my tears were from my happiness that I was still alive, that I hadn't died. Many wounded soldiers were writhing in the rubber forests. But the battle would continue. On the battlefield, the difference between life and death is paper thin.

Source: Gibney, Frank, ed. *Sensō: The Japanese Remember the Pacific War: Letters to the Editor of* Asahi Shimbun, 128. Armonk, NY: M. E. Sharpe, 1995.

As with other nations, the experiences of Japanese servicemen varied enormously. By 1944, as defeat came closer and Allied restrictions hit home, surviving Japanese soldiers, sailors, and fliers were under increasing pressure.

Miyasato Yoshihito, a printer in Chiba, recalls taking part in the June 1942 Battle of Midway as a seaman of twenty.

I participated in the battle of Midway as a navy seaman third class. Stationed as an anti-aircraft gun messenger on the seaplane carrier *Chitose*, my nerves were concentrated on the receiver so as not to miss a single word of the battle commander's orders. With the bugle call to battle blaring out on the bridge, all the antiaircraft and machine guns fired at once.

The carrier first turned right rudder, then left at full speed ahead. We were sprayed by shells hitting near us. The enemy's machine-gun fire burst on the deck. Despite having prepared for the worst, my legs shook violently with my lingering desire for life and my fear of death.

Turning my eyes to the distance after the battle, I saw black smoke rising here and there, indicating the great damage suffered by our warships. The sun tilted toward the west. Planes that had lost the carrier to which they should return made emergency landings near friendly ships. One after another they sank into the sea. It seemed that my ship had received orders to retreat. We sailed northwest in a circular motion.

Source: Gibney, Frank, ed. *Sensō: The Japanese Remember the Pacific War: Letters to the Editor of Asahi Shimbun*, 129–130. Armonk, NY: M. E. Sharpe, 1995.

In January 1943 Ishida Yahachi, then a Japanese soldier in his early thirties, later a Kagoshima merchant, helped to rescue survivors from Guadalcanal.

I was in the army marine transport unit. On 9 January 1943, we landed at Erventa in Bougainville Island in the Solomons. For two weeks from the following day we worked stuffing rice, powdered miso, powdered soy sauce, matches, candles, and other items into oil drums. According to the company commander, these were provisions to send to Japanese soldiers suffering from starvation in the jungles of Guadalcanal some five hundred kilometers south-southeast.

We prepared the oil drums that we had filled, fervently hoping that one more crumb of food would get into the mouths of our starving soldiers. Tied together with cables, they were towed by submarine at night. With buoys set to mark them, they were left offshore. The soldiers who were hiding in the jungle many kilometers from the coast had to go to retrieve them before the sun rose. Our work was terminated at the end of two weeks. It seems that at first this method was effective, but by the time I got there the Japanese soldiers on Guadalcanal were so weak from malnutrition that they couldn't even go to get the supplies.

20 January 1943 was a fateful day. Strangely, on this day there was no rain, and the sea was calm. Several destroyers were anchored right in front of our eyes. It was unclear what time it was. Under the torrid tropical sun the sound of the engines of the transport corps' small iron boats grew loud as the round trips between the destroyers and the shore were repeated in a great hurry. Waiting at the shore, we gently lifted out the soldiers retreating from Guadalcanal one by one and laid them on the sand. What a sad and pitiable sight they presented.

Hardly human beings, they were just skin and bones dressed in military uniform, thin as bamboo sticks. They were so light, it was like carrying infants. Only their eyes were bright; they must have been living on their strong will alone. When I put a spoon with some lukewarm rice gruel to their mouths, large teardrops rolled down their faces, and they said thank you in tiny mosquitolike voices. I, too, felt something hot unexpectedly welling up in my eyes.

My blood roiled with anger at those who had given the orders to these men. Being low-ranking soldiers, we had no way of knowing which company this was or whether the soldiers we fed were able to return safely to Japan.

Source: Gibney, Frank, ed. *Sensō: The Japanese Remember the Pacific War: Letters to the Editor of Asahi Shimbun,* 131–132. Armonk, NY: M. E. Sharpe, 1995.

A veteran of Okinawa, aged seventy-six in 1986 and one of the relatively few troops to surrender there, recalls the battle, in which he was wounded twice.

Receiving a top grade on my draft examination, I was selected to join the Sendai Fourth Regiment Number 2 Machine Gun Company in June 1944. From Narashino in Chiba Prefecture, I was supposed to be sent to Saipan, but the island fell, so it was on to Okinawa for me. Day after day in the fierce heat we cut down trees to construct our encampment.

On 4 January 1945, the port of Motobu was bombed from the air. [Finally, months later,] we faced the American troops at our position in Asato. Seeing several tanks charge toward us, a fifteen- or sixteen-year-old Okinawan volunteer soldier shoved us into a foxhole and saved our lives. Thinking, "Now, we're safe," we were just about to leave the foxhole when a fragment of a trench mortar shell hit me, wounding my armpit and right elbow. I was admitted to the field hospital. The next day I heard that a "bamboo spear" unit of two hundred men had been annihilated. A week after entering the field dispensary I was transferred to Itokazu Hospital. Not eligible to be admitted, I commuted from our camp for treatment.

One day, we got the news that the American forces were only one hundred meters away. We moved to our second-line positions in the middle of the night. Here we were also attacked, so we retreated farther and farther back, walking night and day. Finally we reached the seacoast at the southern edge of the island. We had no provisions and began to live in caves. When we were inside our cave, keeping silent during the day, we heard a voice from a loudspeaker saying, "Japan has lost the War, so come out."

We were so afraid that we couldn't go out. At night we relied on the moonlight to forage for food left in the American positions. Then there were the sweet potato fields. I will never forget the sweetness of the thumb-size sweet potato I bit into.

One morning a soldier who came from that locality said he was going to surrender. So I risked all too. I became a prisoner of war. Guarded by American soldiers, I did construction work for about two months. After that, at the end of 1945, I returned to my parents and wife and children, wearing the coat that the American military had given me. Of the 122 men in my company, there were 24 survivors.

Source: Gibney, Frank, ed. *Sensō: The Japanese Remember the Pacific War: Letters to the Editor of Asahi Shimbun,* 138–139. Armonk, NY: M. E. Sharpe, 1995.

Kobuko Yumio, in 1986 a retiree of sixty-five, in 1945 a teenage soldier, recalls fighting on the Philippine Island of Negros.

On Negros Island in the Philippines. At daybreak on 29 March 1945, the main American forces landed. Our Seventy-seventh Infantry Brigade's 354th Independent Infantry Battalion held our position at 1,100 meters on Higashitarōyama (later renamed Dolan Hill by the U.S. forces).

The fierce bombardment from air and land by the main American forces had scorched the densely foliated deep jungle encampment, rendering it as barren as a volcano. When the artillery bombardment ended, the enemy infantry approached to thirty meters and threw hand grenades in close combat. We struck nightly into the enemy encampment. One after another my war buddies went through the gates of Yasukuni Shrine. We were left with many heavily wounded soldiers. Maggots hatched in our bandages, writhing on our flesh and exuding a foul stench.

Food supplies were cut off. Having eaten up all the stalks of grasses and plants, and all the insects and reptiles, we became malnutrition cases. One's entire body swells, one's strength gives out, and it becomes impossible to control one's bodily functions. Hunger gnawed at people's spirit. There were those who ate human flesh. With the onset of the rainy season, men suffered from malaria, dengue fever, tropical ulcers, and chronic amoebic dysentery. There were those among the seriously wounded and ill soldiers who despaired so much that they killed themselves. Their gunshots echoed in the valley. Some deserted on their way to attack the enemy, or attacked the supply base, fighting against other Japanese soldiers to obtain food.

Higashitarōyama had held out for fifty-two days against a heavy siege. By 23 May, a mere dozen or so men were left under company commander Ishizuka. After ordering his men to assemble at battalion headquarters, Commander Ishikuza received a heavy gunshot wound, which perforated his stomach. I was ordered to escape alone with important documents—reports to battalion headquarters. Giving a sidelong glance at the two hundred heavily wounded and ill soldiers left behind, I made my escape. I thought of the poems "Eyes hot with tears, I see the round eyes of the infant clinging to its mother's dead body"; and "I overtake Japanese women and children carrying children on their backs, pulling children along by the hand and carrying baggage."

I reached brigade headquarters. There they had food—plenty of it. It shocked me to see the well-fed men of the headquarter units line up like ants and carry off provisions into the distance. At the front we had not been sent even a grain of unhulled rice.

Source: Gibney, Frank, ed. *Sensō: The Japanese Remember the Pacific War: Letters to the Editor of Asahi Shimbun,* 152–153. Armonk, NY: M. E. Sharpe, 1995.

Will [Date Unknown, but Late 1944 or Early 1945] of Kamikaze Pilot Ryōji Uehara

Will of Ryōji Uehara

To my dear Father and Mother:

I was so lucky ever since I was given my life some twenty years ago that I was brought up never deprived of anything. Under the love and affection of my loving parents, and with constant encouragement from my wonderful elder brothers and younger sister, I was so fortunate to spend such happy days. I say this in face of the fact that at times I had a tendency to act in a spoiled and selfish manner. Throughout, of all of us siblings, I was the one who caused you, Father and Mother, the most worry. It pains my heart that my time will come before I can return, or try to return, any of these favors I received. But in Japan, where loyalty to the Emperor and filial piety are considered one and the same thing, and total loyalty to the nation is a fulfillment of filial piety, I am confident of your forgiveness.

As a member of the flying staff, I spent each and every day with death as the premise. Every letter and each word I wrote constituted my last will and

---

As defeat came ever closer, the Japanese fought with a ferocity that dismayed and astonished their Western opponents. Specially trained Japanese pilots undertook kamikaze (literally, "divine wind") suicide missions in which they deliberately sacrificed themselves and crashed an airplane into an enemy ship or other major target. The bloodiest Pacific battle of World War II took place on the island of Okinawa, where from April to June 1945 Japanese defenders fought ferociously and suicidally against invading American forces. During the campaign, hundreds of Japanese kamikaze airplanes flying in mass formation repeatedly attacked the 1600 American naval vessels assembled for the Okinawa assault, sinking 30 and damaging a further 164. Among the kamikaze pilots who took part in the Battle of Okinawa was army captain Uehara Ryōji, a student from Keio University in Tokyo who was called up for military service in December 1943, and chosen for what was termed the "Special Attack Unit." He died in action at the age of 22 on May 11, 1945, when he attacked an American mechanized unit in Kadena Bay, Okinawa. Before doing so, Uehara wrote a last will and testament to his parents.

testament. In the sky so high above, death is never a focus of fear. Will I in fact die when I hit the target? No, I cannot believe that I am going to die, and there was even a time when I felt a sudden urge somehow to dive into a target. The fact of the matter is that I am never afraid of death, and, to the contrary, I even welcome it. The reason for this is my deep belief that, through death, I'll be able to get together again with my beloved older brother, Tatsu. To be reunited with him in heaven is what I desire the most. I did not have any specific attitude toward life and death. My reasoning was that the cultivation of a specific attitude toward life and death would amount to an attempt to give a meaning and value to death, something that would have to stem from a person's utter fear of an uncertain death. My belief is that death is a passage leading to reunion with my loved ones in heaven. I am not afraid to die. Death is nothing to be afraid of when you look at it as just a stage in the process of ascending to heaven.

Succinctly speaking, I have always admired liberalism, mainly because I felt that this political philosophy was the only one to follow were Japan really to survive eternally. Perhaps this sort of thinking seems foolish, but it is only because Japan is currently drowned in totalitarianism. Nevertheless, and this state of affairs notwithstanding, it will be clear to any human being who sees clearly and is willing to reflect on the very nature of his or her humanity that liberalism is the most logical ideology.

It seems to me that a nation's probable success in the prosecution of a war would, on the very basis of that nation's ideology, be clearly evident even before the war was fought. It would in fact be so obvious that eventual victory would clearly be seen to belong to the nation that holds a natural ideology, i.e., an ideology which in its way is constitutive of human nature itself.

My hope of making Japan like the British Empire of the past has been utterly defeated. At this point, therefore, I gladly give up my life for Japan's liberty and independence.

While the rise and fall of one nation is indeed a matter of immense importance for any human being, the same shift dwindles to relative insignificance if and when that same human being places it within the context of the universe as a whole. Exactly as the saying has it, "Pride goeth before a fall (or, those who savor victory will soon find themselves in the camp of the defeated)," and even if America and Great Britain turn out to be victorious against us, they will eventually learn that the day of their own defeat is imminent. It pleases me to think that, even if they are not to be defeated in the near future, they may be turned to dust anyway through an explosion of the globe itself. Not only that, but the people who are getting the most fun out of life now are most certainly doomed to die in the end. The only difference is whether it comes sooner or later.

In the drawer, right side of my bookcase, in the annex of the house, you will find the book I am leaving behind. If the drawer does not open, please open the left drawer and pull out a nail—then try the right drawer again.

Well, then, I pray that you will take good care of yourselves.
My very best to my big brother, sister Kiyoko, and to everyone.
Well, then. Good-bye. Farewell. Good-bye forever.

From Ryōji

Source: Kike Wadatsumi no Koe. *Listen to the Voices from the Sea*. Translated by Midori Yamanouchi and Joseph L. Quinn, S.J., 236–238. Scranton: The University of Scranton Press, 2000. Used by permission of the University of Scranton.

American Bombing Raids on Germany: Diary of Robert S. Raymond, January 23, 1943

So much has happened this month that I've had little time to record it. Returned to my squadron on a cold snowy morning and found all my crew glad to see me.

Took them up that afternoon on a night flying test and again that night on a search-light evasion exercise over the south coast of England and London. Flew at 8,000 feet for two hours, and being fatigued from my journey during the whole of the preceding night without sleep, returned to base an hour and a half early. The wing commander had me on the carpet the next morning, but no trouble when I explained the lack of oxygen, and so on.

Operations since my return have been Essen on January 13 and 21 and Berlin on January 10 and 17. Both of them very hot targets. Nearly every other crew was hit by flak or night fighters. The wing commander got hit in the arm and turned back from the first Berlin raid, being barely able to land his plane at base. Haven't been able to get any photos on last four trips due to poor visibility on ground.

Have bombed on flares of selected colors dropped by PFF [Pathfinder Force], which also mark turning points. Were routed over Denmark and near Stettin to Berlin both times. Cloud 10/10 most of the way, icing conditions and condensation trails, all under a full moon. Most who were attacked by night fighters or hit by flak were off track a good way and went over defended areas. The routes given us are never a direct track to the target, and the whole force, usually of less than 200 Lancasters, are pushed over the route at the same time to make interception and radio location more difficult for the enemy.

PFF was late with its flares at Berlin the second night, so we scattered our load of incendiaries on the flak, which was intense and accurate. We could see the little black puffs

---

In the spring of 1940, Robert S. Raymond, a young American from Kansas City, volunteered to serve in the French Army. During the fall of France, he was evacuated to Great Britain, where he joined the Royal Air Force and trained as a bomber pilot, flying a tour of 30 missions on Lancaster bombers. He then transferred to the U.S. Army Air Force, where he remained until the war ended. Bomber crews had a very high casualty rate, and about half failed to complete their full tours but were shot down and killed. This diary entry describes January 1943 bombing raids on Essen and Berlin, Germany, in which Raymond and his crew took part.

of shells bursting very near us in the bright moonlight, so didn't stand upon the order of our departure.

Our loads on two nights were 1,080 4-pound incendiaries, and on the other two nights one 4,000-pound cookie and 720 incendiaries.

We use various radio-jamming devices, which transmit noise from an engine on certain frequencies used by their fighters and searchlights. We bombed on each occasion at 18,000 feet. All northern Europe is covered with snow. It is really indiscriminate bombing, because no attempt is made to light up the target with flares; we are not allowed to carry any, but must depend on the few colored ones dropped by the PFF.

The Ruhr is extensively defended, and you are never free from isolated [antiaircraft] batteries until well out across the North Sea, clear of the flak ships.

Our food becomes progressively worse in quality. No more eggs and bacon before or after operations. We get meat stew every day at noon, but there is very little meat in it.

Crew works well together, but we have had to take freshman gunners on several occasions, because Newton has been sick and Carter went AWOL [absent without leave] for twenty-three days. He went home in the hope that he would be stripped [demoted] and grounded, but was summarily tried today by Group Captain Lewes, was severely reprimanded, and lost twenty-four days' pay. He does not want to fly on operations any more but will not admit it.

Our tonnage record for eleven trips totals 63,720 pounds.

Losses from this squadron and No. 9, based at this same station, have been heavy. I've known only two crews who have completed a tour of thirty trips. None are very keen to go any more, and I can't blame them, although I'd still like to . . .

Operational limitations are never met with in training, hence must be learned quickly during the first few trips if one hopes to survive. The fuel and bomb load carried to any target vary inversely. Short hauls mean big loads. But hauling big loads up to high altitudes in a short time presents another factor that must be balanced with weather and types of bombs carried. Always a very tricky question, which we leave to the experts and tacticians.

Griffiths gets us maximum mileage at all heights by using the supercharger correctly with low revs and high boost. Diversions due to bad weather depend wholly upon his ability to put us up to operational heights and bring us down economically. He also flies the plane well on instruments, and I give him practice on every trip. Have learned how to fly through and recognize beforehand icing conditions, types of cloud, temperatures at which they form, and the frontal weather conditions that are dangerous.

Seventy-three aircraft took off on ops from this station [44 Squadron, based at Waddington, near Lincoln] during the month of December 1942. Four returned early due to mechanical defects. Total ops hours: 486; tonnage carried: 167 tons. Ops undertaken on eleven nights during the month, of which five nights were devoted to mining, which is usually undertaken by new crews for their first op after the captain has done two or three as second pilot with another crew.

No. 9 Squadron, also based here, has had shattering losses and is no longer operational, temporarily being re-equipped with Mark III Lancasters (Packard Merlin engines). It is strange that two separate organizations using the same facilities and same type of aircraft should have such different records. Only three crews remain with two or three ops apiece to their credit. Our losses too have been heavy, so that we are the fifth oldest crew now.

The USAAF [US Army Air Force] bombing has not proved successful. Seventy-one aircraft were dispatched to Lorient [France] on January 23, 1943, and only thirty-one attacked target. Losses: five. Defenses were quickly reorganized to stop their type of attack. From experience, we know how smart the Germans are along those lines.

The Lancasters are carrying the whole weight of Bomber Command's offensive now, and we hear little of the Halifaxes and Stirlings from other groups. One difficulty is coordinating different speeds of other aircraft into times and heights over the same target, both needing to be very exact with the new tactics nowadays.

My crew and I realize the certainty of being shot down or forced down over enemy territory as long as we continue on ops. No experienced crew is anxious to go up against the stiff defenses we meet, but when necessary we go and do our best. And our best is equal to that of a small army in its damaging effect on the enemy.

1. We destroy great areas by bombing.
2. We make accurate observations
3. We maintain a radio transmitter over enemy territory.
4. We have an effect on civilian morale.
5. We disseminate propaganda material direct to the people in the occupied countries.

Source: Raymond, Robert S. *A Yank in Bomber Command*, 155–158. Pacifica, CA: Pacifica Press, 1998.

Appendix: Historical Dilemmas in World War II

WARTIME ALLIANCES

How Did International Geopolitics Evolve during World War II?

During World War II, the international geopolitical climate was in a state of flux. Much of this tumult was the result of the complex relationship between political theory and political reality that was emerging at the time. On the one hand, there were a number of powerful ideologies, including Nazism, fascism, communism, and liberal democracy, that created major rifts between nations. In fact, the vast majority of these political belief systems called for the destruction or conquest of the others. On the other hand, the reality of war forged a number of alliances for purely pragmatic reasons. The opening of the Eastern Front in June 1941 and the development of the Cold War directly after the end of World War II illustrate, however, just how tenuous these alliances could be.

In the two Defining Moments that follow, Dr. Lee Eysturlid explores this interesting intersection of ideology and practicality during World War II. In the first essay, he discusses the German–Soviet Nonaggression Pact, signed between representatives of Nazi Germany and the communist Soviet Union. Although each country distrusted and disliked the other, the agreement benefited both parties. When the pact was no longer expedient, however, Germany was quick to terminate it through its invasion of the Soviet Union (Operation BARBAROSSA). In the second essay, Dr. Eysturlid examines the Allies' conference system, which came to include the Soviet Union after the Germans violated the nonaggression pact. The focus of this conference system evolved during the course of the war, shifting from military strategy at Casablanca to the rebuilding of a postwar world at Potsdam.

Defining Moment 1: German–Soviet Pact of 1939

The German–Soviet Nonaggression Treaty of August 1939 and its secret geopolitical and economic provisions governed the relations of Nazi Germany and the Soviet Union until the German invasion of the Soviet Union on June 22, 1941. The treaty, signed in Moscow between foreign ministers Vyacheslav Molotov of the Soviet Union and Joachim von Ribbentrop of Germany, represents the true nature of the ambitions of Adolf Hitler and Josef Stalin, as well as their political practicalities.

How could Nazi Germany and the Soviet Union create an alliance, in any form? Hitler had clearly stated in *Mein Kampf* that the East was a land of *untermenschen* (subhumans), destined for German conquest and, later, extermination. Soviet communism looked at Nazism as another form of class-ridden capitalism, doomed to failure and eventual conquest. Both states were, therefore, ideological enemies (which they remained), but also short-term natural allies. In this case, perceived geopolitical necessities overcame ideology.

Germany had two key reasons for its alliance with the Soviet Union. The first was a need to have access to Russian resources. This supported the second reason, which was Hitler's wish to avoid a two-front war. He sought to attack and destroy Poland, but such an attack would likely precipitate a war with France and Great Britain. Therefore, Hitler needed a secure eastern border while he defeated his enemies to the west. The fact that secret protocols of the treaty allowed for Soviet domination of Finland, the Baltic states, and a portion of eastern Poland was meaningless in the long term, because German plans called for the eventual conquest of all this territory. The pact was a great success for the Germans, allowing them to conquer Poland and then Western Europe while still having access to Russian resources. It also lulled Stalin into believing that a community of interest existed between Germany and the Soviet Union, making Operation BARBAROSSA in June 1941 a complete surprise and, at least initially, a German success.

The Soviet Union had equally good reasons for its alliance with Germany. Stalin clearly did not trust the democratic West, and even though Nazi Germany was, ideologically, a potential enemy, the two countries had much in common. Both states were keen to aggrandize, especially in their mutually overlapping spheres of influence in Eastern Europe. Stalin believed that his bargain with Hitler had given him a free hand to move into the Baltic states and a portion of Poland, as well as smaller areas such as Bessarabia. Finally, the pact provided the Soviet Union with manufactured goods and military technology in exchange for raw materials.

The pact was a disaster for the French, British, and Poles, as it linked the two most potentially powerful states in Europe. For Poland, it spelled doom, and the combined Soviet–German invasion of September 1939 was unstoppable. For the West, it meant that as long as the pact lasted Germany could concentrate the vast bulk of its forces against them. It also forced Britain and France—and after the fall of France in June 1940, just Britain—to studiously work at avoiding the Soviet Union. Only the German invasion of the Soviet Union, which Nazi ideology made inevitable, ended this international dilemma and paved the way for a Western–Soviet alliance.

Lee W. Eysturlid

Defining Moment 2: The Conference System

The four great conferences held by the Allies between January 1943 and August 1945 can be tied together as the great evolving political event of the war, shaping its course, outcome, and the world that followed. Each successive conference reflects the general nature of the war, with the early meetings dominated by military matters and the later ones, especially Potsdam, dominated by political concerns. The three major participants were the

United States, Great Britain, and the Soviet Union, with China and France playing secondary roles. Each meeting represents the effort of each state and its respective leader to balance the needs and desires of that state with the needs and desires of its allies. As in all wars, success of any alliance comes from the commonality of each player's goals. In this case, all the Allies and all four conferences can be seen as having the same ultimate target: the defeat of Nazi Germany and Imperial Japan. This was, to a great degree, the only unifying focus that existed, and when victory was clearly at hand, the alliance quickly fell apart.

Casablanca Conference

The first of the great conferences, held at Casablanca in French Morocco from January 14 to 24, 1943, brought together Franklin D. Roosevelt (United States) and Winston Churchill (Great Britain), but not Josef Stalin (Soviet Union), as he was wholly occupied with the Battle of Stalingrad. The primary focus of the conference was on future strategy for the war effort. In a battle of wills, Churchill struggled to maintain the "Germany first" strategy and avoid the opening of the "second front" in 1943 with an invasion of France. Of greater strategic impact was the decision to launch the Combined Bomber Offensive against Germany. Most important was the decision that the Allies would only accept unconditional surrender from the Axis. This meant a war to the bitter end, with no potential for negotiation.

Tehran Conference

The Allied meeting at Tehran, Iran, from November 28 to December 1, 1943, was the first personal meeting between Roosevelt, Churchill, and Stalin. The focus moved to the opening of the promised second front in France, with the agreed date of May 1944 (later delayed until June). To assist, Stalin promised a large-scale offensive to coincide (Operation BAGRATION). The Soviets also promised to attack Japan once Germany was defeated. Subsequent discussions involved the future of Poland, support for Josip Tito's Partisans in Yugoslavia, and the postwar division of Germany.

Yalta Conference

The first of two meetings in 1945 happened at Yalta on the Crimean Peninsula during February 4–11. Here, strategy took second place to diplomatic negotiations. The primary military concern was the final phase of attack against Germany. More important was the agreement between Roosevelt and Stalin in order to gain Soviet participation in the fight against Japan. Further talks over the future of Poland and the remainder of Eastern Europe also occurred.

Potsdam Conference

The second meeting of 1945, at Potsdam, Germany, between July 17 and August 2, merely confirmed decisions largely already taken. Harry S. Truman was now president of the United States, and Churchill, having suffered electoral defeat at home, was replaced by Clement Attlee. Much of the discussion centered on the treatment of Germany after the war and ending the war against Japan.

Lee W. Eysturlid

Print Resources

Bennett, Edward M. *Franklin D. Roosevelt and the Search for Victory: American–Soviet Relations, 1939–1945.* Wilmington, DE: Scholarly Resources, 1990.

Berthon, Simon, and Joanna Potts. *Warlords: An Extraordinary Re-Creation of World War II Through the Eyes and Minds of Hitler, Roosevelt, Churchill, and Stalin.* New York: Da Capo Press, 2006.

Black, Jeremy. *Avoiding Armageddon: From the Great War to the Fall of France, 1918–1940.* New York: Continuum, 2012.

Costigliola, Frank. *Roosevelt's Lost Alliances: How Personal Politics Helped Start the Cold War.* Princeton, NJ: Princeton University Press, 2011.

Edmonds, Robin. *The Big Three: Churchill, Roosevelt and Stalin in War and Peace.* New York: Norton, 1991.

Feis, Herbert. *Churchill–Roosevelt–Stalin: The War They Waged and the Peace They Sought.* Princeton, NJ: Princeton University Press, 1957.

Gardner, Lloyd C. *Spheres of Influence: The Great Powers Partition Europe, from Munich to Yalta.* Chicago, IL: I. R. Dee, 1993.

Gormly, James. *From Potsdam to the Cold War: Big Three Diplomacy, 1945–1947.* Wilmington, DE: Scholarly Resources Books, 1990.

Harbutt, Fraser J. *Yalta 1945: Europe and America at the Crossroads.* Cambridge: Cambridge University Press, 2010.

Meacham, Jon. *Franklin and Winston: An Intimate Portrait of an Epic Friendship.* New York: Random House, 2003.

Nadeau, Remi. *Stalin, Churchill and Roosevelt Divide Europe.* New York: Praeger, 1990.

Perlmutter, Amos. *FDR and Stalin: A Not So Grand Alliance, 1943–1945.* Columbia, MO: University of Missouri Press, 1993.

Plokhy, S. M. *Yalta: The Price of Peace.* New York: Viking, 2010.

Read, Anthony, and David Fisher. *The Deadly Embrace: Hitler, Stalin, and the Nazi–Soviet Pact, 1939–1941.* New York: W. W. Norton, 1988.

Reynolds, David. *Summits: Six Meetings that Shaped the Twentieth Century.* New York: Basic Books, 2007.

Sainsbury, Keith. *The Turning Point: Roosevelt, Stalin, Churchill, and Chiang Kai-shek, 1943: The Moscow, Cairo, and Teheran Conferences.* New York: Oxford University Press, 1985.

Stafford, David. *Roosevelt and Churchill: Men of Secrets.* New York: Overlook, 2000.

Steiner, Zara. *The Triumph of the Dark: European International History 1933–1939.* Oxford: Oxford University Press, 2011.

Thomas, Hugh. *Armed Truce: The Beginnings of the Cold War, 1945–1946.* New York: Atheneum, 1987.

Watt, D. C. *How War Came: The Immediate Origins of the Second World War, 1938–1939.* London: Pimlico, 2001.

Williamson, David G. *Poland Betrayed: The Nazi-Soviet Invasions of 1939.* Mechanics-burg, PA: Stackpole Press, 2009.

BATTLE OF THE SEAS

What Role Did Economic Factors Play in World War II?

An important issue facing each of the major nations involved in World War II was how to create enough of the right weapons systems to meet the country's specific strategic needs. In the case of states such as Germany and the Soviet Union, this meant land and air forces—tanks, artillery, and aircraft. For the island nation of Japan, most wartime production centered on ships, both naval and merchant, as well as aircraft. Finally, the United States, and to a lesser degree Great Britain, had to create land, air, and naval forces, as well as equip allies such as France and China. Therefore, winning the "economic war" meant not just making weapons, but allocating the right resources to make enough of the right weapons.

In the first Defining Moment, Dr. Lee Eysturlid examines what is perhaps the greatest logistical or transportation success of the entire war, if not the 20th century. The American ability to organize the production of the so-called Liberty Ships, also known as the "Ugly Ducklings," would serve as a testament to the U.S. industrial system. The fact that these ships, necessary to move the hundreds of thousands of tons of fuel, food, equipment, and men from the United States to war zones in Europe and the Pacific, could be built at a rate never before seen was a logistical triumph. In the second Defining Moment, Dr. Eysturlid explores the German effort to directly attack the economic strength of the Allies with the U-boat. While such attacks were initially successful, it was the superiority of American and British intelligence and weapons technologies, combined with their spectacular production rates, that overwhelmed the Germans. In the end, it was the Germans' industrial inability to produce more—and better—submarines that brought their defeat in the Battle of the Atlantic.

Defining Moment 1: Liberty Ships and American War Production

On a single day in 1943, a shipyard in Portland, Oregon, launched three merchant ships and delivered three more—an incredible feat of industrial production. These ships, known as Liberty ships, were built of prefabricated sections and riveted together. The concept originated with the industrialist Henry Kaiser as a method to meet the tremendous demands for shipping created by overseas conflict. Kaiser's methods reduced the production time for a Liberty ship from 244 days to 72 by the spring of 1942. By the end of the war, it took only about 42 days to build such a ship. Large numbers of these vessels were needed, partly to make up for grievous losses to German U-boats, but also to handle the great bulk of American war material shipped to its allies. During World War II, the United States sent weapons and supplies to Great Britain, North Africa, the Soviet Union, India, China, and the Central and South Pacific—all at the same time. The construction methods of Liberty ships demonstrate the immense capacity of American military production during the war—the very production the ships were designed to carry.

The sheer numbers are staggering. Between 1942 and 1945, the United States produced more than 290,000 airplanes, 86,000 tanks, 319,000 artillery pieces, 11,900 ships of all types, and 42 billion bullets. Civilian industries were converted to wartime production: Westinghouse made torpedoes (among other products); General Motors turned out carrier-based bombers; Chrysler made tank engines. Militarily, the effect of American industrial production was decisive. For example, German armor was superior to American armor on a tank-by-tank basis, but American tanks frequently had a huge numerical superiority. American and Japanese aircraft carrier losses in the Pacific battles of 1942 were serious (by the end of the year only a single American carrier remained in operation), but the United States launched more than a dozen carriers in 1943 and 1944. Japan could not replace its losses with such ease. Antisubmarine efforts against German U-boats in the Battle of the Atlantic were ultimately successful, and new liberty ships rapidly made up for lost tonnage. The Axis was drowned in a wave of American production.

The war transformed the American economy. The stagnant economic picture of the Great Depression vanished with the demands of war production, and unemployment essentially disappeared. Gross national product (GNP) passed $100 billion, then $200 billion. In addition, the increased scale of American military spending created a military–industrial relationship in the United States that did not pass away with the end of the war. The requirements of armies of occupation, the increasing role of the United States in the postwar world, the demands of the Cold War—all contributed to the maintenance of a large military establishment in the United States. While the American military certainly decreased in size substantially after the war, military expenditures remained significant. The days of American isolationism were over.

Lee W. Eysturlid

Defining Moment 2: Submarine Warfare

In April 1943, German U-boats sank a staggering 108 allied merchant ships. At that point in the conflict, the German submarine campaign threatened the entire Allied war effort. U-boats had taken a heavy toll of British and Allied shipping since the war began. By early 1941, submarine sinkings had cut British import tonnage by almost half, and despite significant wartime building of merchant ships, the British merchant fleet was nearly 20% smaller in December 1941 than it had been at the outset of the war. The Allies had to regain control of the vital North Atlantic shipping lanes to prevent the collapse of the British war effort and to allow American war production to exert its influence on the European conflict. However, April 1943 came to represent a high-water mark in the German submarine offensive as British and American antisubmarine measures gained the upper hand in the Atlantic later in the year. The Allies committed significant resources to the Battle of the Atlantic, and their success was crucial to the successful conclusion of the war.

Unrestricted submarine warfare—that is, submarine warfare directed against merchant ships as well as warships—represented the expansion of conflict to include national economies. Modern warfare depends heavily on industrial output, and submarine attacks on maritime British commerce threatened this output. As an island nation, Great Britain was especially susceptible to such a campaign. For example, Britain imported all of its oil and almost half of its food when the submarine war began in 1940. Germany's use of submarines against British shipping during World War I had been extremely effective, but at a heavy price: because of American ship sinkings, the German submarine campaign was a major factor in the decision of the United States to enter the war against Germany. In World War II, Admiral Karl Dönitz determined that an intensive submarine campaign against Britain would be decisive, and Germany pursued such a campaign from the start of the war.

Britain and the United States employed a number of tactics in response to the submarine threat. Merchant ships were organized into convoys at the start of the war. Such convoys made it harder for submarines to find targets in the vast expanse of the Atlantic. Convoys were escorted by warships carrying underwater sound detection equipment (sonar, or ASDIC to the British) and depth charges to be used against detected submarines. These tactics did not succeed in the early years of the war, but increased experience, more numerous escorting vessels, and improvement of the escorts themselves helped Allied performance against submarines as the war proceeded. British success in intercepting and decoding German radio traffic allowed the Allies to follow German submarine traffic and to plan against it. Improved sonar and better antisubmarine weapons—"hedgehog" antisubmarine devices—played a role. Finally, the use of air power against submarines proved highly effective. Land-based planes could patrol coastlines, but obviously could not accompany convoys across the Atlantic. However, large-scale American production of small escort carriers made it possible for convoys to be covered by air surveillance for most of their journey. Together, these countermeasures turned the tide in the antisubmarine campaign by the middle of 1943, and German submarine losses rapidly mounted. By the end of the war, Germany had lost more than three quarters of its submarines, and submarine sailors suffered the highest percentage of deaths of any branch of the German military.

Lee W. Eysturlid

Print Resources

Eiler, Keith. *Mobilizing America: Robert P. Patterson and the War Effort, 1940–1945*. Ithaca, NY: Cornell University Press, 1998.

Elphick, Peter. *Liberty: The Ships that Won the War*. Annapolis, MD: Naval Institute Press, 2001.

Foster, Mark S. *Henry J. Kaiser: Builder in the Modern American West*. Austin, TX: University of Texas Press, 1989.

Gardner, W.J.R. *Decoding History: The Battle of the Atlantic and Ultra*. Annapolis, MD: Naval Institute Press, 1999.

Heitmann, John A. "The Man Who Won the War: Andrew Jackson Higgins." *Louisiana History* 34 (1993): 35–40.

Higgs, Robert. "Wartime Prosperity? A Reassessment of the U.S. Economy in the 1940s." *Journal of Economic History* 52 (1992): 41–62.

Koistinen, Paul A. C. *Arsenal of World War II: The Political Economy of American Warfare, 1940–1945*. Lawrence, KS: University of Kansas Press, 2004.

Milner, Marc. *The Battle of the Atlantic*. Stroud: Tempus Books, 2003.

Niestlé, Axel. *German U-Boat Losses during World War II: Details of Destruction*. Annapolis, MD: Naval Institute Press, 1998.

Offley, Edward. *Turning the Tide: How a Small Band of Allied Sailors Defeated the U-Boats and Won the Battle of the Atlantic.* New York: Basic Books, 2011.

Overy, Richard. *Why the Allies Won.* New York: W. W. Norton, 1995.

Runyan, Timothy J., and Jan M. Copes, eds. *To Die Gallantly: The Battle of the Atlantic.* Boulder, CO: Westview Press, 1994.

Snow, Richard. *A Measureless Peril: America in the Fight for the Atlantic, the Longest Battle of World War II.* New York: Scribner's, 2010.

Syrett, David. *The Defeat of the German U-Boats: The Battle of the Atlantic.* Columbia, SC: University of South Carolina Press, 1994.

Williams, Andrew. *The Battle of the Atlantic: The Allies, Submarine Fight against Hitler's Grey Wolves of the Sea.* London: BBC Books, 2002.

Yenne, Bill. *The American Aircraft Factory in World War II.* Minneapolis, MN: Zenith Press, 2006.

DROPPING THE BOMB

Was the United States Justified in Dropping the Bomb on Hiroshima and Nagasaki?

The ramifications of the U.S. decision to use the atomic bomb against Hiroshima and Nagasaki in 1945 are felt even today. Many saw the bomb as a solution to end the war quickly with the fewest number of casualties. Others worried about the moral obligations inherent in the use of the new weapon, while still others argued that a land invasion would be more effective than using the atomic bomb.

Dr. Spencer C. Tucker contends that the use of the atomic bomb was justified, as the United States did not have conclusive proof that Japan was ready to accept terms of unconditional surrender. Further, a land invasion would have resulted in unacceptably high numbers of casualties on both sides of the conflict. Taking this viewpoint a step further, Dr. J. Samuel Walker makes a distinction between justified and necessary, arguing that dropping the bomb was necessary to end the war much sooner than it otherwise would have ended, but pointing out that President Harry S. Truman was not given casualty estimates in the "hundreds of thousands" and therefore did not take this into account when he made the decision. Last, Dr. Gar Alperovitz is firm in his standpoint that dropping the bomb was not only unnecessary, but was also opposed by several key U.S. military figures at the time. He contends that Japan was on the brink of surrendering, and that a coordinated Soviet attack alone would have been sufficient to end the war. Alperovitz suggests that the United States should have waited until after November 1945, the time scheduled for a land invasion, before deployment, and believes that by that time the war would have ended without the use of the bomb.

Perspective 1: Dropping the Bomb Saved Lives

Dropping the atomic bombs on Japan saved the lives of hundreds of thousands of U.S. soldiers and was the only way to end the war quickly. In the summer of 1945, American planners hoped that a naval blockade and strategic bombing campaign of the Japanese home islands would bring the war to an end. The prospects for an actual invasion appeared dim, as Japanese leaders made major preparations to defend against such an attack. In light of the heavy casualties sustained by U.S. forces in the invasions of Iwo Jima and Okinawa earlier that year, the U.S. Joint Chiefs of Staff were reluctant to carry out Operation DOWNFALL, the planned land invasion of Japan. The Japanese military had a million soldiers, 3,000 Kamikaze aircraft, and 5,000 suicide boats available to defend its home islands. Civilians were also being prepared to fight to the death. With the U.S. invasion scheduled for November 1, 1945, and well aware that the cost of such an enterprise was likely to be high, the Joint Chiefs of Staff pressed President Franklin D. Roosevelt at the February 1945 Yalta Conference to persuade the Soviet Union to enter the war against Japan at any cost.

Following the successful test detonation of an atomic bomb at Alamogordo, New Mexico, on July 16, 1945, sharp debate arose among advisers to U.S. president Harry S. Truman (who had succeeded Roosevelt as president on the latter's death in April) regarding whether to employ the new weapon against Japan. The terror threshold had already been passed in the firebombing of Japanese cities. Indeed, the most destructive single air raid in history was not the atomic bombing of Hiroshima or Nagasaki, but the firebombing of Tokyo on the night of March 9–10, 1945. This was total war. It was always assumed that the bomb would be used if it became available. American planners believed that employing the bomb would, in all likelihood, bring the war to a speedy end, saving many American lives. It would also mean that the United States would not have to share occupation of Japan with the Soviet Union, and hopefully it would deter Soviet leader Josef Stalin from future aggression. The atomic bomb was thus essentially a psychological weapon, rather than a purely military tool, the use of which was designed to influence Japanese political leaders. Dropping it appeared to be the only way to realize the American goal of unconditional surrender.

Revisionist historians have held that the Japanese government was trying desperately to leave the war and that employing the bomb was unnecessary. Intercepts of diplomatic messages indicated, however, that Japan had not yet reached the decision to surrender when the first bomb was dropped. While Emperor Hirohito and his principal advisers had concluded that Japan could not win the war, they still held out hope for a negotiated settlement and believed that a last decisive battle would force the Allies to grant more favorable peace terms.

Post-atomic bomb estimates have claimed the possibility of up to a million casualties in a U.S. invasion of Japan. However, historian Ray Skates concludes in his authoritative study *The Invasion of Japan: Alternative to the Bomb* (1998) that Operation OLYMPIC, the first phase of the invasion of Japan (the conquest of the island of Kyushu planned for November 1945), would alone have taken two months and resulted in 75,000 to 100,000 U.S. casualties. Such losses, while they would not have affected the outcome of the war, might indeed have brought about the political goals sought by the Japanese leaders for more favorable surrender terms.

Prolonging the war would have meant a significantly higher cost in Japanese lives than those actually killed in the atomic bombings. During the war, the Japanese lost 323,495 dead on the home front, the vast majority of them from air attack. With continued strategic bombing this total would have swelled, and many other Japanese would simply have died of starvation. By August 1945, Japan's largest cities had been largely burned out.

Waterborne transportation had been interdicted by airborne mining and submarines, and the Japanese nation was close to starvation. The reduced food supply was highly dependent on railroad distribution, and the railroads would have been the next major strategic bombing target. In effect, dropping the bomb resulted in a net saving of both Japanese and American lives.

The first bomb fell on Hiroshima on August 6, 1945. On August 8, the Soviet Union declared war on Japan, Stalin honoring, to the day, his pledge at Yalta to enter the war against Japan "two or three months after the defeat of Germany," which had occurred on May 8, 1945. On August 9, a second atomic bomb fell on Nagasaki.

After prolonged meetings with his advisers, Hirohito made the decision for peace. The U.S. dropping of the atomic bombs enabled him to take this difficult step in the face of a sharply divided cabinet. Even so, his decision was not without danger, for fanatics determined to fight on to the end plotted to assassinate the emperor to prevent announcement of the decision. To forestall this, Hirohito communicated the decision over radio. On the afternoon of August 15, 1945, in a voice never heard before by the Japanese people, Hirohito told his people that Japan would accept the Potsdam Declaration and surrender. In so doing, he specifically mentioned the atomic bomb: "Moreover, the enemy has begun to employ a new and most cruel bomb, the power of which to do damage is indeed incalculable, taking the toll of many innocent lives." World War II had come to an end, and the atomic bomb played a major role in it, saving both Japanese and American lives.

Spencer C. Tucker

Perspective 2: The Bomb Was Necessary to End the War

The simple answer to the question "Was the United States justified in dropping the atomic bomb on Hiroshima and Nagasaki in World War II?" is *yes*, the United States was justified in using atomic bombs to end World War II in the Pacific at the earliest possible moment. The answer to a closely related question—"Was the use of the bomb necessary?"—is more ambiguous. In my view, the answer to this question is yes, it was necessary in some ways, and no, it was not necessary in other ways.

By the summer of 1945, after three-and-a-half years of cruel and bloody war, American leaders knew that Japan was defeated. It was running desperately short of vital supplies and faced the prospect of mass starvation. But that did not mean that Japan was ready to surrender. Although its leaders recognized that they could not win the war, they fought on in hopes of securing surrender terms that they would find acceptable. President Harry S. Truman and his advisers considered various methods of forcing the Japanese to surrender, including, in the worst case, an invasion of the Japanese home islands that would claim the lives of large numbers of U.S. soldiers, sailors, and Marines. The invasion, if it became necessary, was scheduled to begin around November 1, 1945.

The success of the Manhattan Project in building atomic bombs that became available for the first time in the summer of 1945 greatly eased the dilemma that Truman faced. Here, he hoped, was a means to force the Japanese to quit the war without having to confront the ghastly prospect of an invasion or risk the major drawbacks of the other possible but highly uncertain alternatives. The alternatives included continuing the firebombing of Japanese cities that had already caused massive destruction and loss of life, modifying the U.S. demand for unconditional surrender by allowing the emperor to remain on his throne, and waiting for Soviet entry into the war against Japan. Those options might have brought about a Japanese surrender but they ran the risks of prolonging the war in the first two cases and expanding Soviet influence in East Asia in the third.

Although some Japanese leaders sought to persuade Emperor Hirohito to surrender, he vacillated while the war continued. Therefore, the use of the atomic bomb was essential, and justified, to compel Japan to capitulate promptly. The shock of the bombing of Hiroshima, followed immediately by a Soviet attack on Japanese forces in Manchuria, finally convinced Hirohito that the war must end quickly. After agonizing deliberations in Tokyo, the Japanese government surrendered on the sole condition that the institution of the emperor be preserved.

For many years after the end of World War II, Americans embraced the view that the use of the bomb was necessary because the only alternative was an invasion of Japan that would have cost hundreds of thousands of American lives. But this categorical position has been discredited by the opening of new American and Japanese sources. They show that neither the president nor top military advisers regarded an invasion as inevitable. Further, Truman was not told by his most trusted advisers that an invasion, if it became necessary, would cost hundreds of thousands of lives. The idea that Truman had to choose between the bomb and an invasion to defeat Japan is a myth that took hold in the United States after World War II.

Truman was committed to ending the war at the earliest possible moment, and he wanted to save as many American lives as he could. He did not need estimates of potential losses in the hundreds of thousands to authorize the use of the bomb, and in fact, there is no contemporaneous evidence that he received projections of such staggering losses. For Truman, his advisers, and the vast majority of the American people, ending the war and sparing the lives of a smaller but far from inconsequential number of Americans was ample reason to drop atomic bombs. The Japanese government could have avoided the terrible effects of the atomic bombs by electing to surrender sooner than it did, but it was too divided and too indecisive to take the proper action.

There are many uncertainties and complexities surrounding the end of World War II. But the answer to the fundamental question of whether the use of the bomb on Hiroshima and Nagasaki was necessary appears to be: yes, and no. Yes, it was necessary to end the war as quickly as possible. And yes, it was necessary to save the lives of American troops, perhaps numbering in the several thousands. But no, the bomb probably was not necessary to end the war within a fairly short time without an invasion because Japan was in such dire straits. And no, it was not necessary to save the lives of *hundreds* of thousands of American troops.

J. Samuel Walker

Perspective 3: Dropping the Bomb Was Unjustified

The United States was not justified in using atomic bombs against Japanese cities in 1945. U.S. and British intelligence had already advised that Japan was likely to surrender when the Soviet Union entered the war in early August—and on terms that, in fact, would have been very close to those ultimately accepted by the United States. There are also reasons to believe the decision had as much to do with geopolitics connected with the Soviet Union as it did with the war against Japan.

The conventional wisdom that the atomic bomb saved a million lives is so widespread that most Americans haven't paused to ponder something rather striking to anyone seriously concerned with the issue: most American military leaders didn't think the bombings were either necessary or justified—and many were morally offended by Hiroshima and Nagasaki.

Here is how General Dwight D. Eisenhower reacted when he was told by Secretary of War Henry L. Stimson that the atomic bomb would be used: "During his recitation of the relevant facts, I had been conscious of a feeling of depression and so I voiced to him my grave misgivings, first on the basis of my belief that Japan was already defeated and that dropping the bomb was completely unnecessary, and secondly because I thought that our country should avoid shocking world opinion by the use of a weapon whose employment was, I thought, no longer mandatory as a measure to save American lives."

In another public statement the man who later became president was blunt: "It wasn't necessary to hit them with that awful thing."

General Curtis LeMay, the tough cigar-smoking air force "hawk," was also dismayed. Shortly after the bombings he stated: "The war would have been over in two weeks. . . . The atomic bomb had nothing to do with the end of the war at all."

And Fleet Admiral Chester W. Nimitz, commander in chief of the Pacific Fleet, went public with this statement: "The Japanese had, in fact, already sued for peace. . . . The atomic bomb played no decisive part, from a purely military standpoint, in the defeat of Japan."

The reasons these and many, many military leaders felt this way are both clear and instructive: Japan was essentially defeated, its navy at the bottom of the ocean; its air force limited by fuel, equipment, and other shortages; its army facing defeat on all fronts; and its cities subjected to bombing that was all but impossible to challenge. With Germany out of the war, the United States and Britain were about to bring their full power to bear on what was left of the Japanese military. Moreover, the Soviet Army was getting ready to attack on the Asian mainland.

American intelligence had broken Japanese codes and had advised as early as April 1945 that although a hard-line faction wished to continue the war, when the Soviet Union attacked—expected roughly in the first week of August—Japan would likely surrender as long as assurances were given concerning the fate of the emperor. Combined U.S. and British intelligence reaffirmed this advice a month before the bombings. One reason this option—using the shock of the Soviet attack and giving assurances to the emperor—appeared highly likely to work was that Japanese leaders feared the political consequences of Soviet power. Moreover, there was also little to lose: an invasion could not in any event begin until November, three months after the Soviet attack. If the war didn't end as expected, the bomb could still be used.

Instead, the United States rushed to use two bombs on August 6 and August 9, at almost exactly the time the Soviet attack was scheduled. Numerous studies suggest this was done in part because they "preferred," as Pulitzer Prize–winning historian Martin Sherwin has put it, to end the war in this way. Although the available evidence is not as yet absolutely conclusive, impressing the Soviets also appears to have been a factor.

Many military leaders were offended not only because the bombs were used in these circumstances but because they were used against Japanese cities—essentially civilian targets. William D. Leahy, President Truman's friend, his chief of staff, and a five star admiral who presided over meetings of both the U.S. Chiefs of Staff and the Combined U.S.–British Chiefs of Staff, wrote this after the war: "[T]he use of this barbarous weapon at Hiroshima and Nagasaki was of no material assistance in our war against Japan. The Japanese were already defeated and ready to surrender. . . . [I]n being the first to use it, we . . . adopted an ethical standard common to the barbarians of the Dark Ages."

President Richard Nixon recalled: "[General Douglas] MacArthur once spoke to me very eloquently about it, pacing the floor of his apartment in the Waldorf. He thought it a tragedy that the Bomb was ever exploded. MacArthur believed that the same restrictions ought to apply to atomic weapons as to conventional weapons, that the military objective should always be limited damage to noncombatants. . . . MacArthur, you see, was a soldier. He believed in using force only against military targets, and that is why the nuclear thing turned him off."

Gar Alperovitz

Print Resources

Alperovitz, Gar. *Atomic Diplomacy: Hiroshima and Potsdam: The Use of the Atomic Bomb and the American Confrontation with Soviet Power*. New York: Simon and Schuster, 1994.

Asada, Sadao. "The Mushroom Cloud and National Psyches: Japanese and American Perceptions of the Atomic-Bomb Decision, 1945–1995." In *Living with the Bomb: American and Japanese Cultural Conflicts in the Nuclear Age*, edited by Laura Hein and Mark Selden. Armonk, NY: East Gate Books, 1997.

Bix, Herbert. "Japan's Delayed Surrender: A Reinterpretation." In *Hiroshima in History and Memory*, edited by Michael J. Hogan. Cambridge: Cambridge University Press, 1996.

Bywater, Hector C. *The Great Pacific War: A Historic Prophecy Now Being Fulfilled*. Boston, MA: Houghton Mifflin, 1991.

Frank, Richard B. *Downfall: The End of the Imperial Japanese Empire*. New York: Random House, 1999.

Giangreco, D. M. *Hell to Pay: Operation Downfall and the Invasion of Japan*. Annapolis, MD: Naval Institute Press, 2009.

Hasegawa, Tsuyoshi. *Racing the Enemy: Stalin, Truman, and the Surrender of Japan*. Cambridge, MA: Belknap Press of Harvard University, 2005.

Miscamble, Wilson D. *The Most Controversial Decision: Truman, the Atomic Bombs, and the Defeat of Japan*. Cambridge: Cambridge University Press, 2011.

Moskin, J. Robert. *Mr. Truman's War: The Final Victories of World War II and the Birth of the Postwar World*. New York: Random House, 1996.

Schaffer, Ronald. *Wings of Judgment: American Bombing in World War II*. New York: Oxford University Press, 1985.

Sherwin, Martin J. *A World Destroyed: Hiroshima and Its Legacies*. 3rd ed. Stanford: Stanford University Press, 2000.

Spector, Ronald H. *Eagle against the Sun: The American War with Japan.* New York: Free
    Press, 1987.

Toland, John. *The Rising Sun: The Decline and Fall of the Japanese Empire, 1936–1945.*
    New York: Penguin, 2001.

Wainstock, Dennis D. *The Decision to Drop the Atomic Bomb.* Westport, CT: Praeger,
    1996.

Walker, J. Samuel. *Prompt and Utter Destruction: Truman and the Use of Atomic Bombs
    against Japan.* 2nd ed. Chapel Hill, NC: University of North Carolina Press, 2004.

Willmott, H. P. *The Great Crusade: A New Complete History of the Second World War.* Rev.
    ed. Washington, DC: Potomac Books, 2008.

CHRONOLOGY

January 30, 1933	Adolf Hitler is appointed chancellor of Germany.
August 2, 1934	Hitler merges the offices of chancellor and president, making himself absolute ruler of Germany.
March 12, 1938	German troops enter Austria unopposed.
March 13, 1938	Germany annexes Austria, creating the Anschluss.
September 30, 1938	Germany, France, Britain, and Italy sign the Munich Agreement, which permits German annexation of the Czechoslovakian Sudetenland.
November 9–10, 1938	Approximately 25,000–30,000 Jews are deported to concentration camps in an event that becomes known as Kristallnacht ("Night of Broken Glass").
March 16, 1939	Czechoslovakia falls under German control.
September 1, 1939	Germany invades Poland.
September 3, 1939	Great Britain and France declare war on Germany.
September 7, 1939	French forces cross the German border near Saarbrücken.
September 17, 1939	The Soviet Union invades eastern Poland.
October 5, 1939	Polish organized resistance ends at Kock.
November 30, 1939	The Soviet Union invades Finland.
February 13, 1940	The Soviets breach the Mannerheim Line in Finland.
March 12, 1940	The Soviets and Finns sign a peace treaty, ending the Finnish–Soviet War (Winter War).
April 1940	The Katyń Forest Massacre takes place throughout April and into early May.

Chronology

April 9, 1940	Germany invades Norway and Denmark.
May 3, 1940	Vidkun Quisling becomes leader of Norway as King Haakon VII departs.
May 10, 1940	Germany invades the Netherlands, Belgium, Luxembourg, and France. Winston Churchill becomes British prime minister.
May 15, 1940	The Netherlands Army surrenders to Germany.
May 26, 1940	Operation DYNAMO, the evacuation of British and French forces at Dunkirk, commences.
May 28, 1940	Belgium capitulates to Germany.
June 4, 1940	Operation DYNAMO ends.
June 8, 1940	Allied forces complete their evacuation from Norway.
June 10, 1940	Italy declares war on France and Great Britain. Norway officially surrenders to the Germans.
June 14, 1940	Paris falls to the Germans.
June 15, 1940	Soviet forces invade Estonia.
June 17, 1940	Soviet forces invade Latvia.
June 22, 1940	France signs an armistice with Germany.
June 27, 1940	Soviet forces invade Romania.
June 28, 1940	The British government recognizes Charles de Gaulle as leader of the Free French.
July 1, 1940	German submarines attack merchant ships in the Atlantic Ocean.
July 9, 1940	Vichy becomes the temporary capital of France. The British government rejects Hitler's peace offer.
July 10, 1940	The Battle of Britain commences.
July 16, 1940	Hitler plans Operation SEA LION, the invasion of Great Britain.
July 25, 1940	The United States announces an embargo of strategic materials to Japan.
August 17, 1940	Hitler declares a blockade of Great Britain.
September 3, 1940	The Destroyers for Bases deal between the United States and Britain is announced by U.S. president Franklin D. Roosevelt as an executive order. Britain receives 50 World War I–vintage U.S. destroyers in return for leases on base territory in North America.
September 13, 1940	Italian forces invade Egypt.
September 15, 1940	A major German air attack is made on London.

September 16, 1940	Conscription is introduced in the United States.
September 22, 1940	Vichy France allows Japanese air bases and troops in French Indochina.
September 27, 1940	Germany, Italy, and Japan sign the Axis Tripartite Pact.
October 7, 1940	German forces enter Romania.
October 10, 1940	Operation SEA LION is shelved.
October 28, 1940	Italian forces invade Greece from Italian-occupied Albania.
October 31, 1940	The Battle of Britain ends. The Germans switch to night bombings (the Blitz).
November 5, 1940	Roosevelt wins election to his third four-year term as U.S. president.
November 14–15, 1940	A German air attack on Coventry, England, destroys much of the city.
November 20, 1940	Hungary joins the Axis alliance.
November 23, 1940	Romania joins the Axis alliance.
December 9, 1940	British forces begin to drive the Italians from Egypt.
January 22, 1941	Tobruk falls to Australian and British forces.
February, 1941	*Life* magazine publishes "The American Century" by Henry Luce.
February 5–7, 1941	The British defeat Italian forces in Libya.
February 8, 1941	British forces take Benghazi, Libya.
February 12, 1941	German general Erwin Rommel arrives in North Africa.
March 1, 1941	Bulgaria joins the Tripartite Pact.
March 11, 1941	Roosevelt signs the Lend-Lease Bill.
March 24, 1941	Rommel commences the German offensive in Libya.
March 26, 1941	The pro-Axis Yugoslav government is overthrown.
April 6, 1941	Germany invades Greece and Yugoslavia.
April 11, 1941	The Axis siege of Tobruk commences.
April 13, 1941	A five-year nonaggression pact is signed between Japan and the Soviet Union.
April 17, 1941	The Yugoslavian Army surrenders to the Germans.
April 23, 1941	Greece signs an armistice with Germany.
May 1, 1941	The British repulse the German attack on Tobruk.

May 20, 1941	The Germans mount an airborne assault against Crete.
May 31, 1941	Crete falls to the Germans.
June 4, 1941	A pro-Allied government is installed in Iraq.
June 8, 1941	British and Free French troops attack Syria and Lebanon.
June 14, 1941	The British defeat Vichy French forces in Syria.
June 15, 1941	The British counteroffensive in Libya is defeated.
June 22, 1941	Germany, Italy, and Romania declare war on the Soviet Union. Germany commences Operation BARBAROSSA, the invasion of the Soviet Union.
June 26, 1941	Finland declares war on the Soviet Union, launching the Continuation War.
July 9, 1941	The Germans capture 300,000 Soviet troops near Minsk in the Soviet Union.
July 12, 1941	The Anglo-Soviet Treaty of Mutual Assistance is signed.
July 14, 1941	British forces occupy Syria and Lebanon.
July 24, 1941	Japanese forces occupy Southern French Indochina.
July 26, 1941	The United States suspends trade with Japan.
July 31, 1941	German preparations commence for the so-called Final Solution, a standardized method of annihilating the European Jews, which ultimately results in the Holocaust.
August 12, 1941	Churchill and Roosevelt draw up the Atlantic Charter.
August 25, 1941	Soviet and British troops occupy Iran.
September 3, 1941	Gas chambers are used experimentally at the Auschwitz concentration camp.
September 8, 1941	German forces besiege Leningrad.
September 19, 1941	German forces capture Kiev.
September 29, 1941	The German Army murders nearly 34,000 Jews in Kiev.
October 2, 1941	The Germans commence Operation TYPHOON, the planned capture of Moscow.
October 16, 1941	German and Romanian forces capture Odessa.
October 17, 1941	General Tōjō Hideki becomes premier of Japan.
October 24, 1941	German forces take Kharkov in the Soviet Union.
November 8, 1941	The Germans move onto the Crimean Peninsula.

December 5, 1941	German forces suspend their attack on Moscow.
December 7, 1941	Japanese forces bomb Pearl Harbor in the Hawaiian Islands.
December 8, 1941	The United States, Great Britain, and other Allied powers declare war on Japan. Japanese forces attack Guam, Wake Island, and the Philippines. Japan invades Hong Kong, Malaya, and Thailand.
December 9, 1941	Japan invades the Gilbert Islands. China declares war on Germany and Japan. Hitler issues his "Night and Fog" decree.
December 11, 1941	Italy and Germany declare war on the United States. Japanese forces invade Burma (Myanmar).
December 16, 1941	Japanese forces invade Borneo. Axis forces in North Africa retreat to El Agheila in Libya.
December 19, 1941	Hitler assumes command of the German Army.
December 23, 1941	The Japanese offensive in the Philippines commences.
December 25, 1941	Japanese forces take Hong Kong.
December 31, 1941	Japanese forces occupy Manila in the Philippines.
January 1, 1942	26 nations sign the United Nations (UN) declaration. The Soviets begin an offensive in Finland.
January 2, 1942	The Japanese capture Manila.
January 11, 1942	The Japanese invade the Netherlands East Indies. Japanese forces capture Kuala Lumpur.
January 13, 1942	Germany begins a U-boat offensive along the eastern coast of the United States. Soviet forces recapture Kiev.
January 20, 1942	Japan commences its Burma offensive. The Wannsee Conference, a meeting of German officials, is held in Berlin to discuss implementation of the Final Solution.
January 21, 1942	The Axis offensive against British forces in Libya commences.
January 26, 1942	The first U.S. troops committed to the war effort arrive in northern Ireland and Gilbert islands.
February 8, 1942	Japanese forces take Rangoon, Burma.
February 15, 1942	Singapore surrenders to Japanese forces.
February 19, 1942	Japanese forces capture Bali.
February 23, 1942	Japanese forces capture Timor.
February 27–28, 1942	The Battle of the Java Sea is waged.

March 7, 1942	Japanese troops enter Rangoon.
March 9, 1942	Java surrenders to the Japanese.
March 19, 1942	The gas chamber is first used on human victims at Auschwitz-Birkenau.
April 9, 1942	U.S. forces surrender to the Japanese on the Bataan Peninsula on Luzon in the Philippines.
April 18, 1942	U.S. B-25 bombers raid Tokyo.
May 1, 1942	Mandalay surrenders to Japanese forces.
May 6, 1942	Corregidor falls to the Japanese. U.S. forces surrender in the Philippines.
May 20, 1942	Japanese forces complete the conquest of Burma.
May 26, 1942	Axis forces begin their offensive in Libya.
May 27, 1942	Reichsprotektor of Bohemia and Moravia Reinhard Heydrich is attacked and wounded in Prague.
May 30, 1942	The Royal Air Force (RAF) bombs Köln (Cologne), Germany.
June 4, 1942	Japanese forces attack the Aleutian Islands.
June 4–6, 1942	The Battle of Midway is waged.
June 6, 1942	Heydrich dies in Prague after being attacked by assassins the previous week.
June 7, 1942	The village of Lidice in Bohemia is liquidated in retaliation for Heydrich's death.
June 21, 1942	Axis forces in North Africa capture Tobruk.
June 24, 1942	General Dwight D. Eisenhower is named to command U.S. forces in Europe.
July 1–4, 1942	The First Battle of El Alamein in Egypt is waged.
July 22, 1942	The first Warsaw Ghetto deportations to death camps occur.
August 7, 1942	U.S. Marines land on Guadalcanal.
August 9, 1942	German forces capture oil fields in the Caucasus.
August 13, 1942	General Bernard L. Montgomery becomes commander of the British Eighth Army in Egypt.
August 23, 1942	The Battle for Stalingrad begins.
September 22, 1942	German forces reach Stalingrad.
October 23, 1942	The British Eighth Army attacks Axis forces at El Alamein.

November 1, 1942	British forces break through at El Alamein.
November 4, 1942	Axis forces retreat from El Alamein.
November 8, 1942	In Operation TORCH, Allied forces land in Algeria and Morocco.
November 11, 1942	Axis forces occupy Vichy-administered France.
November 13, 1942	British forces retake Tobruk.
November 19, 1942	The Soviet counteroffensive begins at Stalingrad.
December 16, 1942	German forces try but fail to relieve Stalingrad.
December 24, 1942	Admiral Jean Darlan is assassinated in Algiers.
January 14–24, 1943	The Casablanca Conference, involving Churchill and Roosevelt, takes place.
January 23, 1943	The British Eighth Army takes Tripoli, Libya.
January 31, 1943	German field marshal Friedrich Paulus surrenders at Stalingrad.
February 8, 1943	The Soviet Red Army recaptures Kursk.
February 9, 1943	U.S. forces secure Guadalcanal.
February 16, 1943	Soviet forces retake Kharkov.
February 22, 1943	Rommel exits by the Kasserine Pass in Tunisia.
February 25, 1943	General Jürgen von Arnim replaces Rommel as commander of German forces in North Africa.
April 18, 1943	Japanese admiral Yamamoto Isoroku's plane is shot down in a U.S. aerial ambush.
April 19, 1943	Elements of the German Army begin an effort to liquidate the Warsaw Ghetto.
April 22, 1943	The United States and Great Britain start the Allied offensive in North Africa.
May 13, 1943	The Allies capture Tunis and secure the surrender of 275,000 German and Italian troops in North Africa.
May 16, 1943	The Warsaw Ghetto Uprising ends.
May 16–17, 1943	The RAF makes Ruhr Valley dams a priority target.
June 13, 1943	The Tunisia Campaign ends in defeat for the Axis powers.
July 5–17, 1943	The Battle of Kursk is waged.
July 9, 1943	U.S. and British forces invade Sicily in Operation HUSKY.
July 24, 1943	RAF bombings reduce Hamburg, Germany, to rubble.

July 25, 1943	King Victor Emmanuel III of Italy dismisses Benito Mussolini; Pietro Badoglio succeeds Mussolini as leader of Italy.
August 1, 1943	The Japanese establish a puppet regime in Burma.
August 14–24, 1943	The Allied Quebec Conference is held.
August 17, 1943	British and U.S. forces conclude the conquest of Sicily.
August 23, 1943	Soviet forces retake Kharkov.
September 8, 1943	The Italian government signs an armistice with the Allies.
September 9, 1943	Allied forces land at Taranto and Salerno, Italy, during Operation AVALANCHE.
September 10–11, 1943	German forces occupy Rome.
September 12, 1943	German commandos led by Otto Skorzeny rescue Mussolini.
September 23, 1943	Mussolini establishes a new Fascist government in northern Italy.
September 25, 1943	Soviet forces retake Smolensk and Novorossisk in the Soviet Union.
October 5, 1943	Allied forces capture Corsica.
October 13, 1943	Italy declares war on Germany.
November 5, 1943	The Greater East Asia Conference is held in Tokyo.
November 7, 1943	Soviet forces liberate Kiev.
November 22–26, 1943	The Allies hold the Cairo Conference.
November 28, 1943	The Tehran Conference between Churchill, Roosevelt, and Stalin begins and will run until December 1.
December 3–7, 1943	The Cairo Conference resumes.
December 24, 1943	Eisenhower receives command of the Allied European invasion.
January 22, 1944	The Allied beachhead is established at Anzio, Italy.
January 25, 1944	The Allies begin a counteroffensive in Burma.
January 27, 1944	Soviet forces break the 900-day Siege of Leningrad.
February 20–26, 1944	Allied forces coordinate the "Big Week" air strikes against German factories.
March 18, 1944	The RAF conducts a large-scale raid on Hamburg.
March 30, 1944	The RAF raids Nürnberg (Nuremberg), Germany.
April 2, 1944	Soviet troops enter Romania.

June 4–5, 1944	Allied troops enter Rome.
June 6, 1944	Allied troops land in Normandy, France (D-Day).
June 9, 1944	Soviet forces attack Finland.
June 12–13, 1944	German V-1 buzz bombs hit London.
June 15, 1944	The USAAF bombs Tokyo. U.S. forces invade Saipan in the Mariana Islands.
June 19–21, 1944	The Battle of the Philippine Sea is fought.
July 9, 1944	British and Canadian forces capture Caen, France. U.S. forces declare Saipan secured.
July 20, 1944	An assassination attempt on Hitler is unsuccessful, and the effort by the German Resistance to seize power fails.
July 21, 1944	U.S. forces invade Guam in the Mariana Islands.
July 25, 1944	Soviet forces liberate the Majdanek concentration camp. In Operation COBRA, Allied forces break out from Normandy.
August 1, 1944	The Warsaw Rising against Germans begins. U.S. troops reach Avranches, France.
August 10, 1944	U.S. forces declare Guam secured.
August 15, 1944	In Operation DRAGOON, Allied forces land in southern France.
August 16, 1944	The Allies liberate Falaise, France. The French Resistance stages an uprising in Paris.
August 21, 1944	Allied forces trap 60,000 Germans in the Argentan–Falaise pocket.
August 23, 1944	Romania surrenders to the Allies.
August 24, 1944	Romania declares war on Germany. The Allies liberate Bordeaux, France.
August 25, 1944	Free French forces liberate Paris. The Allies begin an attack on the Gothic Line in Italy.
September 8, 1944	German V-2 rockets hit London.
September 17–26, 1944	Operation MARKET-GARDEN, the effort of the Western Allies to secure a crossing over the Rhine River at Arnhem, fails.
September 25, 1944	Allied forces break through the Gothic Line in Italy. Hitler calls up all remaining 16- to 60-year-old males for military service.

October 2, 1944	The Germans end the Warsaw Rising. The Polish Home Army surrenders to the Germans. The Allies enter western Germany.
October 14, 1944	British forces liberate Athens, Greece. Rommel is forced to commit suicide.
October 18, 1944	Soviet forces enter Czechoslovakia.
October 20, 1944	Yugoslav partisans and Soviet forces enter Belgrade.
October 23, 1944	The United States recognizes Charles de Gaulle as head of the French provisional government.
October 24, 1944	The Japanese employ kamikaze suicide aircraft for the first time, in the Battle of Leyte Gulf.
October 30, 1944	Gas is used for the last time in executions at Auschwitz.
November 20, 1944	French forces reach the Rhine through the Belfort Gap.
November 24, 1944	The USAAF begins the systematic bombing of Japan.
December 16, 1944	The Battle of the Bulge (Ardennes Offensive) commences.
December 17, 1944	Waffen-SS troops murder U.S. prisoners of war (POWs) at Malmedy, Belgium.
January 1–17, 1945	The Germans begin to leave the Ardennes.
January 9, 1945	U.S. forces invade Luzon.
January 16, 1945	The Battle of the Bulge ends in an impasse.
January 17, 1945	Soviet troops occupy Warsaw.
January 20, 1945	The Hungarian government concludes an armistice with Soviet forces.
January 26, 1945	Soviet troops liberate Auschwitz.
February 4–11, 1945	The Yalta Conference, involving Churchill, Roosevelt, and Stalin, takes place in the Crimea.
February 8, 1945	The Allied offensive to the Rhine River begins.
February 13, 1945	The remaining German forces in Budapest surrender to Soviet forces.
February 13–14, 1945	The RAF and USAAF conduct the firebombing of Dresden, Germany.
February 19, 1945	U.S. forces land on Iwo Jima in the Bonin Islands.
March 4, 1945	U.S. forces secure Manila.
March 7, 1945	Allied forces take Köln. U.S. forces seize the Remagen Bridge over the Rhine River.

March 9, 1945	The USAAF firebombs Tokyo.
March 16, 1945	U.S. forces secure Iwo Jima.
March 20–21, 1945	Allied forces capture Mandalay, Burma.
April 1, 1945	U.S. forces land on Okinawa.
April 7, 1945	Soviet forces enter Vienna.
April 10, 1945	Allied forces take Hanover, Germany.
April 12, 1945	Roosevelt dies in Warm Springs, Georgia. Vice President Harry S. Truman becomes U.S. president.
April 13, 1945	Soviet forces secure Vienna. The Allies take Arnhem.
April 15, 1945	British forces liberate the Bergen-Belsen concentration camp.
April 18, 1945	The Germans in the Ruhr Valley surrender.
April 23, 1945	Soviet forces reach Berlin.
April 23–24, 1945	Heinrich Himmler offers surrender to the United States and Britain.
April 25, 1945	U.S. and Soviet forces meet at the Elbe River in Germany. The San Francisco Conference begins.
April 28, 1945	Italian partisans execute Mussolini at Lake Como, Italy. Allied forces take Venice.
April 29, 1945	German forces in Italy surrender. American forces liberate the Dachau concentration camp. Soviet forces liberate the Ravensbrück concentration camp.
April 30, 1945	Hitler commits suicide in Berlin.
May 2, 1945	German forces in Italy surrender. The Soviets capture Berlin.
May 7, 1945	The Battle of the Atlantic ends. The Germans surrender unconditionally at Rheims, France.
May 8, 1945	Victory in Europe Day (V-E Day) is celebrated. The Netherlands are liberated. Soviet forces enter Prague.
June 28, 1945	The U.S. Senate approves the United Nations Charter in a vote of 89–2.
June 30, 1945	U.S. forces liberate Luzon in the Philippines.
July 1, 1945	Allied troops move into Berlin.
July 16, 1945	The first atomic weapon is successfully tested at Alamogordo, New Mexico.
July 17, 1945	The Potsdam Conference between Churchill, Truman, and Stalin opens, running until August 2.

July 21–22, 1945	U.S. forces secure Okinawa.
August 6, 1945	A USAAF B-29 drops an atomic bomb on Hiroshima, Japan.
August 8, 1945	The Soviet Union declares war on Japan.
August 9, 1945	Soviet forces invade Manchuria. The United States drops an atomic bomb on Nagasaki, Japan.
August 14, 1945	Japan capitulates unconditionally.
September 2, 1945	The formal Japanese surrender takes place aboard the U.S. battleship *Missouri* in Tokyo Harbor. Victory over Japan Day (V-J Day) is celebrated.
September 5, 1945	British forces reach Singapore.
September 7, 1945	Japanese forces in Shanghai surrender.
September 9, 1945	Japanese forces in China surrender.
September 13, 1945	Japanese forces in Burma surrender. Japanese forces in New Guinea surrender.
September 16, 1945	Japanese forces in Hong Kong surrender.
October 24, 1945	The UN Charter comes into force with an initial 29 members.

BIBLIOGRAPHY

Beevor, Antony. *The Fall of Berlin 1945.* New York: Viking, 2002.

Beevor, Antony. *The Second World War.* Boston, MA: Little Brown, 2012.

Bergen, Doris L. *War and Genocide: A Concise History of the Holocaust.* Lanham, MD: Rowman and Littlefield, 2009.

Bessel, Richard, ed. *Life in the Third Reich.* New York: Oxford University Press, 1987.

Bullock, Alan. *Hitler and Stalin: Parallel Lives.* New York: Alfred A. Knopf, 1992.

Burleigh, Michael. *The Third Reich: A New History.* London: Macmillan, 2000.

Calvocoressi, Peter, Guy Wint, and John Pritchard. *Total War: The Causes and Courses of the Second World War.* 2nd rev. ed. New York: Pantheon, 1989.

Churchill, Winston. *The Second World War.* 6 vols. London: Cassell, 1948–1953.

Dower, John W. *War Without Mercy: Race & Power in the Pacific War.* New York: Pantheon Books, 1986.

Evans, Richard J. *Lying About Hitler: History, Holocaust, and the David Irving Trial.* New York: Basic Books, 2002.

Evans, Richard J. *The Coming of the Third Reich.* New York: Penguin, 2004.

Evans, Richard J. *The Third Reich in Power.* New York: Penguin, 2006.

Evans, Richard J. *The Third Reich at War: How the Nazis Led Germany from Conquest to Disaster.* New York: Penguin, 2009.

Giangreco, D. M. *Hell to Pay: Operation Downfall and the Invasion of Japan.* Annapolis, MD: Naval Institute Press, 2009.

Gilbert, Martin. *The Second World War: A Complete History.* Rev. ed. New York: Holt, 2004.

Goldhagen, Daniel Jonah. *Hitler's Willing Executioners: Ordinary Germans and the Holocaust.* New York: Alfred A. Knopf, 1996.

Heide, Robert, and John Gilman. *Home Front America: Popular Culture of the World War II Era.* San Francisco: Chronicle Books, 1995.

Iriye, Akira. *Pearl Harbor and the Coming of the Pacific War: A Brief History with Documents and Essays.* Boston, MA: St. Martin's Press, 1999.

Johnson, William Bruce. *The Pacific Campaign in World War II.* New York: Routledge, 2006.

Judt, Tony. *Postwar: A History of Europe Since 1945.* New York: Penguin, 2005.

Kaplan, Marion A. *Between Dignity and Despair: Jewish Life in Nazi Germany.* New York: Oxford University Press, 1999.

Keegan, John. *The Battle for History: Refighting World War II.* New York: Vintage Books, 1996.

Keegan, John. *The Second World War.* London: Hutchinson, 1989.

Kennedy, David M. *Freedom from Fear: The American People in Depression and War, 1929–1945.* New York: Oxford University Press, 2001.

Kershaw, Ian. *Hitler, 1889–1936: Hubris.* New York: W. W. Norton, 1999.

Kershaw, Ian. *Hitler, 1936–1945: Nemesis.* New York: W. W. Norton, 2000.

Lary, Diana. *The Chinese People at War: Human Suffering and Social Transformation, 1937–1945.* Cambridge: Cambridge University Press, 2010.

Longmate, Norman. *How We Lived Then: A History of Everyday Life During the Second World War.* New York: Random House, 2002.

Maiolo, Joseph. *Cry Havoc: How the Arms Race Drove the World to War, 1931–1941.* London: John Murray, 2010.

Mawdsley, Evan. *Thunder in the East: The Nazi-Soviet War 1941–1945.* New York: Bloomsbury, 2005.

Mawdsley, Evan. *World War II: A New History.* Cambridge: Cambridge University Press, 2009.

Mazower, Mark. *Dark Continent: Europe's Twentieth Century.* New York: Alfred A. Knopf, 1999.

Mazower, Mark. *Hitler's Empire: How the Nazis Ruled Europe.* New York: Penguin Press, 2008.

Mercatante, Steven D. *Why Germany Nearly Won: A New History of World War II in Europe.* Westport, CT: Praeger, 2012.

Murray, Williamson, and Allan R. Millett. *A War to be Won: Fighting the Second World War.* Cambridge, MA: Harvard University Press, 2001.

O'Neill, William L. *A Democracy at War: America's Fight at Home and Abroad in World War II.* New York: Free Press, 1993.

Overy, Richard. *The Dictators: Hitler's Germany, Stalin's Russia.* New York: Norton, 2005.

Overy, Richard. *Interrogations: The Nazi Elite in Allied Hands, 1945.* New York: Penguin, 2002.

Overy, Richard. *1939: Countdown to War.* New York: Viking, 2010.

Overy, Richard. *The Origins of the Second World War.* 3rd ed. New York: Longman, 2008.

Overy, Richard. *Russia's War: A History of the Soviet War Effort: 1941–1945.* New York: Penguin, 1998.

Overy, Richard. *Why the Allies Won.* New York: Norton, 1997.

Rees, Laurence. *World War Two: Behind Closed Doors—Stalin, the Nazis and the West.* London: BBC Books, 2009.

Rhodes, Richard. *The Making of the Atomic Bomb.* New York: Simon and Schuster, 1986.

Roeder, George H., Jr. *The Censored War: American Visual Experience During World War II.* New Haven, CT: Yale University Press, 1993.

Roehrs, Mark D., and William A. Renzi. *World War II in the Pacific.* Armonk, NY: M. E. Sharpe, 2004.

Sherwin, Martin J. *A World Destroyed: Hiroshima and Its Legacies.* 3rd ed. Stanford, CA: Stanford University Press, 2000.

Shirer, William L. *The Rise and Fall of the Third Reich: A History of Nazi Germany.* New York: Simon and Schuster, 1960.

Snyder, Timothy. *Bloodlands: Europe Between Hitler and Stalin.* New York: Basic Books, 2010.

Spector, Ronald H. *Eagle Against the Sun: The American War with Japan.* New York: Free Press, 1985.

Steiner, Zara. *The Triumph of the Dark: European International History 1933–1939.* Oxford: Oxford University Press, 2011.

Takaki, Ronald. *Hiroshima: Why America Dropped the Atomic Bomb.* Boston, MA: Little, Brown, 1995.

Tarling, Nicholas. *A Sudden Rampage: The Japanese Occupation of Southeast Asia, 1941–1945.* Honolulu: University of Hawaii Press, 2001.

Terkel, Studs. *"The Good War": An Oral History of World War Two.* New York: Pantheon Books, 1984.

Thorne, Christopher. *Allies of a Kind: The United States, Britain, and the War Against Japan, 1941–1945.* New York: Oxford University Press, 1978.

Thorne, Christopher. *The Issue of War: States, Societies, and the Coming of the Far Eastern Conflict of 1941–1945.* New York: Oxford University Press, 1985.

Walker, J. Samuel. *Prompt and Utter Destruction: Truman and the Use of Atomic Bombs Against Japan.* 2nd ed. Chapel Hill, NC: University of North Carolina Press, 2004.

Waller, Maureen. *London 1945: Life in the Debris of War.* New York: St. Martin's Press, 2005.

Watt, Donald Cameron. *How War Came: The Immediate Origins of the Second World War 1938–1939.* New York: Pantheon Books, 1989.

Weinberg, Gerhard. *The Foreign Policy of Hitler's Germany: Starting World War II, 1937–1939.* Chicago, IL: Chicago University Press, 1980.

Weinberg, Gerhard. *Germany, Hitler, and World War II: Essays in Modern German and World History.* Cambridge: Cambridge University Press, 1995.

Weinberg, Gerhard. *A World at Arms: A Global History of World War II.* 2nd ed. Cambridge: Cambridge University Press, 2005.

WEB SITES

BBC: World Wars in-depth. http://www.bbc.co.uk/history/worldwars/.

The National World War II Museum. http://www.nationalww2museum.org/.

The Second World War 1939–1945. The British National Archives Web site. http://www.nationalarchives.gov.uk/education/world-war-two.htm.

United States Holocaust Memorial Museum. http://www.ushmm.org/museum/.

World War II. EyeWitness to History.com. http://www.eyewitnesstohistory.com/w2frm.htm.

World War II Gallery. National Museum of the US Air Force. http://www.nationalmuseum.af.mil/exhibits/airpower/index.asp.

World War II Multimedia Database. http://www.worldwar2database.com.

WorldWar-2.Net. http://www.worldwar-2.net/.

TELEVISION AND FILM

BBC History of World War II (2009). BBC Warner.
Japan's War in Colour (2005). Rhino Theatrical.
Russia's War: Blood upon the Snow (1997). PBS.
The World at War (1974). BBC.
World War II: Behind Closed Doors (2009). BBC Warner.
WWII in HD (2010). A & E Home Video.

INDEX

ABOUT THE EDITOR

DR. PRISCILLA ROBERTS read history as an undergraduate at King's College, Cambridge, where she also earned her PhD. She then spent four years in the United States on a variety of fellowships, including one year at Princeton University on a Rotary graduate studentship and a year as a visiting research fellow at the Smithsonian Institution, Washington, DC. She then moved to the University of Hong Kong, where she is now an associate professor of history. She is also honorary director of the University of Hong Kong's Centre of American Studies. She spent the year 2003 at George Washington University as a Fulbright scholar and has received numerous other academic awards for research in the United States, Great Britain, and Australia, including a Harold White Fellowship to the National Library of Australia, Canberra, and a Research Fellowship from the Prime Ministers Centre at the Museum of Australian Democracy, Canberra. She specializes in 20th-century diplomatic and international history.

LIST OF CONTRIBUTORS

Editor:
Dr. Priscilla Roberts
Associate Professor of History, School of
    Humanities
Honorary Director, Centre of American
    Studies
University of Hong Kong
Hong Kong, SAR China

Contributors:
Dr. Alan Allport
Department of History
Syracuse University
Syracuse, New York

Dr. Gar Alperovitz
Department of Government and
    Politics
University of Maryland at
    College Park

Dr. Michael Barrett
Department of History
The Citadel
Charleston, South Carolina

Dr. Colin F. Baxter
Department of History
East Tennessee State University
Johnson City, Tennessee

Dr. Keith W. Bird
Chancellor,
Kentucky Community and Technical
    College System

Philip L. Bolté
Brigadier General
U.S. Army, Retired

Dr. Patrick H. Brennan
Department of History
University of Calgary
Calgary, Canada

Dr. Stanley D. M. Carpenter
Professor of Strategy and Policy
U.S. Naval War College
Newport, Rhode Island

Dr. Don M. Coerver
Department of History
Texas Christian University
Fort Worth, Texas

Dr. Paul H. Collier
Independent scholar

Dr. Conrad C. Crane
Director
U.S. Army Military History Institute
Carlisle Barracks, Pennsylvania

Dr. Arthur I. Cyr
Director
A. W. Clausen Center for World Business
Carthage College
Kenosha, Wisconsin

Dr. Bruce J. DeHart
Department of History
University of North Carolina—Pembroke

Dr. Charles M. Dobbs
Department of History
   Iowa State University
Ames, Iowa

Dr. Lee W. Eysturlid
Department of History
Illinois Mathematics and Science Academy
Aurora, Illinois

Pamela Feltus
Accreditation Coordinator
American Association of Museums
Washington, DC

Dr. Arthur T. Frame
U.S. Army Command and General Staff
   College
Fort Leavenworth, Kansas

Dr. Derek W. Frisby
Department of History
Middle Tennessee State University
Murfreesboro, Tennessee

Jack Greene
Independent scholar

Kathleen Hitt
Department of History
Pierce College
Woodland Hills, California

Dr. John M. Jennings
Department of History
U.S. Air Force Academy
Colorado Springs, Colorado

Dr. Ken Kotani
Senior Fellow, International Conflict
   Division
Center for Military History
National Institute for Defense Studies
Tokyo, Japan

Dr. Cole C. Kingseed
Colonel
U.S. Army, Retired

Dr. Thomas Lansford
Academic Dean
University of Southern Mississippi—Gulf
   Coast
Long Beach, Mississippi

Dana Lombardy
Senior Executive Director
World War One Historical Association
San Francisco, California

Britton W. MacDonald
Independent scholar

Rodney Madison
Department of History
Oregon State University
Corvallis, Oregon

Dr. Jack McCallum
Department of History
Texas Christian University
Forth Worth, Texas

Dr. Eric W. Osborne
Department of History
Virginia Military Institute
Lexington, Virginia

Neville Panthaki
Comparative International Education
   and Development Centre
University of Toronto
Toronto, Canada

Dr. Eugene L. Rasor
Emeritus Professor of History
Emory & Henry College
Emory, Virginia

Dr. Annette Richardson
Department of Educational Policy Studies
University of Alberta
Edmonton, Canada

Dr. Priscilla Roberts
Associate Professor of History, School of
    Humanities
Honorary Director, Centre of American
    Studies
University of Hong Kong
Hong Kong, SAR China

Dr. Jürgen Rohwer
Director Emeritus
Library of Contemporary History
Stuttgart University,
Stuttgart, Germany

Wendy A. Maier Sarti
Department of Historical and Policy Studies
Oakton Community College
Des Plaines, Illinois

T. P. Schweider
Independent scholar

T. Jason Soderstrum
Independent scholar

Dr. Eva-Maria Stolberg
Department of History
University of Duisburg-Essen
Essen, Germany

Dr. Donald E. Thomas, Jr.
Independent Scholar

Dr. Spencer C. Tucker
Senior Fellow
Military History, ABC-CLIO, Inc.

Dr. Mark E. Van Rhyn
Department of History

Louisiana School for Math, Science and
    the Arts
Natchitoches, Louisiana

Dr. Patricia Wadley
Historian and Archivist
American Ex-Prisoners of War
    Organization (AXPOW)
Arlington, Texas

Dr. J. Samuel Walker
Historian
U.S. Nuclear Regulatory Commission
Rockville, Maryland

Dr. A.J.L. Waskey
Department of Social Sciences
Dalton State College
Dalton, Georgia

Dr. Thomas J. Weiler
Department of Political Science
University of Bonn
Bonn, Germany

John W. Whitman
Lieutenant Colonel
U.S. Army, Retired

Dr. James H. Willbanks
Director
Department of Military History
U.S. Army Command and General Staff
    College
Fort Leavenworth, Kansas

Dr. Hedley P. Willmott
Honorary Research Associate
Greenwich Maritime Institute
University of Greenwich
Greenwich, London
United Kingdom

Dr. David T. Zabecki
Major General
U.S. Army, Retired